AF344448

INTERNATIONAL TRADE AGREEMENTS AND POLITICAL ECONOMY

INTERNATIONAL TRADE AGREEMENTS AND POLITICAL ECONOMY

Editor

Raymond Riezman

University of Iowa, USA

NEW JERSEY · LONDON · SINGAPORE · BEIJING · SHANGHAI · HONG KONG · TAIPEI · CHENNAI

Published by

World Scientific Publishing Co. Pte. Ltd.

5 Toh Tuck Link, Singapore 596224

USA office: 27 Warren Street, Suite 401-402, Hackensack, NJ 07601

UK office: 57 Shelton Street, Covent Garden, London WC2H 9HE

Library of Congress Cataloging-in-Publication Data
Riezman, Raymond Glenn.
    International trade agreements and political economy / Raymond Riezman.
    pages cm. -- (The tricontinental series on global economic issues : v. 3)
    Includes bibliographical references.
    ISBN 978-9814390118 (hardcover : alk. paper)
    1. Commercial policy. 2. Commercial treaties. 3. International trade. I. Title.
    HF1411.R525 2013
    382'.9--dc23
                                                                    2012046931

British Library Cataloguing-in-Publication Data
A catalogue record for this book is available from the British Library.

In-house Editor: Chye Shu Wen

Printed in Singapore.

CONTENTS

ACKNOWLEDGMENTS

Chapter 1

Reprinted from Journal of International Economics, 9(3), Riezman, R., *A 3X3 Model of Customs Unions*, 341–354, Copyright (1979), with permission from Elsevier.

Chapter 2

This article appears with the permission of the Southern Economic Association, ©1982. *Tariff Retaliation from a Strategic Viewpoint*, Riezman, R., Southern Economic Journal, 48(3), 583–593.

Chapter 3

Reprinted from Journal of International Economics, 19(3/4), Riezman, R., *Customs Unions and the Core*, 355–366, Copyright (1985), with permission from Elsevier.

Chapter 4

Reprinted from Kennan, J. and Riezman, R., *Do Countries Win Tariff Wars?*, International Economic Review, 29(1), 81–85, Copyright (1988), with permission from John Wiley and Sons.

Chapter 5

Reprinted from Kennan, J. and Riezman, R., *Optimal Tariff Equilibria with Customs Unions*, Canadian Journal of Economics, 23(1), 70–83, Copyright (1990), with permission from John Wiley and Sons.

Chapter 6

Reprinted from Journal of International Economics, 30(3/4), Riezman, R., *Dynamic Tariffs with Asymmetric Information,* 267–283, Copyright (1991), with permission from Elsevier.

Chapter 7

Reprinted from Kose, A. and Riezman, R., *Understanding the Welfare Implications of Preferential Trade Agreements*, Review of International Economies, 8(4), 619–693, Copyright (2000), with permission from John Wiley and Sons.

Chapter 8

Reprinted from Journal of International Economics, 64(1), Bond, E.W., Riezman, R. and Syropoulos, C., *A Strategic and Welfare Theoretic Analysis of Free Trade Areas*, 1–27, Copyright (2004), with permission from Elsevier.

Chapter 9

Reprinted from Journal of International Economics, 68(1), Abrego, L., Riezman, R. and Whalley, J., *How Often are Propositions on the Effects of Regional Trade Agreements Theoretical Curiosa?*, 59–78, Copyright (2006), with permission from Elsevier.

Chapter 10

Reprinted from Kowalczyk, C. and Riezman, R., *Free Trade: What are the Terms-of-Trade Effects?*, Economic Theory, 41(1), 147–161, Copyright (2009), with permission from Springer.

Chapter 11

Reprinted from Mayer, W. and Riezman, R., *Voter Preferences for Trade Policy Instruments*, Economics and Politics, 2(3), 259–273, Copyright (1990), with permission from John Wiley and Sons.

Chapter 12

Reprinted from McKelvey, R.D. and Riezman, R., *Seniority in Legislatures*, American Political Science Review, 86(4), 951–965, Copyright (1992), with permission from Cambridge University Press.

Chapter 13

Reprinted from Journal of International Economics, 42(1/2), Riezman, R. and Wilson J.D., *Political Reform and Trade Policy*, 67–90, Copyright (1997), with permission from Elsevier.

Chapter 14

Reprinted from European Economic Review, 49(7), Laussel, D. and Riezman, R., *The Sources of Protectionist Drift in Representative Democracies*, 1855–1876, Copyright (2005), with permission from Elsevier.

Chapter 15

Reprinted from Casella, A., Palfrey, T., and Riezman, R., *Minorities and Storable Votes*, Quarterly Journal of Political Science, 3(2), 1–36, Copyright (2008), reprinted with permission from now publishers, PO Box 1024, Hanover, MA 02339 USA.

Chapter 16

Reprinted from Cooper, R. and Riezman, R., *Uncertainty and the Choice of Trade Policy in Oligopolistic Industries*, Review of Economic Studies, 56(1), 129–140, Copyright (1989), with permission from Oxford University Press.

Chapter 17

Reprinted with permission, Noussair, C., Plott, C. and Riezman, R., (1995). *An Experimental Investigation of the Patterns of International Trade*, The American Economic Review, 85(3), 462–491.

Chapter 18

Reprinted from Noussair, C., Plott, C. and Riezman, R., *The Principles of Exchange Rate Determination in an International Finance Experiment*, Journal of Political Economy, 105(4), 822–861, Copyright (1997), with permission from University of Chicago Press.

Chapter 19

Reprinted from Journal of Development Economics, 65(1), Kose, A. and Riezman, R., *Trade Shocks and Macroeconomic Fluctuations in Africa*, 55–80, Copyright (2001), with permission from Elsevier.

Chapter 20

Reprinted from Journal of International Economics, 73(2), Bougheas, S. and Riezman, R., *Trade and the Distribution of Human Capital*, 421–433, Copyright (2007), with permission from Elsevier.

Part I: Tariffs and Trade Agreements

Part I: Trade Agreements and Tariffs

The first of three sections focuses on the theory of protection and trade agreements. The first paper develops a model to analyze customs unions. "A 3×3 Model of Customs Unions," develops a three-country-three good model of customs unions that shows that two countries can always benefit from forming a customs union provided that their initial level of trade is not too large. The intuition for this result is that both countries benefit from improved terms of trade with the nonmember country. However, the intra-customs union terms of trade always moves in favor of one country and against the other. Hence, if the initial level of trade is not too large within the customs union, the country that loses from worse intra-union terms of trade does not lose much and will gain overall. This paper was one of the first papers to use the terms of trade-volume of trade approach to analyze customs unions.

The second paper "Tariff Retaliation from a Strategic Viewpoint" was one of the first papers to use game theory to study strategic interactions between countries regarding international trade policy. The main result is that strategic considerations make it unlikely that free trade will be chosen as a pure strategy non-cooperative equilibrium. Cooperation between countries however, does not quarantee free trade. If the gains from moving from the initial equilibrium to free trade are unevenly distributed then free trade will not be obtained without inter country transfers.

Applying cooperative game theory to the problem of customs union is the focus of "Customs Unions and the Core." In this paper, I use the core solution concept to solve for which customs unions would emerge as a cooperative equilibrium. Using a three-country model, I compare three equilibria; non-cooperative tariffs, customs union, and free trade. I show that customs unions can emerge as an equilibrium when member countries are better off than at free trade. This result is not surprising, however, what I also show is that there is an equilibrium in which customs unions emerge even though both countries are worse off than free trade. Here, customs unions are a best response to a third country that benefits from the non-cooperative tariff equilibrium.

In the paper, "Do Big Countries Win Tariff Wars?" we revisit a question first raised by Harry Johnson. His paper showed that a country with constant elasticity offer curves can win a tariff war provided that offer curve elasticities line up correctly. Here we build a simple, transparent model in which offer curves are not required to have constant elasticity. We show that big countries win tariff wars. The intuition is simple: tariffs benefit countries by reducing world demand in their import markets and supply in their export markets. This turns terms of trade in their favor. In a two-country world with both countries doing this large countries will have bigger impacts and hence are more likely to turn the terms of trade in their favor. If they are big enough they can improve their terms of trade just enough to make up for the welfare loss from reduced volume of trade.

This model is extended to three countries in "Optimal Tariff Equilibria with Customs Unions." With three countries all setting optimal tariffs, we consider the effect of customs union formation on the equilibrium. We find that "big" customs unions win tariff wars. In other words, if the combined size of a customs union is large enough it can do better than free trade by forming a union. This is significant because it means that when any pair of countries together are large, then free trade is not stable in the sense that countries can make themselves better off by forming a customs union. The model also allows us to distinguish between the tariff reduction effect and the policy coordination effect of customs unions.

All of the above are static models. In fact, tariff policy is set repeatedly over time. This problem is analyzed in "Dynamic Tariffs with Asymmetric Information." In this model, countries cannot observe protection levels of other countries directly. This could be because domestic policies are used to manipulate the terms of trade or policies such as safety regulations, quotas, or currency restrictions make the actual level of protection difficult for an outsider to observe. In this world, agreements to reduce protection take the form of trigger strategies in which countries agree to lower trade barriers if other countries lower their barriers. Since barriers are not observable, the trigger strategies must depend on observables like price and quantity. We show that trigger strategies based on observing quantities work while trigger strategies based on observing prices do not work.

In "Understanding the Welfare Implications of Preferential Trade Agreements", we study the implications of two types of preferential trade agreements, free trade associations and customs unions. In the model, countries have symmetric endowments and identical preferences. Using simulation techniques, we calculate consumption allocations, tariffs, prices, and trade volumes that result from the various trade arrangements. We compare the implications of customs unions and free trade associations with those of free trade and an initial equilibrium for which we use a Nash equilibrium in tariffs. Our study reveals several regularities and differences across preferential trade agreements: first, in a free trade association equilibrium, the nonmember country charges higher tariffs on imports than the member countries of the agreement. In contrast, the member countries charge higher tariffs on imports than the nonunion country in a customs union equilibrium. Second, while formation of a free trade association does not lead to an increase in the tariff rates of member countries, it induces higher tariff rates in the nonmember economy. Strikingly, when countries have sufficiently uneven endowments, i.e., when they have seemingly more market power in their export goods, the member countries reduce their tariff rates in a customs union equilibrium. Third, upon the formation of a customs union, the terms of trade of the members improve at the expense of nonmembers. In contrast, a nonmember economy in a free trade association equilibrium enjoys an improvement, in terms of trade since member economies do not coordinate their tariff policies. Fourth, the formation of free trade associations leads to more trade in both member and nonmember economies than the formation of customs unions.

We use a simple three-country general-equilibrium trade model to analyze how the formation of an FTA between two countries affects the tariff and welfare levels of all trade partners in "A Strategic and Welfare Theoretic Theory of Free Trade Areas." We show that, in response to internal trade liberalization, individual members have an incentive to reduce their external tariffs by an amount that exceeds the Kemp–Wan tariff reduction. We then use this result to show, first, that in the post-integration Nash equilibrium the external tariff of FTA members falls below its level in the pre-integration Nash equilibrium and, second, that ROW's (the Rest of the World) optimal tariff rises above its pre-integration level. Interestingly, these tariff adjustments cause ROW's terms of trade to improve and, as we will see later, imply that the formation of the FTA benefits ROW. The aforementioned findings also provide fresh insights on the differences between FTAs and custom unions. As emphasized by Kennan and Riezman (1990), a key difference between these forms of integration is that custom union members coordinate their external tariff policies and thus internalize the terms of trade externalities they generate for each other. More generally, though, the formation of a custom union creates two opposing effects on the external tariff: a *coordination effect* that causes this tariff to rise and a *complementarity effect* that causes it to fall. Our analysis clarifies that the absence of the coordination effect in FTAs means that the external tariff of members will always be lower in an FTA than in a custom union equilibrium. A second implication of this lack of coordination of external policies is that the optimal internal tariff for an FTA is positive. The above findings unveil the presence of conflicting welfare effects of FTA formation on member states. The removal of internal tariffs expands internal trade and tends to improve member country welfare. However, the FTA terms of trade deteriorate because of the resulting changes in inter-bloc tariffs: in the post-integration equilibrium, the external tariff of the FTA members falls below its Kemp–Wan level and ROW becomes relatively more aggressive. We find that a relatively large FTA is more likely to benefit its members for two reasons. First, internal trade constitutes a relatively larger fraction of total trade for a large FTA, which implies that the beneficial trade volume effects are likely to be relatively larger. Second, a large FTA suffers less from adverse changes in ROW's external tariff because in this case, ROW's market power is less pronounced.

Lastly, our work sheds light on the question of whether FTAs are "building blocks" or "stumbling blocks" to global free trade (Bhagwati, 1992). We show that either the outside country or the FTA members may block the attainment of global free trade in the post-integration equilibrium when they do not in the absence of an FTA; and second, these possibilities arise if there are significant asymmetries in the relative sizes of the two trading blocs.

In "How Often are Propositions on the Effects of Regional Trade Agreements Theoretical Curiosa?", we generate repeated model solutions for alternative numerical specifications of a general equilibrium trade model so as to map out the extent of the parameter space for which each of a series of propositions regarding customs unions is true. Our idea is to blend theory and numerical simulation to determine the frequency with which various results hold so as to obtain an indication of which statements are more likely to hold and which will not. We apply the techniques we develop to the analysis of various propositions in the customs union literature because despite nearly fifty years of research on regional trade agreements, no set of generally accepted propositions regarding the effects of regional trade agreements has emerged to guide policy makers and public officials. Whether individual countries necessarily gain by entering a customs union is unproven, and the use of alternative reference points, such as free trade or non-cooperative Nash, only further clouds the picture. Whether world welfare is higher under a custom union is also unknown, as is whether customs unions generate higher external tariffs compared to a non-cooperative Nash equilibrium in tariffs. Other propositions are widely thought to be true, but without explicit confirmation: such as that custom unions generally improve the terms of trade of member countries; and that nonmember countries prefer that no customs union be formed against them. Taken as a set, our results show that numerical simulation can be an important and useful adjunct to theory in economics. None of the propositions we consider holds unambiguously; some hold over 80% of the time while others hold considerably less frequently.

In "Free Trade: What are the Terms-of-Trade Effects?", we explore, how large the terms of trade effects would be from global free trade to get some idea of how large the international side-payments might have to be to generate world-wide support for free trade. The size of transfers could matter if the notion of international income transfers were to be brought from theory to a world of practical policy. Firstly, some countries may find it difficult in practice to raise the revenue that would correspond to the terms of trade gains from free trade through taxation of domestic producers and consumers. Secondly, international income transfers would be a somewhat novel tool for facilitating multilateral trade liberalization where negotiations have traditionally involved exchanges of market access. Thirdly, it is a possibility that the transfers would be regressive, i.e., they might go from lower-income countries to higher-income countries. Undoubtedly, many would find it difficult to accept the implications for world income distribution of such transfers. We calculate, for varying distributions of world endowments, and find that transfers for free trade vary considerably depending on the economic environment. For countries that are not too dissimilar we find, in our simulations, terms of trade effects of about 10% of gains from trade, while for very dissimilar countries with large initial trade, terms of trade gains may account for almost 60% of a nation's total gains from free trade, and almost 9% of GDP. In the latter case, the international side-payments discussed in this research would be large, and it could be politically difficult to raise the associated revenue.

Journal of International Economics 9 (19) 341–354. © North-Holland Publishing Company

A 3×3 MODEL OF CUSTOMS UNIONS

Raymond RIEZMAN*

The University of Iowa, Iowa City, IA 52242, USA

Received January 1979, revised version received April 1979

In this paper we develop a three-country–three-good model of customs unions. The main result is that a sufficient condition for two countries to benefit from forming a customs union is that they are similar in the sense that their mutual trade is small. This result is obtained by analyzing the terms of trade effects rather than the more traditional emphasis on trade creation–trade diversion effects.

1. Introduction

The customs union theory literature has concentrated on analyzing the trade creation–trade diversion effects of customs unions [see Viner (1950), Meade (1955), Lipsey (1960), Bhagwati (1971)]. While this approach lends insight into the question of how customs unions affect world welfare, it has not produced answers to questions such as the following. Under what circumstances will two countries decide to form a customs union? Will customs unions lead to free trade?

Vanek (1965) and Kemp (1969) were the first to systematically study the terms of trade effects of customs unions. Vanek concentrated on determining the effect of customs unions on world welfare. Kemp directed his attention to individual country's welfare but, rather than determining when two countries would choose to form a customs union, he simply listed the possible outcomes that followed if two countries decided to form a union.

The purpose of this paper is to determine when two countries could benefit from and, thus, would choose to form, a customs union. We follow Kemp in that we focus on the terms of trade effects. Rather than using Kemp's three-country–two-good geometric model, we will analyze the problem in the context of a three-country–three-good mathematical model. The three-country–three-good model has the advantage that there is not the asymmetry that exists in the three-country–two-good case. We assume that, initially, no tariff discrimination is allowed and, in addition, we rule out international transfers.

*This paper is based on a chapter of my Ph.D. dissertation submitted to the University of Minnesota. I wish to thank my adviser, John S. Chipman, for his helpful comments and advice. An anonymous referee also provided helpful comments.

Our main result is that two countries can benefit from a customs union provided that their mutual trade is initially small and does not increase too much as a result of the agreement. Some other conditions must also hold, but they are essentially regularity conditions. The main result has an intuitive explanation. The effect of the customs union is to reduce the prices of the goods imported by the customs union countries relative to their export goods. Therefore, their terms of trade with respect to the rest of the world (the third country in this case) improve. However, in general, the change in intracustoms union trading will benefit one member at the expense of the other. Thus, if intra-union trade is small, any loss *vis-à-vis* a member country would be outweighed by the gain *vis-à-vis* the rest of the world.

This result says that a sufficient condition for two countries to benefit from forming a customs union is that their mutual trade be small. It does not say that countries whose mutual trade is large cannot benefit from a customs union. To determine if a country gains from a customs union for any specific case, one needs to weigh the gain from improvement in a country's terms of trade *vis-à-vis* the nonmember countries against the possible loss due to a deterioration in the terms of trade *vis-à-vis* other member countries. It seems that this theory lends itself easily to empirical tests and could be useful in empirical investigations of related questions.

The basic model is explained in section 2. Sections 3 and 4 contain the main results for the case in which there is a small reduction in tariffs. Section 5 extends these results to the full customs union case. In section 6 we interpret and summarize our results, and briefly relate them to the issue of transfer payments.

2. Notation and assumptions

We use the following notation:

$X^i_j =$ consumption of good j in country i,
$Y^i_j =$ production of good j in country i,
$Z^i_j \equiv X^i_j - Y^i_j$ net imports if positive (exports if negative) of good j in country i,
$Z_j = Z^1_j + Z^2_j + Z^3_j$,
$P^i_j =$ price of good j in country i,
$p^i = (p^i_1, p^i_2, p^i_3)$,
$p = (p^1, p^2, p^3)$,
$t_{jk} =$ tariff charged by country j on imports from country k,
$t = (t_{12}, t_{13}, t_{21}, t_{23}, t_{31}, t_{32})$,
$I^i =$ is the national income of country i.

Our model consists of three countries numbered 1, 2 and 3, and three goods also numbered 1, 2, and 3. For convenience we assume that country 1 imports good 1 and exports goods 2 and 3. Similarly, country 2 imports good 2 and exports 1 and 3 and country 3 imports 3 and exports 1 and 2. Clearly, other trading patterns are possible; however, this one has the advantage that it is symmetrical. The question we wish to answer is: given that initially we have a symmetric situation, under what conditions will it pay two of the countries to form a customs union? A customs union agreement is one in which two or more countries agree to eliminate tariffs between themselves. Hence, in the context of our model, we want to determine when countries 1 and 2 could benefit from eliminating tariffs on their trade with each other.

In each country we assume that all production functions are continuously differentiable, homogeneous of degree one, and strictly convex to the origin. It follows that the supply of good j in country i, Y^i_j, is a single valued function $Y^i_j(p^i_1, p^i_2, p^i_3)$. Assume this function is continuously differentiable.

Aggregate demand for good j in country i, X^i_j, is assumed to be a continuously differentiable function $h^i_j(p^i_1, p^i_2, p^i_3, I^i)$ of domestic prices and national income. This demand function is generated by a Samuelson type social utility function $U^i(X^i_1, X^i_2, X^i_3)$.[1] Aggregate income I^i consists of income from production plus tariff proceeds:

$$I^i = p^i_1 Y^i_1(p^i) + p^i_2 Y^i_2(p^i) + p^i_3 Y^i_3(p^i) + \{\alpha^i(p^j_i t_{ij}) + (1 - \alpha^i)p^k_i t_{ik}\}Z^i_i,$$

$$i = 1, 2, 3, \qquad j = i + 1 \,(\mathrm{mod}\,3), \qquad k = i + 2 \,(\mathrm{mod}\,3) \tag{1}$$

(where α^i is the fraction of imports i receives from country j). From this formulation it is apparent that the demand for good i in country i, X^i_i, depends on I^i which in turn depends on X^i_i. Because of this circularity, we have to prove that the variable X^i_i can be expressed as a function of prices, tariffs, and alphas. We wish to show that there exists a function

$$\hat{X}^i_i(p^i, p^j_i, p^k_i, t_{ij}, t_{ik}, \alpha^i) = h^i_i[p^i, p^i_1 Y^i_1(p^i) + p^i_2 Y^i_2(p^i) + p^i_3 Y^i_3(p^i)$$

$$+ \{\alpha^i p^j_i t_{ij} + (1 - \alpha^i)p^k_i t_{ik}\}$$

$$\times \{\hat{X}^i_i(p^i, p^j_i, p^k_i, t_{ij}, t_{ik}, \alpha^i) - Y^i_i(p^i)\}], \tag{2}$$

$$i, l = 1, 2, 3, \qquad j = i + 1 \,(\mathrm{mod}\,3), \qquad k = i + 2 \,(\mathrm{mod}\,3).$$

We define the marginal propensity to consume good j in country i, m^i_j, by

$$m^i_j = p^i_j \frac{\partial X^i_j}{\partial I^i}. \tag{3}$$

---

[1] It is assumed that income is optimally distributed by the government to maximize this function, or that all individuals in each country have identical, homothetic utility functions.

$\hat{X}_l^i(p^i, p_i^j, p_i^k, t_{ij}, t_{ik}, \alpha^i)$ (for the case $i=l$) exists and is unique if there exists a μ such that

$$0 < m_i^i < \mu < p_i^i/(\alpha^i p_i^j t_{ij} + (1-\alpha^i)p_i^k t_{ik})$$

and if $I^i > 0$ implies that $h_i^i(p^i, I^i) > 0.$[2]

We now define excess demand functions:

$$\hat{Z}_i^i(p^i, p_i^j, p_i^k, t_{ij}, t_{ik}, \alpha^i) = \hat{X}_l^i(p^i, p_i^j, p_i^k, t_{ij}, t_{ik}, \alpha^i) - Y_l^i(p^i), \tag{4}$$

$$i, l = 1, 2, 3, \qquad j = i+1 \,(\text{mod } 3), \qquad k = i+2 \,(\text{mod } 3).$$

We can write income as follows:

$$\begin{aligned}
\hat{I}^i(p^i, p_i^j, p_i^k, t_{ij}, t_{ik}, \alpha^i) = {}& p_1^i Y_1^i(p^i) + p_2^i Y_2^i(p^i) + p_3^i Y_3^i(p^i) \\
& + \{\alpha^i p_i^j t_{ij} + (1-\alpha^i)p_i^k t_{ik}\} \\
& \times \hat{Z}_i^i(p^i, p_i^j, p_i^k, t_{ij}, t_{ik}, \alpha^i),
\end{aligned} \tag{4a}$$

$$i, l = 1, 2, 3, \qquad j = i+1 \,(\text{mod } 3), \qquad k = i+2 \,(\text{mod } 3).$$

Next we assume that all demand and supply functions respond normally to price

$$\frac{\partial \hat{X}_j^i}{\partial p_k^i} \begin{cases} > 0, & \text{if } j \neq k, \\ < 0, & \text{if } j = k. \end{cases} \tag{5}$$

$$\frac{\partial Y_j^i}{\partial p_k^i} \begin{cases} > 0, & \text{if } j = k, \\ < 0, & \text{if } j \neq k, \quad i, j, k = 1, 2, 3. \end{cases} \tag{6}$$

(Note: For the case $i=j=k$ this is not an assumption. It follows from the convexity of the production-possibility set.)

Eqs. (5) and (6) imply

$$\frac{\partial \hat{Z}_j^i}{\partial p_k^i} \begin{cases} > 0, & \text{if } j \neq k, \\ < 0, & \text{if } j = k, \quad i, j, k = 1, 2, 3. \end{cases} \tag{7}$$

---

[2]Two things should be pointed out. First, the proof of this statement can be found in Riezman (1977b). Secondly, in equilibrium

$$p_i^i/(\alpha^i p_i^j t_{ij} + (1-\alpha^i)p_i^k t_{ik}) = (1+t_{ij})/t_{ij},$$

hence the first part of the condition becomes $0 < m_i^i < \mu < (1+t_{ij})/t_{ij}$.

Given the trading pattern, if each country trades every commodity we have the following equalities:

$$
\begin{aligned}
p_1^1 &= p_1^2 (1 + t_{12}),\\
p_1^1 &= p_1^3 (1 + t_{13}),\\
p_2^2 &= p_2^1 (1 + t_{21}),\\
p_2^2 &= p_2^3 (1 + t_{23}),\\
p_3^3 &= p_3^1 (1 + t_{31}),\\
p_3^3 &= p_3^2 (1 + t_{32}).
\end{aligned}
\tag{8}
$$

Using (8) and the condition of material balance, we can write excess demand Z_j^i as a function of $p' = (p_1^1, p_2^2, 1)$ (we assume p_3^3 is the numeraire) and all tariffs, t, i.e., $Z_j^i(p', t)$, $i, j = 1, 2, 3$. The equilibrium conditions are given by

$$
F^1(p', t) = Z_1^1(p', t) + Z_1^2(p', t) + Z_1^3(p', t) = 0,
\tag{9}
$$

$$
F^2(p', t) = Z_2^1(p', t) + Z_2^2(p', t) + Z_2^3(p', t) = 0.
\tag{10}
$$

Hence (9) and (10) define a function $F = (F^1, F^2)$ which maps a vector (p', t) into $0 \in R^2$. Thus, $F(p', t) = 0$. We assume that there exists an equilibrium set of non-negative prices and tariffs.[3] Mathematically, we assume there exists a $\bar{p}' > 0$ and $\bar{t} > 0$ such that $F(\bar{p}', \bar{t}) = 0$. We now use F to determine what happens to p_1^1 and p_2^2 when t_{12} and t_{21} are reduced.

3. The analysis of prices

In this section we establish sufficient conditions for p_1^1 and p_2^2 to fall when t_{12} and t_{21} are reduced. Simple application of the implicit function theorem gives this result.

Let F_x be the matrix with elements $(F_x)_{ij}$ where

$$
(F_x)_{ij} = \frac{\partial F^i}{\partial p_j^j}, \qquad i, j = 1, 2.
\tag{11}
$$

Call the determinant of F_x, D. We wish to determine sufficient conditions for $D > 0$. Let

$$
\eta_{jk}^i = \frac{\partial Z_j^i}{\partial p_k^k} \frac{p_k^k}{Z_j^i}, \qquad i, j = 1, 2, 3, \qquad k = 1, 2.
\tag{12}
$$

[3]The issue of existence of equilibrium is discussed by Shoven (1974) and Sontheimer (1971).

Consider the following condition:

$$\text{I.} \qquad \lambda_{ij}\eta^i_{jj} > -\lambda_{ij}\eta^i_{jk}\left[\frac{p^j_j}{p^k_k}\right], \tag{13}$$

where

$$\lambda_{ij} = \begin{cases} -1, & \text{if } i=j, \\ 1, & \text{if } i \neq j, \end{cases}$$

and $i=1,2,3$, $j=2$ and $k=1$, or $j=1$ and $k=2$. (Condition I is actually six similar conditions on elasticities of excess demands.)

Lemma 3.1.   *If condition I holds then $D>0$.*

Proof.   Directly calculating,

$$D = \frac{\partial F^1}{\partial p^1_1}\frac{\partial F^2}{\partial p^2_2} - \frac{\partial F^1}{\partial p^2_2}\frac{\partial F^2}{\partial p^1_1} > 0. \tag{14}$$

Hence $D>0$ if

$$\frac{\partial F^1}{\partial p^1_1}\frac{\partial F^2}{\partial p^2_2} - \frac{F^1}{\partial p^2_2}\frac{\partial F^2}{\partial p^1_1} > 0.$$

This becomes

$$\left[\frac{\partial Z^1_1}{\partial p^1_1} + \frac{\partial Z^2_1}{\partial p^1_1} + \frac{\partial Z^3_1}{\partial p^1_1}\right]\left[\frac{\partial Z^1_2}{\partial p^2_2} + \frac{\partial Z^2_2}{\partial p^2_2} + \frac{\partial Z^3_2}{\partial p^2_2}\right]$$
$$> \left[\frac{\partial Z^1_1}{\partial p^2_2} + \frac{\partial Z^2_1}{\partial p^2_2} + \frac{\partial Z^3_1}{\partial p^2_2}\right]\left[\frac{\partial Z^1_2}{\partial p^1_1} + \frac{\partial Z^2_2}{\partial p^1_1} + \frac{\partial Z^3_2}{\partial p^1_1}\right]. \tag{15}$$

Condition I says that the first term on the left-hand side is larger than the first term on the right-hand size in absolute value, the second term on the left-hand side is larger than the second term on the right-hand side, etc. Hence, condition I is sufficient to ensure that inequality (15) holds, therefore $D>0$.

By our previous assumptions, given condition I, $F(p',t)$ is continuously differentiable. Applying the Implicit Function Theorem, if there exists a $(\bar{p}',\bar{t})$ such that $F(\bar{p}',\bar{t})=0$, then there exists a neighbourhood $N(\bar{t})$ around $\bar{t}$ in which a function ϕ can be defined such that for all $t \in N(\bar{t})$, $F(\phi(t),t)=0$.

Also, we know that at any point $t \in N(\bar{t})$,

$$\phi_t = -F_x^{-1} \cdot F_t. \tag{16}$$

ϕ_t is a matrix with elements $(\phi_t)_{ij}$ where

$$(\phi_t)_{ij} = \frac{\partial p_i^i}{\partial t_j}, \qquad i = 1, 2, \qquad j = 1, \ldots, 6 \tag{17}$$

$(t_1 = t_{12}, \ t_2 = t_{13}, \ t_3 = t_{21}, \ t_4 = t_{23}, \ t_5 = t_{31}, \ t_6 = t_{32})$. F_t is a matrix with elements $(F_t)_{ij}$ where

$$(F_t)_{ij} = \frac{\partial F^i}{\partial t_j}, \qquad i = 1, 2, \qquad j = 1, \ldots, 6. \tag{18}$$

Let D_{ij} be the cofactor of the ijth element of F_x. Writing out (16) in matrix notation we obtain

$$
\begin{bmatrix}
\dfrac{\partial p_1^1}{\partial t_{12}} & \dfrac{\partial p_1^1}{\partial t_{13}} & \dfrac{\partial p_1^1}{\partial t_{21}} & \dfrac{\partial p_1^1}{\partial t_{23}} & \dfrac{\partial p_1^1}{\partial t_{31}} & \dfrac{\partial p_1^1}{\partial t_{32}} \\[2ex]
\dfrac{\partial p_2^2}{\partial t_{12}} & \cdots & & & & \dfrac{\partial p_2^2}{\partial t_{32}}
\end{bmatrix}
$$

$$
= -\frac{1}{D}
\begin{bmatrix}
D_{11} & D_{21} \\
D_{12} & D_{22}
\end{bmatrix}
\begin{bmatrix}
\dfrac{\partial F^1}{\partial t_{12}} & \dfrac{\partial F^1}{\partial t_{13}} & \dfrac{\partial F^1}{\partial t_{21}} & \dfrac{\partial F^1}{\partial t_{23}} & \dfrac{\partial F^1}{\partial t_{31}} & \dfrac{\partial F^1}{\partial t_{32}} \\[2ex]
\dfrac{\partial F^2}{\partial t_{12}} & \cdots & & & & \dfrac{\partial F^2}{\partial t_{32}}
\end{bmatrix} \tag{19}
$$

Since we wish to determine how p_1^1 and p_2^2 change when both t_{12} and t_{21} are reduced, we need to find the signs of $\mathrm{d}p_1^1/\mathrm{d}\tau$ and $\mathrm{d}p_2^2/\mathrm{d}\tau$, where τ is a parameter[4] and

$$\frac{\mathrm{d}p_1^1}{\mathrm{d}\tau} = \frac{\partial p_1^1}{\partial t_{12}} \frac{\mathrm{d}t_{12}}{\mathrm{d}\tau} + \frac{\partial p_1^1}{\partial t_{21}} \frac{\mathrm{d}t_{21}}{\mathrm{d}\tau},$$

$$\frac{\mathrm{d}p_2^2}{\mathrm{d}\tau} = \frac{\partial p_2^2}{\partial t_{12}} \frac{\mathrm{d}t_{12}}{\mathrm{d}\tau} + \frac{\partial p_2^2}{\partial t_{21}} \frac{\mathrm{d}t_{21}}{\mathrm{d}\tau}.$$

One could make many different assumptions about $\mathrm{d}t_{12}/\mathrm{d}\tau$ and $\mathrm{d}t_{21}/\mathrm{d}\tau$, but for simplicity we assume $\mathrm{d}t_{12}/\mathrm{d}\tau = \xi t_{12}$ and $\mathrm{d}t_{21}/\mathrm{d}\tau = \beta t_{21}$. This means that

[4]For a more complete discussion of this matter see Riezman (1977b).

we consider constant percentage reductions for both tariff rates, although the rates may be different. From (19) we see that

$$\frac{\mathrm{d}p_1^1}{\mathrm{d}\tau} = \frac{-1}{D}\left[D_{11}\frac{\mathrm{d}F^1}{\mathrm{d}\tau} + D_{21}\frac{\mathrm{d}F^2}{\mathrm{d}\tau} \right],$$

$$\frac{\mathrm{d}p_2^2}{\mathrm{d}\tau} = \frac{-1}{D}\left[D_{12}\frac{\mathrm{d}F^1}{\mathrm{d}\tau} + D_{22}\frac{\mathrm{d}F^2}{\mathrm{d}\tau} \right],$$

$$(20)$$

where

$$\frac{\mathrm{d}F^i}{\mathrm{d}\tau} = \frac{\partial F^i}{\partial t_{12}}\xi t_{12} + \frac{\partial F^i}{\partial t_{21}}\beta t_{21}.$$

We can now state our first theorem.

Theorem 1. Given condition I,

II.　　　　$\hat{\eta}_{11}^2 \xi t_{12} > -\hat{\eta}_{12}^1 \left(\frac{(1+t_{12})Z_1^1}{(1+t_{21})Z_1^2} \right)\beta t_{21},$

and

III.　　　　$\hat{\eta}_{22}^1 \beta t_{21} > -\hat{\eta}_{21}^2 \left(\frac{(1+t_{21})Z_2^2}{(1+t_{12})Z_2^1} \right)\xi t_{12},$

and given also that income effects are small, then $\mathrm{d}p_1^1/\mathrm{d}\tau > 0$ *and* $\mathrm{d}p_2^2/\mathrm{d}\tau > 0$

$$\left(\hat{\eta}_{jk}^i \equiv \frac{\partial \hat{Z}_j^i}{\partial p_k^i}\frac{p_k^i}{Z_j^i}, \quad i,j,k = 1,2,3 \right).$$

Proof.   The details of the proof are left to an appendix.

Remark.   Theorem 1 tells us that when conditions I–III hold, member countries 1 and 2 experience a fall in the domestic price of their imported good (i.e. p_1^1 and p_2^2 fall). p_3^1, p_3^2, and p_3^3 are all constant because p_3^3 was assumed to be the numeraire and t_{31} and t_{32} do not change in our analysis. Hence, for each member country, the price of its import good will fall relative to the price of the good which it exports to the nonmember. In this sense we can say that the member country's terms of trade improve relative to the nonmember country. We cannot determine from our analysis what happens to p_2^1 and p_1^2. Therefore, the change in the terms of trade between member countries is indeterminate.

Remark. Conditions I–III can be viewed as regularity conditions. They essentially require that own price elasticities of excess demand dominate the cross price elasticities.

4. Utility analysis

We have shown that, given some mild restrictions, when two countries mutually reduce tariffs the price of their imported good falls, the price of one exported good is constant, and the price of the other exported good is indeterminate. We show in this section that these price changes will imply an increase in utility for the participating countries, provided that their trade with each other is relatively small.

Theorem 2. Given that countries 1 and 2 mutually reduce tariffs, conditions I–III hold, income effects are small, and countries 1 and 2 initially trade relatively little with each other (i.e. for a sufficiently small $-Z_2^1$ and $-Z_1^2$), then utility will increase for both countries 1 and 2.

Proof. We will sketch the proof. [For a complete proof see Riezman (1977b).] Country 1 maximizes a social utility function,

$$U^1(X_1^1, X_2^1, X_3^1) = U^1[\tilde{X}_1^1(p'(t(\tau))), t_{12}(\tau), t_{13}(\tau), t_{21}(\tau), t_{31}(\tau), \alpha^1(t(\tau)),$$

$$\tilde{X}_2^1(\cdot), \tilde{X}_3^1(\cdot)]$$

$$= U^1[\bar{X}_1^1(\tau), \bar{X}_2^1(\tau), \bar{X}_3^1(\tau)].$$

We wish to show that

$$\frac{dU^1[\bar{X}_1^1(\tau), \bar{X}_2^1(\tau), \bar{X}_3^1(\tau)]}{d\tau} < 0. \tag{21}$$

Expression (21) becomes

$$U_1^1 \frac{d\bar{X}_1^1(\tau)}{d\tau} + U_2^1 \frac{d\bar{X}_2^1(\tau)}{d\tau} + U_3^1 \frac{d\bar{X}_3^1(\tau)}{d\tau} < 0. \tag{22}$$

Using the first-order conditions for utility maximization, (22) becomes

$$p_1^1 \frac{d\bar{X}_1^1(\tau)}{d\tau} + \frac{p_2^2}{1+t_{21}} \frac{d\bar{X}_2^1(\tau)}{d\tau} + \frac{1}{1+t_{31}} \frac{d\bar{X}_3^1(\tau)}{d\tau} < 0. \tag{23}$$

Using the balance of payments condition and results from the previous section, it can be shown that for sufficiently small $-Z_2^1$ and $-Z_1^2$, given conditions I–III, and given also that income effects are small, (23) will hold, thus utility increases for country 1. The proof for country 2 is similar. Hence, we have shown that two countries can gain from mutually reducing tariffs provided that their mutual trade is small. This result is somewhat unexpected but can be explained intuitively. We showed in section 3 that the countries entering into the agreement to reduce tariffs both find that their trading position *vis-à-vis* the third country improves. However, their position with respect to each other may improve or deteriorate. Hence, if we require that initially the trade between members is small, any deterioration in their trading position *vis-à-vis* the other member will be outweighed by the improvement with respect to the rest of the world. Therefore, their trading position will improve overall.

This completes our results for small reductions in tariffs. In the next section we extend our results to a full customs union case.

5. The customs union case

We have shown that two countries can gain by mutually reducing their tariffs, provided that their trade with each other is not too large and that certain regularity conditions hold. In this section we show that this result is easily extended to the case of a full customs union. We do this by showing that a path exists along which tariffs are reduced to zero for the participating coun ries and along which utility is always increasing for both countries. Consider the path along which both member countries reduce tariffs by the same constant percentage amount. In terms of our model this implies that $\xi = \eta$. This path will approach the point $t_{12} = t_{21} = 0$, i.e. the customs union point. We now need to show that utility increases at every point along the path.

We first examine conditions I–III. Condition I does not have any terms containing t_{12} or t_{21}. Since it is essentially a regularity condition, there is no reason to believe condition I would not hold as t_{12} and t_{21} are reduced to zero. The counterpart of I in the customs union case is

$$\text{I}'. \quad \lambda_{ij}\eta^i_{jj} > -\lambda_{ij}\eta^i_{jk}\left(\frac{p^j_j}{p^k_k}\right), \qquad i=1,2,3, \quad j=2 \text{ and } k=1,$$

$$\lambda_{ij} = \begin{cases} -1, & \text{if } i=j, \\ 1, & \text{if } i\neq j, \end{cases} \quad \text{or } j=1 \text{ and } k=2,$$

at every point along the path as t_{12} and $t_{21} \rightarrow 0$.

Conditions II and III, which require that own price elasticities dominate cross price elasticities, contain terms with t_{12} and t_{21}. Thus, as t_{12} and t_{21}

are reduced to zero, conditions II and III will become $0>0$, which cannot hold in the limit. However, there is no reason to believe II and III will not hold as the tariffs are reduced. The fact that they cannot hold in the limit simply means that when $t_{12}=t_{21}=0$, then $dp_1^1/d\tau=dp_2^2/d\tau=0$. Conditions II and III become

II'. $\quad \hat{\eta}_{11}^2 t_{12} > -\hat{\eta}_{12}^1 \left(\dfrac{(1+t_{12})Z_1^1}{(1+t_{21})Z_1^2} \right) t_{21},$

III'. $\quad \hat{\eta}_{22}^1 t_{21} > \hat{\eta}_{21}^2 \left(\dfrac{(1+t_{21})Z_2^2}{(1+t_{12})Z_2^1} \right) t_{12},$

at each point along the path as t_{12} and $t_{21}\rightarrow0$.

We can now state our customs union theorem.

Theorem 3.   Given that conditions I', II', and III' hold, and given also that income effects are small, countries 1 and 2 will gain from forming a customs union provided their trade with each other does not increase too much (i.e. for a sufficiently small $-Z_2^1$ and $-Z_1^2$).

Proof.   The proof is simple. If all the conditions hold, then theorem 2 holds at each point along the path of tariff reductions. As a result, utility is increasing at each point on the path. Therefore, both countries are better off at the end point of the path, which is a customs union.

Remark.   The Latin American Free Trade Association (LAFTA) appears to be an example of a customs union which meets the conditions of theorem 3. In particular, the member countries trade primarily with Europe, Japan and the United States. Viewed in this way LAFTA is a device which essentially improves the member countries' terms of trade (i.e. raises the relative price of the member countries' exportables). Obviously, there are other facets to customs unions, but empirical work done by Petith (1977) on the EEC suggests that the terms of trade effects are important.

6. Summary and interpretation

Theorem 3 says that to guarantee that both countries 1 and 2 can benefit from a customs union, their mutual trade cannot be too large. To see how this applies in practice we need to consider the intuitive explanation for this result. After formation of the union, both member countries gain from an improvement in their terms of trade with country 3. However, it may be that country 1's terms of trade with respect to country 2 deteriorate. Hence, country 2 is unambiguously better off as a result of the union. But again, country 1 has both a source of gain and of loss. Therefore, country 1 gains from the union if the gain due to the improvement in terms of trade with country 3 outweighs the loss incurred *vis-à-vis* country 2. This will be the case if countries 1 and 2 trade little with each other.

As a result, one interpretation of this theory is that, to determine if two countries can gain from forming a customs union, one needs to compare the gains *vis-à-vis* the rest of the world with the possible loss *vis-à-vis* the other member countries. This hypothesis seems readily testable by looking at price changes weighted by the volumes of the respective goods flows.[5] This approach should prove useful in explaining the size and composition of existing customs unions. In addition, one could predict what customs unions might be formed in the future.

Theorem 3 can also be used to shed some light on the issue of transfer payments. Another interpretation of theorem 3 is that, in the absence of transfer payments, countries which trade mainly with each other may not find customs unions mutually advantageous. Kemp and Wan (1976), on the other hand, show that if transfer payments are allowed, then any customs union is potentially advantageous for all countries. Therefore, theorem 3 combined with the Kemp and Wan result indicates that if countries trade largely (little) with each other a mutually beneficial customs union probably will (will not) require transfer payments. This result is consistent with the experience of the EEC. The EEC is a customs union consisting of countries whose mutual trade is large, and is characterized by significant transfer payments.

Consequently, the conclusion which emerges is that when members of a potential customs union trade largely with each other it is likely that transfer payments will be necessary to make the union advantageous for all member countries. If intra-union trade is small, transfer payments should be unnecessary. Hence, this model offers an explanation for and could be used to study the issue of transfer payments within a customs union.

Appendix

We wish to show that, if II and III hold and income effects are small, then

$$\frac{\mathrm{d}p_1^1}{\mathrm{d}\tau} > 0 \quad \text{and} \quad \frac{\mathrm{d}p_2^2}{\mathrm{d}\tau} > 0.$$

$$\frac{\mathrm{d}p_1^1}{\mathrm{d}\tau} = -\frac{1}{D}\left(D_{11}\frac{\mathrm{d}F^1}{\mathrm{d}\tau} + D_{21}\frac{\mathrm{d}F^2}{\mathrm{d}\tau}\right).$$

[5]Petith (1977) has investigated similar issues.

$$D_{11} = \frac{\partial Z_2^1}{\partial p_2^2} + \frac{\partial Z_2^2}{\partial p_2^2} + \frac{\partial Z_2^3}{\partial p_2^2} < 0,$$

$$D_{21} = -\left(\frac{\partial Z_1^1}{\partial p_2^2} + \frac{\partial Z_1^2}{\partial p_2^2} + \frac{\partial Z_1^3}{\partial p_2^2}\right) < 0.$$

Therefore, if

$$\frac{dF^1}{d\tau} > 0 \quad \text{and} \quad \frac{dF^2}{d\tau} > 0,$$

then

$$dp_1^1/d\tau > 0.$$

$$\frac{dF^1}{d\tau} = \frac{\partial F^1}{\partial t_{12}} \frac{dt_{12}}{d\tau} + \frac{\partial F^1}{\partial t_{21}} \frac{dt_{21}}{d\tau}$$

$$= \left(\frac{\partial Z_1^1}{\partial t_{12}} + \frac{\partial Z_1^2}{\partial t_{12}} + \frac{\partial Z_1^3}{\partial t_{12}}\right) \xi t_{12} + \left(\frac{\partial Z_1^1}{\partial t_{21}} + \frac{\partial Z_1^2}{\partial t_{21}} + \frac{\partial Z_1^3}{\partial t_{21}}\right) \eta t_{21}.$$

This can be written as

$$\frac{dF^1}{d\tau} = \left(\frac{\partial Z_1^2}{\partial t_{12}} \xi t_{12} + \frac{\partial Z_1^1}{\partial t_{21}} \eta t_{21}\right)$$

$$+ \left(\frac{\partial Z_1^1}{\partial t_{12}} \xi t_{12} + \frac{\partial Z_1^3}{\partial t_{12}} \xi t_{12} + \frac{\partial Z_1^2}{\partial t_{21}} \eta t_{21} + \frac{\partial Z_1^3}{\partial t_{21}} \eta t_{21}\right).$$

The last four terms are all income effects which are assumed to be small. The first two terms are positive if II holds, hence II implies that $dF^1/d\tau > 0$. In a similar manner it can be shown that III implies $dF^2/d\tau > 0$. Thus, II and III imply that $dp_1^1/d\tau > 0$. The proof for $dp_2^2/d\tau$ is similar.

References

Bhagwati, J., 1971, Trade diverting custom union and welfare improvement: A clarification, Economic Journal 81, 580–587.

Bhagwati, J., 1973, A reply to Professor Kirman, Economic Journal 83, 895–897.

Chipman, J.S., 1960, A survey of the theory of international trade, Econometrica 34, 18–76.

Chipman, J.S., 1972, The theory of exploitative trade and investment policies: A reformulation and synthesis, in: L.E. DeMarco, ed., International economics and development (Academic Press, New York).

Chipman, J.S. and J.C. Moore, 1972, Social utility and the gains from trade, Journal of International Economics 2(2), 157–172.

Kemp, M., 1969, A contribution to the general equilibrium theory of preferential trading (North-Holland, Amsterdam).

Kemp, M. and H.Y. Wan, 1976, An elementary proposition concerning the formation of customs unions, Journal of International Economics 6, 95–97.

Kirman, A.P., 1973, Trade diverting customs unions and welfare improvement: A comment, Economic Journal 83, 890–894.

Krauss, M.B., 1972, Recent developments in customs union theory: An interpretive survey, Journal of Economic Literature 10, 413–436.

Lipsey, R.G., 1960, The theory of customs unions: A general survey, Economic Journal 70(279), 496–513.

Meade, J.E., 1955, The theory of customs unions (North-Holland, Amsterdam).

Negishi, T., 1969, The customs union and the theory of second best, International Economic Review 10, 391–398.

Petith, H.C., 1977, European integration and the terms of trade, Economic Journal 87, 262–272.

Riezman, R., 1977a, A theory of customs unions: The three country–two good case, mimeo. Forthcoming in Weltwirtschaftliches Archiv.

Riezman, R., 1977b, A theory of preferential trading agreements (University of Iowa Working Paper no. 77–4A).

Samuelson, P.A., 1956, Social indifference curves, Quarterly Journal of Economics LXX, 1–22.

Shoven, J.B., 1974, A proof of the existence of a general equilibrium with ad valorem commodity taxes, Journal of Economic Theory 8, 1–25.

Sontheimer, K.C., 1971, The existence of international trade equilibrium with trade tax-subsidy distortions, Econometrica 39(6), 1015–1035.

Vanek, J., 1965, General equilibrium of international discrimination (Harvard University Press, Cambridge, Massachusetts).

Viner, J., 1950, The customs union issue (Carnegie Endowment for International Peace, New York).

Reprint from *Southern Economic Journal*
Volume 48   Number 3   January 1982

Tariff Retaliation from a Strategic Viewpoint*

RAYMOND RIEZMAN
The University of Iowa
Iowa City, Iowa

I. Introduction

One of the most perplexing questions in international trade concerns the rationale for the existence of widespread barriers to trade in the current world economy.[1] The numerous explanations that have been offered for the existence of tariffs are generally based on one of the following four arguments: (a) the existence of market imperfections (monopolies, externalities, etc.) invalidates the free trade theorem and thus free trade is not desirable or perhaps not obtainable, (b) sluggish adjustment of the world economy to free trade implies that the existing tariffs are a temporary phase, (c) non-economic phenomena, such as nationalism, induce political or institutional tariff arrangements or (d) protectionist motives to improve the welfare of a country or a group of individuals in that country induce all countries to simultaneously impose tariffs. While all of these factors can be important in the explanation of the existence of tariffs, the purpose of this paper is to develop an extended analysis of the protectionist view.

The protectionist view is based on the optimal tariff theorem which states (under very restrictive assumptions) that a country can improve its welfare by imposing a tariff [5,12]. A serious difficulty with this explanation is that the optimal tariff theorem assumes that no retaliation occurs.

As Scitovsky [12] points out, a country that could benefit from charging a tariff has monopoly power in trade. Surely, a country sophisticated enough to exercise monopoly power in trade would expect its rivals to respond when tariffs are erected. Hence, Scitovsky argues "...that if protection is the monopolistic behavior of a collectivity, two countries raising tariffs against each other are bilateral monopolists—and we know that bilateral monopoly results in the two parties coming to some working agreement, whose terms depend on their bargaining skill and are analytically indeterminate." Scitovsky concluded that a tariff war would result in an indeterminate solution with both countries worse off.

Johnson [6] formalized Scitovsky's agrument by allowing each country to adopt a Cournot-type assumption regarding its rival's reaction to a change in its own tariff. Thus,

* The author wishes to thank the editorial staff of this Journal for many helpful suggestions. J. S. Chipman, R. Jensen, J. F. O'Connor, A. J. Policano, J. T. Rader, M. Thursby and S. Y. Wu also provided helpful comments on an earlier draft.
1. Arguments for free trade are well known and can be found in Bhagwati [1] and Chipman [2].

**584	*Raymond Riezman***

each country sets its tariff assuming that no retaliation takes place. Johnson showed that equilibrium exists when both countries adopt this Cournot assumption and that both countries cold be worse off at the conclusion of the tariff war. However, Johnson also found that the country initiating the tariff war could be better off at the new Cournot equilibrium. Thus, two possibilities emerge. In the first case, which we will refer to as the standard case, both countries are worse off at the end of a tariff war than at free trade. In the second case, which we will refer to as the Johnson case, one country benefits as the result of a tariff war.

Johnson showed that the outcome of a particular tariff war depends on the elasticities of demand and supply. In addition, he presented an example which demonstrated the plausibility of the Johnson case. The possibility that the Johnson case could occur raises some interesting possibilities. Specifically, since countries could benefit from instituting a tariff war, tariffs might exist because it is in the self-interst of some countries. Conversely, if tariffs exist and negotiations ensue to eliminate them, a country which gains from instituting a tariff war would not agree to move to free trade. Therefore, the widespread existence of tariffs might be in the interests of certain countries.

Johnson's original work on tariff retaliation has been extended in a variety of ways.[2] Panchamukhi [10] in a game theoretic framework, showed that Johnson's tariff war equilibrium is equivalent to the solution of a two-person non-zero sum game. We use this result as a point of departure and extend the preivous work in two ways. First, we consider specific solution concepts for both cooperative and non-cooperative games. For each solution concept we examine the outcome of the game to see if free trade is obtained. Second, for each solution concept, we consider both the Johnson case and the standard case. Hence, the focus of this research is to determine if free trade will be chosen when countries take into account the game theoretic nature of the tariff policy problem. This is important because, to the extent that strategic reasons lead countries away from free trade, they constitute an explanation for the existence of tariffs. Thus, these results have policy implications since it is easier to eliminate tariffs once one understands why they exist.

In Section II it is assumed that countries behave non-cooperatively. Our results indicate that free trade will not be chosen when countries do not cooperate. Sections III and IV deal with the cooperative case. When cooperation is allowed, free trade may or may not occur. These results have interesting policy implications which are discussed in a concluding section.

II. Tariffs in a Non-Cooperative Framework

We first assume that countries set their tariff policies without the benefit of prior communication with each other. Thus, selecting a tariff policy can be viewed as the

---

2. Rodriguez [11] shows that tariffs and quotas are not equivalent if retaliation is considered. Tower and Sheer [15] show that a scheme to share tariff revenue could help avert tariff wars. Tower, Sheer and Baas [16] calculate the welfare effects of tariff wars for hypothetical cases. Panchamukhi [10] was agnostic regarding the question of whether or not free trade would occur. Kuga [7] and Otani [9] provide very general models in which tariffs strategy questions can be handled. However, their results are mainly concerned with the existence of equilibrium in their models.

TARIFF RETALIATION FROM A STRATEGIC VIEWPOINT 585

Table I

		Country I	
		θ	$\bar{t}$
Country II	θ	(b,b')	(a,d')
	$\bar{t}$	(d,a')	(c,c')

selection of a strategy in the playing of a game.[3] We consider a model in which there are two countries.

We assume that each country selects a tariff policy or strategy which maximizes its level of welfare. For the moment we leave problems of internal distribution aside by assuming the existence of a Von Neumann type utility function for each country [8]. Furthermore, we simplify the problem by assuming that each country has only two alternative strategies from which to choose, no tariff or the optimal tariff (given the other country's existing tariff). A strategy is a rule which describes a country's tariff rates under all possible circumstances. In our model, the strategy θ indicates that a country charges a zero tariff regardless of the other country's tariff. The strategy $\bar{t}$ indicates that a country will charge a tariff that is optimal relative to the other country's tariff. Since each country has two possible strategies, there are four pairs of strategies possible.

Allowing only two strategies might seem restrictive. In fact, it is not. Essentially, we are assuming that a country can choose free trade or tariff ridden trade. If tariff ridden trade is chosen we require that the choice of actual tariff rates be optimal relative to the other country's tariff. Therefore, although only two tariff strategies are allowed, many tariff rates are possible.

We represent the game with Table I. The elements of Table I indicate the four possible outcomes which correspond to the four pairs of strategies.[4] Thus, if country I chooses strategy $\bar{t}$ and country II chooses strategy θ, the outcome is (a,d'). Country I receives a and country II receives d', where a and d' are measured in utility terms. Using existing results from trade theory, we can determine the relative magnitudes of the elements of Table I.[5]

The optimal tariff theorem says that starting from free trade, if one country charges a tariff and no retaliation takes place, the country which erects the tariff is better off and the other country is worse off. In terms of the elements of Table I this means that $a > b$, $a' > b'$, $b > d$ and $b' > d'$. The outcome (c,c') is obtained when a tariff war occurs. Thus, from

---

3. A tariff policy corresponds to the notion of strategy in a game theoretic sense. Thus, the choice of a tariff policy is a listing of the choice of tariff rates for every possible contingency (in this case for all possible values of the other countries tariffs).

4. Note that if country I chooses strategy $\bar{t}$ and country II chooses strategy θ the actual outcome will be that country I charges the standard optimal tariff and country II charges a zero tariff. If both countries choose strategy t the outcome will be tariffs which are optimal relative to the other coutnry's tariff ridden offer curve. These tariff rates are the ones which Johnson solves for in [6]. If both countries play strategy θ then there will be free trade.

5. One could have modeled the strategy space in different ways. For example, we could have considered ad valorem versus specific tariffs or tariffs versus quotas (see Tower [14]). Our main purpose is to provide a methodology for looking at free trade versus non-free trade. As Tower has shown ad valorem tariffs are better than specific tariffs or quotas for the country imposing protection. Therefore, we restrict our attentin to the case of ad valorem tariffs.

586	*Raymond Riezman*

Johnson's work we know there are two possibilities. In the standard case both countries are worse off than at free trade, $b > c$, $b' > c'$. The Johnson case occurs when one country benefits from a tariff war. In terms of Table I this would mean that $b > c$ and $c' > b'$ (or $c > b$ and $b' > c'$). Putting the optimal tariff theorem results and Johnson's tariff retaliation results together we have two possibilities. In the standard case we have, $a > b > c > d$ and $a' > b' > c' > d'$, both countries lose from the tariff war. In the Johnson case we have $a > c > b > d$ and $a' > b' > c' > d'$, one country gains from the tariff war.[6] Having described the outcomes which occur corresponding to various strategies our next task is to determine for each case which strategies are chosen.

For the standard case this game is commonly called the prisoners dilemma. As is shown in Luce and Raiffa [8], a "rational" player will always choose strategy $\bar{t}$, since for any strategy choice of the opposing player the playing of strategy $\bar{t}$ yields a higher payoff. This can be seen in Table I. Suppose country II chooses strategy θ, then country I gets b for playing θ, and a for playing $\bar{t}$. Since $a > b$, $\bar{t}$ is the best choice for I when II chooses θ. Suppose II chooses $\bar{t}$. Country I obtains d by playing θ and c by playing $\bar{t}$; again $\bar{t}$ is the best choice for I. Thus, country I will choose $\bar{t}$, and the same reasoning applies for country II. For the Johnson case you can use the same reasoning to show that each country will choose strategy $\bar{t}$. Therefore, when countries play non-cooperatively they will select the strategy of charging the optimal tariff, hence free trade will not be reached.[7]

III. Tariffs in a Cooperative Framework: The Negotiation Set

In this section we relax the assumption that cooperation is not allowed. In particular, we assume that countries can communicate and make binding agreements prior to selecting a tariff strategy. No transfer payments are allowed. Considering the case in which transfers are allowed would be a natural extension of this work but is beyond the scope of this paper. Using the framework of Section II we will investigate the issue of the choice of tariff strategy when cooperation is allowed.

Each country approaches the negotiations trying to maximize its own welfare. They both know that they can obtain at least c and c' respectively (the outcome where both countries select strategy $\bar{t}$ since they could select strategy $\bar{t}$ and refuse to negotiate. So, in that sense the point (c, c') is a logical choice for the starting point for negotiations. The next step in the analysis is to determine the set of points that could be chosen in negotiations. This set of points is called the negotiation set.

Referring to Figure 1 we see that the point $0 = (c, c')$ divides the positive quadrant into four regions. From our previous analysis it is reasonable to restrict the negotiation set to region I, since any point in II, III, and IV is dominated by 0 for at least one country. 0 dominates because either country can obtain the utility associated with 0 by refusing to negotiate and erecting the optimal tariff. We now proceed to construct the negotiation set

---

6. We could also consider $a > b > c > d >$ and $a' > c' > b' > d'$, but the results are the same.

7. If this game is played repeatedly, the conclusions may change. Jensen and Thursby [4] consider this problem. They show that when countries take the repeated nature of the game into account, tariff ridden trade will be the Nash equilibrium under certainty. However, if a slightly weaker equilibrium concept is used (or uncertainty introduced) free trade may occur for some finite length of time. Thus, depending on the equilibrium concept used considering a repeated game could change the results.

TARIFF RETALIATION FROM A STRATEGIC VIEWPOINT   587

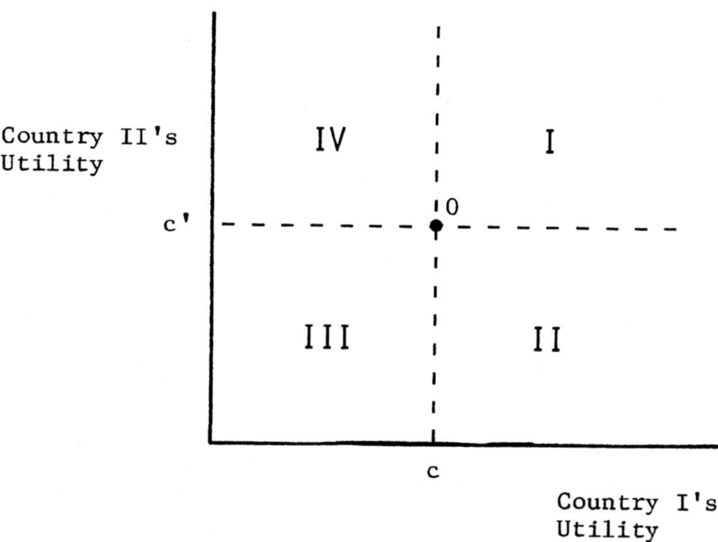

Figure 1.

for the standard case (recall that in the standard case both countries suffer from a tariff war).

From the analysis of Section II, we know that the payoff corresponding to strategy choice $(\theta,\bar{t})$, which is (d,a'), must lie in region IV (because $d < c$ and $a' > c'$). We denote this point, B in Figure 2. By similar reasoning pont C in Figure 2 corresponds to the payoff (a,d') which occurs when the strategy pair $(\bar{t},\theta)$ is chosen. When free trade is chosen (θ,θ), the outcome is (b,b'). From earlier results we know that in the standard case $b > c$, $b' > c'$. Thus, the free trade point, F in Figure 2, will lie in region I. If we consider randomized strategies our search for the negotiation set can be restricted to the shaded area $0EFD$ in

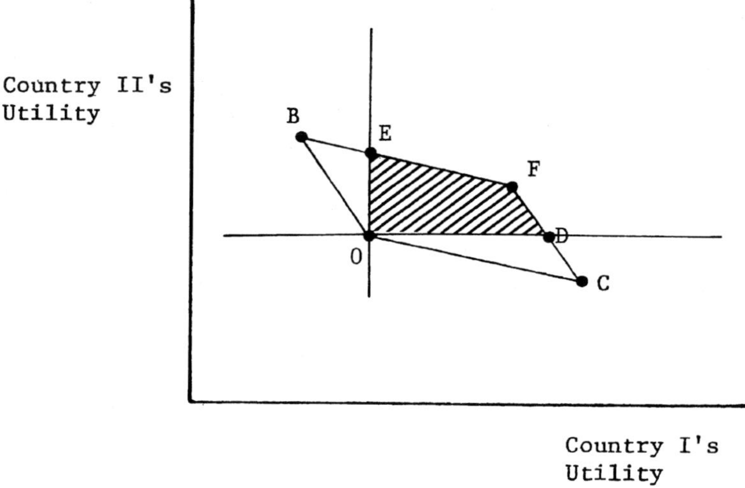

Figure 2. The Standard Case

588   *Raymond Riezman*

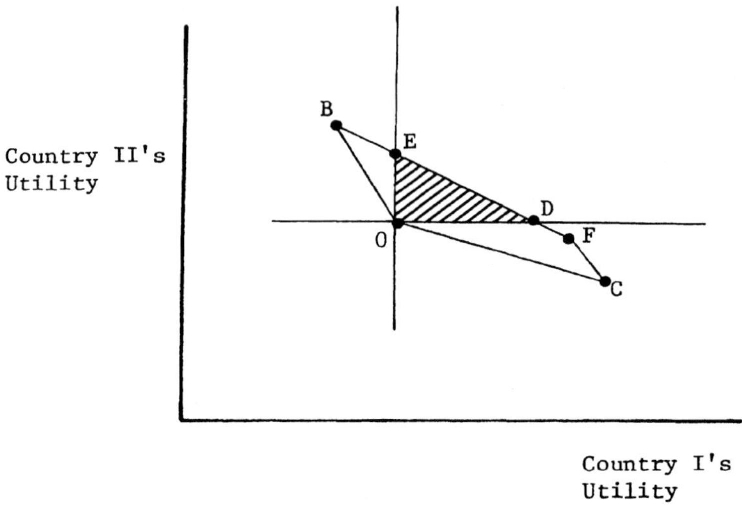

Figure 3. The Johnson Case

Figure 2. If we assume that our solution is Pareto optimal with respect to the negotiation set, then the negotiation set becomes line segment *EFD*, since all other points of 0*EFD* are dominated by some point on *EFD*.[8] This set of points is called the Von Neumann-Morgenstern solution. Therefore, when two countries cooperate they will choose a joint tariff policy that yields utility given by some point on *EFD*. The free trade point *F* is only one of many candidates which could be chosen. To determine which point in the negotiation set is actually chosen we need to specify more precisely how each country plays the game. This will be done after we determine the negotiation set in the Johnson case.

A similar analysis of the Johnson case yields the conclusion that free trade is not an element of the negotiation set and hence will not be chosen. Points 0, *B*, and *C* are determined in the same way as the standard case (see Figure 3). The free trade point, *F*, must lie in either region II or IV. This occurs because when strategy pair (θ,θ) is played the outcome is (b,b'). In the Johnson case we have either $b > c$, $c' > b'$ or $c > b$, $b' > c'$. Hence, one country must be worse off at *F* as compared to 0 and point *F* must lie on either region II or IV. Referring to Figure 3, the negotiation set for the Johnson case is the line segment *ED*. Also note that the farther to the south and west point *F* lies, the smaller the negotiation set. In fact, in the extreme case the negotiation set could shrink to 0, the status quo. This conclusion is not surprising since, in the Johnson case, moving to the free trade point makes one country worse off as compared to the point where both countries charge the optimal tariff. Thus, in the Johnson case free trade as a pure strategy is never chosen, even when cooperation is allowed. We now turn our attention to determining which point in the negotiation set will be selected when the standard case occurs.

8. If a point on *EFD* other than *F* is chosen, the interpretation is that countries agree to randomized strategies with the appropriate probabilities attached to the pure strategies $\bar{t}$ and θ such that the expected utilities correspond to the point chosen on *EFD*.

IV. Tariffs in a Cooperative Framework: The Solution

In this section we will examine a cooperative game solution in an attempt to determine
which point of the negotiation set (line segment *EFD* in Figure 2) is chosen. In particular,
we are most interested in seeing if free trade (point *F*) is more likely to be chosen than
some other point. This will give us some insight into the issue of whether two countries
acting cooperatively have any tendency to move towards free trade. We will consider the
Nash cooperative solution [8, ch.6]. Since it was established in the last section that free
trade will never be chosen with certainty in the Johnson case, we restrict our attention in
this section to the standard case.

To find the Nash cooperative solution begin by first finding the negotiation set using
the non-cooperative equilibrium as the origin, as was done in Section III. The point
chosen from the negotiation set is the one which maximizes the product of the two
country's utilities. In our example, if U_i is the utility of country i, then the Nash solution
chooses the point which maximizes $U = U_I U_{II}$. As shown in Figure 4, the Nash solution
could select free trade (see Figure 4(a)) or a point which is not free trade (see Figure 4(b)).

Using the framework developed in Section II we can determine when free trade will
be chosen. Referring to Figure 4, free trade will be chosen if the slope of the world
indifference surface U_{II}/U_I is greater in terms of absolute value than the slope of line
segment *BF* and less than the slope of *FC*. The slope of *BF* is $a'-b'/b-d$ and the slope of
FC is $b'-d'/a-b$. Thus, free trade is chosen if,

$$a' - b'/b' - d < U_{II}/U_I < b' - d'/a - b.$$

This condition says that free trade is more likely to be chosen as a joint cooperative
strategy the smaller the gain from tariff exploitation ($a-b$ and $a'-b'$) and the larger the
gain to the exploited country of moving to free trade ($b-d$ and $b'-d'$). Also, notice that if

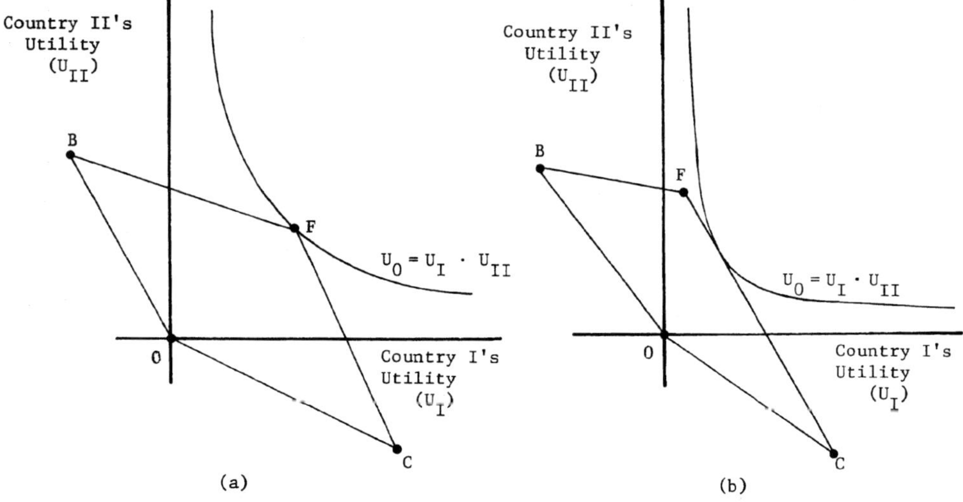

Figure 4.

590   *Raymond Riezman*

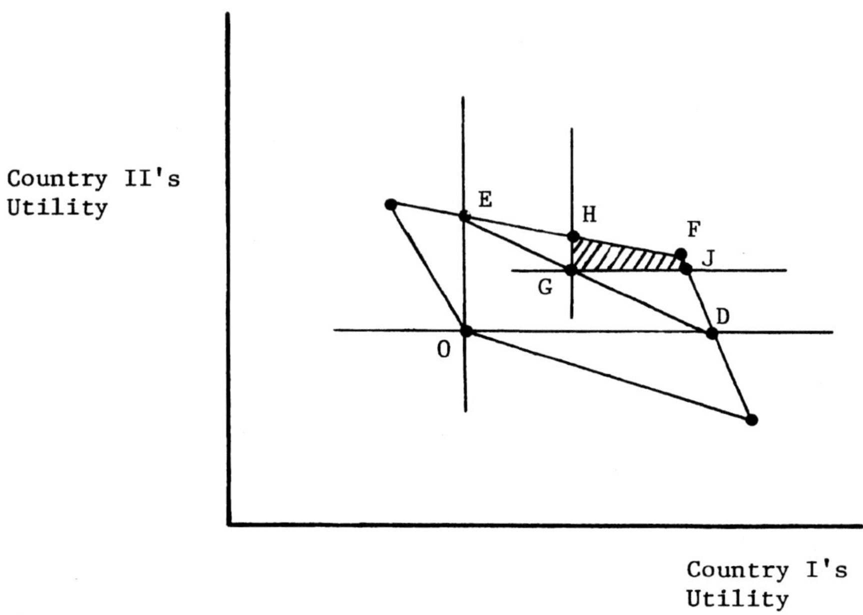

Figure 5.

the countries are symmetric (i.e., $a=a'$, $b=b'$, etc.) then free trade will be chosen (this is ilustrated in Figure 4(a)).

Figure 4(b) illustrates an example in which free trade is not the outcome. In this case, $U_{II}/U_I = b'-d'/a-b$. Here $a-b$ is large, indicating that country I's potential gain from exploiting country II is very large. Thus, intuitively country I is sacrificing a great deal more than country II by accepting free trade. Since the Nash cooperative solution treats each country symmetrically, the solution will not be free trade.

Thus, if the countries are symmetric, free trade will be chosen. More generally, we could say that when the gains from moving to free trade are similar for both countries then free trade is likely to be chosen. When the gains are unevenly distributed the attainment of free trade is more unlikely. These generalizations could be applied to the problem of tariff negotiations.

We begin with some existing tariff structure and consider negotiations to reduce tariffs. If the gains from moving to free trade are evenly distributed, then our results tell us that the international redistribution problem associated with moving to free trade should not be a barrier to the attainment of free trade. We do not mean to imply that this is the only factor in tariff negotiatons which are also complicated by adjustment problems, internal redistribution factors and dynamic considerations. However, this model also tells us that unequal distribution of the gains from moving to free trade may create a significant barrier to its attainment.

In addition to the Nash cooperative solution one could consider other more intuitively plausible arbitration schemes such as Zeuthen's or Raiffa's [8. ch. 6]. Since it can be shown that Zeuthen's scheme is mathematically equivalent to the Nash solution while Raiffa's is not we will consider Raiffa's.

It is an arbitration scheme which, by proceeding in a step-by-step fashion starting from the non-cooprative equilibrium, selects an element of the negotiation set. In each step of the process the negotiation set is reduced until only one point is left. This iterative process starts by each country making its most selfish demand. In Figure 5, we start with negotiation set *EFD*. Country I's most selfish demand is point *D*, because *D* is the best point for country I given the existing negotiation set. Country II's most selfish demand is point *E*. Then, we draw a line connecting *D* and *E* and take its midpoint, *G*. We construct a new negotiation set which consists of the intersection of all points northeast of *G* and the old negotiation set. This is *HFJ* in Figure 5. We repeat the procedure. *H* and *J* are the respective most selfish demands. We connect them and choose the midpoint and further reduce the size of the negotiation set. Using this procedure the negotiation set will converge to one point.

The Raiffa solution yields results similar to the Nash cooperative solution. Again, if both countries are symmetric then free trade will be chosen. If the gains from moving to free trade are unequally distributed then free trade will not be the solution. Hence, our conclusions are esentially the same. If tariffs exist and the gains from removing them are unequally distributed, then, when both countries act strategically this unequal distribution of gain could be a barrier to free trade.

V. Conclusion

This paper uses game theory to analyze the problem of tariff retaliation. Countries selecting tariff strategies can be viewed as players in a game. As players in this game each country recognizes the dynamic nature of the tariff decision and realizes that any change in its tariff rates will evoke a response from its rival. Theefore, instead of choosing tariff rates, each country must decide on an overall tariff strategy which considers the possibility of retaliation.

Different types of solution concepts as well as initial conditions are considered to see if free trade will be obtained. Although free trade is the "best" outcome in the sense that it is the most efficient way to organize use of the world's resources, there is no strong presumption that free trade will be chosen. In fact, free trade will not be chosen as a pure strategy if countries behave non-cooperatively, if countries cooperate and the Johnson case (where one country benefits from a tariff war) occurs, or if the standard case occurs and the gains from free trade are unevenly distributed. Thus, our results indicate that free trade may be difficult to obtain when countries behave strategically.

The framework of bilateral monopoly, as suggested by Scitovsky, is used to interpret these results. Viewing tariff retaliation as essentially a problem of bilateral monopoly, each country uses its tariff policy to secure the greatest possible advantage over its rival. If there is no cooperation, each country can secure the greatest advantage with a tariff-ridden strategy. Specifically, on the one hand, if your rival chooses a free trade strategy the best response is to choose a tariff-ridden strategy. This strategy will result in you charging the optimal static tariff and securing the best possible outcome. On the other hand, if your rival adopts a tariff-ridden policy, again your best response is a tariff-ridden policy since the free trade strategy implies that you would be optimally exploited.

592   *Raymond Riezman*

If the Johnson case occurs and countries are allowed to cooperate, tariff-ridden strategies will likely be chosen. In the Johnson case, where one country benefits from the tariff war, the country that benefits would not agree to return to free trade since by doing so it would be worse off. Therefore, the outcome should involve tariffs being charged.

If the standard case occurs, and cooperation is allowed, free trade may not be chosen if the gains from eliminating tariffs are unequally distributed. Again, using the perspective of bilateral monopoly, the country which gains relatively little from moving to free trade may choose a tariff-ridden strategy in an attempt to secure some of the gains accruing to the other country. this policy can be interpreted as the use of a threat strategy. Hence, tariffs could result from countries using threat strategies to secure some of the gains which accrue to its rival. The implication of this analysis is that free trade is difficult to obtain, because of tariff-ridden strategy usually dominates a free trade strategy for individual countries.

The bilateral analysis can be applied to the problem of multilateral tariff negotiations. In the case of multilateral negotiations, such as the Kennedy and Tokyo rounds, cooperation takes the form of direct negotiation on tariff rates. Our results imply that cooperation will not necessarily result in free trade. Hence, direct negotiations to eliminate tariffs may be unsuccessful in attaining their goal. This interpretation is consistent with recent experience. Although the Kennedy round produced significant reductions in tariffs, the later Tokyo round has been acompanied by increasing non-tariff barriers. Hence, our results indicate that the attempt to attain free trade by direct negotiations may be doomed to failure. The explanation for this failure is that strategic behavior constitutes a barrier to free trade which cooperation (in the form of direct negotiation) may not overcome. Specifically, choosing non-free trade policies is in the individual strategic interest of each country.

While these results seem pessimistic, they suggest a solution to the problem of the existence of tariffs. Using cooperative game theory without side payments, we have shown that free trade will be difficult to obtain because choosing a tariff-ridden strategy will usually be in the best interest of each country. In practical terms, it means that direct negotiations of tariff rates may not lead to free trade. This suggests that to reach free trade a change in the negotiating rules needs to be made so that each country will be led by their strategic interest to choose free trade. Determining new negotiating rules is essentially a problem of cooperative game theory with side payments. Hence, in a sequel we apply cooperative game theory with side payments to the framework developed in this paper. Hopefully, this will shed some light on the problem of determining a negotiating mechanism that will lead to free trade.

References

1. Bhagwati, J., "The Pure Theory of International Trade: A Survey." *Economic Journal*, 74. March 1964, 293.

2. Chipman, J. S., "A Survey of the Theory of International Trade." *Econometrica* XXIV, January 1966, 18–76.

3. Chipman, J. S. and J. C. Moore., "Social Utility and the Gains from Trade." *Journal of International Economics* 2, May 1972, 2.

4. Jensen, R. and M. Thursby. "Free Trade: Two Non-Cooperative Equilibrium Approaches." Ohio State University Working Paper #58, September 1980.

5. Johnson, H. G., "Optimum Welfare and Maximum Revenue Tariffs." *Review of Economic Studies*, 51, 1950–51, 28–35.

6. —,"Optimum Tariffs and Retaliation." *Review of Economic Studies*, 55, 1953-54, 142–53.

7. Kuga, J., "Tariff Retaliation and Policy Equilibrium." *Journal of International Economics*, 3, November 1973, 4.

8. Luce, R. D. and H. Raiffa. *Games and Decisions*. New York: John Wiley & Sons, 1957.

9. Otani, Y., "Strategic Equilibrium of Tariffs and General Equilibrium." *Econometrica* 48, April 1980, 643–62.

10. Panchamukhi, V. R., "A Theory of Optimum Tariff Policy." *Indian Economic Journal*, October 1961, 178–98.

11. Rodriguez, C. A., "The Non Equivalence of Tariffs and Quotas under Retalization." *Journal of International Economics* 4, 1974, 295–98.

12. Scitovsky, T., "A Reconsideration of the Theory of Tariffs." *Review of Economic Studies* 9, Summer 1942, 89–110.

13. Stern, R. M., "Tariffs and Other Measures of Trade Control: A Survey of Recent Developments." *Journal of Economic Literature* 11, September 1973, 3.

14. Tower, E. "The Optimum Quota and Retaliation." *The Review of Economic Studies*, 1975, 623–30.

15. Tower, E. and A. Sheer. "How to End Tariff Wars." Discussion Paper, Duke University, 1978. Summarized in Amacher, Ryan, et al., editors, *Challenges to a Liberal International Economic Order*, Washington: American Enterprise Institute, 1979.

16. Tower, E., A. Sheer, and H. Baas, "Alternative Optimum Tariff Strategies as Devices for Transferrring Real Income." *Southern Economic Journal* 45, 1978, 18–31.

Journal of International Economics 19 (1985) 355–365. North-Holland

CUSTOMS UNIONS AND THE CORE

Raymond RIEZMAN*

University of Iowa, Iowa City, IA 52242, USA

Received March 1984, revised version received November 1984

Customs union formation is modeled as a two-stage game. In the first stage countries make coalitional choices according to core theory. In the second stage optimal tariffs are determined. This yields a theory that predicts which customs unions form. An example shows that a customs union can be an equilibrium even when both member countries do better at free trade.

1. Introduction

It has often been observed that an analogy exists between customs unions and coalition formation in a game theoretic context. In particular, existence of a customs union could be thought of as a coalition in the core of a game. In this sense customs unions might be an equilibrium phenomenon. The purpose here is to pursue this argument by adapting the notion of the core to correspond to a standard view of international equilibrium. The main adaptation is to restrict the amount of cooperation allowed within a coalition so that coalitions conform to the usual definition of a customs union. We view countries as players in a two-stage game.

In the first stage of the game countries make coalitional choices. The choices are conditioned on the second stage in which tariffs are chosen for a given coalition structure. We use this formulation because coalition choice is a simpler and more easily enforced agreement than a tariff agreement. Once the coalition is formed some mechanism can be used to enforce the tariff agreement.

The analysis integrates optimal tariff theory with the theory of economic integration. In the second stage countries set tariffs optimally. This analysis uses results by Kennan and Riezman (1982) which extend Johnson's (1958) work on tariff retaliation to a three-country model. First-stage analysis shows how this can be developed into a theory of economic integration.

Perhaps the key difference between this model and more traditional customs union analysis is that the focus is on explaining which customs

*This paper was written while I was visiting the University of Minnesota. I would like to thank John Kennan, Ed Ray, William Thomson, Henry Wan and two anonymous referees for helpful comments and suggestions on an earlier draft.

unions form rather than on the effects of customs union formation. This requires two important departures from earlier work. First, countries behave optimally. Hence the use of optimal tariff theory. Second, and most importantly, to explain which customs unions form, the focus is on the comparison of customs unions to free trade rather than customs unions and some initial tariff equilibrium. To get a satisfactory explanation of customs unions existence we need to know not only that they are superior to some initial tariff equilibrium but that they are chosen over free trade.

The second stage, optimal tariff equilibrium for a given coalition structure, is defined in section 2. Coalition choice, the first stage, is analyzed in section 3. Illustrative examples are discussed in section 4. Section 5 briefly discusses inter-country transfers and concluding remarks are in section 6.

2. Three-country equilibrium

A three-country–three-good model is the simplest symmetric model one can use to discuss customs unions. The goods and countries are numbered 1 to 3. Suppose that country i exports good i and imports the others. Inter-country transfers are ruled out.

Let $X^i = (X^i_1, X^i_2, X^i_3)$ be the vector of consumption goods for country i. Define t^i_j to be the tariff charged by country i on good j. $t^i \equiv (t^i_1, t^i_2, t^i_3)$ is the vector of country i's tariffs and $t \equiv (t^1, t^2, t^3)$ is the world tariff vector. Assume that consumption is a function of tariffs, $X^i(t)$, so that social utility can be expressed as a function of tariffs:

$$U^i(X^i(t)) = U^i(t). \tag{1}$$

Given fixed endowments, technology and preferences, social utility depends on the vector of tariffs chosen. It is this choice of tariffs that is of interest. Additionally, one can think of tariffs as strategies and (1) as the payoff function. The determination of tariff rates is the outcome of some game whose payoffs are in terms of social utility.

The two-country tariff game has been widely analyzed [Johnson (1958), Riezman (1982), Mayer (1981), Thursby and Jensen (1983), Kennan and Riezman (1984)]. With three countries there is a serious complication. Pairs of countries can cooperate and pursue joint strategies against the third country. How this possibility affects the outcome is the focus of this research.

With three countries there are five distinct cooperation possibilities. There could be no cooperation. All countries could cooperate or any pair of countries (there are three distinct pairs) could cooperate.

Suppose no countries cooperate. Assume they adopt a Nash non-cooperative strategy. They each set their tariff rates to maximize utility assuming other tariffs are fixed. Equilibrium is attained when

$$\frac{\partial U^i(t)}{\partial t^i_j}=0, \quad \text{for } i,j=1,2,3. \tag{2}$$

Call this the optimal tariff equilibrium. This is the same equilibrium analyzed by Johnson (1958) and Kennan and Riezman (1984) in the two-country case. Kennan and Riezman (1982) produce three-country examples that exhibit the same qualitative results. At the optimal tariff equilibrium one country could gain (over free trade) and the others lose or all countries could lose.

We assume that cooperation consists of two or more countries setting tariffs between them to zero and a common tariff to the rest of the world.[1] A two-country coalition conforms to the usual notion of a customs union, and a three-country coalition (complete cooperation) corresponds to free trade. We rule out all inter-country transfers.[2] While it may be that transfers are important, to analyze them one first has to know what happens in their absence. Thus, one could use the model developed here to determine what transfers would take place and what the resulting equilibrium would be.

In general, there is a conflict of interest between members of a customs union on the level of its external tariff. To deal with this problem assume that one member of a customs union determines the joint external tariff.[3] Call this member the dominant country and list it first. For example, in a $\{3,2\}$ customs union countries 2 and 3 are members, 3 is the dominant country which sets the external tariff.

It is now possible to define equilibrium with a customs union. Suppose customs union $\{2,1\}$ forms. t^* is an equilibrium when customs union $\{2,1\}$ form if

(i) $t^{*1}_2 = t^{*2}_1 = 0$;

(ii) $t^{*1}_3 = t^{*2}_3$;

(iii) $\partial U^2(t^*)/\partial t^2_3 = 0$;

(iv) $\partial U^3(t^*)/\partial t^3_j = 0, \quad \text{for } j=1,2.$

Other customs unions are similarly defined.

Assume that for each possible customs union a unique tariff equilibrium and consumption allocation exists. This means that each country can associate a unique payoff to each customs union and to the optimal tariff equilibrium. One could relax this uniqueness assumption, but another source

---

[1] One justification for the zero tariff assumption is the existence of Most Favored Nation treaties which requires this.

[2] I assume that the tariff revenues collected at a country's borders are retained by the collecting country.

[3] This formulation is not critical to the results that follow, merely more convenient. The problem of setting the external tariff is another game which can be analyzed as such. For example, one could analyze the problem as a three-stage game: (1) coalitions chosen; (2) each coalition decides how to set their joint tariff; (3) Nash equilibrium in tariffs occurs.

of uncertainty is introduced. If equilibrium is not unique, then each customs union could yield different outcomes. Any country's utility for a given customs union would be a set of possible values. Countries would then have to evaluate these uncertain payoffs in deciding whether or not to join a particular customs union. Dealing with this complication is left for future research.

In this section optimal tariff equilibrium, free trade and customs union equilibria have been defined. Given the behavioral assumptions made, each country associates a unique outcome with every coalitional possibility. Coalitional choice is analyzed next.

3. Coalition choice

A theory of coalitional choice is defined and discussed below. The core solution concept is adapted to our problem.

For convenience, number the eight possible coalition structures:

1. $\{1\}\ \{2\}\ \{3\}$,
2. $\{1\}\ \{2,3\}$,
3. $\{1\}\ \{3,2\}$,
4. $\{2\}\ \{1,3\}$,
5. $\{2\}\ \{3,1\}$,
6. $\{3\}\ \{1,2\}$,
7. $\{3\}\ \{2,1\}$,
8. $\{1,2,3\}$.

Coalition structure number 1 corresponds to the optimal tariff equilibrium with no customs unions and number 8 is free trade. Each of the other coalition structures involves a particular customs union.

Define $A_j \equiv (X^1, X^2, X^3)$, $j = 1$–8, to be the allocation of consumption goods for all countries when coalition structure j prevails. Each country's utility can be expressed as a function of the allocation, $U^i(A_j)$ being the utility of country i when allocation j (coalition structure j) occurs.

To define the core we need to know how a country evaluates membership in a particular coalition. For two- and three-country coalitions it is straightforward because each such coalition corresponds to a unique allocation. Countries use the utility levels at the relevant allocation to evaluate two- and three-country coalitions. For example,

$$U^2(\{3,\ 2\}) = U^2(A_3). \tag{2}$$

Country 2 uses the utility level it receives under A_3 to evaluate its membership in a $\{3,2\}$ customs union since A_3 must be the result if $\{3,2\}$ forms.

One-country coalitions are more complicated because any of three allocations can occur when a one-country coalition forms. For example, if $\{1\}$ forms than A_1, A_2 or A_3 could occur depending on what countries 2 and 3 do. We assume that countries are pessimistic and act as if they receive the lowest of the three possible utility levels. In the above example,

$$U^1(\{1\}) = \min\,[U^1(A_1),\, U^1(A_2),\, U^1(A_3)].$$

This assumption makes one-country coalitions less likely to block. However, we have an example where a one-country coalition blocks an allocation despite this assumption. We are now able to define the core.

Definition. A_j is in the *core* if it is unblocked by any possible coalition. A coalition S *blocks* allocation j if, for all $i \in S$,

$$U^i(S) \geqq U^i(A_j),$$

with strict inequality for at least one member of S.

Our use of the core concept is different than the usual definition in two respects.[4] Limits are put on the cooperation allowed within a coalition (i.e. they must have free trade within the coalition) and transfers within a coalition are not allowed. The core concept implicitly describes the game of coalitional choice.

It implies that countries cooperate and communicate about the various possibilities and act voluntarily. Countries decide whether to join or not join a customs union depending on payoffs to the various customs unions. This is realistic in the sense that countries are never forced to enter into international agreements, but cannot prevent others from doing so. Allocations in the core are stable in the sense that it does not pay any member of a coalition to change the coalition structure.

The core solution concept has a natural interpretation, namely allocations which are in the core will be observed. If, for example, A_4 is the only allocation in the core, the model would imply a customs union between countries 1 and 3 with country 1 dominant. If A_8 is the only coalition in the core, then the model would predict free trade.

It is possible that the core is empty. This possibility and conditions for nonemptiness are discussed in Riezman (1980). In what follows, unless specified otherwise, assume a nonempty core. We next discuss the impli-

---

[4]See Luce and Raiffa (1957) for further discussion of the core concept.

cations of the core solution concept for customs union formation and attainment of free trade by examining some examples.

4. Examples[5]

Three examples are presented to illustrate how the core solution concept determines a pure exchange equilibrium. Preferences are the same for each country, Cobb–Douglas, and symmetric in the three goods. Each country differs only by endowments of commodities. The examples are chosen so that the trade pattern turns out to be the assumed one. The endowments are given by the matrix Y. For example 1 (table 1):

$$Y = \begin{pmatrix} 2 & 0.6 & 0.6 \\ 0.1 & 1.1 & 0.1 \\ 0.1 & 0.1 & 1.1 \end{pmatrix}.$$

The ijth element of Y is country i's endowment of commodity j. (Notice that countries 2 and 3 are symmetric.) The results are fully reported in tables 1–3.

In this example A_1 is blocked by $\{2,3\}$ and $\{3,2\}$ because 2 and 3 are better off forming a customs union than at the noncooperative optimal tariff equilibrium. Free trade, A_8, is blocked by $\{1\}$, $\{1,2\}$, $\{2,1\}$, $\{1,3\}$ and $\{3,1\}$. Country 1 is better off with tariffs regardless of whether or not 2 and 3 form a customs union. Any customs union with country 1 blocks free trade. All allocations with country 1 in a two-country customs union, A_4, A_5, A_6 and A_7, are blocked by $\{1\}$. Intuitively, country 1 does better by itself because when it forms a customs union it has to share too much of the gains it receives from charging tariffs with its customs union partner. A_2 and A_3 are unblocked and therefore are in the core. Hence, in example 1, we would observe allocations A_2 or A_3, a customs union between countries 2 and 3.

This example is interesting in a number of respects. Notice that both countries 2 and 3 are worse off than free trade. This shows that customs unions do not necessarily improve the members' welfare compared to free trade. Rather, one can interpret this customs union as the best response to a third country who benefits from a tariff war. Also, notice that country 1 gains from any tariff equilibrium as compared to free trade. Thus, in the absence of inter-country transfers country 1 would never agree to free trade.

Compare the $\{1,2\}$ customs union with the $\{2,3\}$ customs union. If country 2 could pay country 1 a small bribe they could both be better off with a $\{1,2\}$ customs union. In this sense $\{1,2\}$ is more beneficial for its members than the $\{2,3\}$ customs union. Thus, the core does not necessarily

---

[5]For more details about these examples, see Keenan and Riezman (1982).

Table 1

$$\text{Example 1: } Y = (Y^i_j) = \begin{pmatrix} 0.2 & 0.6 & 0.6 \\ 0.1 & 1.1 & 0.1 \\ 0.1 & 0.1 & 1.1 \end{pmatrix}.$$

	Utility	Tariffs	Prices	Consumption
(A_8) Free trade equilibrium	$(3001.08, 2921.66, 2921.66)$	$\begin{pmatrix} 0 & 0 & 0 \\ 0 & 0 & 0 \\ 0 & 0 & 0 \end{pmatrix}$	$(0.1515, 0.1852, 0.1852)$	$\begin{pmatrix} 1.1556 & 0.9455 & 0.9455 \\ 0.5222 & 0.4273 & 0.4273 \\ 0.5222 & 0.4273 & 0.4273 \end{pmatrix}$
(A_1) Optimal tariff equilibrium	$(3004.30, 2902.81, 2902.81)$	$\begin{pmatrix} 0 & 2.04 & 2.04 \\ 0.77 & 0 & 0.92 \\ 0.77 & 0.92 & 0 \end{pmatrix}$	$(0.2143, 0.1468, 0.1468)$	$\begin{pmatrix} 1.7020 & 0.8176 & 0.8176 \\ 0.2490 & 0.6455 & 0.3369 \\ 0.2490 & 0.3369 & 0.6455 \end{pmatrix}$
(A_2) CU $\{2,3\}$ equilibrium	$(3002.44, 2907.20, 2907.20)$	$\begin{pmatrix} 0 & 1.90 & 1.90 \\ 0.54 & 0 & 0 \\ 0.54 & 0 & 0 \end{pmatrix}$	$(0.2048, \ 0.1526, \ 0.1526)$	$\begin{pmatrix} 1.7130 & 0.7925 & 0.7925 \\ 0.2435 & 0.5037 & 0.5037 \\ 0.2435 & 0.5037 & 0.5037 \end{pmatrix}$
(A_6) CU $\{1,2\}$ equilibrium (1 sets tariff)	$(3002.39, 2929.04, 2891.27)$	$\begin{pmatrix} 0 & 0 & 1.40 \\ 0 & 0 & 1.40 \\ 0.76 & 0.75 & 0 \end{pmatrix}$	$(0.1762, 0.2156, 0.1246)$	$\begin{pmatrix} 1.3073 & 1.0684 & 0.7692 \\ 0.6278 & 0.5130 & 0.3694 \\ 0.2650 & 0.2186 & 0.6614 \end{pmatrix}$
(A_7) CU $\{2,1\}$ equilibrium (2 sets tariff)	$(3001.73, 2932.31, 2870.39)$	$\begin{pmatrix} 0 & 0 & 3.70 \\ 0 & 0 & 3.70 \\ 0.59 & 0.58 & 0 \end{pmatrix}$	$(0.1952, 0.2387, 0.0782)$	$\begin{pmatrix} 1.3443 & 1.0990 & 0.7129 \\ 0.6714 & 0.5489 & 0.3561 \\ 0.1842 & 0.1521 & 0.7311 \end{pmatrix}$

$U^1(\{1\}) = 3002.44, \ U^2(\{2\}) = U^3(\{3\} = 2870.39,$

$U^1(\{1,2\}) = U^1(\{1,3\}) = 3002.39, \ U^2(\{1,2\}) = U^3(\{1,3\}) = 2929.04,$

$U^2(\{2,3\} = U^2(\{3,2\}) = U^3(\{2,3\}) = U^3(\{3,2\}) = 2907.20,$

$U^1(\{1,2,3\}) = 3001.08, \ U^2(\{1,2,3\}) = U^3(\{1,2,3\}) = 2929.66.$

Note: The utility numbers computed are

$$U^i = 3000 + 100 \sum_{j=1}^{3} 1/3 \ln X^i_j.$$

pick out the most beneficial customs unions. This is because the division of gain between members as well as overall gain both are taken into account in the coalition decision. In section 5, allowing inter-country transfers will be briefly discussed.

Examples 2 and 3 (tables 2 and 3) are examples of symmetric endowment patterns. In example 2, $\{2, 3\}$ blocks both A_1 and A_8. All customs unions allocations A_2–A_7 are unblocked and therefore in the core. The only prediction is that some customs union would be observed. This example is interesting because all countries are completely symmetric yet it still pays any pair of them to form a coalition. The intuition for this can be seen by thinking of the customs union as one country and considering the two-country tariff retaliation game. These two countries are no longer symmetric, the union has most of the world's endowment of two commodities. Therefore, they can turn the terms of trade in their favor by playing a joint strategy against the other country. In this example, it turns out that these terms of trade gains outweigh the efficiency loss that the tariffs induce.

Compare example 2 with example 3. Example 3 has a different symmetric endowment pattern. In this example $\{1, 2, 3\}$ blocks all other allocations, thus free trade is the only member of the core. In this case the efficiency loss outweighs the terms of trade gain and no customs union is beneficial. Again thinking about a customs union as one country these three examples mimic the standard two-country tariff retaliation results. One country could benefit or they both could lose as the result of a tariff war.

5. Transfer payments

Allowing inter-country transfer payments would alter the analysis. Kemp and Wan (1976) show that if transfers are allowed there always exists a transfer scheme that makes enlarging a customs union better for all member countries. The implication of this result is that given any initial tariff equilibrium there exists a set of transfers that makes everyone better off at free trade. This raises the question of whether the existence of transfers between countries would actually lead to free trade. This question arises because Kemp and Wan show that free trade with transfers is better for all countries but not that it is chosen as the equilibrium outcome.

To see the problem consider example 2. Suppose initially the $\{2, 3\}$ customs union forms. If transfers are allowed then country 1 could bribe 2 and 3 to move to free trade. Is this an equilibrium? No, because country 1 could pay a smaller bribe to country 2 to join in a customs union against 3. It is clear that free trade with transfers is not an equilibrium because no country would be willing to be the net transferor at free trade. This follows from symmetry and the fact that all countries do better in a customs union

Table 2

$$\text{Example 2: } Y = \begin{pmatrix} 0.3 & 0.1 & 0.1 \\ 0.1 & 0.3 & 0.1 \\ 0.1 & 0.1 & 0.3 \end{pmatrix}.$$

	Utility	Tariffs			Prices	Consumption		
(A_8) Free trade equilibrium	(2820.82, 2820.82, 2820.82)	0	0	0	(0.6667, 0.6667, 0.6667)	0.1667	0.1667	0.1667
		0	0	0		0.1667	0.1667	0.1667
		0	0	0		0.1667	0.1667	0.1667
(A_1) Optimal tariff equilibrium	(2818.52, 2818.52, 2818.52)	0	0.56	0.56	(0.6667, 0.6667, 0.6667)	0.2192	0.1404	0.1404
		0.56	0	0.56		0.1404	0.2192	0.1404
		0.56	0.56	0		0.1404	0.1404	0.2192
(A_2) CU $\{2, 3\}$ equilibrium	(2814.29, 2821.03, 2821.03)	0	0.46	0.46	(0.5799, 0.7101, 0.7101)	0.2296	0.1287	0.1287
		0.68	0	0		0.1352	0.1856	0.1856
		0.68	0	0		0.1352	0.1856	0.1856

Table 3

$$\text{Example 3: } Y = \begin{pmatrix} 1.1 & 0.1 & 0.1 \\ 0.1 & 1.1 & 0.1 \\ 0.1 & 0.1 & 1.1 \end{pmatrix}.$$

	Utility	Tariffs			Prices	Consumption		
(A_8) Free trade equilibrium	(2916.38, 2916.38, 2916.38)	0	0	0	(0.2564, 0.2564, 0.2564)	0.4333	0.4333	0.4333
		0	0	0		0.4333	0.4333	0.4333
		0	0	0		0.4333	0.4333	0.4333
(A_1) Optimal tariff equilibrium	(2901.91, 2901.91, 2901.91)	0	2.00	2.00	(0.2564, 0.2564, 0.2564)	0.7800	0.2600	0.2600
		2.00	0	2.00		0.2600	0.7800	0.2600
		2.00	2.00	0		0.2600	0.2600	0.7800
(A_2) CU $\{2, 3\}$ equilibrium	(2889.01, 2913.42, 2913.42)	0	1.76	1.76	(0.2075, 0.2809, 0.2809)	0.7967	0.2120	0.2120
		1.93	0	0		0.2516	0.5440	0.5440
		1.93	0	0		0.2516	0.5440	0.5440

than at free trade. Therefore, whether transfers would actually lead to free trade is an open question. Answering it is beyond the scope of this paper but it is an important issue and one that can be addressed using the model developed here.

6. Concluding comments

This paper develops a theory of customs unions in which the emphasis is on determining which customs unions are chosen rather than determining the effects of given customs unions. Most of the results are not surprising. Using examples we show that a customs union could be observed in which both countries are better off than at free trade. Or, as example 3 shows, all countries and customs unions could be worse off with tariffs than at free trade in which case free trade will be the outcome.

One surprising result is that a customs union could be an equilibrium outcome, even though both countries do worse than free trade. In this case, a customs union is the best response to a third country that benefits from a tariff war.

Several interesting extensions remain. Most important is to obtain more complete results on the second-stage analysis. The aim is to develop a theory which relates observable characteristics of economies to specific customs union outcomes. Other worthwhile extensions could be to relax the dominant country assumption and analyze the intra-customs union tariff bargaining problem. Finally, one might want to consider different first-stage solution concepts.

References

Dixit, A. and V. Norman, 1980, Theory of international trade (James Nisbet, Welwyn, UK).

Grinols, E.L., 1981, An extension of Kemp–Wan theorem on the formation of customs unions, Journal of International Economics 11 (2), May, 259–266.

Johnson, H., 1958, Optimal tariffs and retaliation, in: International trade and economic growth, ch. II (Harvard University Press, Cambridge).

Kemp, M. and H. Wan, 1976, An elementary proposition concerning the formation of customs unions, Journal of International Economics 6 (1), February, 95–97.

Keenan, J. and R. Riezman, 1982, Optimal tariff equilibria with customs unions, University of Minnesota discussion paper no. 82-172, December.

Keenan, J. and R. Riezman, 1984, Do big countries win tariff wars?, Mimeo., June.

Krauss, M.B., 1972, Recent developments in customs theory: An interpretive survey, Journal of Economic Literature 10 (2), June 413–426.

Lipsey, R.G., 1970, The theory of customs unions: A general equilibrium analysis (Weidenfeld and Nicolson, London).

Lloyd, P.J., 1982, 3 × 3 theory of customs unions, Journal of International Economics 12 (1/2), February, 41–63.

Luce, R.D. and H. Raiffa, 1957, Games and decisions (John Wiley and Sons, USA).

R. Riezman, Customs unions and the core 365

Mayer, W., 1981, Theoretical considerations on negotiated tariff adjustments, Oxford Economic Papers 33, 135–153.

Riezman, R., 1980, Coalition formation in the international economy, Mimeo.

Riezman, R., 1982, Tariff retaliation from a strategic viewpoint, Southern Economic Journal 48 (3), January, 583–593.

Thursby, M. and R. Jensen, 1983, A conjectural variation approach to strategic tariff equilibria, Journal of International Economics 14 (1/2), February, 145–162.

DO BIG COUNTRIES WIN TARIFF WARS?*

JOHN KENNAN AND RAYMOND RIEZMAN[1]

INTERNATIONAL ECONOMIC REVIEW
Vol. 29, No. 1, February 1988

INTERNATIONAL ECONOMIC REVIEW
Vol. 29, No. 1, February 1988

DO BIG COUNTRIES WIN TARIFF WARS?*

JOHN KENNAN AND RAYMOND RIEZMAN[1]

It is well known that large countries can manipulate the terms of trade to their advantage by using tariffs. It is widely believed, however, that this invites retaliation, and that the post-retaliation equilibrium leaves all countries worse off than they would be at free trade.[2] We present a simple pure exchange model and show which endowment patterns are consistent with this belief. In this model, we find that if one country is substantially bigger it can expect to gain from a tariff war, despite retaliation. Thus we suggest that big countries win tariff wars. We believe that this provides a potentially important explanation for the persistence of tariffs, and the difficulty of attaining free trade. Our model can also be extended to show that when more than two countries trade with each other, the advantage obtained by being part of a large trading unit can help explain the formation of customs unions (see Kennan and Riezman 1987).

Our model is similar to Johnson's (1953).[3] Johnson pointed out the problems that arise in a general model and simplified the analysis by assuming constant elasticity offer curves for each country. This implies that the optimal tariff for one country does not depend on the tariff set by the other.[4] We simplify in a different way, by assuming that each country's preferences generate a linear expenditure system. The main advantage of this is that we obtain explicit solutions, stating results not merely in terms of elasticities, but in terms of more fundamental (endowment) parameters.

We use a model with two countries, A and B, and two goods, X and Y. Each country contains many consumers with identical utility functions

$$(1) \qquad U^A = X^A Y^A \qquad U^B = X^B Y^B$$

where X^A, Y^A, X^B and Y^B denote consumption levels of each good in each country. We use this simple functional form for utility so as to obtain explicit solutions for optimal tariffs in terms of endowments and tastes.[5]

---

* Manuscript received July 1986; revised January 1987

[1] We thank Avinash Dixit and Forrest Nelson for valuable comments on an earlier draft.

[2] For example, Baumol and Blinder (1985, p. 743) assert that "Tariffs can benefit a country that is able to impose them without fear of retaliation. But when every country uses them, everyone is likely to lose in the long run."

[3] Johnson's original contribution led to models with more structure, such as Gorman (1958), Horwell (1966), Kuga (1973), and Otani (1980), or more complicated tariff strategies, such as Thursby and Jensen (1983), Mayer (1981) and Riezman (1982). In addition, Tower (1975) analyzed the use of quotas, while Kennan and Riezman (1987) and Hamilton and Whalley (1983) used simulation techniques to study tariff retaliation.

[4] Hamilton and Whalley (1983) discussed in some detail the restrictive nature of this assumption.

[5] See Kennan and Riezman (1986) for an analysis of logarithmic utility functions in which the goods are not weighted equally.

82   JOHN KENNAN AND RAYMOND RIEZMAN

We define the world endowment of each commodity to be one unit. Country A has γ units of X and B has $1 - \gamma$ units; country B has μ units of Y, and A has $1 - \mu$ units. The endowments are divided equally between consumers within countries. In equilibrium, A exports X to B, and imports Y from B.[6] Country A charges a tariff at the rate $S - 1$ on imports of Y, and B charges a tariff $T - 1$ on imports of X. World prices are denoted by P and Q, so the domestic price of Y in A is SQ, and the price of X in B is TP.

Consumers in A face prices P and SQ, and maximize U^A subject to the budget constraint

$$(2) \qquad PX^A + SQY^A = I^A = P\gamma + SQ(1 - \mu) + (S - 1)QY$$

Tariff revenue is included in income I^A, but individual consumers ignore the (negligible) effect of changes in Y^A on their share of tariff revenue. Utility is maximized by allocating equal expenditures to each good, so that

$$(3) \qquad \pi(\gamma - X) = \pi X^A = SY^A = S(1 - \mu + Y)$$

where π is the world price ratio P/Q. When the budget constraint (2) is used to eliminate π from equation (3) the result is A's offer curve:

$$(4) \qquad \frac{\gamma}{X} = \frac{S(1 - \mu)}{Y} + S + 1$$

Given any tariffs S and T, A's offer curve (4) and the analogous equation for B are linear in the reciprocals of imports and exports, so they can easily be solved to obtain the market-clearing consumption levels. Thus

$$(5) \qquad \begin{aligned} X^A = \gamma - X &= \frac{\gamma + (1 - \mu)T}{1 + (1 - \mu)T + \mu/S} \\[2mm] Y^A = (1 - \mu) + Y &= \frac{\gamma + (1 - \mu)T}{T + (1 - \gamma)ST + \gamma} \end{aligned}$$

Then A's utility level is

$$(6) \qquad U^A = X^A Y^A = \frac{[\gamma + (1 - \mu)T]^2}{[1 + (1 - \mu)T + \mu/S][T + (1 - \gamma)ST + \gamma]}$$

The optimal tariff problem for A is to choose a tariff which maximizes the utility of the representative consumer at the market-clearing levels of X^A and Y^A. From (6), the first-order condition for this problem is

$$(7) \qquad \frac{\mu}{S^2[1 + (1 - \mu)T + \mu/S]} = \frac{(1 - \gamma)}{1 + (1 - \gamma)S + \gamma/T}$$

This can be written as a quadratic equation in S which (implicitly) defines A's tariff reaction function. The reaction functions for the two countries can be solved

---

[6] We will use the symbols X and Y both as commodity labels and as volumes of trade in equilibrium.

DO BIG COUNTRIES WIN TARIFF WARS? 83

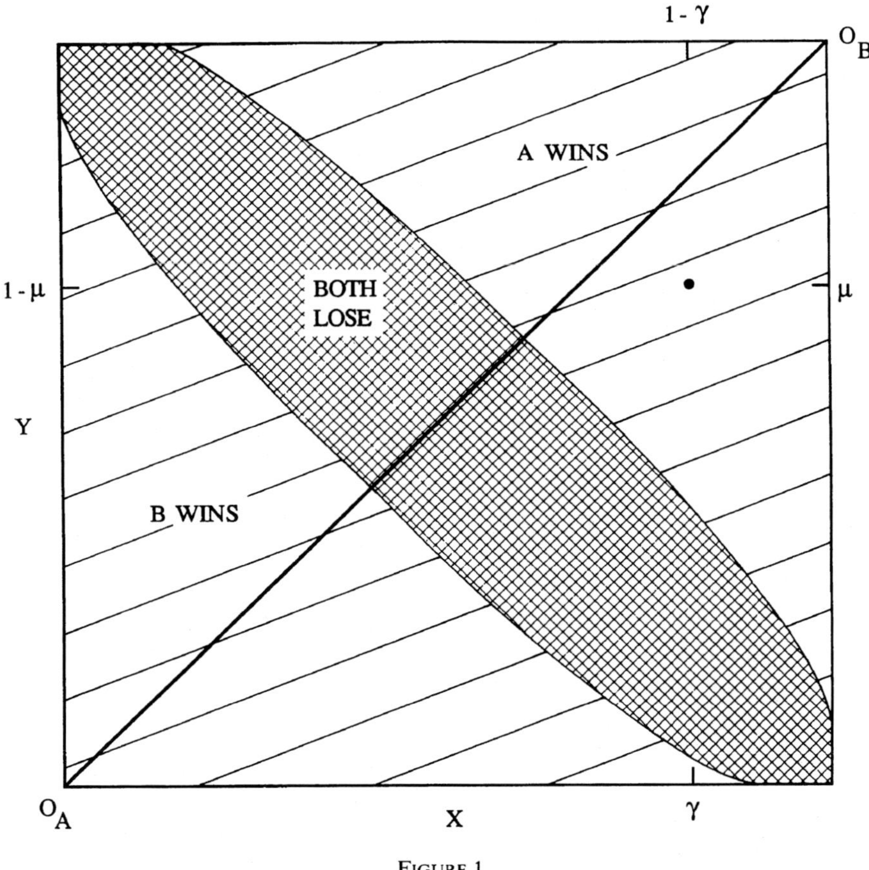

FIGURE 1

An Edgeworth box showing the endowment vectors for which countries A or B win a tariff war. The total world endowment of each good is defined to be one unit, so the box is a unit square. The region to the northeast of the cigar-shaped area is the set of endowment vectors which satisfy inequality (10) in the text: if the endowments are in this region A wins a tariff war. The region to the southwest of the cigar is defined by inequality (10) with the roles of a and b reversed (as if the box were rotated around the NW-SE diagonal). Here B wins a tariff war.

to obtain the Nash equilibrium tariffs, S^N and T^N, as functions of the endowments:

$$(8) \qquad T^N = a = \left[\frac{\gamma}{1-\mu}\right]^{1/2} \qquad S^N = b = \left[\frac{\mu}{1-\gamma}\right]^{1/2}$$

Although the offer curves do not have constant elasticity in our model, the elasticities calculated at the Nash equilibrium are simple: a is the offer curve elasticity for A, and b for B. Also, the equilibrium relative price is just $\pi = b/a$.

The Nash equilibrium utility level for A, U^{AN}, can be found by first expressing μ and γ as functions of a^2 and b^2, and then substituting for the tariffs in equation (6). A's utility level at free trade, U^{AF}, is found by setting $S = T = 1$ in equation

84   JOHN KENNAN AND RAYMOND RIEZMAN

(6). This gives

$$U^{AN} = \frac{a^{1/2}(b-1)}{ab-1} \qquad U^{AF} = \frac{(a^2+1)(b^2-1)}{2(a^2b^2-1)}$$

(9)

Thus A gains from a tariff war if

$$\frac{2a^{1/2}(1+ab)}{(1+a^2)(1+b)} > 1$$

(10)

This condition is interpreted in Figure 1. The endowments μ and γ determine a point in an Edgeworth box, and A wins a tariff war if inequality (10) holds at this point (with a and b defined by equation (8)). We assumed that the endowment vector was below the diagonal in the Edgeworth box (so that A exports X), but the argument can obviously be repeated for points above the diagonal, by interchanging X and Y.[7] Also, interchanging a and b in inequality (10) gives the condition for B to win a tariff war.

The cigar-shaped area in Figure 1 describes the circumstances where both sides lose a tariff war. If the endowment vector lies to the northeast of this area then A wins, and if it is to the southwest then B wins. We conclude that the possibility that one side or the other could win a tariff war is by no means remote. In particular, if one country is substantially bigger than the other, then the big country can expect to gain by starting a tariff war.

The University of Iowa, U.S.A.

REFERENCES

BAUMOL, W. J., AND A. S. BLINDER, *Economics: Principles and Policy*, 3rd edition (San Diego: Harcourt Brace Jovanovich, 1985).

GORMAN, W. M., "Tariffs, Retaliation and the Elasticity of Demand for Imports," *Review of Economic Studies* 25 (June, 1958), 133–162.

HAMILTON, B. AND J. WHALLEY, "Optimal Tariff Calculations in Alternative Trade Models and Some Possible Implications for Current World Trading Arrangements," *Journal of International Economics* 15 (November 1983), 323–348.

HORWELL, D. J., "Optimum Tariffs and Tariff Policy," *Review of Economic Studies* 33 (April 1966), 147–158.

JOHNSON, H. G., "Optimum Tariffs and Retaliation," *Review of Economic Studies* 21 (1953–1954), 142–153; revised version in H. G. Johnson, *International Trade and Economic Growth* (Cambridge: Harvard University Press, 1958).

KENNAN, J. AND R. RIEZMAN, "Do Big Countries Win Tariff Wars?" Economics Working Paper, No. 86-24, University of Iowa (July 1986).

———, "Optimal Tariff Equilibria with Customs Unions," Economics Working Paper, No. 86-23, University of Iowa (revised January 1987).

KUGA, K., "Tariff Retaliation and Policy Equilibrium," *Journal of International Economics* 3 (November 1973), 351–366.

[7] If the endowment vector is exactly on the diagonal, there is no trade in equilibrium. Thus, although A gains from a tariff war when the endowment vector is in the northeast corner of the Edgeworth box, the gains shrink to zero on the diagonal.

DO BIG COUNTRIES WIN TARIFF WARS?   85

MAYER, W., "Theoretical Considerations on Negotiated Tariff Adjustments," *Oxford Economic Papers* 33 (March 1981), 135–153.

OTANI, Y., "Strategic Equilibrium of Tariffs and General Equilibrium," *Econometrica* 48 (April 1980), 643–662.

RIEZMAN, R., "Tariff Retaliation from a Strategic Viewpoint," *Southern Economic Journal* 48 (January 1982), 583–593.

THURSBY, M. AND R. JENSEN, "A Conjectural Variation Approach to Strategic Tariff Equilibria," *Journal of International Economics* 14 (February 1983), 145–161.

TOWER, E., "The Optimum Quota and Retaliation," *Review of Economic Studies* 42 (October 1975), 623–630.

Optimal tariff equilibria with customs unions

JOHN KENNAN and RAYMOND RIEZMAN
University of Iowa

Abstract. We construct a model of customs unions in which countries charge optimal tariffs. Customs unions internalize the externality that exists whenever two countries import the same good. Also, customs unions make several countries into one large unit with more market power. Big customs unions can improve their members' welfare relative to the free trade. Our model of customs unions separates the effects of tariff reduction from the effects of policy co-ordination. The movement from Nash equilibrium to a Free Trade Association improves global resource allocation. Moving from a Free Trade Association to a full customs union has ambiguous resource allocation effects.

Equilibres avec droits de douane optimaux quand il y a union douanière. Les auteurs construisent un modèle d'union douanière dans lequel les pays imposent des droits de douane optimaux. Les unions douanières internalisent l'externalité qui existe quand deux pays importent le même bien. De plus, les unions douanières créent une unité plus grande qui a un pouvoir de marché agrandi en agrégeant plusieurs pays. Les grandes unions douanières peuvent améliorer le bien-être de leurs membres par rapport à ce que procurerait le libre échange. Le modèle d'union douanière proposé sépare l'effet des réductions de droits de douane de l'effet de la coordination de politiques. Le déplacement d'un équilibre à la Nash vers une association de libre-échange améliore l'allocation globale des ressources. Un déplacement d'une association de libre-échange vers une union douanière complète a des effets ambigus sur l'allocation de ressources.

I. INTRODUCTION

Since Jacob Viner's pioneering work (1950), customs union research has focused on isolating characteristics of customs unions that affect worldwide economic efficiency. Customs unions are usually analysed by comparing a particular customs

We thank Forrest Nelson for valuable comments on earlier drafts. The final version of the paper was completed while Kennan was a visiting scholar at the Hoover Institution. Kennan acknowledges funding from the National Science Foundation, under grant SES-8607771.

Canadian Journal of Economics   Revue canadienne d'Economique, XXIII, No. 1
February   février 1990. Printed in Canada   Imprimé au Canada

0008-4085 / 90 / 70–83 $1.50 © Canadian Economics Association union equilibrium with some arbitrarily given tariff equilibrium (e.g., see Lloyd 1982). The choice of the customs union's common external tariff has been extensively discussed using what Corden (1984) calls the 'non-optimality assumption,' which allows customs unions (and also non-member countries) to set non-optimal tariffs. (See, e.g., Vanek 1965, Takayama 1972, Kemp and Wan 1976, and Grinols 1986.)

While this line of research has been useful, it ignores some interesting questions, such as: (1) What are the nationalistic motivations for customs union membership? (2) Will the process of customs union formation lead toward free trade? (3) What determines which countries choose to form a customs union? (4) How does a custom union choose the common external tariff?

In seeking to answer questions of this sort, the natural assumption is that self-interest dictates what tariffs countries choose and which customs unions they join. We view the process as a two-stage game. In the second stage, tariffs are chosen for a given coalition structure.[1] In the first stage, countries chose coalition partners. In this paper we analyse the second stage of this game, since it is logically prior to the first: to understand how coalitions form one must first understand the equilibrium that would result from any given coalition structure.[2]

We construct a model in which all countries charge optimal tariffs, given the coalition structure and the tariffs charged by other countries.[3] Members of a customs union have internal free trade and jointly set a common optimal external tariff. Customs union equilibria are compared with a Nash equilibrium in tariffs, and with free trade. This makes the non-member country's reaction to the customs union's tariff policy explicit.

An inevitable difficulty is that the analysis of optimal tariffs is very complicated, even when customs unions are not considered (see, e.g., Otani 1980). We simplify the problem by considering a pure exchange economy in which commodity demands in each country are generated by a linear expenditure system. This model delivers explicit formulae for the effects of alternative tariff patterns on world prices, trade volumes, and consumption levels, and optimal tariffs can then be calculated by numerical methods for any given specification of preferences and endowments. We use this framework to generate examples with three countries and three goods which illuminate some important strategic issues in customs union theory.

The first issue concerns the circumstances in which a customs union can improve the welfare of its members compared with free trade, even when the non-member country retaliates with its own optimal tariffs. To investigate this we develop an

---

1 See Riezman (1985) for further discussion of the coalition formation game.

2 See Hamilton and Whalley (1983) and Markusen and Wigle (1987) for empirical studies of whether actual tariff rates are at the levels that optimal tariff theory would suggest.

3 Arndt (1968, 1969) presented a general discussion of customs union tariff policy, assuming that pre-union tariffs were optimal, but without solving explicitly for optimal post-union tariffs. Takayama (1972) obtained some results on optimal customs union tariffs: a zero tariff between members is optimal, and the standard optimal tariff formula applies to the union's tariff to the third country. This latter result depends crucially on his assumption that there are only two goods: in our 3×3 model, for example, if customs union members have asymmetric endowments, they will have different optimal external tariffs.

72 John Kennan and Raymond Riezman

example in which endowments are symmetric and all countries have the same preferences. We find that whenever each country's endowment of its export good is not too large, relative to the total world endowment, any pair of countries can benefit (compared with free trade) by forming a customs union. This stands in sharp contrast to the more familiar results for a symmetric two-country model, where both countries lose a tariff war (see Johnson 1958 and Kennan and Riezman 1988). In the three-country case this is still true, but only if countries cannot form customs unions.

This example has some interesting implications. In a symmetric world where any pair of countries can benefit from a customs union it is difficult to see how free trade could be an equilibrium, since each pair of countries has an incentive to defect. Thus the possibility of customs unions may be an additional barrier to free trade rather than a 'stepping stone' toward free trade.

In the symmetric example we can compute the set of endowments for which customs unions are beneficial, albeit for a special case. In this context we show that the size of a customs union relative to the excluded country is important in determining whether the customs union can improve its members' welfare. Thus, one motivation for customs union formation is to make the member countries into one larger country for the purposes of trade policy, so that they can compete more effectively with larger countries and with other customs unions.

Our examples also illustrate a pervasive externality associated with tariffs. When one country imposes tariffs on the goods it imports, the world prices of these goods fall, conferring an uncompensated benefit on all other countries that import the same goods. Customs unions internalize this externality by setting tariffs jointly: this provides another motivation for the formation of customs unions.

Finally, our examples illustrate the effects of customs union formation on prices, tariffs, and the volume of trade. Using these results we discuss the effect of trade agreements on global efficiency and the argument that customs unions are a 'stepping stone' to free trade.

II. A LINEAR EXPENDITURE SYSTEM WITH TARIFFS

We use a model in which n countries, indexed by the superscript i, trade m goods, indexed by the subscript j. Each country contains many consumers with identical utility function:

$$U^i = \sum_{j=1}^{m} \beta_j^i \log X_j^i, \quad \sum_{j=1}^{m} \beta_j^i = 1; \qquad i = 1, 2 \ldots n. \tag{1}$$

where U^i is the utility of country i, with taste parameters β_j^i, and X_j^i is the aggregate consumption of good j in country i, which is divided equally over individuals within the country.

Define the total world endowment of each commodity as one unit. Country i's endowment of good j is ω_j^i, so that $\sum_i \omega_j^i = 1$, for each good j. The endowments are divided equally between consumers within countries. The volume of trade in each good is $Z_j^i \equiv X_j^i - \omega_j^i$, where a negative value of Z_j^i means that country i exports good j, and a positive value denotes an import. Country i charges a tariff at the rate t_j^i on imports of good j.[4] The world price of good j is denoted by P_j, so the domestic price in i is $(1 + t_j^i)P_j$.

Consumers in i maximize U^i subject to the budget constraint

$$\sum_{j=1}^{m} P_j(1 + t_j^i)X_j^i = I^i = \sum_{j=1}^{m} P_j(1 + t_j^i)\omega_j^i + P_j t_j^i Z_j^i, \qquad i = 1, 2 \ldots n. \tag{2}$$

Income I^i includes the value of endowments at domestic prices, plus the net revenue from tariffs,[5] which is divided equally over individuals.[6] We assume that individual consumers ignore the (small) effect of changes in Z_j^i on their share of tariff revenue. The logarithmic form of U^i leads to a linear expenditure system, in which consumers spend a fixed proportion of their income on each commodity. The demand functions are

$$(1 + t_j^i)P_j X_j^i = \beta_j^i I^i, \qquad i = 1, 2 \ldots n, j = 1, 2 \ldots m. \tag{3}$$

Expenditure $E_j^i = P_j X_j^i$ on good j, valued at world prices P_j, and aggregate expenditure E^i, can then be written as $E_j^i = \theta_j^i I^i$ and $E^i = \theta^i I^i$, where

$$\theta_j^i = \frac{\beta_j^i}{1 + t_j^i} \text{ and } \theta^i = \sum_{j=1}^{m} \theta_j^i. \tag{4}$$

Thus expenditure is allocated across goods in the proportions $E_j^i = b_j^i E^i$, where $b_j^i = \theta_j^i / \theta^i$. This has the interpretation that the tariffs charged by country i cause the consumers in i to act as if their loglinear utility function had weights b_j^i instead of β_j^i.

The budget constraint (2) implies that, regardless of tariffs, the aggregate expenditure in each country must equal the value of the endowment vector, at world prices:

$$E^i = \sum_{j=1}^{m} P_j X_j^i = \sum_{j=1}^{m} P_j \omega_j^i \tag{5}$$

The world supply of each good is one unit, so the world price of each good is equal to aggregate world expenditure on that good:

$$\sum_{i=1}^{n} E_j^i = P_j \sum_{i=1}^{n} X_j^i = P_j \sum_{i=1}^{n} \omega_j^i = P_j, \qquad j = 1, 2 \ldots. \tag{6}$$

4 We allow export subsidies (i.e., negative tariffs on exports).

5 In the case of a customs union, we assume that each member country retains the tariff revenue from its own external trade (i.e., the customs union does not pool tariff revenues).

6 It is possible that the tariff system yields negative revenue, in which case the deficit is covered by lump-sum taxation.

74   John Kennan and Raymond Riezman

Thus prices can be written in terms of the expenditure variables E_j^i, and these are proportional to the aggregate expenditures E^i. Then, from equation (5),

$$E^i = \sum_{j=1}^{m} \sum_{s=1}^{n} b_j^s E^s \omega_j^i. \tag{7}$$

Define

$$\alpha_s^i \equiv \sum_{j=1}^{m} b_j^s \omega_j^i \tag{8}$$

Then equation (7) can be rewritten as

$$E^i = \sum_{s=1}^{n} \alpha_s^i E^s, \qquad i = 1, 2 \ldots n. \tag{9}$$

This is a system of n equations in the n variables E^i, but these equations are linearly dependent, since the units of expenditure are arbitrary. We normalize by setting aggregate world expenditure to 1, so that equation (9) can be replaced by the matrix equation

$$\begin{bmatrix} \alpha_1^1 - 1 & \alpha_2^1 & \cdots & \alpha_{n-1}^1 & \alpha_n^1 \\ \alpha_1^2 & \alpha_2^2 - 1 & \cdots & \alpha_{n-1}^2 & \alpha_n^2 \\ \cdots & \cdots & \cdots & \cdots & \cdots \\ \cdots & \cdots & \cdots & \cdots & \cdots \\ \cdots & \cdots & \cdots & \cdots & \cdots \\ \alpha_1^{n-1} & & \cdots & \alpha_{n-1}^{n-1} - 1 & \alpha_n^{n-1} \\ 1 & 1 & \cdots & 1 & 1 \end{bmatrix} \begin{bmatrix} E^1 \\ E^2 \\ \cdots \\ \cdots \\ \cdots \\ E^{n-1} \\ E^n \end{bmatrix} = \begin{bmatrix} 0 \\ 0 \\ \cdots \\ \cdots \\ \cdots \\ 0 \\ 1 \end{bmatrix} \tag{10}$$

The equilibrium expenditure levels are determined by this equation, since the coefficient matrix depends only on preferences, endowments, and tariffs. The equilibrium price vector can then be found from (6), and substitution of the demand functions (3) in the utility function (1) gives the utility levels resulting from any tariff pattern.

Equation (10) illustrates the complications involved in optimal tariff calculations. We did not consider production, and we assumed a nice functional form for preferences, but the effect of tariff variations on equilibrium consumption and utility levels is still far from transparent. Optimal tariffs cannot be determined analytically, except in very special cases (as illustrated in Kennan and Riezman 1988). Equations (10), (6), (3), and (1) do, however, provide an analytical expression for utility as a function of tariffs, for any given preference and endowment pattern, so that optimal tariffs can be determined numerically.

III. SOME ILLUSTRATIVE EXAMPLES

We develop four examples using the model described above, with three countries and three goods. These examples were chosen to highlight the effect of variations in two features of the world economy: the degree of symmetry across countries, and the size of each country in its export market. In the symmetric examples (A and B) the three countries are identical up to a relabelling of the goods. In this set-up we can consider how a customs union can arise for purely strategic reasons, rather than as a response to special features of the economy. In example A each country dominates its export market (in the sense that it has more than half of the world endowment) whereas exporters are not dominant in example B (each has half of the world endowment). The asymmetric examples were chosen to compare a small customs union (example C) with a large one (example D). The endowments in all four examples are such that each country exports one good and imports the other two in all of the equilibria we consider.[7]

In each example the countries' preferences are assumed to be symmetric over goods, in the sense that $\beta^i_j = 1/3$ for all i and j. In examples A and B the endowment matrix $\Omega = (\omega^i_j)$ is also symmetric. In examples C and D the endowment matrix is symmetric with respect to countries 2 and 3 only, with 1 being dominant in example C, and 2 and 3 dominant in example D. For each example we compute utility, optimal tariffs, prices, and consumption at four alternative equilibria: free trade (FT), Nash equilibrium (NE), free trade association (FTA), and customs union (CU). Free trade means that the tariff matrix $T = (t^i_j)$ is zero. Nash equilibrium means that no country could gain by changing its tariffs, given the tariffs charged by the other countries. This equilibrium is characterized by a system of six equations in the six off-diagonal elements of T, which we solved by a cobweb algorithm. The first country uses the procedure outlined in section II to find its optimal tariffs, given the tariffs set by 2 and 3. Then the second country chooses t^2_1 and t^2_3, given the other elements of T, and so on, until T repeats itself, indicating that no country desires to make further tariff adjustments.

An FTA is an agreement between two countries to eliminate tariffs on their two export goods, without restricting the tariffs charged on the third good. Here, the equilibrium tariff matrix is computed as in NE, except that tariffs within the FTA are set to zero. For example, to compute an FTA between countries 2 and 3 we fix t^2_3 and t^3_2 at zero and proceed as in the NE case.

In a customs union there is internal free trade (as in the FTA), and in addition the members jointly set a common tariff on the third good. This poses two new problems. First, a tariff externality exists. Second, members of a customs union will not necessarily agree on what the external tariff should be.

The tariff externality arises whenever two large countries import the same good, because a tariff imposed by one country lowers the price paid by both. A CU differs from an FTA in that this externality is internalized by having the members set the

---

7 This is one of two possible symmetric trade patterns, the other being where each country exports two goods and imports the other one.

76   John Kennan and Raymond Riezman

external tariff jointly. Although this generally involves a conflict of interest between the member countries we avoid this conflict by considering only symmetric cases, so that members of a customs union always agree on what the external tariff should be.[8]

To compute the tariff equilibrium when countries 2 and 3 form a customs union, for example, we fix t_3^2 and t_2^3 at zero. Then we compute tariffs as in NE except that countries 2 and 3 jointly choose both t_1^2 and t_1^3, with the constraint that these must be equal.

For each example, table 1 lists the endowment matrix assumed, and the equilibrium values of utility, tariffs, world prices, and consumption. When a customs union or free trade association exists, the member countries are 2 and 3, and 1 is the non-member. The utility function used is

$$U = 200 + 100 \sum_{j=1}^{3} 1/3 \log X_j^i.$$

IV. THE TARIFF EXTERNALITY

Member countries derive two distinct benefits from a customs union. In this section we discuss examples which illustrate the first of these, which comes from internalizing the tariff externality. In section VI we consider the benefit that comes from being part of a larger trading unit.

The only difference between the FTA and CU equilibria is that CU is computed by letting country 2 choose tariffs for both CU members. In example A, the effect of this is to increase the CU tariff from 42 per cent to 156 per cent. Country 1 responds by lowering its tariff to 134 per cent from 167 per cent. The increased CU tariff and lower non-member tariff are entirely attributable to internalizing the tariff externality. The other examples give similar results.

In all four examples the move from FTA to CU improves the terms of trade for CU members at the non-member's expense. Intra-customs union trade increases and trade between the customs union and the rest of the world decreases. Internalizing the tariff externality results in higher member country welfare and lower non-member welfare.

In examples A and C co-ordination of tariff policy fails to provide enough benefits for CU members to do better than they would at free trade. The co-ordination effect is large enough in examples B and D so that CU is better than FT for the member countries. These examples highlight the policy co-ordination role of customs unions. Next, we consider the effects customs unions have on efficiency.

V. RESOURCE ALLOCATION EFFECTS

Do customs unions improve the allocation of resources, relative to a Nash equilibrium in tariffs? This is a second-best problem with no general answer. A common

---

8 The appendix contains an example with asymmetric endowments, where the CU members disagree on the optimal external tariff.

TABLE 1

Examples

Example A: Symmetric, big exporters

$$\text{Endowments} \quad \Omega = \begin{bmatrix} 0.8 & 0.1 & 0.1 \\ 0.1 & 0.8 & 0.1 \\ 0.1 & 0.1 & 0.8 \end{bmatrix} \begin{array}{ccc} 1 & 2 & 3 \end{array}$$

Eq^m	Country	Utility	Tariffs			Prices	Consumption		
FT	1:	90.14	0	0	0	0.3333	0.3333	0.3333	0.3333
	2:	90.14	0	0	0	0.3333	0.3333	0.3333	0.3333
	3:	90.14	0	0	0	0.3333	0.3333	0.3333	0.3333
NE	1:	79.77	0	1.5414	1.5414	0.3333	0.5596	0.2202	0.2202
	2:	79.77	1.5414	0	1.5414	0.3333	0.2202	0.5596	0.2202
	3:	79.77	1.5414	1.5414	0	0.3333	0.2202	0.2202	0.5596
FTA	1:	86.91	0	1.6672	1.6672	0.3726	0.5534	0.2465	0.2465
	2:	84.95	0.4202	0	0	0.3137	0.2233	0.3767	0.3767
	3:	84.95	0.4202	0	0	0.3137	0.2233	0.3767	0.3767
CU	1:	68.80	0	1.3423	1.3423	0.2727	0.5754	0.1842	0.1842
	2:	88.56	1.5616	0	0	0.3636	0.2123	0.4079	0.4079
	3:	88.56	1.5616	0	0	0.3636	0.2123	0.4079	0.4079

Example B: Symmetric, small exporters

$$\text{Endowments} \quad \Omega = \begin{bmatrix} 0.5 & 0.25 & 0.25 \\ 0.25 & 0.5 & 0.25 \\ 0.25 & 0.25 & 0.5 \end{bmatrix} \begin{array}{ccc} 1 & 2 & 3 \end{array}$$

Eq^m	Country	Utility	Tariffs			Prices	Consumption		
FT	1:	90.14	0	0	0	0.3333	0.3333	0.3333	0.3333
	2:	90.14	0	0	0	0.3333	0.3333	0.3333	0.3333
	3:	90.14	0	0	0	0.3333	0.3333	0.3333	0.3333
NE	1:	89.34	0	0.3028	0.3028	0.3333	0.3944	0.3028	0.3028
	2:	89.34	0.3028	0	0.3028	0.3333	0.3028	0.3944	0.3028
	3:	89.34	0.3028	0.3028	0	0.3333	0.3028	0.3028	0.3944
FTA	1:	89.57	0	0.3099	0.3099	0.3368	0.3927	0.3045	0.3045
	2:	89.85	0.1273	0	0	0.3316	0.3037	0.3477	0.3477
	3:	89.85	0.1273	0	0	0.3316	0.3037	0.3477	0.3477
CU	1:	87.48	0	0.2388	0.2388	0.3022	0.4121	0.2881	0.2881
	2:	90.33	0.3982	0	0	0.3489	0.2940	0.3560	0.3560
	3:	90.33	0.3982	0	0	0.3489	0.2940	0.3560	0.3560

78   John Kennan and Raymond Riezman

TABLE 1 (*concluded*)

Examples

Example C: Asymmetric, small customs union

			Endowments	1	2	3

$$\Omega = \begin{bmatrix} 0.8 & 0.25 & 0.25 \\ 0.1 & 0.5 & 0.25 \\ 0.1 & 0.25 & 0.5 \end{bmatrix}$$

Eq^m	Country	Utility	Tariffs			Prices	Consumption		
FT	1:	116.38	0	0	0	0.3333	0.4333	0.4333	0.4333
	2:	73.89	0	0	0	0.3333	0.2833	0.2833	0.2833
	3:	73.89	0	0	0	0.3333	0.2833	0.2833	0.2833
NE	1:	117.36	0	1.2358	1.2358	0.3971	0.6226	0.3669	0.3669
	2:	67.11	0.4453	0	0.3133	0.3014	0.1887	0.3594	0.2737
	3:	67.11	0.4453	0.3133	0	0.3014	0.1887	0.2737	0.3594
FTA	1:	117.71	0	1.2490	1.2490	0.4003	0.6216	0.3691	0.3691
	2:	67.58	0.2486	0	0	0.2998	0.1892	0.3154	0.3154
	3:	67.58	0.2486	0	0	0.2998	0.1892	0.3154	0.3154
CU	1:	112.63	0	1.0473	1.0473	0.3511	0.6383	0.3375	0.3375
	2:	69.34	0.6920	0	0	0.3244	0.1808	0.3312	0.3312
	3:	69.34	0.6920	0	0	0.3244	0.1808	0.3312	0.3312

Example D: Asymmetric, big customs union

			Endowments	1	2	3

$$\Omega = \begin{bmatrix} 0.5 & 0.1 & 0.1 \\ 0.25 & 0.8 & 0.1 \\ 0.25 & 0.1 & 0.8 \end{bmatrix}$$

Eq^m	Country	Utility	Tariffs			Prices	Consumption		
FT	1:	54.47	0	0	0	0.3333	0.2333	0.2333	0.2333
	2:	104.11	0	0	0	0.3333	0.3833	0.3833	0.3833
	3:	104.11	0	0	0	0.3333	0.3833	0.3833	0.3833
NE	1:	43.33	0	0.4665	0.4665	0.2766	0.3222	0.1680	0.1680
	2:	98.85	1.2857	0	1.4740	0.3616	0.3389	0.5925	0.2395
	3:	98.85	1.2857	1.4740	0	0.3616	0.3389	0.2395	0.5925
FTA	1:	49.79	0	0.5315	0.5315	0.3181	0.3098	0.1888	0.1888
	2:	104.38	0.2592	0	0	0.3409	0.3451	0.4056	0.4056
	3:	104.38	0.2592	0	0	0.3409	0.3451	0.4056	0.4056
CU	1:	36.61	0	0.3900	0.3900	0.2307	0.3417	0.1475	0.1475
	2:	106.11	1.1583	0	0	0.3846	0.3291	0.4262	0.4262
	3:	106.11	1.1583	0	0	0.3846	0.3291	0.4262	0.4262

procedure in analysing customs unions (see Lloyd 1982) is to compare some arbitrary initial tariff equilibrium with a customs union, assuming that the non-member is passive and that the formation of the customs union does not affect the tariffs that members charge to non-members. This procedure is natural in models that do not specify how the tariffs were set in the first place, or how a customs union chooses its tariffs. These decisions are the focus of our model, which requires that pre- and post-union tariffs are optimal given the other tariffs. This implies a comparison between Nash equilibrium and customs union equilibrium.

The comparison between Nash and customs union equilibria can usefully be made in two steps: eliminating tariffs on the two goods that the member countries export (NE to FTA), and co-ordinating the tariffs charged by the CU members on the non-member country's good (FTA to CU). In all four examples moving from NE to FTA decreases the tariffs charged by the FTA members, and increases the non-member's tariffs. The terms of trade shift in favour of the non-member, but everyone is better off at FTA than at NE and both inter- and intra-FTA trade increase. In example A the non-member country actually benefits more from the move to FTA from NE than the members; in example B the members benefit more.[9]

We next consider the second step in the CU process: moving from an FTA to CU. In all the examples this leads to an increase in the tariffs charged by the customs union members and a decrease in the non-member's tariffs. The terms of trade shift in favour of the customs union, and there is more intra-CU trade and less trade between the CU member countries and the non-member country. The members' utility rises, while the non-member's utility falls.[10] Thus, the resource allocation effect of the move from FTA to CU is ambiguous.

The two steps have opposing effects on tariffs and on the terms of trade. The net effect on tariffs is ambiguous, but the terms of trade always move in favour of the customs union. Overall, the customs union increases the welfare of its members, while the non-member gains in the first step (NE to FTA) and loses in the second (FTA to CU). In our examples, the non-member's gains in the first step are outweighed by its losses in the second, so that the customs union benefits its members (relative to NE) at the expense of the non-member country.

VI. DO BIG CUSTOMS UNIONS WIN TARIFF WARS?

Even if endowments are symmetric and preferences are identical across countries, it may yet be true that each pair of countries has an incentive to defect from free trade and form a customs union. This was shown in example B. In this case it is difficult to see how free trade could be an equilibrium.

---

9 These results suggest that moving from NE to FTA is a 'stepping stone' towards freer trade, in that all countries gain from an improvement in the global allocation of resources. Recall, however, that our examples require that the FTA members have symmetric endowments. In the appendix we briefly discuss an example where this requirement is dropped, and we find that one FTA member is made worse off in the move from NE to FTA.

10 Although we do not specifically analyse unilateral tariff reductions (UTR), the external tariff coordination provided by a customs union is an additional reason why a customs union would be superior to UTR (see Wonnacott and Wonnacott 1981, 1984, and Berglas 1983).

80 John Kennan and Raymond Riezman

It can also happen, as was shown in example A, that each country is better off at free trade than it would be in any customs union. In this section we determine the set of symmetric endowments for which this result holds. We show that a customs union can improve welfare over free trade if the member countries are large enough.

When countries are symmetric the endowment matrix can be written as

$$\Omega(y) = \begin{bmatrix} y & 0.5(1-y) & 0.5(1-y) \\ 0.5(1-y) & y & 0.5(1-y) \\ 0.5(1-y) & 0.5(1-y) & y \end{bmatrix},$$

where y is each country's percentage share of the world endowment of their export good.

We let y vary from 0.98 to 0.36 and for each y we compute NE, CU, and FT, where the CU members are countries 2 and 3. The problem reduces to determining which values of y imply that customs unions improve members' welfare over free trade.[11] Since reporting the results for each y would be too cumbersome we report only a summary.

The critical value of y is (approximately) 0.66919. If each country's endowment of y (their export good) is less than 0.66919 then member countries do better at CU than at FT; otherwise they do worse. Of course, the non-member is worse off at CU no matter what the endowment.

This result may seem puzzling, since it means that customs unions are beneficial is y is small. We next show that y's being small is equivalent to the customs union's being large. This can be seen by collapsing the three-country model to two countries, treating the customs union as a single country. This can be done, since the customs union members (countries 2 and 3) decide their tariffs jointly and they are symmetric. In addition, since the relative price of goods 2 and 3 is always unity, these goods can be aggregated into a composite commodity. Note, however, that the customs union's preferences over good 1 and the composite good will not be symmetric.

We combine countries and aggregate goods and renormalize so that there is one unit of both good 1 and the composite good, with the resulting endowment matrix

$$\Omega_2(y) = \begin{bmatrix} y & 0.5(1-y) \\ 1-y & 0.5(1+y) \end{bmatrix}.$$

In a 2×2 version of this model with symmetric preferences Kennan and Riezman (1988) showed that a sufficient condition for a country to win a tariff war is that it be large in the sense that the sum of its endowments is greater than some critical number. It can also be shown that this condition remains approximately valid for a broad range of asymmetric preferences. In the present context this condition means

---

11 Following the discussion in section V above, note that the terms of trade move in favour of the customs union, for all values of y. In addition, the customs union members are always better off relative to NE, at the expense of the non-member.

that the customs union wins a tariff war if $(1 - y) + 0.5(1 + y) > 1.2$. This is equivalent to $y < 0.6$, which is close to the condition we derived in the 3×3 case. The difference is due to the fact that in the aggregated case the correct preferences would not be symmetric over goods. Hence, the condition that customs unions gain if $y < 0.66919$ means that customs unions that are big enough gain compared with free trade. In other words, customs unions can be regarded as a device to increase country size for the purposes of trade policy.

VII. CONCLUSION

The analysis of optimal tariff equilibria with customs unions presents a formidable theoretical puzzle, and general results in this area do not yet exist. As a first step, we have developed a prototype model which illustrates, by means of examples, some important pieces of the puzzle.

Two distinct motivations for customs union formation were demonstrated. First, a custom union enables its members to internalize the tariff externality that exists whenever two countries import the same good. Second, a customs union can make several countries into one larger one for the purpose of trade policy. If the customs union is big enough it can improve its members' welfare over free trade. One implication of this argument is that even if countries are initially symmetric, it may be difficult to sustain free trade as an equilibrium.

Our model was also used to separate the tariff reduction aspect of customs unions from the policy co-ordination aspect. The movement from a Nash equilibrium in tariffs to an equilibrium in which two of the countries form a Free Trade Association with zero internal tariffs improved global resource allocation. Moving from a Free Trade Association to a full customs union in which the member countries agree on a common external tariff had ambiguous resource allocation effects.

There are two obvious directions for further research. First, the robustness of the examples should be investigated, by extending the model to include production and by examining more general preferences. A particularly attractive prospect is that such a model could be used to analyse optimal tariff policies under imperfect competition. Perhaps the best way to do this is to embed our optimal tariff calculations within the computable general equilibrium models of Whalley (1985, 1986) or Harrison (1986). Second, the model can provide a base on which to build a practical framework for empirical applications. For example, it might be used to analyse how the initial formation and subsequent expansion of the European Community affected tariffs charged on U.S. exports to Europe, and tariffs charged by the United States on imports from Europe. The model could also be used to study the effect of the Canada-U.S. free trade agreement on their external tariff policies and the response of the EEC and Japan to these changes.

APPENDIX: AN ASYMMETRIC CUSTOMS UNION

Here we give an example (table A1) in which an FTA makes one of its members worse off, relative to Nash equilibrium. The endowments of countries 2 and 3 are not

82   John Kennan and Raymond Riezman

symmetric, so they do not set the same tariff on good 1 when they form an FTA: country 2 picks 17 per cent and 3 picks 37 per cent. Country 3 is made worse off in the move from NE to FTA. The reason for this is that country 3 is large and can use tariffs to turn the terms of trade in its favour. The FTA restricts this market power, and country 3's terms of trade substantially deteriorate.

The example also illustrates the conflict of interest between CU members when endowments are not symmetric. Two alternative equilibria are shown: in CU_2 country picks the common external tariff, and in CU_3 country 3 picks the tariff. Either version of the customs union makes the members better off relative to both free trade and Nash equilibrium.

TABLE A1

$$\text{Endowments} \quad \Omega = \begin{bmatrix} 0.5 & 0.15 & 0.05 \\ 0.25 & 0.7 & 0.05 \\ 0.25 & 0.15 & 0.9 \end{bmatrix} \quad \begin{matrix} 1 & 2 & 3 \end{matrix}$$

Eq^m	Country	Utility	Tariffs			Prices	Consumption		
FT	1:	54.47	0	0	0	0.3333	0.2333	0.2333	0.2333
	2:	90.14	0	0	0	0.3333	0.3333	0.3333	0.3333
	3:	116.38	0	0	0	0.3333	0.4333	0.4333	0.4333
NE	1:	37.96	0	0.4203	0.5044	0.2580	0.3196	0.1984	0.1220
	2:	74.76	0.8142	0	1.0120	0.2925	0.3043	0.4868	0.1575
	3:	117.92	2.3359	2.5167	0	0.4493	0.3760	0.3146	0.7204
FTA	1:	49.53	0	0.4517	0.6072	0.3160	0.3104	0.1957	0.1802
	2:	91.23	0.1658	0	0	0.3452	0.3206	0.3422	0.3488
	3:	115.93	0.3678	0	0	0.3386	0.3689	0.4620	0.4709
CU_2	1:	42.54	0	0.3878	0.5268	0.2708	0.3242	0.1722	0.1590
	2:	91.26	0.6617	0	0	0.3674	0.2929	0.3587	0.3645
	3:	118.04	0.6617	0	0	0.3616	0.3828	0.4689	0.4764
CU_2	1:	33.63	0	0.2829	0.4145	0.2083	0.3543	0.1444	0.1328
	2:	90.97	1.5341	0	0	0.3984	0.2773	0.3675	0.3725
	3:	119.33	1.5341	0	0	0.3931	0.3682	0.4880	0.4946

REFERENCES

Arndt, Sven (1968) 'On discriminatroy vs. non-preferential tariff policies.' *Economic Journal* 78, 971–9
— (1969) 'Customs unions and the theory of tariffs.' *American Economic Review* 59, 108–18
Berglas, Eitan (1983) 'The case for unilateral tariff reductions: foreign tariffs rediscovered.' *American Economic Review* 73, 1141–2
Corden, Max (1984) 'The normative theory of international trade.' In R. Jones and P. Kenen, *Handbook of International Economics*, vol. 1 (Amsterdam: North-Holland)

Grinols, Earl (1986) 'Foreign investment and economic growth: characterization of a second best policy for welfare gains.' *Journal of International Economics* 21, 165–72

Hamilton, Bob and John Whalley (1985) 'Optimal tariff calculations in alternative trade models and some possible implications for current world trading arrangements.' *Journal of International Economics* 15, 323–48

Harrison, Glenn (1985) 'A general equilibrium evaluation of tariff reductions.' In Srinivasan and Whalley, eds, *General Equilibrium Trade Policy Modeling* (Cambridge, MA: MIT Press)

Johnson, Harry G. (1958) 'Optimum tariffs and retaliation.' *Review of Economic Studies* 21, 142–53; revised version in chap II of H.G. Johnson, *International Trade and Economic Growth* (Cambridge, MA: Harvard University Press)

Kemp, Murray and Henry Wan (1983) 'An elementary proposition concerning the formation of customs unions.' Reprinted in J. Bhagwati, ed., *International Trade: Selected Readings* (Cambridge, MA: MIT Press)

Kennan, John and Raymond Riezman (1988) 'Do big countries win tariff wars?' *International Economic Review* 29, 81–5

Lloyd, Peter J. (1982) '3 × 3 theory of customs unions.' *Journal of International Economics* 12, 41–64

Markusen, James and Randall Wigle (1987) 'Nash-equilibrium tariffs for the U.S. and Canada: the roles of country size, scale economies and capital mobility.' Paper presented at the Sixth Annual Conference on International Trade Theory, London, Ont., 11–12, April

Otani, Yoshihiko (1980) 'Strategic equilibrium of tariffs and general equilibrium.' *Econometrica* 48, 643–62

Riezman, Raymond (1985) 'Customs unions and the core.' *Journal of International Economics* 19, 355–66

Takayama, Akira (1972) *International Trade* (Holt, Rinehart & Winston)

Vanek, Jaroslav (1965) *General Equilibrium of International Discrimination* (Cambridge, MA: Harvard University Press)

Viner, Jacob (1950) *The Customs Union Issue* (New York: Carnegie Endowment for International Peach)

Whalley, John (1985) *Trade Liberalization Among Major World Trading Areas* (Cambridge, MA: MIT Press)

— (1985) 'Impacts of a 50% tariff reduction in an eight-region global trade model.' In Srinivasan and Whalley, eds, *General Equilibrium Trade Policy Modelling* (Cambridge, MA: MIT Press)

Wonnacott, Paul and Ronald Wonnacott (1981) 'Is unilateral tariff reduction preferable to a customs union? The curious case of the missing foreign tariffs.' *American Economic Review* 71, 704–14

— (1984) 'How general is the case for unilateral tariff reduction?' *American Economic Review* 74, 491

Journal of International Economics 30 (1991) 267–283. North-Holland

Dynamic tariffs with asymmetric information

Raymond Riezman*

University of Iowa, Iowa City, IA 52242, USA

Received June 1989, revised version received September 1990

Recent developments in dynamic game theory are applied to determine when two countries can sustain freer trade given that they determine trade policies non-cooperatively. Countries know their own level of protection, but not the other country's level of protection. Using import trigger strategies, cooperation (in the form of low tariffs) can be supported, although there are periodic reversionary (high tariff) episodes. However, if terms of trade trigger strategies are used, cooperation does not occur.

1. Introduction

Recent developments in the theory of repeated games has been applied to try to better understand protection of international trade. This paper's contribution is to view protection as the outcome of a repeated game in which countries cannot perfectly observe other countries' protection policies.[1] The main purpose is to argue that the lack of perfect information about protection policies is central to understanding protection of international trade.

The notion that protection is not perfectly observable can be justified on factual and theoretical grounds. Current U.S. trade legislation includes a new provision called Trade Liberalization Priorities (Super 301) which revises section 301 of the 1974 trade bill. This new provision directs the U.S. Trade Representative to identify trade practices and countries that hinder U.S.

*I thank Pat Conway, Russell Cooper, Avinash Dixit, James Friedman, Howard Gruenspecht, John Kennan, Ramon Marimon, Doug McManus, Roger Myerson, Rob Porter, Jennifer Reinganum, participants at the Mid-West International Economics Group meetings, the University of Western Ontario, and two anonymous referees for helpful comments and suggestions.

[1]An early version of the dynamic problem by Jensen and Thursby (1980) uses the idea of approximate equilibria; a paper by Mayer (1981) focuses on different negotiation schemes to reduce tariffs; Enders (1986) examines different punishment schemes; Dixit (1987) determines when cooperation breaks down; Bagwell and Staiger (1988) have a model in which the level of protection depends on the volume of trade; and Ludema (1989) determines optimal trade agreements. All of these papers assume that protection is observable. Copeland (1989) does consider imperfect observability of protection.

exports the most. These priority countries would then face retaliation from the United States if a negotiated agreement to reduce these barriers to U.S. exports could not be reached. Thus, it is not clear a priori which countries or practices this applies to, and the provision for retaliatory action suggests that the offending countries and the USTR may not agree on what constitutes unfair trade practices.

A provision which failed to be included in the current trade bill took a more direct approach to the same problem. This amendment, which has become known as the Gephardt Bill, proposes punishing Japan with higher U.S. tariffs if the bilateral trade deficit is above some predetermined level. The rationale behind this bill is that the Japan–U.S. trade deficit is due to hidden protection by the Japanese. The Gephardt Bill is a trigger strategy in which the punishment is higher U.S. tariffs which are triggered by certain realizations of the Japan–U.S. trade deficit. This threat of punishment would discourage Japan from using hidden protection to the extent that this protection affects the trade deficit.

This proposed legislation generated a great deal of public discussion during which it became apparent that there is great disagreement over how much Japan actually protects its imports. Japanese tariffs are not especially high and have been substantially reduced in recent years. Yet many feel that Japan effectively keeps out U.S. imports with a variety of non-tariff trade barriers. Opponents of the Gephardt Bill argue that no such hidden protection exists and that the U.S. trade deficit is due to the inability of U.S. industries to compete with the Japanese. This debate suggests that U.S. policy-makers do not know how much Japan protects imports, and it raises the question of how policy should be conducted in light of this fact.

Theory suggests that it may be difficult to know the extent of foreign protection. For example, in simple models a 10% tariff can be replicated by a 10% consumption tax along with a 10% production subsidy. In more complicated models it may be difficult to exactly replicate the effects of tariffs with domestic policies, but one can always use domestic policies to manipulate international trade. Therefore, any agreement to eliminate or reduce tariffs is limited by the fact that countries can cheat on the agreement by using domestic policies or other forms of protection not covered by the agreement. Ray and Marvel (1984) have shown that following the Kennedy round of tariff reductions, U.S. industries were able to replace tariffs that had been negotiated away with other forms of protection.

The theory of political economy explains non-tariff forms of protection by arguing that politicians use them in order to disguise protection from the voters. Then, inadvertently, political considerations might work to make protection less observable to foreigners. Thus, the facts and the theory suggest that viewing protection as not observable to foreigners is appropriate.

The basic model we use comes from Dixit (1987). He develops the standard prisoner's dilemma tariff model and shows that in an infinitely repeated game, cooperation (free trade) can be attained for some period of time provided that the gains from tariffs are not too large and that the discount factor is not too small. We extend his model in two directions. We add uncertainty in the underlying model and non-observability of protection.

We use recent work in game theory which has demonstrated how cooperative outcomes can be sustained when the game is played repeatedly, defectors are punished, but agents play non-cooperatively. Recent papers examine how a group of firms, acting non-cooperatively, can produce the monopoly level of output when they can observe other firms' output levels [Rotemberg and Saloner (1986)] and when they cannot observe other firms' output levels [Green and Porter (1984), Abreu, Pearce and Stacchetti (1986)].

We use the Green and Porter methodology to determine when two countries can sustain freer trade given that they determine trade policies non-cooperatively. The Green and Porter trigger strategies are simple, have a straightforward economic interpretation in our problem, and seem to correspond to practical policy measures (such as Super 301 or the Gephardt Bill).[2]

In section 3 we analyze the effect of adding uncertainty when protection is perfectly observable. This model works much like Dixit's except that certain realizations of the random variable can trigger tariff wars. Rotemberg and Saloner (1986) take a different approach by focusing on how much cooperation can be sustained under varying demand conditions.

Protection is not observable in section 4. Here, using import trigger strategies, cooperation (in the form of low tariffs) can be supported. As in Green and Porter (1984) there are periodic reversionary (high tariff) episodes which necessarily occur. They are not the result of mistakes, attempted manipulation, or misperception. Neither country cheats on the low tariff agreement, but reversions to high tariffs are triggered by the random variable. In spite of this, countries go along with the reversionary episodes because they realize that high tariff periods are necessary to provide each country with the correct incentives to sustain the low tariff episodes. In addition, the high tariff equilibria are short-run Nash equilibria. The extent and duration of cooperation depends on the form of the trigger strategy and the actual parameter values. Thus, it is not clear whether free trade is a possibility, nor is it clear whether cooperative periods or reversionary periods are more prevalent.

---

[2]Recent work by Abreu, Pearce and Stacchetti (1987) and Fudenberg and Maskin (1986) examine more general prisoner's dilemma games. Their results suggest that the Green–Porter strategies may not be optimal. A direction for future research is to characterize optimal protection policies when protection is not observable.

In section 5 we examine a slightly different trigger strategy. Countries' strategies are based on their observations of the terms of trade. This alteration changes the results and in this case cooperation does not occur. This result is in sharp contrast to section 4 and to the results of Green and Porter (1984) who find that in the case of oligopoly, cooperation can be attained for periods of time. However, our result does indicate a major difference between the tariff problem and the oligopoly problem. In the oligopoly problem firms try to cheat in the same direction, namely they all want to produce a little more, selling it at the monopoly price. This pushes the price down, no matter which firm does it. When the price falls below a certain level a reversion to Cournot outputs and prices is triggered. Symmetric punishments make sense since there is no way to determine (even ex post) which firm cheated. In the tariff problem, the countries are trying to push the terms of trade in opposite directions, hence the reversion to Nash tariffs occurs if the terms of trade are too high or too low. It turns out that a country gets punished when it could not have been cheating, and in this case symmetric punishments do not induce cooperation.

These results show that whether protection is observable or not matters. When protection cannot be observed, as in section 4, some cooperation can be achieved, but it may be quite limited. In particular, free trade might not be a possibility. Reversions to high tariffs occur, but for different reasons than when tariffs are observable. In the observable case, reversions occur because a realization of the random variable makes cheating worthwhile. In the model with non-observable protection, countries never cheat, but reversions occur because the observable variable is pushed below some predetermined level by a realization of the random variable. Also, as section 5 makes clear, the choice of the mechanism used to induce cooperation is crucial. If the 'wrong' trigger strategy is chosen, then no cooperation will be achieved.

2. The model

The basic model employed is from Dixit (1987). There are two countries, home and foreign (foreign country variables are denoted by an asterisk) and two competitive industries producing goods x and y. The home country imports x, the foreign country imports y and countries can levy positive or negative tariffs (τ, τ^*) on imports. There are four prices, p_x, p_y, p_x^*, and p_y^*, and they are related by the following:

$$p_x = p_x^*(1+\tau), \qquad p_y^* = p_y(1+\tau^*).$$

Define $\pi = p_x^*/p_y$, the international relative price or terms of trade. Notice that the home country prefers lower values of π, and the foreign country likes higher values. We ignore all intra-country income distribution issues. The justification for this is based on optimal taxation considerations. Since tariffs are far down the list of desirable policies to accomplish any redistribution of income, there is no a priori reason to think that income redistribution considerations will be important in the determination of tariffs.

Each country has a social welfare function, $U(\pi, \tau)$ and $U^*(\pi, \tau^*)$. These give rise to import demand functions $M(\pi, \tau)$ and $M^*(\pi, \tau^*)$. Equilibrium occurs when the balance of payments is zero:[3]

$$\pi M(\pi, \tau) = M^*(\pi, \tau^*).$$

This determines a function $\pi(\tau, \tau^*)$, which we assume to be continuous and differentiable.

We now adopt the view that countries select tariff policies that maximize expected social welfare over an infinite horizon, and hence view the tariff game as an infinitely repeated game. Uncertainty arises because of shocks to preferences or endowments, and is manifested by the fact that home imports have a random component. We assume

$$M_t = \theta_t M(\tau_t, \tau_t^*),$$

where θ_t is i.i.d. with c.d.f. F and continuous density f, $E(\theta_t) = 1$.[4] Substituting this expression for imports into the balance of payments condition, π_t, M_t, and M_t^* can be written as functions of τ_t, τ_t^*, and θ_t.

Social welfare can now be expressed as

$$W(\tau_t, \tau_t^*, \theta_t) = U(\pi_t(\tau_t, \tau_t^*, \theta_t), \tau_t),$$

with a similar expression for the foreign country. The problem facing the home country is

$$\max_{\tau} \sum_{t=0}^{\infty} E \beta^t W(\tau_t, \tau_t^*, \theta_t). \tag{1}$$

where $\tau = (\tau_0, \tau_1, \tau_2, \ldots)$ and β is the discount factor.

Assume that the Marshall–Lerner conditions hold and that all tariff revenues are redistributed to consumers, so that raising tariffs improves the terms of trade:

---

[3]An interesting extension would be to allow for trade imbalances. This will introduce an additional set of intertemporal considerations [see Marimon (1988)].

[4]Different assumptions about the timing and observability of θ_t will be made in other sections of the paper.

$$\frac{\partial \pi_t}{\partial \tau_t} < 0, \qquad \frac{\partial \pi_t}{\partial \tau_t^*} > 0.$$

In addition, assume that starting from a zero tariff a country's welfare improves when it imposes a small tariff, and one country is always hurt by increases in the other country's tariff.[5] As a one-shot game, the tariff game results in a prisoner's dilemma in which charging tariffs is a Nash equilibrium, yet there are gains available if free trade can be attained.[6]

Our approach to cooperation is to assume that countries do not formally cooperate, but adopt strategies that can lead to cooperation over time [see Friedman (1971)]. Such mechanisms involve strategies in which defectors from the cooperative equilibrium are punished. However, the punishments must be credible in the sense that if defection does occur the other country will actually carry out the punishment; that is, the game must be subgame perfect. One convenient way to do this is to make the punishment be a finite reversion to the one-period equilibrium strategies (see, for example, Green and Porter). In our model this would mean that the punishment would involve countries adopting the one-shot Nash equilibrium tariffs for some fixed number of periods.[7] We will analyze two different models: one in which the random shock and tariffs are observable and one in which they are not.

3. Observable tariffs

In this section all tariffs and random variables are observable. We assume that both countries adopt trigger strategies [see Friedman (1971)] which require free trade if free trade occurred in the previous period.[8] Any defection from free trade is punished by a reversion to Nash equilibrium tariffs. In this section, for analytical convenience, we assume that the Nash reversion is infinite. More generally, one could consider finite reversions (which we do later), and other choices for the reversion equilibrium (autarky for example) to determine optimal punishments.

The timing critically affects the results. Suppose tariffs are chosen simultaneously, then θ is revealed. Free trade is sustained as long as it never pays a country to defect. That is, if the one-period gain from defection is less than the discounted stream of losses from having Nash tariffs for ever, then free

---

[5]Once autarky is reached, this last statement has to be modified because further increases in tariffs have no effect.

[6]In what follows we ignore one potential Nash equilibrium, i.e. autarky. As discussed in Enders (1986), this is a weak equilibrium.

[7]These are not necessarily jointly optimal strategies in the sense that harsher punishments might be better because they would induce longer periods of cooperation or a greater degree of cooperation.

[8]We rule out state contingent tariff agreements.

trade is chosen. At time T the home country will choose free trade if (2) holds:

$$\text{E}_{\theta}\,(W(\tau^0, 0, \tau_T) - W(0, 0, \theta_T)) < \sum_{t=T+1}^{\infty} \beta^t\,\text{E}_{\theta}\,(W(0, 0, \theta_t) - W(h, h^*, \theta_t)), \quad (2)$$

where τ^0 is the standard optimal tariff and h, h^* are the one-shot Nash tariffs. The left-hand side gives the one-period expected gain to cheating by charging the optimal tariff. The right-hand side gives the expected discounted losses that occur because from the next period on high tariffs will be charged by both countries instead of free trade. If the LHS is smaller than the RHS, then there is no incentive for the home country to cheat on a free trade agreement. A similar condition exists for the foreign country. This condition is essentially the same as Dixit's. Free trade can be sustained by tacit cooperation, provided β is not too small.

Different timing changes the results. Suppose that θ is revealed first, followed by the simultaneous choice of tariffs. The left-hand side of (2) changes because the value of θ is known when tariffs are chosen. The condition for free trade to be sustained becomes:

$$W(\tau^0, 0, \theta_T) - W(0, 0, \theta_T) < \sum_{t=T+1}^{\infty} \beta^t\,\text{E}_{\theta}\,(W(0, 0, \theta_t) - W(h, h^*, \theta_t)). \quad (3)$$

Interpreting θ as a temporary shock any realization of θ affects only the LHS of (3). Realizations of θ that make the LHS of (3) larger increase the likelihood that tariff reversions are triggered. For example, values of θ that make the foreign offer curve very inelastic would increase the gains from the optimal tariff and hence increase the likelihood of high tariff episodes.

This framework can be used to develop testable models of tariff wars. Specifying particular motivations for protection will yield specific versions of inequality (3). For example, one could suppose welfare depended on employment, or the terms of trade, or one could formulate a political economy version in which the function W is an outcome of a political process [see Feenstra and Lewis (1987)]. Then, differentiating with respect to θ gives predictions about what triggers reversions to high tariffs. This hypothesis can then be tested by examining periods of high and low levels of protection.

4. Non-observable tariffs – import trigger strategy

In this section we assume that countries cannot observe the tariffs of other countries, nor can they observe the random variable, θ. The motivation for this is that since tariffs can be replaced exactly by the correct combination of domestic policies (an equal percentage production subsidy and consumption tax or appropriate behavior on the part of a state trading agency) protection is in a real sense not observable. To some extent the current dispute with Japan over the U.S. trade deficit is an example of this phenomenon. Much of the debate concerns the extent of actual Japanese protection, with the Japanese pointing to their relatively modest tariffs and the United States claiming that the local Japanese price of goods imported from the United States are much higher than they should be based on these tariff rates.

One way to interpret what follows is that there are observable and non-observable forms of protection. Assume that the observable tariffs are zero, for example because of international treaties, so that only non-observable protection can be used. For analytical convenience we will assume that non-observable protection takes the form of tariffs.[9]

We use the model developed in section 2, except that countries now observe only π_t, M_t (and therefore M_t^*) and their own tariff, with the other country's past and current tariffs and past and current θ_t not observable. Countries use the same type of strategy as before, but since they do not know directly what tariff the other country is charging, their strategies have to be conditioned on observables. This problem is similar to the one solved by Green and Porter for an oligopoly. What follows draws heavily from their model.

Countries have trigger strategies, s and s^*, defined by

$$s = (s_0, s_1, \ldots), \quad s^* = (s_0^*, s_1^*, \ldots),$$

$$s_0 = \tau_0, \qquad s_0^* = r_0^*.$$

τ_0 and τ_0^* can be given initial tariffs. The strategy at time t depends only on the history of home imports up to time $t-1$[10]

$$s_t(M_0, \ldots, M_{t-1}) = \tau_t, \qquad s_t^*(M_0, \ldots, M_{t-1}) = \tau_t^*.$$

A Nash equilibrium is a pair $\bar{s}, \bar{s}^*$ for which

$$\mathop{\mathrm{E}}_{s,\,\bar{s}^*} \left\{ \sum_{t=0}^{\infty} \beta^t U(s_t(M_0, \ldots, M_{t-1}), \pi_t) \right\}$$

---

[9]We assume that tariffs are not observable throughout. This would be appropriate, for example, if the non-observable protection is equal percentage production subsidies and consumption taxes. Less efficient methods of protection may have to be used but the qualitative results will be unaffected by this.

[10]Strategies do not depend on past values of tariffs and θ_t, except to the extent that these variables influence M_t.

$$\leq \mathop{\mathrm{E}}_{\bar{s}, \bar{s}^*} \left\{ \sum_{t=0}^{\infty} \beta^t U(\bar{s}_t(M_0, \ldots, M_{t-1}), \pi_t) \right\}, \tag{4}$$

for all possible strategies s, with a similar condition for the foreign country.

An equilibrium occurs when both countries' strategies maximize discounted expected utility, taking the other country's strategy as given. This is the usual definition of Nash equlibrium, except that the strategies are trigger strategies. In this model, both countries realize that they are in a prisoner's dilemma game. They would prefer the low tariff outcome (free trade if possible) and will set low tariffs provided that the other country is also setting low tariffs. However, the other country's tariffs cannot be directly observed, nor, since there is uncertainty, can they be inferred by observing imports or the terms of trade.

What is done is to adopt a trigger strategy which requires them to keep tariffs low unless there is evidence that someone is cheating on the low tariff agreement. Both countries can observe the home country's imports.[11] If either country charges higher tariffs than the low tariff agreement rates, home imports will fall. If home imports fall below some predetermined critical level, then high (one-shot Nash) tariffs are used for a specified period of time. Thus, cheating can be detected, probabilistically, by observing home imports. In this way cheaters are deterred since if the cheating is detected, there will be high tariffs for some finite period of time. The punishment will actually be carried out, because the high tariffs are equilibrium tariffs in the one-shot game.

More formally, call the set of low tariffs (l, l^*) and the high tariffs (h, h^*). The low tariffs are endogenously determined and the high tariffs are the one-shot Nash tariffs. Countries choose the level of home imports, $\hat{M}$, that triggers reversion, and the length of the reversionary period, T. We also require that at the low tariff equilibrium a small change in either tariff reduces home imports: $\partial M(l, l^*)/\partial l$ and $\partial M(l, l^*)/\partial l^*$ are negative.[12] Equilibrium requires that the trigger imports and length of the reversionary period be the same for both countries. Period t is normal if

$t = 0$, or

$t - 1$ normal and $M_t > \hat{M}$,

$t - T$ normal and $M_{t-T} < \hat{M}$.

---

[11]Presumably both countries can observe the foreign country's imports and, therefore, the terms of trade. The analysis would be the same if the punishment were triggered on the foreign country's imports.

[12]A sufficient condition for this is that both offer curves are elastic at the low tariff equilibrium.

Otherwise t is reversionary. We now can determine the tariff at any time t:

$$\tau_t = \begin{cases} l, & t \text{ normal,} \\ h, & t \text{ reversionary,} \end{cases}$$

$$\tau_t^* = \begin{cases} l^*, & t \text{ normal,} \\ h^*, & t \text{ reversionary.} \end{cases}$$

Thus, $(l, l^*, h, h^*, T, \hat{M})$ characterize an equilibrium. The plan of attack is to choose arbitrary T and $\hat{M}$, and use the one-shot Nash tariffs for h and h^* and solve for the l and l^* that will occur in normal periods. Clearly, the choice of T and $\hat{M}$ will affect the actual values of l and l^*, but our goal here is to characterize the equilibrium and show how cooperative trade agreements can be sustained by repetition even when protection is not observable.

Define

$$\hat{V}(\tau_t, \tau_t^*) = \mathop{\mathrm{E}}_{\theta_t} \sum_{t=0}^{\infty} \beta^t(W(\tau_t, \tau_t^*, \theta_t),$$

with a similar definition for the foreign country. Let $V(r)$ $[V^*(r^*)]$ be discounted expected utility when $\tau_t = r$ $(\tau_t^* = r^*)$ in normal periods, that is

$$V(r) = \hat{V}(r, l^*), \qquad V^*(r^*) = \hat{V}^*(l, r^*).$$

Let $\gamma(r)$ be the one-period expected utility of setting the tariff equal to r given that the foreign country sets its tariff low:

$$\gamma(r) = \mathop{\mathrm{E}}_{\theta_t} W(r, l^*, \theta_t) \quad \text{and} \quad \gamma^*(r^*) = \mathop{\mathrm{E}}_{\theta_t} W^*(l, r^*, \theta_t).$$

Expected utility in reversionary periods is δ and δ^*:

$$\delta = \mathop{\mathrm{E}}_{\theta_t} W(h, h^*, \theta_t) \quad \text{and} \quad \delta^* = \mathop{\mathrm{E}}_{\theta_t} W^*(h, h^*, \theta_t).$$

We assume that $\gamma(l) > \delta$ and $\gamma^*(l^*) > \delta^*$, that is, expected utility is higher with low tariffs than high tariffs for both countries. This assumption is restrictive since it assumes that no country can do better with Nash tariffs than at the low tariff equilibrium. As shown in Kennan and Riezman (1988), countries with a big enough size advantage might benefit from high tariffs.

V and V^* satisfy the equations:

$$V(r) = \gamma(r) + \beta \Pr(\theta_t M(r, l^*) > \hat{M})V(r)$$

$$+ [1 - \Pr(\theta_t M(r, l^*) > \hat{M})]\left[\sum_{t=1}^{T-1} \beta^t \delta + \beta^T V(r)\right], \tag{5}$$

$$V^*(r^*) = \gamma^*(r^*) + \beta \Pr(\theta_t M(l, r^*) > \hat{M})V^*(r^*)$$

$$+ [1 + \Pr(\theta_t M(l, r^*) > \hat{M})]\left[\sum_{t=1}^{T-1} \beta^t \delta^* + \beta^T V^*(r^*)\right]. \tag{6}$$

For each country the probability of no reversion, given that the other country charges low tariffs, is a function of its tariff:

$$\Pr(\theta_t M(r, l^*) > \hat{M}) = 1 - F(\hat{M}/M(r, l^*)) \equiv 1 - b,$$

$$\Pr(\theta_t M(l, r^*) > \hat{M}) = 1 - F(\hat{M}/M(l, r^*)) = 1 - b^*. \tag{7}$$

Then (5) becomes:

$$V(r)(1 - \beta(1 - b) - b\beta^T) = \gamma(r) + b \sum_{t=1}^{T-1} \beta^t \delta. \tag{8}$$

With some straightforward algebraic manipulation, this becomes:

$$V(r) = \frac{\gamma(r) + \dfrac{b(\beta - \beta^T)}{1 - \beta}\delta}{1 - \beta + b(\beta - \beta^T)}.$$

This in turn simplifies to

$$V(r) = \frac{\gamma(r) - \delta}{1 - \beta + b(\beta - \beta^T)} + \frac{\delta}{1 - \beta}. \tag{9}$$

The interpretation of (9) is that the home country's expected utility of tariff rate r is the gain from the low tariff agreement plus the utility with high tariffs, appropriately discounted. The corresponding expression for the foreign country is

$$V^*(r^*) = \frac{\gamma(r^*) - \delta^*}{1 - \beta + b^*(\beta - \beta^T)} + \frac{\delta^*}{1 - \beta}. \tag{10}$$

If (l, l^*) is a Nash equilibrium, then given $\hat{M}$, h, h^*, and T:

$$V(r) < V(l), \quad \text{for all } r, \tag{11}$$

and

$$V(r^*) < V(l^*), \quad \text{for all } r^*. \tag{12}$$

The first-order conditions are

$$V'(l) = 0 \tag{13}$$

and

$$V^{*\prime}(l^*) = 0. \tag{14}$$

Using (7), (9) and (10), (13) becomes:

$$[1 - \beta + (\beta - \beta^T)(F(\hat{M}/M(l, l^*)))\gamma'(l)$$

$$+ (\gamma(l) - \delta)(\beta - \beta^T)f(\hat{M}/M(l, l^*))(\partial M(l, l^*)/\delta l)(\hat{M}/M(l, l^*)^2) = 0, \tag{15}$$

and for the foreign country (14) becomes:

$$[1 - \beta + (\beta - \beta^T)(F(\hat{M}/M(l, l^*)))\gamma'(l^*)$$

$$+ (\gamma^*(l^*) - \delta^*)(\beta - \beta^T)f(\hat{M}/M(l, l^*))(\partial M(l, l^*)/\partial l^*)(\hat{M}/M(l, l^*)^2) = 0. \tag{16}$$

Eqs. (15) and (16) give the necessary conditions for equilibrium with trigger strategies to exist under the conditions stated above. These equations are analogous to the equilibrium conditions in Green and Porter [see their eq. (6)]. The first term is the marginal gain from an increase in the tariff given that the other country has low tariffs. For both countries this term is positive. The second term gives the marginal loss due to the expected change in the probability that a reversionary episode is triggered by this increase in tariffs. The components of the second term are all positive except for $\partial M(l, l^*)/\partial l$ in (15) and $\partial M(l, l^*)/\partial l^*$ in (16), which are negative since any increase in tariffs reduces the volume of trade. Thus, no country cheats in equilibrium since the expected one-period gain from doing so is exactly offset by the discounted expected losses that occur because cheating on the low tariff agreement increases the probability that reversion to high tariffs occurs.

However, as in the Green–Porter model, reversions to the punishment phase, i.e. high tariffs, will be triggered by the random variable. Even though each country knows it is not optimal for either country to cheat, it is rational to participate in the high tariff phase because countries understand the incentives of the dynamic equilibrium which require that the punishment phase actually occur. Thus, the empirical prediction of the model is that there will be periods of low tariffs and periods of high levels of protection, i.e. trade wars. In this model, these reversions to high tariffs are not some kind of mistake or miscalculation; rather they are necessary to sustain the low tariff periods. Another interesting feature is that the tariff rates observed in the low tariff phase are affected by tariff rates in the one-shot Nash game. Thus, over time, if the underlying one-shot Nash game changes, so will l and l^*.

There is one aspect of the tariff problem that is different from the oligopoly problem. In the oligopoly case, the punishment phase is triggered by the price falling below some level. Even ex post there would be no way to determine which firm, if any, cheated on the agreement (firm output is only observable to the firms themselves). Thus, having all firms share equally in the punishment makes sense. The same is not true in the tariff case. Presumably the terms of trade are observable. Suppose the punishment is triggered and the terms of trade move in favor of the home country. In this case it seems very unlikely that the foreign country cheated on the low tariff agreement. Yet, the foreign country will be punished. Intuitively, it seems that there is useful information available that is not being used to detect cheating. In the next section we examine this more closely by changing the model of this section to have the punishment triggered by the terms of trade instead of home imports. As we will see, the results are quite different.

5. Non-observable tariffs – terms of trade trigger

In this section, countries use observations of the terms of trade to detect cheating on the low tariff agreement. The model is the same as section 4 with the following modifications. The strategy at time t depends on the history of prices up to time $t-1$:

$$s_t(\pi_0, \ldots, \pi_{t-1}) = \tau_t, \qquad s_t^*(\pi_0, \ldots, \pi_{t-1}) = \tau_t^*.$$

A Nash equilibrium is a pair $\bar{s}, \bar{s}^*$ for which

$$\mathop{\mathrm{E}}_{s, \bar{s}^*} \left\{ \sum_{t=0}^{\infty} \beta^t U(s_t(\pi_0, \ldots, \pi_{t-1}), \pi_t) \right\}$$

$$\leqq \mathop{\mathrm{E}}_{\bar{s}, \bar{s}^*} \left\{ \sum_{t=0}^{\infty} \beta^t U(\bar{s}_t(\pi_0, \ldots, \pi_{t-1}), \pi_t) \right\}, \tag{4'}$$

for all possible strategies s. There is a similar condition for the foreign country.

Countries keep tariffs low if the terms of trade stays within a predetermined range. If world prices are outside that range, then high (one-shot Nash) tariffs are used for a specified period of time. Thus, cheating can be detected, probabilistically, by observing prices. In this way cheaters are deterred since if the cheating is detected, there will be high tariffs for some finite period of time. As before, the punishment will actually be carried out because the high tariffs are equilibrium tariffs in the one-shot game.

As in section 4, call the set of low tariffs (l, l^*) and the high tariffs (h, h^*). Countries choose the price that triggers reversion on the low end π_l, the high end π_h, and the length of the reversionary period T. Equilibrium requires that the trigger prices and length of the reversionary period be the same for both countries. Period t is normal if

$t = 0$, or

$t - 1$ normal and $\pi_l < \pi_t < \pi_h$, or

$t - T$ normal and either $\pi_{t-T} < \pi_l$ or $\pi_{t-T} > \pi_h$.

Otherwise t is reversionary. The tariffs at any time are

$$\tau_t = \begin{cases} l, & t \text{ normal,} \\ h, & t \text{ reversionary,} \end{cases}$$

$$\tau_t^* = \begin{cases} l^*, & t \text{ normal,} \\ h^*, & t \text{ reversionary.} \end{cases}$$

Using the same approach as section 4, V and V^* satisfy the functional equations:

$$V(r) = \gamma(r) + \beta \Pr(\pi_l < \theta_t \pi(r, l^*) < \pi_h) V(r)$$

$$+ [1 - \Pr(\pi_l < \theta_t \pi(r, l^*) < \pi_h)] \left[\sum_{t=1}^{T-1} \beta^t \delta + \beta^T V(r) \right], \tag{5'}$$

$$V^*(r^*) = \gamma^*(r^*) + \beta \Pr(\pi_l < \theta_t \pi(l, r^*) < \pi_h) V^*(r^*)$$

$$+ [1 - \Pr(\pi_l < \theta_t \pi(l, r^*) < \pi_h)] \left[\sum_{t=1}^{T-1} \beta^t \delta^* + \beta^T V^*(r^*) \right]. \tag{6'}$$

Define

$$\Pr\left(\pi_l < \theta_t \pi(r, l^*) < \pi_h\right) = F(\pi_h/\pi(r, l^*)) - F(\pi_l/\pi(r, l^*)),$$

$$\Pr\left(\pi_l < \theta_t \pi(l, r^*) < \pi_h\right) = F(\pi_h/\pi(l, r^*)) - F(\pi_l/\pi(l, r^*)). \tag{7'}$$

Then (5′) becomes exactly the same as eq. (8) before. The analysis proceeds as in section 4, except (15) and (16) become:

$$[1 - \beta + (\beta - \beta^T)(1 - F(\pi_h/\pi(l, l^*)) + F(\pi_l/\pi(l, l^*)))]\gamma'(l)$$

$$+ (\gamma(l) - \delta)(\beta - \beta^T)\frac{\partial \pi(l, l^*)/\partial l}{\pi(l, l^*)^2}$$

$$\times [-f(\pi_h/\pi(l, l^*))\pi_h + f(\pi_l/\pi(l, l^*))\pi_l] = 0, \tag{15'}$$

and for the foreign country we have

$$[1 - \beta + (\beta - \beta^T)(1 - F(\pi_h/\pi(l, l^*)) + F(\pi_l/\pi(l, l^*)))]\gamma^{*\prime}(l^*)$$

$$+ (\gamma^*(l^*) - \delta^*)(\beta - \beta^T)\frac{\partial \pi(l, l^*)/\partial l^*}{\pi(l, l^*)^2}$$

$$\times [-f(\pi_h/\pi(l, l^*))\pi_h + f(\pi_l/\pi(l, l^*))\pi_l] = 0. \tag{16'}$$

Eqs. (15′) and (16′) give the necessary conditions for equilibrium with trigger strategies to exist under the conditions stated above. These equations are analogous to the equilibrium conditions (15) and (16). The first term is the marginal gain from an increase in the tariff given that the other country has low tariffs. For both countries this term is positive. The second term gives the marginal gain or loss due to the expected change in the probability that a reversionary episode is triggered by this increase in tariffs. The second term consists of four components: three are non-negative (by previous assumptions), but the third, which has $\delta\pi(l, l^*)/\partial l$ in (15′) and $\partial\pi(l, l^*)/\partial l^*$ in (16′), has opposite signs in the two equations. An increase in tariffs has opposite effects on the terms of trade. Suppose that $\partial\pi(l, l^*)/\partial l < 0$ and (15′) holds. Then, $\partial\pi(l, l^*)/\partial l^* > 0$ and (16′) cannot hold. Hence, it is impossible that both first-order conditions (15′) and (16′) hold simultaneously, and hence no trigger strategy equilibrium exists.[13]

This result stands in sharp contrast to Green and Porter and to the results of section 4. In the Green–Porter model equilibrium exists because firms

---

[13]The second terms of (15′) or (16′) could be zero, but if this is the case no equilibrium exists, since the first term is unambiguously positive. There are benefits, but no cost to cheating.

always cheat in the same direction. Cheating means selling more, which lowers the price, which in turn increases the probability that a reversionary episode is triggered. In their model the one-period gain from cheating is equated with the expected losses due to a higher probability of reversion. In the section 5 model each country's cheating pushes the relevant price in *opposite* directions. So, for example, if the home country cheats by increasing its non-observable tariff it gets the one-period gain and increases the probability of a reversion being triggered by π being too low. But, reversions are also triggered by π being too high, and the home country's cheating reduces the probability of this happening. What (15′) and (16′) taken together show is that for one of these countries cheating *lowers* the probability that reversion will occur. Hence, for one country it always pays to cheat, and there can be no low tariff equilibrium.

Section 4 fixes things up by having the reversion triggered when imports are too low. This works because any cheating lowers imports (given some restrictions on offer curve elasticities). Hence, any cheating causes the probability of reversion to increase. This suggests that low tariffs could be achieved using terms of trade trigger strategies by introducing asymmetric punishments so that the home (foreign) country only gets punished when π is too low (high). Then any cheating would increase the probability of reversion.

6. Conclusion

We have analyzed dynamic theories of tariffs when there is uncertainty and when protection is both observable and non-observable. If protection is observable, free trade can be sustained over time; however, there will be periodic reversions to high tariffs. This occurs because certain realizations of the random variable make cheating worthwhile. When tariffs are not observable, if countries use the correct trigger strategies, some degree of cooperation can be sustained. Periodic reversions will occur but for different reasons than in the observable case. Reversions occur because a realization of the random variable pushes the observable variable below some critical value. Even though no country cheats, it is still optimal for the reversion to take place. It remains to be determined under what circumstances free trade can be maintained, but the general conclusion is that there will be periods of high and low protection levels when countries use import trigger strategies. The high tariff episodes are necessary to provide the right incentives for countries to cooperate some of the time, and are not the result of irrationality or miscalculation.

Interesting extensions would be to analyze the terms of trade trigger strategy with asymmetric punishments. In addition, other types of strategies can be analyzed. Another important direction for future research is to consider finite horizon models. A longer range goal is to provide more modeling detail to produce a model that can be tested using historical data.

References

Abreu, D., D. Pearce and E. Stacchetti, 1986, Optimal cartel equilibria with imperfect monitoring, Journal of Economic Theory 39, 251–269.

Abreu, D., D. Pearce and E. Stacchetti, 1987, Toward a theory of discounted repeated games with imperfect monitoring, Mimeo.

Bagwell, K. and R. Staiger, 1988, A theory of managed trade, Mimeo.

Copeland, B., 1989, Theory of trade wars, Mimeo.

Dixit, A., 1987, Strategic aspects of trade policy, in: Truman F. Bewley, ed., Advances in economic theory: Fifth world congress (Cambridge University Press, New York) 329–362.

Enders, A., 1986, Strategic aspects of low-tariff agreements, Mimeo.

Feenstra, R. and T. Lewis, 1987, Negotiated trade restrictions with private political pressure, University of California-Davis working paper no. 290.

Friedman, J., 1971, A non-cooperative equilibrium for supergames, Review of Economic Studies 28, 1–12.

Fudenberg, D. and E. Maskin, 1986, Discounted repeated games with unobservable actions, I: One-sided moral hazard, Harvard discussion paper no. 1280.

Green, E. and R. Porter, 1984, Noncooperative collusion under imperfect price information, Econometrica 52, 87–100.

Jensen, R. and M. Thursby, 1980, Free trade: Two non-cooperative equilibrium approaches, Ohio State University working paper no. 58.

Kennan, J. and R. Riezman, 1988, Do big countries win tariff wars?, International Economic Review 29, 81–85.

Ludema, R., 1989, Optimal trade agreements between sovereign nations, Mimeo.

Marimon, R., 1988, Wealth accumulation with moral hazard, Mimeo. (Hoover Institution).

Mayer, W., 1981, Theoretical considerations on negotiated tariff adjustments, Oxford Economic Papers 33, 135–153.

Ray, E. and H. Marvel, 1984, The pattern of protection in the industrialized world, Review of Economics and Statistics 66, 452–458.

Riezman, R., 1982, Tariff retaliation from a strategic viewpoint, Southern Economic Journal 48, 583–593.

Rotemberg, J. and G. Saloner, 1986, A supergame-theoretic model of price wars during booms, American Economic Review 76, 390–407.

Review of International Economics, 8(4), 619–633, 2000

Understanding the Welfare Implications of Preferential Trade Agreements

*M. Ayhan Kose and Raymond Riezman**

Abstract

This paper examines various implications of preferential trade agreements, namely customs unions and free trade areas, in the context of a multicountry general equilibrium model. The model is calibrated to represent countries with symmetric endowments, and aggregate and disaggregate welfare change measures are used to quantify the welfare effects of preferential trade agreements. It is found that free trade areas are better than customs unions on welfare grounds for the world as a whole. Welfare decompositions suggest that a significant fraction of the welfare changes is explained by the volume-of-trade effect for both types of preferential trade agreements.

1. Introduction

The world trading system has been going through many changes in recent years. One important change is that attention has shifted away from the multilateralism of the WTO (formerly GATT) towards preferential trade agreements. In particular, the number of preferential trade agreements (PTAs) has nearly doubled in the last four years. Most of these agreements are free trade areas (FTAs) rather than customs unions (CUs).[1] In this paper, we systematically analyze the various implications of these agreements in a general equilibrium setting. In particular, we examine the following questions. First, what are the effects of different types of PTAs on welfare, tariffs, prices, and the volume of trade? Second, what are the contributions of the variations in the terms of trade and volume of trade to the welfare changes associated with different types of PTAs?

To deal with these questions we construct a highly stylized multicountry general equilibrium model in which tariffs are determined endogenously. Our model is a pure-exchange economy in which trading patterns are determined by comparative advantage considerations. Countries can sign preferential trade agreements, such as CUs and FTAs, with each other. In addition, they can establish free trade (FT), or they can behave non-cooperatively by charging optimal tariffs on the imports from other countries; i.e., Nash equilibrium. We simulate the model and find consumption allocations, prices, terms of trade, and volume of trade for member and nonmember economies and for every trading regime. We utilize two complementary welfare change measures to examine welfare effects of PTAs. The first calculates the aggregate consumption change in member and nonmember countries which occurs with the formation of trade agreements. We then examine a measure which decomposes the welfare effects

Kose: Brandeis University, MS 021, Waltham, MA 02454, USA. Tel: (781) 736-2266; Fax: (781) 736-2269; E-mail: akose@lemberg.brandeis.edu. Riezman: University of Iowa, Iowa City, IA 52242, USA. Tel: (319) 335-0832; Fax: (319) 335-1956; E-mail: raymond-riezman@uiowa.edu. We benefited from the suggestions of Eric Bond, Carsten Kowalczyk, Steve Matusz, and seminar participants at the Econometric Society Meetings (Pasadena), Midwest International Trade Meetings (St Louis), University of Melbourne, Australian National University, University of Munich, University of Stockholm, University of San Andres, University of Warwick, University of Maynooth, EPRU, Brandeis University, City University of Hong Kong, and University of Iowa. The usual disclaimer applies. Riezman gratefully acknowledges the support of the Obermann Center for Advanced Studies at the University of Iowa.

620   *M. Ayhan Kose and Raymond Riezman*

into two components: the variation in aggregate income induced by the movements in terms of trade and the change in aggregate income caused by the change in volume of trade.

Our paper is part of a rapidly growing literature that investigates a variety of issues related to preferential trade agreements. Inspired by the seminal work of Viner (1950), this literature has mostly focused on trade creation and trade diversion effects arising from trade agreements. For example, Krugman (1991) examines these two effects in the context of a monopolistically competitive model and shows that formation of CUs can potentially lead to higher external tariffs and can consequently result in lower world welfare. This result is interpreted as implying that recent PTAs constitute a potential threat to the multilateral trading system, since they increase the possibility of a global trade conflict.[2]

Although a significant fraction of recent PTAs have taken the form of FTAs, the massive body of the literature sparked by Krugman's study has largely ignored FTAs, and exclusively focused on the issues pertaining to CUs. In a recent paper, Krueger (1997) raises this issue, and investigates the differences between FTAs and CUs. Utilizing the Vinerian terminology, she finds that trade-creating CUs are superior to the FTAs on welfare grounds. Her results suggest that an FTA results in more trade diversion than a CU does, since sustainability of FTAs requires a variety of rules of origin requirements.[3]

While our analysis provides some important insights into these debates, our approach to the problems posed above differs in several important ways from others in this literature. First, we construct a fully specified general equilibrium model that requires only the specification of fundamental endowment parameters. We are able to analyze the strategic interactions between member and nonmember economies since tariffs are determined endogenously in our model. Second, FTAs and CUs are easily examined in our framework and the differences and similarities across different types of PTAs are documented. Third, our simple model economy with the symmetric endowment structure isolates the impact of rules-of-origin requirements associated with FTAs from the other fundamental considerations which shape the policies of member and nonmember economies upon the formation of PTAs. Hence, our study asks the same question as Krueger, namely whether CUs are preferred to FTAs, but focuses on how strategic interactions, rather than rules-of-origin requirements, affect welfare.

In particular, we consider terms-of-trade and volume-of-trade effects, and develop a numerical approximation method to decompose the aggregate welfare effects into those two components. In this regard, our analysis constitutes a major departure from the literature that was fostered with the extensive use of the Vinerian trade-creation trade-diversion terminology. While this taxonomy has enlarged our understanding of different effects of trade arrangements, and proven to be useful for simple descriptive arguments, a number of researchers have advanced concerns about the relative merits of it.[4] For example, the trade-creation trade-diversion terminology does not provide unambiguous results about the welfare implications of trade agreements. Further, it ignores the effects associated with the initial tariff levels, and the effect of PTA formation on tariff levels and terms of trade. While accounting for the changes in tariffs and terms of trade, our welfare decomposition also separates the market-power and market-access forces. The former force is associated with the terms-of-trade effect, and the latter described by the volume-of-trade effect.

We first document the regularities associated with the effects of PTAs on tariffs, prices, and the volume of trade: our findings suggest that formation of CUs might not result in higher tariff rates and FTAs induce lower protective barriers. These two results challenge the conventional notion that simultaneous formation of trade agreements results in higher protective barriers that constitute a potential threat to the multilateral trading system. Regarding prices, our findings indicate that in a CU equilibrium, the member country's terms of trade improve at the expense of nonmembers. In contrast, a nonmember economy in an FTA equilibrium enjoys a terms-of-trade improvement, since the member economies do not coordinate their tariff policies.

Unlike Krueger, we find that FTAs are better than CUs on welfare grounds for the world as a whole. While both member and nonmember economies enjoy welfare gains in an FTA, in a CU member economies gain and nonmembers lose. The total welfare gain of the union members exceeds the loss of nonmember economy, and the formation of a CU results in an increase in the world welfare over Nash equilibrium. Our results also suggest that member economies have larger welfare gains in CUs than in FTAs.

Our welfare decompositions suggest that a significant fraction of the welfare changes in both member and nonmember countries is explained by the volume-of-trade effect for both types of PTAs. The terms-of-trade effect accounts for much of the welfare gain of member economies of CUs since the members jointly determine their tariff rates. The absence of policy coordination between the members of FTAs induces welfare losses that are also associated with the terms-of-trade effect.

2. The Model

We construct a general equilibrium model of a representative world economy in which countries set tariffs optimally and can choose to not be part of any trade agreement and charge the optimal tariff, or they could decide to join a coalition with other countries. They could be part of an FTA, a CU, or can mutually agree on establishing FT. In the FTA, member countries agree to free trade between themselves, but are allowed to set their external tariffs independently. A CU is an FTA with the additional provision that the external tariff is set jointly by the members. A CU (or FTA) of all countries is, of course, free trade.[5]

The Environment

Consider a world of n countries. In each country, the agents derive utility by consuming m different goods. Let y_j^i be country i's endowment of good j. Assume that each country consists of individuals with identical Cobb–Douglas preferences. Then the utility function of a representative agent is given by

$$U^i = \sum_{j=1}^{m} \beta_j^i \ln x_j^i,$$

(1)

where U^i is the utility of country i, and β_j^i is the weight country i puts on commodity j $(\Sigma_{j=1}^{m}\beta_j^i = 1, i = 1, \ldots, n)$. x_j^i denotes the aggregate consumption of good j in country i.

The net imports of each good, z_j^i, is defined to be $z_j^i = x_j^i - y_j^i$. As we have already stated above, countries charge optimal tariffs (export taxes or subsidies) on imports (exports). Denote the tariff charged by country i on imports of good j by t_j^i. If the world price for good j is p_j, then the domestic price of good j in country i is $q_j^i = (1 + t_j^i) p_j$.

Aggregate demand is obtained from maximizing the utility subject to the budget constraint

622   *M. Ayhan Kose and Raymond Riezman*

$$\sum_{j=1}^{m} p_j(1+t_j^i)x_j^i = I^i = \sum_{j=1}^{m} p_j(1+t_j^i)y_j^i + p_i t_j^i z_j^i, \quad i=1,\dots,n, j=1,\dots,m. \tag{2}$$

where I^i is income of country i and consists of income from the endowment plus tariff revenue which is rebated to consumers in a lump sum. Since we do not allow trade deficits or surpluses, the balance-of-payments constraint of each country i is given by

$$W^i = \sum_{j=1}^{m} p_j x_j^i = \sum_{j=1}^{m} p_j y_j^i, \quad i=1,\dots,n. \tag{3}$$

W^i is the aggregate expenditure of country i. In addition to this constraint, the world demand for each good should be equal to world supply, Y^i, that is equal to 1:

$$\sum_{i=1}^{n} x_j^i = \sum_{i=1}^{n} y_j^i = Y^i, \quad j=1,\dots,m. \tag{4}$$

The Numerical Solution Method and Calibration

The logarithmic utility results in a linear expenditure system, in which agents allocate a fixed fraction of their income on each good. Using the first-order conditions of the maximization problem, we derive an analytical expression for utility of each country as a function of tariffs, for any given preference and endowment distribution. We employ a recursive numerical solution method to find an approximate solution for equilibrium allocations, prices, and tariffs since we cannot obtain a closed-form solution for each equilibrium.

In order to utilize the numerical solution algorithm, we should specify the number of countries, the number of goods and endowment of each country. We assume that $m = n = 3$ and $\beta_j^i = \frac{1}{3}$ for all $i,j = 1,2,3$. Each country i has an endowment of $y_i^i = s$ units of good i and $y_j^i = 0.5(1 - s)$ units of good j ($j \neq i$). s, which is between zero and one, denotes the degree of symmetry (or similarity) between countries. This endowment structure implies that countries are identical up to a relabeling of the goods. Depending on s, two symmetric trade patterns can occur at any equilibrium: when $s < \frac{1}{3}$, each country exports two goods ($z_j^i < 0$, $i \neq j$), imports the other ($z_i^i > 0$), and charges taxes ($t_j^i < 0$, $i \neq j$) on its exports. When $s > \frac{1}{3}$, each country exports one good ($z_i^i < 0$), imports the other two ($z_j^i > 0$, $i \neq j$), and charges tariffs on its imports ($t_j^i > 0$, $i \neq j$). As s increases, the countries become more dissimilar, and their market power in their export goods increases. When $s = a = \frac{1}{3}$, there is no trade, since countries have identical preferences and endowments. We let s vary from 0.1 to 0.9. For each s, we compute equilibrium allocations in Nash, CU, FTA, and FT equilibria. In CU and FTA equilibria, two countries establish a free trade agreement and leave the third one out.

3. Measuring Welfare Changes

The Aggregate Welfare Change Measure

We use the measure of "compensating variation in consumption" to evaluate the aggregate welfare changes associated with trade agreements.[6] The compensating variation in consumption is the fraction δ by which the consumption allocations should be decreased in a free trade equilibrium, which can be an FTA, CU, or FT, to keep the representative agent with the same utility as the one in the Nash equilibrium. So, the welfare change, δ, is calculated as

WELFARE IMPLICATIONS OF TRADE AGREEMENTS   623

$$U^N(x_1^N, x_2^N, x_3^N) = U^F((1-\delta)x_1^F, (1-\delta)x_2^F, (1-\delta)x_3^F)$$

where U^N (U^F) is utility under a Nash (preferential trade) equilibrium.

The Disaggregate Welfare Change Measure

We decompose the welfare changes into two components which are associated with the variations in the terms of trade and volume of trade of each country. Our measure, which we call the disaggregate welfare change measure, was first carefully worked out by Kowalczyk (1999).[7]

Consider country i which is in a preferential trade arrangement. We denote the aggregate income of country i by I^i. Let q^i be the m-element column vector of domestic prices (i.e., tariff inclusive prices) of country i. z^i is a row vector with m elements listing country i's net imports (i.e., the difference between imports and exports). We can rewrite (2) in terms of country i's net imports, and use the first-order conditions of the optimization problem to get $dI^i = q^i dz^i$. It is possible to rewrite the equation (3) to get the balanced trade condition, $pz^i = 0$, where p is an m-element column vector of world prices (i.e., tariff exclusive prices). Now, totally differentiating this equation and subtracting the change in aggregate income from it yields $dI^i = -z^i dp + (q^i - p)dz^i$. In this expression, the first term is the terms-of-trade (TOT) effect which is the inner product of the vectors of net imports and changes in world prices. The second component denotes the volume-of-trade (VOT) effect that is the inner product of the tariff wedge and the change in net imports. In our framework, the tariff rates are *ad valorem*, $q^i = (1 + t^i)p$, where $(1 + t^i)$ is an $n \times n$ diagonal matrix with zeros on its diagonal.

The above welfare measure disaggregates welfare changes for infinitesimal changes in tariffs. However, in our analysis tariffs change discretely when countries move from one equilibrium to another. In order to adapt this measure for our purposes, we develop a numerical approximation method that allows us to decompose the overall welfare effects associated with discrete changes in tariffs.

To do this we first define a transition path and divide the total change in tariffs into smaller discrete steps. Accordingly, countries go through N steps in which they reduce their tariff rates proportionally. We then calculate $(N - 2)$ intermediate equilibria on the transition path that leads countries from the initial equilibrium to the final one. Let k ($1 \leq k \leq N$) index the equilibrium on the transition path. The initial equilibrium, which is the Nash equilibrium, is denoted by $k = 1$, and the final equilibrium, (FTA, CU, or FT), corresponds to $k = N$. In each step, the countries charge tariff rates which are between the initial and final tariff rates. Next, we solve the model for each intermediate set of tariff rates, and find respective vectors of prices, exports, and imports. Knowing these variables, we calculate the disaggregated welfare gains for each equilibrium along the transition path. Then, we sum the changes in welfare over each equilibrium on the transition path. The summation of changes in welfare produces an approximation to the overall welfare change of country i due to a PTA. As N increases, the accuracy of our approximation gets better. Through simulations we find that for our problem $N = 4$ gets us "sufficiently" accurate answers.[8]

4. Understanding Trade Agreements

Tariffs, Prices, and Trade Volume

Figure 1 presents the equilibrium tariff rates charged by member and nonmember countries in different types of PTAs. For all PTAs, the larger the disparity in endow-

624   **M. Ayhan Kose and Raymond Riezman**

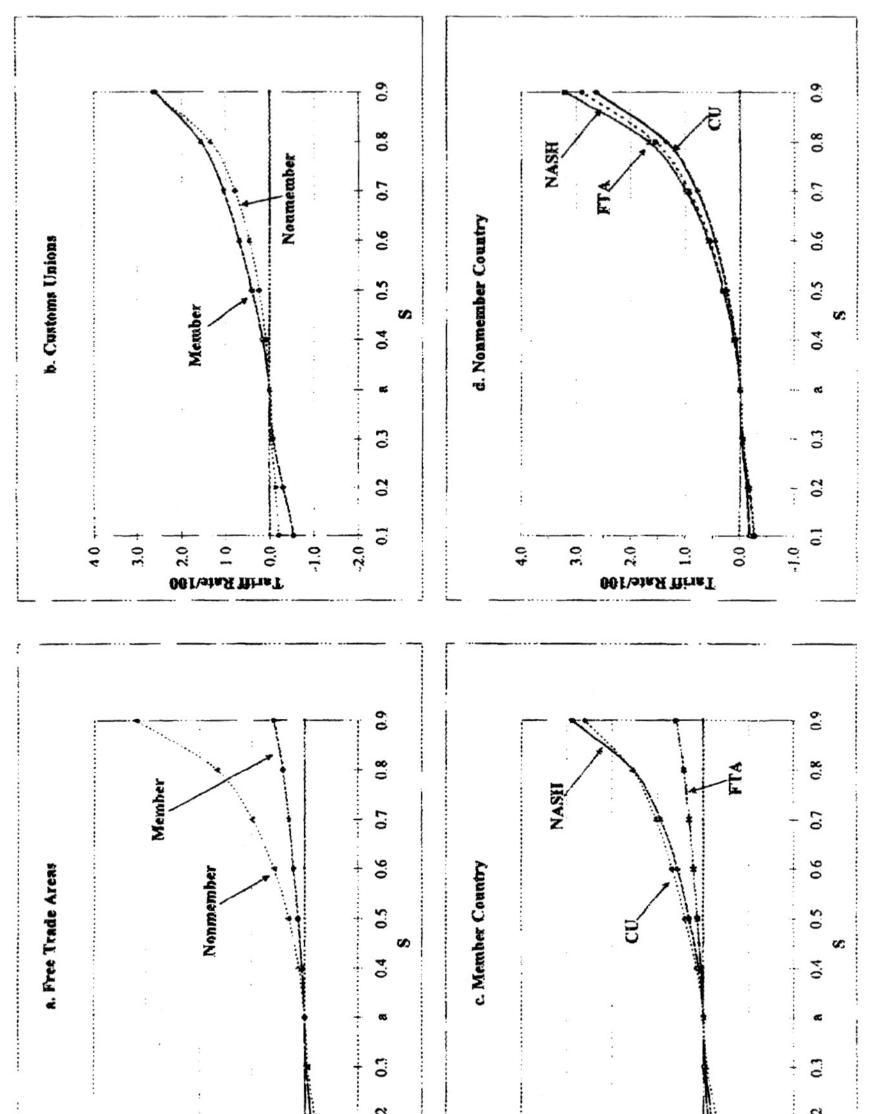

Figure 1. Tariff Rates

WELFARE IMPLICATIONS OF TRADE AGREEMENTS   625

ments, the larger is the equilibrium tariff rate. An increase in s can be interpreted as an increase in the monopoly power of the countries in world trade, since it indicates that each country has a larger share of the world supply of its export good. This induces a rise in equilibrium tariff rates as s rises.

As Figure 1(a) shows, an FTA results in member countries charging lower tariffs than nonmembers. The intuition for this surprising result is that the FTA puts the member countries at a strategic disadvantage. While the nonmember has two strategies (tariff rates) to use, the members have only one since they have agreed to eliminate their tariffs on each other. This results in the nonmember country being more aggressive in equilibrium. A CU, however, results in the opposite result, higher tariffs for member countries (see Figure 1(b)). The strategic advantage gained when the members coordinate their external tariff is more than enough to make up for the disadvantage of being able to use fewer tariff rates. The difference between the tariff policies of CUs and FTAs can be explained with the "externality internalizing" effect: in a CU there is internal free trade (as in the FTA), and in addition, the union members jointly set a common tariff on imports of goods from the nonunion country. This generates a tariff externality whenever two countries import the same good, because a tariff imposed by one country lowers the price paid by both. The CU, unlike an FTA, internalizes the tariff externality and confers a strategic advantage on the members which is enough to outweigh the strategic disadvantage of internal free trade.

In Figures 1(c) and (d), we compare tariff rates across equilibria. For member countries, Figure 1(c) shows that tariffs fall in an FTA but may increase or decrease as the result of a CU. In particular, when s is greater than 0.81, the members of the customs union set a lower tariff rate than they charge independently in a Nash equilibrium. In a recent paper, Syropoulos (1999) argues convincingly that, since the internal free trade among CU members causes an increase in the price elasticities of demand for the exports of all countries, the market power of union members and nonunion members decrease, and they both reduce their tariff rates. Combined with our earlier explanation about the externality-internalizing effect, which increases the tariff rate, Syropoulos' argument on the "trade-liberalizing" effect explains the decrease in the tariff rates of member countries. When s is greater than 0.81, the trade-liberalizing effect outweighs the externality-internalizing force, and drives the tariff rates down in a CU. When s is less than 0.81, the externality-internalizing force becomes more pronounced and induces an increase in the common tariff rate practiced by the union members. This result stands in sharp contrast to Krugman's (1991) claim that member country tariffs increase when they form a customs union.

We can explain the fall in the tariff rates charged by the members of an FTA with the help of the trade-liberalizing effect. In an FTA, there is no externality-internalizing force, and the only present effect is the trade-liberalizing force which provides an incentive to member countries to decrease their tariff rates upon the formation of the FTA.

While formation of an FTA does not lead to an increase in the tariff rates of member countries, it induces higher tariff rates in the nonmember economy. This is because the formation of the FTA has improved the nonmember's strategic position since they now have two strategies (tariffs) to use compared with one each for the member countries. This leads to them being more aggressive and charging higher tariffs in equilibrium. In contrast, nonmember's tariffs fall in CU equilibrium because the tariff coordination of the member countries result in them being more aggressive. It is interesting to note that when $s > 0.81$ both members and the nonmember country reduce tariffs when a CU forms.

626   *M. Ayhan Kose and Raymond Riezman*

These results challenge the notion that simultaneous formation of trade agreements must result in higher protective barriers that constitute a potential threat to the multilateral trading system. Krugman (1991) shows that CUs can potentially increase external tariffs owing to the non-cooperative behavior of large economic units. He considers a model in which each country produces a single good that is differentiable from the other goods produced by other countries and CUs that are formed by symmetrically endowed countries.

Krugman's findings suggest that simultaneous formation of PTAs can cause higher protective barriers, and lead to a global trade conflict. Our results paint a more optimistic picture: first, the formation of a CU can, indeed, lead to lower, not higher, tariff rates even within the context of a model with symmetrically endowed countries that set tariffs optimally. Our model, in which trade is driven by the differences in endowment distributions, illuminates the interaction between the tariff-increasing and tariff-decreasing forces (i.e., the externality-internalizing and trade-liberalizing effects) and shows that a CU arrangement between countries with sufficiently diverse endowments lowers protective barriers. Second, and more importantly, our findings suggest that understanding preferential trade agreements and the new wave of regionalism requires examination of both FTAs and CUs. For example, our results indicate that the formation of FTAs leads to lower tariff rates. In a recent study, the World Trade Organization (1995) reports that most of the regional trade agreements take the form of FTAs, and that the number of CUs is small.

Figure 2 provides information on the behavior of different price measures. It is evident that as countries become more powerful in their export markets (i.e., as s rises), the prices of their export goods increase. Figures 2(a) and (b) show the impact of policy coordination on the terms of trade of member and nonmember economies. In Figure 2(a) the nonmember's terms of trade improve at the expense of the members when an FTA forms. This is due to the strategic disadvantage of the FTA for its members discussed above. In Figure 2(b), upon the formation of a CU, the terms of trade of the members improves at the expense of nonmembers. This occurs because the members of the CU gain from coordinating their tariff policy which more than makes up for the strategic disadvantage they incur because they have only one strategy (one tariff rate) to use. As Figures 2(c) and (d) indicate, agents in the nonmember country receive more protection regardless of whether a CU or FTA forms. In the case of an FTA nonmember, terms of trade improve which tends to reduce domestic prices in the nonmember country and raise them in the member country. However, the nonmember tariff rates are so much higher that the overall effect is that there are higher domestic prices in the nonmember country. When a CU forms, the terms of trade go the opposite way, which raises domestic prices in the nonmember country and lowers them in the member.

We also examine the effect of trade agreements on trade volume measured by a country's trade volume with the ratio of its exports to its GDP. For the sake of brevity we do not present the figures associated with the results of trade volume. We report some of the main findings here: a member country of a PTA has a larger trade volume than does the nonmember economy. The gap between the trading volumes of member and nonmember economies becomes more pronounced as the disparity in endowments increases.[9]

Aggregate Welfare Effects

We first analyze the effects of PTAs on the allocation of resources using the aggregate welfare measure described in section 3. We present the results of our simulations in

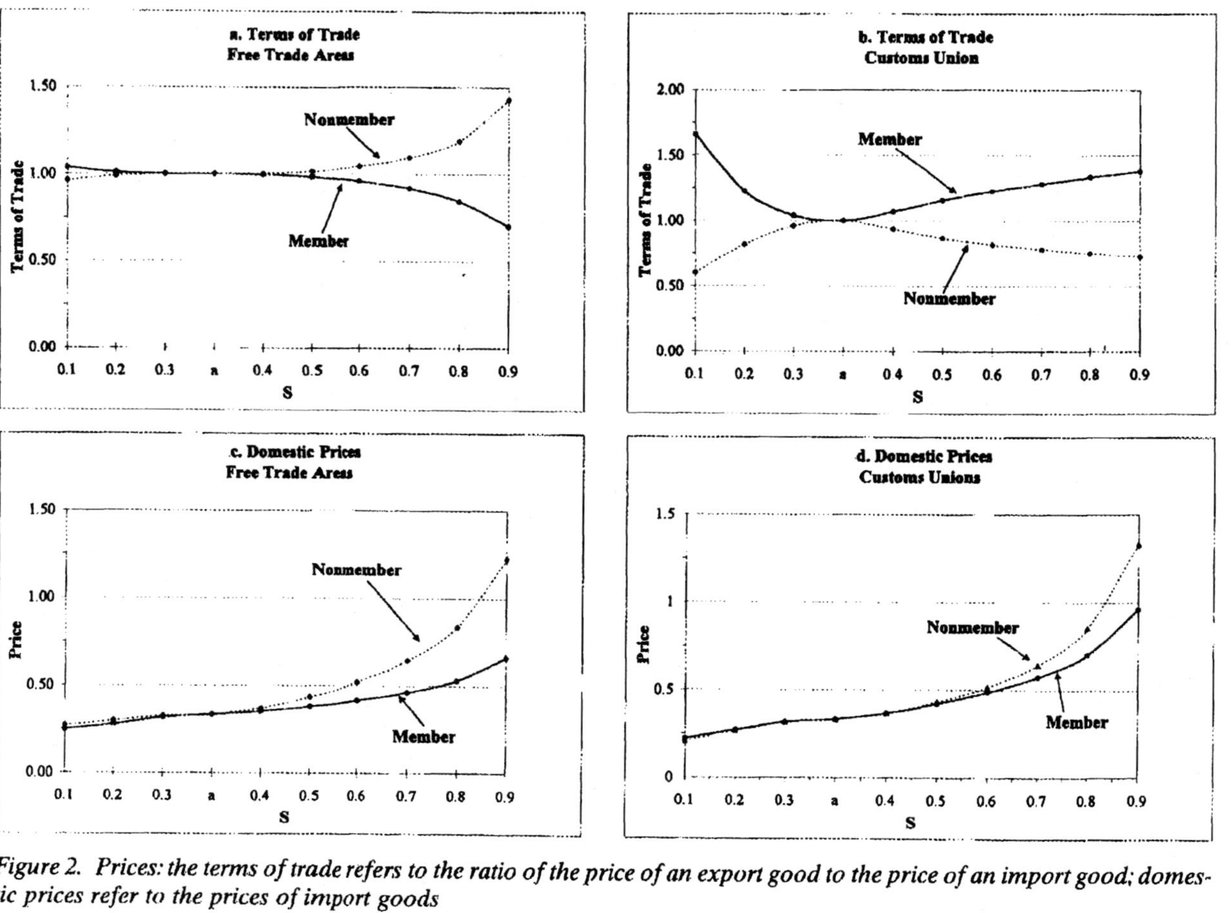

Figure 2. Prices: the terms of trade refers to the ratio of the price of an export good to the price of an import good; domestic prices refer to the prices of import goods

628   *M. Ayhan Kose and Raymond Riezman*

Figure 3. As endowments of countries become more dissimilar, they get larger welfare gains through establishing PTAs. This regularity is an expected one considering that each country consumes all three goods, and as the endowments of countries get more divergent, international trade becomes more important. Figure 3(a) makes clear that when s is less than 0.68, member countries get larger welfare gains than does the non-member. Surprisingly, as the disparity in endowments gets larger, in particular when s is greater than 0.68, the nonmember country gets larger welfare gains than do the members of the FTA. The intuition for this result can be seen by recalling that an FTA results in higher tariff rates in nonmember countries than in member economies. In addition, the terms of trade of the nonmember country improve at the expense of the members and is an increasing function of s. Thus, for high enough values of s there is enough terms-of-trade improvement for the nonmember that their welfare improvement is larger than for the member. Unlike FTAs, CUs are harmful to nonmember countries as it is shown in Figure 3(b). In a CU, the terms of trade turn against the nonmember country; it always loses and the members always gain.

Figures 3(c) and (d) show that CUs (FTAs) are better than FTAs (CUs) for member (nonmember) countries on welfare grounds. Interestingly enough, though, formation of a CU can improve members' welfare over FT. If each country's endowment of its export good is less than 0.67, then member economies are better off with a CU than with FT. This result follows from the fact that formation of CUs helps to generate larger economic units which can, because of their size, manipulate the terms of trade in their favor, and have larger welfare gains than FT. If s is small, that is equivalent to the CUs being large in our framework. On the other hand, as countries become more dissimilar, the formation of a CU does not necessarily increase the welfare of the members over FT.

These results have implications for the current debate about the welfare implications of PTAs, namely, "are PTAs stumbling blocks or stepping stones to the attainment of global free trade?" For certain endowment distributions, (when $s < 0.67$), CUs pose a threat to the multilateral trading system. Member countries can get larger welfare gains at CU than at FT. Therefore, if we rule out transfer payments from the nonmember economies to the member ones, CUs can be considered as stumbling blocks. However, when countries are sufficiently dissimilar, or when they have more market power in their export markets, then CUs do not necessarily constitute a danger to the multilateral trading system, and in fact they can serve as a stepping stone to the attainment of global free trade. The role of FTAs is quite different. Notice that all countries, whether members or not, would prefer a move from NE to any FTA. Starting from any FTA equilibrium all countries would benefit from a move to FT. This suggests that FTAs are indeed a stepping stone to free trade.

Figure 4 presents the results of world welfare calculations. As expected FT is the best outcome for the world as a whole. FTAs are always better than the CUs since while both the member and nonmember economies gain in an FTA, only members gain at the expense of the nonmember country in a CU. The total welfare gain of the members exceeds the loss of nonmember economy in a CU, and the world welfare increases over Nash equilibrium.

Our results also shed light on an important policy debate that has recently gained momentum: "are FTAs better than CUs?" Krueger (1997), using Vinerian trade-creation trade-diversion terminology, argues that CUs are better than FTAs from the viewpoint of welfare economics. Krueger assumes that after the formation a CU, member economies levy a tariff rate which is the average of their pre-agreement tariffs, and the formation of an FTA does not result in any change in tariff rates: i.e., the

WELFARE IMPLICATIONS OF TRADE AGREEMENTS   629

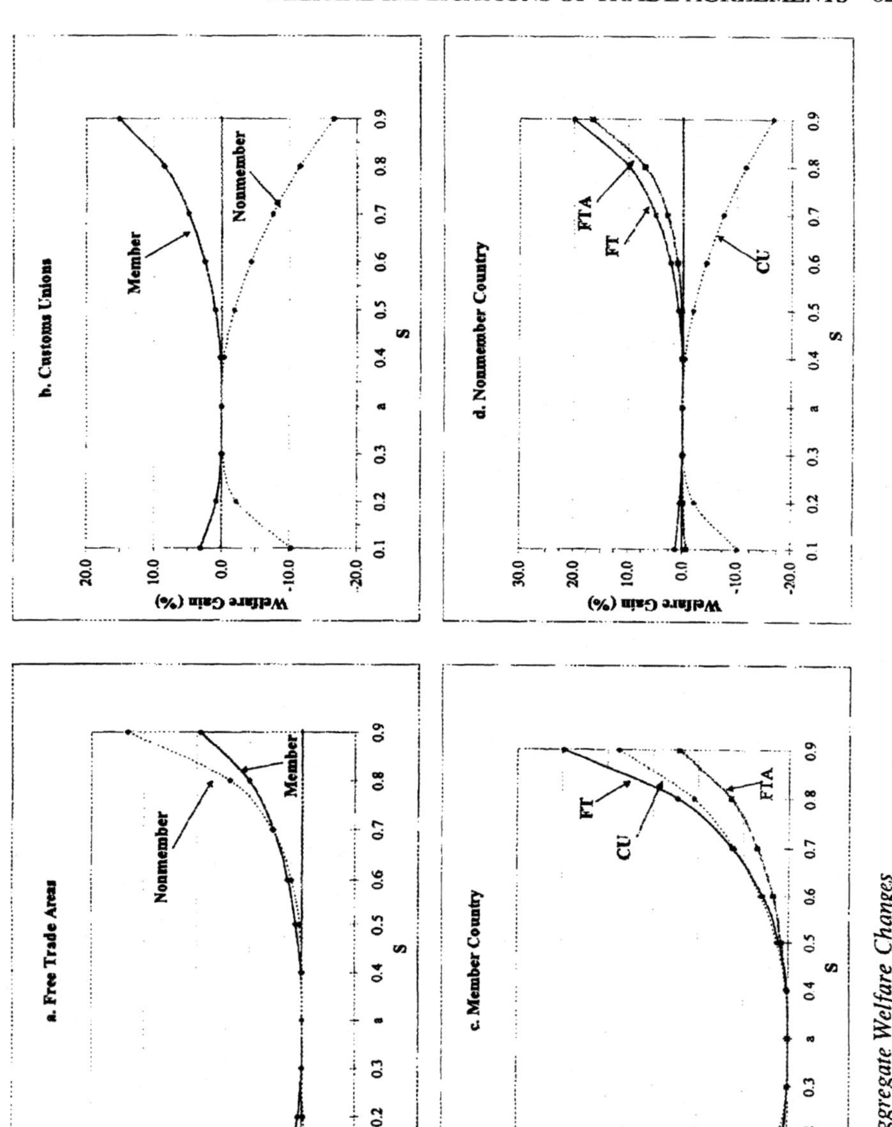

Figure 3. Aggregate Welfare Changes

630 *M. Ayhan Kose and Raymond Riezman*

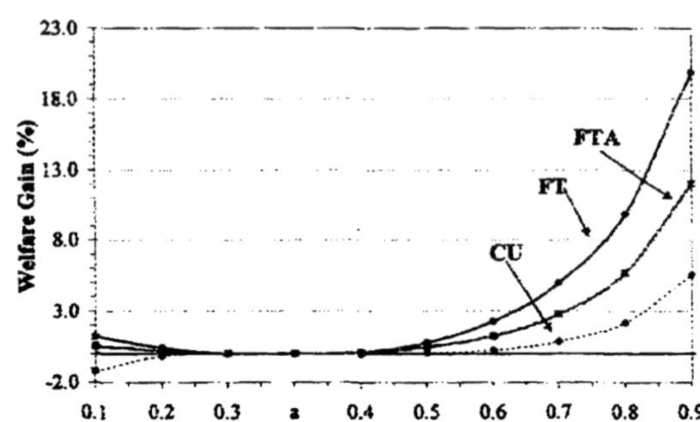

Figure 4. Aggregate Change in World Welfare

member economies maintain their pre-agreement tariffs. Krueger's analysis focuses on the rules-of-origin requirements that are exercised by the members of FTAs to prevent trade deflection when two FTA members charge different tariff rates. These requirements induce more trade diversion in FTAs than in CUs, and thus Krueger's finds that CUs result in higher world welfare than FTAs.

Our analysis is different than Krueger's: first, we exclude rules-of-origin problems by employing a symmetric endowment distribution. While abstracting from the rules-of-origin requirements, our framework emphasizes the strategic interactions between the members and nonmembers to differentiate CUs from FTAs. Second, since tariffs are determined endogenously in our model, we do not impose any a priori assumptions about the pre- and post-agreement tariff rates. The tariffs coming out of the general equilibrium model used here do not justify the assumptions about the tariff rates made by Krueger. Third, while Krueger's study considers only world welfare, we examine the welfare implications of PTAs for the member and nonmember economies as well as for the world.

In contrast to Krueger's conclusion, our findings show that FTAs are better than CUs on welfare grounds for the world as a whole. Nonetheless, our study suggests that member economies have larger welfare gains in CUs than in FTAs. While both member and nonmember economies enjoy welfare gains in an FTA, only the member economies gain and the nonmembers lose in a CU. Further, we show that, for certain endowment distributions, upon formation of an FTA, nonmember economies get larger welfare benefits than do member economies.

Decomposition of the Welfare Effects

We explore the different sources of welfare effects associated with preferential trade arrangements, focusing in this section on the relative contribution of the terms-of-trade and volume-of-trade effects to the welfare changes. These two effects provide further intuitive insight into the welfare changes. For example, the volume-of-trade effect is associated with the welfare changes arising from the fact that with PTAs countries have free access into each others' markets. One might think of this as a "market-access" effect. Similarly, the terms-of-trade effect is a useful instrument for understanding the "market-power" effects of PTAs.

We present the results of our calculations in Table 1. Columns 2 to 5 show that, when two countries establish an FTA (i.e., when they move from a Nash equilibrium to an

WELFARE IMPLICATIONS OF TRADE AGREEMENTS   631

Table I. Welfare Change Decomposition (percentages)

| | FTA | | | | CU | | | |
| | Nonmember | | Member | | Nonmember | | Member | |
s	TOT[a]	VOT[b]	TOT	VOT	TOT	VOT	TOT	VOT
0.1	−49.35	−50.65	19.03	80.98	−50.79	−49.21	53.89	46.11
0.2	−47.25	−52.76	10.58	89.42	−47.08	−52.92	48.34	51.67
0.3	−44.28	−55.73	2.70	97.31	−43.99	−56.01	42.65	57.35
0.4	43.46	56.54	−4.22	104.22	−43.14	−56.86	38.04	61.96
0.5	39.42	60.58	−11.58	111.58	−38.48	−61.52	30.84	69.16
0.6	36.43	63.57	−16.87	116.87	−34.45	−65.55	26.59	73.41
0.7	32.72	67.28	−21.41	121.41	−31.17	−68.83	19.34	80.66
0.8	28.69	71.31	−22.40	122.40	−26.88	−73.12	12.87	87.13
0.9	22.55	77.45	−20.38	120.38	−21.19	−78.81	6.56	93.44

[a] Percentage fraction of the welfare gain attributable to changes in terms of trade.
[b] Percentage fraction of the welfare gain attributable to changes in volume of trade.
Negative numbers correspond to decomposition of welfare losses.

FTA equilibrium), a significant fraction of the welfare gains in both, member and non-member countries is explained by the volume-of-trade effect. Consider the economy with s equal to 0.5: in the nonmember country, the terms-of-trade effect explains approximately 39% of the welfare gain, and the volume-of-trade effect accounts for the remaining 61%. Earlier we documented that, upon the formation of the FTA, the nonmember economy enjoys a terms-of-trade improvement, whereas the members face a decline in their terms of trade. We can clearly see the implication of this regularity on the disaggregated changes of the welfare of member economies. While the volume-of-trade effect explains roughly 112% of the aggregate welfare gain, 12% welfare loss is attributed to the terms-of-trade effect. The latter is an indicator of the changes in market power. Since FTAs do not increase the market power of the member economies, they face welfare losses resulting from the fall in their terms of trade.

Our results suggest that volume-of-trade effects explain a larger fraction of the welfare changes in member economies of FTAs than it does in the nonmember country. This result has also an intuitive interpretation: a member country has a larger trade volume than the nonmember economy does in an FTA. Further, as s increases, the gains associated with the volume-of-trade effect become more pronounced. As s rises, countries control more of the world supply of their export goods. This increases the fraction of the welfare gains resulting from the free market access, since international trade becomes more important for the members as well as the nonmember.

In columns 6 to 9 of Table 1, the results corresponding to CUs are presented. CUs result in a welfare loss in nonmember economies in our model. As in FTAs, the volume-of-trade effect accounts for a larger fraction of the welfare change in both union and nonunion countries in CUs. This indicates that having free market access is quite important even if countries can coordinate their tariff policies and gain terms-of-trade improvements. Surprisingly, the change associated with the terms-of-trade effect is smaller in a CU member than the nonmember. Table 1 also suggests that the decomposition of welfare changes yields similar results for the nonmember economy in both CU and FTA equilibria. Comparison across endowment distributions indicates that as

632   *M. Ayhan Kose and Raymond Riezman*

countries become more dissimilar (i.e., as s rises), the fraction of total welfare change explained by the volume-of-trade effect gets larger, since international trade, for each country, becomes more important.

5. Concluding Comments

We have constructed a general equilibrium model to study various implications of different types of PTAs, namely FTAs and CUs. The results suggest that FTAs are better than CUs on welfare grounds for the world as a whole. Further, while member economies have larger welfare gains in CUs than in FTAs, FTAs benefit the nonmember country more than the member countries. FTAs also could conceivably be a stepping stone to FT in the sense that every country benefits from the move from NE to any FTA and all countries also benefit from the further move to FT. CUs, on the other hand, benefit member countries at the expense of the nonmember. Our welfare decompositions indicate that a significant fraction of the welfare gains in both member and nonmember countries is explained by the volume-of-trade effect for both types of PTAs. The terms-of-trade effect generates relatively large welfare gains in the member economies of CUs since the members jointly determine their tariff rates. The absence of policy coordination between the members of FTAs decreases their market power and this produces welfare losses that are also associated with the terms-of-trade effect.

References

Baldwin, Richard E. and Anthony J. Venables, "Regional Economic Integration," in Gene N. Grossman and Kenneth Rogoff (eds), *Handbook of International Economics*, Vol. III, Amsterdam: North-Holland (1995):1597–644.

Bond, Eric W., "The Optimal Tariff Structure in Higher Dimensions," *International Economic Review* 31 (1990):103–16.

Hamilton, Bob and John Whalley, "Geographically Discriminatory Trade Arrangements," *Review of Economics and Statistics* (1985):446–55.

Harrison, Glenn W., Thomas F. Rutherford, and Ian Wooton, "An Alternative Welfare Decomposition for Customs Unions," *Canadian Journal of Economics* 26 (1993):961–8.

Kennan, John and Raymond Riezman, "Optimal Tariff Equilibria with Customs Unions," *Canadian Journal of Economics* 90 (1990):70–83.

Kowalczyk, Carsten, "Welfare and Customs Unions," manuscript, Tufts University (1996).

Krueger, Anne O., "Free Trade Agreements Versus Customs Unions," *Journal of Development Economics* 54 (1997):169–87

Krugman, Paul, "Is Bilateralism Bad?" in E. Helpman and A. Razin, (eds.), *International Trade and Trade Policy*, Cambridge, MA: MIT Press (1991):9–23.

Perroni, Carlo and John Whalley, "How Severe is Global Retaliation Risk under Increasing Regionalism?" *American Economic Review* 86 (1996):57–61.

Pomfret, Richard, "Are Free Trade Areas Better than Customs Unions?" manuscript, University of Adelaide (1996).

Riezman, Raymond, "Can Bilateral Trade Agreements Help Induce Free Trade?" *Canadian Journal of Economics* (1999, forthcoming).

Shibata, Hirofumi, "The Theory of Economic Unions: A Comparative Analysis of Customs Unions, Free Trade Areas, and Tax Unions," in Carl S. Shoup (ed.), *Fiscal Harmonization in Common Markets*, Vol. 1, New York: Columbia University Press (1967):145–264.

Srinivasan, T. N., John Whalley, and Ian Wooton, "Measuring the Effects of Regionalism on Trade and Welfare," in Kym Anderson and Richard Blackhurst (eds.), *Regional Integration and the Global Trading System*, Brighton: Harvester Wheatsheaf (1993):52–79.

WELFARE IMPLICATIONS OF TRADE AGREEMENTS   633

Syropoulos, Constantinos, "Customs Unions and Comparative Advantage," *Oxford Economic Papers* 51:2 (1999):239–66.
Viner, Jacob, "The Customs Union Issue," *Carnegie Endowment for International Peace* (1950).
Winters, L. Alan, "Regionalism and the Rest of the World," *Review of International Economics* 5 (1997):134–47.
World Trade Organization. "Regionalism and the World Trading System," Geneva: WTO (1995).

Notes

1. The WTO (1995) reports that "most notifications made to GATT have involved free trade areas, and the number of customs union agreements is small." Riezman (1999) provides an extensive discussion of the question whether or not the new spate of preferential trade agreements are a help or hindrance in the goal of attaining free international trade. Perroni and Whalley (1996) provide several results associated with CUs and FTAs using a general equilibrium model calibrated to represent major trading regions in the world.
2. A number of studies, following Krugman, analyze the impact of the simultaneous formation of CUs on tariffs and welfare by relaxing a variety of his assumptions. Riezman (1999) and Baldwin and Venables (1995) provide a review of this literature.
3. This result is in sharp contrast with the traditional argument advanced by Shibata (1967) who claims that FTAs result in larger welfare gains than CUs. Pomfret (1996) claims that the rules-of-origin requirements, while they could be detrimental to the welfare of member and non-member countries, are unable to justify Krueger's conclusion.
4. Kowalyczyk (1999) provides a critical analysis of the literature and illustrates the potential problems which might arise with the "misuse" of it. Harrison et al. (1993), Srinavasan et al. (1993), and Hamilton and Whalley (1985) also discuss several shortcomings of this terminology.
5. Our model draws from work by Kennan and Riezman (1990). As discussed in Riezman (1999), a number of researchers have recently used this setup to analyze different issues.
6. This measure is slightly different from the Equivalent Income Variation measure which looks at the change in income at constant prices. The measure of Compensating Variation in Consumption is widely used in macroeconomics and finance literature to evaluate the costs of business cycles and of the lack of international consumption risk-sharing.
7. There were some earlier studies suggesting this type of disaggregate welfare change calculation, but Kowalczyk was the first one who convincingly argued that this type of welfare taxonomy is superior to the traditional trade-creation and trade-diversion terminology. See Bond (1990) for the derivation of this measure. See Baldwin and Venables (1995), and Winters (1997) for surveys on different types of welfare decompositions. Harrison et al. (1993) also provide a welfare decomposition method.
8. An extensive discussion of the derivation of the disaggregated welfare change measure can be found in the working paper version of the paper that is available from the authors.
9. The formation of FTAs leads to more trade in both member and nonmember economies than the formation of CUs. While FT (Nash) equilibrium results in the largest (smallest) trade volume, CUs "divert" trade from the nonmember country to the member country relative to an FTA.

ELSEVIER

Journal of International Economics 64 (2004) 1–27

Journal of INTERNATIONAL ECONOMICS

www.elsevier.com/locate/econbase

A strategic and welfare theoretic analysis of free trade areas

Eric W. Bond[a,1], Raymond G. Riezman[b,2], Constantinos Syropoulos[c,*]

[a] *Department of Economics, Pennsylvania State University, University Park, PA 16802, USA*
[b] *Department of Economics, W360 PBB, University of Iowa, Iowa City, IA 52242, USA*
[c] *Department of Economics, Florida International University, University Park, DM-321, Miami, FL 33199, USA*

Received 20 April 2001; received in revised form 9 April 2002; accepted 1 December 2002

Abstract

We construct a three-country model to determine how the formation of free trade areas (FTAs) affects optimal tariffs and welfare. We find that, at constant rest of the world (ROW) tariffs, the adoption of internal free trade induces union members to reduce their external tariffs below the Kemp–Wan [J. Int. Econom. 6 (1976) 95–97] level, and causes ROW's terms of trade to improve and its welfare to rise. When ROW also behaves optimally, its policy response to the formation of the FTA is to raise tariffs. Generally, FTA members prefer to liberalize internal trade partially and find regional integration appealing only if their collective size is sufficiently large. We also demonstrate how FTAs may undermine the attainment of global free trade.

Keywords: Regionalism; Free trade areas; Kemp–Wan tariff adjustments; Strategic interactions; Welfare

JEL classification: F11; F13; F15; F42

---

* Corresponding author. Tel.: +1-305-348-2592; fax: +1-305-348-1524.
  E-mail addresses: ewb1@psu.edu (E.W. Bond), raymond-riezman@uiowa.edu (R.G. Riezman), syropoul@fiu.edu (C. Syropoulos).
  [1] Tel.: +1-814-863-0315.
  [2] Tel.: +1-319-335-0832.

2   *E.W. Bond et al. / Journal of International Economics 64 (2004) 1–27*

1. Introduction

A World Trade Organization (2000) report on preferential trade agreements identified 172 trade accords in force as of June 2000, with an additional 68 agreements under negotiation. Free trade areas (FTAs) accounted for 148 of the agreements in force and 67 of the agreements under negotiation. Yet, despite the overwhelming predominance of FTAs in practice, the theoretical literature on preferential trade arrangements (PTA) has tended to focus primarily on the analysis of customs unions[3].

This paper takes a step toward redressing this imbalance in attention by providing new insights on the strategic aspects and welfare effects of FTAs. We use a simple three-country general-equilibrium trade model to analyze how the formation of an FTA between two countries affects the tariff and welfare levels of all trade partners. Since recent research on PTAs examines their effects under a variety of assumptions regarding the setting of inter-bloc tariffs and the structure of regional agreements, it is useful to place our analysis in the literature by highlighting two of our assumptions. First, we assume that external tariffs rates are endogenously determined with countries choosing these rates independently to maximize national welfare in a non-cooperative, single-period, tariff-setting game[4]. Second, we consider situations in which two exogenously chosen countries of equal size form an FTA. The fact that two of the three countries considered form an FTA means that the agreement expands the size of member states relative to the rest of the world (ROW). This enables us to identify the strategic effects of tariff cuts within the FTA and obtain sharp predictions on how its relative size is likely to affect the costs and benefits of regional integration. We adopt the assumption of symmetric FTA members for tractability and because it places the relative size of trading blocs at center stage while abstracting from internal distributional issues within the FTA[5].

In evaluating the effects of FTAs, one of the theoretical difficulties is that tariff changes are discrete. Typically, in such settings, one is concerned with how pre- and post-integration Nash tariff equilibria compare. However, because this comparison involves discrete changes in tariffs, the use of traditional calculus-based methods is difficult. We overcome this problem by decomposing the entire change into two separate steps. We first

---

[3] The theoretical literature on regional trade agreements is now 50 years old. Beginning with Viner (1950), Meade (1955) and Lipsey (1970), and continuing with the modern contributions by Riezman (1979), Kennan and Riezman (1990), Krugman (1991), Bond and Syropoulos (1996a), Syropoulos (1999) and others, this literature has primarily focused on customs unions.

[4] A number of authors have examined this question under alternative assumptions regarding both the objective functions of policymakers and the nature of the tariff-setting game between them. For example, Bagwell and Staiger (1997) and Bond and Syropoulos (1996b) assume that inter-bloc tariffs are the outcome of a repeated game between the trading blocs. Richardson (1993) examines the case in which the objective function of the bloc members attaches a positive weight to special interests. See Baldwin and Venables (1995) for a survey of the recent literature on regional economic integration.

[5] The importance of the relative size of a trading bloc has been extensively examined for the case of customs unions, but is relatively unexplored in the case of FTAs. Kennan and Riezman (1990) numerically studied the role of country size in regional trading arrangements. Krugman (1991) divided the world into an equal number of customs unions to explore the effects of simultaneously expanding the (absolute) size of all CUs. The role of relative versus absolute size in many country models of CUs is emphasized by Bond and Syropoulos (1996a). Kose and Riezman (2000) presented some additional numerical results for CUs and FTAs.

E.W. Bond et al. / Journal of International Economics 64 (2004) 1–27   3

solve for the relationship between trade liberalization within the FTA and the FTA members' optimal external tariffs—which are identical due to symmetry. We then solve for the relationship between inter-bloc tariffs. This decomposition is appealing because it allows us to capture the empirically relevant point that trade liberalization within FTAs (e.g. NAFTA) often takes place gradually with internal free trade being attained only after periods of 10 or more years. We can thus analyze how tariffs and welfare vary along the transition path of internal liberalization. A further benefit of this two-stage approach is that it allows to us to compare the welfare effect of internal liberalization both in the absence and the presence of optimal tariff adjustments by ROW. The former case is relevant for illustrating the welfare effects of trade liberalization when ROW cannot raise its tariff against the FTA members, as may be the case if ROW is constrained by multilateral trade obligations.

We now highlight several of the key results of our analysis. The first concerns the impact of internal trade liberalization on the external tariff of the individual members, assuming that ROW tariffs remain constant. A useful benchmark for this analysis is the Kemp–Wan tariff adjustment, which is a reduction in the external tariff of the FTA that would leave ROW's terms of trade unaffected by the reduction in internal tariffs. We show that, in response to internal trade liberalization, individual members have an incentive to reduce their external tariffs by an amount that exceeds the Kemp–Wan tariff reduction[6]. This result is key to our welfare analysis. Several researchers have established a result similar to ours, namely that internal liberalization in the context of a PTA results in a decline in the PTA's optimal external tariff. Bagwell and Staiger (1998) call this 'tariff complementarity'. Ours is stronger in that it establishes that the fall in the external tariff of FTA members is so large that it improves ROW's terms of trade and hence makes it better off (at constant ROW tariffs)[7].

We then use this result to show, first, that in the post-integration Nash equilibrium the external tariff of FTA members falls below its level in the pre-integration Nash equilibrium and, second, that ROW's optimal tariff rises above its pre-integration level. Interestingly, these tariff adjustments cause ROW's terms of trade to improve and, as we will see later, imply that the formation of the FTA benefits ROW.

The aforementioned findings also provide fresh insights on the differences between FTAs and CUs. As emphasized by Kennan and Riezman (1990), a key difference between these forms of integration is that CU members coordinate their external tariff policies and

---

[6] Our definition of the Kemp–Wan tariff adjustment is based on the well-known result of Kemp and Wan (1976) that there exists an external tariff structure that leaves ROW unaffected by the formation of a customs union. Similarly, in the symmetric trade model we consider, there exists an external tariff of the FTA members that leaves ROW unaffected by regional integration.

[7] Syropoulos (1999) and Bond et al. (2001) also show the presence of tariff complementarity in a trade model similar to the one considered here but with the PTA being a customs union. Bagwell and Staiger (1998) examine a partial equilibrium trade model with identical countries and linear demand functions and find that tariff complementarity holds for both FTAs and CUs. Freund (2000) obtains a similar result in a model with imperfectly competitive firms. Richardson (1995) also establishes that internal liberalization may result in a reduction in external tariffs in an FTA with and without rules of origin. This occurs because member countries reduce their external tariffs below those in the partner country to capture tariff revenues on imports that will ultimately be sold in the partner country's market. Our analysis differs in that we abstract from such competition for tariff revenues.

thus internalize the terms of trade externalities they generate for each other. More generally, though, the formation of a CU creates two opposing effects on the external tariff: a coordination effect that causes this tariff to rise and a complementarity effect that causes it to fall[8]. Our analysis clarifies that the absence of the coordination effect in FTAs means that the external tariff of members will be lower in an FTA than in a CU equilibrium. A second implication of this lack of coordination of external policies is that the optimal internal tariff for an FTA is positive. Intuitively, this is so because an increase of the internal tariff in the neighborhood of free internal trade raises welfare of FTA members by causing them to behave more aggressively in their external tariff policies and thereby improve their extra-union terms of trade.

The above findings unveil the presence of conflicting welfare effects of FTA formation on member states. The removal of internal tariffs expands internal trade and tends to improve member country welfare. However, the FTA terms of trade deteriorate because of the resulting changes in inter-bloc tariffs: in the post-integration equilibrium, the external tariff of the FTA members falls below its Kemp–Wan level and ROW becomes relatively more aggressive. This suggests that the relative size of the FTA ought to play an important role in determining whether FTA members benefit from the agreement.

We find that a relatively large FTA is more likely to benefit its members for two reasons. First, internal trade constitutes a relatively larger fraction of total trade for a large FTA, which implies that the beneficial trade volume effects are likely to be relatively larger. Second, a large FTA suffers less from adverse changes in ROW's external tariff because in this case ROW's market power is less pronounced. We show that there exists a sufficiently large (threshold) FTA size such that FTA members gain from internal liberalization, and provide simulation results to illustrate how large an FTA has to be for these gains to materialize. Our analysis reveals that while, in general, the threshold size is small, it can be large if ROW retaliates, especially when the elasticity of substitution in consumption is small and the degree of inter-country differences in comparative advantage large[9]. In contrast, the formation of the FTA benefits its members and the optimal degree of internal liberalization is quite large if ROW remains passive.

Lastly, our work sheds light on the question of whether FTAs are 'building blocks' or 'stumbling blocks' to global free trade (Bhagwati, 1992). Previous work on this issue showed that PTAs may undermine the attainment of global free trade if external tariffs are prohibitive (Levy, 1997) or fixed (Krishna, 1998). Our analysis reveals that the formation of an FTA may also undermine multilateral trade liberalization if countries intervene in world markets with (individually) optimal external tariffs. More specifically, we show, first, that either the outside country or the FTA members may block the attainment of global free trade in the post-integration equilibrium when they do not in the absence of an

---

[8] Whether external tariffs rise or fall upon the formation of a CU depends, among other things, on inter-country differences in endowments (Syropoulos, 1999).

[9] Kose and Riezman (2000) simulate a three-good version of our model but with identically sized countries and find that the formation of an FTA raises welfare of both members and nonmembers when trade patterns are similar to the ones considered here. Our results indicate that the latter result is a general property of FTAs in this type of model, but that the former result hinges on the assumption that all countries are of equal size.

E.W. Bond et al. / Journal of International Economics 64 (2004) 1–27 5

FTA; and, second, that these possibilities arise if there are significant asymmetries in the relative sizes of the two trading blocs.

In the next section, we present the formal trade model and derive analytic results on the effects of integration on tariffs and welfare under the assumption that ROW's tariff remains fixed. In Section 3, we extend the analysis to examine the effects of allowing ROW to adjust its tariff optimally. In Section 4, we offer some concluding remarks. The proofs to propositions and most algebraic details can be found in Appendix A.

2. The model and analysis

In this section, we present our basic trade model and define equilibrium between the FTA and ROW for an arbitrary degree of internal integration for the FTA. We then solve for the equilibrium of the model in the case where the FTA members are symmetric, and characterize the effects of eliminating internal trade barriers on the inter-bloc tariffs and welfare of all parties.

2.1. The trade model

We examine an endowment model in which there are N regions and N goods[10]. Consumers have Cobb–Douglas preferences represented by the utility function $u^i = \prod_{j=1}^{N} c_j^i$, where c_j^i is consumption of good j in region i. Region i has an endowment of $1 + \alpha$ units of good i and 1 unit of good $j \neq i$, where $\alpha > 0$, so region i has acomparative advantage in good i. We assume that these N regions are divided into three countries, with β_i denoting the fraction of the regions contained in country i. This symmetric configuration of endowments and preferences ensures that country i has comparative advantage in all of the goods $j \in N_i$, where N_i is the set of indices of all regions contained in country i. Choosing good 1 as the numeraire, this model has a free trade equilibrium in which the prices of all goods equal unity and country i exports $(1 - \beta_i)\alpha$ units of good $j \in N_i$. Since the volume of trade is increasing in parameter α for all countries, in this model α serves as a measure of the degree of comparative advantage.

Let τ_k^i and q_k, respectively, denote country i's tariff (plus unity) on its imports of good k and the world price of the same product. The domestic price of good k in country i will be $p_k^i = \tau_k^i q_k$. We will assume that: (i) there are no export taxes, and (ii) country i imposes the same ad valorem tariffs on all goods imported from country j[11]. Assumption (ii) and our assumption of symmetric preferences ensure that, if goods k and l are exported by some country j, then $c_k^i / c_l^i = q_l / q_k$ for every importing country i. Since world

---

[10] Our model is a variant of the model used by Bond and Syropoulos (1996a).

[11] It is shown in Bond and Syropoulos (1996a) that the assumed symmetry in endowments and preferences renders identical the optimal tariffs on all goods from a particular country. Therefore, this assumption is inconsequential when tariffs are set optimally. When tariffs are not set optimally, as in the case of internal tariff cuts in an FTA considered below, the symmetry of regions within a country makes the equal tariff assumption seem natural.

6   *E.W. Bond et al. / Journal of International Economics 64 (2004) 1–27*

endowments of the two goods are equal, this can be consistent with world market equilibrium only if $q_k = q_l$ and $c_j^i = c_k^{i}$[12]. Since the relative prices of all goods from a given country are constant, we can treat goods exported by country j as a Hicksian composite commodity j and define $C_j^i = \sum_{k \in N_j} c_k^i$ to be country i's consumption of good j originating in country j. It can be shown that the direct utility function in country i associated with these composite commodities is a monotonic transformation of the following function[13]:

$$U^i = \prod_{j=1}^{j=3} \left(\frac{C_j^i}{\beta_j} \right)^{\beta_j}, \quad i = 1, 2, 3 \tag{1}$$

The country size parameters β_j appear in the utility function in the composite commodity formulation because the number of goods in which a country has comparative advantage is proportional to its size. Consumer optimization then implies that $(p_j^i C_j^i)/(p_k^i C_k^i) = (\beta_j/\beta_k)$ for $i, j \neq k = 1, 2, 3$, so the relative budget shares (evaluated at domestic prices) are equal to relative country size.

Aggregating the endowments of the individual regions within a country, country i will have an endowment of $\beta_i \beta_j N^2$ of good $j \neq i$ and $\beta_i(\beta_i + \alpha)N^2$ of good i. It can be shown that the equilibrium prices in this model are homogeneous of degree 0 in N so we can simplify the following discussion by choosing $N = 1$[14].

Country i's budget constraint requires its expenditure at world prices to equal the value of its income, Y^i, also evaluated at world prices; that is,

$$\sum_{j=1}^{j=3} q_j C_j^i = Y^i \equiv \beta_i \left(\alpha q_i + \sum_{j=1}^{j=3} \beta_j q_j \right), \quad i = 1, 2, 3 \tag{2}$$

The necessary conditions for consumer optimization yield the following demand functions:

$$C_j^i = s_j^i \left(\frac{Y^i}{q_j} \right), \quad i, j = 1, 2, 3 \tag{3a}$$

---

[12] Consider two goods j and k associated with the same country. The market-clearing condition for good j requires $\sum_{i=1}^{N} c_j^i = x(N + \alpha)$. With Cobb Douglas preferences, consumer optimization implies $c_j^i p_j^i = c_k^i p_k^i$ for each region i. Our assumption of equal tariff rates for goods from the same bloc then yields $c_k^i = c_j^i q_j/q_k$, so the market-clearing condition for good k can be written as $\sum_i c_k^i = (q_j/q_k)(\sum_i c_j^i) = x(N + \alpha)$, which requires $q_j = q_k$.

[13] Letting p_j^i denote the common price of goods coming from country j into country i and Y^i consumer income in a region in country i, the budget constraint requires that $\sum_{j=1}^{j=3}(p_j^i \sum_{k \in N_j} c_k^i) = Y^i$. The indirect utility function is $v^i(p_1^i, p_2^i, p_3^i, Y^i) = (Y^i/N)^N \prod_{j=1}^{j=3} (p_j^i)^{-\beta_j N}$. The corresponding direct utility function can then be obtained by solving $\tilde{U}^i(C_1^i, C_2^i, C_3^i) = \min v^i(p_1^i, p_2^i, p_3^i, Y^i)$ subject to $\sum_{j=1}^{j=3} p_j^i C_j^i = Y^i$. Eq. (1) is obtained by a monotonic transformation of this direct utility function, $U = \tilde{U}^{(1/N)}$.

[14] This is simply another way of scaling world supply. We begin with $\beta_i(\beta_i + \alpha)N^2$ of good i and $\beta_i \beta_j N^2$ of good $j \neq i$. Suppose instead we started with $x(1 + \alpha)$ units of good i and x units of good $j \neq i$. This would yield the same equilibrium prices, because prices are homogeneous of degree 0 in x for the same reason they are homogeneous of degree 0 in N. The supply of the composite commodities would then be $x\beta_i(\beta_i + \alpha)N^2$ and $x\beta_i \beta_j N^2$. $x\beta_i \beta_j N^2$. The normalization of setting $N = 1$ would then be the same as choosing $x = 1/N^2$.

E.W. Bond et al. / Journal of International Economics 64 (2004) 1–27 7

where

$$s_j^i \equiv \frac{\beta_j q_j (p_j^i)^{-1}}{\sum_{k=1}^{k=3} \beta_k q_k (p_k^i)^{-1}} = \frac{\beta_j / \tau_j^i}{\sum_{k=1}^{k=3} (\beta_k / \tau_k^i)}, \quad i, j = 1, 2, 3 \tag{3b}$$

Denote with $\mathbf{T}^i$ the vector of tariffs imposed by country i. Utilizing (3a) and (3b) and the endowment structure described above, the excess demand function of good i in country i is $M_i^i(q_2, q_3, \mathbf{T}^i) = C_i^i - \beta_i(\beta_i + \alpha)$ whereas the excess demand of good j in country i is $M_j^i(q_2, q_3, \mathbf{T}^i) = C_j^i - \beta_i \beta_j$. The market clearing prices will be the values of q_2 and q_3 that solve

$$\sum_{i=1}^{i=3} M_j^i(q_2, q_3, \boldsymbol{T}^i) = 0, \quad j = 2, 3 \tag{4}$$

Under the symmetry conditions on tariffs we impose below, this equilibrium can be shown to be unique (Bond and Syropoulos, 1996a), so we can write the associated world relative prices, $q_i(\mathbf{T})$, as functions of tariffs, where $\mathbf{T} \equiv (\mathbf{T}^1, \mathbf{T}^2, \mathbf{T}^3)$ is the vector of tariffs in the world economy.

Let $V^i(q_2, q_3, \mathbf{T}^i)$ denote the indirect utility function of country i obtained by substituting (3a) and (3b) into (1). We can substitute the equilibrium price relations into the indirect utility functions to obtain the preferences of country i, $W^i(\mathbf{T}) = V^i(q_2(\mathbf{T}), q_3(\mathbf{T}), \mathbf{q}_3(\mathbf{T}), q_3(\mathbf{T}), \mathbf{T}^i)$, over all tariff rates.

2.2. Equilibrium with an FTA

Our next objective is to utilize the trade model to analyze the effect of the formation of an FTA on the welfare of members and ROW. The FTA members set their tariffs on imports from ROW independently. Both the FTA members and ROW adjust their tariffs so as to maximize national welfare. Henceforth, we assume that it is countries 1 and 2 that form an FTA; therefore, country 3 is ROW.

One of the difficulties in deriving analytic results on the formation of FTAs is that this process involves discrete reductions in the tariff levels, $\{\tau_2^1, \tau_1^2\}$, on internal trade. We overcome this problem by introducing the concept of a conditional FTA equilibrium:

Conditional FTA equilibrium:. A tariff vector $\{\tau_3^1, \tau_3^2, \tau_1^3, \tau_2^3\}$ is an FTA equilibrium, conditional on internal tariffs $\{\tau_2^1, \tau_1^2\}$, if the external tariffs of FTA members satisfy

$$\frac{\partial W^1(\boldsymbol{T})}{\partial \tau_3^1} = 0, \quad \frac{\partial W^2(\boldsymbol{T})}{\partial \tau_3^2} = 0 \tag{5a}$$

and the tariffs of the nonmember country (ROW) satisfy

$$\frac{\partial W^3(\boldsymbol{T})}{\partial \tau_j^3} = 0, \quad \text{for } j = 1, 2 \tag{5b}$$

Thus, according to this definition, the pre-integration Nash equilibrium is a particular conditional FTA equilibrium in which the internal tariffs also satisfy the conditions

8   *E.W. Bond et al. / Journal of International Economics 64 (2004) 1–27*

$\partial W^1(\mathbf{T})/\partial \tau_2^1 = \partial W^2(\mathbf{T})/\partial \tau_1^2 = 0$. The effects of the formation of an FTA can be derived by first establishing the existence of equilibrium for a conditional FTA. The effects of reducing internal tariffs from their initial Nash equilibrium levels all the way to zero can then be determined with the use of comparative statics analysis. In addition to tractability, the concept of a conditional FTA generates two additional benefits. First, we can investigate how welfare changes along the adjustment path. In practice, FTA members do not eliminate their internal trade barriers immediately; usually, they reduce these barriers gradually. Second, we can examine whether it is optimal for the FTA members to completely eliminate their internal tariffs, or whether they would prefer partial elimination.. It is now convenient to change our notation slightly and let a star '*' identify ROW variables. (For example, $\tau_j^*(j=1, 2)$ will denote ROW's tariff on its imports of good j from country j). We now adopt the following additional assumption.

Symmetry of partner countries:. Suppose the FTA members are of equal size (i.e. $\beta_1 = \beta_2$). Then we can restrict the analysis to solutions to (5a) and (5b), which satisfy the following symmetry conditions for tariffs:

(C1) $t \equiv \tau_2^1 = \tau_1^2$

(C2) $\tau \equiv \tau_3^1 = \tau_3^2$

(C3) $\tau^* \equiv \tau_1^* = \tau_2^*$

It should be noted that the symmetry conditions on tariffs are introduced to simplify the exposition[15]. Bond and Syropoulos (1996a) establish the existence of a pre-integration Nash equilibrium in which (C1), (C2) and (C3) are satisfied, so it is natural to focus on a path to internally free trade along which (C1) is satisfied. With $\beta_1 = \beta_2$ our analysis of the conditional FTA equilibrium is simplified to solving for tariffs $\tau^*(t)$ and $\tau(t) \equiv \tau_3^1(t) = \tau_3^2(t)$ that satisfy (5a) and (5b).

2.3. Kemp–Wan tariff adjustments

The Kemp–Wan adjustment is defined as the change in the external tariff of the FTA members that leaves welfare of ROW unaffected by a change in the internal tariff. The Kemp–Wan tariff adjustment is normally associated with the theory of customs unions,

---

[15] Symmetry is a useful simplification because it allows us to analyze the behavior of a representative FTA member and tariff interactions can be reduced to those between two (as opposed to three) policymakers in the pre- and post-integration Nash equilibria. It can be shown that, given (C1) and (C3), the best-response external tariffs of the FTA members that solve (5a) will satisfy (C2). Similarly, if (C1) and (C2) are satisfied, the best-response tariffs of ROW will satisfy (C3). Therefore, if internal tariffs satisfy (C1), an equilibrium in which (C2) and (C3) are satisfied will continue to be an equilibrium in the absence of these restrictions.

E.W. Bond et al. / Journal of International Economics 64 (2004) 1–27 9

where union members have a common external tariff (CET). However, by symmetry, the FTA members will end up choosing the same level of external tariff here as well. The Kemp–Wan adjustment provides a useful benchmark for our welfare analysis because (it can be shown that) trade liberalization within the FTA improves the terms of trade of ROW, at given ROW tariffs, iff the external tariffs of FTA members are reduced by more than the Kemp–Wan adjustment.

The following result establishes that adjustments in tariffs of FTA members result in a terms of trade improvement for ROW iff they reduce Ψ, where

$$\Psi \equiv \frac{\tau(1 + t^{-1})}{2} \tag{6}$$

Lemma 1, which is proven in Appendix A, is established using (3a), (3b) and (4).

Lemma 1. *If (C1), (C2) and (C3) hold, then*

(a) $q_2 = 1$
(b) $q_3 = q(\Psi(\tau, t), \tau^*)$, *where* $-1 < (\partial q / \partial \Psi)(\Psi / q) < 0$ *and* $0 < (\partial q / \partial \tau^*)(\tau^* / q) < 1$.

The terms of trade of the FTA relative to ROW are improved by an increase in the external tariff, τ, of the FTA, and are worsened by an increase in the internal tariff, t. These results follow from the fact that, at given world prices, an increase in the external (internal) tariff results in substitution toward (away from) exports of the member partner. Our assumptions of symmetry in endowments and preferences eliminate the possibility of a Metzler or Lerner paradox due to tariff changes. We can then invert (6) and define the Kemp–Wan tariff adjustment as follows:

$$\tau = \kappa(\Psi, t) \quad \text{where} \quad \frac{\partial \kappa / \partial t}{\kappa / t} = \frac{1}{1 + t} \tag{7}$$

Under a Kemp–Wan adjustment, a reciprocal and symmetric cut in the FTA members' internal tariffs must be met by a less than proportionate reduction in their external tariffs for the world price, q_3, to remain at its initial level. By Lemma 1, ROW's terms of trade improve iff internal trade liberalization is accompanied by an external tariff change that exceeds the Kemp–Wan adjustment. Lemma 1 also shows that ROW can improve its terms of trade by raising its tariff, τ^*.

The effect of changes in t and τ on welfare of FTA members can be illustrated with the help of Fig. 1 and the results of Lemma 1. The Ψ_N schedule reflects a Kemp–Wan tariff adjustment path, as defined by (7), starting from the initial Nash tariff equilibrium, N. The Ψ_G schedule depicts a Kemp–Wan tariff adjustment path associated with a lower value of Ψ, which by Lemma 1 reflects a higher initial value of q_3 (and hence worse terms of trade for FTA members). The Ψ loci also represent ROW indifference curves in (t, τ) space because the terms of trade and trade volume for ROW remain constant along each Ψ.

Under our symmetry assumptions, we can substitute the demand functions (3a) and (3b) and equilibrium relations from Lemma 1 into (1) to obtain welfare of a representative

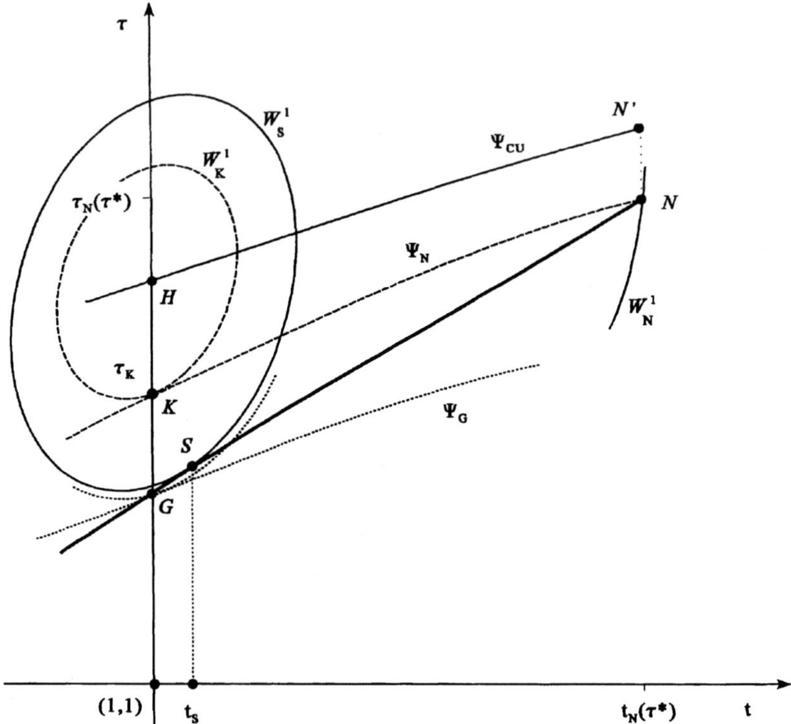

Fig. 1. Tariff adjustments and welfare under an FTA and a CU for fixed ROW tariffs.

FTA member. Normalizing welfare to be that of a representative region within a country, which has income Y^i/β_i from (2), we obtain

$$\tilde{W}^1(\tau, t, \tau^*) = W^1(\tau, \tau, t, t, \tau^*, \tau^*)$$

$$= \frac{2^\beta[\alpha + \beta + \beta^* q(\Psi, \tau^*)]\Psi^\beta q(\Psi, \tau^*)^{\beta-1}[t/(1+t)^2]^{\beta/2}}{\beta^* + \beta\Psi} \tag{8}$$

where $\beta = 2\beta_1$ is the relative size of the FTA and $\beta^* = 1 - \beta$ is the relative size of ROW. With this normalization, the free trade welfare is $W^1_{FT} = 1 + \alpha$.

Totally differentiating (8) with respect to t and Ψ and using the comparative statics results from Lemma 1 yields

$$\frac{d\tilde{W}^1}{\tilde{W}^1} = \beta\left[\left(\frac{\beta^*}{\beta^* + \beta\Psi}\right)\left(\frac{\varepsilon^* - 1}{\varepsilon + \varepsilon^* - 1}\right)\left(\frac{\varepsilon^*}{\varepsilon^* - 1} - \Psi\right)\hat{\Psi} - \frac{1}{2}\left(\frac{t-1}{t+1}\right)\hat{t}\right] \tag{9}$$

where $\varepsilon > 1$ ($\varepsilon^* > 1$) is the price elasticity of the FTA (ROW) import demand function and a hat ($^\wedge$) over variables denotes percentage change. The second term in (9) shows that, at a given Ψ, a reduction in t will raise welfare in the FTA iff $t > 1$. Thus, holding the external terms of trade of the FTA constant, internal tariff adjustments in the direction of free trade must raise welfare of FTA members. This is due to the favorable trade volume effect that

E.W. Bond et al. / Journal of International Economics 64 (2004) 1–27 11

results from this (reciprocal) tariff reduction at given terms of trade. This idea is captured in Fig. 1 by the fact that welfare of the FTA members is decreasing in t along a constant Ψ locus for $t>1$, and by the fact that the constant Ψ locus is tangent to a member iso-welfare contour at $t=1$.

The first term in (9) shows that welfare of the FTA will be increasing in Ψ iff $\Psi < \varepsilon^*/(\varepsilon^*-1)$. Note that the welfare of union members is maximized by choosing a CET that satisfies $\Psi = \varepsilon^*/(\varepsilon^*-1)$, which corresponds to the familiar optimal tariff formula when internal tariffs are zero, ($t=1$.) This is the external tariff that would be chosen if member states formed a customs union and chose the external tariff to maximize joint welfare (as discussed in Bond et al., 2001), and is illustrated by the Ψ_{CU} locus in Fig. 1. On this locus, member country iso-welfare contours will be vertical. Further, member country welfare will be increasing (decreasing) in Ψ for values below (above) Ψ_{CU}[16]. However, since members do not coordinate in their choice of external tariffs in an FTA, they do not take into account the favorable terms of trade effects of increases in their external tariff on the partner country. Specifically, since $\partial \tilde{W}^1/\partial \tau = \partial W^1/\partial \tau_3^1 + \partial W^1/\partial \tau_3^2$, a favorable terms of trade spillover between member countries (i.e. $\partial W^1/\partial \tau_3^2 > 0$) will mean that the member iso-welfare contour will be positively sloped at the conditional FTA equilibrium where $\partial W^1/\partial \tau_3^1 = 0$. We now turn to a characterization of the external tariffs chosen in the conditional FTA equilibria.

2.4. Best-response tariff for the representative FTA member

The best-response function for the FTA members will be the optimal choice of tariffs $\{\tau_3^1, \tau_3^2\}$ that satisfies (5a) given $\tau_2^1 = \tau_1^2 = t$ and $\tau_1^3 = \tau_2^3 = \tau^*$[17]. As a result of our symmetry assumptions, the best-response external tariff of an FTA member will be the value of τ that satisfies

$$\frac{\partial W^{-1}(\tau,\ \tau,\ t,\ t,\ \tau^*,\ \tau^*)}{\partial \tau_3^1} = 0 \tag{10}$$

If (10) holds, the symmetry assumptions ensure that $\partial W^2/\partial \tau_3^2 = 0$ when evaluated at the same tariff vector.

In our derivation of the properties of the best-response function, we will limit attention to values of $t < t_E(\tau^*)$, where $t_E(\tau^*)$ satisfies $\partial W^1(\tau,\ \tau,\ t,\ t,\ \tau^*,\ \tau^*)/\partial \tau_2^1 = 0$ when evaluated

---

[16] Using the result for ε^* derived in the Proof of Lemma 1 in Appendix A, the value of Ψ that maximizes member welfare satisfies $\Psi = (\alpha + \beta^*)q(\Psi,\ \tau^*)/\beta^*\tau^*$. It then follows from Lemma 1(b) that for $\Psi < \Psi_{CU}$ ($\Psi > \Psi_{CU}$), welfare of the FTA members will be increasing (decreasing) in τ.

[17] The type of an FTA we consider here is one in which trade deflection is absent. In other words, we abstract from the possibility of transshipment and the potential problems that may arise with respect to the sustainability of external tariffs. In addition, we abstract from the possible competition for tariff revenues that may arise between FTA policymakers when producers attempt to capitalize on arbitrage opportunities across national borders due to differential external tariffs. See Richardson (1995) for an argument establishing how such competition may induce both FTA members to dismantle their external tariffs as they adhere to internally free trade. As will become clear later on, we could modify the analysis appropriately to consider this possibility. It is useful to keep in mind though that the FTA we consider here will provide an upper bound to the external tariffs FTA members can sustain.

12   *E.W. Bond et al. / Journal of International Economics 64 (2004) 1–27*

at τ satisfying (10). Since the purpose of the formation of the FTA is to achieve mutual gains among members through reciprocal tariff reductions, we can limit attention to internal tariffs that are less than the values that would be optimal for a country acting unilaterally. Our first result establishes the properties of the FTA external tariff rates.

Proposition 1. (*Tariffs*) *Assume (C1), (C3), and suppose ROW tariffs remain fixed at a non-prohibitive level* τ^*. *Then there will exist an aggregate best-response function,* $\varphi(\tau^*, t)$, *for the FTA with the following properties:*

(a) $\partial \varphi(\tau^*, t)/\tau^* < 0$
(b) (*Tariff Complementarity*) $\partial \varphi(\tau^*, t)/\partial t > 0$
(c) *If* $t_2 < t_1$ *and* $\tau_1 = \varphi(\tau^*, t_1)$, *then* $\varphi(\tau^*, t_2) < \kappa(\Psi(\tau_1, t_1), t_2)$.

Part (a) of Proposition 1 shows that τ and τ^* are strategic substitutes. Higher ROW tariffs induce the FTA members to lower their external tariffs. Part (b) establishes tariff complementarity between internal and external tariffs for the FTA, so that reductions in internal tariffs reduce the external tariff of the member countries. Part (c) strengthens this result by showing that the external tariff falls below the Kemp–Wan tariff. Thus, complete internal liberalization by the FTA induces its members to reduce their external tariff so much that their external terms of trade deteriorate. These results are illustrated in Fig. 1. The *NG* locus indicates the path of best-response external tariffs of the FTA members as the internal tariff falls from t_N to 1. By part (c) of Proposition 1, this line lies below the Kemp–Wan schedule, *NK*, so point *G* represents a worsening of the FTA terms of trade relative to point N^{18}.

We next consider the welfare effects of an FTA. Proposition 1 can be used to derive the impact of internal liberalization of an FTA on welfare for a given level of the ROW tariff, τ^*.

Proposition 2. (*Welfare for a given* τ^*) *Assume (C1), (C3), and suppose ROW's tariff remains fixed at a non-prohibitive level* $\tau*$ *while FTA countries 1 and 2 set their external tariffs optimally.*

(a) *Internal trade liberalization within the FTA raises ROW welfare, and may either raise or lower welfare of the FTA members.*
(b) *There exists an internal tariff* $t_S > 1$ *that leaves every FTA member better off as compared with internal free trade, i.e.* $W^1(\varphi(\tau^*, t_S), t_S, \tau^*) > W^1(\varphi(\tau^*, t=1), t=1, \tau^*)$.

The fact that ROW gains from the formation of the FTA follows immediately from Proposition 1(c), which indicates that ROW's terms of trade improve with internal

---

18 In contrast, it is shown in Syropoulos (1999) and Bond et al. (2001) that members of a CU adopt a more aggressive stance externally so that their CET exceeds the Kemp–Wan tariff that is associated with the initial Nash equilibrium (illustrated by the $N'H$ locus in Fig. 1). Members of a CU choose higher tariffs because they internalize the effects of one member's tariff on the welfare of other members. As a consequence, the CU improves its terms of trade as compared with the Nash equilibrium.

E.W. Bond et al. / Journal of International Economics 64 (2004) 1–27 13

liberalization. The effect of tariff reduction on member welfare consists of two effects, which can be illustrated with the help of Fig. 1 and the welfare decomposition in (9). The first effect is the trade volume effect, which is favorable to the FTA members. To see this consider the effect of complete elimination of internal trade barriers starting from the Nash equilibrium (point N). If the external tariff were adjusted so as to maintain world prices constant, the elimination of internal trade barriers would involve a movement along the Ψ_N locus from point N to point K in Fig. 1, which must be welfare-improving for FTA members. The second effect is the terms of trade effect resulting from the external tariff adjustment, illustrated by the movement from K to G, which must be welfare-reducing for FTA members. Thus, the overall effect on welfare of the movement from N to G appears to be ambiguous for FTA members. It is interesting to note that this decomposition of a favorable trade volume effect and unfavorable terms of trade effect also applies to partial reductions of internal tariffs. We will revisit these points later when we will allow ROW to behave strategically.

Part (b) of Proposition 2 illustrates that welfare of FTA members could be improved if they stopped short of totally dismantling their (symmetric) internal trade barriers. This can be shown by using the fact that an iso-welfare contour of an FTA member is tangent to an iso-Ψ contour at $t=1$, as noted in the discussion above. Therefore, an increase in t and τ that raises Ψ will raise welfare of an FTA member if the external tariff is below the welfare-maximizing tariff at H. This is illustrated by the movement in the direction of point N along GN in Fig. 1, with the welfare of each FTA member rising throughout the interval GS. The desirability of stopping short of completely eliminating internal barriers results from the fact that FTA members do not take into account the impact of their external tariff on the welfare of other members, so that FTA members adopt external tariffs that are lower than the ones that would maximize joint welfare. Due to the complementarity between internal and external tariffs identified in Proposition 1, the internal tariff provides an indirect means of coordinating their external tariff policies[19].

The size of the FTA members relative to ROW plays an important role in determining the relative importance of the terms of trade and trade volume effects, and hence the response of member welfare to trade liberalization. For very large blocs, the internal liberalization effect will dominate and the FTA will be welfare-improving. This can be seen by noting that, in the limiting case in which $\beta \to 1$, trade with ROW becomes insignificant—the terms of trade effect disappears and only the benefits to trade liberalization matter. This limiting case is equivalent to the gains from tariff reduction in a two-country world, so welfare of members rises monotonically as the internal tariff t is reduced (i.e. $t_S \to 1$ as $\beta \to 1$ in part (b)). On the other hand, for small blocs the benefits of internal liberalization approach zero as $\beta \to 0$ because internal trade becomes an insignificant share of total trade. However, terms of trade

---

[19] As compared with the case of customs unions, this finding resembles the one due to Ethier and Horn (1984) who showed that internal free trade is not optimal for a small customs union with positive CETs, but differs from the one due to Bond et al. (2001) who proved that internal free trade is optimal when the CET maximizes union welfare.

effects also disappear as $\beta \to 0$ because the impact of changes in Ψ on world prices goes to zero. (It can be shown, for example, that $\lim_{\beta \to 0} (dW^1/dt)(W^1/t) = 0$).

2.5. Optimal policies in ROW

We next turn to an examination of how ROW's optimal tariff responds to changes in the FTA internal tariff, t. The tariff reaction function for ROW is derived by finding the value of τ^* that satisfies (5b) for given FTA tariffs. Using our symmetry assumptions and the results of Lemma 1, the excess demand functions of the FTA members can be expressed as $M_j^i(\Psi, q_3)$ for $i = 1, 2$ and $j = 1, 2, 3$. The optimal tariff of ROW will thus be a function of Ψ, so its best-response function can be expressed as $\varphi^*(\tau, t) = f(\Psi(\tau, t))$. We can establish the following properties for this function.

Proposition 3. *Assume (C1), (C2), and suppose the tariffs of FTA members 1 and 2 are below their prohibitive levels. Then, ROW will have a best-response tariff, $\varphi^*(\tau, t) = f'(\Psi(\tau, t))$, such that $f(\Psi(\cdot)) < 0$. Therefore,*

(a) $\partial \varphi^*(\tau, t)/\partial \tau < 0$
(b) $\partial \varphi^*(\tau, t)/\partial_t > 0$

Part (a) of Proposition 3 says that ROW responds to an increase in the FTA external tariff τ by lowering its own external tariff τ^*. In other words, the external tariff of the FTA is a strategic substitute for ROW's tariff. The intuition for this result can be seen by considering Lemma 1 which shows that q_2 is independent of ROW's tariff policy and implies that we can think of this as a two-good model in which ROW imports a composite commodity from the FTA. An increase in the FTA's external tariff reduces the FTA's import demand for ROW goods thereby raising the price elasticity of demand for ROW exports and diminishing its market power in trade. This induces ROW to reduce its tariff. An increase in the FTA's internal trade barriers would have the opposite effect on ROW's optimal tariff (part (b) of Proposition 3) because it would raise the demand for ROW exports and reduce the elasticity of demand. This, of course, would induce ROW to raise its tariff. Hence, the internal tariff of the FTA is a strategic complement for ROW's tariff.

These results identify another reason as to why FTA members find the complete removal of internal tariffs unappealing. By inducing FTA members to behave less aggressively externally, on balance internal trade liberalization enhances ROW's market power and thus exacerbates the inability of FTA members to internalize their (external) tariff externality. In other words, as internal tariffs approach zero, the additional benefits of liberalization get smaller, but the terms-of-trade losses due to lower FTA external tariffs and higher ROW tariffs do not. We are now in a position to determine equilibrium.

3. Equilibrium tariffs and welfare

Proposition 2 derived the welfare effects of internal liberalization for the FTA under the assumption that ROW tariffs do not change. Now that we have derived the properties of the

E.W. Bond et al. / Journal of International Economics 64 (2004) 1–27 15

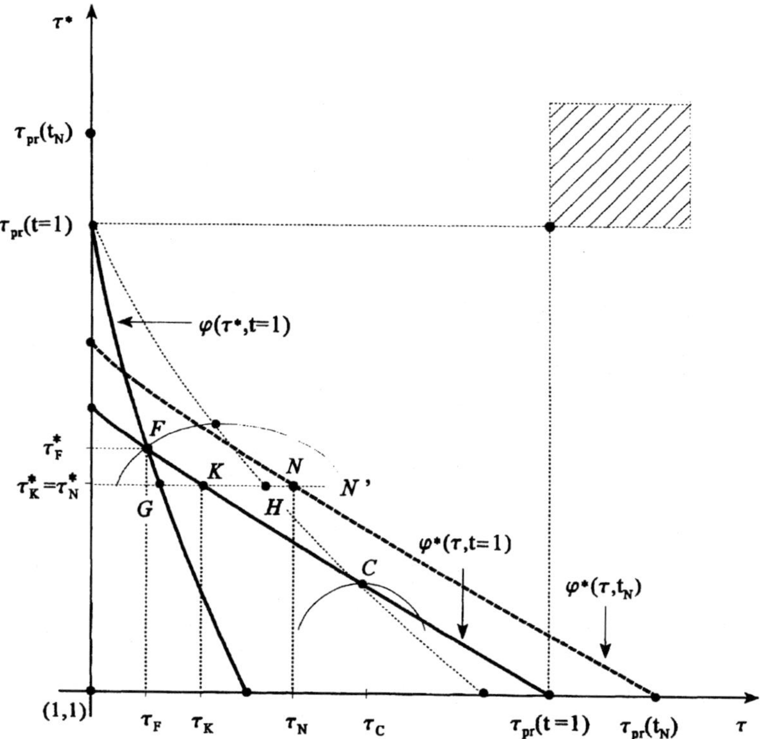

Fig. 2. Best-response tariff functions and policy equilibria.

reaction functions of the FTA members and ROW, we can obtain results on the equilibrium tariffs between ROW and the FTA when ROW reacts optimally to the liberalization of trade within the FTA. These results on tariffs will then be used to study how internal trade liberalization affects welfare of FTA members and ROW.

3.1. Inter-bloc tariff adjustments

Starting from the three-country (pre-integration) Nash equilibrium, where the initial tariffs are denoted $\{\tau_N, \tau_N^*, t_N\}$, we consider the effects of eliminating internal barriers in the context of Fig. 2 whose two axes are the external tariff of a representative FTA member and of ROW. The pre-integration Nash equilibrium is captured by point N, the intersection of ROW's best-response function (dashed-line curve) and the best-response function of the representative FTA member (not shown). These functions are drawn for a given t, and in this case we set t at t_N.

It follows from Propositions 1 and 3 that the elimination of internal barriers will cause a leftward shift in both best-response functions. In order to compare the magnitude of these shifts, we can compare these best responses to the situation that would arise if the FTA external tariff adjusted in a Kemp–Wan fashion relative to the pre-integration equilibrium instead; that is, if $\tau = \kappa(\Psi_N, t=1)$ where $\Psi_N \equiv \Psi(\tau_N, t_N)$. Proposition 3 showed that ROW's best response is a function of Ψ alone; that is, $\varphi^*(\kappa(\Psi_N, t=1), t=1) = \tau_N^*$, $t=1) = \tau_N^*$, as illustrated by point K in Fig. 2. Furthermore, Proposition 1(a) established that $\varphi(\tau_N^*, t=1) < \kappa(\Psi_N, t=1)$, therefore, the FTA members' best-response tariff must lie to the left of point K. Since the best-response functions of both parties are downward sloping and intersect uniquely when $t=1$, the conditional FTA equilibrium tariff pair at internal free trade (i.e. $\{\tau_F, \tau_F^*\}$) must be at a point like F in Fig. 2 where $\tau_F < \kappa(\Psi_N, t=1) < \tau_N$ and $\tau_F^* > \tau_N^*$.

The above discussion focused on the case in which the initial equilibrium was the pre-integration Nash equilibrium. Interestingly, however, the same argument can be made starting from any conditional Nash equilibrium with $t \in (1, t_N]$. This yields the following result.

Proposition 4. (*Tariffs*) *Suppose an FTA has an internal tariff of $t_1 \in (1, t_N]$. Let $\tau_1 = \varphi(\tau_1^*, t_1)$ and $\tau_1^* = \varphi^*(\tau_1, t_1)$ denote a conditional FTA tariff equilibrium. If the FTA members completely eliminate their internal tariff, the tariffs $\{\tau_F, \tau_F^*\}$ in the resulting Nash equilibrium will satisfy*

(a) $\tau_F < \kappa(\Psi(\tau_1, t_1), t=1) < \tau_1$
(b) $\tau_F^* > \tau_1^*$.

Part (a) shows that, along a path of internal tariff reductions to free internal trade, the external tariff of the FTA members will always be above the level chosen when $t=1$. This means that for FTA members the Kemp–Wan external tariff is below its initial level and, furthermore, the optimal external tariff at the full-integration equilibrium is less than the Kemp–Wan tariff level. Part (b) shows that ROW responds by charging a higher tariff. Thus, FTA formation results in lower tariffs for members and higher tariffs for ROW.

3.2. Welfare effects of complete trade liberalization

What do the changes in external tariffs identified in Proposition 4 mean for welfare of ROW and FTA members? Combining Propositions 3 and 4, we may answer this question as follows.

Proposition 5. (*Welfare*) *Suppose we have a conditional equilibrium $\{\tau_1, \tau_1^*\}$ for $t_1 \in (1, t_N]$. An FTA between symmetric countries that leads to a complete elimination of internal trade barriers always benefits ROW. The FTA benefits its members if their combined size is sufficiently large relative to ROW. However, small FTAs may be welfare-reducing for its members. Specifically,*

(a) $W^*(\tau_F, t=1, \tau_F^*) > W^*(\tau_1, t_1, \tau_1^*)$
(b) *There exists a $\bar{\beta} \in (0, 1)$ such that $W^i(\tau_F, t=1, \tau_F^*) > W^i(\tau_1, t_1, \tau_1^*)$ for $\beta > \bar{\beta}$.*

To see why ROW welfare must rise, consider the effect of a reduction in the internal tariff from $t = t_N$ to 1, as shown in Fig. 2. ROW welfare at point K will be equal to that at the initial point N by the definition of the Kemp–Wan tariff reduction. However, ROW welfare at point F must exceed the level at point K because ROW welfare is decreasing in τ along its

E.W. Bond et al. / Journal of International Economics 64 (2004) 1–27   17

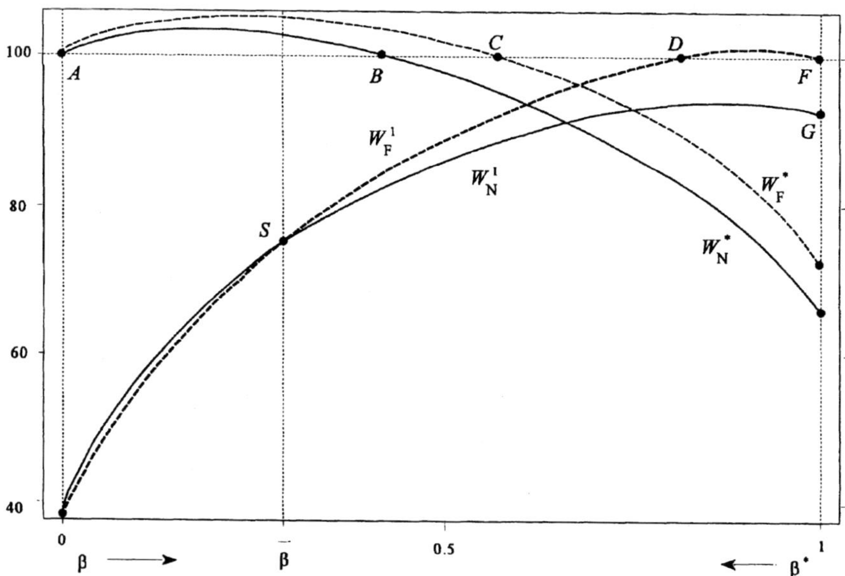

Fig. 3. Welfare of ROW and the representative FTA member as functions of relative size.

best-response function. Thus, the movement from N to F must raise ROW welfare. By Proposition 2(a), we know that the movement from N to G affects welfare of an FTA member ambiguously. Moreover, the movement from G to F is welfare-reducing because the typical member's welfare is decreasing in τ^* along its reaction function. Therefore, when ROW tariffs adjust optimally in response to trade liberalization in the FTA it becomes more likely that FTA members will lose from this form of regional integration. Still, the net effect of integration on welfare of FTA members remains ambiguous.

Part (b) says that, if the FTA members are large enough they will benefit from the formation of the FTA. The intuition for this result is that, for FTA members whose combined size relative to ROW is sufficiently large, the benefits from internal liberalization are large while the welfare losses due to terms of trade deterioration with ROW are small. One can also see this result by considering the limiting case in which the FTA members become arbitrarily large by letting $\beta \to 1$. The welfare level of FTA members with internal free trade will approach the level with global free trade level, because the tariff-distorted trade with ROW is an insignificant fraction of world trade. In contrast, prior to internally free trade, member welfare will approach the level in the Nash equilibrium of a two (symmetric) country tariff-setting game, which is lower than the free trade level. Since the respective payoffs are continuous in the FTA's size, β, the FTA payoff with internal free trade must be higher than the Nash equilibrium payoff for β sufficiently close to 1. In contrast, when the FTA is small, the gains from internal liberalization are also small because of the small volume of internal trade. However, the welfare loss from deteriorating terms of trade with ROW will be large because of the large volume of trade with the outside country.

Fig. 3 provides some further insights about the role of relative FTA size, as suggested in Proposition 5(b). The reported calculations suppose $\alpha = 2$ and the payoffs are normalized so

18   *E.W. Bond et al. / Journal of International Economics 64 (2004) 1–27*

that the free trade welfare level of the representative region in a country equals 100[20]. The solid-line curves show the welfare of FTA members (W_N^1) and ROW (W_N^*) in the pre-integration Nash equilibrium as a function of the relative size of the FTA. For β below the value associated with point B, ROW's market power is sufficiently large so that its welfare in the pre-integration Nash equilibrium exceeds the free trade level[21]. The dashed-line curves show the welfare level of FTA members (W_F^1) and ROW (W_F^*) in the FTA equilibrium with complete internal liberalization. As indicated by Proposition 5(a), ROW gains from the formation of the FTA for all values of β, with the percentage gains being largest when the FTA is relatively large. For FTA members, the critical value $\bar\beta$ identified in Proposition 5(b) is about 0.3. However, the simulations suggest a stronger result than the one obtained in Proposition 5, since they show that there is a relative size $\bar\beta$ such that FTA members benefit from formation of the FTA iff $\beta > \bar\beta$.

An interesting feature of Fig. 3 is that the formation of the FTA enlarges the set of relative sizes under which a global free trade equilibrium becomes undesirable. Specifically, for sizes associated with the range of points B and F, global free trade is preferred by all countries over the pre-integration Nash equilibrium, and is thus feasible. The FTA formation reduces this set of sizes to those that are associated with interval CD, as the FTA members (ROW) now prefer(s) the FTA regime over global free trade for all configurations along segment DF (AC). This clearly suggests that while, in the short-run, FTAs may be welfare-improving in the Pareto sense, they may end up being 'stumbling blocks' (Bhagwati, 1992) to the attainment of global free trade in the longer run[22]. Lastly, it should be noted that FTA welfare does not rise monotonically with FTA size either in the pre-integration equilibrium or in the FTA equilibrium. Using techniques similar to those in Bond and Syropoulos (1996a), it can be shown that W_F^1 approaches the free trade welfare level from above as $\beta \to 1$. A similar point is valid for ROW welfare as $\beta \to 0$.

With the help of the analysis in Bond et al. (2001), we can contrast the aforementioned results with those obtained in the customs union case. It can be shown that, the optimal CET of a CU between countries 1 and 2 is related to their (common) internal tariff, t, as indicated by schedule $N'H$ in Fig. 1. Further, it can be shown that this schedule does not lie below the Kemp–Wan path through point H' (not drawn). Pulling these ideas together, it can also be shown that, even if ROW behaved optimally, the CET of the CU would be larger than the Kemp–Wan tariff that would keep the world price at the pre-integration level; therefore, the formation of an (unconstrained) CU would benefit its members but would hurt ROW (Syropoulos, 1999).

3.3. Determining the critical size for welfare improvement with an FTA

The analytic results in Proposition 5 suggest an important role for the size of FTA members in determining the benefits of FTA formation. For policy purposes, it would be

---

[20] The payoffs are transformed by multiplying the utility of each country by $100/(1+\alpha)$. It is easy to verify then, that under globally free trade, we would have $W^i = 100$ for the representative region in country i ($=1, 2, 3$).

[21] These possibilities arise for extreme size configurations thereby confirming the idea that sufficiently large countries are likely to win tariffs wars, as pointed out in Kennan and Riezman (1988) and Syropoulos (2002).

[22] In independent but related work, Ornelas (2001) obtained a similar result in the context of a reciprocal dumping model in which policymakers also have (domestic) distributional concerns.

E.W. Bond et al. / Journal of International Economics 64 (2004) 1–27 19

Table 1
Values of $\bar{\beta}$ for alternative parameter values

α	σ				
	1	2	5	10	20
1	0.212	0.137	0.087	0.071	0.062
2	0.283	0.184	0.114	0.091	0.079
5	0.341	0.225	0.135	0.105	0.090
10	0.359	0.240	0.138	0.107	0.092

useful to have an idea of what factors determine how large an FTA has to be to ensure that its members benefit from complete liberalization of internal trade. In addition, it would also be useful to know whether partial internal liberalization can be beneficial for FTAs whose size falls below the critical value. In this section, we provide some additional simulations to address each of these issues.

Table 1 illustrates how $\bar{\beta}$ varies with two parameters: the degree of comparative advantage (α) and the elasticity of substitution in consumption (σ). To derive analytical results, the latter parameter was restricted to $\sigma = 1$ in the formal analysis, but here we allow it to vary to highlight the sensitivity of our findings to this assumption. The results reported in Table 1 indicate that $\bar{\beta}$ is increasing in α and decreasing in σ. Therefore, small FTAs are most vulnerable to adverse effects of internal liberalization when the degree of comparative advantage is large and the elasticity of substitution between products is low. In Bond and Syropoulos (1996a) it was shown that trading blocs will set higher external tariffs when α is high and σ is low because the prices elasticities of the offer curves are lower in this case. This suggests that the losses of the small trading blocs are largely due to the exercise of market power by ROW in adjusting its external tariff.

Figs. 4a and b can be used to see how the welfare of FTA members is affected along the path of internal trade liberalization. In these figures, we consider two cases: a high elasticity of substitution ($\sigma = 5$ in Fig. 4a) and a low elasticity of substitution ($\sigma = 1$ in Fig. 4b). For both cases we choose a value of $\beta = 0.1 < \bar{\beta}$ so that an FTA with complete internal liberalization is welfare-reducing. We choose this value to show that partial liberalization can be beneficial when complete liberalization is not. The dashed-line curves in Figs. 4a and b illustrate how welfare varies with the internal tariff under the assumption that ROW's tariff remains fixed at its pre-integration level. In the spirit of Proposition 2, notice that FTA members can increase their welfare by raising the internal tariff rate above its free trade level. In fact, the welfare of FTA members is maximized at some $t = t_S > 1$ (as in Proposition 2(b)), although the benefit from stopping short of complete internal liberalization is relatively small. The dashed-line curves in Figs. 4a and b also show that, starting from the pre-integration Nash equilibrium, the formation of an FTA would benefit its members if ROW were constrained not to raise its external tariff, even when the aggregate size of the FTA is small[23].

---

[23] The validity of this observation appears to remain intact under a wide range of parameter values. In fact, our simulations failed to identify parameter values under which FTA welfare falls below its pre-integration level when ROW does not behave strategically.

20   *E.W. Bond et al. / Journal of International Economics 64 (2004) 1–27*

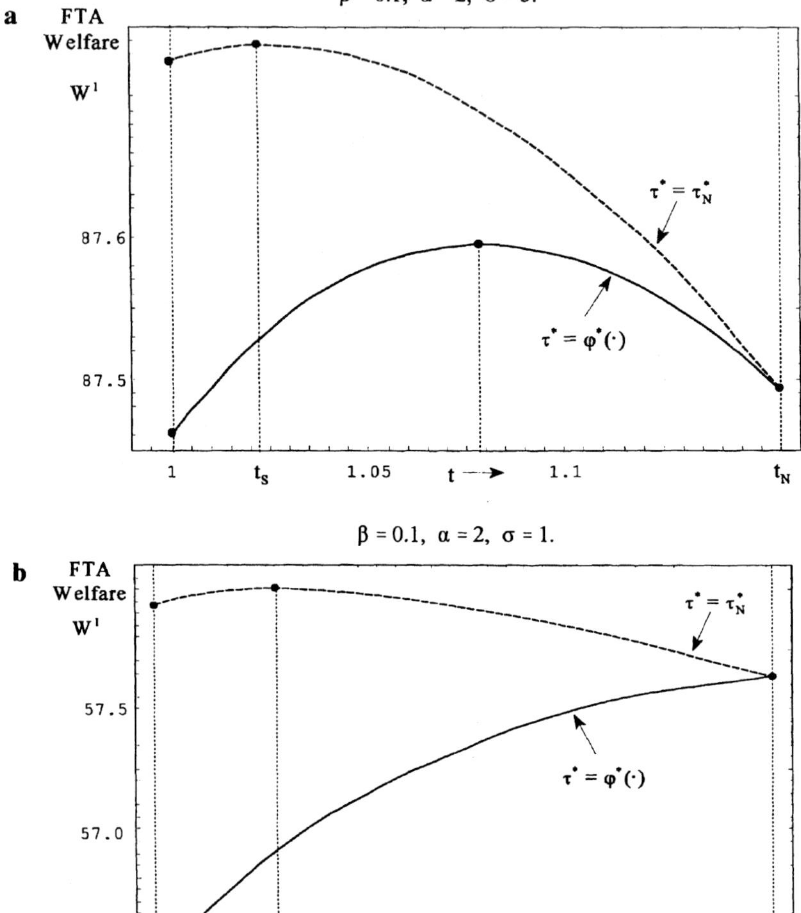

Fig. 4. (a) Welfare of the representative FTA member as a function of the internal tariff for fixed and optimal ROW tariffs ($\sigma = 5$). (b) Welfare of the representative FTA member as a function of the internal tariff for fixed and optimal ROW tariffs ($\sigma = 1$).

The solid-line curves in Figs. 4a and b illustrate the effect of internal liberalization on welfare when ROW's tariff is set optimally. Since $\beta = 0.1 < \bar{\beta}$, we know that the formation of an FTA (with complete internal trade liberalization) would not benefit its members relative to the pre-integration Nash equilibrium. Fig. 4a shows that, when the elasticity of substitution is high, partial liberalization can be welfare-improving. This figure also shows that welfare is maximized at a significantly higher value of the internal tariff, t, than would be the case when ROW's tariff is held constant. Interestingly, when the elasticity of

E.W. Bond et al. / Journal of International Economics 64 (2004) 1–27 21

substitution in consumption is low, all degrees of internal liberalization are welfare-reducing for the FTA.

4. Concluding remarks

Our results indicate that the formation of an FTA improves the terms of trade and welfare of nonmember countries because it creates an incentive for members to reduce their external tariffs[24]. However, for member states, there are two opposing effects. In equilibrium, their terms of trade vis-a-vis ROW deteriorate and this is welfare-reducing. At the same time, the liberalization of internal trade causes intra-union trade to expand and this is welfare-improving. We have shown that, as long as member countries are sufficiently large, the latter effect will dominate and the formation of an FTA will benefit both members.

These findings differ from those that arise under a CU where typically there is a smaller external tariff reduction (or even an increase). This occurs because CU members jointly choose the external tariff to maximize union welfare, thus internalizing the positive tariff externality that exists whenever two countries import the same good from ROW. With the objective function that we consider, a CU will always be preferred to an FTA for symmetric member countries because of its more favorable market power effects[25]. Thus, while this model does not provide a positive theory of FTA formation, it does point out how international distributional effects differ between FTAs and CUs. It also suggests that, in the short run, FTAs are more appealing from a world welfare perspective because they imply relatively less aggressive tariff setting for their members.

Our analysis has several interesting implications for the desirability of Article XXIV of the GATT that binds PTA members to remove substantially all tariffs on internal trade and constrains them to keep external tariffs at or below their pre-integration levels. Depending on comparative advantage, the constraint on external tariffs may be binding for CU members (Syropoulos, 1999) but, as we have seen, it is not binding for FTA members. This suggests that, since ROW may behave relatively more aggressively in the post-integration equilibrium, rules that prevent ROW from raising tariffs may be as important in practice as Article XXIV itself. On the other hand, the requirement to completely liberalize internal trade is incentive-compatible for optimally behaving CUs (Bond et al., 2001) but not for FTA members (Proposition 2). Since this limits the welfare benefits of FTA

---

[24] An empirical implication of our results is that the formation of FTAs should also be associated with unilateral liberalization by the participating countries, with the causation running from the formation of FTAs to unilateral tariff reduction. However, while there are numerous instances where countries have signed preferential trade agreements and engaged in unilateral liberalization, the direction of causation is difficult to determine. An alternative explanation for this correlation would be that there is a change in government preferences that favors both unilateral and bilateral liberalization. Thus, a more thorough empirical analysis would be required to identify the direction of causation.

[25] In practice, an important reason of why countries prefer an FTA over a CU is that they enjoy greater flexibility in conducting their trade policy vis-a-vis ROW.

22   *E.W. Bond et al. / Journal of International Economics 64 (2004) 1–27*

members relative to partial trade liberalization, the possibility arises that fewer FTAs may form and, as a consequence, global free trade may be easier to attain in the long run.

Our results are contingent on the assumptions that the structure of FTAs is exogenously given and that direct trade liberalization between the FTA members and ROW is not possible. Still, our analysis is relevant for the analysis of endogenous coalition formation and has interesting implications for whether FTAs are 'stepping stones' or 'stumbling blocks' to the attainment of global free trade. As we have seen, an FTA may be welfare-improving in the Pareto sense relative to no cooperation at all. However, these welfare gains may very well undermine global free trade because, depending on the relative size of trading blocs, they may render global free trade less attractive either to FTA members or to ROW. Future work could consider in finer detail how the formation of an FTA might affect the appeal of multilateral trade liberalization, paying special attention to incentive constraints, Article XXIV of the GATT, and intra-union asymmetries in relative size[26].

We abstracted from special interest politics and how they might affect tariff-setting incentives. However, our analysis could be extended in this direction by reformulating the payoff functions of national policymakers appropriately to consider these possibilities. We think this is important because a richer model of this type would provide a more solid theoretical benchmark for the growing empirical literature on the subject and, hopefully, help test the hypotheses we have advanced in this paper.

Acknowledgements

For their helpful comments, we wish to thank Richard Chisik, Earl Grinols, Pascalis Raimondos-Møller, two referees, and seminar participants at McGill University, University of Missouri, the Midwest International Economics Meetings at Purdue University, the Southeastern Economic Theory and International Economics Conference at Georgetown University, and the Southern Economic Association Meetings in New Orleans. Syropoulos thanks the FIU Foundation/Provost Office for a summer grant.

Appendix A

Proof of Lemma 1. The fact that $q_2 = 1$ is an equilibrium can be seen by substituting the symmetry assumptions into (3a), (3b) and (4). The uniqueness result from Bond and Syropoulos (1996a) ensures that this is the only equilibrium. If the symmetry assumptions are substituted into (3a) and (3b), the excess demand functions for good 3 by FTA

---

[26] In a previous version of this paper (Bond et al., 2000), we numerically explored the effects of intra-union asymmetries in size and found that, in the absence of compensatory transfers, small countries favor the formation of an FTA with large partners while the latter may not. This differs from McLaren's (1997) finding that the anticipation of a trade agreement (with side payments) between two countries may leave the "small" partner worse off, as compared to non-cooperation. The key reason for this difference in results is that McLaren allows private agents in the small country to undertake irreversible investments under the prospect of free trade that amplify the country's dependence on trade and erode its (strategic) bargaining position in future negotiations.

E.W. Bond et al. / Journal of International Economics 64 (2004) 1–27 23

members can be written as $M_3^i/N^2 = \beta\beta^*(\alpha + \beta - \beta\Psi q)/[2q(\beta^* + \beta\Psi)]$ for $i = 1, 2$ and the excess demand for FTA goods by ROW as $M^*/N^2 = \beta(1 - \beta)[(\alpha + \beta^*)q - \beta^*\tau^*]/(\beta + \beta^*\tau^*)$. The price elasticities of these demands are $\varepsilon \equiv -(\partial M_3^i/\partial q)/(M_3^i/q) = (\alpha + \beta)/(\alpha + \beta - \beta\Psi q) >$ 1 and $\varepsilon^* = (\alpha + \beta^*)q/[(\alpha - \beta^*)q - \beta^*\tau^*] > 1$, respectively. Moreover, $\gamma \equiv -(\partial M_3^i/\partial\Psi)(M_3^i/\Psi)$ $= \Psi\beta(\alpha + \beta + \beta^*q)/((\beta\Psi + \beta^*)(\alpha + \beta - \beta\Psi q)) > 0$ and $\gamma^* \equiv -(\partial M^*/\partial\tau^*)(\tau^*/M^*) = \beta^*\tau^*(q(\alpha$ $+ \beta^*) + \beta)/[(\beta + \beta^*\tau^*)((\alpha + \beta^*)q - \beta^*\tau^*)] > 0$, we have $\varepsilon > \gamma$ and $\varepsilon^* > \gamma^*$. Now, using the budget constraint, the market-clearing condition for good 3 can be written as $2qM_3^1 = M^*$. Totally differentiating this expression and using the definitions above yields the comparative statics results of Lemma 1(b): $-1 < \hat{q}/\hat{\Psi} = -\gamma/(\varepsilon + \varepsilon^* - 1) < 0$ and $0 < \hat{q}/\hat{\tau}^* = \gamma^*/(\varepsilon + \varepsilon^* - 1) < 1$. $\quad\square$

Proof of Proposition 1. To establish existence and the postulated properties of the FTA's aggregate reaction function $\varphi(\tau^*, t)$ it is convenient to work with variables Ψ and t (instead of τ and t). Going back to country 1's welfare decomposition in (9), attribute the changes in world prices q_2 and q_3 to a change in the external tariff τ_3^1. These price changes can be derived by utilizing the definitions of the import demand functions (which follow from Eqs. (2), (3a) and (3b)) in the balanced trade condition (4), and imposing conditions (C1)–(C3) after differentiating (4) appropriately. Doing so leads to Eq. (10) which describes country 1's first-order condition (FOC) for welfare maximization and defines $\varphi(\tau_1^*, t)$ implicitly. After some cumbersome algebra, it can be shown that $\partial W^1(\cdot)/\partial\tau_3^i = 0$ with symmetry is equivalent to the requirement that

$$\Psi = \Omega(\Psi, t, \tau^*) \equiv q(\Psi, \tau^*)\left[\frac{\mu(\Psi, t, \tau^*)}{\lambda(\Psi, t, \tau^*)}\right] \tag{A.1}$$

where

$$q(\cdot) = \left[\frac{\alpha + \beta}{\beta^* + \beta\Psi} + \frac{\beta^*\tau^*}{\beta + \beta^*\tau^*}\right]\left[\frac{\beta\Psi}{\beta^* + \beta\Psi} + \frac{\alpha + \beta^*}{\beta + \beta^*\tau^*}\right]^{-1} \tag{A.2}$$

$$\mu(\cdot) = (1 + \alpha)\left[\frac{\beta\Psi}{2(\beta^* + \beta\Psi)} + \frac{\alpha + \beta^*}{\beta + \beta^*\tau^*}\right](t + 1)$$
$$- \left[\frac{\alpha(\alpha + \beta^*)\beta\Psi}{2(\beta^* + \beta\Psi)(\beta + \beta^*\tau^*)}\right](t - 1) \tag{A.3}$$

$$\lambda(\cdot) = (1 + \alpha)\left[\frac{\alpha + \beta}{\beta^* + \beta\Psi} + \frac{2\beta^*\tau^*}{\beta + \beta^*\tau^*}\right]$$
$$+ \left[\frac{\alpha + \beta}{2(\beta^* + \beta\Psi)} + \frac{\beta^*\tau^*}{\beta + \beta^*\tau^*} + \frac{\alpha(\beta^*)^2\tau^*}{2(\beta^* + \beta\Psi)(\beta + \beta^*\tau^*)}\right](t - 1) \tag{A.4}$$

The $q(\Psi, \tau^*)$ function in (A.2) describes the world price for good 3 (ROW's exportable) that clears world markets. It is useful to keep in mind that, by symmetry, $q_1 = q_2 = 1$ and that differentiation of $q(\Psi, \tau^*)$ gives the properties described in Lemma 1.

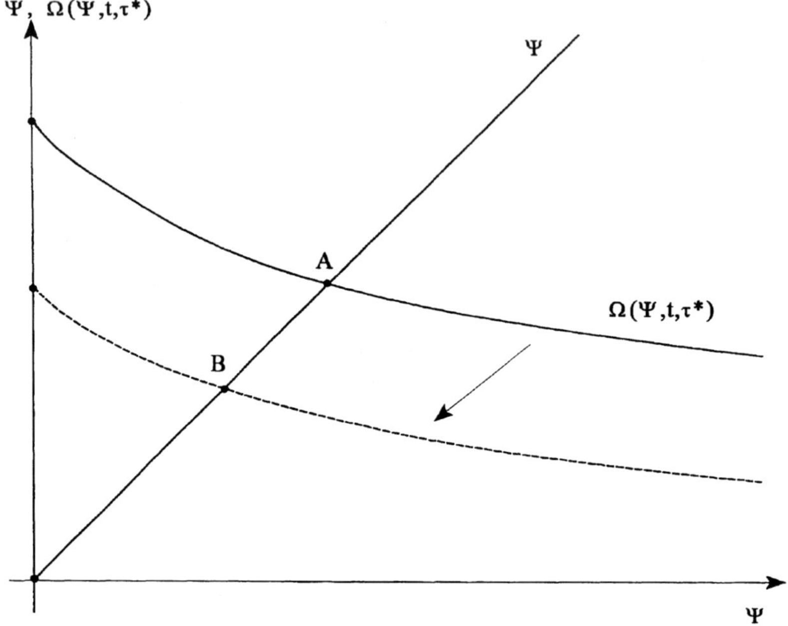

Fig. A1. Determination of the FTA optimal external tariff as a function of the internal tariff.

We now note the following points: First, it can be easily verified that $\Omega(0,\ t,\ \tau^*) > 0$ for any given t and τ^* that do not eliminate internal and external trade flows. Second, $\Omega_\Psi < 0$, as shown below. Thus, for given t and τ^*, there exists a value for Ψ that solves (A.1). To illustrate this point consider Fig. A.1 which depicts $\Omega(\Psi,\ t,\ \tau^*)$ and Ψ (the solid-line curves) as functions of Ψ. The properties of $\Omega(\Psi,\ t,\ \tau^*)$ ensure that it will intersect the Ψ schedule uniquely, as shown by point A.

To establish that $\Omega_\Psi < 0$, we differentiate (A.1) with respect to Ψ logarithmically to find

$$\frac{\Psi\Omega_\Psi}{\Omega} = \frac{\Psi q_\Psi}{q} + \frac{\Psi\mu_\Psi}{\mu} - \frac{\Psi\lambda_\Psi}{\lambda}$$

Differentiating (A.2) with respect to Ψ allows us to rewrite the above expression as

$$\frac{\Psi\Omega_\Psi}{\Omega} = \left\{ -\frac{\beta^*\beta\Psi}{(\beta^* + \beta\Psi)^2}\left[\frac{\beta\Psi}{\beta^* + \beta\Psi} + \frac{\alpha + \beta^*}{\beta + \beta^*\tau^*}\right]^{-1} + \frac{\Psi\mu_\Psi}{\mu}\right\}$$
$$+ \left\{ -\frac{\beta\Psi(\alpha + \beta)}{(\beta^* + \beta\Psi)^2}\left[\frac{\alpha + \beta}{\beta^* + \beta\Psi} + \frac{\beta^*\tau^*}{\beta + \beta^*\tau^*}\right]^{-1} - \frac{\Psi\lambda_\Psi}{\lambda}\right\}$$

It is now easy to check by differentiating (A.3) and (A.4) that both expressions in the curly brackets above are negative. Part (a): To prove this part it is sufficient to show that

E.W. Bond et al. / Journal of International Economics 64 (2004) 1–27 25

$\Omega_{\tau^*} < 0$. Following a procedure similar to the one described above it is direct but tedious to check by differentiating (A.1) and (A.2)–(A.4) appropriately that indeed

$$\frac{\tau^*\Omega_{\tau^*}}{\Omega} = \frac{\tau^* q_{\tau^*}}{q} + \frac{\tau^* \mu_{\tau^*}}{\mu} - \frac{\tau^* \lambda_{\tau^*}}{\lambda} < 0$$

In terms of Fig. A.1, an increase in τ^* causes the $\Omega(\cdot)$ schedule to shift downward. This is shown by the dashed-line schedule which intersects Ψ at the new point B. Since the increase in τ^* causes Ψ to fall while t remains fixed, by (6), it will be the case that the best-response tariff τ falls thereby establishing part (a).

Parts (b) and (c): Logarithmic differentiation of $\Omega(\Psi, t, \tau^*)$ in (A.1) with respect to t gives

$$\frac{t\Omega_t}{\Omega} = \frac{t\mu_t}{\mu} - \frac{t\lambda_t}{\lambda} = \frac{t\alpha(1+\alpha)}{\mu\lambda}\left[\frac{(\alpha+\beta)\beta\Psi}{2(\beta^* + \beta\Psi)^2} + \frac{(\alpha+\beta^*)\beta^*\tau^*}{(\beta + \beta^*\tau^*)^2}\right]$$

$$+ \frac{t\alpha(1+\alpha)}{\mu\lambda}\left[\frac{(\alpha+\beta)(\alpha+\beta^*)(2\beta^* + \beta\Psi) + (\beta\Psi)(\beta^*\tau^*)(\beta^* + 2\beta\Psi)}{2(\beta^* + \beta\Psi)^2(\beta + \beta^*\tau^*)}\right] > 0$$

In the context of Fig. A.1, the above implies that a reduction in the internal tariff t causes the $\Omega(\cdot)$ curve to shift downward, as shown by the dashed-line curve that intersects the Ψ curve at point B. Since this implies that Ψ falls, by the definition of Ψ in (6), the best-response external tariff τ falls below its Kemp–Wan level thereby establishing parts (b) and (c). $\square$

Proof of Proposition 2. Proposition 2 follows immediately from the welfare decomposition in (9) and the results of Proposition 1, as discussed in the text. $\square$

Proof of Proposition 3. According to the optimal tariff formula $\tau^* = \varepsilon/(\varepsilon - 1)$. Substituting into this result for ε as derived in the Proof of Lemma 1, we obtain the best-response function for ROW to be $\tau^* = (\alpha + \beta)/(\beta\Psi q)$, where $q = q(\Psi, \tau^*)$ by Lemma 1. It follows from Lemma 1 that the elasticity of q with respect to τ^* is contained in (0, 1), so ROW will have a unique optimal tariff that is decreasing in Ψ. Proposition 3 then follows from this result and the properties of Ψ. $\square$

Proof of Proposition 5. Derivation of results for an arbitrarily large FTA The case of an arbitrarily large FTA is considered by letting $\beta \to 1$. Using the elasticity formulas derived in Lemma 1, we obtain $\lim_{\beta \to 1} \varepsilon_* = 1$, $\lim_{\beta \to 1} \varepsilon = (1 + \alpha)/\alpha$ and $\lim_{\beta \to 1} q = 1/\Psi$. The external tariff imposed by the FTA members in this case can be obtained by solving (A.1)–(A.4) and using $\beta \to 1$, which yields an optimal external tariff of FTA members of

$$\lim_{\beta \to 1} \tau = \frac{2t(1 + 3\alpha + 3\alpha^2 + t + 3\alpha t + \alpha^2 t)}{(1 + \alpha)(1 + t)(1 + \alpha + t)}$$

In contrast, the optimal external tariff for a customs union is the solution to $\Psi_{\text{CU}} = \varepsilon^*/(\varepsilon^* - 1)$, which yields $\lim_{\beta \to 1} \tau = \infty$. The optimal tariff of ROW is $\lim_{\beta \to 1} \tau^* = 1 + \alpha$. Note that, in this model, small countries maintain some market power in the limit because they are the sole exporters of the goods in which they have a comparative advantage.

26   *E.W. Bond et al. / Journal of International Economics 64 (2004) 1–27*

Substituting these results in (8) yields $\lim_{\beta \to 1} W^1 = 2(1 + \alpha)t^{1/2}/(1 + t)$. As the FTA becomes arbitrarily large, the payoff to the FTA is maximized at $t = 1$ where it reaches the free trade level. Terms of trade have an insignificant effect on welfare as $\beta \to 1$ because the volume of trade becomes insignificant. In the pre-integration Nash equilibrium, $\lim_{\beta \to 1} t = (1 + 2\alpha)^{1/2}$, which is the optimal tariff in a two-country trade war. Thus, in the limit, internal trade liberalization is unambiguously beneficial because it raises welfare from the Nash equilibrium level to the free trade level. $\square$

References

Bagwell, K., Staiger, R.W., 1997. Multilateral tariff cooperation during the formation of regional free trade areas. International Economic Review 38, 291–319.

Bagwell, K., Staiger, R.W., 1998. Regionalism and multilateral tariff cooperation. In: Piggott, J., Woodland, A. (Eds.), International Trade Policy and the Pacific Rim. Macmillan, London.

Baldwin, R.E., Venables, A.J., 1995. Regional economic integration. In: Grossman, G., Rogoff, K. (Eds.), Handbook of International Economics. vol. 3 North-Holland, Amsterdam.

Bhagwati, J.N., 1992. Regionalism versus multilateralism. The World Economy 15, 535–555.

Bond, E.W., Syropoulos, C., 1996a. The size of trading blocs: market power and world welfare effects. Journal of International Economics 40, 411–438.

Bond, E.W., Syropoulos, C., 1996b. Trading blocs and the sustainability of inter-regional cooperation. In: Canzoneri, M., Ethier, W.J., Grilli, V. (Eds.), The New Transatlantic Economy. Cambridge University Press, London.

Bond, E.W., Syropoulos, C., Riezman, R.G., 2000. A Theory of Free Trade Areas. Florida International University, Manuscript.

Bond, E.W., Syropoulos, C., Winters, L.A., 2001. Deepening of regional integration and multilateral trade agreements. Journal of International Economics 53 (2), 335–361.

Ethier, W., Horn, H., 1984. A new look at economic integration. In: Kierzkowski, H. (Ed.), Monopolistic Competition and International Trade. Oxford University Press, Oxford.

Freund, C.L., 2000. Multilateralism and the endogenous formation of PTAs. Journal of International Economics 52 (2), 359–376.

Kemp, M.C., Wan Jr, H., 1976. An elementary proposition concerning the formation of customs unions. Journal of International Economics 6, 95–97.

Kennan, J., Riezman, R.G., 1988. Do big countries win tariff wars? International Economic Review 29, 81–85.

Kennan, J., Riezman, R.G., 1990. Optimal tariff equilibria with customs unions. Canadian Journal of Economics 23, 70–83.

Kose, M.A., Riezman, R.G., 2000. Understanding the welfare implications of preferential trade agreements. Review of International Economics 8 (4), 619–633.

Krishna, P., 1998. Regionalism and multilateralism: a political economy approach. Quarterly Journal of Economics CXII, 227–251.

Krugman, P., 1991. Is bilateralism bad. In: Helpman, E., Razin, A. (Eds.), International Trade and Trade Policy. MIT Press, Cambridge.

Levy, P.I., 1997. A political–economic analysis of free trade agreements. American Economic Review 87, 506–519.

Lipsey, R.G., 1970. The Theory of Customs Unions: A General Equilibrium Analysis. London School of Economics and Political Science, London.

McLaren, J., 1997. Size, sunk costs, and judge Bowker's objection to free trade. American Economic Review 87, 400–420.

Meade, J., 1955. The Theory of Customs Unions. North-Holland, Amsterdam.

Ornelas, E., 2001. Trade Creating Free Trade Areas and the Undermining of Multilateralism. Department of Economics, University of Wisconsin–Madison, Manuscript.

E.W. Bond et al. / Journal of International Economics 64 (2004) 1–27   27

Richardson, M., 1993. Endogenous protection and trade diversion. Journal of International Economics 34, 309–324.

Richardson, M., 1995. Tariff revenue competition in a free trade area. European Economic Review 39, 1429–1437.

Riezman, R., 1979. A 3 × 3 model of customs unions. Journal of International Economics 9 (3), 341–354.

Syropoulos, C., 1999. Customs unions and comparative advantage. Oxford Economic Papers 51 (2), 239–266.

Syropoulos, C., 2002. Optimum tariffs and retaliation revisited: how country size matters. Review of Economic Studies 69, 707–727.

Viner, J., 1950. The Customs Union Issue, Carnegie Endowment for International Peace, New York.

World Trade Organization, 2000. Mapping of Regional Trade Agreements, WT/REG/W/41.

ELSEVIER

Journal of International Economics 68 (2006) 59–78

Journal of
INTERNATIONAL
ECONOMICS

www.elsevier.com/locate/econbase

How often are propositions on the effects of regional trade agreements theoretical curiosa?

Lisandro Abrego[a], Raymond Riezman[b], John Whalley[c,d,e,*]

[a]*IMF, Brazil*
[b]*University of Iowa, United States*
[c]*University of Warwick, United Kingdom*
[d]*University of Western Ontario, Canada*
[e]*NBER, United States*

Received 8 April 2002; received in revised form 19 November 2003; accepted 23 March 2005

Abstract

This paper uses computational techniques to assess whether or not various propositions that have been advanced as plausible in the literature on regional trade agreements may actually hold. The idea is to make probabilistic statements as to whether propositions of interest might hold, rather than to restrict assumptions so they unambiguously hold. Our aim is to blend theory and numerical simulation and go beyond the ambiguous analytically derived propositions that dominate the theoretical literature so as to assess the likelihood of propositions holding for particular model specifications.
© 2005 Published by Elsevier B.V.

Keywords: Regional trade agreement; Customs union; Tariff equilibrium

JEL classification: F10; F13; F15

1. Introduction

In this paper, we generate repeated model solutions for alternative numerical specifications of a simple (few countries and commodities) general equilibrium trade

---

* Corresponding author. University of Western Ontario, Canada.
E-mail address: jwhalley@uwo.ca (J. Whalley).

0022-1996/$ - see front matter © 2005 Published by Elsevier B.V.
doi:10.1016/j.jinteco.2005.03.003

60   *L. Abrego et al. / Journal of International Economics 68 (2006) 59–78*

model so as to map out the extent of the parameter space for which each of a series of propositions regarding customs unions is true.[1] The idea is to blend theory and numerical simulation, in contrast to theoretical work in this area which sets out assumptions under which propositions unambiguously hold, and demonstrates their validity using analytical techniques. Here we take a different approach of trying to determine the frequency with which various results hold so as to obtain an indication of which statements are more likely to hold and which not.

We apply the techniques we develop to the analysis of various propositions in the customs union literature because despite nearly 50 years of research on regional trade agreements, which originates with Viner's (1950) work on Customs Unions, no set of generally accepted propositions regarding the effects of regional trade agreements has yet emerged to guide policy makers and public officials. Whether individual countries necessarily gain by entering a customs union (CU) is unproven, and the use of alternative reference points, such as free trade or non-cooperative Nash, only further clouds the picture. Whether world welfare is higher under a CU is also unknown, as is whether customs unions generate higher external tariffs compared to a non-cooperative Nash equilibrium in tariffs. Other propositions are widely thought to be true, but without explicit confirmation; such as that CUs generally improve the terms of trade of member countries; and that non-member countries prefer that no customs union be formed against them.

Specifically, we consider a three-country, three-good, pure exchange model with CES preferences, and use both random draws and a grid search over the space defining preference parameters and endowments. We compare both free trade and three-country non-cooperative (Nash) equilibria to partial cooperation regional agreement equilibria where two countries form a regional agreement and play non-cooperatively against the third country (CU). If we assume a uniform prior over the parameter space (admittedly a strong assumption) and then calculate the percentage of cases for which certain results hold, our sample frequencies can be interpreted as the probability of particular propositions holding conditional on both the model and the assumed prior.

Taken as a set, our results show that numerical simulation can be an important and useful adjunct to theory in economics. None of the propositions we consider holds unambiguously; some hold over 80% of the time, others considerably less frequently. We also investigate the reasons why particular propositions seem to hold more frequently than others using additional model analyses. Thus, where theory does not yield clear and unambiguous results, numerical simulation can be used to generate insights as to the likelihood of and reasons for particular propositions holding and, we believe, yield significant benefits in many other areas.

---

[1] This differs from previous work on systematic sensitivity analysis for general equilibrium models due to Pagan and Shannon (1986) and Harrison et al. (1993) which focuses on the sensitivity of counterfactual equilibrium results to key parameters, such as elasticities, in calibrated models for which parameter estimates are scarce. Sample frequencies for propositions are our objective more so than sensitivity analysis of central case results. In the process we compute non-cooperative game theoretic solutions as well as cooperative solutions for draws from the entire parameter space and we also go beyond existing literature in this dimension.

L. Abrego et al. / Journal of International Economics 68 (2006) 59–78   61

2. Customs union literature and theory–simulation interactions

Because of our focus on ambiguous propositions in the customs union literature, prior to presenting our analyses it is helpful to provide some background. Ambiguity in theoretical outcomes has been a constant in this literature since its inception. In 1950 Jacob Viner, the initiator of subsequent customs union literature, pointed out that regional trade agreements do not necessarily result in gains to members, even though some tariffs are eliminated by the agreement. He developed what later became known as the trade creation-trade diversion approach to regional trade agreements to help understand this ambiguity. Following Viner's work, for many years trade creating regional agreements were seen as good, and trade diverting regional agreements were seen as bad.[2]

Viner's work was also the driving force behind later literature that subsequently sought to set out the conditions under which regional trade agreements would either improve or worsen welfare. This work was still based on trade creation-trade diversion considerations; but Meade (1955), Lipsey (1957) and others discovered that preference considerations also enter in trying to make such determinations; this was to lead to Lipsey and Lancaster's (1956) characterization of the general theory of the second best; confirmation that no general customs union results were possible. Dissatisfaction with the trade creation-trade diversion dichotomy resulted in Lipsey (1970), Kemp (1969), Riezman (1979) and others trying to develop other approaches that would yield clear propositions.[3] A new approach known as the terms of trade–volume of trade approach became popular, under which the impact of a regional trade agreement can be summarized by its effects on both terms of trade (prices) and trade volumes.[4] This terms of trade–volume of trade approach uses general equilibrium instead of Vinerian partial equilibrium analysis, and emphasizes the impacts of the union on individual countries as integration occurs, instead of on world welfare.

However, even with the adoption of a new approach the same lack of general results has continued to characterize the literature. Indeed, few if any propositions are true for all parameter values even in highly simplified models. Consider the conjecture: "In a 3-country pure exchange economy, any pair of countries can benefit by forming a regional trade agreement". In a world where countries are of the same size this conjecture is true, but as Riezman (1999) shows, this conjecture fails to hold more generally. In a world with one large and two smaller countries, a regional trade agreement between the large country and either smaller country can result in the large country doing worse than in the initial equilibrium. In the initial equilibrium the large country benefits from its use of tariffs

---

[2] These two forces can be explained with a simple example. Suppose countries 1 and 2 initially have no tariffs, but form a customs union while country 3 remains outside the agreement. If we suppose that before the agreement country 1 imports clothing from country 3, a low cost producer of clothing, and that as a result of the agreement, 1 imports clothing instead from 2 because 2 had the advantage of tariff-free access to 1's market, trade into 1 is diverted from low cost producer 3 to high cost producer 2 and welfare may be lowered. However, if 1 formed a union with 3, 1 would import more from low cost producer 3 and less from high cost producer 2; trade would be created and welfare increased.

[3] See Lloyd (1982), Wooton (1986), Riezman (1985), Kemp and Wan (1976).

[4] Kowalczyk (2000) provides a comprehensive critique of the trade diversion and trade creation methodology, and argues that the terms of trade and volume of trade approach constitutes an attractive alternative.

62   *L. Abrego et al. / Journal of International Economics 68 (2006) 59–78*

against both countries, while small countries lose. When the large country forms a customs union it shares some of its tariff advantages with the other union partner, but foregoes the opportunity to play strategically against the small partner. Thus, even in a very simple model there are still no general results even for a more restricted set of questions.[5]

In other literature, such as Kennan and Riezman (1990), strategic considerations underlying the formation of regional trade agreements have served to further cloud the picture. Thus, one objective behind the formation of the EU in the late-1950s was to enhance joint country bargaining in the GATT with the US; and Mercosur was, in part, an attempt by four countries (Brazil, Argentina, Uruguay, Paraguay) to strengthen their bargaining position for an eventual accession negotiation with NAFTA. Such considerations naturally suggest treating countries as strategic players in a multi-country mixed cooperative–non-cooperative trade policy game, but such considerations have made the search for clear propositions as to the effects customs unions even more difficult.

This paper begins then from the ambiguity of most, if not all, theoretical propositions as to what happens when regional trade agreements form. Whether individual countries benefit, whether trade volumes expand, whether tariffs rise globally are all uncertain. Such propositions are further complicated by whether a regional agreement is to be compared to free trade or a multi-country Nash outcome. Our approach is to build on the applied general equilibrium modelling literature and use numerical simulation methods to investigate the frequency with which various propositions hold. Since Miller and Spencer (1971), Shoven and Whalley (1974) and Whalley (1985), researchers have used numerical equilibrium models to simulate the effects of regional trade agreements as well as to address a range of policy questions. They were used extensively in the WTO Uruguay Round process (see Harrison et al., 1996; Francois et al., 1996) as well as in the earlier Tokyo Round. They have also been used to explicitly model the effects of regional trade agreements (Hamilton and Whalley, 1985; Perroni and Whalley, 2000). These models are richer (more countries, production, more commodities) than the trade models that theorists frequently use. However, propositions of the form we investigate here are not explored.

Our blend of theory and numerical simulation seeks to assess whether propositions hold most of the time, and thus stand as reasonable working hypotheses; or whether they hold seldom, and are thus largely theoretical curiosa. We do this by using numerical simulation techniques to compute equilibria for a large number of model parameterizations, and then to assess the likelihood of a given proposition holding generally by computing sample frequencies.

3. Implementing propositional analysis

The literature on customs unions has focused on the effects of the formation of customs unions on the welfare of individual countries, as well as on the world as a

---

[5] There has nonetheless been intense recent policy debate over whether or not regional trade agreements are desirable in which strong positions are advanced (Bhagwati and Panagariya, 1996; Summers, 1991; Riezman, 1999).

L. Abrego et al. / Journal of International Economics 68 (2006) 59–78 63

whole. In addition, there has been work on the effects of customs union formation on the terms of trade and volume of trade of both member and non-member countries. Understanding how customs union formation affects country terms of trade and their volume of trade helps in understanding the welfare effects of customs unions. Older literature concentrates on comparing customs unions to an exogenously given initial equilibrium. More recent literature endogenizes the initial equilibrium and also compares customs union equilibria to free trade.[6] We follow more recent literature and focus on comparisons of customs union equilibria with three-country Nash equilibria and free trade. For each of these three equilibria we compare welfare, terms of trade and volume of trade. We assume countries 1 and 2 in a 3-country world are the union members. We do not consider the added complication of endogenous membership of the union (see Footnote 10).

We consider eight propositions as to the effects of regional trade agreements that we feel reflect central themes that the theoretical literature in the area has explored. They are widely discussed in the previously cited literature, are of theoretical interest, and have important policy implications. These are that:

1. Both members benefit from a customs union relative to free trade.
2. Both members benefit from a customs union relative to a Nash equilibrium.
3. A customs union increases world welfare relative to a 3-country Nash equilibrium.
4. Customs unions are a "stepping stone" to free trade (i.e. members are better off in CU relative to Nash, and members gain from free trade).
5. A customs union results in higher external tariffs for member countries relative to a Nash equilibrium.
6. A customs union improves member countries' terms of trade relative to a Nash equilibrium.
7. A customs union increases member countries' volume of trade relative to free trade.
8. A customs union increases member countries' volume of trade relative to a Nash equilibrium.

We assess the likelihood that each of these propositions hold in a particular case; a 3-country pure exchange model based on Kennan and Riezman (1990) and specify functional forms and admissible ranges of parameter values. We consider both random parameterizations of the model drawn from the admissible parameter space and parameterizations represented by a lattice of grid points in the parameter space. For each parameterization, we compute equilibria in the presence of regional trade agreements, as well as three-country non-cooperative Nash equilibria, and free trade equilibria.[7] From these computed equilibria we calculate the impacts on world welfare, individual country

---

[6] See Kennan and Riezman (1990) and Krugman (1991), for example.

[7] We assume uniqueness of these equilibria, and have done various ad hoc tests (changing the speed of approach and the initial starting point) to search for multiple equilibria. None have been found, although Kehoe's (1980) discussion suggests that, for competitive equilibria, even in small dimensional examples multiple equilibria can occur.

64   *L. Abrego et al. / Journal of International Economics 68 (2006) 59–78*

welfare, prices, tariff levels, and trade volumes as regional agreements form, and hence assess whether each of the propositions holds for that parameterization.[8]

3.1. Model structure

Each country has a single representative consumer with endowments of three goods, and a utility function of the form

$$U^i = U^i\left(X_1^i, X_2^i, X_3^i\right) \qquad (i = 1,\dots,3) \tag{1}$$

where X_1^i, X_2^i, X_3^i represent consumption of goods 1, 2 and 3 in country i and U^i is country i's utility. Endowments are given by $\bar{E}_1^i$, $\bar{E}_2^i$, $\bar{E}_3^i$, where i denotes the country, and 1, 2 and 3 denote the goods.

Because each country can impose non-negative tariffs at rate t_j^i on good j imported by country i, we define the sellers prices (i.e. net of tariff prices) as P_j for any good j. This implies that internal (gross of tariff) prices π_j^i in any country are

$$\pi_j^i = \left(1 + t_j^i\right)P_j. \tag{2}$$

Tariffs are set to zero on any good exported by country i. Countries (or regions) set tariffs on all imported goods, typically in some optimal fashion although we also consider free trade cases with zero tariffs. Tariff revenues collected by country i are

$$T^i = \sum_{j=1}^{3} t_j^i P_j \max\left\{ \left(X_j^i - \bar{E}_j^i\right), 0 \right\}. \tag{3}$$

The income of country i is thus given by

$$I^i = \sum_{j=1}^{3} \pi_j^i \bar{E}_j^i + T^i \tag{4}$$

It is easily shown that (2), (3) and (4) imply that the balance of trade for each country is zero.

We use constant elasticity of substitution (CES) (and in special cases Cobb-Douglas) preferences to represent the utility functions (1), for which (in the CES case) utility maximizing demands are given by

$$X_j^i = \frac{\alpha_j^i I^i}{\left(\pi_j^i\right)^{\sigma^i} \sum_{j=1}^{3} \alpha_j^i \pi_j^{i(1-\sigma^i)}} \tag{5}$$

where the α_j^i are CES preference shares on good j in country i, and the σ^i are country i CES substitution elasticities in preferences. Eq. (2) presumes knowledge of the direction of

---

[8] We use Hicksian equivalent money metric measures by country which we aggregate as necessary across countries for this purpose.

L. Abrego et al. / Journal of International Economics 68 (2006) 59–78 65

trade for any country in any commodity. In the theoretical literature this is assumed to be given and unchanging as we move between alternative equilibria (free trade; three-country Nash; with regional trade agreements).

In the model we use, the direction of trade is endogenously determined as part of the equilibrium solution. This endogeneity of trade patterns is an important feature of this model and differentiates it from previous work in this area. We achieve\endogeneity by performing sequential equilibrium calculations in which the direction of trade is given by the previous iteration and then checked for consistency with the resulting model solution.[9] Only when full consistency is achieved do we accept this as a bona fide equilibrium solution. We find that changes in the direction of trade across equilibria occur surprisingly frequently (see Abrego and Whalley, 2001), calling into question the use of this assumption in theoretical work.

3.1.1. Equilibrium solution concepts

We examine a range of solution concepts for our model, each relevant to the propositions listed above whose frequency we analyze.

3.1.1.1. Competitive free trade equilibria.

In free trade, tariff rates are all zero on all products in all countries, and equilibrium prices clear markets globally, i.e. equilibrium prices (P_1^*, P_2^*, P_3^*) are determined such that for each good j

$$\sum_{i=1}^{3} X_j^i - \sum_{i=1}^{3} \bar{E}_j^i = 0 \tag{6}$$

and global excess demands are all zero for all three commodities. Given that only relative prices matter in such a structure; we can normalize prices to sum to unity i.e.

$$\sum_{j=1}^{3} P_j = 1; P_j \geq 0. \tag{7}$$

3.1.1.2. Three-country non-cooperative Nash equilibria.

We also compute 3-country non-cooperative Nash equilibria. In these, each country takes other countries' tariffs as given and computes its own optimal tariffs by commodity. In equilibrium country computations of optimal tariffs are mutually consistent. The t_j^{i} are thus endogenously determined for country i.

Specifically, each country determines its own optimal tariff vector $(t_j^i)^*$ by maximizing U^i subject to the constraint that their balance of trade equals zero. Equilibrium occurs where global markets clear and each country charges optimal tariffs given the tariffs of other countries. Tariff revenues, T^i, enter this version of the model, and affect demands since they are redistributed to the country's representative consumer in lump sum fashion.

---

[9] Initially, we use the base case trade pattern.

Equilibrium requires consistent optimizing behavior with tariffs by country, market clearing and government budget balance in each country. Thus each country i solves an optimization problem

$$\max U^i$$

subject to

$$\sum_{j=1}^{3} P_j \left(X_j^i - \bar{E}_j^i \right) = 0. \tag{8}$$

In problem (8), t_j^i for $j \neq i$ are taken as given and denoted by $\hat{t}_j^i$. In a Nash equilibrium, optimal tariff rates $t_j^{i*} = \hat{t}_j^i$ for all i, j and markets clear, i.e.

$$\sum_{j=1}^{3} X_j^i - \sum_{j=1}^{3} \bar{E}_j^i = 0 \ \forall i \tag{9}$$

3.1.1.3. Customs union equilibria. We also compute customs union equilibria for this model. In these, we assume that country 1 and country 2 form a customs union with zero tariffs between them, and set a common external tariff against country 3.[10] Thus, countries 1 and 2 jointly set an optimal tariff against country 3, and country 3 sets an optimal tariff against the other two countries. Members of the Union receive the tariff revenues collected on their own imports.

In this mixed cooperative, non-cooperative case, countries 1 and 2 set zero tariffs against each other, i.e. $t_j^1 = t_j^2 = 0$ if the supplying country is 1 or 2, but jointly set optimal tariffs against country 3. Since countries 1 and 2 typically have a conflict of interest over how their joint external tariff is set, we assume that this tariff is set to maximize the sum of country 1 and 2's utilities. We then use different weights on country utilities in this joint sum in subsequent sensitivity analyses.

The customs union optimization problem is given by

$$\max U^1 + U^2$$

subject to

$$\sum_{i=1}^{2} \sum_{j=1}^{3} P_j \left(X_j^i - \bar{E}_j^i \right) = 0. \tag{10}$$

3.2. Implementing the approach

To compute sample frequencies for the propositions we list above, we use two different procedures for generating alternative model parameterizations. One is a randomization which, in our central case analysis, we implement across both preference parameters (both

---

[10] We have not considered cases where customs unions are themselves endogenously determined, but this is clearly an important issue. We assume that countries 1 and 2 are exogenously chosen as the countries which form a union.

Table 1

Key features of the procedures used in propositional analysis in the central case

Dimensionality	3 countries, 3 goods
Preferences	Randomization: CES
	Grid search: Cobb-Douglas-symmetric identical preferences across countries, with shares equal to 1/3 for each good.
Endowments	Randomization: randomly drawn from the interval 0.05–1.0 for each good for each country.
	Grid search: lattice grid of model specifications, with country endowment intervals for each good of 0.1. Off diagonal elements are treated as symmetric. Thus, each model specification given by a 3-dimensional vector (see below) from a range of endowments is generated.
Number of cases	Randomization: we consider 2000 draws from the range of potential parametric specifications.
	Grid search: we consider 769 different model specifications reflecting a single integer grid in own endowments.
Equilibria computed for each case for each method	Competitive equilibria, three-country Nash equilibria, Customs Union equilibria (the sum of member utilities is maximized).

shares and elasticities) and endowments. In this we consider CES preferences and generate share and substitution parameters in preferences for all three countries as well as endowments normalized to lie in a unit interval for each good for each country. The other uses a search over a grid defined only on endowment configurations since the dimensionality of the grid becomes unworkably large if we also include preference parameters.

The reason for using these two methods is both to check that they yield comparable results, and to provide a better understanding of the factors underlying computed sample frequencies. Since our central case involves randomizing over both preference parameters and endowments, for comparability to our grid search in which we only consider endowment configurations we later analyze randomizations restricted to endowment configurations only. In our grid search, we focus on the case where share parameters are identically symmetric across countries (all one third), and substitution elasticity values are common to all countries. We search across equilibria associated with parametric specifications of the model given by a lattice grid of points in the parameter space. In these cases we first restrict ourselves to Cobb-Douglas preference functions, and later to CES sensitivity analysis with different preference share parameters across goods and use varying elasticities of substitution.

Table 1 sets out the key features of the procedures we use in computing equilibria on which our sample frequencies are based. Table 2 sets out in more detail an example of the parametric variations we make over the endowment parameter space in the grid search

Table 2

An example of a model parametric specification generated by the grid search procedure

Endowment of goods	Country		
	1	2	3
1	0.10	0.45	0.45
2	0.35	0.30	0.35
3	0.30	0.30	0.40

cases we have constructed. We assume that the global endowment of each good is 1 by choice of units, and consider own country endowments of goods that range between 0.1 and 0.9. We consider diagonal elements of the endowment array to be symmetric. Table 2 indicates how a case of (0.1, 0.3, 0.4) translates into the endowment array by good by country given in Table 2.

The grid search procedure we consider involves all possible own endowment configurations across the three countries with single digit decimals; a total of 769 cases. Cases which by construction are symmetric are excluded (e.g. (0.2, 0.4, 0.6) gives the same equilibrium solution as (0.4, 0.2, 0.6)).

In randomization cases we limit our parametric specification to the relevant range for each parameter, e.g. 0.1 for share parameters. We consider 2000 draws in our central case analysis. For all the specifications generated by both methods we compute free trade, three-country Nash, and customs union equilibria and compare across these to assess sample frequencies as to how often the propositions we list above hold in the cases we consider. Assuming a uniform prior, we can interpret the computed sample frequencies in probabilistic form as the likelihood of whether or not any particular proposition holds. As noted above, an important difference between the randomization and grid search procedures is that the grid search is limited to endowments, while the randomization is over all model parameters.

In three-country Nash cases, we encounter difficulties in computing equilibria reflecting a lack of monotonicity in the individual country utilities when they are maximized with respect to their own tariff vector. Such problems are confined to the three-country Nash cases (and occur in between 17% and 20% of cases in our central case). They do not arise with customs union or free trade equilibrium computations. These problems manifest themselves in the GAMS optimization code we use in the form of cycling between local equilibria. They are more common in cases where trade patterns change.[11]

4. Results

4.1. Central case results

Table 3 presents results for the central case where all model parameters (preferences and endowments) are randomized. In these, we randomly draw preference (share and elasticity) parameters and endowment configurations for 2000 cases, and for each compute free trade, customs union, and Nash equilibria. We compile sample frequencies for the eight propositions holding that we listed earlier in Section 3.

Results in Table 3 indicate that some propositions hold in a clear majority of computed cases (Proposition 6, whether a CU improves the members' terms of trade relative to Nash) while others hold less frequently. For instance, both members benefit by forming a customs union relative to the three-country Nash outcome in only 48% of the cases. A

---

[11] In the cases in which we cannot compute Nash equilibrium we drop all results for that endowment and preference specification.

*L. Abrego et al. / Journal of International Economics 68 (2006) 59–78*69

Table 3
Central case analyses of customs unions propositions under randomization over both preference parameters and endowments

Proposition	Sample frequencies of computed model parameterizations for which the proposition is true
1. Both members benefit from a customs union relative to free trade	22.9
2. Both members benefit from a customs union relative to a Nash equilibrium	47.6
3. Customs union increases world welfare relative to a 3-country Nash equilibrium	76.0
4. Customs unions are a "stepping stone" to free trade (i.e. members are better off in CU relative to Nash, and members gain from free trade)	3.6
5. Customs union results in higher external tariffs for member countries relative to a Nash equilibrium	72.2
6. Customs union improves member countries' terms of trade relative to a Nash equilibrium	88.6
7. Customs union increases member countries' volume of trade relative to free trade	27.1
8. Customs union increases member countries' volume of trade relative to Nash equilibrium	86.9

customs union improves world welfare relative to a Nash equilibrium in 76% of computed cases. Customs unions result in higher external tariffs for member countries compared to Nash in 72% of cases. Customs unions lead to more international trade for member countries (relative to Nash) 87% of the time. At the other end of the spectrum only in 4% of the cases are customs unions a "stepping stone" to free trade. We next discuss each of the results in more detail.

Propositions 1 and 2 look at welfare changes between equilibria. Proposition 1 suggests that both members of a customs union do better than at free trade in about 20% of the cases while that number jumps to almost 50% (Proposition 2) when the comparison is made to Nash equilibrium rather than free trade. Moving from a Nash equilibrium (or free trade) to a customs union improves the union member's bargaining power and the members should gain vis-a-vis the non-member. From Johnson (1953) and Kennan and Riezman (1988) we know that only where there are significant asymmetries of size in a two-country case will a country gain in Nash equilibrium relative to free trade. The same logic applies to the union–nonunion distinction and in our computations both members gain (i.e. the customs union is big enough) about 20% of the time.

To see the intuition for these results it helps to decompose the change into a terms of trade effect and a volume of trade effect. Moving to a customs union from either free trade or a Nash equilibrium will usually improve the terms of trade of union members with respect to the rest of the world (see Proposition 6). However, within the customs union one country will see its terms of trade improve at the expense of the other member.[12] So, for

---

[12] Riezman (1979) stresses the importance of this effect.

70 *L. Abrego et al. / Journal of International Economics 68 (2006) 59–78*

one member the terms of trade improve with respect to all trading partners while for the other the change in overall terms of trade is ambiguous and will depend on what percentage of its trade is within the customs union. The volume of trade will usually fall moving from free trade to customs union (Proposition 7) and increase moving from Nash equilibrium to customs union (Proposition 8). Putting these effects together it follows that welfare gain for both members of a customs union is more likely when the comparison is to a Nash equilibrium rather than to free trade.

The fundamental significance of Proposition 1 lies in the fact that it gives a measure of the stability of free trade. If free trade existed, more than 20% of the time there would be a customs union that would benefit both member countries. In those cases, free trade would not be very stable in the sense that there would be a tendency to defect and form a customs union. Proposition 2 implies that about half the time in a tariff ridden world there will be at least one pair of countries that can benefit from forming a customs union. Hence, in this situation there would be a strong tendency to move towards regionalism.

The world welfare results for Proposition 3 suggest a bias in favor of customs unions over three-country Nash equilibria when one looks at world welfare. Theoretically, here we are comparing two distorted equilibria, and moving from a Nash equilibrium to a customs union gives some tariff reduction. However, members of the customs union coordinate their external tariffs which leads to higher protection. The results therefore indicate that from a global point of view the benefits of tariff reduction outweigh the costs of tariff coordination, with a sample frequency of considerably more than half.

One traditional view of regional trade agreements is that starting from an initial tariff equilibrium, one could view customs unions as an intermediate step or "stepping stone" on the path to free trade. In the context of our model, this means that starting at Nash equilibrium two countries could benefit from forming a customs union (and would presumably do so) and starting from the customs union equilibrium all countries would do better at free trade (and would presumably move to free trade). In this context, customs unions facilitate the attainment of free trade by providing a path along which countries gain each step of the way until free trade is obtained.[13] In our numerical analysis we start with the result that in 48% of the cases both members benefit by moving from a three-country Nash equilibrium to a customs union. Result 4 tells us that starting from the customs unions equilibrium in less than 10% of these cases will all countries benefit from a further move to free trade. The view that customs unions are likely to be an intermediate step on the way to free trade is not supported by our results.

Results for Proposition 5 suggest that in more than 70% of the cases, customs unions raise common external tariff rates relative to three-country Nash levels. Krugman (1991) shows that customs unions always increase tariffs, a proposition that is not generally true

---

[13] Starting at Nash equilibrium the country excluded from the customs union would probably be worse off, but they would be unable to stop the customs union from forming. GATT/WTO rules under Article 24 require a regional agreement both to broadly cover all trade and not to raise barriers against third parties. These rules, in practice, could restrain the formation of a customs union.

L. Abrego et al. / Journal of International Economics 68 (2006) 59–78 71

once asymmetric cases are considered. The intuition for why customs unions lower tariffs some of the time can be found in a paper by Syropoulos (1999). Here he argues that when two countries form a customs union there are two effects working against each other in determining the optimal external tariff for the union. First, there is a tariff reduction effect. As customs unions members eliminate tariffs between them the optimal external tariff falls. Second, there is a tariff increasing effect as the customs union internalizes the tariff externality that occurs when members import the same good. Thus, there are two forces working in opposite directions. This intuition suggests that customs union external tariffs fall when the tariff externality is small accounting for the results here, generally cases where the customs union members do not import much of the same good.

Results for Proposition 6 suggest that customs unions improve their external terms of trade relative to Nash in a large majority of cases. Subsequent sensitivity analysis suggests that this result depends on country size, since a customs union's external terms of trade deteriorates when the customs union is small relative to the third country. This result is not surprising if one views the problem from non-member country's point of view. In Nash equilibrium they compete against two other countries that are setting their tariffs independently. When those two countries form a customs union the third country now faces what is essentially one country from the point of view of trade policy. Hence it is not surprising that the non-member's terms of trade deteriorate vis-a-vis the member countries.

Propositions 7 and 8 indicate the extent to which customs unions are pro-trade, in the sense that they lead to more trade among member countries. Proposition 7 shows that a quarter of time customs union countries trade more than they would at free trade. Proposition 8 results suggest that if we compare customs union to Nash equilibria nearly 87% of the time members trade increases moving to the customs union. Theory suggests that with a customs union the volume of internal trade increases while external trade falls, but provides no guidance as to which effect will dominate. These results indicate that at least compared to Nash equilibrium the increase in internal trade will usually dominate.[14]

4.2. Discriminant analysis

We have also undertaken further analyses of our results in which we impose various conditions in an attempt to ascertain whether these conditions make it more or less likely that particular propositions will hold. We term this discriminant analysis. Results in Table 4 show the deviation in sub-sample frequencies where propositions hold from full sample frequencies.

In the intra-customs union country size cases, for example, we calculate the number of cases for which the income of country 1 exceeds that of country 2 and then determine the sample frequency for each proposition in that sub-sample. We then deduct the full sample

---

[14] It is possible that a customs union, due income effects, can lead to increased trade with non-members (see Kowalczyk and Wonnacott, 1992).

L. Abrego et al. / Journal of International Economics 68 (2006) 59–78

Table 4
Discriminant analysis of customs union proposition frequencies[a] (results show percentage deviation of sub-sample frequencies for propositions from full sample frequencies)

	Proposition 1	Proposition 2	Proposition 3	Proposition 4	Proposition 5	Proposition 6	Proposition 7	Proposition 8
Full sample percentage relative frequency	18.8	44.6	75.3	3.0	71.3	90.1	23.8	89.1
A. Member country relative size								
1. Income of country 1 exceeds that of country 2	−0.6	10.0	2.0	−3.0	1.4	−1.5	−10.1	−5.0
2. Income of country 1 exceeds 1.5 times that of country 2	−2.1	−2.9	12.3	−3.0	3.7	−2.6	−15.4	−9.9
3. Income of country 1 exceeds twice that of country 2	−5.5	−17.9	18.1	−3.0	−4.6	−3.4	−10.4	−9.1
B. Union–Nonunion Relative Size								
4. Income of CU countries combined exceeds twice income of country 3	4.1	7.5	12.3	−3.0	−10.9	−6.8	5.4	4.6
5. Income of CU countries combined exceeds 4 times income of country 3	−18.8	−6.1	17.1	−3.0	−17.4	−13.2	14.7	10.9
6. Income of CU countries combined exceeds 6 times income of country 3	−18.8	−4.6	4.8	−3.0	8.7	9.9	36.2	10.9

These are P1: CU welfare compared to FT, P2: CU welfare compared to Nash, P3: World welfare compared to Nash, P4: Stepping stone, P5: External tariff, P6: TT improvement for CU as a whole, P7: CU trade volume increase relative to FT, P8: CU trade volume increases relative to Nash.

[a] We consider 2000 randomization cases in generating these results.

L. Abrego et al. / Journal of International Economics 68 (2006) 59–78 73

frequency from this sample frequency, giving the deviations (in percentages) of sub-sample from full sample frequencies. Numbers which are small (closer to zero) indicate that the discriminant has little impact on sample frequencies. We consider two types of discriminants in Table 4; some relating to the relative incomes of member countries in a union to capture the importance of country size within the union, and others relating to relative incomes across the union and nonunion countries. We impose conditions of increasing stringency in applying these tests, and as we do so the number of cases in the larger sample meeting those restrictions falls.

Consider for example, Proposition 7 which implies that in 23.8% of cases customs union increases member countries' volume of trade relative to free trade. If we then take our 2000 randomizations and select all those in which the income of country 1 exceeds the income of country 2 then that percentage of cases for which Proposition 7 holds falls by 10.1% so that for that particular sub-sample, trade volume increases in 13.7% of cases. For the case in which income of country 1 exceeds 1.5 times the income of country 2 the percentage of cases for which Proposition 7 holds falls by 15.4% meaning that it holds 12.4% of the time. Using this discriminant analysis in this way we try and get some insight into the role that relative incomes play, both internal and external to the customs union, in driving the results we have. The discriminant analysis for Propositions 7 and 8 provide some interesting results. Taken together these results suggest that size inequality within the customs union make it less likely that customs unions increase trade volume, while size inequality between union and nonunion members make it more likely. This is an intriguing finding that suggests interesting directions for future theoretical research.

4.3. Sensitivity analysis

The results we report above for the various customs union cases will also produce different frequencies for different parameterization procedures. In Table 5 we report results in which the number of randomizations used to generate frequency results is varied. Our central case results in Table 2 use 2000 randomizations. Here, we report additional cases for 500, 1000 and 3000 randomizations. Results indicate minor variations in results across these different procedures. This suggests that the frequencies obtained using 2000 randomizations have small standard errors.

4.4. Grid search versus randomization

In Table 6 we report results which compare grid search and randomization procedures. Because the grid search is restricted only to endowments, for the reasons of tractability noted above, we undertake a randomization analysis only over endowments using 2000 randomizations as in the central case. We also report the full randomization results from Table 3, and a case in which randomization is restricted to preference parameters only rather than endowments.

These results show a high degree of similarity between grid search and endowment restricted randomization. There are, however, large differences between these cases and the complete randomization case. Taken together, these results suggest that the method

74   *L. Abrego et al. / Journal of International Economics 68 (2006) 59–78*

Table 5
Sensitivity analysis to full randomization sample frequencies (percentage sample frequencies for which the proposition holds)

Proposition	Central case	3000 Randomizations	1000 Randomizations	500 Randomizations
1. Both members benefit from a customs union relative to free trade	22.9	22.2	23.3	25.0
2. Both members benefit from a customs union relative to a Nash equilibrium	47.6	47.2	47.4	48.1
3. Customs union increases world welfare relative to a 3-country Nash equilibrium	76.0	76.3	74.8	77.9
4. Customs unions are a "stepping stone" to free trade (i.e. members are better off in CU relative to Nash, and members gain on free trade)	3.6	3.6	2.9	3.3
5. Customs union results in higher external tariffs for member countries relative to a Nash equilibrium	72.2	72.0	73.2	72.2
6. Customs union improves member countries' terms of trade relative to a Nash equilibrium	88.6	89.8	88.9	88.4
7. Customs union increases member countries' volume of trade relative to free trade	27.1	27.4	27.7	24.9
8. Customs union increases member countries' volume of trade relative to a Nash equilibrium	86.9	87.7	88.2	88.4

used to generate sample frequencies may be less important than the restrictions placed on the search made, independent of the method used. In other words, it may not make much difference whether grid search or randomization is used, but inclusion of different variables appears to have an important effect on the outcome.

4.5. The size of gains and losses

While our analysis has concentrated on purely qualitative propositions of gain and loss and their likelihood of occurring, we are also able to make statements about the size of gains and losses across the cases we consider. In Table 7, we consider the same cases as for our central case analyses in Table 3 but now report the mean welfare gain and loss across gaining and losing cases comparing free trade, customs union and Nash equilibrium. We calculate a money metric measure of the welfare change (the Hicksian equivalent variation) which we report as a percentage of base case income, and also give ranges of effects. These results are dependent on the parametric specification used for the model, but provide quantitative instead of qualitative information. The results indicate that, on

L. Abrego et al. / Journal of International Economics 68 (2006) 59–78   75

Table 6
Proposition sample frequencies computed using both grid search and randomization techniques (percentage sample frequencies for which the proposition holds)

Proposition	Using grid search procedure	Randomization over endowments only	Using full randomization procedure (central case)	Randomization over preference parameters only
1. Both members benefit from a customs union relative to free trade	30.3	29.9	22.9	23.2
2. Both members benefit from a customs union relative to a Nash equilibrium	81.6	75.7	47.6	57.4
3. Customs union increases world welfare relative to a 3-country Nash equilibrium	95.4	87.0	76.0	78.9
4. Customs unions are a "stepping stone" to free trade	21.9	22.4	3.6	4.6
5. Customs union results in higher external tariffs for member countries relative to a Nash equilibrium	79.5	83.6	72.2	72.4
6. Customs union improves member countries' terms of trade relative to a Nash equilibrium	98.5	98.2	27.1	96.2
7. Customs union increases member countries' volume of trade relative to free trade	8.1	3.1	27.1	19.4
8. Customs union increases member countries' volume of trade relative to a Nash equilibrium	91.6	89.1	86.9	88.9

Table 7
Quantitative orders of magnitude of gains and losses from cases considered in Table 3 (welfare effects (EV) as % of income) (percentage sample frequencies for which the proposition holds)

Comparisons	Mean gain	Max gain	Smallest gain	Mean loss	Max loss	Smallest loss
	Across gaining cases			Across losing cases		
1. Customs union versus free trade	0.53	8.52	$2.00e-05$	0.74	9.17	$1.00e-05$
2. Customs union versus a Nash equilibrium	2.58	10.21	$5.00e-07$	1.34	11.72	$7.00e-09$
3. Nash equilibrium versus free trade	0.21	9.63	$1.00e-10$	2.07	14.17	$2.00e-06$

average, the welfare effects of the changes we consider are significant. In addition, in some instances the welfare effects are quite large.

5. Conclusion

In this paper we use computational methods to calculate sample frequencies for parameterizations for which various propositions in the customs union literature hold for a given model. Our motivation is that despite 50 years of research, most if not all propositions in customs union literature remain ambiguous. These include whether customs unions raise world welfare, the welfare of particular countries, tariff levels, and other variables, and for each relative proposition alternative base cases as the reference point are investigated. The usual argument made against numerical analysis is that only statements conditional on a particular numerical specification be made. Here we examine equilibria associated with different parameterizations drawn from the admissible parameter space using both randomization and grid search techniques. We use a 3-country, 3-good Cobb-Douglas/CES pure exchange economy. Our results show, for example, that for the model we consider, world welfare increases under a customs union relative to a Nash equilibrium more than 70% of the time.

Taken as a set we interpret our results as suggesting that few (or none) of the propositions we investigate are extrema; they are neither theoretical curiosa, nor largely true. Whether they hold depends on model characteristics that are amenable to investigation. Results seem robust to alternative procedures for analysis, and constraints are applied in propositional analysis to demonstrate this. Blending theory and numerical simulation thus provides useful insights as to when propositions may hold in these cases, and we suggest that this may also be so in other cases where theory does not yield unambiguous conclusions.

Acknowledgement

We are grateful to the Centre for the Study of Globalisation and Regionalisation at the University of Warwick and the ESRC for financial support and we acknowledge comments at Centre seminars. The paper was mostly written while the first author was a research fellow at the University of Warwick. Jon Eaton, Scott Page, Carlo Perroni, Danny Tsiddon, Chuck Whiteman, Ben Zissimos and a referee have also provided helpful comment and input. An earlier version was presented to a conference on the WTO and World Trade held in Seattle, December 4, 1999, the Ecole de Printemps held in Aix-en-Provence, May 2000 and the CESifo conference on Globalisation, Inequality and Well-Being, November 2002. We thank participants in these conferences for useful comments.

References

Abrego, L., Whalley, J., 2001. How reasonable are the assumptions used in theoretical models? Computational evidence of the likelihood of trade pattern changes (mimeo), NBER WP #W8169, March 2001.

L. Abrego et al. / Journal of International Economics 68 (2006) 59–78　　　77

Bhagwati, J., Panagariya,, 1996. Preferential trading areas and multilateralism: strangers, friends or foes? In: Bhagwati, J., Panagariya, A. (Eds.), Free Trade Areas or Free Trade? The Economics of Preferential Trading Agreements. AEI Press, Washington, D.C.

Francois, J.F., MacDonald, B., Nordstrom, H., 1996. The Uruguay Round: a numerically based qualitative assessment. In: Martin, W., Winters, A. (Eds.), The Uruguay Round and the Developing Countries. Cambridge University Press, Cambridge, New York.

Hamilton, R., Whalley, J., 1985. Geographically discriminatory trade arrangements. Review of Economics and Statistics 67, 446–455.

Harrison, G., Jones, R., Kimbell, L., Wigle, R., 1993. How robust is general equilibrium analysis. Journal of Policy Modelling 15 (1), 99–115.

Harrison, G.W., Rutherford, T.F., Tarr, D.G., 1996. Quantifying the Uruguay round. In: Martin, W., Winters, L.A. (Eds.), The Uruguay Round and the Developing Economies, World Bank Discussion Paper No.307, 1995; Martin, W., Winters, L.A. (Eds.), The Uruguay Round and the Developing Countries, Cambridge University Press 1996; and Economic Journal, September 1997, vol. 107, no. 44, pp. 1405–1430.

Johnson, H.G., 1953. Optimum tariffs and retaliation. In C. Kowalczyk, (Ed.), Elgar Reference Collection. International Library of Critical Writings in Economics, vol. 115. Economic integration and international trade. Cheltenham, U.K. and Northampton, Mass.: Elgar; distributed by American International Distribution Corporation, Williston, Vt., 1999; 140–151. Previously published: 1953.

Kehoe, T., 1980. An index theorem for general equilibrium models with production. Econometrica 48, 1211–1232.

Kemp, M., 1969. The Pure Theory of International Trade and Investment. Prentice-Hall, London.

Kemp, M., Wan, H., 1976. An elementary proposition concerning the formation of customs unions. Journal of International Economics 6, 95–97.

Kennan, J., Riezman, R., 1988. Do big countries win tariff wars? International Economic Review 29 (1), 81–85.

Kennan, J., Riezman, R., 1990. Optimal tariff equilibria with customs unions. Canadian Journal of Economics 90, 70–83.

Kowalczyk, C., 2000. Welfare and integration. International Economic Review 41 (2), 483–494.

Kowalczyk, C., Wonnacott, R., 1992. Hubs and spokes, and free trade in the Americas, NBER WP#4198, October.

Krugman, P., 1991. Is bilateralism bad? In: Helpman, E., Razin, A. (Eds.), International Trade and Trade Policy. MIT Press, Cambridge.

Lipsey, R.G., 1957. The theory of customs unions: trade diversion and welfare. Economica 24, 40–46.

Lipsey, R.G., 1970. The Theory of Customs Unions: A General Equilibrium Analysis. Weidenfeld and Nicholson, London.

Lipsey, R.G., Lancaster, K., 1956. The general theory of second best. Review of Economic Studies 24, 11–32.

Lloyd, P.J., 1982. A 3×3 theory of customs unions. Journal of International Economics 12, 41–63.

Meade, J.E., 1955. The Theory of Customs Unions. North-Holland, Amsterdam.

Miller, M.H., Spencer, J.E., 1971. The static economic effects of the UK joining the EEC: a general equilibrium approach. Review of Economic Studies 44, 71–93.

Pagan, A., Shannon, T., 1986. Sensitivity analysis for linearized computable general equilibrium models. In: Piggott, J., Whalley, J. (Eds.), New Developments in Applied General Equilibrium Analysis, vol. 1985. Cambridge University Press, Cambridge, pp. 104–118.

Perroni, C., Whalley, J., 2000. The new regionalism: trade liberalization or insurance? Canadian Journal of Economics 33.

Riezman, R., 1979. A 3×3 model of customs unions. Journal of International Economics 9, 341–354.

Riezman, R., 1985. Customs unions and the core. Journal of International Economics 19, 355–365.

Riezman, R., 1999. Can bilateral agreements help induce free trade? Canadian Journal of Economics 32, 751–766.

Shoven, J.B., Whalley, J., 1974. On the computation of competitive equilibrium on international markets with tariffs. Journal of International Economics 4, 341–354.

Summers, L., 1991. Regionalism and the world trading system. Policy Implications of Trade and Currency Zones. Federal Reserve Bank of Kansas City, pp. 295–301.

Syropoulos, C., 1999. Customs unions and comparative advantage. Oxford Economic Papers 51, 239–266.
Viner, J., 1950. The Customs Union Issue. Carnegie Endowment for International Peace, New York.
Whalley, J., 1985. Trade Liberalization Among Major World Trading Areas. MIT Press, Cambridge. MA.
Wooton, I., 1986. Preferential trading agreements: an investigation. Journal of International Economics 21, 81–97.

Econ Theory (2009) 41:147–161
DOI 10.1007/s00199-008-0407-z

SYMPOSIUM

Free trade: what are the terms-of-trade effects?

Carsten Kowalczyk · Raymond Riezman

Received: 14 September 2007 / Accepted: 31 July 2008 / Published online: 22 August 2008
© Springer-Verlag 2008

Abstract   Changes in trade policy affect a nation's economic welfare through terms-of-trade and volume-of-trade effects. A move to global free trade would imply higher world economic welfare equal to the sum of all nations' volume-of-trade, or efficiency, effects. Since the sum of the terms-of-trade effects across all nations is zero, terms-of-trade effects are contentious. Konishi, Kowalczyk and Sjöström (2003) have shown that if customs unions do not affect trade with non-member countries, immediate global free could be achieved if free trade were proposed together with international sidepayments equal to the terms of trade effects. How large would these terms of trade effects, and hence transfers, be? This paper presents estimates from a simple computable general equilibrium model of a world economy of perfect competition. We show that, in some cases, terms-of-trade effects are small compared to

Prepared for the conference "New Directions in International Trade Theory" at the University of Nottingham's Leverhulme Center. We are grateful to our discussant, Eric Bond, to conference participants, and to two anonymous referees for helpful comments. We also appreciate comments at Vanderbilt, Buffalo, the Midwest Trade Meetings, Singapore Management University, City University of Hong Kong, and Copenhagen Business School. This paper is part of the Globalization Project at the University of Aarhus.

C. Kowalczyk (✉)
The Fletcher School, Tufts University, Medford, MA 02155, USA
e-mail: carsten.kowalczyk@tufts.edu

R. Riezman
Department of Economics, University of Iowa, Iowa City, IA 52242, USA
e-mail: raymond-riezman@uiowa.edu

R. Riezman
GEP, University of Nottingham, Nottingham, UK

R. Riezman
CES-ifo, Ludwig Maximilian University, Munich, Germany

 Springer

efficiency gains, and transfers are not necessary for free trade. In other cases, terms-of-trade gains may account for more than 50% of a country's gains from free trade and transfers could be large.

Keywords   WTO · Multilateralism · Free trade · Customs unions · Free trade areas · Transfers

JEL Classification   F00 · F02 · F10 · F11 · F13 · F15

1 Introduction

Even as the Doha Round multilateral negotiations, which were launched in 2001, have been ongoing, many WTO member countries have continued to establish new free trade areas or customs unions.

Free trade areas and customs unions reduce trade barriers, but they also pose potential problems: surprisingly, they may reduce the economic welfare of the participants, and, indeed, of the world by making world trade more distorted.[1] They may also affect adversely non-member countries. Finally, they may discourage further liberalization, and hence prevent global free trade, if they imply a situation where some member countries would prefer to stay in a world of preferential trading areas because a move to free trade would imply losing existing valuable preferential access to some markets.

Is it possible to get global free trade in a world of trading blocs? Until recently, the strongest theoretical result on free trade in a world of preferential trade was due to Ohyama (1972) and Kemp and Wan (1976) who showed that if the members of a customs union are required to set their common external tariff such that trade with non-members remains constant, then there exist income transfers between members such that no country loses. It follows that global free trade can be achieved through a sequence, or through parallel sequences, of continual expansions of such Ohyama–Kemp–Wan customs unions.

Konishi, Kowalczyk, and Sjöström have identified a more direct approach to global free trade: recognizing that the long-standing negotiating principle in GATT/WTO for a multilateral agreement to be reached is that no group of members object, and maintaining the Ohyama–Kemp–Wan requirement that customs unions must not affect trade with non-members, they show in Konishi et al. (2003b) that there exists a proposal for immediate global free trade with international income transfers that would be blocked by no group of countries. They show, in particular, in Konishi et al. (2003a) that free trade with international income transfers equal to any terms-of-trade effects is not blocked. In other words, free trade with international income transfers equal to the terms of trade effects is in the core of the customs union trade policy game.

One line of research has considered the possibility of global free trade without international income transfers and has found that if important asymmetries between countries exist, in particular with respect to differences in ability to affect own terms of trade, global free trade may be impeded by nations who have an ability to obtain

---

[1] This was the insight of Viner (1950).

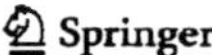 Springer

better terms of trade with protection. In a two-country world, Johnson (1953-54) showed that if the two countries' import elasticities are relatively similar both will lose from deviating from free trade, but that if one country has relatively more elastic import demand than its trading partner then the former country may obtain higher economic welfare from levying its optimal tariff rather than from free trade even if its trading partner retaliates. Kennan and Riezman (1988) presented numerical examples to illustrate how differences in preferences or in endowments could upset the balance between countries required for both to desire free trade. Syropoulos (2002) has identified how differences in country size impact optimal tariffs and hence the ability to sustain free trade through their effect on trade elasticities .

In a world of three countries, Riezman (1985), in an early application of the core in international trade, and Kennan and Riezman (1990), Bond and Syropoulos (1996), and Riezman (1985) explore how the ability of countries to form customs unions or free trade areas may further affect the incentives of countries to agree to free trade. They find that the effect is ambiguous: customs unions or free trade areas may deter deviation from free trade by raising relatively weak countries' ability to retaliate, or they may induce deviation by reducing already stronger countries' vulnerability to retaliation through their partnership.

Once international sidepayments are possible then, as shown by Kowalczyk and Sjöström (1994) in a model of international monopoly trade, there exist income transfers such that no country objects to a multilateral agreement to eliminate all distortions. And they show, in Kowalczyk and Sjöström (2000), that transfers equal to terms-of-trade changes, originally discussed by Grinols (1981) as between-member transfers that would make an Ohyama–Kemp–Wan customs union beneficial for all its members, would prevent any blocking of a proposal to eliminate all trade distortions. Konishi, Kowalczyk and Sjöström (2003a,b) extend that work to the standard model of international trade in a competitive world economy. It is a critical assumption in both lines of research, i.e., both for the monopoly trade model result and the competitive economy result, that if some nations wish to enter into preferential trading arrangements rather than agreeing to the grand coalition of world-wide undistorted trade or instead of staying at the *status quo*, that such arrangements not alter the trade of the member countries relative to non-members. In the monopoly trade model, this no-spillover feature is obtained through assumptions on preferences and monopoly costs; in the perfect competition world, the requirement that customs unions be Ohyma–Kemp–Wan ensures that customs unions have no spill-over effects onto non-members.[2]

In this paper, we explore, in the world of perfect competition, how large the terms-of-trade effects would be from global free trade to get some idea of how large the international sidepayments to generate world-wide support for free trade might be. While the theoretical rationale for the possible benefits from the use of sidepayments does not depend on the answer to this question—a country never pays more than it

---

[2] The assumption of no spill-overs is obviously restrictive. However, it has allowed substantial progress and results on how to obtain globally undistorted trade in general equilibrium rather than partial equilibrium models. If, for example, customs unions were instead assumed always to set their welfare-maximizing optimal external tariffs, it would become exceedingly difficult to calculate equilibria in many-country, many-good world economies.

gains from free trade—the size of transfers could matter if the notion of international income transfers were to be brought from theory to a world of practical policy: first, some countries may find it difficult in practice to raise through taxation of domestic producers and consumers the revenue that would correspond to the terms of trade gains from free trade. And it would, presumably, be harder to raise a large rather than a small amount of revenue. Secondly, while the notion of paying trading partners for market access is not entirely unknown in the context of negotiating free trade areas or customs unions—witness, for example, the EU's agricultural, regional, and structural funds—international income transfers would be a somewhat novel tool for facilitating multilateral trade liberalization where negotiations have traditionally involved exchanges of market access. Thirdly, since, in theoretical work, transfers would tend to go from countries with relatively small domestic markets to countries with relatively large domestic markets, it is a possibility—although not a certainty—that the transfers be regressive, i.e., they might go from lower-income countries to higher-income countries.[3] In short, governments might find it difficult to obtain domestic political support for engaging in international income transfers addressing terms-of-trade effects.

We consider, in this paper, a three-country model of international trade in which key economic variables such as consumption, prices, and utility, can be calculated both before and after changes in trade policy. Assuming an initial situation where countries apply their non-cooperative Nash optimal tariffs, we calculate the change in each nation's real income from global free trade. Decomposing this change into a terms-of-trade effect and an efficiency effect, and quantifying these effects, we then have estimates for the transfers discussed above that would support global free trade. We conduct these calculations for varying distributions of world endowments, and find that transfers for free trade vary considerably depending on the economic environment: for countries that are not too dissimilar we find, in our simulations, terms-of-trade effects of about ten percent of gains from trade, while for very dissimilar countries with large initial trade, terms-of-trade gains may account for almost 60% of a nation's total gains from free trade, and almost nine percent of GDP. In the latter case, the international sidepayments discussed in this research would be large, and it could be politically difficult to raise the associated revenue.[4]

Section 2 states an expression for evaluating the change in national economic welfare from a change in trade policy in a competitive world economy. Section 3 introduces the roles of terms-of-trade effects and international income transfers in obtaining global free trade. Section 4 offers calculations of how large terms-of-trade effects from free trade might be in a three-country, three-good general equilibrium model. Section 5 concludes and offers suggestions for further research.

---

[3] Undoubtedly, many would find it difficult to accept the implications for world income distribution of such transfers. It should be stressed, though, that the sidepayments discussed here are not inconsistent with foreign aid which nations might still wish to undertake for reasons not considered in this work.

[4] Of course, without such sidepayments, the same countries might not experience these larger gains as other countries might block the very trade that would induce them.

 Springer

2 National economic welfare in perfect competition

Consider a country i ($i = 1,\ldots,n$) where price-taking consumers and producers trade a finite number of goods with price-taking producers and consumers in other countries. Assuming that preferences can be expressed by the utility function of a representative consumer, that international trade is initially subject to tariffs the revenue of which is redistributed lump-sum to domestic households, and that trade is balanced, it is possible to express the change in country i's national income, $\Delta\eta^i$, from a change in tariffs, whether own or trading partners', as:[5]

$$\Delta\eta^i = -\Delta(p^e)^i m_A^i + (p_B^i - (p_B^e)^i)\Delta m^i + S^i. \tag{1}$$

With subscript A denoting pre-change values and subscript B post-change values, and Δ denoting a change, Eq. (1) states that the change in real income, $\Delta\eta^i = \eta_B^i - \eta_A^i$, measured in units of some numéraire good, can be expressed as the sum of three terms: a terms-of-trade effect, $-\Delta(p^e)^i m_A^i$, where m_A^i is country i's pre-change trade vector and $\Delta(p^e)^i = (p_B^e)^i - (p_A^e)^i$ is the vector of changes in country i's tariff-exclusive trade prices. A tariff-revenue effect, $(p_B^i - (p_B^e)^i)\Delta m^i$, where $\Delta m^i = m_B^i - m_A^i$, and p_B^i is the vector of domestic prices in country i, and hence $p_B^i - (p_B^e)^i$ is the vector of post-change specific tariffs, t_B^i, or the vector $\tau_B^i(p_B^e)^i$, where τ_B^i is a matrix of post-change ad valorem tariffs. The final term, S^i, is the non-negative sum of production and consumption effects in country i due to substitution by domestic producers and consumers as they face changed domestic prices. If y_A^i and y_B^i are profit-maximizing pre- and post-change production, respectively, the production efficiency effect is $p_B^i(y_B^i - y_A^i) \geq 0$, and if c_A^i is initial consumption, and if $c^i(p_B^i, u_A^i)$ would be the consumption at the new domestic price vector p_B^i that would preserve the initial level of utility u_A^i, the consumption efficiency effect is $p_B^i(c_A^i - c^i(p_B^i, u_A^i)) \geq 0$.

This approach allows for a comparison of a nation's real income from different policy strategies and, in particular, for a comparison of national welfare from free trade versus from customs unions or free trade areas.

While GATT/WTO emphasizes non-discrimination between its members, GATT Article XXIV allows WTO members to form free trade areas, which eliminate the barriers on mutual trade between the free trade area members while leaving each member's tariffs on its trade with non-members to that member country to decide, or customs unions, which eliminate the barriers to mutual trade on the union members while setting common external tariffs on trade with non-members.[6]

As mentioned in the "Introduction," Ohyama (op. cit.) and Kemp and Wan (op. cit.) consider a variation of the Article XXIV customs union, namely a union where the common external tariffs be such that aggregate trade of members with non-members

---

[5] See Ohyama (1972) or Grinols and Wong (1991) for a derivation of this expression. For small changes this expression becomes the terms-of-trade and volume-of-trade effects formalized by Jones (1969). Kowalczyk (2000) demonstrates that this is a better approach to analyzing the welfare effects of free trade areas or customs unions than is Viner's trade diversion and trade creation approach.

[6] Additional requirements are that internal barriers must be eliminated on "substantially all trade" and that the average rate of protection on trade with non-members must not increase.

not be affected, and they show the existence of intra-union sidepayments such that no member country would be hurt from the formation of such a customs union. Konishi et al. (op. cit.) prove that if customs unions are required to satisfy that trade with non-members not be affected then there exist sidepayments such that a proposal for immediate free trade with such sidepayments will not be blocked by any nation or by any Ohyama–Kemp–Wan customs union. They show, specifically, that international sidepayments that off-set countries' terms-of-trade losses or gains, together with global free trade, constitute an outcome in the core of the customs union game. Thus, if T_B^i is the (aggregate) net transfer to country i associated with moving from the initial situation A to global free trade in B, the sidepayment mechanism that transfers to country i the amount

$$T_B^i = (p_B^e - p_A^e)m_A^i \tag{2}$$

supports global free trade as an outcome in the core.

How large would these transfers be? This is the question we consider next.

3 Computing the terms-of-trade effects

We construct a general equilibrium model where three endowment economies trade three goods. Since we wish to derive the transfers that would compensate for terms-of-trade effects, we calculate the terms of trade effects from global free trade assuming that transfers do not take place.[7]

We assume that countries set their individually non-cooperative optimal tariffs initially, and that they consider as alternatives whether to join a free trade area (FTA) or a customs union (CU), or whether to establish global free trade (FT).

We assume that each country i is endowed with a fixed amount of commodity j, ω_j^i $(i, j = 1, 2, 3)$. We assume also that the utility function of the representative consumer in country i is given by

$$U^i = \sum_{j=1}^{3} \beta_j^i \ln c_j^i \tag{3}$$

where U^i is the utility of the country i consumer, and β_j^i is the weight this consumer puts on consumption of good j, c_j^i. This preference formulation results in a linear expenditure system which allows us to employ numerical methods to solve the model.

---

[7] In the papers by Konishi et al. (op. cit.), the post-change free trade prices p_B^e are "full" equilibrium prices inclusive of all effects from the transfers assuming they were realized; in other words, the theoretical analyses incorporate any effects from the so-called "transfer problem" and the transfers are derived from prices that incorporate these effects. In the present paper, post-change free trade prices are not calculated inclusive of any potential feedback effects if transfers were effected. The transfers derived in this paper are thus most appropriately viewed as approximations to the theoretically correct transfers.

Further, with this structure we do not have to specify elasticities, and can state our results in terms of fundamental endowment parameters.

The net imports of good j into country i are $m^i_j = c^i_j - \omega^i_j$. When acting individually, countries charge optimal tariffs on imports. Tariffs are assumed to be *ad valorem* with τ^i_j denoting the rate charged by country i on imports of good j. If the world price for good j is p^e_j, the domestic price of good j in country i is $p^i_j = (1+ \tau^i_j)\, p^e_j$.

Given that each country consists of identical individuals, aggregate demand is obtained from maximizing the utility subject to the budget constraint where I^i is income of the representative consumer in country i which consists of income from the endowment plus any tariff revenue which is rebated to consumers lump-sum.

At world market prices, balanced trade implies that aggregate expenditure in each country i must equal the value of country i's endowment in equilibrium. Thus

$$W^i = \sum_{j=1}^{3} p^e_j c^i_j = \sum_{j=1}^{3} p^e_j \omega^i_j \tag{4}$$

where W^i is the aggregate expenditure of country i. In addition, in equilibrium, world demand for each good equals world supply:

$$\sum_{i=1}^{3} c^i_j = \sum_{i=1}^{3} \omega^i_j \tag{5}$$

This system of equations allows us to solve for p^e_j, c^i_j, and U^i.

Treating the Nash equilibrium as the benchmark, we are interested in seeing how large the terms of trade effects are relative to the change in real income from a move to global free trade.

With free trade there is no revenue effect, and expression (1) simplifies to:

$$\Delta \eta^i = -\Delta (p^e)^i m^i_A + S^i. \tag{6}$$

We illustrate how the terms-of-trade and consumption effects impact real income in Fig. 1 where we assume that only two goods, X and Y, are consumed:

Let E be the endowment point, C_1 the initial consumption bundle with Nash tariffs, and C_3 the free trade consumption bundle. The point C_2 is the consumption bundle that has equal utility with the Nash equilibrium consumption and that would be chosen at post-change free trade prices if utility were to be constant. In Sect. 2 of this paper, we wrote C_2 as $c^i(p^i_B, u^i_A)$ when introducing the consumption effect from a price change. Evaluating changes at post-change prices, and assuming good X is the numéraire, we then have that the distance $X_2 X_3$ represents the total increase in real income associated with a move from Nash equilibrium to free trade. We can decompose this change into

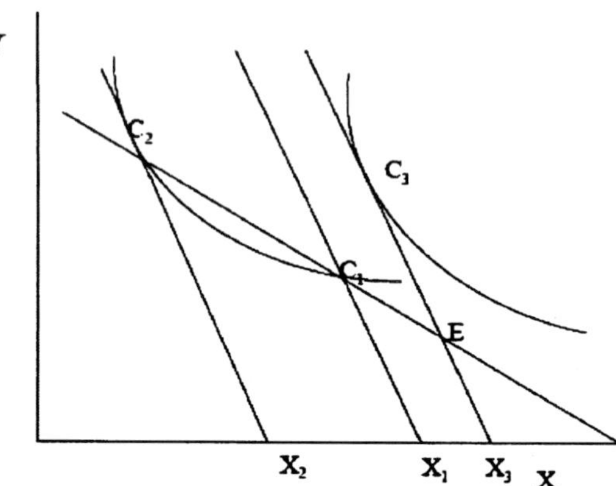

Fig. 1 Nash equilibrium to free trade

a change due to a substitution effect, $X_2 X_1$, which is the consumption effect, and a change due to a terms of trade effect, $X_1 X_3$.

If we call the terms-of-trade effect ΔTOT and the substitution effect S, then the total effect on real income caused by the move from the benchmark to free trade, $\Delta \eta$, is

$$\Delta \eta = \Delta TOT + S \tag{7}$$

We are particularly interested in learning how much of the welfare change, $\Delta \eta$, is due to terms-of trade-changes, ΔTOT. For that purpose, we consider four examples that differ in assumptions regarding country sizes and in how (dis-)similar countries are, and hence how much they trade.

The calculations are derived as follows: For the initial equilibrium, we calculate optimal tariffs, world market prices (and by implication domestic prices), consumption, and utility of each country corresponding to point C_1. For the free trade equilibrium, we calculate world market prices, consumption, and utility of each country corresponding to point C_3. To calculate the welfare decomposition as expressed in expression (6), we then apply the post-change free trade prices to calculate the real value of the initial consumption point C_1 to yield X_1, and the real value of the final consumption point C_3 to yield X_3. We identify consumption point C_2 by solving for the point of tangency between the equation for the indifference curve through C_1 and free trade world market prices, and calculate the real value of C_2 by applying the free trade prices to yield X_2.

4 Examples

4.1 Country 1 is large

In all examples in this paper we assume that preferences are identical and symmetric across countries and goods, and we normalize the world endowment of each good to

Free trade: what are the terms-of-trade effects?   155

be one. It follows that expenditure shares will be identical across all goods, and free trade world market prices will be the same and equal to 1/3. We will then consider four examples that differ in country i's relative endowment of good i ($i = 1, 2, 3$), and we will associate the term "large" with a large value of that endowment.[8]

The endowment matrix in our first example is given by:

	Good 1	Good 2	Good 3
Country 1	0.8	0.25	0.25
Country 2	0.1	0.5	0.25
Country 3	0.1	0.25	0.5

Letting τ_j^* denote the optimal tariff on good j ($j = 1, 2, 3$) by the country indicated by the row entry, key endogenous variables in the Nash equilibrium are:

	τ_1^*	τ_2^*	τ_3^*	c_1	c_2	c_3	Utility
Country 1	0	1.2358	1.2358	0.6226	0.3669	0.3669	117.36
Country 2	0.4453	0	0.3133	0.1887	0.3594	0.2737	67.11
Country 3	0.4453	0.3133	0	0.1887	0.2737	0.3594	67.11

We normalize world market prices so that their sum is one. In this first case, Nash equilibrium prices are:

Good 1	Good 2	Good 3
0.3971	0.3014	0.3014

In free trade, we have the following consumption, utility, and income (which from balanced trade equals the value of the endowment, GDP) evaluated at free trade prices:

	c_1	c_2	c_3	Utility	GDP
Country 1	0.4333	0.4333	0.4333	116.38	0.43329
Country 2	0.2833	0.2833	0.2833	73.89	0.283305
Country 3	0.2833	0.2833	0.2833	73.89	0.283305

The changes in economic welfare and its components are hence:

	$\Delta\eta$	ΔTOT	S
Country 1	-0.004321461	-0.01883145	0.014509989
Country 2	0.0185298	0.00936573	0.00916407
Country 3	0.0185298	0.00936573	0.00916407

Or, in relative terms:

	$\Delta TOT/\Delta\eta$	$S/\Delta\eta$	$\Delta TOT/GDP$	S/GDP	$\Delta\eta/GDP$
Country 1	435.77%	-335.77%	-4.35%	3.35%	-1.00%
Country 2	50.54%	49.46%	3.31%	3.23%	6.54%
Country 3	50.54%	49.46%	3.31%	3.23%	6.54%

---

[8] We recognize that raising a country's endowment of some but not all goods may change the size of comparative advantage which in turn may affect countries initial optimal tariff rates and have consequences for the size of the terms-of trade effects from free trade. Syropoulos (2002) offers an analysis of these issues.

By moving to free trade, the large country would forego the terms of trade gains from applying its optimal tariff, and it would require a transfer to agree to free trade. The smaller countries experience terms of trade improvements that are about the same size as their consumption gains.

If transfers were implemented, the smaller countries would surrender about half of their gains from free trade as payments to the large country. We note also that, in this example, terms-of-trade effects, and hence any transfers, would be less than four percent of GDP for the paying countries, and less than five percent of GDP for the receiving country.

Finally, we note that the gains from free trade relative to income, $\Delta\eta/GDP$, are quite large for the smaller countries: If no transfers take place, they are over 6% of GDP; with transfers, they are about 3%, still a substantial gain.

4.2 Countries 2 and 3 are large

The endowment matrix is assumed to be:

	Good 1	Good 2	Good 3
Country 1	0.5	0.1	0.1
Country 2	0.25	0.8	0.1
Country 3	0.25	0.1	0.8

Nash equilibrium yields:

	τ_1^*	τ_2^*	τ_3^*	c_1	c_2	c_3	Utility
Country 1	0	0.4665	0.4665	0.3222	0.168	0.168	43.33
Country 2	1.2857	0	1.474	0.3389	0.5925	0.2395	98.85
Country 3	1.2857	1.474	0	0.3389	0.2395	0.5925	98.85

World market Nash prices are:

Good 1	Good 2	Good 3
0.2766	0.3616	0.3616

At free trade:

	c_1	c_2	c_3	Utility	GDP
Country 1	0.2333	0.2333	0.2333	54.47	0.23331
Country 2	0.3833	0.3833	0.3833	104.11	0.383295
Country 3	0.3833	0.3833	0.3833	104.11	0.383295

Changes in welfare and terms of trade and consumption effects are:

	$\Delta\eta$	ΔTOT	S
Country 1	0.024564678	0.01389861	0.010666068
Country 2	0.019624977	−0.0069993	0.026624277
Country 3	0.019624977	−0.0069993	0.026624277

implying:

	$\Delta TOT/\Delta\eta$	$S/\Delta\eta$	$\Delta TOT/GDP$	S/GDP	$\Delta\eta/GDP$
Country 1	56.58%	43.42%	5.96%	4.57%	10.53%
Country 2	−35.67%	135.67%	−1.83%	6.96%	−5.12%
Country 3	−35.67%	135.67%	−1.83%	6.96%	−5.12%

In this example, two countries, 2 and 3, are relatively large due to a skewed world endowment that makes each country almost a monopoly seller of its export good. While both countries would experience terms of trade losses from global free trade as compared to the Nash equilibrium both countries would gain from free trade since their consumption effects are larger than their terms of trade losses.

In this case, transfers would not be necessary for countries to agree to free trade. If, nevertheless, transfers equal to the terms-of-trade changes were implemented, country 1 would surrender about 57% of its gains from free trade. This transfer would be about the same relative magnitude as in example 1. When viewed as a fraction of income, the donor country would pay almost six percent of GDP, a substantial transfer, while the receiving countries would receive less than two percent of their GDP as transfers. In this example too, the gains to the small country from free trade relative to GDP if transfers take place are about 5% and almost 7% for each of the two larger countries who gain primarily due to liberalization relative each other.

4.3 Countries 1, 2, and 3 are of different size

The endowment matrix is given by:

	Good 1	Good 2	Good 3
Country 1	0.5	0.15	0.05
Country 2	0.25	0.7	0.05
Country 3	0.25	0.15	0.9

Nash equilibrium yields:

	τ_1^*	τ_2^*	τ_3^*	c_1	c_2	c_3	Utility
Country 1	0	0.4203	0.5044	0.3196	0.1984	0.122	37.96
Country 2	0.8142	0	1.012	0.3043	0.4868	0.1575	74.76
Country 3	2.3359	2.5167	0	0.376	0.3146	0.7204	117.92

World market Nash prices are:

Good 1	Good 2	Good 3
0.258	0.2925	0.4493

At free trade:

	c_1	c_2	c_3	Utility	GDP
Country 1	0.2333	0.2333	0.2333	54.47	0.23331
Country 2	0.3333	0.3333	0.3333	90.14	0.3333
Country 3	0.4333	0.4333	0.4333	116.38	0.43329

158   C. Kowalczyk, R. Riezman

Changes in welfare and terms of trade and consumption effects are:

	$\Delta\eta$	ΔTOT	S
Country 1	0.035476897	0.01996467	0.015512227
Country 2	0.047477242	0.01709829	0.030378952
Country 3	−0.006778772	−0.03702963	0.030250858

implying:

	$\Delta TOT/\Delta\eta$	$S/\Delta\eta$	$\Delta TOT/GDP$	S/GDP	$\Delta\eta/GDP$
Country 1	56.58%	43.42%	8.56%	6.65%	15.21%
Country 2	36.01%	63.99%	5.13%	9.11%	14.24%
Country 3	546.26%	−446.26%	−8.55%	6.98%	−1.57%

In this example, no two countries are of equal size. Global free trade hurts the largest of the countries, country 3, and benefits the smaller ones. The smallest country would surrender about 56% of its gains from free trade as a transfer, while the mid-sized country would surrender only about 36% of its gains from free trade.

Transfers are almost 9% and about 5% of GDP for both of the potentially paying countries, 1 and 2, and almost 9% for the receiving country 3. Gains from free trade relative to GDP even after transfers are about 6% for smallest country 1, and a substantial 9% for next smallest country 2.

4.4 Countries 2 and 3 are symmetric

The endowment matrix is:

	Good 1	Good 2	Good 3
Country 1	0.5	0.2	0.2
Country 2	0.25	0.6	0.2
Country 3	0.25	0.2	0.6

Nash equilibrium yields:

	τ_1^*	τ_2^*	τ_3^*	c_1	c_2	c_3	Utility
Country 1	0	0.36	0.36	0.372	0.261	0.261	73.499
Country 2	0.501	0	0.554	0.314	0.450	0.289	93.404
Country 3	0.501	0.554	0	0314	0.289	0.450	93.404

World market Nash prices:

Good 1	Good 2	Good 3
0.323	0.339	0.339

At free trade:

	c_1	c_2	c_3	Utility	GDP
Country 1	0.3	0.3	0.3	79.603	0.29997
Country 2	0.35	0.35	0.35	95.018	0.349965
Country 3	0.35	0.35	0.35	95.018	0.349965

 Springer

Free trade: what are the terms-of-trade effects?   159

Changes in real income, and terms of trade and consumption effects are:

	$\Delta\eta$	ΔTOT	S
Country 1	0.01776175	0.0019998	0.01576195
Country 2	0.005602365	−0.0009999	0.006602265
Country 3	0.005602365	−0.0009999	0.006602265

Hence:

	$\Delta TOT/\Delta\eta$	$S/\Delta\eta$	$\Delta TOT/GDP$	S/GDP	$\Delta\eta/GDP$
Country 1	11.26%	88.74%	0.67%	5.25%	5.92%
Country 2	−17.85%	117.85%	−0.29%	1.89%	1.60%
Country 3	−17.85%	117.85%	−0.29%	1.89%	1.60%

In this, final, example, countries are made more symmetric, and terms-of-trade effects become relatively less important.[9] Every country gains from free trade and no sidepayments would be necessary for countries to agree to free trade.

If, however, transfers were implemented, they would only be about 11% of the gains of the country whose terms-of-trade improve. When calculated as a fraction of GDP, terms-of-trade effects, and hence potential transfers, are about zero for both paying and receiving countries. The smallest country has the largest gains relative to GDP at about 5% if transfers are enacted.

5 Conclusion and further research

Terms-of-trade effects are contentious as their sum is zero across all the world's nations. Indeed, if the world were one of perfect competition, elimination of all the world's trade barriers would imply positive contributions to every nation's economic welfare from adjustments in production (which we do not consider in this paper) and consumption, yet some nations might experience lower income, and hence object to global free trade, if they face terms-of-trade losses that are even larger than the gains from any production and consumption effects.

We have presented estimates of terms-of-trade effects from moving from a non-cooperative tariff equilibrium to global free trade in a world trade model of perfect competition, and we have found that these terms-of-trade effects can be large. For countries whose real income falls from free trade, the terms-of-trade effects are so large that they dominate any positive contribution from the consumption effects. For countries whose terms-of-trade improve, they may constitute more than half of their total gains from free trade. When calculated as a fraction of a nation's GDP, terms-of-trade effects do not exceed 9% in our examples.

---

[9] In a completely symmetric world economy, there would be no terms-of-trade effects from moving from Nash tariffs to global free trade.

The terms-of-trade effects and hence potential payments that we derive in this paper are larger than those derived under monopoly trade by Kowalczyk and Sjöström (1994) who find that transfers account for about 14% of the payees' gains from trade, and less than 1% of their GDP. In the monopoly trade model, the underlying sources of gains are efficiency gains and the distortions due to mark-up pricing, hence terms-of-trade effects should reasonably account for a smaller share of the total welfare gains from eliminating all distortions than in the competitive model where the underlying sources of aggregate gains are only the efficiency gains. In other estimates of welfare gains from free trade in a competitive world economy, Hertel (2000), for example, finds, from calculations derived from the GTAP model, that those regions of the world that would experience particularly large efficiency gains (more than 2% of GDP) also would tend to experience worse terms of trade. He also reports that terms of trade losses may be large—up to 60% of efficiency gains for some major emerging market economies. However, only in one instance does the terms-of-trade loss exceed the efficiency gains. One likely reason why terms-of-trade effects are relatively less important in Hertel's estimates than in ours is that our calculations are relative to Nash equilibrium tariffs, which in some of our examples exceed 100%, while Hertel's are relative to estimates of actual rates of protection which are calculated to be substantially smaller, frequently less than 20%.

It would be a useful extension of the work in the present paper to explore the robustness of our findings by undertaking a grid search over all possible parameter values, and calculating the corresponding terms-of-trade effects and associated income transfers. Furthermore, our analysis assumes no substitution in production allowing only for consumption effects. It would be another interesting extension to consider whether introducing substitution in production would make terms-of-trade effects from free trade, and hence international sidepayments, larger or smaller relative to any total income change. On the one hand, added substitution would tend to imply that adjustments between equilibria are more in quantities than in prices, suggesting smaller terms-of-trade effects. On the other hand, additional substitution might raise the initial trade volume in the non-cooperative Nash equilibrium, and thereby imply that terms-of-trade effects relative to free trade would be larger. Sorting these out would be useful.

Finally, it is an interesting question how transport cost would affect our findings. For given endowments and preferences, introducing transport costs would presumably reduce trade flows in the optimal tariff equilibrium, and hence reduce one of the components of any terms-of-trade effects from free trade while, at the same time, reducing the responsiveness of import-demand functions and hence reducing the relative magnitudes of volume responses but raising those of price responses. Thus transport costs could have ambiguous overall effects for the size of terms-of-trade effects and thus of any transfers. A quantitative investigation of these would be necessary to determine whether transport costs would raise or lower the importance of international sidepayments.

We conclude by suggesting that since terms-of-trade effects may constitute a significant cause for some nations' resistance to free trade, exploring these effects further may prove to be a productive approach to unlocking the gains that could be earned from trade.

 Springer

References

Bond, E., Syropoulos, C.: The size of trading blocs: market power and world welfare effects. J Int Econ **40**, 411–438 (1996)

Grinols, E.L.: An extension of the Kemp–Wan theorem on the formation of customs unions. J Int Econ **6**, 95–97 (1981)

Grinols, E.L., Wong, K.-y.: An exact measure of welfare change. Can J Econ **24**, 61–64 (1991)

Hertel, T.W.: Potential gains from reducing trade barriers in manufacturing, services and agriculture. Fed Reserve Bank St. Louis Rev 4, 77–99 (2000)

Johnson, H.G.: Optimum tariffs and retaliation. Rev Econ Stud **XXI**, 142–153 (1953)

Jones, R.W.: Tariffs and trade in general equilibrium: comment. Am Econ Rev **59**, 418–424 (1969)

Kemp, M.C., Wan, H.Y.: An elementary proposition concerning the formation of customs unions. J Int Econ **6**, 95–97 (1976)

Kennan, J., Riezman, R.: Do big countries win tariff wars? Int Econ Rev **29**, 81–85 (1988)

Kennan, J., Riezman, R.: Optimal tariff equilibria with customs unions Can J Econ **23**, 70–83 (1990)

Konishi, H., Kowalczyk, C., Sjöström, T.: Free trade, customs unions, and transfers. Social Science Research Network, July; http://ssrn.com/abstract=428346 (2003a)

Konishi, H., Kowalczyk, C., Sjöström, T.: Global free trade is in the core of a customs union formation game. Rev Int Econ (2003b, forthcoming)

Kowalczyk, C.: Welfare and integration. Int Econ Rev **41**, 483–494 (2000)

Kowalczyk, C., Sjöström, T.: Bringing GATT into the core. Economica **61**, 301–317 (1994)

Kowalczyk, C., Sjöström, T.: Trade as transfers, GATT and the core. Econ Lett **66**, 163–169 (2000)

Ohyama, M.: Trade and welfare in general equilibrium. Keio Econ Stud **9**, 73 (1972)

Riezman, R.: Customs unions and the core. J Int Econ **19**, 355–365 (1985)

Riezman, R.: Can bilateral trade agreements help to induce free trade? Can J Econ **32**, 751–766 (1999)

Syropoulos, C.: Optimum tariffs and retaliation revisited: how country size matters. Rev Econ Stud **69**, 707–727 (2002)

Viner, J.: The Customs Union Issue. New York: Carnegie Endowment for International Peace (1950)

Part II: Political Economy and Voting Models

Part II: Political Economy and Voting Models

In "Voter Preferences for Trade Policy Instruments", we consider the choice of tariffs versus production subsidies as a method for redistributing income in a simple political economy model. We find that voters with high direct tax burdens tend to prefer tariffs to subsidies. This is because tariffs create revenue lessening the burden on high tax bracket people while subsidies use revenue thereby increasing the burden on these same people. So despite the fact that tariffs are less efficient the deadweight loss effect is outweighed by the revenue effect for high tax bracket voters. In an uncertain environment it is shown that if actual tariff and subsidy rates are chosen from the set of individually optimal rates, then tariffs will have a smaller range than subsidies. In this case, tariffs might be preferred to subsidies. Finally, for large countries, voters whose income share declines with more protection actually prefer tariffs to subsidies.

"Seniority in Legislatures" constructs a model to answer the following questions: why do most legislative institutions have a seniority system? Why are incumbents re-elected so often and by such large margins? In our model there is a legislature that, in each session that it meets, endogenously determines whether or not there will be a seniority system. We model the behavior of the individual legislators as well as voters in their districts. In an infinitely repeated divide-the-dollar game, we show that there exists a stationary equilibrium with the property that the legislature always imposes a seniority system on itself. Voters understanding the equilibrium behavior of the legislators always re-elect incumbents. Thus, the seniority system is responsible for very strong incumbency effects.

The paper "Political Reform and Trade Policy" develops a model that includes important elements of both electoral competition and pressure-group competition. The economic model is an amended version of Rodrik's specific-factor trade model, but we replace his political model with an amended version of Baron's model of informed and uniformed voters. The critical feature of the political reforms is that they take the form of partial restrictions on political behavior. It is this partialness that distinguishes policy reforms in our model from the traditional welfare analysis, where policy instruments are fully controlled. Our model allows for two types of partial restrictions: ceilings on allowable contributions per interest group and restrictions on the number of groups that is allowed to contribute. The results demonstrate that both types of restrictions may be ineffective. The ability of candidates to seek out additional contributors in response to contribution ceilings can easily lead to a higher level of overall deadweight loss from trade protection. We identify the "contributor elasticity" as an important consideration in this regard. Restrictions on the access of contributors to candidates may also lead to a more distortionary trade policy by causing candidates to seek greater contributions from a small set of industries, thereby raising the level of trade protection in the protected industries. Taken as a whole, our results suggest that the behavioral responses to partial restrictions on political competition often overwhelm the direct effects.

In "The Sources of Protectionist Drift in Representative Democracies", we use a representative democracy framework (where voters vote for candidates) in which candidates are chosen endogenously *a la* Besley and Coate. We find that there is a "protectionist drift" in a representative democracies framework. We borrow from Besley and Coate, and Osborne and Slivinski the idea of "citizen candidates": the future policymaker is chosen in each country among the citizens who are willing to run for election and these citizens are unable to commit to a given policy. Rather, citizens elected implement the policy associated with their given "type" as in Mayer's model. This leads to a "delegation effect". Since the election stage takes place before trade policy is selected, the "type" of the policymaker has strategic effects on the trade policy equilibrium. Hence, voters generally favor the election of somebody whose type differs from their own. We show that there exists a one-candidate-per-country equilibrium in which the selected policymaker is the ideal candidate of the median voter and is unambiguously more protectionist than her. Thus, delegation effects produce "protectionist drift". We go on to show however, that besides delegation effects, there is an additional source for protectionist drift in a representative democracy when candidates are purely outcome-motivated. This is what we call the "abstention effect". Not only do candidates wish to delegate to more protectionist colleagues, but these more protectionist colleagues who can win the election, prefer still more protectionist candidates than themselves. In two-candidates-per-country equilibria, this abstention effect prevents policy convergence. We also introduce the possibility that there may be costs and benefits associated with holding office. In one-candidate equilibria, the larger the net benefits from holding office the smaller the set of possible equilibria. With two-candidate equilibria, more benefits mean less dispersion in candidate types. The interesting implication of this result is that as holding office becomes more unpleasant (larger negative net benefits) there will be more dispersion between candidates.

"Storable Votes and Minorities" shows that from a practical point of view, storable votes seem particularly well-suited to the protection of minority interests. The use of storable votes was initially proposed by Alessandra Casella. The desirable efficiency properties of storable votes stem from the fact that voters who have an allocation of storable votes will use them to vote on more salient decisions. In equilibrium, this means that the probability of obtaining the desired outcome shifts away from decisions that matter little and towards decisions that matter more, with positive welfare effects. Namely, storable votes have the potential to increase efficiency while improving equity at the same time. In the first part of the paper, we explicitly study the efficiency properties of the storable votes mechanism, as well as its distributional effects on minorities. The desirable properties of storable votes are features of the equilibrium of the resulting voting game — they emerge if every voter chooses the correct number of votes, given what she expects others to do. The second part of the paper presents the results of a set of experiments showing that under storable votes, the minority does indeed win on a significant number of issues. Both the minority payoff and the aggregate efficiency of the mechanism match the theoretical predictions, indicating that the equity gains accrue with little or no loss of efficiency. Voters use responsive strategies, consistently casting more votes when valuations are higher, and such behavior gets voters close to their equilibrium payoffs.

ECONOMICS AND POLITICS 0954-1985

Volume 2 November 1990 No. 3

VOTER PREFERENCES FOR TRADE POLICY INSTRUMENTS*

WOLFGANG MAYER AND RAYMOND RIEZMAN

We analyze voter preferences for tariffs and production subsidies. The distribution of tax revenues argument shows that voters with high direct tax burdens prefer tariffs to subsidies. The uncertainty argument demonstrates that if actual tariff and subsidy rates are chosen from the set of individually optimal rates then the range of tariff rates is smaller than the range of subsidy rates. Thus, tariffs might be preferred even though they are less efficient. Finally, the large country argument shows that if a country is large then voters whose income shares decline with more protection prefer tariffs to subsidies.

I. INTRODUCTION

WHEN REDISTRIBUTION of income through commercial policies is considered, which instrument is preferred by voters? This question is of particular interest in an open economy when the choice is between tariffs and production subsidies.[1] Concerning the voters' preferences between these instruments, Mayer and Riezman (1987) have shown that production subsidies dominate tariffs, if people's policy preferences are based on differences in factor ownership.[2] Domination means that every person is better off with a production subsidy than a tariff of the same value, independent of the rate of protection. Consequently, one would expect that neither individual voters nor policy platforms of politicians call for tariffs. Empirical evidence, however, reveals that voters, lobbying groups, and politicians frequently favor tariffs over production subsidies, with the primary objective of redistributing income.

A variety of arguments has been suggested to reconcile theory and practice. Most frequently mentioned is the *transparency argument*.[3] It states that governments prefer tariffs to subsidies because the welfare-reducing effects of tariff intervention are less transparent to individuals. People are less informed about the cost of a tariff, through a loss in consumer surplus, than about the cost of the subsidy, which requires higher taxes to finance it.

---

[1] Other, potentially more efficient, instruments, such as lump-sum transfers and factor income taxes, are precluded by assumption.

[2] This proposition at the individual's level corresponds to the more basic proposition at society's level that subsidies are better than tariffs in correcting domestic distortions, as demonstrated by Bhagwati and Ramaswami (1963) and Bhagwati (1971).

[3] Hillman (1989) discusses the essence of the argument and refers to its role in the history of Australian tariff formation.

*Comments by Jagdish Bhagwati, Dani Rodrik, and participants in the Columbia Conference on Political Economy and International Economics, as well as by Costas Syropoulos and seminar participants at Pennsylvania State University and the University of Western Ontario are greatly appreciated.

260   MAYER AND RIEZMAN

Feenstra and Lewis (1990) also focus on incomplete information in explaining the choice of tariffs. However, it is not the people who are less informed than the government, but the government has incomplete information about the losses of individuals from import competition. A nonlinear tariff becomes the optimal instrument to protect them.

An alternative asymmetry assumption is introduced by Rodrik (1986) in developing what may be called the *public goods argument*. Tariffs, which affect a wider grouping of firms, are more of a public good than subsidies, which tend to be more firm specific. Consequently, the free rider problem is more serious in the case of tariffs and interest groups tend to underpursue them. The public, in turn, wants to minimize injury from trade intervention and pushes politicians into precommitting to the less damaging tariff regime.

Wilson (1990) questions the conclusion of Rodrik's public goods argument and suggests that a given politician should prefer subsidies to tariffs since the former generate higher political contributions. However, he goes on to show that in a political game of several politicians they still may prefer tariffs since the game for subsidies leads to excessive protection.

Staiger and Tabellini (1987) specify a model with fully immobile capital and partially immobile labor in which a terms of trade shock occurs. These adjustment difficulties prevent the government from precommitting to free trade, and tariffs rather than subsidies are likely to be adopted.

Finally, there is a *political process argument*, suggested by Nelson (1987) and elaborated by Mayer and Riezman (1989). It postulates that people differ with respect to more than one feature, in which case multidimensional policy preferences emerge. Even if a tariff is not the ideal point for any person, the social choice process still may yield tariffs as the adopted instrument.

This paper introduces three additional arguments to question the domination of tariffs by production subsidies at the level of voter preferences. The arguments emphasize that the Mayer-Riezman (1987) model, where voters differ with respect to factor ownership only, represents just one polar case. When tax collection and revenue redistribution systems are no longer unbiased, when voters are uncertain about which rates of protection will eventually be adopted, and when the choice is restricted to either tariff or subsidy in case of a large country, subsidies no longer dominate.[4] In each of the three situations at least some individuals consider tariffs superior to production subsidies as an instrument for redistributing income. Given these preferences of voters with respect to policy instruments, this also opens the possibility that society as a whole will choose tariffs rather than subsidies as a regime for protection.

---

[4] This breakdown of subsidy domination at the level of individual voters is similar to the breakdown of the first-best production subsidy argument at the level of a benevolent government, when there are not just production distortions but also government revenue constraints [Corden (1986, pp. 96–101)], uncertainty [Eaton and Grossman (1985)], revenue-seeking by individuals or groups [Bhagwati, Brecher, and Srinivasan (1984)], or non-economic objectives [Johnson (1965) and Bhagwati and Srinivasan (1969)].

VOTER PREFERENCES FOR TRADE POLICY INSTRUMENTS 261

First, we discuss the *distribution of tax revenues argument*. It rests on the assumption that many income tax systems, on which production subsidies draw and to which tariff revenues contribute, are progressive. When a person's tax share is higher than his or her income share, tariffs reduce the individual's direct tax burden while subsidies raise it. There exists an asymmetry with respect to cost, as the cost of a subsidy is borne by a small group of upper-income people while the cost of the tariff, in terms of lost consumer surplus, is spread across the whole population.

Second, there is the *uncertainty argument*. It deals with situations where people must express their preferences for a policy regime, such as tariffs or subsidies, before they know which rates will actually be adopted. It is shown that the potential range of rates is narrower for tariffs than subsidies, under the assumption that actual rates are chosen from the set of individually optimal rates. This implies that individuals consider a tariff regime to be less efficient, but also less risky than a production subsidy regime, and the less risky tariff regime may be preferred.

Finally, there is the *large country argument*. As was indicated in Mayer and Riezman (1987), when a country has control over the terms of trade, each person likes a combination of tariffs and subsidies. All people want the same tariff rate to exploit the country's monopoly position, but individually optimal subsidy rates differ depending on factor ownership. Here, we deal with the more realistic situation that people have to choose between either tariffs or subsidies, excluding the possibility of a combination of the two. It is shown that all people whose income shares decline with more protection of the import industry prefer tariffs to subsidies. Even gainers from the protective measures may be better off with the tariff.

II. REAL INCOME UNDER TARIFFS AND SUBSIDIES

The economy under consideration is assumed to consist of I risk-neutral individuals who possess homothetic, identical preferences, but differ from each other with respect to their fixed factor endowments. These differences in factor ownership are the underlying cause for people's differences in policy preferences. There are two factors of production which are employed by two competitive industries producing commodities X_1 and X_2. Unless stated otherwise, the economy under consideration is small.

For the risk-neutral ith person, welfare is measured by real income,

$$R^i = y_d^i / e^i(p), \tag{1}$$

where y_d^i is disposable income of individual i, p is the domestic price of the second in terms of the first commodity as faced by consumers, and $e^i = e$ is a price index which, under identically homothetic preferences, is the same for all consumers. We also note that $-\partial R^i / \partial p = R^i e_p / e = (\partial R^i / \partial y_d^i) D_2^i = D_2^i / e$, where D_2^i is the ith consumer's demand for the second commodity.

262   MAYER AND RIEZMAN

The second commodity, whose world price is π, is imported. Under a production subsidy, domestic consumers face this world price. Under a tariff, on the other hand, the price becomes:

$$p = \pi(1 + t), \tag{2}$$

where t is an *ad valorem* tariff rate on the import good. Disposable income of the ith person, y_d^i, is income received from factor ownership, y^i, adjusted for redistributed tariff revenues received, τ^i, or taxes paid to finance the subsidy, σ^i:

$$y_{dt}^i = y_t^i + \tau^i \qquad \text{and} \qquad y_{ds}^i = y_s^i - \sigma^i, \tag{3}$$

where subscripts t and s refer to the tariff and subsidy regimes respectively.

It is convenient to define the ith person's share of total factor income by $\phi^i = y^i/Y$ and the shares of total tariff revenues received by $\psi_t^i = \tau^i/T$ and of subsidies financed by $\psi_s^i = \sigma^i/S$. In these expressions, $Y = (X_1 + pX_2)$ is national income produced (total factor income earned), X_j denotes industry output of commodity j, $T = \pi t [D_2(p) - X_2(p)] = \pi t M_2(p)$ is total tariff revenues, $S = \pi s X_2 [\pi(1 + s)]$ measures total subsidy payments, $D_2(p)$ is total domestic demand, and $M_2(p)$ expresses import demand for good two at domestic price p. Using the share definitions, we express the ith person's real income under a tariff and subsidy regime respectively as:

$$R_t^i = [\phi_t^i(Y_t + T) - (\phi_t^i - \psi_t^i)T]/e(p) \tag{4}$$

$$R_s^i = [\phi_s^i(Y_s - S) + (\phi_s^i - \psi_s^i)S]/e(\pi). \tag{5}$$

Each person's real income is proportionate to real national income, R, after it has been adjusted by a term which reflects the divergence between factor income and tax shares, whereby real national income under tariff and subsidy respectively equals:

$$R_t = (Y_t + T)/e(p) \qquad \text{and} \qquad R_s = (Y_s - S)/e(\pi).$$

We finally note that, at $t = s$ of a small country, $Y_t = Y_s$, $\phi_t^i = \phi_s^i$, and $(Y_t + T) = (Y_s - S + \pi t D_2) = [Y_s - S]/[1 - m_2 t/(1 + t)]$, where $m_2(p) = pD_2/(Y_t + T)$ is the marginal and average propensity to consume the second good under a tariff.

III.   THE DISTRIBUTION OF TAX REVENUES ARGUMENT

The purpose of this section is to show that in a small economy a person may be better off under a tariff than equal-value production subsidy if the person's shares of taxes paid and of tariff revenues received exceed the share of factor income.[5] In many less developed countries in which a large segment of below-average income people pays no or very little income tax, these conditions are likely to be encountered.

---

[5] It is explicitly assumed that the choice between tariffs and subsidies is made given the existing income tax system. The model does not explain how the income tax structure has come about and how preferences for various taxes would be determined if the entire tax structure were to be chosen.

VOTER PREFERENCES FOR TRADE POLICY INSTRUMENTS   263

We assume that initially, when protection of the import industry is considered, free trade prevails. At issue is whether the ith person will fare better with a tariff or an equal-value production subsidy; that is, whether R_t^i is greater or smaller than R_s^i, given that $t = s$. Using the earlier stated definitions of real national income, R_t and R_s, we subtract (5) from (4) and obtain:

$$R_t^i - R_s^i = \phi^i [R_t - R_s] + [\psi^i - \phi^i] [T/e(p) + S/e(\pi)], \tag{6}$$

where we set $\phi_t^i = \phi_s^i = \phi^i$ and for simplicity's sake assume that $\psi_t^i = \psi_s^i = \psi^i$.[6] The ith person's real income change from selecting a tariff rather than production subsidy depends on two effects. First, there is the real income change for the entire country weighted by the person's factor income share. Second, there is the real value of government savings, as it replaces an expenditure-causing subsidization policy by a revenue-generating tariff policy, when weighted by the difference between the person's tax and income shares. Clearly, the second effect is positive (negative) if the ith person's tax share is high (low) relative to his or her factor income share.

An interpretation of $(R_t - R_s)$ can be given for situations where policy changes are large. Recalling that $R_t = [Y_t + T]/e(p)$ and $R_s = [Y_s - S]/e(\pi)$, where $Y_t = Y_s$ for $s = t$, and writing $e(p) = e(\pi) + \Delta e$, we obtain:

$$R_t - R_s = \{T + S - [Y_s - S] [\Delta e/e(\pi)] \}/e(p) = [T + S - R_s \Delta e]/e(p), \tag{7}$$

where the change in price index, Δe, is due to a tariff which, starting from a free trade position, can be expressed as $(\Delta e/\Delta p)\pi t$. For large tariffs, the index change is approximated by:

$$\Delta e/\Delta p \cong [e_p(\pi) + e_p(p)]/2, \tag{8}$$

where we average the price index responses in the neighbourhood of initial and new consumption points respectively. Since $e_p(\pi) = D_2(\pi)/R_s$ and $e_p(p) = D_2(p)/R_t$, we can write:

$$R_s \Delta e = \pi t \{D_2(\pi) + D_2(p) - [D_2(p)/R_t] [R_t - R_s]\}/2. \tag{9}$$

Substitution of $(T + S) = \pi t D_2(p)$, when $t = s$, and of (9) in (7), and using $m_2 = [\pi(1 + t)D_2(p)]/[R_t e(p)]$, yields:

$$R_t - R_s = \{\pi t [D_2(p) - D_2(\pi)]\}/\{2e(p)[1 - m_2 t/(2 + 2t)]\}, \tag{10}$$

which is always negative since $D_2(p) < D_2(\pi)$ for $p > \pi$ and $1 > m_2 t/(2 + 2t)$. Consequently, no matter what the rate's value, protection of an industry through a tariff makes the nation as a whole always worse off than protection through an equal-rate production subsidy.

---

[6] This simplification does not affect the argument in a fundamental way.

264 MAYER AND RIEZMAN

Knowing that $R_t < R_s$ always, we now return to (6) to draw the following conclusions concerning the ith person's welfare effects of a tariff relative to a production subsidy:

(1) If the tax system is unbiased, in the sense that tax shares are the same as income shares, a production subsidy is preferred by every individual independent of factor ownership. This reaffirms the result that tariffs are dominated by subsidies.
(2) If the tax system is biased such that some people's tax shares exceed their income shares, they may find tariffs to be superior to production subsidies as an instrument of protection. The superiority of tariffs is more likely the greater the difference between tax and income shares.

The *distribution of tax revenues argument* rests on the assumption that a country's tax system is such that high-income groups have tax shares which exceed their factor income shares. When high-income people consider protection, they realize that a tariff generates revenues whose distribution would be of primary benefit to them, while production subsidies require higher taxes which fall on them disproportionately. Looked at the two instruments' cost side, subsidization translates into higher income taxes for upper income groups, while tariff costs, in form of reduced consumer surplus, are distributed much more evenly across the population.[7] The argument, therefore, involves an asymmetry concerning the identity of cost bearers; subsidy costs fall on a small group of high income tax payers, while tariff costs are borne by all consumers of the import good.

IV. THE UNCERTAINTY ARGUMENT

This argument rests on the assumption that the voters' choice between employment of a tariff or subsidy regime has to be made before actual rates of protection are to be selected. For example, in a two-candidate race for political office, candidates may express positions only on the type of instrument but not on the rates to be chosen. What we are going to show is that under this uncertainty about future rates of protection many voters, especially those with moderate preferences for or against protection, may prefer a tariff to a subsidy regime. In presenting the argument, we assume that there is no bias in distributing tariff revenues or collecting taxes to finance the subsidy; that is, we assume that $\psi^i = \phi^i$.

---

[7] In reality it may not be the case that consumer surplus shrinks in proportion to a person's income, as preferences may not be identical and homothetic. In less developed countries, the share of income spent on imported goods frequently is larger for upper-income than lower-income groups. In such a case, the distribution of tax revenues argument would be weakened.

[8] Nothing is said about the political process itself through which the rate is chosen, as even this process may not be known yet. Loosely speaking, the assumption states that a person considers a certain rate of protection more likely the more people look at it as their best rate.

VOTER PREFERENCES FOR TRADE POLICY INSTRUMENTS 265

The uncertainty argument rests on the assumption that the probability of a given rate of protection getting adopted equals the fraction of people which considers this rate to be best.[8] The probability that rate of protection x will be adopted is expressed by $f(x,t)$ and $f(x,s)$ for the alternatives of tariff and subsidy regime respectively. If we define $R^i(x,t)$ and $R^i(x,s)$ as the ith person's welfare under tariff and subsidy regimes when rate x prevails, then the person's expected utility under a tariff regime is higher than under a subsidy regime if:

$$B^i = \int_{\underline{x}}^{\bar{x}} R^i(x,t)\,dF(x,t) - \int_{\underline{x}}^{\bar{x}} R^i(x,s)\,dF(x,s) > 0, \tag{11}$$

where $F(x,.)$ is the cumulative distribution function under a given policy regime and $\bar{x}$ and $\underline{x}$ are the finite limits on the rates of protection under either policy regime. The values of $\bar{x}$ and $\underline{x}$ are given by the highest and lowest individually optimal rates of protection from all the people of the country.

To evaluate B^i, we first add and subtract $\int_{\underline{x}}^{\bar{x}} R^i(x,s)\,dF(x,t)$ to obtain:

$$B^i = \int_{\underline{x}}^{\bar{x}} [R^i(x,t) - R^i(x,s)]\,dF(x,t) - \int_{\underline{x}}^{\bar{x}} R^i(x,s)[dF(x,s) - dF(x,t)]. \tag{12}$$

The first term on the RHS of (12) must always be negative when $\psi^i = \phi^i$ since we know from (6) that $R^i(x,t) \leq R^i(x,s)$ for all x, with equality holding at $x = 0$ only. This term measures the expected loss in utility due to a switch from a subsidy to a tariff regime when the probabilities of tariff rates are employed as weights. Hence, a necessary condition for B^i to become positive is that the second term on the RHS of (12), including the minus sign, is positive.

Using integration by parts, this second term can be rewritten as:

$$-\int_{\underline{x}}^{\bar{x}} R^i(x,s)[dF(x,s) - dF(x,t)] = \int_{\underline{x}}^{\bar{x}} R'^i(x,s)[F(x,s) - F(x,t)]\,dx, \tag{13}$$

where $R'^i(x,s)$ is the marginal utility of a subsidy change.[9] For a person whose utility maximizing rate is $\bar{x}^i$, the term R'^i is positive for $\underline{x} < x < \bar{x}^i$, whereas R'^i is negative for $\bar{x}^i < x < \bar{x}$. What we are going to show is that the expression in (13) must always be positive for a voter whose optimal policy is free trade, as the distribution $F(x,t)$ dominates $F(x,s)$[10] in the first-order stochastic sense. For voters whose optimal rate of protection deviates from free trade, the value of this expression becomes smaller with the degree of deviation.

First-order stochastic dominance of $F(x,t)$ over $F(x,s)$ is due to the fact that each person's optimal tariff rate, whether positive or negative, is always less extreme than the same person's optimal subsidy rate. In order to show this, we rewrite (4) and (5) under the assumption that $\phi^i = \psi^i$, as:

$$R_t^i = \phi^i(Y_t + T)/e(p) = \phi^i\{X_1(p) + pX_2(p) + \pi t[D_2(p) - X_2(p)]\}/e(p) \tag{4'}$$

---

[9] Note that $F(\underline{x},t) = F(\underline{x},s) = 0$ and $F(\bar{x},t) = F(\bar{x},s) = 1$.

[10] See Laffont (1989) for definitions of stochastic dominance.

266   MAYER AND RIEZMAN

$$R_s^i = \phi^i(Y_s - S)/e(\pi) = \phi^i\{X_1(p) + pX_2(p) - \pi s X_2(p)\}/e(\pi), \tag{5'}$$

where $p = \pi(1 + t) = \pi(1 + s)$. The responses of real income to tariff and subsidy rate changes are:

$$\partial R_t^i/\partial t = \pi\phi^i\{\pi t(\partial M_2/\partial p) + [Y_t + T](\partial\phi^i/\partial p)/\phi^i\}/e(p) \tag{14}$$

$$\partial R_s^i/\partial s = \pi\phi^i\{-\pi s(\partial X_2/\partial p) + [Y_s - S](\partial\phi^i/\partial p)/\phi^i\}/e(\pi), \tag{15}$$

where $M_2 = (D_2 - X_2)$ is import demand, $(\partial M_2/\partial p) < 0$, $(\partial X_2/\partial p) > 0$, and $(\partial\phi^i/\partial p)$ measures the change in the ith person's factor income share as the second good's domestic price rises. Both real income responses reveal that a person can gain from an increase in either tariff or subsidy rate only if his factor income share rises as the domestic price of the import good goes up. Figure 1 portrays the real income curves for two alternative persons, a winner from protection indicated by superscript w and a loser from protection with superscript L. The $R^i(t)$ curve is uniformly below the $R^i(s)$ curve except for the free trade point, where $s = t = 0$. Assuming that the second order conditions for a maximum are satisfied, the ith individual maximizes real income by choosing a subsidy rate $\tilde{s}^i$ such that:

$$\tilde{s}^i = [(Y_s - S)(\partial\phi^i/\partial p)]/[\pi\phi^i(\partial X_2/\partial p)]. \tag{16}$$

Clearly, the optimal subsidy rate is positive for a winner from protection, since $\partial\phi^w/\partial p > 0$, and negative for a loser, as $\partial\phi^L/\partial p < 0$. But what is the slope of

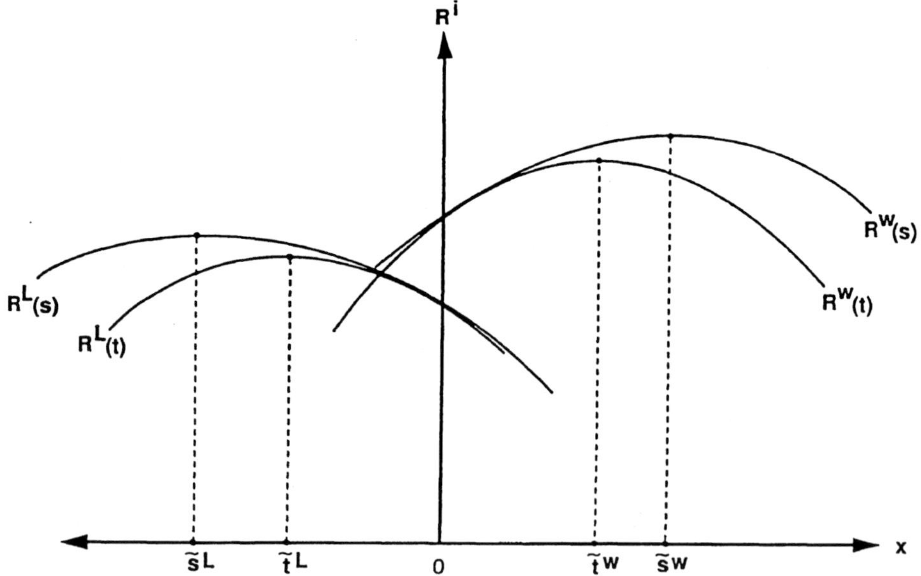

Figure 1

VOTER PREFERENCES FOR TRADE POLICY INSTRUMENTS 267

the $R^i(t)$ locus at tariff rate $t = \bar{s}^i$? If one can show that it is negative at $\bar{s}^w$, then the individually optimal tariff rate $\tilde{t}^w$ occurs at a lower value than $\bar{s}^w$, as drawn in the diagram for the winner. And if the slope of $R^L(t)$ is positive at $\bar{s}^L$ then $\bar{s}^L < \tilde{t}^L < 0$. In demonstrating this we note again that, at a given rate x, $Y_s = Y_t$ and $(\partial X_2 / \partial p)$ is the same under both regimes. Then, we recall that $(Y_t + T) = (Y_s - S)/[1 - m_2 t/(1 + t)]$. Substituting (16) for t and the expression for $(Y_t + T)$ in (14), one can see after some manipulations that:

$$\partial R^i / \partial t = \frac{\{\pi[Y_s - S][\partial \phi^i / \partial p]\}\{(\partial D_2 / \partial p)|_U / (\partial X_2 / \partial p)\}}{e(p)[1 - m_2 t/(1 + t)]}, \tag{17}$$

where $(\partial D_2 / \partial p)|_U < 0$ is the pure substitution effect of the own price change.[11] This implies that, evaluated at $t = \bar{s}^i$, $\partial R_t^i / \partial t < 0$ if $\partial \phi^i / \partial p > 0$ and $\partial R_t^i / \partial t > 0$ if $\partial \phi^i / \partial p < 0$. In words, for people who gain (lose) from protection, real income under the tariff regime is already (still) decreasing (increasing) at the rate where the optimal production subsidy is attained. This means that the optimal import tariff rate is lower than the optimal production subsidy rate for gainers from protection, while the optimal import subsidy (implying a negative value for t) falls short of the optimal production tax for losers from protection; that is, $\bar{s}^i < \tilde{t}^i < 0$ for all people with $\bar{x}^i < 0$ and $0 < \tilde{t}^i < \bar{s}^i$ for all people with $\bar{x}^i > 0$.

The fact that the range of individually optimal tariff rates around the free trade point is narrower than the range of subsidy rates furthermore implies that:

$$[F(x,s) - F(x,t)] > 0 \text{ for } x < 0$$
$$[F(x,s) - F(x,t)] < 0 \text{ for } x > 0, \tag{18}$$

given our assumption that the probability of a certain rate of protection being adopted equals the fraction of the population which considers this rate to be optimal. As we examine the case of a person whose optimal policies favor free trade, $\bar{x}^i = 0$, such that $R'^i > 0$ for $x < 0$ and $R'^i < 0$ for $x > 0$, one can see from (18) that

$$R'^i(x,s)[F(x,s) - F(x,t)] > 0 \tag{19}$$

always. Hence, the expression of (13) is positive and the second term in (12), which states the expected utility gain from a subsidy to tariff switch, is positive. Provided the second term's magnitude is sufficient to outweigh the negative first term in the B^i expression, the person will favor a tariff regime.

The case for preferring a tariff regime under uncertainty is weakened when the person's optimal subsidy rate under certainty is not zero. For example, let us consider the case when $\bar{x}^i = \bar{s}^i > 0$. Then one can rewrite (13) as:

$$\int_{\underline{x}}^{0} R'^i[F(x,s) - F(x,t)]\,dx + \int_{0}^{\bar{x}^i} R'^i[F(x,s) - F(x,t)]\,dx$$

$$+ \int_{\bar{x}^i}^{\bar{x}} R'^i[F(x,s) - F(x,t)]\,dx, \tag{13'}$$

[11] In deriving this expression we made use of $(\partial M_2 / \partial t)/\pi = \partial D_2 / \partial p - \partial X_2 / \partial p = [(\partial D_2 / \partial p)|_U - (\partial X_2 / \partial p)]/[1 - m_2 t/(1 + t)]$.

268   MAYER AND RIEZMAN

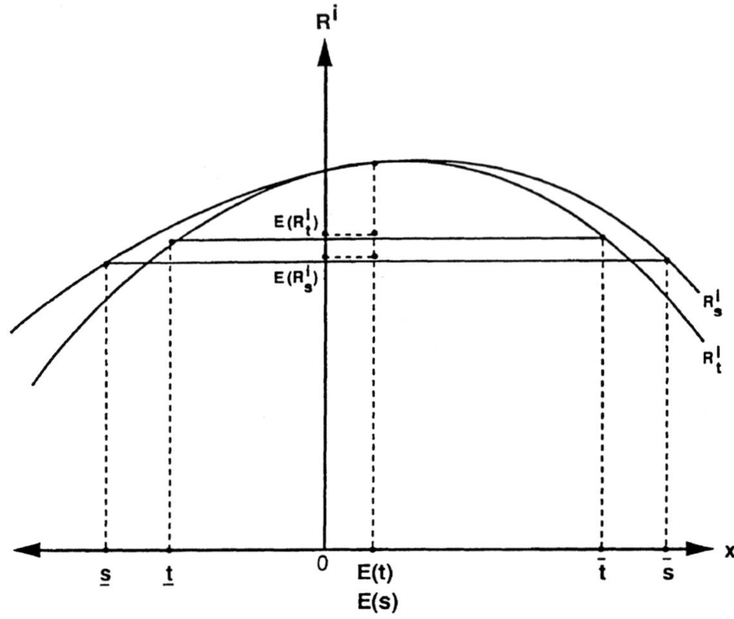

Figure 2

where $R'^i > 0$ for $x < \bar{x}^i$ and $R'^i < 0$ for $x > \bar{x}^i > 0$. Using (18), one can see that the first and last terms in (13') are still positive while the second term becomes negative. The more extreme the optimal subsidy for the individual under consideration, the larger is the impact of this middle relative to the last term and the less likely it is that the person prefers a tariff regime.

Figure 2 provides a simple illustration of the possibility that a person prefers a tariff to a subsidy regime when rates of protection are not known yet. It is assumed that individual i believes that actual trade policy is going to be dictated either by those who strongly favor protection of the second industry, with $\bar{t}$ and $\bar{s}$ as their optimal respective rates, or by those who strongly favor assistance to the first industry, implying $t̲$ and $s̲$ as their choices. Assuming subjective probabilities of 1/2 for each possible outcome, the ith person's real income at the expected subsidy rate $E(s)$ exceeds real income at the expected tariff rate $E(t)$. However, expected real income under the tariff regime, $E(R^i_t)$, is larger than expected real income under the subsidy regime, $E(R^i_s)$, making individual i prefer the tariff regime.

V. THE LARGE COUNTRY ARGUMENT

The earlier made assertion that, at each rate of protection and for each individual, a production subsidy leads to a higher level of welfare than a tariff applies only to the case when world prices are fixed. The purpose of this section is to show that, with variable world prices, all people whose factor income shares shrink with import protection prefer a tariff to a

VOTER PREFERENCES FOR TRADE POLICY INSTRUMENTS 269

subsidy. Even people whose income shares rise in response to protective action may prefer tariffs to subsidies.

Under variable world prices, equal-valued tariffs and subsidies no longer result in the same domestic prices as faced by producers. The decrease in world excess demand for the second good is larger when a tariff is imposed than when an equal-value subsidy is granted, as can be seen from differentiation of the import functions, $M_2(s)$ and $M_2(t)$, under subsidy and tariff respectively, where:

$$M_2(s) = D_2 [\pi, \ X_1(p) + pX_2(p) - \pi s X_2(p)] - X_2(p)$$

$$M_2(t) = D_2\{p, \ X_1(p) + pX_2(p) + \pi t [D_2(p) - X_2(p)]\} - X_2(p). \tag{20}$$

These differentiations, assuming that initially $s = t = 0$, yield:

$$\partial M_2/\partial s = -\pi \partial X_2/\partial p < 0 \qquad \text{and}$$
$$\partial M_2/\partial t = \pi [(\partial D_2/\partial p)|_U - (\partial X_2/\partial p)] < 0. \tag{21}$$

The import response expression tell us that, evaluated at the initial world price, the decline in world excess demand for the import good is greater in case of a tariff than a subsidy. Consequently, world and domestic prices of the import good will be lower under a tariff than an equal-value subsidy; that is:

$$\pi(s) > \pi(t) \qquad \text{and} \qquad p(s) > p(t) \text{ for } s = t. \tag{22}$$

A second consideration under variable world prices is that each person's optimal instrument use involves now a combination of a tariff and production subsidy rather than use of only one instrument. Independent of factor ownership, all people are in full agreement that the same tariff rate, namely the one which maximizes social welfare for a large country, should be employed. On the other hand, the accompanying optimal subsidy depends on relative factor ownership.[12]

In a situation of instrument choice, a person is not given the option of combining the two instruments. Each individual has to express a preference for either tariffs or subsidies. It is obvious that neither instrument is preferred at all rates and by all people to the other instrument. Some may like tariffs better while others prefer production subsidies. Broadly speaking, however, there exists a bias towards tariffs, as all people whose income shares decline with import protection are better off with a tariff for a large range of protection rates, and even some people whose income shares expand in response to protection are better served by a tariff.

To show this, we express the ith individual's real income under instrument use $k = t,s$ as:

$$R_k^i = \phi_k^i R_k, \tag{23}$$

---

[12] For more details see Mayer and Riezman (1987) and references therein.

270   MAYER AND RIEZMAN

where it is assumed that $\psi^i = \phi^i$. Instrument use affects both income share, ϕ^i_k, and real national income, R_k. The latter is maximized when the chosen instrument is a tariff and the rate which is optimal for the whole country, $\bar{t} = 1/(\epsilon^* - 1)$, is employed, where ϵ^* is the import elasticity of demand for the foreign country. Furthermore, one can show that real national income under the tariff regime, R_t, is larger than real national income under the subsidy regime, R_s, for a wide range of rates of protection.[13]

The relationship between a person's income share under a tariff and equal-value subsidy depends on whether the person is a gainer or loser from protection. We first look at people whose income shares are reduced by import protection. As they consider the choice between tariffs and subsidies, tariffs result in smaller losses in income shares, since $p(t) < p(s)$ implies that $(\partial\phi^i_s/\partial p)(\partial p/\partial s) < (\partial\phi^i_t/\partial p)(\partial p/\partial t) < 0$ for all $s = t > 0$. For individuals whose income shares rise with the adoption of protective measures, on the other hand, the gains in income shares are more pronounced in the case of a production subsidy since $(\partial\phi^i/\partial p)(\partial p/\partial s) > (\partial\phi^i/\partial p)/(\partial p/\partial t) > 0$.

Returning to (23), we now examine which instrument is preferred by a given person. If the person's income share is reduced by import protection then, except for some very high rates, $R_t > R_s$ and $\phi_t > \phi_s$ for $t = s > 0$. Consequently, 'losers' from protection are better off with the tariff than the subsidy. If the person's income share rises with import protection then, except for very high rates, $R_t > R_s$ but $\phi_t < \phi_s$ for $t = s > 0$. Hence, 'gainers' from protection are better off with a tariff only if the tariff advantage in raising national income is not offset by the tariff disadvantage in raising one's income share. This is more likely to be the case for small rather than large gainers from protection.

VI.   SOME THOUGHTS ON THE TRANSPARENCY ARGUMENT

Incomplete information is at the core of the *transparency argument*. The argument states that the public can more easily be persuaded to accept a tariff than production subsidy since the detrimental ramifications of the latter are more transparent. The reason for this asymmetry in transparency is, however, not easy to pinpoint. Intuitively, one can argue that tariffs work in a more complicated way than subsidies. In particular, the former require an assessment of how much consumer surplus a person loses while the latter deals with the simpler task of figuring out how much more taxes have to be paid to finance the subsidy. People not only understand the impact of subsidies better than that of tariffs, but they

---

[13] As long as the rate of protection is less than the socially optimal tariff rate, real national income under a tariff is at least as large as under a production subsidy. This can be seen by adding a consumption tax to a preexisting production subsidy and evaluating the overall welfare change. For very high rates of protection beyond the socially optimal tariff rate, however, it is possible that real national income under the subsidy is higher than under the tariff.

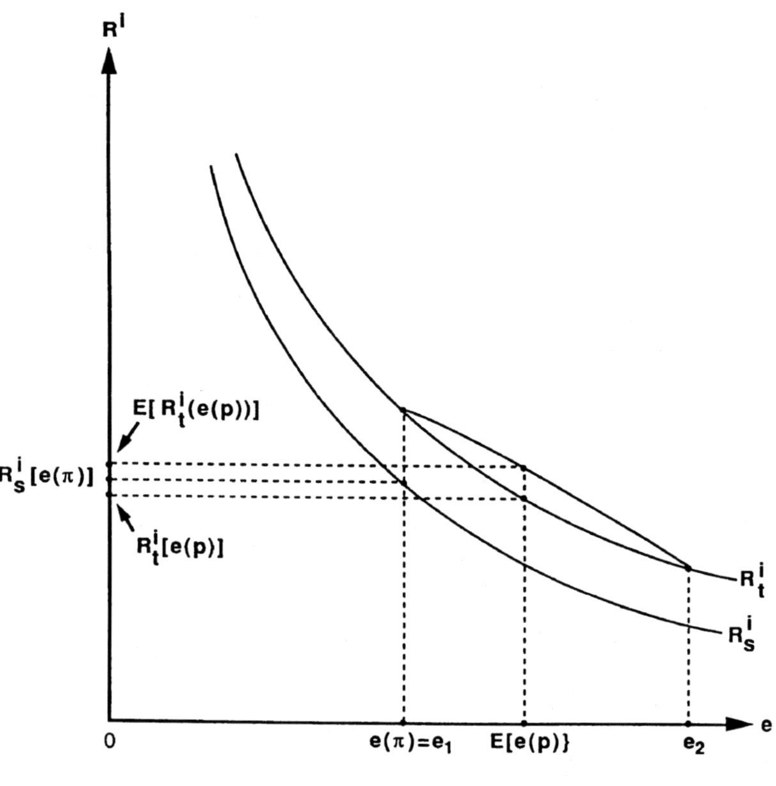

VOTER PREFERENCES FOR TRADE POLICY INSTRUMENTS 271

Figure 3

also receive clearer messages from news services and politicians about the costs of these instrument uses.[14]

Let us examine the essence of the transparency argument with more rigor. We return to the earlier made assumption of a small country and employ $(4)-(5)$ to express the ith person's real income under tariff and subsidy respectively, assuming that factor income and tax shares are identical; that is, $R_t^i = \phi_t^i (Y_t + T)/e(p)$ and $R_s^i = \phi_s^i (Y_s - S)/e(\pi)$. Now let us assume that the ith person is not sure how, starting from an initial free trade position, the tariff would affect his price index $e(p)$. On the other hand, there would be no change in $e(\pi)$ under a subsidy. This uncertainty under the tariff has the following implications for the choice of instruments. As Figure 3 illustrates, R^i is convex in the price index, whereby R_t^i lies uniformly above R_s^i since $(Y_t + T) > (Y_s - S)$ and both disposable incomes are evaluated at the same level of e. For a subsidy, real income at $e(\pi)$ would be $R_s^i[e(\pi)]$ which is larger than real income with an equal value tariff

---

[14] The real complicated question, namely how a given rate of protection affects the factor income of individuals under different protection instruments, does not enter the comparison since in a small country a person's factor income, whatever its value, would be the same under both tariff and subsidy of the same value.

272   MAYER AND RIEZMAN

which amounts to $R_t^i[e(p)]$. When $e(p)$ is random, however, then it is possible that $E\{R_t^i[e(p)]\} > R_s^i[e(\pi)]$ since, using Jensen's inequality, $E[1/e(p)] > 1/E[e(p)]$. In the diagram this is illustrated for the case where the person attaches probabilities of ½ to the possible price indices of e_1 and e_2. The person would prefer a tariff with its unclear effect on consumer surplus over a subsidy with its much more transparent cost.

Unfortunately, the above presented reasoning is flawed. The assumption that people have difficulty in evaluating the price index under the new tariff rate must rest on the premise that people do not know with certainty what their consumption demand would be at the tariff-ridden domestic price. As Drèze (1974), however, points out in his discussion of the foundations of expected utility theory, "uncertainty of the decision-maker about his own tastes at a future date cannot be described through distinct events corresponding to distinct preference structures, since this would violate the condition of interpersonal objectivity."

VII. CONCLUDING REMARKS

The starting point for this paper was the observation that, with factor ownership the only distinguishing characteristic, tariffs are dominated by production subsidies from an individual's point of view. We added to the growing list of arguments in support of individual preferences for tariffs by allowing for biased income tax systems, by introducing uncertainty about what rates will actually come about, and by doing away with the small country assumption when choice is restricted to one instrument. The objective of the paper was to show that under each of these modifications individuals may indeed express a preference for tariffs. We have talked about individual preferences only and do not want to leave the impression that a given argument automatically explains the social choice of tariffs. One has to add a complete specification of the political process to explain the social choice. However, one could show that for appropriate choices of voter eligibility rules, majority voting can bring about a tariff regime as the social choice under each of the three arguments presented.

WOLFGANG MAYER   RAYMOND RIEZMAN
Economics Department   *University of Iowa*
University of Cincinnati   *Iowa City*
Cincinnati   *Iowa 52242*
OH 45221-0371

REFERENCES

Bhagwati, J. N., 1971, "The generalized theory of distortions and welfare," in J. N. Bhagwati, et al. (eds.), *Trade, balance of payments, and growth*, North-Holland, Amsterdam, 69–90.

Bhagwati, J. N., R. A. Brecher and T. N. Srinivasan, 1984, "DUP activities and economic theory," *European Economic Review*, 24, 291–307.

VOTER PREFERENCES FOR TRADE POLICY INSTRUMENTS　　273

Bhagwati, J. N. and V. K. Ramaswami, 1963, "Domestic distortions, tariffs and the theory of the optimum subsidy," *Journal of Political Economy*, 71, 44–50.

Bhagwati, J. N. and T. N. Srinivasan, 1969, "Optimal intervention to achieve noneconomic objectives," *Review of Economic Studies*, 36, 27–38.

Corden, W. M., 1986, "The normative theory of international trade," in R. W. Jones (ed.), *International trade: surveys of theory and policy*, Elsevier Science, Amsterdam, 63–130.

Drèze, J. H., 1974, "Axiomatic theories of choice, cardinal utility and subjective probability:" A review, in J. Drèze (ed.), *Allocation under uncertainty*, Equilibrium and optimality, Wiley, New York and Toronto, 3–23.

Eaton, J. and G. M. Grossman, 1985 "Tariffs as insurance: optimal commercial policy when domestic markets are incomplete," *Canadian Journal of Economics*, 18, 258–272.

Feenstra, R. C. and T. R. Lewis, 1990, "Distributing the gains from trade with incomplete information," Mimeo, University of California, Davis.

Hillman, A. L., 1989, *The political economy of protection*, Harwood Academic, New York.

Laffont, J.-J., 1989, *The economics of uncertainty and information*, MIT Press, Cambridge, MA.

Mayer, W. and R. Riezman, 1987, "Endogenous choice of trade policy instruments," *Journal of International Economics*, 23, 377–381.

———, and ———, 1989, "Tariff formation in a multidimensional voting model," *Economics and Politics*, 1, 61–79.

Nelson, D., 1987, "Endogenous tariff theory: A critical survey," Mimeo, Washington University, St Louis.

Rodrik, D., 1986, "Tariffs, subsidies, and welfare with endogenous policy," *Journal of International Economics*, 21, 285–299.

Staiger, R. W. and G. Tabellini, 1987, "Discretionary trade policy and excessive protection," *American Economic Review*, 77, 823–837.

Wilson, J. D., 1990, "On the political choice between tariffs and production subsidies," Mimeo, Indiana University, Bloomington.

American Political Science Review   Vol. 86, No. 4   December 1992

SENIORITY IN LEGISLATURES

RICHARD D. MCKELVEY *California Institute of Technology*
RAYMOND RIEZMAN *University of Iowa*

We construct a stochastic model of a legislature with an endogenously determined seniority system. We model the behavior of the legislators as well as their constituents as an infinitely repeated divide-the-dollar game. The game has a stationary equilibrium with the property that the legislature imposes on itself a non-trivial seniority system, and that incumbent legislators are always reelected.

Why do legislatures have seniority systems? Why do incumbent legislators tend to be reelected by wide margins? These are questions that have engaged legislative scholars for some time.

On the issue of the incumbency advantage, a large empirical literature has advanced a number of explanations for this effect. Jacobson (1983) gives a good review of this literature. The explanations range from the increased access of incumbents to money and the media (see, e.g., Mayhew 1974a), to the effects of gerrymandering (Erikson 1972; Jacobson 1983, 13–15), to the decline of the party system and consequent increased use of incumbency, rather than party, as a voting cue (Ferejohn 1977), to constituency service and expertise built up by veteran legislators (e.g., Fiorina 1977a, 1977b; Mayhew 1974b).

Although the question of incumbency advantage and its relation to legislative organization have received considerable attention in the empirical literature on Congress, we know of no attempt to see if any of these explanations can be derived from a full-equilibrium, dynamic model. All of these explanations of the incumbency effect are nondynamic, partial equilibrium explanations. In other words, it is not clear that all individuals at all points in time are behaving rationally. For example, the explanations of the incumbency effect in terms of money and the media typically do not explain why voters should be swayed repeatedly by advertising and campaign literature. The explanation based on gerrymandering assumes that voters' behavior can be determined by certain socioeconomic characteristics of the voters, such as party identification, race, sex, income and religion. It ignores the possibility that both voters and candidates may have incentives to alter their behavior based on the new district characteristics. The explanation based on the decline of parties has no well worked-out theory as to why voters should use cues such as party or incumbency in the first place. The explanation based on constituency service has some weaknesses when one considers the timing of voter and candidate decisions. For example, why should voters vote for candidates who have done a lot for them in the past if the voters have already collected the rewards of the candidate's behavior? These models are a rich source of ideas; and some of the ideas

could undoubtedly be made part of a consistent theory in which all participants are behaving rationally and timing issues are dealt with explicitly. However, this has not yet been done.[1]

From our perspective, the most interesting observation in this literature is that many of these variables are determined endogenously by the legislature. It has been argued persuasively by Mayhew (1974b) and Fiorina (1977b) that *Congress organizes itself to serve the reelection goals of its members.* Thus, the franking privilege, the specialized committee system, the norm of reciprocity, and so on are all seen as ways in which Congress advances the reelection goals of its members. Fiorina has taken this argument to its extreme in his thesis that big government is partially a result of the fact that members of Congress benefit from the increased opportunities to intervene in the bureaucracy on the behalf of their constituents.

We shall consider one particular aspect of legislative organization, namely, the seniority system, and build a theoretical model connecting the seniority system with the reelection goals of the legislators: we formulate a full-equilibrium, dynamic model of policy formation in a representative system in which a seniority system emerges endogenously.[2] We develop a model in which both voters and legislators are acting rationally both on and off the equilibrium path. Voters take into account the fact that their representative is only a member of a legislative body and legislators realize that their actions will affect voters' behavior in subsequent elections. All agents take into account the dynamic effects of all of their actions.

Our approach is to model the representative process as an $\mathcal{L} + n$–player stochastic game, where $\mathcal{L}$ is the number of legislators, and n is the number of voters, partitioned into $\mathcal{L}$ distinct districts. The game alternates back and forth between the voter game and the legislative game. The voter game will consist of a game in which all the voters in each of the $\mathcal{L}$ legislative districts vote to determine who will be their representative for the next legislative session. The legislative game will consist of a game in which the legislators decide whether or not to have a seniority system for the current session and then proceed to select a policy. The policy selected is a decision on a distribution of a fixed amount of money among the legislative districts. We shall model the legislative game using the approach of Baron and Ferejohn (1989), who consider the legislative game as a form of a Rubinstein bargaining game: a random recognition rule, which depends on seniority, determines the legislator who makes a proposal. The legislators then vote, by majority rule, whether to accept or reject the proposal. The process continues until the legislature accepts a proposal—at which time the legislature adjourns, and new elections are held (i.e., we return to the voter game).

We show that an equilibrium exists in which the legislature always votes to impose on itself a nontrivial seniority system. In the proposal stage, the proposer selects a minimum winning coalition, retaining $(\mathscr{L} + 1)/2\mathscr{L}$ for its own district and allocating $1/\mathscr{L}$ to the districts of the remaining coalition members. Districts that are not part of the winning coalition get nothing. This proposal passes and the game proceeds to the voter game. Voters always reelect incumbents. The intuition behind the results is that voters, understanding the incentives in the legislative game, realize that their representative will be disadvantaged without seniority.

These results contrast with those found in most formal models of voting. Most formal voting models predict tied elections, with no incumbency effects. In our model the incumbent always wins by a unanimous margin. In addition, we have an endogenously chosen seniority system. These two phenomena are related to each other in that the seniority system and the incumbency effect support each other in equilibrium.

It is tempting to interpret the equilibrium of this model as a situation in which legislators blackmail voters to reelect them through the imposition of the seniority system. However, note that that is not exactly what happens in the model. In our model, the legislators cannot commit future legislatures to adopt a seniority system. The future legislature is free to vote against the seniority system if it is not in the interest of the legislators in that legislature to do so. What drives the incumbency effect in our model is the recognition by voters that self-interested legislators with seniority will vote for a seniority system. If a sufficient number of the other legislators have seniority, then it is in the self-interest of a district to make sure that its legislator does also, since the legislature will undoubtedly impose a seniority system. If all voters think this, it becomes a self-fulfilling prophecy.

THE GENERAL FRAMEWORK

Before introducing the model, we develop some general notation for stochastic games. Our model will be a special case of such a general model. Assume that there is a set N of *players*, a set X of *alternatives*, and for each player $i \in N$, a Von Neumann Morgenstern *utility function* $u_i: X \to \mathbb{R}$ over the set of alternatives. We assume that X contains a *null outcome*, x_0 with $u_i(x_0) = 0$ for all $i \in N$. Let $\mathscr{T}$ be a set of *states*. We

now define a *stochastic game*, $\Gamma = \{\Gamma^t: t \in \mathscr{T}\}$ to be a collection of *game elements* $\Gamma^t = (S^t, \pi^t, \psi^t)$. Here $S^t = \Pi_{i \in N} S_i^t$ is an n-tuple of *pure strategy sets*. Next $\pi^t: S^t \to \mathscr{M}(\mathscr{T}) = \Delta^{|\mathscr{T}|}$ is a *transition function* specifying for each $s^t \in S^t$ a probability distribution, $\pi^t(s^t)$ on $\mathscr{T}$, which determines for each $s^t \in S^t$ and $y \in \mathscr{T}$, the probability $\pi^t(s^t)(y)$ of proceeding to game element Γ^y. Finally, $\psi^t: S^t \to X$ is an *outcome function* that specifies for each $s^t \in S^t$ an outcome $\psi^t(s^t) \in X$. We let $S = \Pi_{t \in \mathscr{T}} S^t$ be the collection of pure strategy n-tuples, one for each game element. We write $\Sigma_i^t = \mathscr{M}(S_i^t)$, where $\mathscr{M}(S_i^t)$ is the set of probability distributions over S_i^t, and then define $\Sigma_i = \Pi_{t \in \mathscr{T}} \Sigma_i^t$ to be the set of *stationary strategies* for player i. Elements of Σ are written in the form $\sigma = (\sigma_1, \sigma_2, \ldots, \sigma_n)$. We also use the abusive notation $\sigma^t(s^t) = \Pi_{i \in N} \sigma_i^t(s_i^t)$ and $\sigma(s) = \Pi_{t \in \mathscr{T}} \sigma^t(s^t)$ to represent the probability under σ of choosing the pure strategy profile $s^t \in S^t$ and $s \in S$, respectively.

For stationary strategies, we can define the payoff function $M^t: \Sigma \to \mathbb{R}^n$ by

$$M_i^t(\sigma) = \sum_{\tau = 1}^{\infty} \sum_{r \in \mathscr{T}} \pi_\tau^t(\sigma)(r) \cdot u_i(\psi^r(\sigma^r)), \qquad (1)$$

where $\pi_\tau^t(\sigma)(r)$ is defined inductively by

$$\pi_1^t(\sigma)(r) = \pi^t(\sigma^t)(r) = \sum_{s^t \in S^t} \sigma^t(s^t) \cdot \pi^t(s^t)(r)$$

$$\pi_\tau^y(\sigma)(r) = \sum_{y \in Y} \pi_{\tau - 1}^t(\sigma)(y) \cdot \pi_\tau^y(\sigma^t)(r)$$

and $u_i(\psi^t(\sigma^t))$ is defined by

$$u_i(\psi^t(\sigma^t)) = \sum_{s^t \in S^t} \sigma^t(s^t) \cdot u_i(\psi^t(s^t)).$$

Note that this is only well defined if the sum in equation 1 converges for all σ, t, and i.

A strategy n-tuple, $\sigma \in \Sigma$ is said to be a *Nash equilibrium* if $M_i(\sigma_i', \sigma_{-i}) \le M_i(\sigma)$ for all $\sigma_i' \in \Sigma_i$. Applying Bellman's optimality principle (see, e.g., Sobel 1971, theorem 3), it follows that any stationary Nash equilibrium can be characterized by a collection $\{v^t\}_{t \in \mathscr{T}} \subseteq \mathbb{R}^n$ of values for each game element Γ^t and a strategy profile, $\sigma \in \Sigma$ satisfying two properties.

P1. For all $t \in \mathscr{T}$, σ^t is a Nash equilibrium to the game with payoff function $G^t: \Sigma^t \to \mathbb{R}^n$ defined by

$$G^t(\sigma^t) = u(\psi^t(\sigma^t)) + \sum_{y \in \mathscr{T}} \pi^t(\sigma^t)(y) \cdot v^y$$

$$= E_{\sigma^t}\left[u(\psi^t(s^t)) + \sum_{y \in \mathscr{T}} \pi^t(s^t)(y) \cdot v^y \right]$$

$$= \sum_{s^t \in S^t} \sigma^t(s^t) \cdot \left[u(\psi^t(s^t)) + \sum_{y \in \mathscr{T}} \pi^t(s^t)(y) \cdot v^y \right].$$

P2. For all $t \in \mathscr{T}$, $v^t = G^t(\sigma^t)$.

American Political Science Review   Vol. 86, No. 4

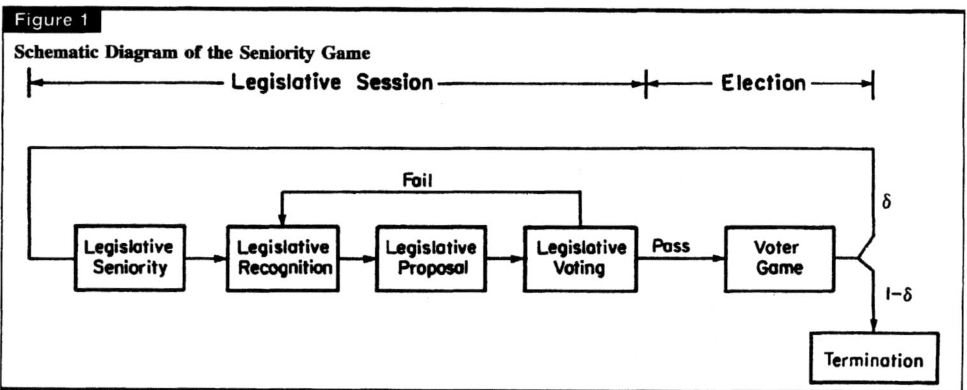

We will use this result to characterize equilibria in the stochastic game we consider. Finally, it also follows from Sobel's (1971) results that a Nash equilibrium in the set of stationary strategies is also a Nash equilibrium in the larger class of nonstationary strategies.

THE GAME

We consider an infinitely repeated game between legislators and their constituents.[3] The game alternates back and forth between a legislative session and an election, as illustrated in Figure 1. In the legislative session, the actors are the legislators (one from each legislative district), and the job of the legislature is to divide a dollar between the legislative districts. The legislative session consists of four parts: a vote on the seniority structure, random recognition of a member, a proposal by the randomly selected member, and a vote on the proposal. In the vote on the seniority structure, if a majority of the legislators vote for a seniority system, a seniority system is imposed; otherwise, there is no seniority system. Next, a random recognition rule, like that of Baron and Ferejohn (1989) is used to select a legislator as a proposer. If no seniority system was passed, all legislators have equal probability of being selected. On the other hand, if a seniority system was passed, then the probability of recognition is an increasing function of i's relative seniority. The proposer then proposes a division of the dollar by legislative district. Finally, the legislature votes on the proposal. If the proposal is defeated, a new proposer is selected and the game continues as before, except that in the second round and thereafter seniority is ignored in selecting the proposer.[4] Once a proposal passes the legislature, the legislative session ends, and the game moves to the election.

In the election, the actors are the voters in the legislative districts. In each district, the voters can choose to reelect their incumbent legislator (in which case the legislator has seniority in the next session and receives a salary c) or not to reelect the incumbent (in which case their legislator receives no salary and goes to the next session with no seniority).[5] After each election the legislative game begins again with the new seniority structure.

All agents have utility functions that are the discounted present value of their lifetime stream of utility. For the legislators, in each period, payoffs consist of a salary, which depends on whether they are reelected, and a percentage $(1 - \theta)$ of what they secure for their district. Thus, they skim some exogenously given portion of their district's payoff. In each period, the voters get θ times their share of what their legislator is able to secure for the district.

Figure 1 gives a schematic diagram that illustrates the basic components and the sequence of events for the seniority game. We now define the legislative seniority game more formally as a special kind of stochastic game. Each of the aforementioned components will be a game element in the stochastic game. We will specify the strategy sets, transition functions, and outcome functions for each of these game elements. The reader may find it useful to refer to Figure 2 in understanding the following definitions. This figure illustrates the extensive form game tree for each of the game elements in the case in which there are just three legislative districts, one voter per district, and five possible policy choices.

We let $N = L \cup V$, where L is the set of *legislators*, with $\mathscr{L} = |L| \geq 3$ odd, and V is the set of *voters*. We assume that $X' = \Delta^{\mathscr{L}} \times \{0, 1\}^{\mathscr{L}}$, and $X = X' \cup \{x_0\}$. Elements of X' are written in the form $x = (z, q)$, where $z = (z_1, \ldots, z_{\mathscr{L}}) \in Z = \Delta^{\mathscr{L}}$ and $q = (q_1, \ldots, q_{\mathscr{L}}) \in Q = \{0, 1\}^{\mathscr{L}}$. We assume that there is a function $\phi: V \to L$ identifying the legislative districts, such that voter v is in legislator ℓ's district if $\phi(v) = \ell$. We assume that $n_\ell = |\phi^{-1}(\ell)|$ is odd for all $\ell \in L$. We assume that utility functions over X' are of the form $u_i(x) = (1 - \theta)z_i + cq_i$ for $i \in L$, and $u_i(x) = (\theta/n_{\phi(i)})z_{\phi(i)}$ for $i \in V$. So $Q = \{0, 1\}^{\mathscr{L}}$ represents the seniority

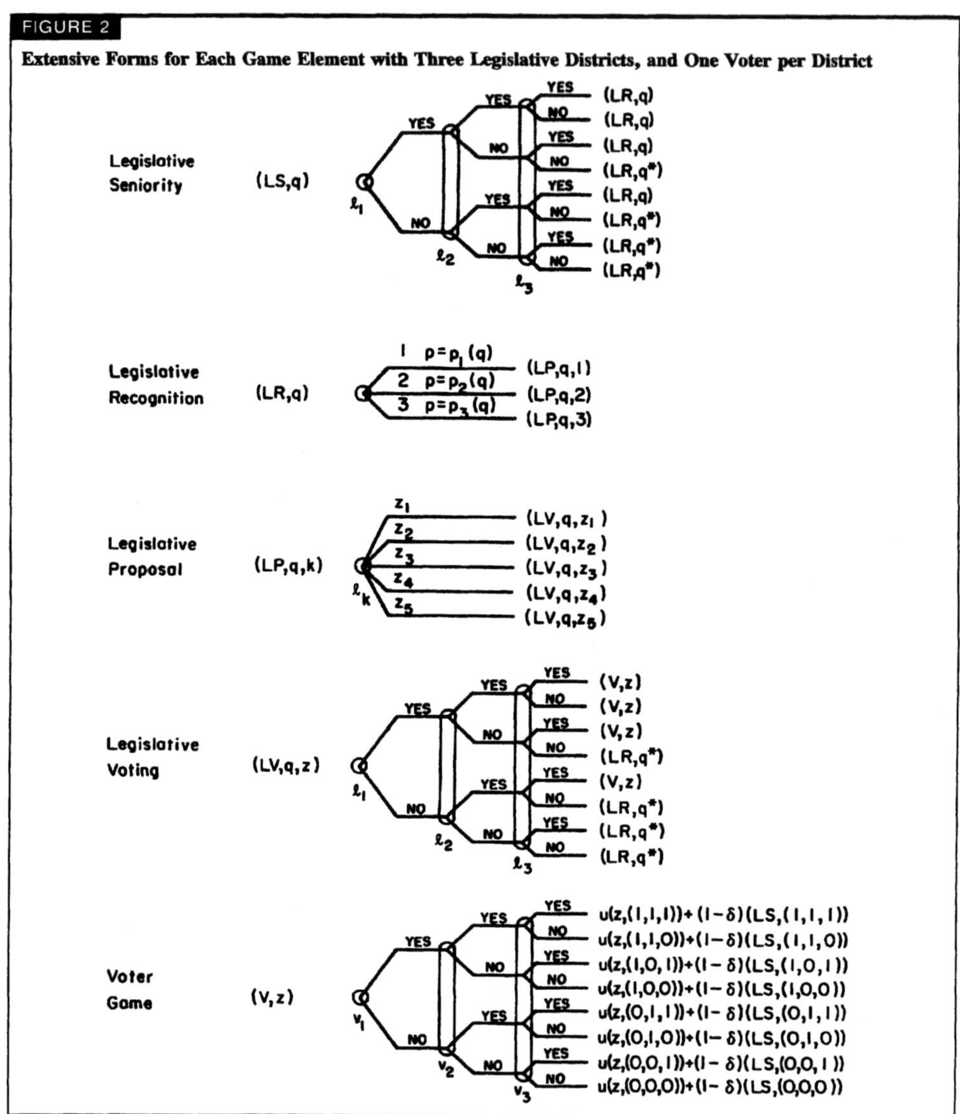

FIGURE 2

Extensive Forms for Each Game Element with Three Legislative Districts, and One Voter per District

structure of the legislature, with typical element $q = (q_1, \ldots, q_{\mathscr{L}})$. Thus, $q_i = 1$ indicates that legislator i has seniority, whereas $q_i = 0$ indicates it does not have seniority.

Let $0 < \delta < 1$ be a fixed discount rate and q^* be the element of Q satisfying $q_i^* = 1$ for all i. Let $p: Q \to \Delta^{\mathscr{L}}$

be a function which indicates the proposal power of each legislator as a function of its seniority (if a seniority system is adopted). We assume that p is strictly monotonic in each component: for all $q \in Q$ and $i \in L$, $q_i > q_i' \Rightarrow p_i(q) > p_i(q_i', q_{-i})$ and that $q_i = q_j \Rightarrow p_i(q) = p_j(q)$. Thus, more seniority means a higher

American Political Science Review   Vol. 86, No. 4

probability that a legislator will be selected as the proposer; and legislators with the same seniority have equal probability of being selected.

There are a total of six game elements, referred to as Termination Game, Legislative Seniority Game, Legislative Recognition Game, Legislative Proposal Game, Legislative Voting Game, and Voter Game. These games are indexed by the corresponding element in the set $\{T, LS, LR, LP, LV, V\}$. Each game element can be further indexed on a state variable. The state spaces for these games are $\emptyset$, Q, Q, $Q \times L$, $Q \times Z$, and Z, respectively. In order to be able to distinguish the difference between the games by means of the state variable we append the identifying element as the first element of the state for each game element. Thus, $\mathcal{T} = (\{T\}) \cup (\{LS\} \times Q) \cup (\{LR\} \times Q) \cup (\{LP\} \times Q \times L) \cup (\{LV\} \times Q \times Z) \cup (\{V\} \times Z)$ is the set of possible states.[6] We now define the strategy sets and transition functions for the game elements.

Termination Game

For $t = T \in \{T\}$,

$$S_i^t = \{0\} \quad \text{if} \quad i \in N.$$

For all $s^t \in S^t$,

$$\pi^t(s^t)(T) = 1$$

and

$$\psi^t(s^t) = x_0.$$

The Termination Game is just a dummy game element that occurs when the game ends. It is indicated by $t = T$. After each election, the stochastic game proceeds to the termination game with probability $1 - \delta$. In the termination game, each agent has a dummy strategy set, consisting of the singelton $\{0\}$; and the transition function π^t specifies that for any strategy choice, we remain in Termination Game with probability 1. In each period, the null outcome occurs, giving all agents utility 0. Hence, once the Termination Game is reached, all agents get 0 ever after. This is a formal way of introducing discounting into the model. In expected value, this makes utility in other parts of the game equal to the discounted current value of the future utility stream, where players discount future payoffs by a factor δ.

Legislative Seniority Game

For $t = (t_0, t_1) \in \{LS\} \times Q$,

$$S_i^t = \begin{cases} \{0, 1\} & \text{if } i \in L \\ \{0\} & \text{if } i \in N - L. \end{cases}$$

For all $s^t \in S^t$,

$$\pi^t(s^t)(LR, t_1) = 1 \quad \text{if} \quad \Sigma_{i \in L}\, s_i^t > \frac{\mathcal{L}}{2},$$

$$\pi^t(s^t)(LR, q^*) = 1 \quad \text{if} \quad \Sigma_{i \in L}\, s_i^t \le \frac{\mathcal{L}}{2},$$

and

$$\psi^t(s^t) = x_0.$$

The Legislative Seniority Game is the first stage of the legislative session. In this game, the legislature votes whether or not to have seniority for the current session. This game is indexed by $t = (S, t_1)$, where $t_0 = S$ indicates that we are in the Legislative Seniority Game, and t_1 is the current seniority vector. Since this game is a game between legislators, only the legislators have nontrivial strategy sets in the game. The strategy set for a legislator i is the set $\{0, 1\}$, where 0 represents a *no* vote, and 1 represents a *yes* vote. The transition function π^t indicates that we proceed with probability 1 to the Legislative Recognition Game. The vote determines which seniority vector is used in the Legislative Recognition Game. If a majority of the legislators vote for seniority, then the current seniority vector, t_1, is used in the Legislative Recognition Game. If there is not a strict majority for seniority, then the seniority vector q^*, which assigns equal weight to all legislators, is used.

Legislative Recognition Game

For $t = (t_0, t_1) \in \{LR\} \times Q$,

$$S_i^t = \{0\} \quad \text{if} \quad i \in N.$$

For all $s^t \in S^t$ and $y \in L$,

$$\pi^t(s^t)(LP, t_1, y) = p_y(t_1)$$

and

$$\psi^t(s^t) = x_0.$$

The Legislative Recognition Game is the second stage of the legislative session. This game is indexed by $t = (LR, t_1)$, where $t_0 = LR$ indicates we are in the Legislative Recognition Game, and t_1 is the current seniority vector. All agents have singleton strategy sets in this game. Thus, this game is just a chance move, which selects the legislator to make a proposal. From this game, we go with probability 1 to the Legislative Proposal Game. The probability that any legislator is selected is determined by the function $p_y(t_1)$. If seniority passed in the Legislative Seniority Game, the argument of p_y is t_1, which is the vector of seniorities of the legislators. If seniority failed, then $t_1 = q^*$ is used for the seniority vector. A legislator is selected by a random recognition rule to make a proposal for consideration by the legislature. This rule is similar to the Baron–Ferejohn recognition rule, except that we let the recognition rule be a function of seniority. Assumptions made above about p_y guarantee that higher seniority leads to higher probability of being selected.

Legislative Proposal Game

For $t = (t_0, t_1, t_2) \in \{LP\} \times Q \times L$,

$$S_i^t = \begin{cases} Z & \text{if } i = t \\ \{0\} & \text{if } i \in N - \{t\}. \end{cases}$$

For all $s^t \in S^t$,

$$\pi^t(s^t)(LV, t_1, s_t^t) = 1$$

and

$$\psi^t(s^t) = x_0.$$

The Legislative Proposal Game is the third stage of the legislative session. This game is indexed by $t = (LP, t_1, t_2)$, where $t_0 = LP$ indicates that we are in the Legislative Proposal Game; $t_1 \in Q$ is the current seniority structure that has been approved by the legislature; and $t_2 \in L$ represents the legislator who has been selected to make a proposal. In this game element, the only legislator with a nontrivial strategy set is legislator $j = t_2$, whose strategy set is Z, the set of possible divisions of the dollar between the legislative districts. If the legislator proposes the division z, then we proceed with probability 1 to the Legislative Voting Game (LV, t_1, z).

Legislative Voting Game

For $t = (t_0, t_1, t_2) \in \{LV\} \times Q \times Z$,

$$S_i^t = \begin{cases} \{0, 1\} & \text{if } i \in L \\ \{0\} & \text{if } i \in V. \end{cases}$$

For all $s^t \in S^t$,

$$\pi^t(s^t)(V, t_1) = 1 \quad \text{if } \Sigma_{i \in L} s_i^t > \frac{\mathcal{L}}{2},$$

$$\pi^t(s^t)(LP, q^*) = 1 \quad \text{if } \Sigma_{i \in L} s_i^t \leq \frac{\mathcal{L}}{2},$$

and

$$\psi^t(s^t) = x_0.$$

The Legislative Voting Game is the fourth and last stage of the legislative session. This game is indexed by $t = (LV, t_1, t_2)$, where $t_0 = LV$ indicates that we are in the Legislative Voting Game, $t_1 \in Q$ indicates the current seniority vector, and $t_2 \in Z$ indicates the proposal for division of the dollar that was selected by the proposer in the Legislative Proposal Game. In this game, each legislator has the strategy set $\{0, 1\}$. Here, a zero represents a *no* vote, a one a *yes* vote, on the proposal t_1. If the legislators vote to accept the proposal, the legislative session ends, and we proceed with probability 1 to the Voter Game. If the legislators reject the proposal, then we return with probability 1 to the Legislative Recognition Game,

with the exception that seniority is ignored in selecting the proposer. We shall discuss what happens if seniority is used in subsequent proposal rounds. Note that the Legislative Proposal and Legislative Voting Games together are similar to the closed rule version of the Baron–Ferejohn model.

Voter Game

For $t = (t_0, t_1) \in \{V\} \times Z$,

$$S_i^t = \begin{cases} \{0, 1\} & \text{if } i \in V \\ \{0\} & \text{if } i \in L. \end{cases}$$

For all $s^t \in S^t$,

$$\pi^t(s^t)(y) = \begin{cases} \delta & \text{if } y = (S, q(s^t)) \\ 1 - \delta & \text{if } y = T \end{cases}$$

and

$$\psi^t(s^t) = (t_1, q(s^t)),$$

where $q(s^t) = (q_1(s^t), q_2(s^t), \ldots, q_{\mathcal{L}}(s^t)) \in Q$ is defined by

$$q_i(s^t) = \begin{cases} 1 & \text{if } \Sigma_{j \in \phi^{-1}(i)} s_j^t > \dfrac{n_\ell}{2} \\ 0 & \text{if } \Sigma_{j \in \phi^{-1}(i)} s_j^t \leq \dfrac{n_\ell}{2} \end{cases}$$

and where $0 < \theta < 1$ and $0 < c$ are constants. The Voter Game consists of a set of simultaneous elections in all of the legislative districts. This game is indexed by $t = (V, t_1)$, where $t_0 = V$ indicates that we are in the Voter Game, and $t_1 \in Z$ represents the outcome of the Legislative Voting Game. In each legislative district, the voters of that district vote whether or not to reelect their legislator. In the version of the game as it is presented here, there is only one legislator in each district and no challenger. So the effect of a negative vote in a given district is that the legislator from that district does not get a salary for the next period and loses seniority.

This completes the description of the stochastic game. Note that there are no payoffs except in the voter game. At that point policy $x = (t_1, q(s^t))$ is implemented. Thus, the pie is divided up among the districts according to $z = t_1 \in \Delta^{\mathcal{L}}$, and $q(s^t) \in Q$ determines which legislators get reelected and which do not. Given the utility functions we have specified, it follows that the output $t_{1\ell}$ to district ℓ is first divided up with $\theta t_{1\ell}$ actually delivered to the voters and $(1 - \theta)t_{1\ell}$ being skimmed off by legislator ℓ. The voters each get an even share of the delivered output. The legislators, in addition to their share of the output, get a salary that is dependent on whether they are reelected or not.

Figure 2 presents a schematic depiction of the game for the case of three legislators, three voters (one per district), and five possible proposals. The Legislative Seniority vote determines the probabilities in the Legislative Recognition Game. A proposer is selected who makes a proposal in the Legislative Proposal Game. The legislature votes on this proposal. If it passes, the game proceeds to the Voter Game and a new election is held leading to a new session of the legislature. (The discounting comes in here.) If the proposal fails, the game goes back to the Legislative Recognition Game, with seniority not used to determine the probabilities of recognition. From here, the game proceeds as before.

RESULTS

Our main result is that there exists an equilibrium to the stochastic game in which a seniority system is adopted and incumbent legislators always get re-elected.

PROPOSITION 1. *The following is a stationary equilibrium to the stochastic game defined in the previous section:*

1. *Legislative Seniority Game. For $t \in \{LS\} \times Q$, and $i \in L$,*

$$\sigma_i^t(t_{1i}) = 1$$

2. *Legislative Proposal Game. For $t \in \{LP\} \times Q \times L$,*

$$\sigma_t^t = \frac{1}{|\Omega_t|} \sum_{w \in \Omega_t} \delta_{z_t(w)},$$

where $\Omega_t = \{\omega \in \{0, 1\}^{\mathcal{L}} : \Sigma_i \omega_i = (\mathcal{L} + 1)/2, \omega_t = 1\}$, δ_x is the Dirac delta at x, and $z_t : \Omega_t \to \mathbb{R}^{\mathcal{L}}$ is defined by

$$z_{ti}(\omega) = \begin{cases} \dfrac{\mathcal{L} + 1}{2\mathcal{L}} & \text{if } i = t \\[2mm] \dfrac{1}{\mathcal{L}} & \text{if } i \neq t,\ \omega_i = 1 \\[2mm] 0 & \text{otherwise.} \end{cases}$$

3. *Legislative Voting Game. For $t \in \{LV\} \times Q \times Z$, and $i \in L$,*

$$\sigma_i^t(1) = \begin{cases} 1 & \text{if } t_{1i} \geq \dfrac{1}{\mathcal{L}} \\[2mm] 0 & \text{if } t_{1i} < \dfrac{1}{\mathcal{L}}. \end{cases}$$

4. *Voter Game. For $t \in \{V\} \times Z$, and $i \in V$,*

$$\sigma_i^t(1) = 1.$$

Proof. The formal proof is in the Appendix. The proof is straightforward, and simply consists of verifying that these strategies satisfy the Bellman conditions that characterize a Nash equilibrium of a stochastic game. These conditions are given as conditions P1 and P2. To verify this, we first specify values, v^t, for each game element. These values represent the value of the game element if equilibrium behavior is followed forever after. The Bellman conditions require that if we replace all game elements by their values, then for each game element, fixing the values of the other game elements, the specified strategies are a Nash equilibrium for that game element (P1), and the computed value of each game element at the equilibrium strategies is equal to the specified value (P2). While the proof is straightforward, it is tedious, since each of these conditions must be verified for all of the six game elements.

Remarks. The proposition gives equilibrium strategies for both the legislators and voters in the stochastic game. We first describe the equilibrium and then provide some intuition for the result. In the Legislative Seniority Game all legislators who have seniority vote in favor of the seniority system, and those who do not have seniority vote against the seniority system. Since in equilibrium all legislators get reelected the, seniority system always passes.

In the Legislative Proposal game, the proposer selects a minimal winning coalition of legislators, which includes itself. The proposer retains $(\mathcal{L} + 1)/2\mathcal{L}$ for its own district, leaving $1/\mathcal{L}$ to be allocated to the districts of each of the remaining members of the coalition. Districts that are not a part of the winning coalition are allocated 0. Thus, the proposer obtains a premium of $(\mathcal{L} + 1)/2\mathcal{L} - 1/\mathcal{L} = (\mathcal{L} - 1)/2\mathcal{L}$ due to its proposal power. As $\mathcal{L} \to \infty$, the premium increases with a limit of one-half.

In the Legislative Voting Game, a legislator votes for a proposal if and only if the legislator receives at least $1/\mathcal{L}$. Thus, if the proposer has proposed an equilibrium proposal, it will pass. Finally, in the Voter Game, the voters always vote to reelect their legislators. It should be noted that although the proof shows only that this is a Nash equilibrium for the voters, in fact, the strategy of voting for the incumbent is a dominant strategy for the voters in any given legislative district, taking the behavior in the remainder of the game as fixed.

Several features of this equilibrium stand in sharp contrast to the results that come out of the traditional voting literature. Most voting models predict tied elections, with no incumbency effects. Here, we obtain instead equilibrium behavior by the voters in which the incumbent wins by a large (unanimous) margin. The intuition behind the result is simple: the voters know that in equilibrium the seniority system will pass and thus that it is in the their best interest to reelect the incumbent, since a senior legislator will be more easily able to serve the constituency than a junior legislator. Note that voters do not know that there will be a seniority system in the next session but, rather, know that in the steady-state equilibrium, seniority will be voted in each session.

Finally, we emphasize that we have only identified one equilibrium of this model. There may be other equilibria. In fact, we believe that there would also be an equilibrium in which seniority is rejected by the legislature and all legislators are defeated for reelection. This later equilibrium may be able to be refined away by appropriate equilibrium refinements, since voters would all be indifferent, in equilibrium, between voting for the incumbent and voting for the challenger.

EXTENSIONS

The Power of the Initial Proposal

In our model the seniority system works through the proposal stage, by influencing the probability that legislators will get chosen to be the proposer. We assumed that seniority is only used for selecting the proposer in the first round of any legislative session. Thus, if a proposal is turned down in the legislature, seniority is no longer used to select the proposer during that legislative session. In a companion paper we analyze the case in which seniority is in effect throughout the legislative session (McKelvey and Riezman (n.d.)). One might think that this system (which, on its face, gives more power to the senior members) would make them better off and hence would be selected by them. However, we show that the opposite is the case. When seniority is in effect for the entire session, there is no symmetric stationary equilibrium in which senior and nonsenior legislators have different values and in which voters always reelect incumbents. In other words, when seniority is used throughout the session, there is no equilibrium in which seniority has benefits for legislators. Thus, legislators would be indifferent between having, and not having, such a seniority system and would hence prefer a seniority system in which seniority is used only for the first proposal in each legislative session. Thus, we get the rather paradoxical result that legislators who have seniority would choose a seniority system that on its face gives less power to senior members.

It is worth pointing out that a seniority system that gives only initial proposal power is a realistic description of the seniority system for the U.S. Congress in the sense that seniority is embodied in the committee system. The committees make proposals by sending bills to the floor. Once the bills go to the floor, the committees lose most of their power, since bills that are amended or defeated generally do not go back to committee in that session. Hence, our model might explain certain features about how seniority systems are set up—in particular, the importance of initial proposal power.

We briefly describe the result from the companion paper. The game is altered by changing the Legislative Voting Game so that when a proposal is rejected, the subsequent Legislative Recognition Game will use the original seniority vector. The rest of the stochastic game is as before. In other words, the Legislative Voting Game is

The Revised Legislative Voting Game

For $t \in \{LV\} \times Z$,

$$S_i^t = \begin{cases} \{0, 1\} & \text{if } i \in L \\ \{0\} & \text{if } i \in V. \end{cases}$$

For all $s^t \in S^t$,

$$\pi^t(s^t)(V, t_1) = 1 \quad \text{if} \quad \Sigma_{i \in L}\, s_i^t > \frac{\mathscr{L}}{2},$$

$$\pi^t(s^t)(LR, t_1) = 1 \quad \text{if} \quad \Sigma_{i \in L}\, s_i^t \le \frac{\mathscr{L}}{2},$$

and

$$\psi^t(s^t) = x_0.$$

Consider the stochastic game of the previous section, substituting the above game for the previous Legislative Voting Game. Call this the Revised Game. The following proposition is proved in McKelvey and Riezman (n.d.).

PROPOSITION 2. *In the Revised Game there is no symmetric stationary equilibrium with the following two properties:*

1. *Voters always reelect incumbents:*

   For $t \in \{V\} \times Z$, and $i \in V$: $\sigma_i^t(1) = 1$ for all i.

2. *The value of senior and nonsenior members in the Legislative Seniority Game is different.*

The intuition behind this result has to do with how proposers choose coalition partners. Once chosen, proposers want to include in the coalition those with the lowest continuation values, because they can be given less and will still vote for the proposal. It follows, then, when seniority is used throughout the legislative session, that if seniority benefits senior members, they will be less likely to be included in coalitions. Proposition 2 shows that this effect of being chosen less often swamps any other advantages of using seniority throughout the session. Thus, once the proposer is chosen, senior members want to look like nonsenior members so they are as likely to be included in the coalition.

Ordinal Seniority

Our model assumes a binary seniority system: a legislator either has seniority or does not. The next step is to introduce the possibility of ordinal seniority, where a legislator's seniority measures the number of times the legislator has been reelected. The congressional seniority system is an ordinal system.

American Political Science Review   Vol. 86, No. 4

If each legislator has an independent probability of dying or retiring, then at any point in time, the distribution of seniority, even in equilibrium, could be heterogeneous. Depending on the distribution of seniority and exactly how seniority affects the probability of being selected as the proposer, a seniority system would not necessarily be adopted by the legislature in the first place. Hence, with ordinal seniority, it appears that seniority system may occasionally be defeated. We plan to explore this issue in future work.

CONCLUSION

We have developed a formal model of voter behavior and legislative decision making in which the seniority system and the incumbency effects emerge as an equilibrium. There are a number of weaknesses in this model. We have assumed an unrealistically simple model of the legislative session and of how seniority plays a role; that is, the legislative session is characterized by a random recognition voting game similar to the Baron–Ferejohn model. Second, we assume that the only decision made by the legislature is a decision on the division of a fixed pie. We also assume that legislators' preferences are a function of how much they get for their constituents, rather than just whether they are reelected. We hope to remedy some of these weaknesses in the future. Despite these obvious weaknesses of the model, the model illustrates that it is possible to construct consistent formal models that connect legislative organization with reelectoral goals of legislators. Within the context of this model we have shown that when the effect of seniority is to change the probability of recognition on the first round, seniority has value. If seniority changes the probability of recognition on every round, then senior members get no benefits from seniority.

APPENDIX: PROOF OF PROPOSITION 1

We first specify the values, v^t, associated with these strategies. We then verify that for these values, property P1 and P2 are satisfied. For the following equations, we set $w_1 = (\mathcal{L} + 1)/2\mathcal{L}$, and $w_2 = 1/\mathcal{L}$. Also, we define $Z^1 = \{z \in Z: |\{j \in L: z_j \geq w_2\}| > \mathcal{L}/2\}$, and $Z^0 = Z - Z^1$. Similarly, define $Q^1 = \{q \in Q: |\{i \in L: q_i = 1\}| > \mathcal{L}/2\}$, and $Q^0 = Q - Q^1$.

The values of the games are defined below. To interpret these values, go to the definitions of the individual games. For example, for $t \in \{LS\} \times Q$, you are in the Legislative Seniority Game. $v_i^t = v_i^{(R, t_1)}$ means that the value of the seniority game given that seniority has passed ($t_1 \in Q^1$) is the value in the Legislative Recognition Game with seniority vector t_1. If seniority does not pass ($t_1 \in Q^0$), then the value of the game is given by the value in the Legislative Recognition Game with seniority vector q^*. Other values are defined in a similar way.

For $t \in \{T\}$,
$$v_i^t = 0 \text{ for all } i \in N.$$

For $t \in \{LS\} \times Q$,
$$v_i^t = v_i^{(R,\, t_1)} \text{ if } t_1 \in Q^1,$$
$$v_i^t = v_i^{(R,\, q^*)} \text{ if } t_1 \in Q^0.$$

For $t \in \{LR\} \times Q$,
$$v_i^t = (1 - \theta)\left[p_i(t_1)w_1 + \frac{1}{2} \sum_{y \in \mathcal{L} - \{i\}} p_y(t_1)w_2 \right] + c + \delta v_i^* \quad \text{if } i \in L,$$
$$v_i^t = \frac{\theta}{n_{\phi(i)}}\left[p_{\phi(i)}(t_1)w_1 + \frac{1}{2} \sum_{y \in \mathcal{L} - \{\phi(i)\}} p_y(t_1)w_2 \right] + \delta v_i^* \quad \text{if } i \in V,$$

where
$$v_i^* = v_i^{(R,\, q^*)} = \begin{cases} \dfrac{1}{1 - \delta}\left[\dfrac{1}{\mathcal{L}}(1 - \theta) + c \right] & \text{if } i \in L, \\[3ex] \dfrac{1}{1 - \delta}\left[\dfrac{\theta}{\mathcal{L}n_{\phi(i)}} \right] & \text{if } i \in V. \end{cases}$$

For $t \in \{LP\} \times Q \times L$,
$$v_i^t = (1 - \theta)w_1 + c + \delta v_i^* \quad\quad \text{if } i = t,$$
$$v_i^t = \frac{1}{2}(1 - \theta)w_2 + c + \delta v_i^* \quad\quad \text{if } i \neq t,$$
$$v_i^t = \frac{\theta}{n_{\phi(i)}} w_1 + \delta v_i^* \quad\quad \text{if } \phi(i) = t,$$
$$v_i^t = \frac{1}{2}\frac{\theta}{n_{\phi(i)}} w_2 + \delta v_i^* \quad\quad \text{if } \phi(i) \neq t.$$

For $t \in \{LV\} \times Q \times Z^1$,
$$v_i^t = (1 - \theta)t_{1i} + c + \delta v_i^* \quad \text{if } i \in L,$$
$$v_i^t = \theta t_{1\phi(i)} + \delta v_i^* \quad \text{if } i \in V.$$

For $t \in \{LV\} \times Q \times Z^0$,
$$v_i^t = v_i^* \quad \text{if } i \in N.$$

For $t \in \{V\} \times Z$,
$$v_i^t = (1 - \theta)t_{1i} + c + \delta v_i^* \quad \text{if } i \in L,$$
$$v_i^t = \frac{\theta}{n_{\phi(i)}} t_{1\phi(i)} + \delta v_i^* \quad \text{if } i \in V.$$

The next step in the proof is to verify property P2, which requires that for each game and each player the payoffs correspond to the values we have specified. To do this, we start with the definition of G and then, using the definitions of the game elements and the equilibrium strategies, show that the payoffs equal the appropriate values.

For $t \in \{T\}$,

$$G^t(\sigma^t) = E_{\sigma^t}\left[u(\psi^t(s^t)) + \sum_{y \in \mathcal{F}} \pi^t(s^t)(y)v^y\right]$$

$$= u(x_0) + \pi^t(\sigma^t)(t)v^t = v^t.$$

For $t \in \{LS\} \times Q$,

$$G_i^t(\sigma^t) = E_{\sigma^t}\left[u_i(\psi^t(s^t)) + \sum_{y \in \mathcal{F}} \pi^t(s^t)(y)v_i^y\right]$$

$$= u_i(\psi^t(t_1)) + \sum_{y \in \mathcal{F}} \pi^t(t_1)(y)v_i^y$$

$$= \begin{cases} v_i^{(LR,\, t_1)} & \text{if } \sum_{i \in L} t_{1i} > \dfrac{\mathcal{L}}{2} \\[2ex] v_i^{(LR,\, q^*)} & \text{if } \sum_{i \in L} t_{1i} \le \dfrac{\mathcal{L}}{2} \end{cases}$$

$$= \begin{cases} v_i^{(LR,\, t_1)} & \text{if } |\{i \in L: t_{1i} = 1\}| > \dfrac{\mathcal{L}}{2} \\[2ex] v_i^{(LR,\, q^*)} & \text{if } |\{i \in L: t_{1i} = 1\}| \le \dfrac{\mathcal{L}}{2} \end{cases}$$

$$= \begin{cases} v_i^{(LR,\, t_1)} & \text{if } t_1 \in Q^1 \\ v_i^{(LR,\, q^*)} & \text{if } t_1 \in Q^0. \end{cases}$$

$$= v^t.$$

For $t \in \{LR\} \times Q$,

$$G^t(\sigma^t) = E_{\sigma^t}\left[u(\psi^t(\sigma^t)) + \sum_{y \in \mathcal{F}} \pi^t(\sigma^t)(y)v^y\right]$$

$$= u(x_0) + \sum_{y \in L} p_y(t_1)v^y.$$

So, for $i \in L$,

$$G_i^t(\sigma^t) = p_i(t_1)v_i^i + \sum_{y \in \mathcal{L} - \{i\}} p_y(t_1)v_i^y$$

$$= p_i(t_1)[(1 - \theta)w_1 + c + \delta v_i^*]$$

$$+ \sum_{y \in \mathcal{L} - \{i\}} p_y(t_1)\left[\frac{1}{2}(1 - \theta)w_2 + c + \delta v_i^*\right]$$

$$= (1 - \theta)\left[p_i(t_1)w_1 + \frac{1}{2} \sum_{y \in \mathcal{L} - \{i\}} p_y(t_1)w_2\right]$$

$$+ c + \delta v_i^* = v_i^t$$

and for $i \in V$,

$$G_i^t(\sigma^t) = p_{\phi(i)}(t_1)v_i^{\phi(i)} + \sum_{y \in \mathcal{L} - \{\phi(i)\}} p_y(t_1)v_i^y$$

$$= p_{\phi(i)}(t_1)\left[\frac{\theta}{n_{\phi(i)}} w_1 + \delta v_i^*\right]$$

$$+ \sum_{y \in \mathcal{L} - \{\phi(i)\}} p_y(t_1)\left[\frac{\theta}{2n_{\phi(i)}} w_2 + \delta v_i^*\right]$$

$$= \frac{\theta}{n_{\phi(i)}}\left[p_{\phi(i)}(t_1)w_1 + \sum_{y \in \mathcal{L} - \{\phi(i)\}} \frac{1}{2} p_y(t_1)w_2\right]$$

$$+ \delta v_i^* = v_i^t.$$

For $t \in \{LP\} \times Q \times L$,

$$G^t(\sigma^t) = E_{\sigma^t}\left[u(\psi^t(s^t)) + \sum_{y \in \mathcal{F}} \pi^t(s^t)(y)v^y\right]$$

$$= u(x_0) + E_{\sigma^t}[v^{(LV,\, s_i^t)}].$$

But since $\sigma_i^t(Z^1) = 1$, we have, for $i \in L$,

$$G^t(\sigma^t) = E_{\sigma^t}[(1 - \theta)s_t^t + c + \delta v^*]$$

$$= (1 - \theta)E_{\sigma^t}[s_t^t] + c + \delta v^*.$$

But

$$E_{\sigma^t}[s_t^t] = E_{\sigma^t}\left[\frac{1}{|\Omega_t|} \sum_{w \in \Omega_t} \delta_{z_t(w)}\right] = \frac{1}{|\Omega_t|} \sum_{w \in \Omega_t} E_{\sigma^t}[\delta_{z_t(w)}]$$

$$= \frac{1}{|\Omega_t|} \sum_{w \in \Omega_t} z_t(\omega).$$

So

$$E_{\sigma^t}[s_{ti}^t] = \frac{1}{|\Omega_t|} \sum_{w \in \Omega_t} z_{ti}(\omega) = \frac{1}{|\Omega_t|} \cdot |\Omega_t| \frac{\mathcal{L} + 1}{2\mathcal{L}}$$

$$= \frac{\mathcal{L} + 1}{2\mathcal{L}} = w_1 \text{ if } i = t$$

$$E_{\sigma^t}[s_{ti}^t] = \frac{2\left[\dfrac{\mathcal{L} - 1}{2}\right]!}{(\mathcal{L} - 1)!} \cdot \frac{(\mathcal{L} - 2)!}{2\left[\dfrac{\mathcal{L} - 3}{2}\right]!} \cdot \frac{1}{\mathcal{L}}$$

$$= \frac{\left[\dfrac{\mathcal{L} - 1}{2}\right]}{(\mathcal{L} - 1)} \cdot \frac{1}{\mathcal{L}} = \frac{1}{2\mathcal{L}} = \frac{1}{2}w_2 \text{ if } i \ne t.$$

Thus,

$$G_i^t(\sigma^t) = \begin{cases} (1 - \theta)w_1 + c + \delta v_i^* & \text{if } i = t \\[1ex] \dfrac{1}{2}(1 - \theta)w_2 + c + \delta v_i^* & \text{if } i \ne t \end{cases}$$

$$= v_i^t$$

American Political Science Review   Vol. 86, No. 4

and for $i \in V$,

$$G_i^t(\sigma^t) = E_{\sigma^t}\left[\frac{\theta}{n_{\phi(i)}} s_{ti}^t + \delta v_i^*\right] = \frac{\theta}{n_{\phi(i)}} E_{\sigma^t}[s_{ti}^t] + \delta v_i^*$$

$$= \begin{cases} \dfrac{\theta}{n_{\phi(i)}} w_1 + \delta v_i^* & \text{if} \quad \phi(i) = t \\[2ex] \dfrac{1}{2}\dfrac{\theta}{n_{\phi(i)}} w_2 + \delta v_i^* & \text{if} \quad \phi(i) \neq t \end{cases}$$

$$= v_i^t.$$

For $t \in \{LV\} \times Q \times Z^1$, since $t_1 \in Z^1$, it follows that

$$\sigma^t\left(\sum_{i \in L} s_i^t > \frac{\mathscr{L}}{2}\right) = 1.$$

So $\pi^t(\sigma^t)(V, t_1) = 1$. Hence,

$$G_i^t(\sigma^t) = E_{\sigma^t}\left[u_i(\psi^t(s^t)) + \sum_{y \in \mathscr{T}} \pi^t(s^t)(y)v_i^y\right]$$

$$= u(x_0) + \pi^t(\sigma^t)(t_1, V)v_i^{(V, t_1)} + \pi^t(\sigma^t)$$

$$(q^*, 2)v_i^{(LR, q^*)}$$

$$= v_i^{(V, t_1)} = \begin{cases} (1 - \theta)t_{1i} + c + \delta v_i^* & \text{if} \quad i \in L \\ \theta t_{1\phi(i)} + \delta v_i^* & \text{if} \quad i \in V \end{cases}$$

$$= v_i^t.$$

For $t \in \{LV\} \times Q \times Z^0$, since $t_1 \in Z^0$, it follows that

$$\sigma^t\left(\sum_{i \in L} s_i^t \leq \mathscr{L}/2\right) = 1,$$

so $\pi^t(\sigma^t)(q^*, 2) = 1$. Hence,

$$G_i^t(\sigma^t) = E_{\sigma^t}\left[u_i(\psi^t(s^t)) + \sum_{y \in \mathscr{T}} \pi^t(s^t)(y)v_i^y\right]$$

$$= u(x_0) + \pi^t(\sigma^t)(t_1, V)v_i^{(V, t_1)}$$

$$+ \pi^t(\sigma^t)(q^*, 2)v_i^{(LR, q^*)}$$

$$= v_i^{(LR, q^*)} = v_i^* = v_i^t.$$

For $t \in \{V\} \times Z$,

$$\pi^t(s^t)(y) = \begin{cases} \delta & \text{if} \quad y = (S, q(s^t)) \\ 1 - \delta & \text{if} \quad y = T, \end{cases}$$

$$\sigma_i^t(1) = 1 \text{ for all } i.$$

$$G^t(\sigma^t) = E_{\sigma^t}\left[u(\psi^t(s^t)) + \sum_{y \in \mathscr{T}} \pi^t(s^t)(y)v^y\right]$$

$$= E_{\sigma^t}[u(t_1, q(s^t))] + \delta \pi^t(\sigma^t)(q(s^t), 1)v^{(S, q(s^t))}$$

$$= u(t_1, q^*) + \delta v^{(S, q^*)} = u(t_1, q^*) + \delta v^*$$

So, for $i \in L$,

$$G_i^t(\sigma^t) = (1 - \theta)t_{1i} + cq_i^* + \delta v_i^*$$

$$= (1 - \theta)t_{1i} + c + \delta v_i^* = v_i^t$$

and for $i \in V$,

$$G_i^t(\sigma^t) = \frac{\theta}{n_{\phi(i)}} t_{1\phi(i)} + \delta v_i^* = v_i^t.$$

We next verify that property P1 is satisfied, that is, that σ^t is a Nash equilibrium. For each game element we show that no player can benefit from playing a different strategy.

For $t \in \{V\} \times Z$, we want to show that σ^t is a Nash equilibrium to the game with payoff function G^t, where $\sigma_i^t(1) = 1$ for all $i \in V$. It suffices to show that for each $i \in V$, σ_i^t is at least as good as any pure strategy $s_i' \in S_i^t$. So,

$$G_i^t(\sigma^t) \geq G_i^t(\sigma_i', \sigma_{-i}^t)$$

$$\Leftrightarrow E_{\sigma^t}\left[u_i(\psi^t(s^t)) + \sum_{y \in \mathscr{T}} \pi^t(s^t)(y)v_i^y\right]$$

$$\geq E_{\sigma_{-i}^t}\left[u_i(\psi^t(s_i', s_{-i}^t)) + \sum_{y \in \mathscr{T}} \pi^t(s_i', s_{-i}^t)(y)v_i^y\right]$$

for all $s_i' \in S_i^t$. Writing $\underline{1}$ for the $|V|$ component vector of ones, we can rewrite this inequality as

$$u_i(\psi^t(\underline{1})) + \sum_{y \in \mathscr{T}} \pi^t(\underline{1})(y)v_i^y$$

$$\geq u_i(\psi^t(s_i', \underline{1}_{-i})) + \sum_{y \in \mathscr{T}} \pi^t(s_i', \underline{1}_{-i})(y)v_i^y$$

$$\Leftrightarrow \delta v_i^{(S, q(\underline{1}))} \geq \delta v_i^{(S, q(s_i', \underline{1}_{-i}))} \Leftrightarrow v_i^* \geq v_i^{(S, q(s_i', \underline{1}_{-i}))}$$

But $q(s_i', \underline{1}_{-i}) \geq \underline{1} - \varepsilon_\ell$, where $\ell = \phi(i)$, and ε_ℓ is the ℓth standard basis vector. Further, since $\underline{1} - \varepsilon_\ell \in Q^1$, we have $q(s_i', \underline{1}_{-i}) \in Q^1$. So $v_i^{(S, q(s_i', \underline{1}_{-i}))} = v_i^{(LR, q(s_i', \underline{1}_{-i}))}$. Hence, the above inequality can be written

$$v_i^* \geq \frac{\theta}{n_{\phi(i)}}\left[p_{\phi(i)}(q(s_i', \underline{1}_{-i}))w_1\right.$$

$$\left. + \frac{1}{2}\sum_{y \in \mathscr{L} - \{\phi(i)\}} p_y(q(s_i', \underline{1}_{-i}))w_2\right] + \delta v_i^*$$

$$\Leftrightarrow \frac{\theta}{\mathscr{L}n_{\phi(i)}} \geq \frac{\theta}{n_{\phi(i)}}\left[p_{\phi(i)}(q(s_i', \underline{1}_{-i}))w_1\right.$$

$$\left. + \frac{1}{2}(1 - p_{\phi(i)}(q(s_i', \underline{1}_{-i})))w_2\right]$$

$$\Leftrightarrow \frac{1}{\mathscr{L}} = p_i(q_0)w_1 + \frac{1}{2}(1 - p_i(q_0))w_2$$

$$\geq p_i(q(s_i', \underline{1}_{-i}))w_1 + \frac{1}{2}(1 - p_i(q(s_i', \underline{1}_{-i})))w_2$$

$$\Leftrightarrow [p_i(q_0) - p_i(q(s_i', s_{-i}))]\left(w_1 - \frac{1}{2}w_2\right) \geq 0.$$

Now if $n_{\phi(i)} = |\phi^{-1}(\phi(i))| > 1$ (there is more than one voter in district i), then $q_0 = q(s_i', \underline{1}_{-i})$; thus, one voter changing a vote does not affect the outcome. Hence, the above expression equals 0, and it follows that σ^t is a Nash equilibrium for G^t. If $n_{\phi(i)} = 1$ (there is a single voter in district i), then since $\sigma_i^t(1) = 1$ and $s_i' \leq 1$, it follows that $q_{0i} = 1$ and $q_i(s_i', \underline{1}_{-i}) = s_i' \leq 1$. In this case, one voter changing a vote changes the outcome. Hence, monotonicity of p implies that $[p_i(q_0) - p_i(q(s_i', \underline{1}_{-i}))] \geq 0$, and the last inequality holds if and only if

$$\left[w_1 - \frac{1}{2}w_2\right] = \frac{\mathcal{L}+1}{2\mathcal{L}} - \frac{1}{2\mathcal{L}} = \frac{1}{2} \geq 0.$$

Since all terms in the last expression are positive, this inequality holds; and it follows that s^t is a Nash equilibrium for G^t. This demonstrates that from the voter's point of view, changing a vote either does not change the outcome or changes the outcome in such a way as to make that voter worse off.

For $t \in \{LS\} \times Q^1$, we want to show that σ^t is a Nash equilibrium to the game with payoff function G^t, where $\sigma_i^t(t_{1i}) = 1$ for all $i \in L$. It suffices to show that for each $i \in L$, σ_i^t is at least as good as any pure strategy $s_i' \in S_i^t$. So,

$$G_i^t(\sigma^t) \geq G_i^t(\sigma_i', \sigma_{-i}^t)$$

$$\Leftrightarrow E_{\sigma^t}\left[u_i(\psi^t(s^t)) + \sum_{y \in \mathcal{T}} \pi^t(s^t)(y)v_i^y\right]$$

$$\geq E_{\sigma_{-i}^t}\left[u_i(\psi^t(s_i', s_{-i}^t)) + \sum_{y \in \mathcal{T}} \pi^t(s_i', s_{-i}^t)(y)v_i^y\right]$$

for all $s_i' \in S_i^t$. Using $\sigma_i^t(t_{1i}) = 1$, this can be reduced to

$$u_i(\psi^t(t_1)) + \sum_{y \in \mathcal{T}} \pi^t(t_1)(y)v_i^y \geq u_i(\psi^t(s_i', (t_1)_{-i}))$$

$$+ \sum_{y \in \mathcal{T}} \pi^t(s_i', (t_1)_{-i})(y)v_i^y.$$

Since $t_1 \in Q^1$, it follows that $\Sigma_{j \in L}t_{1j} > \mathcal{L}/2 \Rightarrow \pi^t(t_1)(LR, t_1) = 1$. So we get

$$v_i^{(LR,\,t_1)} \geq \pi^t(s_i', (t_1)_{-i})(LR, t_1)v_i^{(LR,\,t_1)}$$

$$+ \pi^t(s_i', (t_1)_{-i})(LR, q^*)v_i^{(LR,\,q^*)}.$$

Clearly, if $\pi^t(s_i', (t_1)_{-i})(LR, t_1) = 1$, legislator i is not pivotal and the above is an equality. So we consider the case when legislator i is pivotal, $\pi^t(s_i', (t_1)_{-i})(LR, t_1) \neq 1$. In this case, we must have $\Sigma_{j \in L} t_{1j} > \ell/2$ and $s_i' + \Sigma_{j \in L - \{i\}}t_{1j} < \mathcal{L}/2$. So $t_{1i} = 1$, and $s_i' = 0$. Thus, $\pi^t(s_i', (t_1)_{-i})(LR, q^*) = 1$, and the above inequality can be rewritten

$$v_i^{(LR,\,t_1)} \geq v_i^{(r,\,q^*)}$$

$$\Leftrightarrow (1 - \theta)\left[p_i(t_1)w_1 + \frac{1}{2}\sum_{y \in \mathcal{L}-\{i\}} p_y(t_1)w_2\right] + c + \delta v_i^*$$

$$\geq (1 - \theta)\left[q_i^* w_1 + \frac{1}{2}\sum_{y \in \mathcal{L}-\{i\}} q_y^* w_2\right] + c + \delta v_i^*$$

$$\Leftrightarrow p_i(t_1)w_1 + \frac{1}{2}(1 - p_i(t_1))w_2 \geq q_i^* w_1 + \frac{1}{2}(1 - q_i^*)w_2$$

$$\Leftrightarrow p_i(t_1)\left(w_1 - \frac{1}{2}w_2\right) \geq q_i^*\left(w_1 - \frac{1}{2}w_2\right)$$

$$\Leftrightarrow p_i(t_1) \geq q_i^*.$$

Now $p_i(t_1)$ is the probability that i will be selected, given that seniority is used and that $(\mathcal{L} + 1)/2$ members (including i) have seniority and $(\mathcal{L} - 1)/2$ do not have seniority. The seniority assumption implies that for all $q \in Q$, and $i, j \in L$, $q_i > q_i' \Rightarrow p_j(q) < p_j(q_i', q_{-i})$, $i \neq j$; that is, higher (lower) seniority for legislator i means that every other legislator now has a lower (higher) probability of being selected than the proposer. Now begin at q^* (assume every legislator has seniority) and remove seniority for $(\mathcal{L} - 1)/2$ legislators (not including i). At each step, p_i increases. Therefore, the last inequality is satisfied. Hence, σ^t is a Nash equilibrium for G^t.

For $t \in \{LS\} \times Q^0$, as above, we have

$$G_i^t(\sigma^t) \geq G_i^t(\sigma_i', \sigma_{-i}^t)$$

$$u_i(\psi^t(t_1)) + \sum_{y \in \mathcal{T}} \pi^t(t_1)(y)v_i^y \geq u_i(\psi^t(s_i', (t_1)_{-i}))$$

$$+ \sum_{y \in \mathcal{T}} \pi^t(s_i', (t_1)_{-i})(y)v_i^y$$

for all $s_i' \in S_i^t$. Since $t_1 \in Q^0$, it follows that $\Sigma_{j \in L}t_{1j} \leq \mathcal{L}/2 \Rightarrow \pi^t(t_1)(LR, q^*) = 1$. So we get

$$\Leftrightarrow v_i^{(LR,\,q^*)} \geq \pi^t(s_i', (t_1)_{-i})(LR, t_1)v_i^{(LR,\,t_1)}$$

$$+ \pi^t(s_i', (t_1)_{-i})(LR, q^*)v_i^{(LR,\,q^*)}.$$

Clearly, if $\pi^t(s_i', (t_1)_{-i})(LR, q^*) = 1$, legislator i is not pivotal and the above is an equality. So we consider the case when legislator i is pivotal, $\pi^t(s_i', (t_1)_{-i})(LR, q^*)) \neq 1$. In this case, we must have $\Sigma_{j \in L}t_{1j} \leq \mathcal{L}/2$ and $s_i' + \Sigma_{j \in L-\{i\}} t_{1j} > \mathcal{L}/2$. So $t_{1i} = 0$, and $s_i' = 1$. Thus, $\pi^t(s_i', t_{1-i})(LR, t_1) = 1$, and the above inequality can be rewritten

$$v_i^{(LR,\,q^*)} \geq v_i^{(LR,\,t_1)}$$

$$\Leftrightarrow (1 - \theta)\left[q_i^* w_1 + \frac{1}{2}\sum_{y \in \mathcal{L}-\{i\}} q_y^* w_2\right] + c + \delta v_i^*$$

$$\geq (1 - \theta)\left[p_i(t_1)w_1 + \frac{1}{2}\sum_{y \in \mathcal{L}-\{i\}} p_y(t_1)w_2\right] + c + \delta v_i^*$$

American Political Science Review   Vol. 86, No. 4

$$\Leftrightarrow q_i^* w_1 + \frac{1}{2}(1 - q_i^*)w_2 \geq p_i(t_1)w_1 + \frac{1}{2}(1 - p_i(t_1))w_2$$

$$\Leftrightarrow q_i^*\left(w_1 - \frac{1}{2}w_2\right) \geq p_i(t_1)\left(w_1 - \frac{1}{2}w_2\right)$$

$$\Leftrightarrow q_i^* \geq p_i(t_1).$$

But $p_i(t_1)$ is the probability that i will be selected, given that seniority is used and that $(\mathcal{L} - 1)/2$ members have seniority and $(\mathcal{L} - 1)/2$ (including i) do not have seniority. Using reasoning similar to that above, begin at q^* (assume no legislator has seniority) and add seniority for $(\mathcal{L} - 1)/2$ legislators (not including i). At each step, p_i decreases. Therefore, the last inequality is satisfied. Hence, σ^t is a Nash equilibrium for G^t.

For $t \in \{LV\} \times Q \times Z^1$, we want to show that σ^t is a Nash equilibrium to the game with payoff function G^t, where

$$\sigma_i^t(1) = \begin{cases} 1 & \text{if } \quad t_{1i} \geq \dfrac{1}{\mathcal{L}} \\[2ex] 0 & \text{if } \quad t_{1i} < \dfrac{1}{\mathcal{L}} \end{cases}$$

for all $i \in L$. It suffices to show that for each $i \in L$, σ_i^t is at least as good as any pure strategy $s_i' \in S_i^t$. So,

$$G_i^t(\sigma^t) \geq G_i^t(\sigma_i', \sigma_{-i}^t)$$

$$\Leftrightarrow E_{\sigma^t}\left[u_i(\psi^t(s^t)) + \sum_{y \in \mathcal{I}} \pi^t(s^t)(y)v_i^y\right]$$

$$\geq E_{\sigma_i^t}\left[u_i(\psi^t(s_i', s_{-i}^t)) + \sum_{y \in \mathcal{I}} \pi^t(s_i', s_{-i}^t)(y)v_i^y\right]$$

for all $s_i' \in S_i^t$. Since $t_1 \in Z^1$, $|\{j \in L: t_{1j} \geq w_2\}| > \mathcal{L}/2$. But $\sigma_i^t(1) = 1$ if $t_{1i} \geq 1/\mathcal{L} = w_2$. So, define $r \in \{0, 1\}^{\mathcal{L}}$ by $r_i = 1$ if $t_{1i} \geq w_2$ and $r_i = 0$ if $t_{1i} < w_2$. Then $\sigma(r) = 1$ and $\sigma_{-i}(r_{-i}) = 1$. Since $\Sigma_{i \in L}\, r_i > \mathcal{L}/2$, $\pi^t(r)(t_1, V) = 1$, and the above equation can be reduced to

$$u_i(x_0) + \sum_{y \in \mathcal{I}} \pi^t(r)(y)v_i^y \geq u_i(x_0) + \sum_{y \in \mathcal{I}} \pi^t(s_i', r_{-i})(y)v_i^y$$

$$\Leftrightarrow \sum_{y \in \mathcal{I}} \pi^t(r)(y)v_i^y \geq \sum_{y \in \mathcal{I}} \pi^t(s_i', r_{-i})(y)v_i^y$$

$$\Leftrightarrow v_i^{(V,\, t_1)} \geq \pi^t(s_i', r_{-i})(V, t_1)v_i^{(V,\, t_1)}$$

$$+ \pi^t(s_i', r_{-i})(LR, q^*)v_i^{(LR,\, q^*)}.$$

Clearly, if $\pi^t(s_i', r_{-i})(V, t_1) = 1$, legislator i is not pivotal and the above is an equality. So we consider the case when legislator i is pivotal, $\pi^t(s_i', r_{-i})(V, t_1) \neq 1$. In this case, we must have $\Sigma_{j \in L}\, r_j > \mathcal{L}/2$ and $s_i' + \Sigma_{j \in L - \{i\}}\, r_j < \mathcal{L}/2$. So $r_i = 1$, and $s_i' = 0$. Thus, $\pi^t(s_i', r_{-i})(LR, q^*) = 1$, and the above inequality can be rewritten

$$v_i^{(V,\, t_1)} \geq v_i^{(LR,\, q^*)} \Leftrightarrow (1 - \theta)t_{1i} + c + \delta v_i^* \geq v_i^*$$

$$\Leftrightarrow t_{1i} \geq \frac{1}{(1 - \theta)}[(1 - \delta)v_i^* - c].$$

$$\Leftrightarrow t_{1i} \geq \frac{1}{(1 - \theta)}\left[\left[\frac{1}{\mathcal{L}}(1 - \theta) + c\right] - c\right].$$

$$\Leftrightarrow t_{1i} \geq \frac{1}{\mathcal{L}}.$$

But $s_i^t = 1 \Rightarrow t_{1i} \geq w_2 = 1/\mathcal{L}$. Hence, the above inequality holds; and we have shown that $G_i^t(\sigma^t) \geq G_i^t(\sigma_i', \sigma_{-i}^t)$, so σ^t is a Nash equilibrium for G^t.

For $t \in Z^0$, define r as above. Since $t_1 \in Z^0$, $|\{j \in L: t_{1j} \geq w_2\}| \leq \mathcal{L}/2$, we get $\Sigma_{i \in L}\, r_i \leq \mathcal{L}/2$, implying $\pi^t(r)(LR, q^*) = 1$. Then arguing as above,

$$G_i^t(\sigma^t) \geq G_i^t(\sigma_i', \sigma_{-i}^t)$$

$$\Leftrightarrow v_i^{(LR,\, q^*)} \geq \pi^t(s_i', r_{-1})(V, t_1)v_i^{(V,\, t_1)}$$

$$+ \pi^t(s_i', r_{-i})(LR, q^*)v_i^{(LR,\, q^*)}$$

for all $s_i' \in S_i^t$. Clearly, if $\pi^t(s_i', r_{-i})(LR, q^*) = 1$, legislator i is not pivotal and the above is an equality. So we consider the case when legislator i is pivotal, $\pi^t(s_i', r_{-i})(LR, q^*) \neq 1$. In this case, we must have $\Sigma_{j \in L}\, r_j < \mathcal{L}/2$ and $s_i' + \Sigma_{j \in L - \{i\}}\, r_j > \mathcal{L}/2$. So $r_i = 0$, and $s_i' = 1$. Thus, $\pi^t(s_i', r_{-i})(V, t_1) = 1$, and the above inequality can be rewritten

$$v_i^{(LR,\, q^*)} \geq v_i^{(V,\, t_1)} \Leftrightarrow v_i^* \geq (1 - \theta)t_{1i} + c + \delta v_i^*$$

$$\Leftrightarrow \frac{1}{(1 - \theta)}[(1 - \delta)v_i^* - c] \geq t_{1i}.$$

$$\Leftrightarrow \frac{1}{(1 - \theta)}\left[\left[\frac{1}{\mathcal{L}}(1 - \theta) + c\right] - c\right] \geq t_{1i}.$$

$$\Leftrightarrow \frac{1}{\mathcal{L}} \geq t_{1i}.$$

But $s_i^t = 0 \Rightarrow t_{1i} < w_2 = 1/\mathcal{L}$. Hence, the above inequality holds; and it follows that σ^t is a Nash equilibrium for G^t.

For $t \in \{LP\} \times Q \times L$, we want to show that σ^t is a Nash equilibrium to the game with payoff function G^t, in which

$$\sigma_t^t = \frac{1}{|\Omega_t|}\Sigma_{w \in \Omega_t}\, \delta_{z_t}(w),$$

where $\Omega_t = \{\omega \in \{0, 1\}^{\mathcal{L}}: \Sigma_i \omega_i = (\mathcal{L} + 1)/2, \omega_t = 1\}$ and $z_t: \Omega_t \to \mathbb{R}^{\mathcal{L}}$ is defined by

$$z_{ti}(\omega) = \begin{cases} \dfrac{\mathcal{L} + 1}{2\mathcal{L}} & \text{if } \quad i = t \\[2ex] \dfrac{1}{\mathcal{L}} & \text{if } \quad i \neq 1, \omega_i = 1 \\[2ex] 0 & \text{otherwise} \end{cases}$$

for all $i \in L$. It suffices to show that σ_t^t is at least as good as any pure strategy $s_i' \in S_i^t$. So, for all $s_t' \in S_t^t$,

$$G_t^t(\sigma^t) \geq G_t^t(\sigma_t', \sigma_{-t}^t)$$

$$\Leftrightarrow E_{\sigma^t}[u_t(\psi^t(s^t)) + \sum_{y \in \mathcal{G}} \pi^t(s^t)(y)v_t^y]$$

$$\geq E_{\sigma_{-i}^t}[u_t(\psi^t(s_t', s_{-t}^t)) + \sum_{y \in \mathcal{G}} \pi^t(s_t', s_{-t}^t)(y)v_t^y]$$

$$\Leftrightarrow u_t(x_0) + \frac{1}{|\Omega_t|} \sum_{w \in \Omega_t} \sum_{y \in \mathcal{G}} \pi^t(z_t(\omega), \underline{0}_{-t})(y)v_t^y$$

$$\geq u_t(x_0) + \sum_{y \in \mathcal{G}} \pi^t(s_t', \underline{0}_{-t})(y)v_t^y$$

$$\Leftrightarrow \frac{1}{|\Omega_t|} \sum_{w \in \Omega_t} v_t^{(LV,\, z_t(\omega))} \geq v_t^{(LV,\, s_t)}.$$

But now, for all $\omega, \omega' \in \Omega_t$, $z_{tt}(\omega) = z_{tt}(\omega')$. So, writing $z_{tt} = z_{tt}(\omega)$, then the above inequality becomes

$$\frac{1}{|\Omega_t|} \sum_{w \in \Omega_t} v_t^{(LV,\, z_t(\omega))} = (1 - \theta)z_{tt} + c + \delta v_t^* \geq v_t^{(LV,\, s_t)}$$

Now if $s_t' \in Z^0$, which means that the proposal will not pass, then $v_t^{(LV,\, s_t')} = v_t^*$. So the above inequality becomes

$$(1 - \theta)\frac{\mathcal{L} + 1}{2\mathcal{L}} + c \geq (1 - \delta)v_t^* = (1 - \theta)\frac{1}{\mathcal{L}} + c$$

$$\Leftrightarrow \frac{\mathcal{L} - 1}{2\mathcal{L}} \geq 0 \Leftrightarrow \mathcal{L} \geq 1.$$

Since this inequality holds, σ^t is a Nash equilibrium for G^t in this case. On the other hand, if $s_t' \in Z^1$, the proposal is one that will pass; then in order to have $|\{j \in L: s_{tj} > w_2\}| \geq \mathcal{L}/2$, we must have $s_{tt}' \leq s_{tt}^t$. But then

$$\frac{1}{|\Omega_t|} \sum_{w \in \Omega_t} v_t^{(LV,\, z_t(\omega))}$$

$$= (1 - \theta)s_{tt}^t + c + \delta v_t^* \geq (1 - \theta)s_{tt}' + c + \delta v_t^* = v_t^{(LV,\, s_t')}.$$

Hence, σ^t is a Nash equilibrium for G^t.

Notes

This paper was funded in part by National Science Foundation Grants SES–864348 and SES–9022932 to the California Institute of Technology and SES–9023056 to the University of Iowa. This paper was written in part while Raymond Riezman was a visiting professor at the California Institute of Technology. We thank Ken Shepsle and Jeff Banks for useful comments on earlier drafts.

1. There have been partial attempts in this direction. Austen-Smith and Banks (1988) develop a full-equilibrium model of voter and legislative behavior in a parliamentary system. However, their model is not dynamic, since it deals with a one-shot game. Kramer (1977), Baron (1989), and Ferejohn (Baron and Ferejohn 1989) have developed dynamic models of policy formation and legislative organisation; but these models are not full-equilibrium, since they do not explicitly consider voter and legislative interactions.

2. On the issue of seniority, there has been remarkably little formal work in the political science literature. One exception is Shepsle and Nalebuff (1990), which develops a model explaining the existence of seniority systems in the group provision of public or private goods. Their explanation is based on a model of overlapping generations, in which agents need to have incentives to participate throughout their lifetime. This explanation does not depend on any characteristics of the group that are unique to legislative bodies and hence is equally applicable to firms and legislative bodies. Although there has not been a lot of explicit work on seniority, there has been a substantial body of formal work looking at the role of specialized committees in legislative organization (e.g., Gilligan and Krehbiel 1990; Shepsle 1979).

3. We model the infinitely repeated game as a stochastic game and only consider stationary solutions, thus avoiding the usual problems associated with the folk theorems in repeated games.

4. It is important to note that in our formulation, the seniority system only matters on the initial proposal. An interesting variation to consider would be the case in which seniority counts not only on the first proposal but on all successive proposals, as well. We believe that our formulation makes sense for two reasons. First, it captures an aspect of how congressional rules operate—namely, seniority is embodied in the committee system, which gives higher-than-average influence to ranking committee members to specify the proposed legislation. But if a majority of the legislators oppose a committee proposal on the floor, then the committee effectively loses its power, and the proposal of the committee can be amended by the full legislature at will. Second, suppose one defines the status quo to be fair division (each district gets $1/\mathcal{L}$). Then our model is equivalent to a model in which the failure of a proposal leads to a reversion to the status quo.

5. While this is not completely realistic, it captures the idea that voters can punish their representatives who they feel are not acting in their best interests. Our formulation allows more limited punishments than would be the case if voters could remove the legislator from office permanently.

6. Elements of $\mathcal{G}$ will be denoted by t. If t has two components, then we write $t = (t_0, t_1)$. The reader is cautioned that t is a variable indexing the games and thus can represent different things in different games.

References

Austen-Smith, David, and Jeffrey Banks. 1988. "Elections, Coalitions, and Legislative Outcomes." *American Political Science Review* 82:405–22.

Baron, David. 1989. "A Noncooperative Theory of Legislative Coalitions." *American Journal of Political Science* 33:1048–84.

Baron, David, and John Ferejohn. 1989. "Bargaining in Legislatures." *American Political Science Review* 83:1181–1206.

Erikson, Robert S. 1972. "Malapportionment, Gerrymandering, and Party Fortunes in Congressional Elections." *American Political Science Review* 66:1234–45.

Ferejohn, John. 1977. "On the Decline of Competition in Congressional Elections." *American Political Science Review* 71:166–76.

Fiorina, Morris P. 1977a. "The Case of the Vanishing Marginals: The Bureaucracy Did It." *American Political Science Review* 71:177–81.

Fiorina, Morris P. 1977b. *Congress: Keystone of the Washington Establishment*. New Haven: Yale University Press.

Gilligan, Thomas W., and Keith Krehbiel. 1990. "Organization of Informative Committees by a Rational Legislature." *American Journal of Political Science* 34:531–64.

Jacobson, Gary. 1983. *The Politics of Congressional Elections*. Boston: Little, Brown.

American Political Science Review   Vol. 86, No. 4

Kramer, Gerald H. 1977. "A Dynamic Model of Political Equilibrium." *Journal of Economic Theory* 16:310–44.

McKelvey, Richard D., and Raymond Riezman. N.d. "Initial Versus Continuing Proposal Power in Legislative Seniority Systems." In *Political Economy: Institutions, Information, Competition, and Representation,* ed. William Barnett, Mel Hinich, Norman Schofield, and Howard Rosenthal. Forthcoming.

Mayhew, David R. 1974a. "Congressional Elections: The Case of the Vanishing Marginals." *Polity* 6:295–317.

Mayhew, David R. 1974b. *Congress: The Electoral Connection.* New Haven: Yale University Press.

Rubinstein, Ariel. 1982. "Perfect Equilibrium in a Bargaining Model." *Econmetrica* 50:97–110.

Shepsle, Keneth A. 1979. "Institutional Arrangements and Equilibrium in Multidimensional Voting Models." *American Journal of Political Science* 23:23–59.

Shepsle, Kenneth A., and Barry Nalebuff. 1990. "The Committment to Seniority in Self-Governing Groups." *Journal of Law, Economics, and Organization* 6:45–72.

Sobel, Matthew J. 1971. "Noncooperative Stochastic Games." *Annals of Mathematical Statistics* 42:1930–35.

Richard D. McKelvey is Professor of Political Science, California Institute of Technology, Pasadena, CA 91125.

Raymond Riezman is Professor of Economics, University of Iowa, Iowa City, IA 52242.

ELSEVIER   Journal of International Economics 42 (1997) 67–90

Journal of
INTERNATIONAL
ECONOMICS

Political reform and trade policy

Raymond Riezman[a], John Douglas Wilson[b,*]

[a]University of Iowa, USA
[b]*Department of Economics, Wylie Hall, Indiana University, Bloomington, IN 47405, USA*

Received December 1995

Abstract

The welfare effects of partial restrictions on political competition are investigated in a model in which two candidates receive campaign contributions from import-competing industries in return for tariff protection. Ceilings on allowable contributions per industry may be welfare-worsening, particularly if the "contributor elasticity" is high, because they induce candidates to seek additional contributors. Restrictions that reduce the number of industries allowed to contribute may also worsen welfare, because candidates respond by increasing contributions (and tariff protection) for each active contributor. The results suggest that the ability of candidates to circumvent partial restrictions may eliminate any potential benefits.

Key words: Tariffs; Lobbies; Trade protection; Campaign contributions; Political reform

JEL classification: F1

1. Introduction

The literature on political economy and trade has emphasized the endogenous determination of trade policies via a political process.[1] Much of this literature takes a "black-box" approach to the modeling of political processes, making it difficult

*Corresponding author: Mailing Address: John D. Wilson, Department of Economics, Wylie Hall, Indiana University, Bloomington, IN 47405. Phone: 812-855-8035, FAX: 812-855-3736, Email: Wilsonj@Indiana.edu

[1]Riezman and Wilson (1995) and Hillman (1989) review the literature. See also the influential work of Magee et al. (1989).

68   *R. Riezman, J.D. Wilson / Journal of International Economics 42 (1997) 67–90*

to examine "institutional reforms" in these processes. For example, Rodrik (1986) argues that tariffs may dominate firm-specific production subsidies, because free-rider problems in coordinating industry-wide lobbying efforts lead to a lower equilibrium tariff rate than subsidy rate (see also Wilson (1990)). He assumes an exogenous relationship between each trade policy instrument and lobbying activities. In this way, he is able to compare production subsidies with tariffs, but only by assuming that these functions are "similar", albeit in a natural way. Grossman and Helpman (1994) significantly improve upon the black-box method by developing a model that "focuses on the political interactions between a government that is concerned both with campaign contributions and with the welfare of the average voter and a set of organized special-interest groups that care only about the welfare of their members" (p. 848). They use this approach to explain the structure of tariffs across different industries. One of the modeling compromises they make is to view the government as a single entity, rather than explicitly consider electoral competition between different candidates. Mayer (1984) examines tariff formation as the outcome of majority voting, but his model ignores pressure group politics.

The goal of this paper is to develop a model that includes important elements of *both* electoral competition and pressure-group competition, with enough structure to enable us to examine political reforms as a means of reducing trade protection. Following normal practice, our modeling strategy is to merge an "economic model" with a "political model". The economic model is an amended version of Rodrik's (1986) specific-factor trade model, but we replace his political model with an amended version of Baron's (1989) model. The critical feature of the political reforms is that they take the form of *partial* restrictions on political competition, by which we mean that ways will still exist to partially circumvent restrictions on the abilities of politicians to obtain contributions in return for trade protection. It is this partialness that distinguishes policy reforms in our model from the traditional welfare analysis, where policy instruments are fully controlled. A basic concern of our analysis will be to more fully understand the circumstances under which the behavioral responses allowed by partial restrictions thwart the intended goals of these restrictions.

Our model allows for two types of partial restrictions: ceilings on allowable contributions per interest group and restrictions on the number of groups allowed to contribute. Both types imposed together would represent total restrictions. Alone, however, they are partial. Such reforms are empirically relevant for the United States. Federal election reforms adopted in the early 1970s limited the amounts that groups could contribute and excluded some groups from contributing at all (corporations, for example). Only the use of aggregate spending limits for Presidential campaigns as a condition for receiving any federal election funds appears not to have been partial in nature. Since the 1970s, some of the many proposed election reforms would limit aggregate spending, but most involve

R. Riezman, J.D. Wilson / Journal of International Economics 42 (1997) 67–90 69

limiting contribution levels or restricting the types of groups that are allowed to contribute.[2]

The results reported here demonstrate that both types of restrictions may be ineffective. The ability of candidates to seek out additional contributors in response to contribution ceilings can easily lead to a higher level of overall deadweight loss from trade protection. We identify the "contributor elasticity" as an important consideration in this regard. Restrictions on the access of contributors to candidates may also lead to a more distortionary trade policy, by causing candidates to seek greater contributions from a small set of industries, thereby raising the level of trade protection in the protected industries. For such restrictions, we identify a key difference between candidates that allows these welfare losses to occur (see Prop. 4). Taken as a whole, our results suggest that the behavioral responses to partial restrictions on political competition often overwhelm the direct effects.

The plan of this paper is as follows. The next section describes the model. Then, Section 3 demonstrates the benefits of small restrictions on political competition. Section 4 shows that a sufficiently high "contributor elasticity" can eliminate the benefits of contribution ceilings. Section 5 then presents conditions under which restrictions on the number of contributors are harmful, and Sections 6 and 7 describe several extensions to the analysis. Appendix A contains some of the proofs.

2. The model

Consider an election game played between two candidates, "1" and "2". Each candidate collects "political contributions" from a large number of competitive import-competing industries and provides trade protection in return. The behavior of these industries is first considered, followed by a discussion of the behavior of candidates and the resulting political equilibrium.

To start, we assume that there are two types of import-competing industries, those that are potential contributors to candidate 1 ("type 1") and those that are potential contributors to candidate 2 ("type 2"). The number of type-i industries that actually contribute is denoted n_i. For our analysis of contribution ceilings, n_1 and n_2 are endogenous to the model. However, we also analyze the effects of exogenous restrictions on n_1 and n_2. In Section 6, we eliminate the exogenous assignment of industries to different candidates and instead let the candidates compete for contributions from the same set of industries; this extension is shown

---

[2]For example, there have been proposals to limit contributors geographically, so that politicians could only accept contributions from home districts or home state constituents. These reforms have not been adopted.

70   *R. Riezman, J.D. Wilson / Journal of International Economics 42 (1997) 67–90*

to reinforce some of our main results. In either case, our framework allows us to distinguish between reductions in the contributors to a single candidate and reductions in contributors to both.

The assumption that each industry contributes to only one candidate is empirically relevant. Sabato (1984) argues that there are very few instances of PACs contributing to both candidates in an election. This finding is understandable in the context of the political-support-maximizing candidates of our model. We shall see that what matters to a candidate is how much money she spends relative to her opponent. Therefore, the value of contributions that are matched by contributions to the opponent should be minimal. Presumably, a candidate would not be willing to offer much protection for such contributions.

Each import-competing industry uses a constant-returns-to-scale technology to produce a single good from mobile labor and an industry-specific input (e.g., a type of capital). Following Rodrik (1986), all exported goods are aggregated into a single composite good, which is produced with labor by means of a Ricardian technology. Since the marginal product of labor is then constant, the wage rate is technologically determined, and we may normalize it to equal one.

Factor costs equal revenue in a competitive equilibrium. Thus, the return on an import-competing industry's specific factor equals the difference between revenue and labor costs, as represented by the following "profits function" for type-i industries:

$$r_i(q_i) = \text{Max } q_i f_i(L_i) - L_i, \tag{1}$$

where $f_i(L_i)$ is the industry's production function (with the specific factor omitted as an explicit argument), L_i is labor and q_i is the domestic producer price for the industry's output. Since differences between industries per se are not the focus of our analysis, we assume that all potential contributors to a given candidate possess identical production functions and face identical world prices for their products, denoted p_i for a type-i industry.

In return for an industry's contributions, a candidate commits to provide the industry with a tariff at a specified level, if elected. A tariff rate t_i provides type-i industries with an effective income transfer, $T_i = r_i[p_i + t_i] - r_i[p_i]$. This transfer equals the change in "producers' surplus", as measured by the area to the left of the output supply curve, between p_i and $p_i + t_i$. To simplify the analysis, we shall assume linear demand and supply curves, $D_i(q_i)$ and $X_i(q_i)$, in which case T_i is found by subtracting a triangle from a rectangle:

$$T_i = t_i X_i(p_i + t_i) - 0.5 t_i^2 X_i', \tag{2}$$

where X_i' is the constant supply derivative. The linearity assumption also enables us to use the familiar "Harberger Triangle" expression to measure the deadweight loss from a tariff imposed at the rate t_i on a type-i industry:

$$b_i(t_i) = 0.5[t_i]^2[X_i' - D_i']. \tag{3}$$

R. Riezman, J.D. Wilson / Journal of International Economics 42 (1997) 67–90 71

Both of the constant derivatives, X_i' and D_i', enter the deadweight loss expression, because a tariff distorts both production and consumption decisions. Given that all n_i type-i industries receive the same tariff rate, t_i, the total excess burden is

$$B_i(t_i) = n_i b_i(t_i). \tag{4}$$

Consider now the structure of the market for protection. Candidate i offers type-i industries the tariff rate t_i in return for contributions c_i. The choice facing an industry is whether or not to enter the market for protection and "purchase" protection. Because the number of contributors is "large", each potential entrant treats the candidate's probability of election, denoted π_i, as independent of its decision to enter the market. If an industry does enter, then it must incur a fixed "entry cost", k_i, which may be thought of as representing the costs associated with solving the "free-rider" problem that arises from the public good nature of lobbying for an industry-wide tariff [see Rodrik (1986) for an analysis of this problem].

Throughout much of the paper, we allow these entry costs to differ across industries, with $n_i(k)$ representing the number of type-i industries with entry costs less than or equal to k. It will be convenient to work with the inverse of this function, $k_i(n)$. Then $k_i(n_i)$ represents the highest entry cost among the n_i type-i industries that choose to seek protection. The "marginal contributor" receives an expected transfer net of contributions, $\pi_i T_i - c_i$, that is exactly offset by entry cost $k_i(n_i)$. In other words, we have the following "zero-profit condition" for the marginal contributor:

$$\pi_i T_i - c_i = k_i(n_i). \tag{5}$$

As the expected net transfer rises, the entry cost possessed by the marginal contributor rises to satisfy Eq. (5). Thus, heterogeneity of entry costs produces an upward-sloping "supply" of contributors. Some of our results will use the reasonable assumption that this supply function is convex at the equilibrium in question, in which case, $d^2 k_i / dn_i^2 \geq 0$. To illustrate the importance of the elasticity of the contributor supply, we will also consider the special case of an infinite elasticity, where $k_i(n_i)$ is replaced with a constant, k_i.

The zero-profit condition (Eq. (5)) enables us to derive an important relation between deadweight loss and both the level of contributions and the number of contributors. Define $t_i = t_i^*(T_i)$ as the tariff needed to increase specific-factor income by T_i, i.e., the t_i that solves Eq. (2) for a given T_i. Implicit differentiation and the envelope theorem give

$$t_i^{*\prime}(T_i) = \frac{1}{X_i(p_i + t_i)}. \tag{6}$$

Define the composite function,

$$b_i^*(T_i) = b_i[t_i^*(T_i)]. \tag{7}$$

72   *R. Riezman, J.D. Wilson / Journal of International Economics 42 (1997) 67–90*

This new function relates the excess burden from a type-i industry's trade protection to T_i. Using Eq. (4) and the zero-profit condition (Eq. (5)), we have

$$B_i = n_i b_i^* \left[\frac{c_i + k_i(n_i)}{\pi_i} \right]. \tag{8}$$

Consider now the game played between the two candidates. Each candidate is assumed to maximize the probability of being elected. Following the framework of Baron (1994), this probability is determined by the voting behavior of "uninformed voters", who are influenced solely by political contributions, and "informed voters," who vote according to their assessments of the actual policies of the candidates. In symbols, candidate i's probability of election is expressed,

$$\pi_i = \kappa u_i + (1 - \kappa) v_i, \tag{9}$$

where u_i denotes the expected proportion of uninformed voters who vote for i, v_i is the expected proportion of informed voters voting for i, and κ is an exogenously given proportion of voters who are uninformed. As in Baron, the expected number of votes is assumed to be a good measure of the probability of winning. For the determination of u_i, we borrow the following specification from the work of both Baron (1989, 1994); Hillman and Ursprung (1988):

$$u_i(C_i, C_j) = \frac{e_i C_i}{e_1 C_1 + e_2 C_2}, \tag{10}$$

where parameters e_1 and e_2 reflect differences in the relative efficiencies of the two candidates' contributions, subscripts identify the candidate (i,j = 1,2), and C_i equals candidate i's total contributions, $n_i c_i$. The specification of v_i is given by

$$v_i(B_i, B_j) = \alpha_i + a[B_j - B_i] \tag{11}$$

for deadweight loss levels B_i and B_j associated with i and j's trade policies, and positive constants α_i and a (where $\alpha_1 + \alpha_2 = 1$ so that election probabilities sum to one). This specification may be justified by assuming that each voter assigns some value, s_i, to candidate i's "platform" on non-trade issues, and supports candidate i when the difference in excess burdens, $B_i - B_j$, is no greater than the difference in $s_i - s_j$. Assuming that $s_i - s_j$ is uniformly distributed across voters, the proportion of voters supporting candidate i can be written in the form given by Eq. (11).

An alternative to Eq. (11) would be to assume that informed voters object not only to the deadweight loss created by a candidate's trade policy, but also to the transfers, totaling $n_i T_i$ for candidate i. The current specification reflects the interpretation of informed voters as including the "specific-factor owners". In this case, the transfers do not represent a loss of income for informed voters and are therefore excluded from Eq. (11). This explanation ignores conflicts between different informed voters who own different amounts of the specific factors, but such conflicts also point to the possibility that informed voters will not be

R. Riezman, J.D. Wilson / Journal of International Economics 42 (1997) 67–90 73

effectively united against the transfers per se. If, on the other hand, the specific-factor owners differ from the informed voters, then it can be argued that deadweight losses and transfers should be treated equally in the specification of the informed voters' welfare function. Most of the results in this paper carry over to this alternative specification.[3]

The two candidates play a Nash game. The strategy variables are the contribution level c_i and the number of contributors n_i. This leaves t_i to adjust to satisfy the zero-profit condition (Eq. (5)). Thus, when candidate i adjusts c_i and n_i, she treats c_j and n_j as fixed. Since such marginal adjustments from i's optimum have no impact on the election probabilities (since π_i is maximized and π_j is minimized), they do not change the t_j that satisfies j's zero-profit condition for the given c_j and n_j. Thus, candidate i also effectively treats t_j as fixed for purposes of calculating her first-order conditions.

Candidate i's maximization problem may now be stated as follows:

$$(P.1)\ \ \text{Max}\ \kappa\left\{\frac{e_i C_i}{e_i C_i + e_j C_j}\right\}$$
$$+ (1 - \kappa)\left\{\alpha_i + a\left[n_j b_j^*\left(\frac{c_j + k_j(n_j)}{\pi_j}\right) - n_i b_i^*\left(\frac{c_i + k_i(n_i)}{\pi_i}\right)\right]\right\},\tag{12}$$

where c_i and n_i are the control variables. To state the first-order condition for c_i, differentiate Eq. (12) with respect to c_i, set the derivative equal to zero and multiply through by c_i:

$$\kappa u_1 u_2 - (1 - \kappa)a n_i b_i^{*\prime}(T_i)\frac{c_i}{\pi_i} = 0.\tag{13}$$

The first-order condition for n_i is similarly obtained by differentiating Eq. (12) with respect to n_i, setting the derivative equal to zero and multiplying through by n_i:

$$\kappa u_1 u_2 - (1 - \kappa)a\left[B_i + n_i b_i^{*\prime}(T_i)\frac{dk_i}{dn_i}\frac{n_i}{\pi_i}\right] = 0.\tag{14}$$

It will prove useful to state the optimality conditions in a different way by decomposing the optimization problem into two suboptimization problems. First, we consider the problem of choosing c_i and n_i to minimize B_i, given the desired level of total contributions, C_i. The first-order condition for this problem is obtained by subtracting Eq. (14) from Eq. (13):

---

[3]We have investigated this alternative specification and found that it does not change our main results through Prop. 3. However, the proof of Prop. 4 is no longer valid, due to required modifications in the first-order condition given by Eq. (A.10).

74   *R. Riezman, J.D. Wilson / Journal of International Economics 42 (1997) 67–90*

$$B_i + n_i b_i^{*\prime}(T_i)\left[\frac{dk_i}{dn_i}n_i - c_i\right]\pi_i^{-1} = 0. \tag{15}$$

This condition places an important bound on the marginal impact of n_i on entry cost k_i at the optimum:

$$\frac{dk_i}{dn_i}n_i < c_i. \tag{16}$$

Violation of this condition means that candidate i could lower B_i without changing C_i by collecting a higher c_i from fewer contributors, thereby obtaining the gains associated with lower entry costs. On the other hand, an optimum could not exist if there were no entry costs ($k_i = 0$). To see this, set $k_i = 0$ in the zero-profit condition (Eq. (5)) and then substitute this condition into Eq. (15) for $dk_i/dn_i = 0$:

$$B_i = n_i b_i^{*\prime}(T_i)T_i. \tag{17}$$

Using Eqs. (3), (6) and (7),

$$b_i^{*\prime}(T_i) = b_i'[t_i^*(T_i)] \cdot t_i^{*\prime}(T_i) = \frac{t_i^*(T_i)}{X_i}[X_i' - D_i'], \tag{18}$$

where, by the assumption of linear supply curves,

$$X_i = \eta_i + [p_i + t_i^*(T_i)]X_i' \tag{19}$$

for some positive constant η_i. Inspection of Eqs. (18) and (19) shows that $b_i^{*\prime}(T_i)$ rises with T_i. But then the linear approximation for B_i given by the right side of Eq. (17) overestimates B_i, implying that Eq. (17) cannot be true. Basically, the absence of entry costs provides a candidate with an incentive to take advantage of the convexity of the deadweight loss function by collecting an infinitesimal contribution in return for infinitesimal tariff from an infinite number of industries, or, more realistically, to go to a corner solution, where all available industries contribute to the campaign. The following two sections will assume an interior solution for n_i.

To construct the second suboptimization problem, we use the first-order condition for the first problem, Eq. (15), to define the minimized B_i as a function of C_i and π_i: $B_i = B_i(C_i, \pi_i)$, where the equilibrium π_i is now a function of C_i and the strategy variables chosen by the other candidate, $\pi_i = \pi_i(C_i, c_j, n_j)$.[4] Substituting these functions into problem (P.1) then produces a problem with only C_i as the control variable. The first-order condition is

---

[4] This function is implicitly defined by substituting the function $B_i(C_i, \pi_i)$ for $n_i b_i$ in Eq. (12), and noting that the entire expression in Eq. (12) equals π_i.

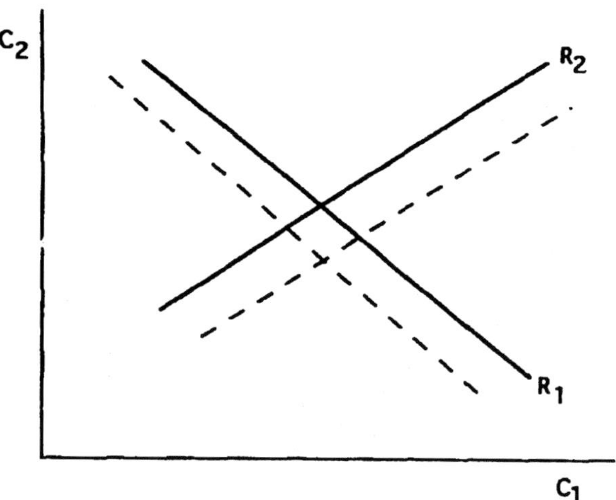

Fig. 1. Determination of contribution levels.

$$\kappa u_1 u_2 - (1 - \kappa)a\frac{\partial B_i}{\partial C_i}C_i = 0. \tag{20}$$

Using Eq. (20), candidate i's chosen C_i may be defined as a function of C_j and π_i: $C_i = R_i(C_j, \pi_i)$. Fig. 1 graphs this function for each candidate in total contributions space, holding the election probabilities fixed at their equilibrium levels. We shall refer to these curves as "reaction curves", although it should be noted that candidate i's best response to a change in C_j will generally depend on the individual changes in c_j and n_j through their impact on π_i. Observe, however, that *marginal* departures from the equilibrium have no first-order impact on π_i, since candidate i seeks to maximize π_i, whereas candidate j minimizes π_i. Hence, candidate i's best response to a marginal increase in C_j from its equilibrium value is given by the slope of our reaction curve, i.e., the *partial* derivative, $\partial R_i / \partial C_j$. The difference in these slopes is discussed shortly.

Partial restrictions on industry lobbying are modeled as restrictions on either the number of contributors (n_i) or the contribution level (c_i). In the next two sections, we consider restrictions targeted towards one of the two candidates. This alters the candidate's reaction curves by making the restricted variable a parameter, e.g., $C_i = R_i(C_j, \pi_i, n_i)$ in the case where n_i is restricted.[5] Two interpretations may be given to these restrictions: (1) A uniform ceiling is placed on both candidates' contributors or contribution levels, but it is binding for only one of the two candidates; or (2) the restrictions are imposed indirectly by specifying particular attributes of the industry to which they apply, but only one candidate's potential

---

[5] We shall limit attention to those cases where the equilibrium values of the unrestricted variables are continuously differentiable functions of the restricted variables, over the relevant range.

76   *R. Riezman, J.D. Wilson / Journal of International Economics 42 (1997) 67–90*

contributors possess these attributes. In either case, a major theme of the results will be that the impact of partial restrictions on trade protection depends on the candidate towards which they are targeted. In particular, the critical difference between the two candidates is their popularity with the uninformed voters. Fig. 1 depicts the case where candidate 2 is more popular, i.e., $u_2 > u_1$. As illustrated, we now prove that the more popular candidate's curve slopes up, whereas the other is downward-sloping:

Lemma 1. If $u_2 > u_1$, then the slopes of the candidates' reaction curves satisfy the following property at the equilibria C_1 and C_2, regardless of whether the number of contributors or contributions per contributor are restricted:

$$\partial R_1 / \partial C_2 < 0 \text{ and } \partial R_2 / \partial C_1 > 0. \tag{21}$$

Proof. For candidate 2's reaction curve, note that a rise in C_1 affects Eq. (20) for i=2 only by raising $u_1 u_2$, which equals $u_1(1-u_1)$ and is therefore maximized at $u_1 = u_2 = 1/2$. The second-order condition for candidate 2's optimal C_2 then implies that C_2 must increase to restore Eq. (20) to equality. This proves that $\partial R_2 / \partial C_1 > 0$. Similar reasoning signs the slope of candidate 1's reaction curve. Q.E.D.

Magee et al. (1989) present a very different model of endogenous tariff policy but nevertheless obtain the same conclusion that the two candidates possess reaction curves with different slopes. In both models, the essential reason for this result is that one candidate is attempting to minimize the function that the other candidate is attempting to maximize; candidate j tries to minimize candidate i's probability of election, since doing so is equivalent to maximizing j's election probability. Thus, candidate j's first-order condition for C_j (Eq. (20)) is minus the derivative of i's election probability with respect to j's control variable: $-\partial \pi_i / \partial C_j = 0$. The slope of j's reaction curve then has the same sign as the derivative of this first-order condition with respect to C_i: $-\partial^2 \pi_i / \partial C_j \partial C_i$. But this is minus the derivative of i's first-order condition with respect to C_j. Thus, the reaction curves must differ in sign.

The specific structure that we place on the probability-of-election functions enables us to assign the positively-sloped curve to the more popular candidate. The proof of Lemma 1 shows that this slope is positive because if $C_2 > C_1$ initially, then an increase in candidate 1's spending (C_1) raises the marginal impact of 2's spending on the support that 2 receives from uninformed voters. Candidate 2 responds to this higher marginal impact by increasing C_2.

3. Small restrictions

The main point of this section is that there exists a role for partial restrictions on industry lobbying as a welfare-improving device. Consideration is given both to

R. Riezman, J.D. Wilson / Journal of International Economics 42 (1997) 67–90 77

"ceilings" on allowable levels of c_1 and c_2 and to "entry restrictions" on the numbers of active contributors. It turns out that both types of restrictions are desirable, if they are sufficiently small in size, and if they actually lead to a reduction in total contributions. The latter qualification need not always hold, however.

We begin with a lemma that ties changes in total deadweight losses to changes in total contribution levels.

Lemma 2. Starting from the unrestricted equilibrium, suppose that one or both candidates are forced to lower by a small amount either the number of contributors (n_i) or the contribution level (c_i). For each i, these changes cause a (first-order) decline in B_i if, and only if, they lower C_i.

Proof. This is basically an envelope-theorem result. Candidate i chooses n_i and c_i to minimize B_i, given her choice of total contributions, C_i. Thus, marginal changes in n_i and c_i that leave C_i fixed have a zero first-order impact on B_i. If, however, these marginal changes reduce (raise) C_i, then the minimized B_i must also decline (rise) at the margin. Finally, Eq. (8) shows that any marginal changes in c_j and n_j do not alter B_i, because they only enter the determination of B_i through π_i, which is not affected by marginal changes in c_j and n_j (since candidate j minimizes π_i). Thus, we may conclude that B_i declines as C_i declines. Q.E.D.

Turning now to the specific methods of limiting total contributions, we now show that the benefits of such methods depend on which candidate they are targeted towards.

Proposition 1. Assume that $u_2 > u_1$ and $dk_i/dn_i > 0$ at the initial equilibrium. If candidate 2 is required to reduce either n_2 or c_2 by a small amount, then C_2 and B_2 decline, and C_1 and B_1 rise. If candidate 1 is required to reduce either n_1 or c_1 by a small amount, then C_1, B_1, C_2 and B_2 all decline.

Proof. Reducing c_i or n_i by marginal amounts from their equilibrium values does not have a first-order impact on the election probabilities, since c_i and n_i are chosen to maximize π_i. However, Appendix A shows that reducing n_i or c_i shifts down candidate i's reaction curve, $\partial R_i / \partial n_i < 0$ and $\partial R_i / \partial c_i < 0$, but does not change candidate j's reaction curve ($j \neq i$). For $i = 1$ and 2, these shifts are illustrated by the dashed lines in Fig. 1. It is clear from the figure that reducing either n_2 or c_2 lowers the equilibrium C_2 and raises the equilibrium C_1, whereas both C_1 and C_2 fall if either n_1 or c_1 is reduced. Lemma 2 then signs the changes in deadweight losses. Q.E.D.

An interesting aspect of Prop. 1 is that the one case where contribution ceilings or entry restrictions may raise deadweight losses (depending on who is elected) is the case where they are targeted towards the candidate who is *most* popular among those voters who are swayed by contributions. As shown in Fig. 1, such

78   *R. Riezman, J.D. Wilson / Journal of International Economics 42 (1997) 67–90*

restrictions reduce candidate 2's reaction curve, thereby raising C_1 along candidate 1's negatively-sloped reaction curve. To attract these additional contributions, candidate 1 chooses a more distortionary trade policy (i.e., B_1 increases). Thus, attempts to restrict the behavior of contributors as a means of obtaining a "more level playing field" in election campaigns can potentially be costly in terms of increased deadweight losses. We return to this possibility in Section 4.

4. The contributor elasticity

Partial restrictions on industry lobbying may reduce total contributions, but they can be expected to do so in a wasteful way. If a candidate faces a ceiling on contributions per industry, for example, then it faces an incentive to obtain its chosen contribution level by providing inefficiently low tariff rates to an inefficiently high number of industries. In other words, the same total amount of contributions could be obtained at a lower cost in terms of deadweight loss, if the candidate provided higher tariff rates to fewer industries. The size of this inefficiency should depend on the elasticity of contributors with respect to the expected net return on contributions (given by the left side of Eq. (5)). In line with this intuition, this section demonstrates that a high contributor elasticity can cause contribution ceilings to adversely affect trade policies. The inefficiencies associated with entry restrictions are discussed in the following section.

To find out what happens for sufficiently high contributor elasticities, we can examine the infinite-elasticity case, which occurs when entry costs do not vary across potential contributors $(\mathrm{d}k_i / \mathrm{d}n_i = 0)$. The results for this case are stated in the form of a lemma and a proposition.

Lemma 3. Assume that the supply of contributors is infinitely elastic. If restrictions on c_1 and c_2 move support levels u_1 and u_2 closer to (farther from) each other, then B_1 and B_2 rise (decline). If u_1 and u_2 do not change, neither do B_1 and B_2.

Proof. With $\mathrm{d}k_i / \mathrm{d}n_i = 0$, the first-order condition for n_i given by Eq. (14) becomes

$$\kappa u_1 u_2 - (1 - \kappa)aB_i = 0. \tag{22}$$

This completes the proof, since a decline in $u_2 - u_1$ implies a rise in $u_1 u_2$, given that u_1 and u_2 sum to one. Q.E.D.

Proposition 2. Assume that the supply of contributors is infinitely elastic. Then:
(a) Small restrictions on c_1 and c_2 cause no first-order changes in total contributions and total deadweight losses.
(b) Assume that $u_2 > u_1$ before and after any restrictions are imposed on c_1 or

R. Riezman, J.D. Wilson / Journal of International Economics 42 (1997) 67–90 79

c_2. *Then a reduction in c_2 raises both B_1 and B_2, whereas a reduction in c_1 lowers both B_1 and B_2.*

Proof. To prove (a), reduce c_1 and/or c_2 by marginal amounts from their equilibrium values, and change n_1 and n_2 so that C_1 and C_2 remain fixed. Then u_1 and u_2 do not change. Since candidate i's initial choice of c_i and n_i minimized the B_i associated with her choice of C_i, it is also true that B_i does not change to a first-order approximation. But then the first-order condition given by Eq. (22) remains satisfied, implying that these changes in n_1 and n_2 were optimal. Since they leave B_1 and B_2 fixed, the proof is complete.

To prove the first part of (b), we first demonstrate that a forced reduction in c_2 from its (unrestricted) equilibrium level must lower the equilibrium π_2, denoted $\pi_2(c_2)$. This is done by showing that $\pi_2(c_2)$ has a positive derivative at each c_2 below its equilibrium level. Since n_2 remains chosen to maximize π_2, whereas c_1 and n_1 are chosen to minimize π_2, the changes in these variables that accompany a marginal reduction in c_2 have no first-order impact on π_2. Hence, we may prove the claim by calculating the marginal change in the election probability from a marginal reduction in c_2 accompanied by an increase in n_2 that leaves C_2 unchanged. Specifically, let $(dc_2, dn_2) = (-c_2/n_2, 1)$. Then the resulting differential of Eq. (12) is

$$d\pi_2 = \frac{1}{\mu}\left\{ b_2^{*\prime}\left(\frac{c_2 + k_2}{\pi_2}\right)\frac{c_2}{\pi_2} - b_2^{*}\left(\frac{c_2 + k_2}{\pi_2}\right)\right\}, \tag{23}$$

where μ equals one minus the derivative of Eq. (12) with respect to π_i (with $\pi_j = 1 - \pi_i$ for $j \neq i$ and $i = 1$ or 2), which must be positive to satisfy the second-order condition for candidate 2's choice of n_2. This expression equals zero at the unrestricted value of c_2 [see the first-order condition given by Eq. (15)] and it is easy to show that it falls and stays below zero as c_2 declines.[6] Thus, reducing c_2 must lower π_2.

Now the first-order condition given by Eq. (22) implies that $B_1 = B_2$ before and after the reduction in c_2. Thus, the fall in π_2 implies that the support candidate 2 receives from uninformed voters falls, in which case C_2/C_1 falls towards one. It follows that u_2u_1 rises and we may then conclude from Eq. (22) that B_1 and B_2 both rise.

---

[6]Using the zero-profit condition (Eq. (5)), this expression may be seen to be a positive multiple of $\pi_2[T_2 - b_2^{*}(T_2)/b_2^{*\prime}(T_2)] - k_2$. It follows from Eqs. (3), (6) and (7) that this expression reduces to $\pi_2(T_2 - (t_2/2)X_2) - k_2$. Using Eqs. (2) and (19) to solve for T_2, we obtain $\pi_2(t_2/2)(\eta_2 + p_2 X_2') - k_2$. The sign of this expression equals the sign of $d\pi_2$ and we have noted in the text that $d\pi_2 = 0$ at the unrestricted value of c_2. As c_2 falls, t_2 falls to keep the zero-profit condition satisfied, thereby reducing the magnitude of this last expression. Consequently, it is possible to conclude that $d\pi_2 < 0$ at all c_2 below the unrestricted value.

By similar reasoning, a fall in c_1 raises C_2/C_1, enabling us to conclude from Eq. (22) that B_1 and B_2 both fall. Q.E.D.

The potential ineffectiveness of contribution ceilings may be understood by drawing an analogy to the ineffectiveness of price floors in a competitive market with no entry barriers. The price floor may succeed in raising the market price above its free-market level, but the resulting entry may then prevent firms from achieving abnormal profits. In the present instance, candidates respond to small restrictions in contributions by seeking out new contributors in an effort to maintain their existing contribution levels. As a result, there is no (first-order) change in total contributions or deadweight losses, i.e., the changes in C_i and B_i identified in Prop. 2a all become zero when infinite contributor elasticity is assumed. For a discrete restriction in c_i, however, B_i will rise even in the case where candidate i responds by increasing n_i enough to maintain C_i at its previous level, because the candidate is being forced to obtain this C_i using an inefficient mix of protected industries and tariff rates. Thus, we obtain the welfare losses identified in Prop. 2b, despite the absence of first-order welfare changes in part (a).

This proposition also suggests that a uniform ceiling on both candidates may be undesirable, even though no explicit "targeting" of the ceiling takes place. Consider the reasonable case where the candidate who is more popular with uninformed voters also raises the largest amount of contributions per candidate, i.e. $u_2 > u_1$ and $c_2 > c_1$. Suppose that an attempt is made to "level the playing field" by imposing a uniform contribution ceiling. Prop. 2b implies immediately that this ceiling will raise both B_1 and B_2 if it does not bind for candidate 1's chosen c_1.

The harmful effects of contribution ceilings identified in Prop. 2 depend on the existence of differences between politicians. In particular, if the candidates are identical and face identical contribution ceilings (keeping $u_1 = u_2$), then contribution ceilings have no effect on deadweight losses under an infinite contributor elasticity. This observation leads to the hypothesis that contribution ceilings will lower deadweight losses if the contribution elasticity is finite and the candidates are sufficiently similar. The following proposition confirms this reasoning:

Proposition 3. Assume that the two candidates are identical and $dk_i/dn_i > 0$. Then, restricting c_1 and c_2 to any common level below the Nash equilibrium levels must lower B_1 and B_2.

Proof. See Appendix A.

To summarize, the conditions under which contribution ceilings are beneficial involve assumptions about how the candidates differ, how the ceilings are targeted and how high contributor elasticity is set. There seems to be no simple way of knowing when these ceilings will have desirable effects.

R. Riezman, J.D. Wilson / Journal of International Economics 42 (1997) 67–90 81

Yet another complication, which we have ignored, is the social cost of the resources expended on lobbying. The issue of whether to count contributions as a social cost is perhaps open to debate. If they represent real resources spent on election campaigns, then the social-cost view seems appropriate. But they could, at least partially, represent transfer payments (e.g., dinners for campaign supporters), in which case the social-cost view seems inaccurate. In contrast, the costs required to collect and distribute contributions (our "entry costs") should be viewed as a social cost, and they definitely rise in our model as the number of contributors rise. Thus, their presence enforces the view that contribution ceilings are often undesirable. Take, for example, the case identified in Prop. 2, where small restrictions on c_1 or c_2 have no effects on total contributions or total deadweight losses. Since candidates seek out more contributors to offset these restrictions, total entry costs also rise. Thus, contribution ceilings look even less desirable, if one considers the resource costs associated with lobbying.

5. The potential undesirability of entry restrictions

We saw in the previous section that contribution ceilings can fail to produce more efficient trade policies, because the candidates respond by increasing the numbers of contributors. The theme of the current section is that restrictions on the numbers of contributors may also be undesirable, because candidates then provide higher tariff rates to the protected industries, in an effort to obtain more contributions from this restricted set of industries. As before, the problem is that partial restrictions force candidates to obtain their contributions in an inefficient way. For the present case, the severity of this inefficiency should depend on the level of the fixed costs associated with making contributions. If these "entry costs" are absent, then reductions in the numbers of contributors may be harmful, because there are no reductions in entry costs to offset their harmful effects.

In this section, we show not only that the absence of entry costs implies that entry restrictions are often harmful from a social welfare point of view (in terms of increased deadweight losses), but also that no single candidate would want to unilaterally restrict its number of contributors. We first provide a formal proof of this latter result and then use it to examine the issue of deadweight losses:

Lemma 4. If n_1 and n_2 are initially fixed where $k_i(n_i) = dk_i(n_i)/dn_i = 0$, then a marginal reduction in n_i must reduce candidate i's probability of election.

Proof. Following the proof of Prop. 2b, the marginal impact of n_i on π_i is given by the expression in Eq. (23), evaluated at $k_i = 0$:

$$\frac{\partial \pi_i}{\partial n_i} = \frac{1}{\mu}\left\{ b_i^{*\prime}\left(\frac{c_i}{\pi_i}\right)\frac{c_i}{\pi_i} - b_i^{*}\left(\frac{c_i}{\pi_i}\right)\right\}, \tag{24}$$

where μ is positive. By the arguments involving Eq. (17) in Section 2, the term in the curly brackets is positive. Q.E.D.

The basic idea here is that forcing candidate i to reduce the number of protected industries means that the tariff rate must now be raised to induce the remaining industries to provide enough additional contributions to keep C_i from falling. Under the convexity properties of the deadweight loss function, this substitution of a higher t_i for a lower n_i causes the B_i associated with the given C_i to rise. As a result, candidate i's probability of election goes down.

Consider now the equilibrium changes in deadweight losses from entry restrictions. Because of the inefficiencies such restrictions impose on the manner in which given levels of C_1 and C_2 are collected, we find that they can result in higher deadweight losses. Specifically, we now prove–

*Proposition 4. If n_i and n_j are initially fixed where $k_i(n_i)=dk_i(n_i)/dn_i=0$, then
(a) Any further reductions in n_1 and n_2 that either move support levels u_1 and u_2 closer to each other or do not change them must raise B_1 and B_2.
(b) If $u_2>u_1$, then a further reduction in n_2 raises B_1 and B_2, whereas a fall in n_1 must lower B_2.*

Proof. See Appendix A.

Thus, B_1 and B_2 rise in cases where entry restrictions achieve a more "level playing field" by moving u_1 and u_2 closer together. In terms of the first-order condition for c_i, these movements raise $u_1 u_2$, which, by itself, increases the marginal impact of c_i on political support, holding fixed the tariff rate [see the first-order condition given by Eqs. (A.6)]. This consideration tends to cause the candidates to respond by offering more distortionary trade policies in order to attract more contributions per contributor. However, Prop. 4 shows that B_1 and B_2 also rise in response to entry restrictions that have little or no effect on u_1 and u_2. For example, identical reductions in n_1 and n_2 raise B_1 and B_2 when both candidates are identical in all respects. In this case, both candidates increase the tariff rates they offer contributors more than enough to offset the reductions in n_1 and n_2.

What is more likely to be beneficial, contribution ceilings or entry restrictions? Our results do not suggest a definitive answer, but two observations do favor entry restrictions. First, if entry costs are present, then one benefit of entry restrictions is that these costs decline, whereas contribution ceilings raise this cost by causing candidates to seek out additional contributors. Second, whereas we saw that an infinite contributor elasticity eliminates the deadweight loss changes from small restrictions on contributions (Prop. 2a), small entry restrictions continue to reduce

R. Riezman, J.D. Wilson / Journal of International Economics 42 (1997) 67–90   83

deadweight losses. It appears then that entry restrictions are often more desirable than contribution ceilings.

6. Competition for contributors

We have so far ignored competition among candidates for contributors. However, extending the model in this direction adds additional concerns about the desirability of contribution ceilings. To see this, let us now allow candidates to compete for the same set of contributors. In this case, the marginal "entry cost" required to become an active contributor is now a function of the total number of contributors, i.e., the single function $k = k(n_1 + n_2)$, replaces the separate functions, $k_i = k_i(n_i)$ for $i = 1,2$. Competition for contributors then results in an equalization of net transfers, with entry occurring until this common value equals the marginal entry cost:

$$\pi_1 T_1 - c_1 = \pi_2 T_2 - c_2 = k(n_1 + n_2). \tag{25}$$

This specification introduces a new external effect into the analysis. When the two candidates play a Nash game in contribution levels (c_i) and the number of contributors (n_i), an increase in n_i raises the tariff rate t_j that the other candidate must offer to attract its current n_j contributors, thereby raising B_j. This rise in B_j benefits candidate i by raising π_i. Recognizing this benefit, candidate i raises n_i beyond the point where B_i is minimized, given the candidate's chosen total contribution level, $C_i = c_i n_i$. Thus, we have the following result: Starting from the Nash equilibrium, both B_1 and B_2 can be reduced without changing either C_1 or C_2 by lowering n_1 and n_2, and raising c_1 and c_2. In this sense, the candidates obtain contributions from an inefficiently large number of contributors. Given that contribution ceilings cause candidates to substitute towards even more contributors, they worsen this type of inefficiency. We therefore have another argument for the relative undesirability of contribution ceilings.

The externality just identified eliminates the simple positive relation between total contributions and total deadweight losses in Lemma 2, on which Prop. 1 is based, thereby calling into further question the desirability of partial restrictions on political competition. There is no change in the subsequent results, but they provide evidence against the desirability of partial restrictions. Most of these results concern the case of infinite contributor elasticity, for which the current specification reduces to the original one [i.e., $k(n_1 + n_2)$ is a constant function]. Proposition 3, which concerns finite elasticities, remains valid under the new specification.[7] Thus, the desirability of contribution ceilings continues to depend critically on the size of contributor elasticity.

---

[7]The proof in Appendix A, which relies on Eq. (A.5), remains unchanged.

7. Other extensions

In this final section, we discuss some additional extensions of the analysis, beginning with those that are straightforward and ending with more speculative possibilities.

Although our model has been specified in terms of tariff protection, the results also apply to other distortionary means of transferring income to special-interest groups. In particular, none of our results would change if we replaced our tariff with a production subsidy. The only modification required of the analysis would be the replacement of $X_i' - D_i'$ with X_i' in the deadweight loss expressions. Similarly, the results extend to the case of industry subsidies in a closed economy, if we again assume linear demand and supply curves. In this case, the market clearing condition, $X(q) = D(q - s)$ for subsidy s, can be solved to obtain dX/ds, which now replaces $X_i' - D_i'$ in the deadweight loss expressions. Thus, the potentially harmful effects of entry restrictions and contribution ceilings apply not only to open-economy trade policies, but also to closed-economy subsidy policies.

Once alternative policy instruments are introduced, a natural question to ask is: Which is better? If we consider the choice between tariffs and production subsidies, then an obvious answer is that the latter is better, since it distorts only production, whereas tariffs also distort consumption decisions. However, this reasoning ignores the possibility that the higher deadweight losses associated with tariffs represent an additional cost to the candidates, in terms of reduced support from informed voters. Because of this cost, the candidates are likely to restrict tariff rates to levels below the equilibrium subsidy rates. For the case of identical candidates, it is in fact possible to show that tariff rates are so much lower than the subsidy rates that total deadweight losses are also lower.[8] Paradoxically, then, tariffs are preferred to production subsidies precisely because they are more distortionary. This example illustrates the usefulness of considering not only the economic equilibrium, but also the political equilibrium, when comparing the welfare effects of different policy instruments.

Another type of policy that would be useful to examine is a tax on campaign contributions. Some countries pursue the reverse policy of providing tax deductions for campaign contributions, thus implicitly subsidizing them. Eliminating this tax deduction should therefore have incentive effects similar to the imposition of a positive tax on contributions. Unlike the contribution ceilings discussed in this paper, a tax on total contributions does not appear to create the incentive to inefficiently substitute more protected industries for less protection per industry, thereby raising the deadweight loss per dollar of contributions. In particular, there should be no tax savings from making this substitution, if total contributions do not change. For this reason, such a tax might be more likely to lower the

---

[8]Wilson (1990) obtains a similar result for a model with a different specification of the objective functions for candidates.

R. Riezman, J.D. Wilson / Journal of International Economics 42 (1997) 67–90 85

deadweight loss from trade policies, through the incentives it creates to reduce total contributions. Moreover, an advantage of a tax over a move to less efficient policy instruments is that the tax payments represent a private cost of obtaining additional contributions, but not a social cost. A complete analysis would include the effect of this tax on the relative campaign contributions of different candidates. As we have seen, differences between candidates have important implications for the desirability of particular restrictions on political competition.

A related policy initiative is the use of public funds to help finance political campaigns. If matching grants are provided, then their welfare effects should be similar to a subsidy on contributions. Given our argument that a positive tax may reduce the deadweight losses associated with trade policy, the desirability of a subsidy (negative tax) is at least open to question. A system of lump-sum grants would seem to be preferable, because it does not directly reduce the effective price of obtaining contributions from private sources. But such grants may again affect the relative contributions obtained by different candidates, producing higher deadweight losses from one candidate's policies. One might try to prevent possible adverse effects by accompanying public financing with restrictions on the candidates' fundraising activities, but the ability to enforce such restrictions then becomes an important issue. Public financing of campaigns raises other issues such as incumbency advantages. These issues remain to be explored in future work.

These extensions, along with the exercises conducted in this paper, may be viewed as examples of "institutional comparative statics". Specifically, government policies are determined endogenously as part of a political equilibrium, subject to specific institutional specifications. In our exercise, changes in the allowable policy instruments are considered. Another possible exercise would be to consider an increase in the number of voters who are informed. Brecher (1982) touches on this issue in his comment on Findlay and Wellisz (1982) when he argues that greater "government resistance to lobbying" generally has an ambiguous effect on the equilibrium tariff rate. In our model, this "greater resistance" occurs when more voters are informed (a decrease in κ), in which case their opposition to distortionary trade policies exercises greater influence over the candidates. In the case of identical candidates, a decrease in κ does lower total contributions and the level of protection. However, differences between candidates complicate the story. Once a decline in κ has shifted the relevant reaction curves, one candidate's total contributions will be higher in the new equilibrium, in which case, that candidate's protection level may rise. Thus, the ambiguity identified by Brecher appears to persist.

The framework used in this paper might also be applicable to government decisions about public expenditure programs. At the local level, differences in property ownership and moving costs produce different incentives to become informed about government policy choices. If a resident owns no property and is able to costlessly switch communities (as assumed in standard "Tiebout models"), then he or she should care little about the efficiency of the community's tax and expenditure policies. On the other hand, a renter who lacks opportunities to move elsewhere has an important stake in these policies. Moreover, property owners should be particularly concerned with these policies, given their potential impacts on property values. Indeed, one justification for the favorable treatment of homeownership under the U.S. federal income tax is that homeownership leads to a more informed citizenry. It would be useful to examine local government decision-making in a system of communities where labor mobility and home-ownership patterns have implications for the degree to which individuals play a role as informed participants in their communities' political processes.

Finally, it would be useful to allow campaign contributions themselves to play an explicit informational role in the model. One interpretation of the current set-up is that campaign contributions "inform" the (initially) "uninformed voters" about desirable features of the candidates' platforms. An alternative specification would be to formally incorporate uncertainty about tariff rates into the model and allow campaign contributions to reduce the level of uncertainty.[9] The approach taken in the current paper has contained sufficient structure to enable us to identify the potential undesirability of various partial restrictions on political competition. However, further illuminating the "black-box" that typically characterizes the link between campaign contributions and trade policy in the endogenous-tariff litera-ture should be an important goal for future research.

Acknowledgments

We thank Phil Sprunger, Larry Rothenberg, and seminar participants at Carleton University, Johns Hopkins University, and the Midwest International Economics Meeting in Pittsburgh for useful comments and suggestions. Riezman acknowl-edges the financial support of the National Science Foundation under grant no. SES 90-23056. Wilson acknowledges the financial support of the National Science Foundation under grant no. SES-9209168.

Appendix A

Shifts in the reaction curves

Proposition 1 relies on several results about how marginal changes in n_i or c_i from their (unrestricted) equilibrium values shift the reaction curves. This section provides the proofs.

None of these marginal restrictions have first-order impacts on the election probabilities. Thus, restricting c_i or n_i will not alter the location of candidate j's

---

[9] Mayer and Li (1994) pursue this approach in their analysis of how probabilistic voting affects the conclusions of the Magee-Brock-Young model of endogenous trade policy.

R. Riezman, J.D. Wilson / Journal of International Economics 42 (1997) 67–90 87

reaction curve in Fig. 1, which continues to be defined by the function $C_j = R_j(C_i, \pi_j)$. On the other hand, the restricted c_i or n_i now enters the function describing i's reaction curve: $C_i = R_i(C_j, \pi_i, c_i)$ or $C_i = R_i(C_j, \pi_i, n_i)$.

To investigate how candidate i's curve shifts in response to a marginal reduction in n_i, we use the first-order conditions for c_i given by Eq. (13):

$$\kappa u_1 u_2 - (1 - \kappa) a n_i b_i^{*\prime}(T_i)\frac{c_i}{\pi_i} = 0.$$

As n_i declines, let us initially hold C_1 and C_2 fixed by raising c_i. Since the initial c_i and n_i are chosen to minimize the B_i associated with the chosen C_i, these changes cause no first-order change in B_i. To keep B_i fixed, t_i must rise following the fall in n_i. Thus, T_i rises, in which case the convexity of $b_i^{*}(T_i)$ implies that the left side of Eq. (13) falls. Using the second-order condition for c_i, it follows that c_i must decline to restore the equality in Eq. (13). Thus, C_i declines, enabling us to conclude that

$$\frac{\partial R_i}{\partial n_i} > 0. \tag{A.1}$$

Consider next a marginal reduction in c_i. In this case, the choice of n_i and, hence, C_i is described by the first-order condition given by Eq. (14). Using Eq. (18), this first-order condition can be rewritten as follows:

$$\kappa u_1 u_2 - (1 - \kappa) a \left\{ B_i + (n_i)^2 \frac{t_i}{X_i} \frac{k_i'}{\pi_i}[X_i' - D_i'] \right\} = 0. \tag{A.2}$$

It will be useful to use Eqs. (3) and (4) to further manipulate this first-order condition to obtain

$$\kappa u_1 u_2 - (1 - \kappa) a B_i \left[1 + 2\frac{n_i}{t_i X_i} \frac{k_i'}{\pi_i} \right] = 0. \tag{A.3}$$

As c_i declines, let us initially raise n_i to keep C_i fixed. Then $u_1 u_2$ in Eq. (A.3) stays fixed. Since candidate i was initially minimizing the B_i associated with this C_i, there is no first-order change in B_i. It follows that t_i declines to keep B_i fixed as n_i increases. As a result, $n_i/(t_i X_i)$ rises in Eq. (A.3), and the assumed convexity of $k_i(n_i)$ implies that $k_i'(n_i)$ cannot fall. Thus, the left side of Eq. (A.3) rises. Applying the second-order condition for n_i, it follows that n_i rises further to restore Eq. (A.3) to equality. Thus, the reduction in c_i causes C_i to rise. In other words,

$$\frac{\partial R_i}{\partial c_i} > 0. \tag{A.4}$$

Proof of Proposition 3. Consider the first-order condition for n_i given by Eq.

(A.3). By the assumption of identical candidates, $u_1 = u_2 = \pi_1 = \pi_2 = 1/2$ always, in which case Eq. (A.3) becomes

$$\kappa/4 - (1 - \kappa)aB_i\left[1 + 4\frac{n_i}{t_iX_i}k_i'\right] = 0. \tag{A.5}$$

To prove the proposition, initially hold n_1 and n_2 fixed while lowering c_1 and c_2. Then t_1 and t_2 fall to re-establish the zero-profit conditions for marginal contributors, thereby reducing B_1 and B_2. Now raise n_1 and n_2, with accompanying increases in t_1 and t_2 to maintain the zero-profit conditions, until B_1 and B_2 are at their original levels. These original levels are now obtained with higher levels of n_1 and n_2 and lower levels of t_1 and t_2. As a result, $[n_i/(t_iX_i)]\cdot k_i'$ is higher than before, implying that the left side of Eq. (A.5) is now negative. This side is increasing in both n_i and t_i (since it is also given by Eq. (A.3) above). Thus, the equality in Eq. (A.5) is restored by reducing n_i, with t_i falling to maintain the zero-profit condition. It follows that B_1 and B_2 are lower in the new equilibrium. Q.E.D.

Proof of Proposition 4. Using Eqs. (5) and (18) and the assumption that $k_i = 0$, rewrite first-order condition (Eq. (13)) for c_i as follows:

$$\kappa u_1 u_2 - (1 - \kappa)n_i a\frac{t_i}{X_i}T_i[X_i' - D_i'] = 0. \tag{A.6}$$

To prove (a), suppose that n_1 and n_2 are both reduced, and note that u_1u_2 rises or remains fixed under our assumptions. Thus, at fixed tariff rates, the left side of Eq. (A.6) rises for each i. Since t_i/X_i and T_i are both increasing in t_i (using the assumption of linear supply curves), the left side declines with t_i. Thus, both t_1 and t_2 must rise to restore the equality in Eq. (A.6) for i = 1 and i = 2.

Recall that the assumption of linear supply curves implies that

$$T_i = t_iX_i(p_i + t_i) - 0.5t_i^2X_i'. \tag{A.7}$$

Substituting Eq. (A.7) into Eq. (A.6) and rearranging yields

$$\kappa u_1 u_2 = (1 - \kappa)an_i t_i^2[1 - 0.5t_iX_i'/X_i]\cdot[X_i' - D_i'], \tag{A.8}$$

or, using the definition of excess burden,

$$\frac{\kappa u_1 u_2}{1 - 0.5t_iX_i'/X_i} = 2a(1 - \kappa)B_i. \tag{A.9}$$

Having observed that u_1u_2 and t_i both rise as n_i falls, we may conclude immediately from Eq. (A.9) that B_1 and B_2 both rise. This proves (a).

Turning to the first part of (b), reduce n_2 by a marginal amount, and consider its impact on the first-order condition for c_i obtained by substituting $T_i = C_i/(n_i\pi_i)$ into Eq. (13):

R. Riezman, J.D. Wilson / Journal of International Economics 42 (1997) 67–90 89

$$\kappa u_1 u_2 - (1 - \kappa)ab_i^{*\prime}\left(\frac{C_i}{n_i \pi_i}\right)\frac{C_i}{\pi_i} = 0. \tag{A.10}$$

We shall use this condition to prove that $u_1 u_2$ increases, in which case part (a) of the proposition completes the proof. Suppose instead that $u_1 u_2$ fails to increase. By Lemma 4, the reduction in n_2 lowers π_2. Thus, C_2 must fall to restore the equality in Eq. (A.10) for $i = 2$. It follows that C_1 must fall by a greater percentage amount to insure that $u_1 u_2$ does not increase. Holding c_1 fixed, the fall in C_2 and rise in π_1 increase the left side of Eq. (A.10) for $i = 1$. Then the second-order condition for c_1 implies that c_1 must rise to restore Eq. (A.1) to equality, thereby contradicting the previous conclusion that C_1 falls. Thus, $u_1 u_2$ rises, and Prop. 4a completes the proof.

Consider finally the second part of (b). We shall first prove that a reduction in n_1 must lower $u_1 u_2$. Suppose instead that $u_1 u_2$ fails to decline. By Lemma 4, the fall in n_1 lowers π_1 and raises π_2. With n_2 being held fixed, C_2 must then rise to restore the equality in Eq. (A.10) for $i = 2$. It follows that C_1 must rise by a greater percentage to prevent $u_1 u_2$ from declining. Given c_1, the rise in C_2, combined with the reductions in π_1 and n_1, cause the left side of Eq. (A.10) to decline for $i = 1$. Then the second-order condition for c_1 implies that c_1 falls to maintain the equality in Eq. (A.10), which contradicts our finding that C_1 rises. Thus, $u_1 u_2$ declines. By Eq. (A.6), t_2 also declines, and we may then conclude from Eq. (A.9) that B_2 falls. Q.E.D.

References

Baron, D., 1994, Spatial electoral competition and campaign contributions with informed and uninformed voters, American Political Science Review 88, 33–47.

Baron, D., 1989, Service-induced campaign contributions and the electoral equilibrium, Quarterly Journal of Economics 104, 45–72.

Brecher, R.A., 1982, Comment on "Endogenous tariffs, the political economy of trade restrictions, and welfare," by Ronald Findlay and Stanislaw Wellisz, in: J. Bhagwati, ed., Import competition and response (University of Chicago Press, Chicago) 234–238.

Grossman, G.M. and E. Helpman, 1994, Protection for sale, American Economic Review 84, 833–850.

Hillman, A.L., 1989, The political economy of protection (Harwood, Chur, Switzerland).

Hillman, A.L. and H.W. Ursprung, 1988, Domestic politics, foreign interests, and international trade policy, American Economic Review 78, 729–745.

Magee, S.P., W.A. Brock and L. Young, 1989, Black hole tariffs and endogenous policy theory (Cambridge University Press, Cambridge).

Mayer, W., 1984, Endogenous tariff formation, American Economic Review 74, 970–985.

Mayer, W. and J. Li, 1994, Interest groups, electoral competition, and probabilistic voting for trade policies, Economics and Politics 6, 59–78.

Riezman, R. and J.D. Wilson, 1995, Politics and trade policy, in: J. Banks and E. Hanushek (eds.), Modern political economy, (Cambridge University Press, New York), 108–144.

90   *R. Riezman, J.D. Wilson / Journal of International Economics 42 (1997) 67–90*

Rodrik, D., 1986, Tariffs, subsidies, and welfare with endogenous policy, Journal of International Economics 21, 285–299.

Sabato, L., 1984, PAC power: Inside the world of political action committees (Norton, New York).

Wilson, J.D., 1990, Are efficiency improvements in government transfer policies self-defeating in political equilibrium?, Economics and Politics 2, 241–258.

Available online at www.sciencedirect.com

SCIENCE  DIRECT•

European Economic Review 49 (2005) 1855–1876

www.elsevier.com/locate/econbase

The sources of protectionist drift in representative democracies

Didier Laussel[a], Raymond Riezman[b],*

[a]*GREQAM, University of Aix-Marseille 2, Marseille, France*
[b]*Department of Economics, University of Iowa, Iowa City, IA 52242, USA*

Received 14 February 2003; accepted 9 June 2004
Available online 25 August 2004

Abstract

We analyze a two country–two good model of international trade in which citizens in each country differ by their specific factor endowments. The trade policy in each country is set by the politician who has been elected by the citizens in a previous stage. Due to a delegation effect citizens generally favor candidates who are more protectionist than they are. The one-candidate-per-country equilibria exhibit a "protectionist drift" owing to this delegation effect. In addition, we find an additional source of protectionist drift that we call the "abstention effect". Not only do candidates wish to delegate to more protectionist colleagues, but these more protectionist colleagues who can win election, prefer still more protectionist candidates than themselves. Therefore, they have an incentive to abstain, that is, not run for election. We show that because of this abstention effect there exists a range of electable citizens all of whom are more protectionist than the median voter's most preferred candidate. We extend the analysis allowing two-candidate equilibria and the possibility that there are costs and benefits of holding office.
© 2004 Published by Elsevier Ltd.

JEL classification: F10; F13

Keywords: Tariffs; Political economy; Commercial policy

*Corresponding author. Tel.: + 1-319-335-0832.
E-mail addresses: laussel@univ-aix.fr (D. Laussel), raymond-riezman@uiowa.edu (R. Riezman).

0278-4319/$ - see front matter © 2004 Published by Elsevier Ltd.
doi:10.1016/j.euroecorev.2004.06.002

1. Introduction

It is well known that a one-shot Nash equilibrium between benevolent governments independently setting their trade policies exhibits strictly positive taxes on imports (or exports) in each country.[1] This "tariff war" equilibrium result generalizes the classical "optimum tariff argument" in which governments use tariff policy in order to take advantage of the country's collective market power on international commodities markets and modify the equilibrium terms of trade with the rest of the world.

While this line of research undoubtedly gives insight into the basic incentives existing in actual economies it has been criticized because it relies on the assumption that governments maximize social utility. Trade policy decisions are made by political entities and there has been a vast literature (surveyed superbly by Rodrik (1995)) examining the link between trade policy and political decision making.

What we do is to merge the "tariff war" equilibrium concept with political economy considerations to come up with an explanation for tariffs that is based on political economy motivations, but which is driven by terms-of-trade effects of tariffs. The political economy approach we follow has its roots in a paper by Wolfgang Mayer (1984). Mayer's paper marked an important step towards a positive approach to trade policy. He showed that if the indirect utility functions of the citizens in each country are single-peaked and the trade policy is determined by direct democracy (voters vote directly for a policy), then the equilibrium tariff in country i is the tariff preferred by the median voter. The "Mayer equilibrium" is hence equivalent to a two country Nash equilibrium in trade policies where the policies are the ones preferred by the two median voters. In a classical 2X2X2 framework where the distribution of capital is more skewed than the distribution of labor in the capital-rich country then the equilibrium trade policy is more protectionist in the capital-rich country and less protectionist in the capital-poor country.[2] Hence, at a "Mayer equilibrium" there is more protection than at the equilibrium between social utility maximizing governments. In this case, considering the influence of political decision making results in a general tendency toward more protectionist equilibria.

We build on Mayer's work by changing the direct democracy framework to a representative democracy framework (voters vote for candidates) in which candidates are chosen endogenously à la Besley and Coate (1997). We find that there is a "protectionist drift" in a representative democracies framework. We borrow from Besley and Coate (1997,1998a,b) and Osborne and Slivinski (1996) the idea of "citizen candidates": the future policymaker is chosen in each country among the citizens who are willing to run for election and these citizens are unable to commit to a given policy. Rather, citizens elected implement the policy associated with their given "type" as in Mayer's model. This leads to a "delegation effect".

---

[1]See Johnson (1953–1954) and Kennan and Riezman (1988).

[2]In what follows we assume that the mean and median voter are the same so our results do not rely on the skewness of the distribution of labor.

D. Laussel, R. Riezman / European Economic Review 49 (2005) 1855–1876　　　1857

Since the election stage takes place before the trade policy selection and changes in the "type" of the policymaker does have strategic effects on the trade policy equilibrium, voters generally favor the election of somebody whose type differs from their own.

We show that there exists a one-candidate-per-country equilibrium in which the selected policymaker in country i ($i = 1, 2$) is the ideal candidate of the median voter and is unambiguously more protectionist than her and that in every two-candidates-per-country equilibrium the *expected* type of the elected policymaker in country i ($i = 1, 2$) is the preferred type of the median voter. Thus, delegation effects produce "protectionist drift". This result is similar to those found by others who have investigated delegation effects in a representative democracy framework for different policy questions (Persson and Tabellini, 1992, 1994, 1996; Chari et al., 1997; Besley and Coate, 1998a). In addition, Willmann (2002) studies delegation in a Grossman–Helpman framework with political decisions made by a legislature. Gatsios and Karp (1991, 1995) show that in the context of a customs union, delegation can lead to more protection because members of a customs union may benefit from delegating the power to set external tariffs to one of its members.

We go on to show, however, that besides delegation effects, there is an additional source for protectionist drift in a representative democracy when candidates are purely outcome-motivated. This is what we call the "abstention effect". Not only do candidates wish to delegate to more protectionist colleagues, but these more protectionist colleagues who can win election, prefer still more protectionist candidates than themselves. Therefore, they have an incentive to abstain, that is, not run for election. We show that because of this "abstention effect" there exists in one-candidate-per-country equilibria a range of electable citizens all of whom are more protectionist than the median voter's most preferred candidate. Thus, candidates who are more protectionist than the ideal candidate of the median voter may run unopposed for election because the only citizens who could defeat them choose not to run. Moreover, in two-candidates-per-country equilibria, this abstention effect prevents policy convergence: the two candidates in country i ($i = 1, 2$) have to be far apart in order that one of them does not find it worthwhile to withdraw her application.

We also introduce the possibility that there may be costs and benefits associated with holding office. In one-candidate equilibria, the larger the net benefits from holding office the smaller the set of possible equilibria. With two-candidate equilibria, more benefits mean less dispersion in candidate types. The interesting implication of this result is that as holding office becomes more unpleasant (larger negative net benefits) there will be more dispersion between candidates.

2. The model

There are two countries, 1 and 2, producing two goods, A and B, with the help of specific factors. In each sector one unit of specific factor is needed to produce one unit of the good under perfect competition. Hence y_{ij} will denote both the output of

1858   *D. Laussel, R. Riezman / European Economic Review 49 (2005) 1855–1876*

good i in country j and the overall stock of the specific factor in sector i of country j. There are N_j citizens in country j. Each citizen k is endowed with $(y_{Aj}/N_j) + \theta_k$ units of factor A and y_{Bj}/N_j units of factor B such that $\sum_{k=1}^{k=N_j} \theta_k = 0$. We suppose for the sake of simplicity that, in each country, the average and median endowments of factor A do coincide. In other words if m is the median voter $\theta_m = 0$. In the following, θ_k will be the citizen k's "type".

Citizen k has a quasi-linear utility function $U(c_{Ak}, c_{Bk}) = \alpha c_{Ak} - \frac{1}{2}c_{Ak}^2 + c_{Bk}$, $\alpha > 0$, which is the same in both countries. In equilibrium all consumers in country j will have the same demand for good A which will be denoted c_{Aj}.

Under free trade it is straightforward to show that country i is a net exporter of good A if and only if its output per head in sector A is larger than in country j, i.e. $y_{Ai}N_j - y_{Aj}N_i \geqslant 0$. Without any loss of generality we will assume that the output of good A per head is larger in country 1, hence country 1 exports good A.

Assumption 1. Under free trade $N_2 y_{A1} - N_1 y_{A2} > 0$.

Let good B be the numeraire good. The price of the good A in country j is p_j. Throughout we assume that each country levies import taxes or export taxes on good A. The respective specific taxes on exports and imports of good A in countries 1 and 2 are t_1 and t_2 and the international price of good A is defined by $p = p_1 + t_1 = p_2 - t_2$. This is the price which one country must pay to the other in order to receive one unit of good A (or the price which it receives when it sells one unit of good A to the other country). In country j citizens receive a uniform lump-sum transfer f_j and the government budget constraints in countries 1 and 2 are respectively

$$t_1(y_{A1} - N_1 c_{A1}) = N_1 f_1,$$
$$t_2(N_2 c_{A2} - y_{A2}) = N_2 f_2. \tag{1}$$

In country j each citizen k has the same demand $\alpha - p_j$ for good A. Hence the market-clearing equilibrium condition for good A is easily derived as

$$(N_1 + N_2)(\alpha - p) + N_1 t_1 - N_2 t_2 = y_{A1} + y_{A2} \tag{2}$$

and then we obtain the equilibrium international price as

$$p = \alpha + \frac{N_1 t_1 - N_2 t_2 - y_A}{N_1 + N_2}, \tag{3}$$

where $y_A = y_{A1} + y_{A2}$. It follows that in country 1 we obtain

$$c_{A1} = \frac{N_2(t_1 + t_2) + y_A}{N_1 + N_2} \tag{4}$$

for all $k = 1, 2, \ldots, N_1$, while in country 2,

$$c_{A2} = \frac{-N_1(t_1 + t_2) + y_A}{N_1 + N_2} \tag{5}$$

for all $k = 1, 2, \ldots, N_2$.

D. Laussel, R. Riezman / European Economic Review 49 (2005) 1855–1876   1859

The budget constraint for individual k in country i is given by

$$p_i c_{Ai} + c_{Bi} = p_i\left(\frac{y_{Ai}}{N_i} + \theta_k\right) + \frac{y_{Bi}}{N_i} + f_i. \tag{6}$$

Using (1) and (6) the indirect utility function of a citizen k in country 1 is now obtained as

$$U_k^1(t_1, t_2) = \alpha c_{A1} - \frac{1}{2}c_{A1}^2 + p\left(\frac{y_{A1}}{N_1} - c_{A1}\right) + \frac{y_{B1}}{N_1} + (p - t_1)\theta_k$$

with p and c_{A1} given respectively by Eqs. (3) and (4).

In country 2 the indirect utility function of a citizen k is obtained as

$$U_k^2(t_1, t_2) = \alpha c_{A2} - \frac{1}{2}c_{A2}^2 + p\left(\frac{y_{A2}}{N_2} - c_{A2}\right) + \frac{y_{B2}}{N_2} + (p + t_2)\theta_k,$$

where p and c_{A2} given respectively by Eqs. (3) and (5).

Let us now define the game which is played. In the first stage, and in each country, each citizen decides whether or not she will run for election in order to represent the community. The entry decisions are strategic: the citizens decide whether to run or not by evaluating the potential benefit from running which, for each of them, depends on the entry decisions of all the other citizens in the same country and in the other country. In the second stage, and in each country, the polity selects its representative in an election. All citizens have one vote which, if used, must be cast for one of the self-declared candidates. Candidates cannot credibly commit to anything other than implementing their most preferred policies. Voters know this and vote accordingly. The candidate who receives the most votes is elected and, when the candidates tie, all tied candidates win with equal probability. The types of the candidates (i.e. their endowments of the specific factor A) are perfectly observable both inside and outside the country. In the third stage the representative selected in the second stage in country j selects the country's trade policy (i.e. the value of t_j). If nobody runs for office the default policy $t_j = 0$ (*laissez faire*) is applied.

Note that we follow Besley and Coate (1997) in supposing that there is no exogenous benefit from holding office[3] (such as ego rents, resource diversion and the like): candidates are only outcome-motivated. We will indicate below how the removal of this assumption can modify some of our results.

In this paper we will first focus on the one-candidate equilibria, i.e. the equilibria where, in each country, one and only one candidate runs unopposed, and on two-candidate equilibria where, in one country at least, two winning candidates run against each other. Besides convenience, there are also some good theoretical arguments for giving less attention to n-candidate equilibria when $n > 2$. In the first place, assuming that people vote *strategically*, contrary to Osborne and Slivinski (1996) who assume *sincere* voting, Besley and Coate (1997) have been able to show that, in a one-dimensional model, some very mild assumptions are enough to rule out elections where more than two *winning* candidates run. The basic argument is

---

[3]For a different assumption see for instance Osborne and Slivinsky (1996).

rather intuitive. If three or more candidates tie and if there is a subset of citizens nearly indifferent between two nearby candidates, it is always true (in a large country with continuous variations in endowments) that they will prefer the sure election of one of these two to the lottery between all the candidates.

We can also rule out equilibria with two winning and one or several losing candidates. The argument runs as follows: with two winning candidates the losing candidate incurs the (even infinitesimal) cost of running only if this prevents the election of her less-preferred candidate and it follows that she must be in-between the two candidates and that the median voters are voting for her. If she dropped out the medians voters would split equally their votes between the two remaining candidates and thus her presence, which is costly, can have no effect. The only remaining possibility is the existence of equilibria with one winning and three or more losing candidates. They correspond however to rather strange bootstrap equilibria which will not be considered here.

3. Trade policy selection

Let the citizens r and s be the representatives chosen respectively in countries 1 and 2 and θ_r and θ_s their respective "types". The first-order conditions for the trade policy game are derived as

$$-t_1 N_2 + \frac{N_2 y_{A1} - N_1 y_{A2} - N_1 N_2 (t_1 + t_2)}{N_1 + N_2} - \theta_r N_2 = 0 \tag{7}$$

for country 1 and

$$-t_2 N_1 + \frac{N_2 y_{A1} - N_1 y_{A2} - N_1 N_2 (t_1 + t_2)}{N_1 + N_2} - \theta_s N_1 = 0 \tag{8}$$

for country 2.

It is easy to check that these conditions are both necessary and sufficient (i.e. U_r^1 and U_s^2 are respectively strictly concave with respect to t_1 and t_2) and that t_1 and t_2 are *strategic substitutes*.[4] A Nash equilibrium of the trade policy game is any couple $(t_1(\theta_r, \theta_s), t_2(\theta_r, \theta_s))$ that is a solution of Eqs. (7) and (8). It is straightforward to show that these equations have a unique solution:

$$t_1(\theta_r, \theta_s) = \frac{1}{2} \frac{(N_2 y_{A1} - N_1 y_{2A}) - \theta_s N_2 N_1 - \theta_r (2N_2 + N_1) N_2}{N_2 (N_1 + N_2)}, \tag{9}$$

$$t_2(\theta_r, \theta_s) = \frac{1}{2} \frac{(N_2 y_{A1} - N_1 y_{2A}) + \theta_r N_2 N_1 + \theta_s (N_2 + 2N_1) N_1}{(N_1 + N_2) N_1}. \tag{10}$$

As can be seen from Eq. (9) introducing distributional considerations will tend to reduce the export tax in country 1 since the owners of factor A are hurt by the tax. Hence, the larger is the country 1 policymaker's factor A endowment the lower is the

---

[4]In other types of models in which t_1 and t_2 are strategic complements the results could change.

D. Laussel, R. Riezman / European Economic Review 49 (2005) 1855–1876 1861

specific tax on country 1 exports of good A. The same considerations (see Eq. (10)) will tend to increase the tariff in country 2 since the tariff increases incomes of specific factor A owners in country 2.

We next solve for the equilibrium when each country's median voter is elected. One could think of this as a result of Downsian political competition.[5] The equilibrium values of t_1 and t_2 can be obtained from (9) and (10) simply by setting $\theta_r = \theta_s = 0$.

$$t_1(0,0) = \frac{1}{2}\frac{(N_2 y_{A1} - N_1 y_{2A})}{N_2(N_1 + N_2)}, \tag{11}$$

$$t_2(0,0) = \frac{1}{2}\frac{(N_2 y_{A1} - N_1 y_{2A})}{N_1(N_1 + N_2)}. \tag{12}$$

In each country the trade policy is the optimal trade policy of *the median voter* as in Mayer (1984). In this case, country 1 sets a positive export tax and country 2 has a positive tariff. They differ only depending on country size, *the larger country setting the larger tax*. Thus, the larger the country 2 policymaker's factor A endowment the larger is the specific tax on imports of good A in country 2. It is, moreover, easy to compare the median voter utility at a "Mayer equilibrium" to her utility under free trade. Subtracting the latter from the former one obtains for country 1:[6]

$$\frac{(2N_1 - 3N_2)(N_2 y_{A1} - N_1 y_{A2})^2}{8N_1^2 N_2(N_1 + N_2)^2}.$$

Obviously the median voter's utility in country 1 is larger at the Mayer equilibrium iff $N_1 > \frac{3}{5}(N_1 + N_2)$, i.e. country one is large enough. This result is consistent with Kennan and Riezman (1988). The utility function of any given citizen in either country is indeed strictly concave (and hence single-peaked) and the median voter theorem can be applied. In the next section we determine whether this is an equilibrium in a "citizen candidate" model of political equilibrium.

It is also possible to determine the conditions under which country 1 is a net exporter of good A. Net exports of good A by country 1 are easily obtained as

$$\frac{1}{2}\frac{(\theta_r - \theta_s)N_2 N_1 + (N_2 y_{A1} - N_1 y_{A2})}{(N_1 + N_2)}.$$

It is thus a priori possible that the natural (i.e. free-trade) specialization of countries (determined by the sign of $(N_2 y_{A1} - N_1 y_{A2})$) be reversed by a biased choice of policymakers in one or both countries:[7] this could occur for instance if the country 2 policymaker's endowment in factor A was much larger than country 1 policymaker's. Of course this can't occur under direct democracy. We will show below that this never occurs in equilibrium under representative democracy.

---

[5]In each country two office-motivated candidates who care only about winning the elections both commit in equilibrium to the policy preferred by the median voter.

[6]Symmetric results for country 2 are readily obtained.

[7]"Natural" specialization occurs not only under free trade but also when the policies are set in each country by the median voters ($\theta_r = \theta_s = 0$).

1862   *D. Laussel, R. Riezman / European Economic Review 49 (2005) 1855–1876*

4. Voting

In this section we examine a model of "citizen candidates". We assume that, in each country, the citizens can anticipate the utility imputations which arise from the policies selected by each possible couple (θ_r, θ_s) of policymakers. In country 1 for instance, a citizen k will receive a utility level $U_k^1(t_1(\theta_r, \theta_s), t_2(\theta_r, \theta_s), \theta_k) = V^1(\theta_r, \theta_s, \theta_k)$ which depends on its own endowment and on the types of the domestic and the foreign policymakers. We show in the appendix that V^1 and V^2 are strictly concave respectively with respect to θ_r and θ_s. We first analyze the delegation effect.

4.1. The delegation effect

In this section we show that each policymaker wants to delegate the authority to make trade policy to a more protectionist candidate. It is now straightforward to derive explicitly who is the "ideal" policymaker for a θ_k-type citizen of country j given the policymaker's type in the other country. In country 1

$$\theta_r(\theta_k, \theta_s) = \frac{2N_1\theta_k(N_1 + N_2) - (N_2 y_{A1} - N_1 y_{A2}) + \theta_s N_2 N_1}{(3N_2 + 2N_1)N_1}. \tag{13}$$

Eq. (13) clearly shows that the policymaker type which is preferred by a type θ_k-citizen generally differs from θ_k. The source of this difference lies in the strategic effect of the choice of a policymaker. Selecting a candidate with a lower factor A endowment leads (see Eq. (9)) to a higher equilibrium value of the export tax t_1 in the country 1. Since from Eq. (7) t_1 and t_2 are strategic substitutes this elicits from the foreign country policymaker a *lower equilibrium tariff* t_2 (see Eq. (10)). This is beneficial for all citizens whose types are larger than some critical value since, as net sellers of good A, they benefit from the resulting higher international price for it.[8]

In Fig. 1 we show how the desired θ_r varies with θ_k for a given value of θ_s (drawn for $\theta_s > 0$). $\hat{\theta}_k(\theta_s) = \theta_s - ((y_{A1}/N_1) - (y_{A2}/N_2))$ is the critical endowment value in country 1: any citizen with an endowment θ_k larger (resp. lower) than this value favors a candidate with a lower (resp. larger) factor A endowment than her own (see Fig. 1). In Fig. 1, all factor owners who own more than $\hat{\theta}_k$ of factor A want to delegate the power to make trade policy to a candidate who owns less factor A than they do. These types will clearly be in the majority whenever $\theta_s \leqslant 0$. θ_r^* is the type preferred by the median voter in country 1.

In country 2

$$\theta_s(\theta_k, \theta_r) = \frac{2N_2\theta_k(N_1 + N_2) + (N_2 y_{A1} - N_1 y_{A2}) + \theta_r N_2 N_1}{(2N_2 + 3N_1)N_2} \tag{14}$$

and the corresponding critical endowment value $\hat{\theta}_k(\theta_r) = \theta_r + ((y_{A1}/N_1) - (y_{A2}/N_2))$. This case works differently than the export case. In country 2, owners of factor A benefit from higher tariffs in two ways. First, they improve the terms of

---

[8]The receipts from export taxes are distributed in a uniform lump-sum fashion to the citizens so that the domestic agents do care about the international price p (see the definition of U_k^1 in Section 2).

D. Laussel, R. Riezman / European Economic Review 49 (2005) 1855–1876   1863

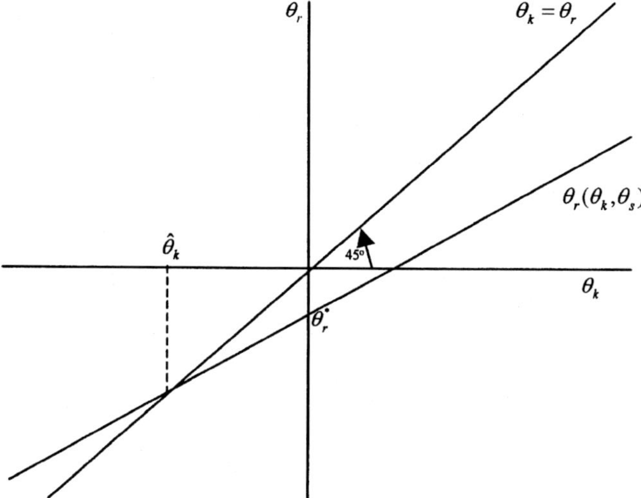

Fig. 1.

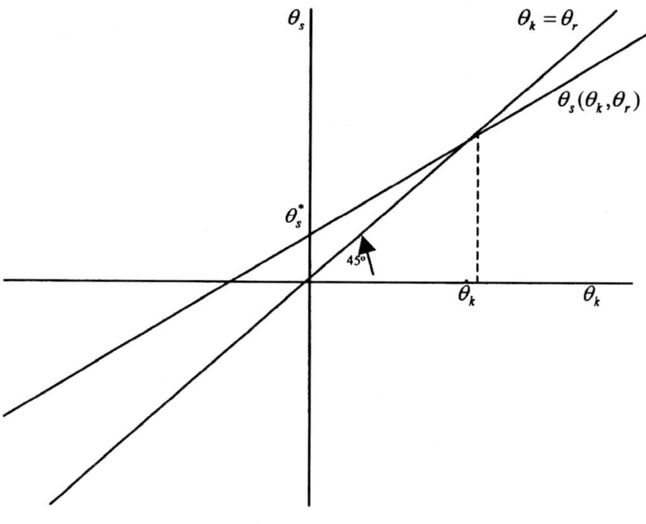

Fig. 2.

trade as before, but now increases in the tariff increase the domestic price of good A leading to an increase in income for voters who own large amounts of factor A. So, in the case of the importing country, most factor owners prefer a policymaker who owns more A than they do. Fig. 2 illustrates this. Here all factor owners to the left of $\hat{\theta}_k$, clearly a majority whenever $\theta_r \geqslant 0$, wish to delegate the power to make trade policy to someone who owns more factor A than they do. θ_s^* is the type preferred by the median voter in country 2.

1864   *D. Laussel, R. Riezman / European Economic Review 49 (2005) 1855–1876*

We now define single candidate equilibria.

Definition. (θ_r^*, θ_s^*) is a *single candidate equilibrium* if:

(i) given that candidates θ_r^* and θ_s^* are willing to serve no other candidate who could beat (θ_r^*, θ_s^*) in their respective country wants to serve;

(ii) candidates θ_r^* and θ_s^* prefer serving rather than have nobody serve.

It is now straightforward to see that there exists an equilibrium where, in each country, there is one and only one candidate who is the "ideal policymaker" of the median voter. To solve for this equilibrium set $\theta_k = 0$ in (13) and (14) and solve the resulting equations to get

$$\theta_r^* = \frac{1}{3}\frac{N_1 y_{A2} - N_2 y_{A1}}{N_1(N_1 + N_2)}, \tag{15}$$

$$\theta_s^* = \frac{1}{3}\frac{N_2 y_{A1} - N_1 y_{A2}}{N_2(N_1 + N_2)}. \tag{16}$$

This equilibrium is illustrated in Fig. 3. $\theta_r(0, \theta_s)$ is a reaction curve that indicates the desired type of the median voter in country 1 given that country 2 has selected a type θ_s as its political decision maker. This function is obtained from Eq. (13) by setting $\theta_k = 0$. $\theta_s(0, \theta_r)$ is country 2's reaction function obtained by setting $\theta_k = 0$ in Eq. (14).

Moreover, *these candidates are more protectionist than the respective median voters of their countries: in the exporting country they own less factor A than average and in*

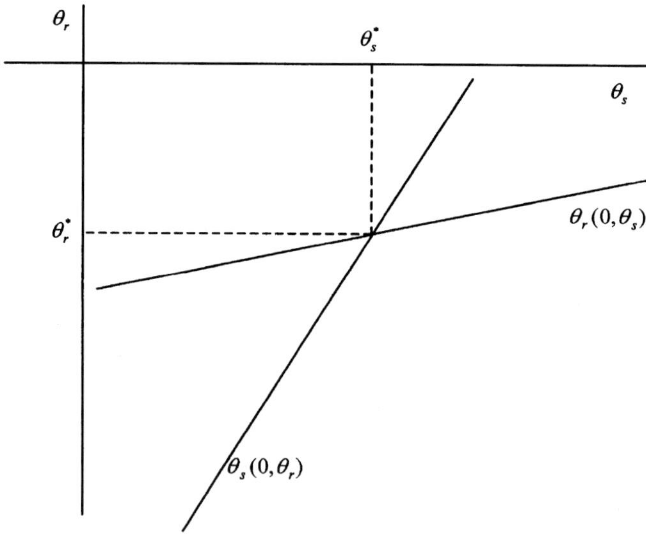

Fig. 3.

D. Laussel, R. Riezman / European Economic Review 49 (2005) 1855–1876　　　1865

the importing country they hold a larger than average amount of factor A. This follows from a pure delegation effect in each country: delegating the trade policy choice to somebody more protectionist than themselves is a convenient way for the median voters to credibly commit their respective countries to more aggressive trade policies.

Proposition 1. *There exists a one-candidate-per-country-equilibrium* (θ_r^*, θ_s^*) *where*

$$\theta_r^* = \frac{1}{3}\frac{N_1 y_{A2} - N_2 y_{A1}}{N_1(N_1 + N_2)}, \tag{17}$$

$$\theta_s^* = \frac{1}{3}\frac{N_2 y_{A1} - N_1 y_{A2}}{N_2(N_1 + N_2)}, \tag{18}$$

$$t_1^* = t_2^* = \frac{1}{3}\left(\frac{y_{A1}}{N_1} - \frac{y_{A2}}{N_2}\right). \tag{19}$$

Proof. (i) Clearly $\theta_r^* = \theta_r(0, \theta_s^*)$ and $\theta_s^* = \theta_s(0, \theta_r^*)$, i.e. (θ_r^*, θ_s^*) is a Nash equilibrium where the policymaker selected in each country is the best reply of the median voter of this country to the policymaker chosen in the other country; straightforwardly it is a best reply for the other citizens in both countries to stay outside the electoral competition since they would win with zero probability;

(ii) It remains to show that it is better for the candidates in both countries to run for office rather than to not run; remember that we assumed that if there is no candidate, the default policy in the country i is *laissez faire* (i.e. $t_i = 0$).

Let us consider country 1: *laissez faire* (and hence not running for office) is formally equivalent to having a policymaker of type $\tilde{\theta}_r$ who would select $t_1(\tilde{\theta}_r, \theta_s^*) = 0$, i.e. such that

$$\tilde{\theta}_r = \frac{1}{3}\frac{(N_2 y_{A1} - N_1 y_{A2})(2N_1 + 3N_2)}{(N_1 + N_2)N_2(2N_2 + N_1)} > 0. \tag{20}$$

It is then straightforward to show that $\hat{\theta}_k(\theta_s^*) - \theta_r^* = \frac{2}{3}((-N_2 y_{A1} + N_1 y_{A2})/N_1 N_2) < 0$ and hence $\theta_r(\theta_r^*, \theta_s^*) < \theta_r^* < 0 < \tilde{\theta}_r$: the strict concavity of $V^1(\theta_r, \theta_s, \theta_k)$ with respect to θ_r now implies that $V^1(\theta_r^*, \theta_s^*, \theta_r^*) > V^1(\tilde{\theta}_r, \theta_s^*, \theta_r^*)$;

In country 2, *laissez faire* is equivalent to having a default policymaker of type

$$\tilde{\theta}_s = \frac{1}{3}\frac{-(3N_1 + 2N_2)(N_2 y_{A1} - N_1 y_{A2})}{(N_1 + N_2)N_1(N_2 + 2N_1)} < 0, \tag{21}$$

where $\hat{\theta}_k(\theta_r^*) - \theta_s^* = \frac{2}{3}((N_2 y_{A1} - N_1 y_{A2})/N_1 N_2) > 0$ and hence $\theta_s(\theta_r^*, \theta_s^*) > \theta_s^* > 0 > \tilde{\theta}_s$. Once again, the strict concavity of $V^2(\theta_s, \theta_r, \theta_k)$ with respect to θ_s implies that $V^2(\theta_s^*, \theta_r^*, \theta_s^*) > V^2(\tilde{\theta}_s, \theta_r^*, \theta_s^*)$. □

It is interesting to compare the values of t_1 and t_2 at the above equilibrium with their equilibrium values under direct democracy. This can be thought of as measuring the delegation effect. It is straightforward to show that *the import and export taxes are both larger under representative democracy, if and only if,* $N_i/(N_1 + N_2) < \frac{2}{3}$, $i = 1, 2$. That is, if countries are roughly the same size the delegation effect results in a higher export tax and a higher tariff. However, if countries are different sizes the delegation effect will reflect country size. Suppose, for example, that country one is relatively large. In particular, suppose, $N_1/(N_1 + N_2) > \frac{2}{3}$. It is easy to show that the equilibrium value of t_1 is *smaller* than $t_1(0,0)$ but the equilibrium value of t_2 is now *larger* than $t_2(0,0)$. Thus, when countries are different sizes delegation leads to higher tariffs (or export taxes) for "smaller" countries and lower tariffs (or export taxes) for "bigger" countries. The overall level of protection is, nevertheless, higher under delegation than under direct democracy. While it is true that the equilibrium export tax may be lower under delegation (representative democracy) when country 1 is large enough, i.e. $N_1/(N_1 + N_2) > \frac{2}{3}$ this is more than compensated for by a much larger import tariff. Comparing $t_1 + t_2$ in both cases one finds $\frac{1}{2}((N_2 y_{A1} - N_1 y_{A2})/N_1 N_2)$ in the case of direct democracy versus $\frac{2}{3}((N_2 y_{A1} - N_1 y_{A2})/N_1 N_2)$ in the case of a representative democracy (delegation). Since the volume of trade is unambiguously decreasing in $(t_1 + t_2)$ we can reasonably conclude that trade policy is globally more protectionist under representative democracy.

Strategic commitment through the election of a policymaker who is more protectionist than the median voter allows a "small" country to obtain a less protectionist trade policy from the bigger country. The intuition can be seen by comparing (11) and (12) with (19). In the direct democracy equilibrium ((11) and (12)) the large country charges a higher tariff/export tax than the smaller country. This accords with standard theoretical results. Once countries can delegate the power to set tariffs we see from (19) that the tariff/export tax is the same regardless of country size. Thus, it follows that moving from the direct democracy case to the delegation case results in the large country tariff/export tax falling while the small country's rises.

The possibility of delegating means that the "small" country can effectively negate the advantage that the "big" country has at the direct democracy equilibrium. Why does this occur? It follows from Eqs. (9) and (10) that the equilibrium value of the export tax of the large country (t_1) is much more sensitive to variations in the policymaker's type in the small country than the equilibrium value of the import tariff in the small country (t_2) is sensitive to variations in the policymaker's type in country 1, i.e. $|\partial t_1/\partial \theta_s| = N_1/(N_1 + N_2) > |\partial t_2/\partial \theta_r| = N_2/(N_1 + N_2)$. Moreover, from Eq. (3) the equilibrium terms of trade (i.e. international price of good A) are more sensitive to variations in the export tax than to variations in the import tariff. *It follows that the strategic effect of delegation is larger for the smaller country.*

The effect on welfare of moving from direct democracy to a delegation equilibrium follow from the results on tariffs. "Small" countries benefit from the delegation effect as follows from a comparison of the utility of the median voter at the Mayer equilibrium with her utility at the "delegation equilibrium" of Proposition 1. Subtracting the former from the latter one obtains for country 1

$$\frac{(3N_2 - 10N_1)(N_2 y_{A1} - N_1 y_{A2})^2}{72N_1^2(N_1 + N_2)^2}.$$

D. Laussel, R. Riezman / European Economic Review 49 (2005) 1855–1876   1867

Thus, the median voter in country 1 is better off at the "delegation equilibrium" than at the "Mayer equilibrium" iff $N_1 < \frac{3}{13}(N_1 + N_2)$ i.e., country one is small enough.

4.2. The abstention effect

In contrast with the model of representative democracy developed by Besley and Coate (1997,1998a,b) (see also Osborne and Slivinski, 1996) in which the preferred candidate of any given citizen is a citizen of the same type, there exist here other one-candidate equilibria than the equilibrium where the policymakers who are chosen are the preferred candidates of the median voters. Implicit in Proposition 1 is the notion that voters θ_r^* and θ_s^* are willing to run for office and serve if elected. There is one difficulty with this assumption. Both type θ_r^* and θ_s^* voters prefer a citizen of different type than themselves to run (see Fig. 1). Let us consider for instance the electoral competition process in country 2 (the same analysis can be applied to the electoral competition in country 1). In country 2, for a given type θ_r-policymaker selected in country 1, a type θ_s candidate such that $\theta_s \neq \theta_s(0, \theta_r)$ runs unopposed. For this to happen it is necessary and sufficient that (a) this candidate prefers the political outcome following her election to the default (*laissez faire*) outcome, (b) there exists no citizen who would prefer her own election to the election of the single candidate and who would be preferred to her opponent by a majority of citizens.

Note that the first condition is satisfied if and only if the single candidate strictly prefers her own election to the election of some other citizen who would favor *laissez faire* (i.e. $t_2 = 0$). It is straightforward from (10) to derive the type $\tilde{\theta}_s(\theta_r)$ of such a citizen:

$$\tilde{\theta}_s(\theta_r) = \frac{-N_2 y_{A1} + N_1 y_{A2} - \theta_r N_2 N_1}{N_1(N_2 + 2N_1)} = -\frac{N_2}{N_2 + 2N_1}\hat{\theta}_k(\theta_r). \tag{22}$$

We will come back to this condition below. Let us now determine exactly who are the citizens who would prefer their own election to the election of a θ_s-type citizen. One has to determine the type θ_k^* of citizen who is indifferent between herself and the type θ_s. Given the linear-quadratic nature of the indirect utility functions V, the value of θ_k^* is determined by solving the equation $\theta_s - \theta_s(\theta_k^*, \theta_r) = \theta_s(\theta_k^*, \theta_r) - \theta_k^*$. Using Eq. (14) we obtain

$$\theta_k^* = \frac{\theta_s N_2(2N_2 + 3N_1) - 2(y_{A1}N_2 - N_1 y_{A2}) - 2\theta_r N_2 N_1}{(2N_2 + N_1)N_2}. \tag{23}$$

There are now only two cases to be considered:

(i) $0 < \theta_s(0, \theta_r) < \hat{\theta}_k(\theta_r)$.[9]

A sufficient condition for a θ_s-type candidate to run unopposed is simply that $\theta_s(0, \theta_r) \leqslant \theta_s \leqslant 2\theta_s(0, \theta_r)$. In Fig. 4, let $A = \theta_s(0, \theta_r)$ and $B = 2\theta_s(0, \theta_r)$ and for simplicity call a candidate with an endowment of $\theta_s(0, \theta_r)(2\theta_s(0, \theta_r))$ candidate $A(B)$.

---

[9]Note that a sufficient condition for this set of inequalities is $\hat{\theta}_k(\theta_r) > 0$ since $\theta_s(0, \theta_r) = \hat{\theta}_k(\theta_r)N_1/(2N_2 + 3N_1)$.

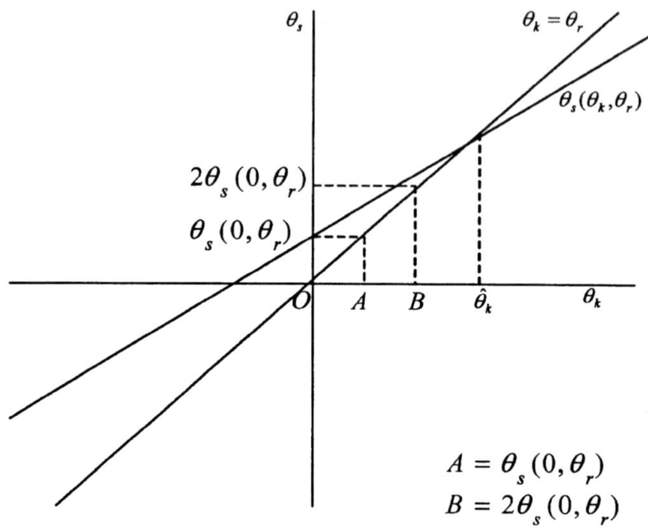

Fig. 4.

We first show that if any candidate between A and B chooses to run they will win. To see this consider candidate B. If candidate B runs she gets all votes to the right of the median voter. Candidates to the left of B do even better. Using Eq. (23) one can easily show that A prefers any candidate in the AB range to running herself. Extending that logic, all voters in the AB range would prefer a candidate to their *right* to themselves. But, they would prefer to run themselves rather than have someone to their *left* win. Therefore, any candidate between A and B is a one candidate equilibrium. Candidates closer to A get larger winning vote shares but would always prefer that someone to their right actually be elected.

We next show that candidates to the left of A or to the right of B cannot win. Any candidate to the left of A ($\theta_s < \theta_s(0,\theta_r)$) would be defeated by candidate A since the median voter (type $\theta_s(0,\theta_r)$) and all voters to the right of the median voter would prefer A. In addition, A would serve herself rather than have someone to her left be elected. For a candidate to the right of B ($\theta_s > 2\theta_s(0,\theta_r)$), one can show using Eq. (23) that the median voter would prefer to run herself (and would clearly win) rather than have a candidate to the right of B in office. That leaves candidates between A and B as possible winners of single candidate elections.

The distance OA in Fig. 4 measures the delegation effect. The median voter wants to delegate authority to a voter with OA more of the specific factor than she has. The distance from A to B measures the abstention effect. The voter at A, although in some sense the most "popular" candidate, actually prefers someone to her right to run. In fact, she prefers any voter between A and B to herself. So, any of those voters represent potential one-candidate equilibria. As you move from A to B the candidates are decreasing in "popularity" and increasing in their "eagerness" to run for election.

D. Laussel, R. Riezman / European Economic Review 49 (2005) 1855–1876 1869

(ii) When $\hat{\theta}_k(\theta_r) < \theta_s(0, \theta_r) < 0$ a sufficient condition for a θ_s-type candidate to run unopposed is simply that $\theta_s \leqslant \theta_s(0, \theta_r)$ and $\theta_k^* \leqslant 0$, i.e. $2\theta_s(0, \theta_r) \leqslant \theta_s \leqslant \theta_s(0, \theta_r)$. The logic is the same as case (i) above so we will not repeat the argument.

The same analysis can be applied to the electoral competition in country 1. Using Eqs. (13), (14), and (23) we can obtain a complete characterization of the set of one-candidate equilibria.

Proposition 2. *Given Assumption 1 any pair* (θ_r, θ_s) *such that*

$$\frac{-2(N_2 y_{A1} - N_1 y_{A2}) + 2\theta_s N_2 N_1}{(3N_2 + 2N_1)N_1} \leqslant \theta_r \leqslant \frac{-(N_2 y_{A1} - N_1 y_{A2}) + \theta_s N_2 N_1}{(3N_2 + 2N_1)N_1},$$

$$\frac{(N_2 y_{A1} - N_1 y_{A2}) + \theta_r N_2 N_1}{(2N_2 + 3N_1)N_2} \leqslant \theta_s \leqslant \frac{2(N_2 y_1 - N_1 y_2) + 2\theta_r N_2 N_1}{(2N_2 + 3N_1)N_2}.$$

is a one-candidate-per-country-equilibrium.

Obviously the equilibrium of Proposition 1 (where the single candidate in each country is the preferred candidate of the median voter) is one of these equilibria. There are, in addition, infinitely many other equilibria as shown in Fig. 5: any point belonging to the area ACBD corresponds to a possible equilibrium. At the more "extremist" of the symmetric equilibria (point B in Fig. 5) one obtains

$$\theta_r^{**} = -\frac{2}{3} \frac{(N_2 y_{A1} - N_1 y_{A2})(N_1 + 2N_2)}{(3N_1 N_2 + 2N_2^2 + 2N_1^2)N_1}, \tag{24}$$

$$\theta_s^{**} = \frac{2}{3} \frac{(N_2 y_{A1} - N_1 y_{A2})(N_2 + 2N_1)}{N_2(3N_1 N_2 + 2N_2^2 + 2N_1^2)}. \tag{25}$$

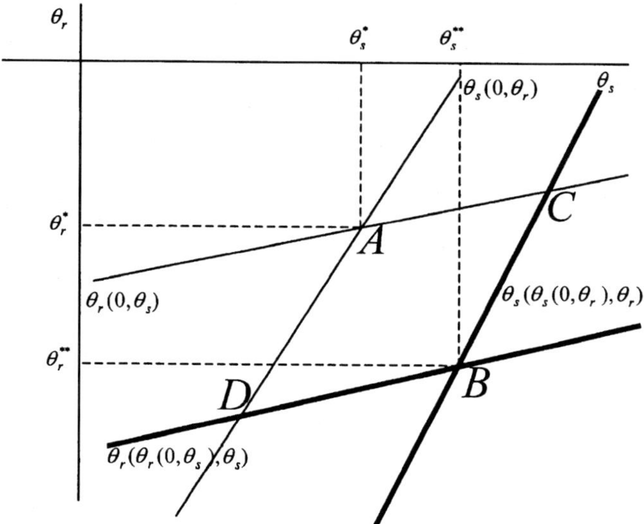

Fig. 5.

If these most "extremist" candidates are chosen the resulting tariff and export tax is (substituting Eqs. (24) and (25) into Eqs. (9) and (10))

$$t_1 = \frac{(2N_2 + N_1)(2N_1^2 + 5N_1N_2 + 4N_2^2)(N_2 y_{A1} - N_1 y_{A2})}{6N_1(2N_2^2 + 3N_1N_2 + 2N_1^2)N_2(N_1 + N_2)}, \tag{26}$$

$$t_2 = \frac{(N_2 + 2N_1)(4N_1^2 + 5N_1N_2 + 2N_2^2)(N_2 y_{A1} - N_1 y_{A2})}{6N_1(2N_2^2 + 3N_1N_2 + 2N_1^2)N_2(N_1 + N_2)}. \tag{27}$$

Note that the extent of the "protectionist drift" depends not only on the extent of the delegation and abstention effects in both countries but also on the strategic interaction between the two countries. In fact, the strategic complementarity between the policymakers limits the impact of the delegation and abstention effects as can be seen by noting that the value of θ_s^* above is less than twice the value of θ_s^{**}. However, it is still the case that if the country sizes are not too dissimilar then both the export tax and the tariff are higher than when only the delegation effect is considered (Proposition 1). Thus, both the delegation and abstention effects tend to result in higher protection levels.

We do obtain clearer results regarding the welfare of the median voter. The utility levels of the median voters in *both* countries are unambiguously lower at the "extremist" equilibrium B than at any of the other equilibria, the "delegation equilibrium," point A, at the Mayer equilibrium, point O and at the free trade equilibrium point.

5. Two-candidate equilibria

We now consider the case when, at the first stage of the game, there are, at least in one country, two candidates who decide to run for election. This may correspond either to equilibria in which in both countries there are two candidates or to equilibria in which two candidates run for election in one country and one candidate in the other country. Our analysis has to be modified in order to account for the possibility of two candidates running in one country, each of them having a probability 0.5 of winning.

Suppose that there are two candidates in each country. In country 1 the two candidate types are given by (θ_r^1, θ_r^2) and in country 2 they are (θ_s^1, θ_s^2). The *expected* utility $E(V^1((\theta_r^1, \theta_r^2), (\theta_s^1, \theta_s^2), \theta_k))$, of a citizen k in country 1 is then

$$E(V^1((\theta_r^1, \theta_r^2), (\theta_s^1, \theta_s^2), \theta_k)) = \tfrac{1}{4}(V^1(\theta_r^1, \theta_s^1, \theta_k) + V^1(\theta_r^1, \theta_s^2, \theta_k)$$
$$+ V^1(\theta_r^2, \theta_s^1, \theta_k) + V^1(\theta_r^2, \theta_s^2, \theta_k)). \tag{28}$$

The expected utility of citizen k when there are two candidates in one country and one candidate in the other country is easily derived in the same way. A very useful feature of our model is the linearity of the function V^1 with respect to θ_s (and, at the same time, of the function V^2 with respect to θ_r). This linearity allows us to write (28)

D. Laussel, R. Riezman / European Economic Review 49 (2005) 1855–1876 1871

more simply as

$$\mathrm{E}(V^1((\theta_r^1,\theta_r^2),(\theta_s^1,\theta_s^2),\theta_k)) = \tfrac{1}{2}(V^1(\theta_r^1,\theta_s,\theta_k) + V^1(\theta_r^2,\theta_s,\theta_k)),$$

where $\theta_s = (\theta_s^1 + \theta_s^2)/2$.

The decisions in one country in the first stage of the game need then to be only functions of the *expected* type of the policymaker in the other country. This greatly simplifies the analysis. We can now proceed to the (partial equilibrium) analysis of two-candidate equilibria in one country (country 1 without loss of generality), given the expected type of the foreign policymaker.

If two candidates of different types θ_r^1 and θ_r^2 run against each other then two conditions must be met. First, each of them should have a positive probability (equal to $\tfrac{1}{2}$) of being elected and second, no candidate prefers to let the other run unopposed. The first condition amounts to stipulating that the election of the two candidates must give the median voter the same utility level. Given the linear-quadratic nature of the function V^1 this simply means that they must be equidistant from the median voter's preferred candidate, i.e., given Eq. (13),

$$\frac{\theta_r^1 + \theta_r^2}{2} = \frac{\theta_s N_2 N_1 - (N_2 y_{A1} - N_1 y_{A2})}{(3N_2 + 2N_1)N_1}. \tag{29}$$

The second condition is equivalent to the condition that the candidates' types should not belong to the interval $[2(\theta_s N_2 N_1 - (N_2 y_{A1} - N_1 y_{A2}))/(3N_2 + 2N_1)N_1,$ $(\theta_s N_2 N_1 - (N_2 y_{A1} - N_1 y_{A2}))/(3N_2 + 2N_1)N_1]$. Given Eq. (29) above, if the first condition is satisfied, this condition means that the leftist candidate's type $\theta_r^1 < 2(\theta_s N_2 N_1 - (N_2 y_{A1} - N_1 y_{A2}))/(3N_2 + 2N_1)N_1$, since, otherwise, she would run unopposed (see Section 4.2). Hence the existence of a delegation effect implies that the two candidates be far apart to guarantee that the rightist candidate does not find it worthwhile to withdraw. A similar argument holds for country 2. As a result, we obtain the following Proposition.

Proposition 3. *Given Assumption 1 the pairs* $((\theta_r^1,\theta_r^2),(\theta_s^1,\theta_s^2))$ *that satisfy*

$$\frac{\theta_r^1 + \theta_r^2}{2} = \frac{1}{3}\frac{(N_1 y_{A2} - N_2 y_{A1})}{(N_2 + N_1)N_1},$$

$$\frac{\theta_s^1 + \theta_s^2}{2} = \frac{1}{3}\frac{(N_2 y_{A1} - N_1 y_{A2})}{(N_2 + N_1)N_2},$$

$$\theta_r^1 < \frac{2}{3}\frac{(N_1 y_{A2} - N_2 y_{A1})}{(N_2 + N_1)N_1},$$

$$\theta_r^2 > \frac{1}{3}\frac{(N_1 y_{A2} - N_2 y_{A1})}{(N_2 + N_1)N_1},$$

$$\theta_s^2 > \frac{2}{3}\frac{(N_2 y_{A1} - N_1 y_{A2})}{(N_2 + N_1)N_2},$$

$$\theta_s^1 < \frac{1}{3}\frac{(N_2 y_{A1} - N_1 y_{A2})}{(N_2 + N_1)N_2}$$

is a two-candidates-per-country equilibrium.

Note that a two-candidates-per-country equilibrium is, when one considers the *expected values* of the policymakers' equilibrium types, equivalent to the one-candidate-per-country equilibrium of Proposition 1 (it corresponds to point A in Fig. 5). When there are two candidates in one country the delegation effect only determines the expected type of the policymaker. This is not to say that the abstention effect disappears completely since it is the reason why, contrary to what happens in the citizen's candidate model without delegation effects (Besley and Coate, 1997), the two candidates must be far apart, *preventing policy convergence* even if there are no costs/benefits of running for office.

The following Proposition characterizes the equilibria in which two candidates run for office in one country and one candidate runs unopposed in the other.

Proposition 4. *Given Assumption 1,*

(i) *any triple* $(\theta_r^1, \theta_r^2, \theta_s)$ *such that*

$$\frac{\theta_r^1 + \theta_r^2}{2} = \frac{\theta_s N_2 N_1 - (N_2 y_{A1} - N_1 y_{A2})}{(3N_2 + 2N_1)N_1} = \theta_r,$$

$$\theta_r^1 < 2\theta_r, \quad \theta_r^2 > \theta_r,$$

$$\frac{\theta_r N_2 N_1 + (N_2 y_{A1} - N_1 y_{A2})}{(3N_1 + 2N_2)N_2} \leqslant \theta_s \leqslant 2 \frac{\theta_r N_2 N_1 + (N_2 y_{A1} - N_1 y_{A2})}{(3N_1 + 2N_2)N_2}$$

is an equilibrium with two candidates in country 1 and one candidate in country 2;

(ii) *any triple* $(\theta_r, \theta_s^1, \theta_s^2)$ *such that*

$$\frac{\theta_s^1 + \theta_s^2}{2} = \frac{\theta_r N_2 N_1 + (N_2 y_{A1} - N_1 y_{A2})}{(3N_1 + 2N_2)N_2} = \theta_s,$$

$$\theta_s^1 < \theta_s, \quad \theta_s^2 > 2\theta_s,$$

$$2 \frac{\theta_s N_2 N_1 - (N_2 y_{A1} - N_1 y_{A2})}{(3N_2 + 2N_1)N_1} \leqslant \theta_r \leqslant \frac{\theta_s N_2 N_1 - (N_2 y_{A1} - N_1 y_{A2})}{(3N_2 + 2N_1)N_1}$$

is an equilibrium with one candidate in the country 1 and two candidates in country 2.

In the country with two candidates, the *expected type* of the policymaker is the preferred type of the median voter. In the other country, the single candidate could take any value between the preferred type of the median voter and twice this value. Looking at Fig. 5, the policymakers' expected equilibrium types lie somewhere on AC (two candidates in country 1, one in country 2) or AD (one candidate in country 1, two in country 2).

Thus, the results change when we consider two-candidates-per-country equilibria. With two candidates the *expected type* of the policymaker is the preferred type of the median voter. The abstention effect is still present, but manifests itself in a different way. The abstention effect determines how far apart the two candidates are from each other.

D. Laussel, R. Riezman / European Economic Review 49 (2005) 1855–1876   1873

6. Rents from office and entry costs

In this section we show how our previous analysis and results are modified when there are rents from office R and entry costs C. The rents from office, otherwise called "spoils of office", are the direct *net* benefits from being in charge. These benefits do not include the gains from being able to implement one's most preferred policy. Instead, they include the wage and all the specific advantages, both material and psychological (the "ego rents") from being in office *minus* the income and advantages foregone. Note that there is nothing to guarantee a priori that rents from office are always positive.[10] The entry costs, C would include personal wealth spent on the campaign and income foregone while campaigning. For one-candidate-per-country equilibria three cases should be considered.

When $R = C$ the results of the previous sections go through without any change. The set of one-candidate-per-country-equilibria remains as it is characterized by Proposition 2: nobody who wanted to run is discouraged from running and nobody who wanted to stay out is encouraged to run.

When $R < C$ the set of one-candidate-per-country-equilibria is enlarged and *includes* the set defined by Proposition 2 provided that $C - R$ is not so large that some previous candidates now prefer the implementation of the *default policy* to running for office. To see why the set of one-candidate equilibria is enlarged consider Fig. 4. Given that a candidate of type θ_r is elected in country r it remains true that any $\theta_s \in [\theta_s(0, \theta_r), 2\theta_s(0, \theta_r)]$ may run unopposed in country s. However, given that $C - R > 0$, it is even less profitable (compared to the case of $C = 0$ and $R = 0$) than before to run against her. Moreover, candidates immediately to the right of B (i.e. of types larger than $2\theta_s(0, \theta_r)$) or to the left of A (i.e. of types lower than $\theta_s(0, \theta_r)$) can now run unopposed since it is no longer profitable for candidate A or for the median voter to oppose (and defeat) them. The equilibrium correspondences are thus enlarged and so is the equilibrium set.

When $R > C$ *there is no other possible one-candidate-per-country-equilibrium than the one described by* Proposition 1, namely in each country the type most preferred by the median voter is elected. To see why this is the case, suppose that in country s a candidate of type $\theta_s > \theta_s(0, \theta_r)$ runs for office. Clearly from the continuity of the distribution of types and of the indirect utility functions there is an $\varepsilon > 0$ such that a candidate of type $\theta_s - \varepsilon$, immediately on the left of θ_s but on the right of $\theta_s(0, \theta_r)$, is willing to run (since the benefits from office minus the cost of running exceed the loss from a less favorable policy outcome). This type $\theta_s - \varepsilon$ is clearly preferred by a majority to θ_s. This result means that when the benefits from office exceed the cost of running, the abstention effect disappears, leaving only the delegation effect.

Therefore, in the one candidate case, if there are net costs of holding office the set of equilibria expands. When there are net benefits from office the set of equilibria contract. In particular, the abstention affect disappears.

---

[10]The wage of the former US President Bill Clinton was about $200,000 per year, much less than he could have earned in the private sector.

What about two-candidate equilibria? The introduction of rents from office and/ or costs of running does not change the basic result that the *expected* policymaker's type is the preferred type of the median voter. Hence, the expected policymakers' types in two-candidates-per-country equilibrium remain unchanged. The only thing which changes is the equilibrium distance between the two candidates. Intuitively, this distance is inversely related to $R - C$. When $R - C$ is not only positive but also very large, the distance between the two candidates goes to zero. If $R - C$ is negative then the distance between candidates increases as the net benefits to holding office become increasingly negative.

7. Concluding remarks

In this paper we used a two-country framework to show that a majority of citizens in both countries favor the election of representatives who are more protectionist than themselves. The key for this result is that the election of a representative is a way for the citizens to commit their country to a more aggressive trade policy.

We demonstrated the existence of an infinite number of one-candidate-per-country equilibria. Provided that the countries sizes are not too dissimilar, all countries are unambiguously more protectionist than in the "Mayer equilibrium" (the median voter in each country selects trade policy). This "protectionist drift" may be ascribed to a *delegation effect* and an *abstention effect*. The delegation effect occurs because all citizens want to choose a policymaker who is more aggressive (protectionist) than they are. The abstention effect is more subtle. This more protectionist citizen who is chosen policymaker herself wishes to delegate to one more protectionist still. What we show is that since there are other viable candidates, the candidate most preferred by the median voter may choose to "abstain" from running for office in order to allow someone more protectionist than herself to run. This results in even greater protectionist drift than would be present with only the delegation effect.

Two-candidate equilibria work a bit differently. The *expected* types of the elected policymakers are always those preferred by the median voters, i.e. more protectionist than them, so that the delegation effect is clearly at work. The abstention effect is still present though it operates in a different way by preventing a convergence of the political positions of the two candidates in a given country.

The introduction of costs and/or benefits from holding office modifies the results in a very simple way. If the spoils of office are larger than the cost of running[11] the abstention effect vanishes in one-candidate-per-country equilibria: the only possible equilibrium of this type is the one where in each country the running candidate is the ideal candidate of the median voters. In two-candidate equilibria, net benefits from office reduces the distance between the two candidates. If, however, the cost of running for office is larger than the rents from office, the set of one-candidate-per-country equilibria is enlarged and the distance between candidates in two-candidate

---

[11]It is not sufficient that they are positive.

D. Laussel, R. Riezman / European Economic Review 49 (2005) 1855–1876 1875

equilibria is increased. These results suggest that as office holding becomes unpleasant more extremism will be observed.

Acknowledgements

We thank participants at the World Congress of the Econometric Society in Seattle and at the Leitner Conference on the Political Geography of Trade at Yale University for helpful comments on an earlier draft.

Appendix

Lemma 5. V^1 *(resp. V^2) is strictly concave with respect to θ_r (resp. θ_s).*

Proof. It will be enough to prove the strict concavity of V^1 (the concavity of V^2 is proved using a similar argument). From the definition of $V^1(\theta_r, \theta_s, \theta_k)$ and Eqs. (3), (4), (7) and (8) we obtain

$$\frac{\partial V^1}{\partial \theta_r} = \frac{N_1 N_2(\theta_k + 2t_1(\theta_r, \theta_s) + t_2(\theta_r, \theta_s)) - (y_{A1} N_2 - N_1 y_{A2})}{N_1(N_1 + N_2)}$$

and then, using again Eqs. (7) and (8),

$$\frac{\partial^2 V^1}{\partial \theta_r^2} = \frac{-N_2(3N_2 + 2N_1)}{(N_1 + N_2)^2} < 0. \qquad \square$$

References

Besley, T., Coate, S., 1997. An economic model of representative democracy. Quarterly Journal of Economics 112, 85–114.

Besley, T., Coate, S., 1998a. Centralized vs decentralized position of local public goods: A political economy analysis. Mimeo., London School of Economics.

Besley, T., Coate, S., 1998b. Sources of inefficiency in a representative democracy: A dynamic analysis. American Economic Review 88, 139–156.

Chari, V.V., Jones, L.E., Marimon, R., 1997. The economics of split-ticket voting in representative democracies. American Economic Review 87, 957–976.

Gatsios, K., Karp, L., 1991. Delegation games in customs unions. Review of Economic Studies 58, 391–397.

Gatsios, K., Karp, L., 1995. Delegation in a general equilibrium model of customs unions. European Economic Review 39, 319–333.

Johnson, H., 1953–54. Optimum tariffs and retaliation. Review of Economic Studies 21, 142–153.

Kennan, J., Riezman, R., 1988. Do big countries win tariff wars? International Economic Review 29, 81–85.

Mayer, W., 1984. Endogenous tariff formation. American Economic Review 74, 970–985.

Osborne, M., Slivinski, A., 1996. A model of political competition with citizen candidates. Quarterly Journal of Economics 111, 65–96.

Persson, T., Tabellini, G., 1992. The politics of 1992: Fiscal policy and European integration. Review of Economic Studies 59, 689–701.

Persson, T., Tabellini, G., 1994. Representative democracy and capital taxation. Journal of Public Economics 85, 53–70.

Persson, T., Tabellini, G., 1996. Federal fiscal constitutions: Risk-sharing and moral hazard. Econometrica 64, 623–646.

Rodrik, Dani, 1995. Political economy of trade policy. In: Grossman, G., Rogoff, K. (Eds.), Handbook of International Economics, vol. 3, Elsevier, Amsterdam, pp. 1457–1494.

Willmann, G., 2002. Why legislators are such protectionists: The role of majoritarian voting in setting tariffs. Mimeo., The University of Kiel.

Quarterly Journal of Political Science, 2008, 3: 1–36

Minorities and Storable Votes*

Alessandra Casella[1], Thomas Palfrey[2] and Raymond Riezman[3]

[1] *Columbia University, Greqam, NBER, CEPR, ac186@columbia.edu*
[2] *Caltech, trp@hss.caltech.edu*
[3] *University of Iowa, GEP, CES-ifo, raymond-riezman@uiowa.edu*

ABSTRACT

The paper studies a simple voting system that can increase the power of minorities without sacrificing aggregate efficiency or treating voters asymmetrically. *Storable votes* grant each voter a stock of votes to spend as desired over a series of binary decisions and thus elicit voters' intensity of preferences. The potential of the mechanism is particularly clear in the presence of systematic minorities: by accumulating votes on issues that it deems most important, the minority can win occasionally. But because the majority typically can outvote it, the minority wins only if its strength of preference is high and the majority's strength of preference is low. The result is that the minority's preferences are represented, while aggregate efficiency either falls little or in fact rises, relative to simple majority voting. The theoretical predictions of our model are confirmed by a series of experiments: the frequency of minority victories, the relative payoff of the minority versus the majority, and the aggregate payoffs all match the theory.

Recent decades have witnessed historic efforts at designing democratic institutions, at many levels. New constitutions were created in much of Eastern Europe and the former Soviet Republics. International organizations such as the European Union and the World Trade Organization have been evolving rapidly, and many developing countries

---

* We gratefully acknowledge financial support from the National Science Foundation, PLESS, CASSEL, and SSEL. We acknowledge helpful comments from participants of the Conference in Tribute to Jean-Jacques Laffont in Toulouse, the Econometric Society World Congress, and seminars at the Institute for Advanced Study in Princeton, Georgetown, NYU, the University of Venice, the European University Institute, and CORE.

MS submitted 24 October 2007; final version received 16 April 2008
ISSN 1554-0626; DOI 10.1561/100.00007048

have moved from autocratic regimes to regimes based on elected representation with majoritarian principles.

While majoritarian principles provide a solid foundation for democracy, there are imperfections. This paper focuses on one particular imperfection that has presented a challenge to designers of democratic institutions for centuries: the *tyranny of the majority*, or the risk of excluding minority groups from representation. At least since Madison, Mill, and Tocqueville, political thinkers have argued that a necessary condition for the legitimacy of a democratic system is for no group with socially acceptable goals to be disenfranchised. In the history of US constitutional law, ensuring fair representation to each group is seen as the crucial second step in the evolution of democratic institutions, after granting the franchise: once all individuals are guaranteed the right to participate in the political process, should separate weights be given to each group's political interest? The core of the difficulty is that the two goals seem inherently contradictory.

The 1965 Voting Rights Act and the debate that continues to accompany its implementation focus on the need to guarantee that minorities, in particular racial minorities, have some direct representation. The obstacle is the possibility that their vote be *de facto diluted* by their minority status in all districts. In this paper, we study a related but different problem: the respect of minority preferences not in the choice of representatives, but in the very act of decision-making. We argue for it not only on the basis of fairness and legitimacy, but also on grounds of aggregate efficiency. Chwe (1999) took a similar perspective and proposed granting special voting power to the minority to ensure its participation when voting aggregates diffuse information. The voting system we analyze treats everyone identically, and we base our analysis on private value considerations — voting in our model aggregates divergent preferences, not diffuse information. But the efficiency rationale remains. A simple example illustrates why.

Suppose there are just two groups in a polity comprised of 100 citizens. Group A has 55 members and group B has 45 members. There are 3 proposals on the table. All citizens in group A have identical preferences and strictly prefer to pass all proposals; all citizens in group B have identical preferences and strictly prefer the *status quo* on all 3 issues. The table below gives a specific utility function for each member on each issue, and preferences are assumed to be additive. For each citizen, the utility of the less preferred option is normalized to 0.

Issue	U_A (pass)	U_A (sq)	U_B (pass)	U_B (sq)
1	3	0	0	1
2	2	0	0	2
3	1	0	0	3

Note that the *intensity* of preferences varies across the issues, and on a given issue the preference intensity for a group A member may be different from the intensity of a group B member. That is, some issues are more important to one group than to the other group — issue 1 is important to group A but not to group B, and issue 3 is important to group B but not to group A.

Now consider what would happen with simple majority rule when issues are decided independently: since group A has a majority, all three proposals pass. Indeed, even if there were a million different issues, group A would always have a majority on all issues, so the B citizens are effectively disenfranchised — the outcome is exactly the same as it would be in a political system where only A citizens were allowed to vote.

Why is this outcome undesirable? First, equity considerations demand that the minority be able to win on at least some issues. But in addition, from a purely utilitarian standpoint, there are plausible welfare criteria according to which the outcome is socially inefficient. In our example, if each individual is treated equally and decisions are evaluated *ex ante*, before membership into the groups is known, the *status quo* should prevail on issue 3. Thus, the tyranny of the majority imposes costs both in terms of equity and in terms of efficiency. The equity problem stems from the existence of a smaller group whose preferences are systematically in the opposite *direction* of the larger group's preferences. The efficiency problem stems from differences in the *strength* of preferences of the two groups. Nothing fundamental depends on all citizens in a group having the same intensity of preferences on every issue, a simplification adopted only to keep the example transparent.[1]

How can the tyranny of the majority problem be solved, or at least mitigated? Any solution must deviate from issue-by-issue simple majority voting system. An immediate possibility might be vote trading or some corresponding log-rolling scheme: members of one group could trade their vote on one issue in exchange for votes on other issues. But, in the simple example we constructed above, there are no gains to trading across groups, because every A citizen is already winning on all issues. Any system that allows the minority group to win on even one issue will make all A citizens worse off, and thus would not emerge spontaneously. With the perfect correlation of preferences we have posited above, an explicit institution re-enfranchising the minority is necessary.

Consider then endowing every voter with an initial stock of votes, and rather than requiring voters to cast exactly one vote on each issue, allowing them to lump their votes together, casting heavier votes on some issues and lighter votes on other issues. It is this voting mechanism, called *storable votes*, that we study in this paper. Even if the initial stock of votes is identical for all voters, storable votes allow the minority to win some of the time, and in particular, to win when its preferences are most intense. But because the majority generally holds more votes, it is in a position to overrule the minority if it cares to do so: the minority can win only those issues over which its strength of preferences is high *and*, at the same time, the majority's preference intensity is weak. These are exactly the issues where the minority *should* win from an efficiency viewpoint: the equity gains resulting from the possibility of occasional minority's victory need not come at a cost to aggregate efficiency.

In most of the specifications of the environment that we study in this paper, we find that standard economic measures of aggregate efficiency rise with storable votes. The main contribution of this paper then is not to suggest a new reason to increase minority's

---

[1] The central idea also does not depend on the direction of preferences within the group being *perfectly* correlated either — there may be some conflicting preferences within groups.

representation but to propose a specific voting scheme with the potential to achieve this goal even in the case of a systematic minority, when other voting mechanisms would fail, and to do so without violating the equal treatment of all voters.

The topic of minorities is felt so intensely, and the terms are so emotionally loaded, that there is a need to be scrupulously clear in terminology. As the example makes clear, we define a minority as a clearly identifiable group characterized by two features: first, a relatively small numerical size; second, preferences that are systematically different from the preferences of the rest of the polity. Thus, a minority in this paper is a political minority, which may, but need not, correspond to a minority according to racial, ethnic, religious or any other type of considerations. In terms of political decisions, what matters in the present context are the coherent and idiosyncratic preferences of the group, as opposed to the specific source of its identity.

The use of storable votes was initially proposed in Casella (2005), in a model that ignored systematic minorities. The desirable efficiency properties of storable votes remain true there, because the basic principle of bunching ones votes on more salient decisions continues to apply, with the implication that the probability of obtaining the desired outcome shifts away from decisions that matter little and toward decisions that matter more, with positive welfare effects. Storable votes are a particularly natural application of the idea that preferences can be elicited by linking independent decisions through a common budget constraint, an idea that can be exploited quite generally, as shown by Jackson and Sonnenschein (2007).[2] From a practical point of view, storable votes seem particularly well-suited to the protection of minority interests, where they have the potential to increase efficiency while improving equity at the same time.

A voting system similar to storable votes is *cumulative voting*, a mechanism used in single multi-candidate elections. It grants each voter a budget of votes, with the proviso that the votes can spread or concentrated on as many or few of the candidates as the voter wishes. Cumulative voting has been advocated for the protection of minority rights (Guinier 1994) and has been recommended by the courts to redress violations of fair representation in local elections (Issacharoff *et al.* 2002). There is theoretical (Cox 1990), experimental (Gerber *et al.* 1998), and empirical (Pildes and Donoghue 1995; Bowler *et al.* 2003) evidence that cumulative voting does indeed help minorities. The general motivation behind the storable votes mechanism is similar to cumulative voting, but storable votes applies to a sequence of independent binary decisions, a substantively different strategic problem, with different applications. In addition, we explicitly study the efficiency properties of the mechanism, as well as its distributional effects on minorities.

The desirable properties of storable votes are features of the equilibrium of the resulting voting game — they emerge if every voter chooses the correct number of votes, given what he rationally expects others to do. In practice there is a need to consider

---

[2]   Jackson and Sonnenschein propose a specific mechanism that converges to the first best allocation as the number of decisions grows large. The mechanism allows individuals to assign different priority to different actions but constrains their choices in a tightly specified manner. The design of the correct menu of choices offered to the agents is complex, but the mechanism achieves the first best. Storable votes are simple but in general do not achieve the first best.

the robustness of the mechanism. Could the outcome be much worse if voters made mistakes? This is an appropriate concern here because the storable votes game is quite complex: voters need to trade-off the different probabilities of casting the pivotal vote along the full logical tree of possible scenarios, a task further complicated by coordination problems within the two groups, and multiple equilibria. If actual voters were confronted with the problem, what type of decisions would they make?

The second part of the paper presents the results of a set of experiments showing that under storable votes, the minority does indeed win on a significant number of issues. Both the minority payoff and the aggregate efficiency of the mechanism match the theoretical predictions, indicating that the equity gains accrue with little or no loss of efficiency. Voters use responsive strategies, consistently casting more votes when valuations are higher, a behavior that appears sufficient to take them most of the way toward their equilibrium payoffs, even when the number of votes they cast differs from the theoretical equilibrium. Previous experiments with storable votes in symmetric environments (Casella *et al.* 2006) had found a similar robustness of efficiency properties to strategic mistakes. Here the introduction of minorities complicates the game very significantly, and the robustness we observe in the experiments is qualified by the different cost of mistakes faced by majority members, who are likely to win anyway, and minority members, whose deviations are particularly costly (and rarer in the data). Whether because of the inherent robustness of storable votes, or because the minority made few mistakes, we see the minority's success in appropriating a significant share of the surplus with little if any aggregate cost as an encouraging sign of the practical viability of the mechanism.

THE MODEL

A committee with n members meets for T periods to vote over a series of binary proposals $\{P_1, \ldots, P_T\}$, each of which can either pass or fail. Voter i's preferences over proposal P_t are summarized by a valuation $v_{it} \in \mathbb{R}$. A positive valuation means that the voter is in favor of the proposal, a negative valuation means that the voter is against, and voter i's payoff from each proposal is given by $|v_{it}| \equiv v_{it}$ if the outcome of the vote is as he desires, and 0 otherwise. Thus voter i's utility function has the form:

$$U_i(P_1, \ldots, P_T) = \sum_{t-1}^{T} u_{it}(P_t),$$

where

$$u_{it}(P_t) = v_{it} \text{ if } \begin{cases} v_{it} > 0 & \text{and} \quad P_t \text{ passes} \\ v_{it} < 0 & \text{and} \quad P_t \text{ fails} \end{cases}$$
$$= 0 \text{ otherwise.}$$

The magnitude of the valuation, v_{it}, is called the preference *intensity* of voter i on proposal t. The profile of valuations, $v = (v_{11}, \ldots, v_{1T}, \ldots, v_{n1}, \ldots, v_{nT})$, is a random variable that is distributed according to the commonly known distribution $\Gamma(v)$, satisfying the assumptions we detail below.

The committee is composed of two *groups*, the *Majority group* **M**, with M members and the *Minority group* **m**, with $m < M$ members. The two groups differ systematically in their preferences: members of **m** are in favor of all proposals, and members of **M** are against. For all t:

$$v_{it} > 0 \quad \text{if } i \in \mathbf{m}$$
$$v_{it} < 0 \quad \text{if } i \in \mathbf{M}.$$

All members of the minority have valuations drawn from a distribution G_m with support $[0, 1]$, identical across proposals, while all members of the majority have valuations drawn from a distribution G_M with support $[-1, 0]$, again identical across proposals. We assume symmetry in the distributions across the two groups and call $G'_M = G_m \equiv F$ defined over the support $[0, 1]$ the distribution of intensities for each group. F is common knowledge.

Intensities are always drawn independently across proposals and across the two groups. With respect to the correlation of the intensities *within* each group, we consider two polar cases. In the first case (case B), intensities are drawn independently for each member of a group; in the second case (case C) intensities are identical for all members within a group. Hence, although all members of a group always agree on the preferred outcome, in the B case they may have conflicting priorities, while they do not in the C case. The correlation of within group intensities (or lack thereof) is common knowledge, as is the independence of intensities across proposals and groups.

At the beginning of period t, i privately observes v_{it} but does not observe $v_{it'}$ for $t' > t$: intensities are revealed privately and sequentially. Because draws are independent across issues, voter i's observation of v_{it} does not provide information about $v_{it'}$, and because draws are independent across groups, observation of $v_{it}, i \in m$, does not provide information about $v_{jt}, j \in M$ (and vice versa). Whether it provides information about the intensity of other voters in the same group, v_{jt}, with $j \in m$, depends on which case we consider. In case C, members of the same group have identical preferences and observation of their own intensity allows them to perfectly infer the preferences of the other members of their group. In case B, a voter's own intensity provides no information about any other voter's intensity.

The Storable Votes Mechanism

At the beginning of period 1, each voter is endowed with an account of B_0 *bonus* votes, where B_0 is an integer.[3] In the first period, the voter casts his regular vote plus as many discrete bonus votes as he wishes out of his endowment. The bonus votes cast are deducted from his endowment, which is then carried over to the next period. The current

---

[3]   Because we want to study the effect of bonus votes *per se* in strengthening the minority's position, it seems appropriate to give the same initial allocation to all voters.

endowment of bonus votes for every voter in period t, denoted $B_t = (B_{1t}, \ldots, B_{nt})$, is common knowledge at the beginning of period t. Thus each voter i independently decides how many votes, x_{it}, to cast after observing his private intensity v_{it} and B_t, subject to $x_{it} \leq 1 + B_{it}$. The proposal passes if there are more votes in favor of the proposal than against, and fails in the opposite case. Ties are resolved randomly. In the next period, $t + 1$, voters' intensities over the new proposal are again privately observed, and voting proceeds as before, now subject to the constraint, $x_{it+1} \leq 1 + B_{it+1} = 2 + B_{it} - x_{it}$. Since $x_{it} \geq 1$, this is at least as tight a constraint as in period t. The voting continues in this fashion until the end of period T.

THEORETICAL RESULTS

Given F, m, M, B_0, T, the storable votes mechanism defines an asymmetric multistage game of incomplete information. We study the properties of the Perfect Bayesian equilibria of this game, where at each period t and for each possible intensity, v_{it}, and profile of endowments, B_t, individuals choose how many votes to cast so as to maximize expected utility, given the strategies of the other players. Because the sign of each group's preferences is common knowledge and intensities are independent over time, voting decisions cannot be used to manipulate other players' beliefs about future preferences. Assuming, in addition, that players do not use weakly dominated strategies, the direction of each individual vote is always chosen sincerely: all the minority members' votes are cast in favor of each proposal, and all majority votes are cast against each proposal. The *state* of the game at t is defined to be the profile of bonus votes each voter has still available, B_t, and the number of remaining periods, $T - t$. We focus on strategies such that, given F, m, and M, the number of votes each individual chooses to cast each period, x_{it}, depends only on i's intensity of preferences at time t, v_{it}, and on the state of the game. We denote such strategies by $x_{it}(v_i, B_t, t)$.

The $C2$ Game

When characterizing the equilibria of our model, the correlation of intensities within each group in model C can be a source of complications. But matters can be simplified by a simple observation. Consider the following 2-player storable votes game, which we call $C2$. Voter M has M regular votes each period and a stock of MB_0 bonus votes; his valuation over each proposal is Mv_{Mt}, where v_{Mt} is independently drawn from the distribution function G_M with support $[-1, 0]$. Voter m has m regular votes each period and a stock of mB_0 bonus votes; his valuation over each proposal is mv_{mt}, where v_{mt} is independently drawn from the distribution function G_m with support $[0, 1]$. Then the following result holds:

Lemma 1 *If game $C2$ has an equilibrium, then the game described by model C also has an equilibrium. In addition, call $x^*_{Mt}(v_i, B_t, t)$ and $x^*_{mt}(v_i, B_t, t)$ the equilibrium strategies of voter M and voter m in game $C2$, and $\{x^*_{it}(v_i, B_t, t)\}$ the equilibrium strategies in C. If $C2$ has an* *equilibrium, then there exist equilibrium strategies of model C such that $\sum_{i \in m} x_{it}^*(v_i, B_t, t) = x_{mt}^*(v_i, B_t, t)$ and $\sum_{i \in M} x_{it}^*(v_i, B_t, t) = x_{Mt}^*(v_i, B_t, t)$.*

Proof: See Appendix.   ∎

Lemma 1 makes a simple point. In model C voters' interests within each group are perfectly aligned; if there is an equilibrium where each group coordinates its strategy so as to maximize the group's payoff, given the aggregate strategy of the other group, then no individual voter can gain from deviating.[4] In the n-person game described by model C, we will call equilibrium *group strategies* the equilibrium individual strategies of the 2-voter game $C2$.

Equilibrium

The particular feature of storable votes is that they allow individuals to reflect the intensity of their preferences in the number of votes they cast. Lemma 1 allows us to show:

Lemma 2 *For any F, M, m, and T, both model B and model C have an equilibrium in monotone cutpoint strategies: at any state (B_t, t) and for any i with $B_i + 1$ available votes there exists a set of cutpoints $\{c_{i1}(B_t, t), c_{i2}(B_t, t), \ldots, c_{iB_i+1}(B_t, t)\}$, $0 \leq c_{ix} \leq c_{ix+1} \leq 1$, such that i will cast x votes if and only if $v_{it} \in [c_{ix}, c_{ix+1}]$. In model B, the strategies are individual equilibrium strategies and $i \in \{1, \ldots, n\}$; in model C, the strategies are group strategies and $i \in \{M, m\}$.*

Proof: See Appendix.   ∎

Lemma 2 establishes that an equilibrium exists, although it does not rule out the possibility of multiple equilibria. Notice also that the lemma states that strategies may respond to valuations, as we expect intuitively, but allows for equilibria where the monotonicity is only weak — for example, possible equilibria where bonus votes are equally split among proposals, or where strategies depend on the timing of the proposals alone.

Storable votes open the possibility of minority victories. We can derive:

Theorem 1 *In both models B and C: (i) For any F, T, M, and $m > 1$ there is a finite $B_0'(M, m, T)$ such that for all $B_0 > B_0'$ there exist equilibria of the storable votes mechanism where the minority wins some of the time with strictly positive probability. (ii) If $T > M$ and $B_0 > B_0'$, then the minority wins some of the time with strictly positive probability in all equilibria of the mechanism.*

Proof: See Appendix.   ∎

---

[4]   This is the logic exploited by McLennan (1998) to show that whenever *sincere* voting is efficient in common value decision problems, then it must be a Nash equilibrium.

The first part of the theorem establishes the existence of equilibria with a positive probability of minority victories, in direct contrast to the outcome with simple majority voting. The potential of storable votes to help the minority is very intuitive, although for arbitrary T the result cannot be established for all equilibria. The problem is coordination: in both models B and C (although not in $C2$, where coordination is imposed) if the other members of the minority follow a given strategy, it is difficult for a single deviating voter to be able to affect the final outcome, and thus strategies where the minority always loses can be supported in equilibrium. As an illustration, consider one possible equilibrium mentioned above, where every voter, both in the majority and in minority, distributes the bonus votes equally over all proposals: $x_i = 1 + B_0/T$ for all $i \in \{1, \ldots, n\}$. Because everyone always casts the same number of votes, the game becomes identical to simple majority voting, and the minority always loses. But unless a single minority voter deviating alone can lead to at least one proposal passing, the strategies are an equilibrium for both models B and C.[5] Notice that if $T = 2$ this equilibrium exists for all values of B_0: a deviating minority voter can shift at most $B_0/2$ votes, but over each proposal the majority is always winning by at least $1 + B_0/2$ votes (since $M \geq m + 1$). Thus, for $T = 2$ there is always at least one equilibrium where the minority always loses, regardless of the existence and of the number of bonus votes (although, as the theorem states, for appropriate values of B_0 there are also equilibria where the minority can win with positive probability).

Efficiency

Making it possible for the minority to win occasionally favors fairness and representation, but in principle could have efficiency costs because it implies that the larger group occasionally loses. However, even from a pure efficiency criterion, storable votes can be desirable. In equilibria where strategies are strictly monotonic, the minority wins when minority intensities outweigh majority intensities: the minority wins *when it should.*

We measure the efficiency of the storable votes mechanism in terms of *ex ante* efficiency: a voter's expected utility from all T proposals before any of his valuations is realized, and before knowing whether he belongs to **M** or to **m**. We call our efficiency measure EV_0 and contrast it with the equivalent measure under simple majority voting, denoted by EW_0.[6]

---

[5] As mentioned, the strategies described are not equilibrium strategies for model $C2$. Lemma 1 states that the equilibria of model $C2$ are equilibria of model C; the reverse does not hold.

[6] An important question is whether the cardinal valuations and our notion of efficiency force us into comparisons of interpersonal utilities. This is where our assumption of symmetrical distributions of intensities across all voters plays its role. The intensity draws over any specific decision should be read as normalized by a common numeraire. In our model with multiple decisions, the natural numeraire is the individual's mean intensity over the universe of all decisions that could be brought to a vote. In fact, by imposing not only the same mean but the same distribution, we are forcing the voters to adopt an equal scale and to organize the different decisions according to a fixed ordinal ranking, with the same proportion of decisions in any given subinterval of the support. It is this normalization that allows us to avoid interpersonal comparisons. In this model, granting individual

The positive impact on efficiency of monotonic strategies applies to both models, but the properties of the voting mechanism are more robust and easier to characterize in model C.

Theorem 2 *In model C, for all F, M, and $m > M/2$, if $T < \overline{T}(M, m)$ there exists a value of B_0 and an equilibrium of the storable votes mechanism such that storable votes are ex ante superior to simple majority voting (i.e., $EV_0 > EW_0$).*

Proof: See Appendix.   ■

A few remarks will clarify the result. Note first of all that the difference in expected utility can occur only if the minority is expected to win some of the times; thus, in the equilibrium discussed in the theorem the minority itself necessarily fares better, in expected utility terms, than under simple majority voting. Note too that the minority could never win if the horizon were shorter than 2 periods; thus, again trivially, $\overline{T}(M, m) > 2$ for all M and m. The existence of an upper bound on T comes not from the logic of the mechanism but from the need to respect integer constraints: for all M and m, we require that the number of votes cast be always an integer. The proof shows that if integer constraints are ignored, $\overline{T}(M, m)$ can be made arbitrarily large for all M and m, and the result then holds for arbitrary T.

The result in the theorem requires not only that the minority be expected to win with positive probability, but also that equilibrium strategies be responsive to valuations: at least in some states strategies must be strictly monotonic. The difficulty in establishing the theorem is identifying equilibrium majority and minority cutpoints at each state such that expected minority gains and majority losses can be computed and compared for all F, M, m, and T. This is particularly true for model B, where the lack of information about the valuations of other members of one's own group makes coordination impossible. If we specialize our assumptions on F, M, m, and T the task is made much easier. The next subsection discusses the theoretical properties of the model when we restrict the set of parameter values, in line with the choices that we make in the experiment.

Theoretical Properties of the Experimental Design

In designing the experiment, the challenge is to specify a class of environments simple enough to be easily understood and replicated in the laboratory, but rich enough to preserve the main properties of the mechanism. The following specification satisfies these requirements: the total number of voters n is odd; the distribution F is Uniform; there are two consecutive proposals and each voter is endowed with two bonus votes: $T = B_0 = 2$. The strategy chosen by each voter is simply the number of bonus votes to cast over the first proposal, as a function of his valuation. The proposition

---

voters different distributions would be equivalent to taking a stance on the relative intensity of their preferences.

below characterizes equilibria for our experimental environment, where strategies are responsive to intensities and are an equilibrium not only for models B and C but also for model $C2$.[7] Its proof can be found in Casella *et al.* (2007) and in the supplementary material on the *Quarterly Journal of Political Science* web page.

Proposition 1 *Suppose n odd; F Uniform, and $T = B_0 = 2$. Then:*

In model B :

a. *There is an equilibrium where: $x_{i1} = 1$ if $v_{i1} < 0.5$ and $x_{i1} = 3$ if $v_{i1} > 0.5$ for all i.*
In such an equilibrium:

b. *If $M > 3m$, the majority always wins, but for all $M < 3m$ the minority wins one of the two proposals with probability $\sum_{s=k}^{m} \left[\sum_{r=0}^{m-s} \binom{M}{r} \binom{m}{r+s} 2^{-n} \right] > 0$, where $k \equiv (M - m + 1)/2$. Ex ante, each of the two proposals has the same probability of a minority victory.*

c. *If $M > 3m$, storable votes are identical to simple majority voting, and $EV_0 = EW_0$. But for $M < 3m$, there exist m', m'' and, M' with $m'' > m'$ such that $EV_0(m', M') < EW_0(m', M')$ but $EV_0(m'', M') > EW_0(m'', M')$.*

In model C:

a. *There is an equilibrium where the minority's strategy is: $x_{m1} = m$ if $v_{m1} < 0.5$ and $x_{m1} = 3m$ if $v_{m1} > 0.5$. The majority's strategy is: if $2M > 3m$, $x_{M1} = 2M$ for all v_{M1}; if $2M \leq 3m$, $x_{M1} = \max\{M, m+3\}$ if $v_{M1} < 0.5$ and $x_{M1} = \min\{3M, 4M - (m+3)\}$ if $v_{M1} > 0.5$.*
In such an equilibrium:

b. *If $2M > 3m$, the majority always wins, but for all $2M \leq 3m$ the minority wins one of the two proposals with probability 0.25. Ex ante, each of the two proposals has the same probability of a minority victory.*

c. *Storable votes are always ex ante weakly superior to simple majority voting: $EV_0 = EW_0$ if $2M > 3m$, and $EV_0 > EW_0$ if $2M \leq 3m$.*

Together, restricting n, F, and T allows us to identify the equilibrium cutpoints and derive stronger efficiency results than in the general case discussed in Theorem 2.

The properties of these equilibria are illustrated in Figure 1, using the case of $M = m + 1$ as an example. Efficiency is maximized when each decision is resolved in favor of the side with higher total valuation, and in the figure we compare equilibrium and efficient outcomes.

Figure 1(a) shows, for both models, the probability of a minority victory over one of the two proposals in equilibrium — the black dots — and in the first best — the grey dots. The minority can never win both proposals because the majority always has a larger total number of votes. As m increases, the equilibrium probability of a minority victory increases. In model B, the increase is smooth, and the probability of a minority victory converges to 0.5 as the number of voters becomes large and the relative

---

[7] Recall, from earlier discussion, that there can also be nonresponsive equilibria.

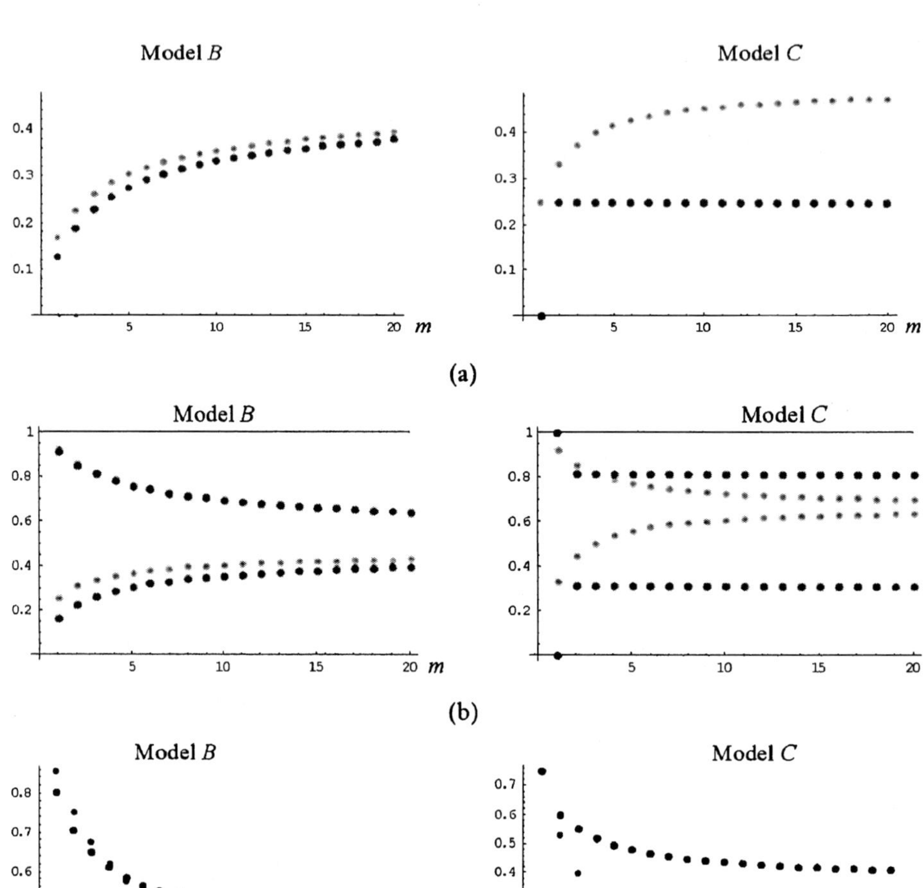

Figure 1. $T = B_0 = 2$; $F(v)$ Uniform; $M = m + 1$. (a) Frequency of minority victories. (b) Expected payoff for majority and minority members (per capita). (c) Expected aggregate payoff as share of the available surplus. The large black dots plot equilibrium payoffs with storable votes; the grey dots efficient payoffs, and the small black dots payoffs with simple majority voting.

difference in size between the majority and the minority becomes negligible. The efficient frequency of minority victories is slightly higher than the equilibrium frequency. In model C, the change in the equilibrium probability of minority victories is discontinuous, jumping from 0 to 0.25 when the majority becomes unable to guarantee itself victory on both proposals, and then remaining constant at that level. The point at which the jump occurs depends on the absolute difference between the two groups, $M - m$. The efficient frequency of minority victories on the other hand increases smoothly with the relative size of the minority and again is always higher than the equilibrium frequency.

Figure 1(b) plots the expected per capita payoff for majority and minority members. With simple majority rule, the respective values are 1 and 0 in both models. With storable votes, the expected payoffs of the two groups are closer, unless the majority can ensure itself victory, although the minority's payoff remains lower than under efficiency (the grey dots in Figure 1(b)). In model C, equilibrium per capita payoffs remain constant for each group, regardless of m, once the threshold where the majority always wins has been passed.[8]

Figure 1(c) plots a normalized measure of expected surplus for both models, where expected aggregate payoff is expressed as a share of the expected first best payoff. The figure compares storable votes and simple majority voting to each other and to first best efficiency. Because we want to measure the added value over purely random decision-making (where each proposal is equally likely to pass or fail), we normalize both numerator and denominator by the expected payoff in the random mechanism. Thus if we call EV_0^* the expected efficient aggregate payoff and R the expected payoff under random decision-making, we define the *normalized aggregate surplus* as $(EV_0 - R)/(EV_0^* - R)$ with storable votes and $(EW_0 - R)/(EV_0^* - R)$ with simple majority. Over the two proposals, $EW_0 = M$ and $R = (M + m)/2$ in both models, while EV_0 and EV_0^* can be found in the Appendix of Casella *et al.* (2007) and in the supplementary material on the *Quarterly Journal of Political Science* web page. As the figure shows, when the number of voters is small and the difference in size between the two groups relatively important, the possibility of minority victories in the storable votes mechanism is accompanied by some loss of efficiency in model B, but not in model C, where efficiency is always at least as high as under simple majority rule. The loss in model B is not large and disappears as the number of voters and the relative size of the minority increases. For most sizes of the electorate, storable votes allow voters to appropriate a larger share of the total surplus in both models.[9]

---

[8] In fact, they remain unchanged for any absolute difference between the two groups, once the threshold $3m < 2M$ has been passed. It is the threshold itself that depends on $(M - m)$.

[9] The main difference between the two models emerges in the limit, and is not visible in the figure. In model B, the intensity draws are independent; hence, as the population becomes very large the law of large numbers guarantees that the empirical average intensity of preferences in both groups converges to the mean of the F distribution. This means that random choice, simple majority voting and storable votes all converge to first best efficiency and any efficiency-based argument for protecting the minority disappears. In model C, on the other hand, the valuation draws within each group are perfectly correlated, and the law of large numbers does not apply. As the number of voters increases, the difference in size between the two groups becomes negligible and simple majority voting again converges to random choice, but random choice remains inferior to efficient decision-making and to storable votes. In very large populations, only minorities whose intensities are correlated should be protected on efficiency grounds.

EXPERIMENTAL DESIGN

Protocol

All sessions of the experiment were run in laboratories either at the California Institute of Technology (SSEL), the University of California at Los Angeles (CASSEL), or Princeton (PLESS). Subjects were registered students, recruited through the laboratory web sites. No subject participated in more than one session. All sessions focussed on the specification just discussed: subjects voted on two consecutive proposals ($T = 2$) and were allocated 2 bonus votes ($B_0 = 2$), in addition to the regular vote they were required to cast over each proposal. With the exception of one session, committees were composed of 5 voters, divided into two groups of 3 and 2 voters with systematically opposed preferences.[10] The experiment's primary treatment variable was the correlation of intensities within each group — the distinction between model B and model C.

After entering the laboratory, the subjects were seated randomly in booths separated by partitions and assigned ID numbers corresponding to their computer terminal; when everyone was seated, the experimenter read aloud the instructions, and any question was answered publicly. The session then began.[11] Subjects were matched randomly into committees and within each committee were assigned randomly to the majority or the minority group. Each subject was then shown his valuation for the first proposal and asked to choose how many votes to cast in the first election. Valuations were restricted to integer values and were drawn by the computer, with equal probability, from the support $[-100, -1]$ for majority members, and from $[1, 100]$ for minority members. In both treatments, the valuations were drawn independently for majority and minority members.

In treatment B each member of each group was assigned a valuation drawn independently from the specified support; in treatment C all members of the same group in the same committee were assigned the same valuation (i.e., all majority members in a given committee shared the same valuation, as did all minority members in a committee). The independence of the intensities within each group in treatment B and their perfect correlation in treatment C were common knowledge. After everyone in a committee had voted, the computer screen showed to each subject the number of votes cast by each of the two groups in the subject's committee, whether the proposal had passed or not, and the subject's own payoff from that election. Valuations over the second proposal were then drawn, the remaining votes were automatically cast, and the outcome determined.

After the second proposal had been voted upon, subjects were rematched; each was assigned a new budget of bonus votes, and the game was replayed. Experimental sessions consisted of between 15 and 30 rounds, each round a pair of consecutive proposals. In the rematching, minority members always remained minority members, and majority members always remained majority members, but the composition of each group and

---

[10] One session had committees of 9 voters, each divided into two opposite groups of sizes 5 and 4.

[11] A sample of the instructions can be downloaded from http://www.hss.caltech.edu/~trp/ MINORI-TIES. The experiments were conducted using the Multistage Game open-source software (http://multistage.ssel.caltech.edu/).

of each committee was randomly determined. Subjects were paid privately at the end of each session their cumulative valuations for all proposals resolved in their preferred direction, multiplied by a pre-determined exchange rate and complemented by a fixed show-up payment of $10. Average earnings were about $17 per experiment for minority subjects and about $31 for majority subjects.

Equilibrium

We found no evidence of non-responsive equilibria, and our analysis of the experimental data focuses exclusively on the equilibrium described in the previous section. Here we derive the details of the equilibrium for the specific case $M = 3$, and $m = 2$ (and for a robustness control in one experimental section, for $M = 5$, and $m = 4$). Individual equilibrium strategies in treatment B and corresponding equilibrium outcomes are in Table 1. The equilibrium cutpoints — the threshold intensities where individual voters switch from casting 0 to casting 1 bonus vote, and from casting 1 to casting 2 — are reported in row 2 of Table 1 and are denoted c_1 and c_2.[12] Rows 3 and 4 in the table report the expected frequency of minority victories in equilibrium and under efficiency, respectively. Rows 5 and 6 report the expected share of per capita payoff for a minority voter, relative to a majority voter, again in equilibrium and under efficiency. So, for example, in the $\{3, 2\}$ experiment with storable votes a minority subject is expected to win on average 26 percent of what a majority subject earns, if everybody plays the equilibrium strategy. Finally, the last two rows report the expected share of normalized aggregate surplus appropriated with storable votes (row 7) and with simple majority voting (non-storable votes, in row 8).

Storable votes in the B treatment are slightly less efficient from an aggregate point of view than simple majority voting, but the equilibrium efficiency loss is minor, relative to the effect of storable votes on the welfare of minorities.

Table 1. Equilibrium strategies and outcomes

B Treatment		
M, m	3, 2	5, 4
c_1, c_2	50, 50	50, 50
% min wins, sv	19	25
% min wins, eff	22.5	28.5
% (min/maj) payoff, sv	26	36
% (min/maj) payoff, eff	35.5	45
% surplus sv	71	61
% surplus nsv	75	62

[12] Because the equilibrium cutpoints are identical for minority and majority voters, we use the symbols c_1 and c_2 for both groups.

Equilibrium strategies in treatment C pose a coordination problem. As described in the previous section, if the two groups are of size $\{3, 2\}$, in equilibrium the minority uses no bonus votes if its intensity is smaller than 50, and all its bonus votes if it is above; the majority casts a total of 5 votes if its intensity is smaller than 50, and 7 votes if it is larger than 50.[13] Any individual strategy compatible with these group strategies is an equilibrium. Hence, each minority voter has a simple symmetrical strategy that aggregates to the equilibrium group strategy: cast no bonus votes if the intensity is below 50 and cast all bonus votes if the intensity is 50 or above. But the coordination problem for majority voters is more difficult. The group strategy described above cannot be supported by *symmetric* individual strategies, and coordination on asymmetric strategies is hampered by the random rematching in our experimental design. In fact, in our experimental environment, not only is there no symmetric individual strategy that aggregates to the equilibrium group strategy, but there is no asymmetric strategy that each majority voter can adopt consistently and that would always aggregate to the equilibrium group strategy, for any possible rematching.

In practice, our basic C treatment is then a test of the robustness of storable votes' outcomes to coordination problems. To evaluate the role of coordination more precisely, we designed two additional treatments that replicate model C but where coordination problems are absent by construction.

Treatment $C2$ mirrored the $C2$ game: for each group, a single voter cast votes on behalf of all members of that group. Each majority group representative had 3 indivisible regular votes to cast on each of the two proposals and 6 bonus votes to cast as desired. Each minority group representative had 2 indivisible regular votes to spend on each of the two proposals and 4 bonus votes to cast as desired. Each committee then consisted of one minority and one majority representative. For each proposal, valuations were drawn independently with equal probability, from the support $[-100, -1]$ for the majority representative, and from $[1, 100]$ for the minority one. The timing of the game proceeded as described earlier. After each two-proposal round, group representatives were rematched. When we discuss experimental payoffs from this treatment, we multiply the minority representative's payoff by 2 and the majority's by 3, to make them comparable to the theoretical predictions and to the experimental payoffs for the C case and for the following treatment, which we call *CChat*.

In treatment *CChat* (*correlated valuations, chat option*) we replicated the C treatment, with each group composed of multiple individual voters rather than just two representatives. Before the vote on the first proposal, voters could exchange messages via computer with other members of the same group. Voters were instructed not to identify themselves, and the messages were anonymous but otherwise unconstrained. In particular,

---

[13]   When the two groups are of size $\{3, 2\}$, the majority has other valuation-responsive equilibrium strategies, but all are payoff-equivalent and all are monotonic, and we treat them as identical when reporting the experimental results. All equilibrium strategies satisfy: cast 0, 1, or 2 bonus votes with probabilities p_0, p_1, p_2 if the absolute valuation is smaller than 50, and 4, 5, or 6 bonus votes with probabilities q_0, q_1, q_2 if the absolute valuation is larger than 50, where $p_2 \geq q_2$ and $p_1 = q_1$. The strategy described in the text corresponds to $p_0 = p_1 = 0$, and $q_1 = q_2 = 0$.

Table 2. Equilibrium group strategies and outcomes

C Treatments	
M, m	3, 2
g_L, g_H	50, 50
% min wins, sv	25
% min wins, eff	33
% (min/maj) payoff, sv	38.5
% (min/maj) payoff, eff	52
% surplus sv	60
% surplus nsv	53

they allowed subjects to coordinate on their preferred group strategy. Everything else in the experiment — the stochastic properties of the valuation draws, the timing, the random re-matching — followed exactly the C treatment, with perfectly correlated values within a group.

Equilibrium group strategies and expected outcomes are identical in the three C treatments — C, $C2$, and *CChat*. They are reported in Table 2, where g_L and g_H denote the cutpoints where the minority switches from casting 0 bonus votes to casting 2, and from casting 2 to casting 4, and the majority from casting 2 bonus votes to casting 3, and from casting 3 to casting 4.

The outcome is more favorable to the minority in model C than in model B, both in terms of the expected frequency of minority victories and of its expected payoff, relative to the majority. In contrast with the B treatment, storable votes in the C treatment lead to efficiency gains over simple majority voting.

The experimental design is summarized in Table 3. In all b, c, and *CChat* sessions the majority was formed by 3 subjects and the minority by 2, with the exception of session b_3

Table 3. Experimental design

Session	Groups size	Subject pool	# Subjects	Rounds
b1	3, 2	CIT	15	30
b2	3, 2	UCLA	20	30
b3	5, 4	UCLA	27	30
c1	3, 2	UCLA	15	30
c2	3, 2	PU	15	20
c3	3, 2	PU	10	20
c21	3, 2	CIT	12	30
c22	3, 2	UCLA	16	30
c23	3, 2	PU	12	20
CChat1	3, 2	PU	10	20
CChat2	3, 2	PU	15	15

where the number of subjects in each group was 5 and 4, respectively. Session b_3 serves us as a control on the sensitivity of the experimental results to the size of the groups. In all $c2$ sessions, a single subject represented each group, but the design was equivalent to two fully coordinated groups of 3 and 2 members, respectively.

EXPERIMENTAL RESULTS

The experiment has two principal goals. First, we want to verify whether voting *outcomes* match the theoretical predictions: are minority subjects able to win some of the votes? Are they able to do so without loss of aggregate efficiency? Second, to what extent does voting *behavior* match the theoretical predictions?

Voting Outcomes and Efficiency

How often do minority groups win?

The diagram on the left of Figure 2(a) summarizes the answer to this question. The vertical axis is the percentage of times the minority prevailed in the experimental sessions, and the horizontal axis is the percentages of times it would have prevailed if all subjects had played the equilibrium strategy, given the valuations drawn during the experiments. Different treatments are indicated by different symbols, as described in the figure's legend.

The figure can then be read in several ways. The vertical height tells us that the minority won between 22 and 26 percent of the time in C, $C2$, and $CChat$, with little dispersion among them; it won less frequently in the B sessions (around 15 percent of the time) with the exception of the one experiment of size $\{5, 4\}$ where the minority won about 23 percent of the time.

Clearly, storable votes helped the minority win. The difference in this effect across treatments matches the theoretical predictions, as is evident from the way the points align along the 45-degree line. The closer to the line a point is, the closer the experiment's results are to the equilibrium predictions. If we estimate a simple regression line, the hypotheses of a unitary slope parameter and a zero constant term cannot be rejected at standard confidence values.[14] On average, the frequency of minority victories in the experiments differs from the equilibrium predictions by 3 percentage points, without clear outliers and without systematic treatment effects. We find this surprising because the complexity of the individual equilibrium strategies in the basic C treatment (as opposed to $C2$ and $CChat$) would suggest a larger discrepancy from equilibrium predictions in that specific treatment, a discrepancy the data do not show.

---

[14] The estimated parameters are: 0.76 for the slope (standard error 0.23), and 3.4 for the constant term (standard error 5.8).

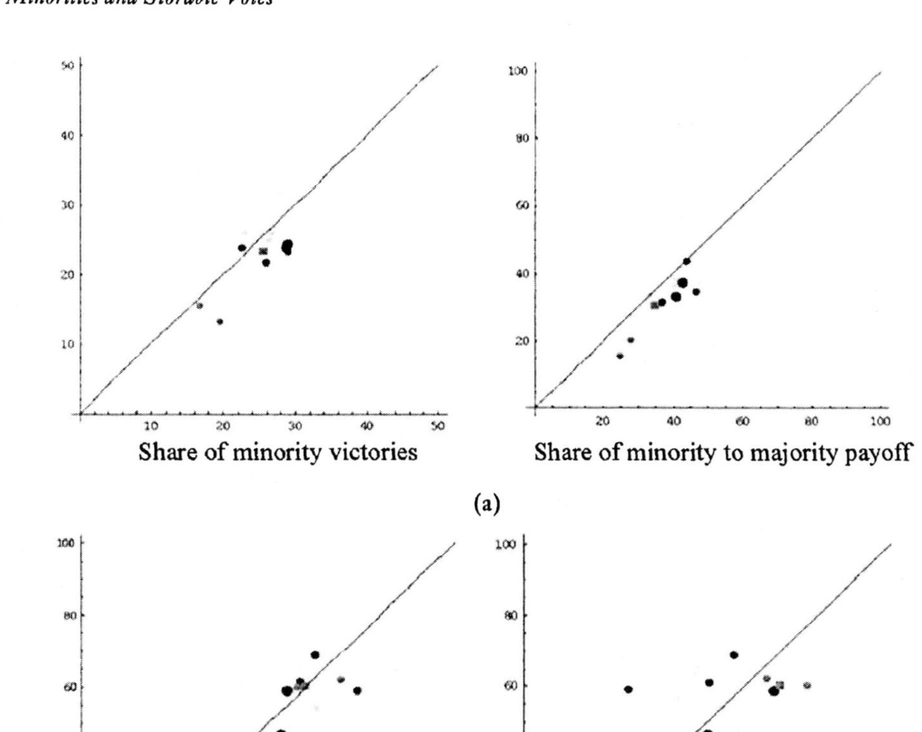

Figure 2. Experimental outcomes. (a) Minorities' outcomes. Experiments vs. equilibrium (b) Aggregate payoff share of surplus over randomness.

Did the experimental payoff to the minority match the theoretical predictions?

The diagram on the right of Figure 2(a) plots per capita minority payoff as a percentage of per capita majority payoff in the experiments on the vertical axis, and in equilibrium on the horizontal axis, using the symbols of the previous figure to identify the different experimental sessions. In all C, $C2$, and *CChat* treatments the relative minority payoff was higher than in any B treatments, as predicted by the theory, ranging between 32 and 44 percent of the average majority payoff, versus 16 to 20 percent in the B treatments of size $\{3, 2\}$ and 30 percent in the B treatment of size $\{5, 4\}$. Again, the effect of the voting mechanism in raising the minority's payoff was significant. Out of 11 experimental sessions, all but two are below the 45-degree line, suggesting that the minority was unable to fully exploit the opportunity presented by storable votes. But the discrepancy is not large — the average distance from the 45-degree line is 5 percentage points, again without clear outliers or treatment effects, which is small in comparison to the differences across treatments.[15] Again, if we estimate a regression line, we cannot reject the hypotheses of unitary slope and zero constant.[16]

*At what cost to the majority were the minority's gains? At what
cost to overall efficiency?*

The left-hand side of Figure 2(b) plots the normalized total surplus in each session on the vertical axis, against the equilibrium predictions on the horizontal axis. The equilibrium predictions are calculated using the actual valuation draws in the experiment. Points on the 45-degree line indicate a perfect match to the theory. The mean distance from the 45-degree line is only 7 percentage points, again with little evidence of outliers, versus a mean equilibrium surplus share of 60 percent. As in the previous figures, we cannot reject a regression line with unitary slope and zero constant, although the fit is poorer.[17]

The central question is how the efficiency of storable votes compares to the efficiency of alternative voting systems — in our case to simple majority voting. In the diagram on the right of Figure 2(b), the vertical axis is again the normalized total surplus in each session, now plotted against the equivalent measure with simple majority voting calculated from the experimental valuation draws. Theory predicts that data from C, $C2$, and *CChat* sessions should lie above the 45-degree line, while B data should lie below. The prediction is confirmed by the C and by the B experiments. Surprisingly, it is the *easier* treatments with coordination, $C2$ and *CChat*, that fall short of the prediction. Once again, two of the three most significant losses relative to non-storable votes occur in $C2$ sessions. Pooling all C, $C2$, and *CChat* data, the mean difference in normalized surplus is $+2$ percentage points, compared to the theoretical prediction of $+7$. Pooling all B data, the mean difference is -10 percentage points, compared with the theoretical prediction of -9.

The data from our experiment can be summarized in three main points. First, storable votes help minorities substantially, both in terms of the frequency with which minorities won decisions and in terms of the resulting benefits. Second, correlation of intensities

---

[15]   Note that a plausible range of values in Figure 2(b) is between 0 (the outcome with simple majority voting) and 100 (the expected outcome with random decision-making). In Figure 2(a), the corresponding range is between 0 and 50.

[16]   The estimated parameters are: 1.03 for the slope (standard error 0.19), and -6.2 for the constant term (standard error 7.1).

[17]   The estimated parameters are: 0.7 for the slope (standard error 0.40), and 14.1 for the constant term (standard error 24.1).

works to the advantage of the minority. Third, the efficiency costs associated with the increased representation of minority interests were small in magnitude. Without correlation, storable votes induced (small) aggregate welfare losses, but with perfectly correlated intensities, storable votes produced (small) welfare gains over simple majority voting.

Voting Behavior

We begin by studying individual behavior in the treatments that did not allow group members to coordinate their strategies (B and C). Later we turn to group behavior and discuss the effects of explicit coordination (treatments $C2$ and $CChat$).

Individual behavior

Storable votes allow voters to express intensity of preference by casting more votes, at any given state, when they have stronger preferences. Hence, *monotonicity of voting strategies is at the core of the mechanism*, and it is natural to analyze subject behavior in our experiments by studying this property first.

To obtain a measure of monotonicity of individual behavior, we estimate *monotonicity violations* and *cutpoints* for each subject. For each subject we have K pairs of observations, where K equals either 20 or 30 depending on the session.[18] Each pair consists of a first proposal intensity value and the number of votes cast for (or against) the first proposal. In treatments B and C, the number of votes cast by each subject is always 1, 2, or 3. A perfectly monotone strategy is one for which we can find two cutpoints, $c1 \leq c2$ such that whenever the subject's first period intensity was below $c1$ the subject cast 1 vote, whenever his intensity was above $c2$, the subject cast 3 votes, and for intermediate values between $c1$ and $c2$ the subject cast 2 votes. We calculate the number of monotonicity violations as the minimum number of voting choices that would have to be changed, for each subject, to make the strategy perfectly monotonic. We then identify the pair of cutpoints that is consistent with such a monotonic strategy. In some cases, multiple cutpoints are consistent with the same number of monotonicity violations; when this happens, we select the pair that is closest to the equilibrium cutpoints.

Figure 3(a) presents histograms of individual monotonicity violations in treatments B and C. The horizontal axis is divided into deciles representing the percentage of violations over the total number of voting decisions, and the vertical axis reports the fraction of subjects that belong to each decile.

In the B treatment, 50 percent of the subjects had 3 or fewer violations out of 30 voting decisions (10 percent). In the C treatment, 57 percent of subjects had violation rates less than or equal to 10 percent. As comparison, a voter choosing randomly whether to cast 0, 1, or 2 bonus votes would have a violation rate converging to 67 percent as the number of decisions becomes very large.[19] The comparison makes clear that, although there is some noise, individual choices indeed tended to be monotonic for most subjects.

---

[18] With the exception of session *CChat2*, with 15 rounds.

[19] To account for the smaller number of violations that would result from the small sample and the free cutpoints, we simulated random behavior with 21 subjects and 30 rounds. We found that no

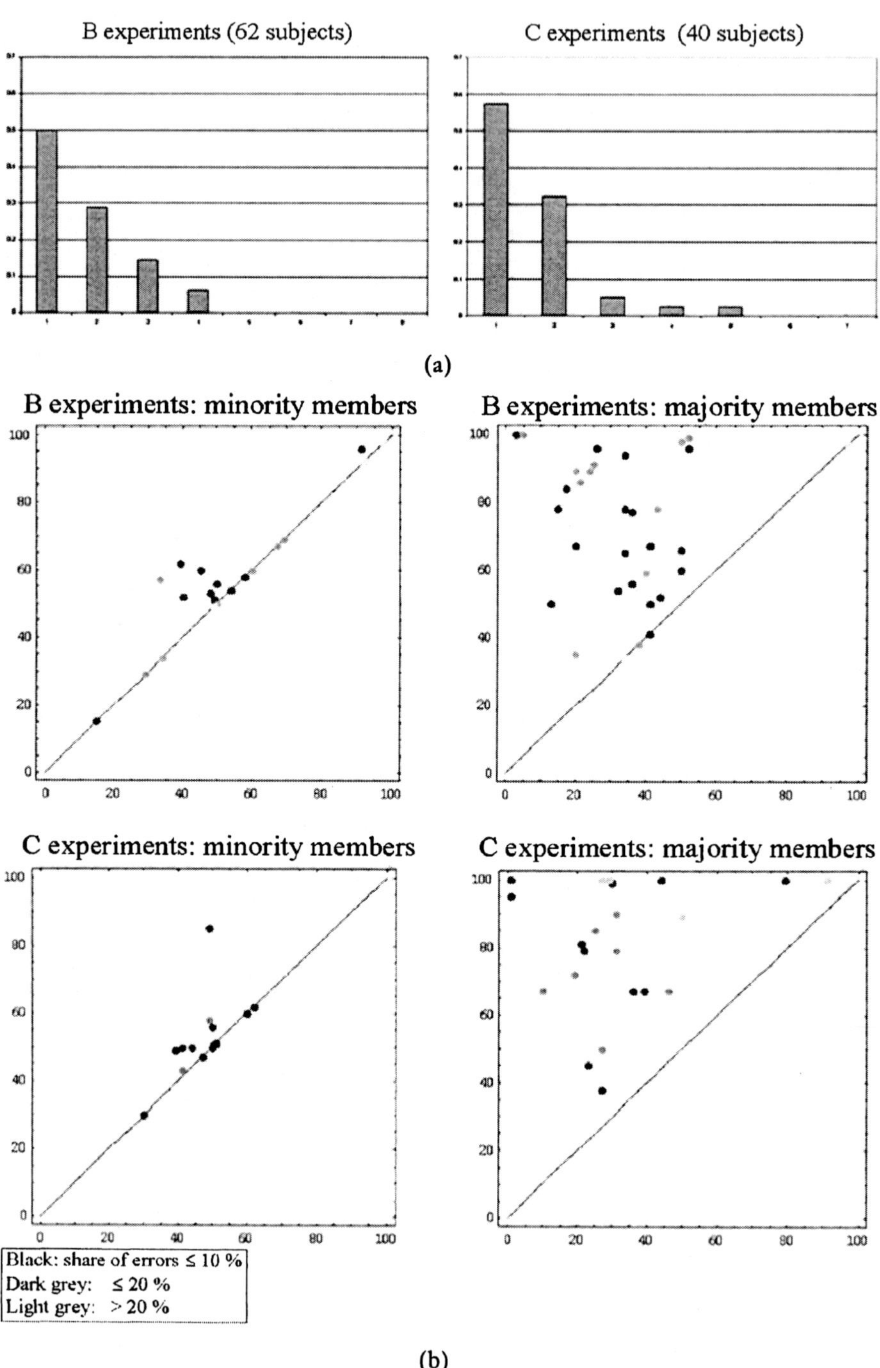

Figure 3. Individual behavior. (a) Monotonicity violations. (b) Cutpoints.

The estimated cutpoints for all individual subjects in the B and C sessions are displayed in Figure 3(b). Each point represents one subject's estimated pair of cutpoints, with $c1$ on the horizontal axis and $c2$ on the vertical axis. All cutpoints lying on the 45-degree line involve no splitting of bonus votes: always casting either both or neither of the bonus votes over the first decision. Moving to the upper left corner of the graph are cutpoints that involve more and more splitting of bonus votes, i.e., using one bonus vote in each period for a range of values that increases as one approaches the corner. The upper left corner of the graph, at $(0, 100)$ corresponds to always casting one bonus vote. Cutpoints for subjects in the minority group are in the left graph and cutpoints for the subjects in the majority group are in the right graph. The rates of monotonicity violations are indicated by shading the points, with the darkest points having the fewest monotonicity violations.

In the B treatments, the equilibrium cutpoints for both majority and minority subjects are $(50, 50)$: if everyone played the equilibrium strategies all points would be on the 45-degree line at 50. In the C treatments, $(50, 50)$ remains an equilibrium for individual minority subjects, but not for subjects in the majority, whose asymmetrical strategies are contingent on the behavior of the other members of the group and cannot be identified unambiguously in the figure.

Two features of the distribution of cutpoints appear in both treatments. First, the minority cutpoints do cluster around $(50, 50)$, and on average minority subjects whose cutpoints are closer to equilibrium have lower violation rates. Second, bonus votes are much more frequently split by majority voters, with little difference between the two treatments in spite of the different theoretical predictions. Intuitively, even in model B, majority voters have less to lose from splitting their bonus votes — their larger number implies that they are guaranteed to always win one of the two decisions, and one single vote more or less plays a smaller role than in the case of the minority. Consider the parameter values used in the experiments and a committee of size $(3, 2)$. The expected loss to a voter deviating from his equilibrium strategy and always casting one bonus vote over each proposal is 15 percent in model B and 50 percent in model C for a minority voter, versus 4 percent in model B and 8 percent in model C for a majority voter (relative to the expected equilibrium payoff).[20] The difference in the cost of splitting one's bonus votes in the two models may play some role in the more pronounced clustering of the minority cutpoints around the 45-degree line, and particularly around $(50, 50)$ in the C treatment.

Group behavior

The monotonicity of the individual strategies provides only a partial picture. Efficiency requires *group* strategies to be monotonic in the group intensity. In the B treatment the

---

subjects had violation rates less or equal to 30 percent; 2 subjects were in the fourth decile; 8 in the fifth, and 11 in the sixth.

[20] Supposing that all other voters play the equilibrium strategy. In model C, we consider the case where the individual majority voter's deviation causes the majority group strategy to switch from casting either 5 or 7 votes to always casting 6.

notion of *group intensity* is not clearly defined because different subjects within a group have different intensities. But we can check for *group monotonicity* in the C treatment, that is, we can check whether the sum of the votes by members of one group is monotone in their (common) intensity. If there is heterogeneity in behavior, monotonicity at the individual level need not imply monotonicity at the group level because individuals are continuously rematched. The problem is particularly severe for the majority whose individual equilibrium strategies are asymmetric.[21]

The histograms in the first row of Figure 4(a) illustrate the difficulty that groups had in the C treatment. Out of a total of 16 groups, 7 had error rates above 20 percent, compared to only 10 percent of individual subjects in the same experimental sessions (see Figure 3(a)). As expected, and as shown by the histogram on the right, most errors are associated with the majority, where 5 of the 8 groups had more than 20 percent error rates.

A comparison of these results to monotonicity violations in the $C2$ and *CChat* treatments allows us to study the role of explicit coordination. According to the histograms in the second row of Figure 4, the open communication in *CChat* reduced group violations dramatically: *all* minority groups and 2 out of 5 of the majority groups had fewer than 10 percent violations. More surprising is the poor performance of the $C2$ treatment, where perfect coordination is imposed by the experimental design.[22]

These results leave us with a puzzle: if the aggregate group behavior of the experimental subjects in sessions C often violates monotonicity, why did the outcomes of these experiments — in terms of minority victories and efficiency — still conform to the theory? Why did these sessions outperform, on average, the $C2$ sessions with a apparently comparable record of monotonicity violations. The answer comes from the underlying monotonicity of the *individual* behavior in treatment C. Intuitively, because individual subjects did cast their vote monotonically, the violations resulting from the uncoordinated aggregation of the votes are numerous, but not large: they tend to be concentrated around the cutpoints values. To verify this, the histograms in Figure 4(b) summarize the distribution of the average distance of *mistaken* (i.e., non-monotonic) voting choices from the cutpoints, as a percentage of the expected distance if voting choices were random.[23] The *CChat* experiments show the greatest consistency: with one outlier, all groups have error distances below 20 percent of the random case. But it is the comparison between the C and the $C2$ treatments that is particularly revealing in explaining the differences in

---

[21]   We identify a group by the label in the experiment (group 1, group 2, etc.), but rematching implies that the composition of each group continues to change. Note that if equilibrium strategies were symmetrical, the changing composition of the group would not matter.

[22]   This appears to be the result of a single experimental session: session c22 conducted at UCLA (where 25 percent of the subjects had a rate of violations approaching 50 percent).

[23]   Following this logic, these cutpoints are estimated so as to minimize the average distance (both in the experimental data and in the theoretical random case). With a very large number of random voting choices, the two cutpoints that minimize the expected errors' distance are $(50, 50)$. The frequency of error is $2/3$, with an average distance of 25, yielding an expected distance of $50/3$. The corresponding number in the experimental data is, for a given pair of cutpoints, the sum of all errors' distances, divided by K, the number of rounds in the experiment.

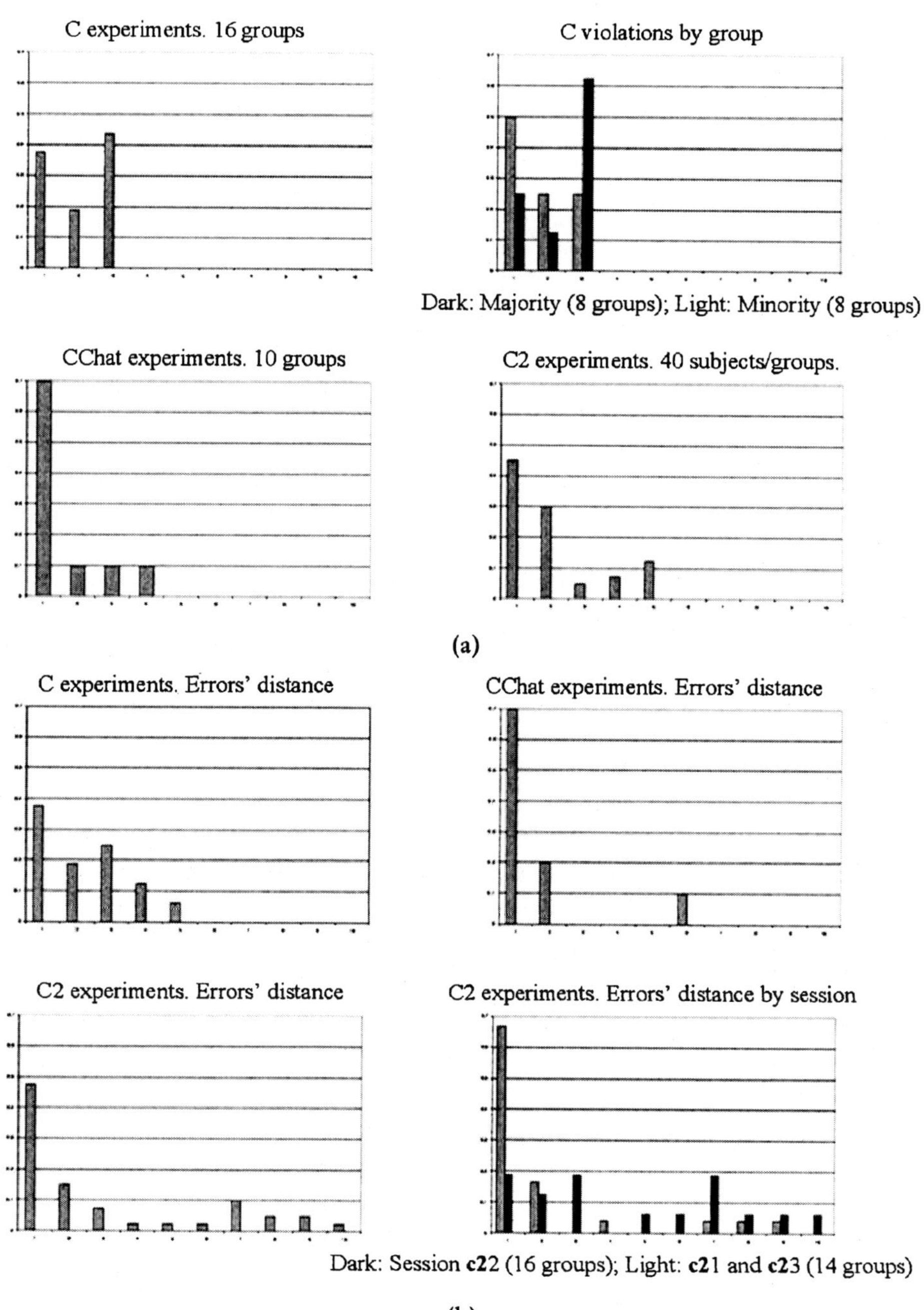

Figure 4. Group behavior — monotonicity violations. (a) Percentage of violations. (b) Average errors' distance relative to random voting.

experimental outcomes: one-fourth of all $C2$ groups have error distances that are closer to the purely random case than *any* of the C groups. As mentioned, this reflects mostly one outlier session, **c22**, and how much of an outlier **c22** is made clear in the diagram on the right, in the bottom row of Figure 4(b). The **c22** session had 16 subjects, each representing one group; of these, 7 had error distances that were closer to the purely random case than *any* of the C groups, and only 3 had distances that were less than 10 percent of the random case, a very different result from the other two $C2$ sessions. This explains why the aggregate experimental payoff of session **c22** falls short both of the theoretical prediction and of the payoff with simple majority. The other $C2$ sessions were much better behaved, although they too presented a few instances of almost random behavior, something we do not observe in the C sessions. As shown in Figure 2(b), these few cases were sufficient to exact a cost in terms of efficiency, lowering the overall performance of the $C2$ treatment. Why the treatment proved difficult to our subjects is an open question, although we can speculate that the problem may come from the larger size of the individual strategy space: each minority voter had 5 different choices of how many votes to use in the first period $(2, 3, 4, 5, 6)$, and each majority voter had 7 different choices $(3, 4, 5, 6, 7, 8, 9)$.

As in the analysis of individual behavior, the monotonicity analysis generates cutpoints estimates.[24] Group cutpoints are depicted in Figure 5, with minority cutpoints on the left and majority cutpoints on the right. In line with the equilibrium predictions, we can summarize the strategies of each group through two cutpoints, represented by a point in the diagrams and equal to $(50, 50)$ for both the minority and the majority.[25]

The first row of diagrams in Figure 5 refers to C treatments; the second row to $C2$ and the last to *CChat*. As in Figure 3(b), darker points indicate fewer monotonicity violations. Coordination affects the cutpoints of the minority groups: none of the estimated cutpoints in treatments $C2$ and *CChat* lies outside the 45–degree line, as opposed to what we observe in treatment C. Thus in treatments $C2$ and *CChat*, in accordance with equilibrium the behavior of all minority groups is best described as voting either 2 (at lower values) or 6 (at higher values), with some dispersion around the equilibrium cutpoints $(50, 50)$. The majority's behavior, on the other hand, is best described as splitting the bonus votes for some intermediate range of values. In addition, the light shading of most points in the majority figures reflects the relatively large number of monotonicity violations for any estimate of cutpoints. The relatively greater deviation from equilibrium by the majority groups may reflect their relative low cost of such deviations. With a single coordinated strategy, the expected percentage loss to the majority from always splitting the bonus votes is about 8 percent when the minority plays the equilibrium

---

[24] The cutpoints estimates that minimize the number of monotonicity violations need not be identical to those that minimize the errors' distance. In practice, they differ mostly in the case of those subjects with more random behavior. The substance of the results does not change, and we report here the cutpoints that minimize the number of violations, for consistency with the discussion of individual behavior.

[25] For the majority groups, we treat as identical all payoff-equivalent strategies, i.e., voting either 3, or 4, or 5 below g_l, and voting either 7, or 8, or 9 above g_h.

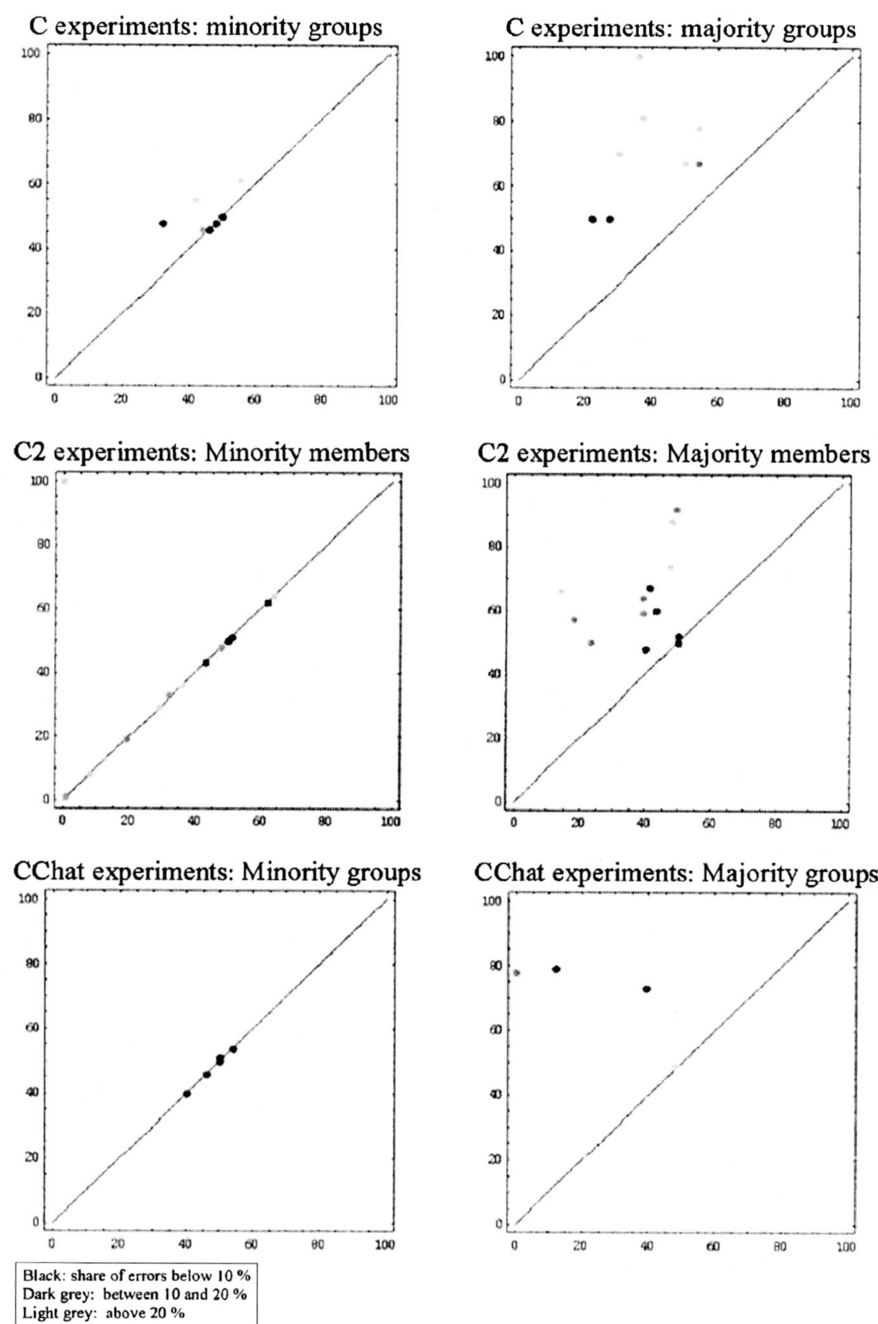

Figure 5. Group behavior — group cutpoints.

strategy.[26] For the minority, on the other hand, splitting the bonus votes can be very costly: a minority always casting 4 votes *always* loses against a majority casting 5 votes at valuations below 50 and 7 at valuations above 50.

CONCLUSIONS

Majoritarian principles are a fundamental ingredient of democratic institutions. But they carry with them the risk of disenfranchising minority groups and endangering the stability of the system, by violating principles of both equity and efficiency. In a well-designed democracy, a judicial system protecting the rights of minority groups needs to be supplemented by political remedies that ensure the minority a voice through the daily, ordered exercise of political rights. This paper has analyzed the potential of a simple voting system — storable votes — to fulfill this function. By granting voters a stock of votes to be divided as desired over a series of multiple binary decisions, storable votes allow the minority to cumulate votes on specific issues and to win sometime. Because the minority wins only if its strength of preferences is high, and the majority's is low, the gains in terms of equity have little, if any, cost in terms of efficiency.

We have studied two related models where two groups of different size have consistently opposite preferences. In our *correlated* model, C, all members of a group — whether the majority or the minority — agree not only on the direction of their preferences but also on the strength of their preferences. If we think in terms of political parties, these would be parties with strong discipline; more generally, the model is best suited to represent groups with some level of organization, sufficient to agree on the set of priorities. In our *basic* model, model B, on the other hand, all members of a group agree on the direction of their preferences, and the two groups have opposite preferences, but within a group the members' priorities may differ. The groups are not organized.

There are many directions for further research. We limit ourselves to mentioning two. First, it would be interesting to compare storable votes to a larger set of alternative mechanisms, both theoretically and experimentally. These alternative mechanisms should include vetoes, serial dictatorship, and even more complex systems such as the one proposed in Jackson and Sonnenschein (2007). Storable votes are more flexible but more complicated than vetoes, and less flexible and less complicated than the Jackson and Sonnenschein mechanism. Serial dictatorship requires a secondary mechanism to allocate decisions to specific individuals or groups in a somewhat efficient fashion. What can the theory tell us, and how would all compare experimentally?[27] Second, the sensitivity of storable votes to agenda manipulation is an open question. The agenda setting procedure should be part of the overall game, and voters will decide how many votes

---

[26] In fact, in this model the majority's maximin strategy entails splitting the bonus votes. It corresponds to cutpoints (25, 100): cast no bonus votes for values below 25, but split the bonus votes for all values above 25.

[27] Two recent experimental analyses are Engelmann and Grimm (2006) on the Jackson–Sonnenschein mechanism, and Kagel *et al.* (2005) on veto power. Neither paper compares different mechanisms.

to cast knowing how new issues are brought to a vote. *A priori* it is not clear whether problems will arise: having multiple votes that can be shifted across proposals may make the order of the proposals more important, but also increase the ability to resist possible manipulations of this order. On the other hand, the additional consideration of political minorities may exacerbate possible problems, either because majority losses are particularly expensive in terms of efficiency or because the minority may end up unable to ever control any outcome.

APPENDIX

Proof of Lemma 1 Suppose that $x^*_{Mt}(v_i, B_t, t)$ and $x^*_{mt}(v_i, B_t, t)$ exist. Consider candidate equilibrium strategies $\{x'_{it}(v_i, B_t, t)\}$ for model C, where $\sum_{i \in m} x'_{it}(v_i, B, t) = x^*_{mt}(v_i, B, t)$ and $\sum_{i \in M} x'_{it}(v_i, B, t) = x^*_{Mt}(v_i, B, t)$. Because preferences between the two groups are always opposed, at any state only the aggregate voting choice of the opposite group affects voters' payoffs. In addition, because in model C preferences within each group are always perfectly correlated, by definition $\{x'_{it}(v_i, B, t)\}, i \in m$ maximize the expected payoff of each individual minority member, given $x^*_{Mt}(v_i, B, t)$ (and similarly for $\{x'_{it}(v_i, B, t)\}, i \in M$, given $x^*_{mt}(v_i, B, t)$). It follows that no individual deviation from the prescribed strategies can be profitable and $\{x'_{it}(v_i, B_t, t)\}$ must be equilibrium strategies. Note that in general the equilibrium will not be unique: any permutation of individual strategies that leaves the aggregate vote for the group unchanged, at given state, is an equilibrium. ∎

Proof of Lemma 2 (i) *Existence of equilibrium in pure strategies.* Milgrom and Weber (1985) discuss conditions for existence of an equilibrium in distributional strategies. In particular, conditional on a publicly observed variable, individual types are required to be independent. The publicly observed information in our case is each voter's membership in one of the two groups, and hence the support of the distribution from which valuations are drawn. Conditional on such support, individual valuations are independent in case B. The arguments in Casella (2005) remain applicable here. Hence an equilibrium in pure strategies exists for model B. Conditional on public information on the support of each distribution, valuations are independent in the two-voter version of model C. Again, the arguments in Casella (2005) apply, and an equilibrium in pure strategies exists. But since such an equilibrium must be an equilibrium of the n-voter C game, it follows that an equilibrium in pure strategies of the n-voter C game exists. (ii) *Monotonicity of the equilibrium strategies.* Call a strategy *monotonic* if, at a given state, the number of votes cast is monotonically increasing in the intensity of preferences v_{it}. Casella *et al.* (2006) shows that at any given state all individual best response strategies must be monotonic when members of each group do not play correlated strategies. Thus the argument applies immediately to equilibria of model B. It also applies to the two-voter version of model C, and hence to group strategies, as opposed to individual strategies, in the equilibrium we focus on in the n-voter C game. If, at any given state, all best response strategies must be monotonic and an equilibrium exists, it follows that equilibrium strategies must be monotonic. Because there is a continuum of types and a finite set of strategies, then it must be that monotonic equilibrium strategies must take the form of monotone cutpoint strategies. ∎

Proof of Theorem 1 We begin by proving the second part of the theorem. Consider any candidate equilibrium where the minority is expected to lose with probability 1 over each decision. A minority member cannot be worse off by cumulating all his bonus votes on one decision. Over all decisions, there must be at least one where with positive probability the majority casts no more than MB_0/T bonus votes, and since the minority can never cast fewer than m total votes, a deviating minority member can always find a decision where with positive probability the difference in votes cast is at most $M(1 + B_0/T) - m$. Thus with positive probability the outcome of that decision changes and deviation is profitable if $M(1 + B_0/T) \leq m + B_0$, or $B_0(1 - M/T) \geq M - m$. This condition requires $T > M$, and in this case becomes $B_0 \geq T(M - m)/(T - M)$. For all M and m, the condition is sufficient and applies to both models B and C. Since we know by Lemma 2 that an equilibrium exists for arbitrary F, T, M, and m, it must be that if $T > M$, and $B_0 \geq T(M - m)/(T - M)$ the minority is expected to win sometime with strictly positive probability in all equilibria. We now prove the first part of the theorem. Suppose $T \leq M$. Consider the following candidate equilibrium: at time $t = 1$, $x_{i1} = 1 + B_0$ for $i \in \mathbf{m}$ and $x_{j1} = 1$ for $j \in \mathbf{M}$; at all other times $t \neq 1$, $x_{it} = 1$, and $x_{jt} = 1 + B_0/(T - 1)$. If $m(1 + B_0) > M$ or $B_0 > (M - m)/m$ the minority always wins the first vote, while the majority always wins all other votes. No individual minority member can gain from deviation, for all possible realizations of his valuations, if $m + B_0 < M[1 + B_0/(T - 1)]$, or $B_0[1 - M/(T - 1)] < M - m$, a condition always satisfied when $T \leq M$. No majority member can gain from deviating, again for all possible realizations of his valuations, if $m(1 + B_0) > M + B_0$ or $B_0 > (M - m)/(m - 1)$, a threshold that is finite for all $m > 1$. Thus if $T \leq M$, $m > 1$, and $B_0 > (M - m)/(m - 1)$, the strategies described are an equilibrium, and the minority always wins the first vote. ∎

Proof of Theorem 2 Consider the following strategies. Over the first $T - 2$ proposals, each minority member always casts only the regular vote; each majority member casts $1 + b$ votes. At $T - 1$, each minority member casts only his regular vote if $v_m < \alpha$, for a fixed $\alpha > 0$, and all bonus votes otherwise; each majority members casts $1 + b$ votes if $v_M < \alpha$ and $1 + h$ otherwise, where $b + h + (T - 2)b = B_0$. In the last election, all remaining votes are cast.

We show in step (i) that for all M and $m \geq 2$ there exist non-negative values of B_0, b, h, and T for which such strategies are equilibrium strategies, and the minority wins at $T - 1$ if $(v_{mT-1} > \alpha, v_{MT-1} < \alpha)$, and at T if $(v_{mT-1} < \alpha, v_{MT-1} > \alpha)$, but always loses otherwise. We then show in (ii) that in such an equilibrium $EV_0 > EW_0$ if $m > M/2$. Because the theorem requires $m > M/2$, it cannot apply to $m = 1$.

(i) The minority wins at $T - 1$ if $(v_{mT-1} > \alpha, v_{MT-1} < \alpha)$, and at T if $(v_{mT-1} < \alpha, v_{MT-1} > \alpha)$ if:

$$m(1 + B_0) > M(1 + b) \tag{A.1}$$

and loses in all other cases if:

$$M(1 + h) > m(1 + B_0). \tag{A.2}$$

Any unilateral deviation by a minority voter is ruled out if:

$$m + B_0 < M(1 + b). \tag{A.3}$$

Similarly, any unilateral deviation by a majority voter is ruled out if:

$$M + (M - 1)b + B_0 < m(1 + B_0). \tag{A.4}$$

If there exist values of B_0, b, h, and T for which these four inequalities are satisfied simultaneously, and the budget constraint $b + h + (T - 2)b = B_0$ holds, then the strategies are an equilibrium, delivering the outcomes described above. It is immediate that (A.4) implies (A.1). Hence, substituting the budget constraint in (A.2), three conditions must be satisfied:

$$T < 1 + \frac{(B_0 + 1)(M - m)}{Mb} \tag{A.2$'$}$$

$$B_0 < (M - m) + Mb \tag{A.3$'$}$$

$$B_0 > \frac{M - m}{m - 1} + \frac{M - m}{m - 1}b. \tag{A.4$'$}$$

If we ignore integer constraints, then for all $m \geq 2$ (A.3$'$) and (A.4$'$) are satisfied for any positive b. With b arbitrarily small, T can be arbitrarily large, and the equilibrium can be supported for any positive finite T. Integer constraints are however part of the environment, and in general impose an upper bound on T, $\overline{T}$, which depends on M and m. The following observations follow immediately from (A.2$'$), (A.3$'$) an (A.4$'$): (a) if $m > 2$, then for all $M > m$, there is an equilibrium with $b = 1$, B_0 integer $\in (2(M - m)/(m - 1), 2M - m)$, and $\overline{T}(M, m) > 2$; (b) if $m = 2$, then the only relevant case satisfying the constraint $M < 2m$ is $M = 3$. For $m = 2$ and $M = 3$, there is an equilibrium with $b = 2$, $B_0 = 6$, and $\overline{T} = 13/6 > 2$.

(ii) In any equilibrium of this type, $EV_0 > EW_0$ iff:

$$F(\alpha)\left[M\int_0^\alpha vdF(v) + F(\alpha)M\int_0^1 vdF(v)\right]$$

$$+ \left[1 - F(\alpha)\right]\left[M\int_\alpha^1 vdF(v) + [1 - F(\alpha)]M\int_0^1 vdF(v)\right]$$

$$+ F(\alpha)\left[M\int_\alpha^1 vdF(v) + [1 - F(\alpha)]m\int_0^1 vdF(v)\right]$$

$$+ F(\alpha)\left[m\int_\alpha^1 vdF(v) + [1 - F(\alpha)]M\int_0^1 vdF(v)\right] > 2M\int_0^1 vdF(v)$$

Simplifying:

$$F(\alpha)\left[MF(\alpha) + m(1 - F(\alpha))\right] \int_0^1 v\,dF(v)$$

$$+ \left[mF(\alpha) + M(1 - F(\alpha))\right] \int_\alpha^1 v\,dF(v) > M \int_0^1 v\,dF(v). \tag{A.5}$$

Note that the left-hand side simplifies to $M \int_0^1 v\,dF(v)$ when evaluated at either $\alpha = 0$ or $\alpha = 1$, since in both cases the majority always wins (and thus $EV_0 = EW_0$). Taking the derivative of (A.5) with respect to α and evaluating it at $\alpha = 0$, we obtain:

$$\left.\frac{\partial(EV_0 - EW_0)}{\partial \alpha}\right|_{\alpha=0} = f(0)\int_0^1 v\,dF(v)(2m - M) > 0 \Leftrightarrow m > M/2$$

Thus if $m > M/2$ there exists a threshold $\alpha > 0$ such that the strategies described above lead to higher *ex ante* welfare than simple majority voting.   ∎

SUPPLEMENTARY MATERIAL
MINORITIES AND STORABLE VOTES

PROOF OF THE PROPOSITION

Model B

(a) *Equilibrium.* To verify that the strategy described is an equilibrium, consider the best response for voter i. If i casts x_{i1} votes in the vote over the first proposal, his expected utility over the whole game is: $EU_i|x_{i1} = v_{i1}\mathrm{prob}(W_1|x_{i1}) + E(v)\mathrm{prob}(W_2|4 - x_{i1})$, where $\mathrm{prob}(W_t|x_{it})$ is i's probability of obtaining the desired outcome in period t conditional on casting x_{it} votes, and from the symmetry of F, $E(v) = 0.5$. Since $(n - 1)$ is an even number, and every other voter is casting either 1 or 3 votes, the difference in votes between the two sides, excluding i, must be even for both proposals. Thus, when i considers the choice between casting 3, 2 or 1 votes, the only case in which the choice matters is a difference of 2 votes in his side disfavor, either over proposal 1 or proposal 2:

$$EU_i|3 > EU_i|2 \Leftrightarrow v_{i1}[\mathrm{prob}(\Delta x_{1-i} = 2)] > 0.5[\mathrm{prob}(\Delta x_{2-i} = 2)]$$

$$EU_i|2 > EU_i|1 \Leftrightarrow v_{i1}[\mathrm{prob}(\Delta x_{1-i} = 2)] > 0.5[\mathrm{prob}(\Delta x_{2-i} = 2)],$$

where Δx_{t-i} indicates the number of votes by which i's side is losing over proposal P_t, absent i's vote. Given the symmetry of F, in the candidate equilibrium the probability of any other voter casting 1 or 3 votes is identical, implying: $\mathrm{prob}(\Delta x_{1-i} = 2) = \mathrm{prob}(\Delta x_{2-i} = 2)$. Thus i's best response is to cast 1 vote if $v_{i1} < 0.5$ and 3 votes if

$v_{i1} > 0.5$; the conclusion holds for all i, and the strategy is indeed an equilibrium. If $M > 3m$, $\text{prob}(\Delta x_{1-i} = 2) = \text{prob}(\Delta x_{2-i} = 2) = 0$, and the number of votes cast is irrelevant.

(b) *Frequency of minority victories.* Write the majority size as $M = m + 2k - 1$, with $k \geq 1$ (recall than n is odd). The minority wins the first vote if there are at least k more valuations above 0.5 among the minority than the majority. Given the symmetry of F, the probability of this event is given by the formula in the lemma. The minority wins the second vote if there are at least k more valuations below 0.5 over the first proposal among the minority than the majority, an event that again, given the symmetry of F, has the probability given in the lemma. Note that the two events are mutually exclusive and that the probability can be positive only if $k < m$, implying that the majority always wins if $M > 3m$.

(c) *Expected equilibrium payoff.* With n odd and the equilibrium strategies described above, the difference in votes cast by the two groups is always an even number. In addition, the symmetry of F guarantees that the probability of any given difference in votes is equal over the two proposals. If we call $\text{prob}(W_M|x)$ the probability of obtaining the desired outcome for $i \in M$, conditional on casting x votes, then, given F Uniform, we can write the *ex ante* expected payoff of a majority member as:

$$EV_{Bi} = (3/8)\text{prob}(W_M|1) + (5/8)\text{prob}(W_M|3), \quad \forall i \in M$$

where $\text{prob}(W_M|1) = \text{prob}(x_{M-i} \geq x_m)$ and $\text{prob}(W_M|3) = \text{prob}(x_{M-i} \geq x_m - 2)$. Recall that $M = m + 2k - 1$. Given the equilibrium strategies, the symmetry of F, and the independence of the valuation draws, if we call *high* a valuation above 0.5, $\text{prob}(x_{M-i} \geq x_m)$ equals the probability that the number of high draws in the minority group is at most $k - 1$ higher than for the majority group, excluding voter i:

$$\text{prob}(W_M|1) = 1 - \sum_{s=k}^{m} \left[\sum_{r=0}^{m-s} \binom{M-1}{r} \binom{m}{r+s} \right] 2^{-(M-1+m)}.$$

Similarly, $\text{prob}(x_{M-i} \geq x_m - 2)$ equals the probability that the number of high draws in the minority group is at most k higher than for the majority group, excluding voter i:

$$\text{prob}(W_M|3) = 1 - \sum_{s=k+1}^{m} \left[\sum_{r=0}^{m-s} \binom{M-1}{r} \binom{m}{r+s} \right] 2^{-(M-1+m)}.$$

Analogous calculations yield the *ex ante* expected payoff of a minority member:

$$EV_{Bj} = (3/8)\text{prob}(W_m|1) + (5/8)\text{prob}(W_m|3), \quad \forall j \in m$$

where:

$$\text{prob}(W_m|1) = \sum_{s=k}^{m-1} \left[\sum_{r=0}^{m-s-1} \binom{M}{r} \binom{m-1}{r+s} \right] 2^{-(M+m-1)}$$

and

$$\text{prob}(W_m|3) = \sum_{s=k-1}^{m-1} \left[\sum_{r=0}^{m-s-1} \binom{M}{r} \binom{m-1}{r+s} \right] 2^{-(M+m-1)}.$$

Ex ante aggregate expected payoff in equilibrium is then: $EV_B = M(EV_{Bi}) + m(EV_{Bj})$, $i \in M, j \in m$. The expressions can be simplified slightly, and after some manipulations we derive:

$$EV_B > EW_0 = M \Leftrightarrow \frac{5}{8} \frac{(M+m)}{\left(\frac{3m-M-1}{2}\right)! \left(\frac{3M-m-1}{2}\right)!}$$

$$> \sum_{s=k}^{m} \frac{M}{(m-s)!(M-1+s)!} - \sum_{s=k}^{m-1} \frac{m}{(m-s-1)!(M+s)!},$$

where $k = (M - m + 1)/2$. It is then simple to verify that for all $M = 3m - 1$ (i.e., $k = m$) or $M = 3m - 3$ (i.e., $k = m - 1$), $EV_B < EW_0$. At the same time, for M large enough it is not difficult to find values of $m = M - 1$ ($k = 1$) such that $EV_B > EW_0$, and generate examples that satisfy the statement in the lemma. $M' = 8$, $m' = 3$, and $m'' = 7$ is one such example; $M' = 6$, $m' = 3$, and $m'' = 5$ is another.

Model C

(a) *Equilibrium.* If $2M > 3m$, by setting $x_{M1} = 2M$ for all v_{M1} the majority can guarantee itself victory over both proposals. All minority strategies are equivalent, including $x_{m1} = m$ if $v_{m1} < 0.5$ and $x_{m1} = 3m$ if $v_{m1} > 0.5$. No deviation can be profitable for a member of either group, and the strategies are an equilibrium. Suppose then $2M \leq 3m$. When $x_m = m$, the minority always loses ($m < \max\{M, m + 3\} < \min\{3M, 4M - (m + 3)\}$). The only possible deviation for a minority member is to cast 2 or 3 votes when $x_{m-i} = m - 1$, but $m + 2 < \max\{M, m + 3\} < \min\{3M, 4M - (m+3)\}$: the deviation cannot be profitable. The majority always wins when casting $\min\{3M, 4M - (m + 3)\}$ votes, but loses when $x_M = \max\{M, m + 3\}$ if $x_m = 3m$. A majority member could deviate and use his bonus votes when $x_{M-i} = \max\{M - 1, m + 2\}$. But casting 2 votes cannot be profitable: with $2M \leq 3m$, $\max\{M+1, m+4\} < 3m$. And neither can casting 3: with $2M \leq 3m$, either $\max\{M + 2, m + 5\} < 3m$ and $\min\{3M - 2, 4M - (m + 5)\} > 3m$, in which case the outcomes are unchanged; or $\max\{M+2, m+5\} > 3m$ and $\min\{3M - 2, 4M - (m+5)\} < 3m$, in which case the certainty of winning at $v_M > 0.5$ is traded for the certainty of winning in the future, with $E(v) = 0.5$ — a net loss in expected utility. Hence $x_{m1} = m$ if $v_{m1} < 0.5$ and $x_{m1} = 3m$ if $v_{m1} > 0.5$; and $x_{M1} = \max\{M, m + 3\}$ if $v_{M1} < 0.5$ and $x_{M1} = \min\{3M, 4M - (m + 3)\}$ if $v_{M1} > 0.5$ are equilibrium strategies.

(b) *Frequency of minority victories.* If $2M \leq 3m$ the minority wins the first vote if $(v_{m1} > 0.5 \cap v_{M1} < 0.5)$ and the second if $(v_{m1} < 0.5 \cap v_{M1} > 0.5)$ — given the symmetry of F, it wins each vote with probability 0.25.

(c) *Expected equilibrium payoff.* If $2M > 3m$, the majority always wins and the expected aggregate payoff over the two proposals equals M. If $2M \leq 3m$, the expected aggregate payoff equals: $(1/4)(M/4 + M/2) + (1/4)(3M/4 + M/2) + (1/4)(3M/4 + m/2) + (1/4)(3m/4 + M/2) = (13M + 5m)/16$ (where the first term is the expected payoff over the two proposals when $(v_{m1} < 0.5 \cap v_{M1} < 0.5)$, the second when $(v_{m1} > 0.5 \cap v_{M1} > 0.5)$, the third when $(v_{M1} > 0.5 \cap v_{m1} < 0.5)$, and the fourth when $(v_{m1} > 0.5 \cap v_{M1} < 0.5)$ — all events with probability $1/4$). With simple majority voting, the majority always wins and over the two proposals $EW_0 = M$ for all M, m. In this storable votes equilibrium, $EV_0 = M$ if $2M > 3m$, but $EV_0 = (13M + 5m)/16 > M$ for all $2M \leq 3m$, establishing the result in the lemma.

CONSTRUCTION OF FIGURE 1

Model B

(a) *Efficient frequency of minority victories.* According to our efficiency criterion, the minority should win whenever the sum of its valuations is larger than the sum of the majority's valuations. Call $y(z)$ the sum of m (M) independent random variables, each distributed Uniformly over $[0, 1]$. The efficient frequency of minority victories is then given by $\int_0^m \left(\int_z^m P_m(y)dy \right) P_M(z)dz$ where:

$$P_m(y) = \frac{1}{2(m-1)!} \sum_{s=0}^{m} (-1)^s \binom{m}{s} (y-s)^{m-1} \mathrm{sign}(y-s) \qquad (A.6)$$

(and correspondingly for $P_M(z)$).

(b) *Expected aggregate payoff under first best efficiency.* For each proposal, the *ex ante* efficient aggregate payoff EU_B^* is easily derived, given (A.6):

$$EU_B^* = \int_0^m \left(\int_z^m y P_m(y)dy \right) P_M(z)dz + \int_0^m \left(\int_y^M z P_M(z)dz \right) P_m(y)dy. \qquad (A.7)$$

Over the two proposals, the *ex ante* efficient payoff is $2EU_B^*$. The first term in (A.7) corresponds to the efficient expected payoff for the minority group, and the second for the majority group. The corresponding per capita values (multiplied by 2) are plotted in Figure 1(b).

(c) *Random choice.* If each group has a 50 percent chance of winning any vote, Given $E(v) = 1/2$, the aggregate expected payoff is $1/2(M/2) + 1/2(m/2)$ over each proposal, or $(M + m)/2$ for the 2-proposal game.

Model C

(a) *Efficient frequency of minority victories.* Given the perfect correlation of valuations within each group, the efficient frequency of minority victories is given by $\mathrm{prob}(Mv_M < mv_m) = \int_0^1 \int_0^{(m/M)v_m} dv_M dv_m = m/(2M)$.

(b) *Expected aggregate payoff under first best efficiency.* In model C, we can represent the total valuation of the minority (majority) group by a random variable y (z), Uniformly distributed over $[0, m]$ ($[0, M]$). The efficient aggregate expected payoff, per proposal, is given by

$$EU_C^* = \int_0^m \left(\int_z^m \frac{y}{m} dy \right) \frac{1}{M} dx + \int_0^m \left(\int_y^M \frac{z}{M} dz \right) \frac{1}{m} dy = \frac{m^2 + 3M^2}{6M}. \quad \text{(A.8)}$$

Over the two proposals, the *ex ante* efficient payoff is $2EU_C^*$. The first term in (A.8) corresponds to the efficient expected payoff for the minority group ($m^2/(3M)$), and the second for the majority group (($3M^2 - m^2)/6M$). The corresponding per capita values (multiplied by 2) are plotted in Figure 1(b).

REFERENCES

Bowler, S., T. Donovan, and D. Brockington. 2003. *Electoral Reform and Minority Representation: Local Experiments with Alternative Elections.* Columbus: Ohio State University Press.

Casella, A. 2005. "Storable Votes." *Games and Economic Behavior* 51(May): 391–419.

Casella, A., A. Gelman, and T. R. Palfrey. 2006. "An Experimental Study of Storable Votes." *Games and Economic Behavior* 57(October): 123–154.

Casella, A., T. R. Palfrey, and R. Riezman. 2007. "Minorities and Storable Votes," Social Science Working Paper #1261, California Institute of Technology: Pasadena, October (http://www.hss.caltech.edu/SSPapers/sswp1261R.pdf).

Chwe, M. 1999. "Minority Voting Rights Can Maximize Majority Welfare." *American Political Science Review* 93(March): 85–97.

Cox, G. 1990. "Centripetal and Centrifugal Incentives in Electoral Systems." *American Journal of Political Science* 34(November): 903–935.

Engelmann, D., and V. Grimm. 2006. "Overcoming Incentive Constraints: The (In-)effectiveness of Social Interaction." unpublished paper. University of London.

Gerber, E. R., R. B. Morton, and T. A. Rietz. 1998. "Minority Representation in Multimember Districts." *American Political Science Review* 92(March): 127–144.

Guinier, L. 1994. *The Tyranny of the Majority.* New York: Free Press.

Hortala-Vallve, R. 2004. "Qualitative Voting." Mimeo: London School of Economics.

Issacharoff, S., P. Karlan, and R. Pildes. 2002. *The Law of Democracy: Legal Structure and the Political Process.* 2nd edition. Foundation Press.

Jackson, M., and H. Sonnenschein. 2007. "Overcoming Incentive Constraints by Linking Decisions." *Econometrica* 75(January): 241–257.

Kagel, J., H. Sung, and E. Winter. 2005. "Veto Power in Committees: An Experimental Study." Unpublished paper, Ohio State.

McLennan, A. 1998. "Consequences of the Condorcet Jury Theorem for Beneficial Information Aggregation by Rational Agents." *American Political Science Review* 92(June): 413–418.

Milgrom, P. R., and R. J. Weber. 1985. "Distributional Strategies for Games with Incomplete Information." *Mathematics of Operations Research* 10(November): 619–632.

Pildes, R. H., and K. A. Donoghue. 1995. "Cumulative Voting in the United States." *The University of Chicago Legal Forum* 1995: 241–313.

Part III: International Trade Topics

Part III: International Trade Topics

The final section of the book explores a variety of topics: from using laboratory experiments to study whether comparative advantage determines trade patterns, to using real business cycle theory to study how trade shocks are transmitted across countries. The first paper "Uncertainty and the Choice of Trade Policy in Oligopolistic Industries", looks at strategic trade policy when there are oligopolistic industries. We focus on the question of how uncertainty affects the choice of trade policy instruments in an uncertain world. In this paper, governments are trying to shift profits toward their firms by using either export taxes/subsidies or quantitative restrictions. We first show that in a world of perfect certainty, governments would use quantitative restrictions rather than export taxes/subsidies as their preferred policy. We then allow uncertainty; at low levels of uncertainty quantitative restrictions are still preferred, but after the uncertainty reaches a certain level, taxes/subsidies are the preferred instrument.

The next two papers represent the first attempt to use laboratory experiments to study principles of international trade. In "An Experimental Investigation of the Patterns of International Trade", we study a laboratory economy that has the essential features of an international economy. Factors can only be traded within a country but goods produced from them can be traded internationally. We find that the patterns of output, consumption, and trade predicted by the theory of comparative advantage evolve in these experimental markets. Factor–price equalization occurs despite the fact that factors of production receive less than the value of their marginal product. We introduce tariffs into the experiments and find that their effect is to reduce trade and efficiency as predicted by theory.

The next experimental paper "The Principles of Exchange Rate Determination in an International Finance Experiment", follows up on the first set of experiments by introducing domestic currencies. When countries have their own currency, there needs to be a way to convert one currency into another in order for international trade to take place. This is normally done with a foreign exchange market which we introduce into these experiments. The introduction of domestic currencies does not change the results obtained from our earlier experiments regarding trade flows; the law of comparative advantage still explains trade patterns. In terms of prices, goods prices generally converged to their predicted equilibrium and the exchange rate converged as well. However, purchasing power parity and in some cases, the law of one price, is rejected by the experimentally generated data.

In "Trade Shocks and Macroeconomic Fluctuations in Africa", we develop a dynamic, stochastic, multi-sector, small open economy model to examine the effect of trade shocks on macroeconomic performance in African countries. The results from our calibration show that trade shocks play a significant role in driving macroeconomic fluctuations in African countries. More specifically, more than 44% of fluctuations in aggregate output are explained by trade shocks. These trade shocks also explain 86% of the volatility in investment and 80% of labor supply fluctuations. We also find that negative trade shocks cause prolonged recessions since they induce a significant decrease in investment. Looking at interest rate shocks, we find that interest rate shocks tend to be relatively unimportant, except in countries that have significant foreign debts.

The final paper in the volume "Trade, and the Distribution of Human Capital", examines the effect of the distribution of human capital on international trade. We begin by considering two countries that are identical except for their distribution of human capital. Their aggregate human capital, technology and preferences are the same. We find that if the home country's distribution of human capital stochastically dominates foreign capital, then the home country will export the high-tech (human capital intensive) product and the distribution of income will be more unequal in the home country. Next, we show that in this model trade does not necessarily increase welfare. Then, we introduce a simple political economy model that relies on majority voting. Using this model, we show that autarky, free trade with winners compensating losers, and free trade with no compensation are all possible equilibria.

Review of Economic Studies (1989) **56**, 129–140
0034-6527/89/00090129$02.00

Uncertainty and the Choice of Trade Policy in Oligopolistic Industries

RUSSELL COOPER
University of Iowa and Hoover Institution

and

RAYMOND RIEZMAN
University of Iowa

First version received July 1987; *final version accepted June* 1988 (*Eds.*)

This paper investigates the design of trade policies in an uncertain world. Governments in each of two countries select between direct quantity controls and subsidies in an attempt to shift profits in favour of domestic, imperfectly competitive firms. The equilibrium of this bilateral policy game depends critically on the variability of the environment. In a world of certainty, both governments would choose to regulate the behaviour of their firms through direct quantity controls. With a sufficient amount of uncertainty, both governments regulate their firms through subsidies. This result reflects an important tradeoff between the strategic advantages of direct quantity controls and flexibility gained by the use of subsidies.

I. INTRODUCTION

Strategic trade policies provide a means of shifting profits towards domestic firms when export markets are imperfectly competitive. Through these policies, governments influence the behaviour of domestic firms in their subsequent strategic interaction with foreign firms. These government policies are advantageous principally because they provide a means of precommitment not otherwise available to individual firms. Brander and Spencer (1985) demonstrate that this "profit shifting" role of trade policies rationalizes observed export subsidization.[1] Related are Krishna (1984) and Cooper and Riezman (1986) which show that direct quantity constraints on exports can perform a similar role.[2] Thus this approach of strategic trade policy provides a basis for understanding interventions which appear to be against the interest of a country when product markets are competitive.[3]

One weakness of these results is that these models explicitly constrain the government's policy choice. For example, in the Brander and Spencer model, governments can choose to subsidize or tax exports but other policies are not considered. Thus one must be cautious in interpreting those results as providing a basis for observed trade policies. Analysis of a broader menu of policy tools is warranted as a basis for obtaining predictions about trade policies in these settings.

---

1. See Hufbauer (1983) for a discussion of the role subsidization plays in current trade policy debates. Throughout we will refer to this policy as one of export subsidization. However, in some cases we find that governments would actually prefer to tax the exports of their firms.

2. An example of direct quantity controls would be the Japanese use of voluntary export restrictions in the automobile market.

3. As Brander and Spencer state, it is difficult to rationalize the observed subsidization of exports under the hypothesis that product markets are perfectly competitive as these policies simply benefit foreign consumers.

Cooper and Riezman provide a step in this direction by contrasting the use of export subsidies with direct quantity interventions. These two modes of intervention lead to identical results when only a single government is intervening.[4] However, when two (or more) exporting countries pursue profit shifting policies the outcomes are quite dependent on the means of intervention. As discussed below, direct quantity controls are *dominant* forms of policy intervention in a certain market. Thus, in this setting, profit shifting does not explain observed subsidization if quantity controls are feasible.

The purpose of this paper is to consider the robustness of this result to the introduction of market uncertainty. The spirit of our comparison of price incentives (i.e. export subsidies) with direct quantity controls (export quotas) follows the seminal paper by Weitzman (1974) which brought to light an important weakness of direct quantity intervention. In an uncertain environment, the flexibility provided by price incentives is potentially desirable and is lost when direct quantity controls are imposed.

Using a model similar to that proposed by Brander and Spencer, we explore the tradeoff between the strategic advantages of quantity controls and the costs from their inflexibility. In markets with highly volatile demands, governments will control the actions of their firms with subsidies. Countries with a large number of firms will tax their exports while countries with few firms will subsidize. Further, total output is higher than when the governments do not intervene in the market. As a consequence, countries with many firms are worse off in the bilateral subsidy game than in the game with no government intervention while countries with few firms are better off.

In more stable markets, governments will choose to use quantity controls and total market output, on average, will be less than the equilibrium output without intervention. In this case, both countries are better off than in the equilibrium without intervention since output is restricted.

II. UNCERTAINTY AND TRADE POLICIES: AN OVERVIEW

Consider the market for a homogenous good which is produced by a relatively small number of firms (F) and consumed by a large group of consumers. N_1 of the firms produce in one ("domestic") country and the remainder, N_2, produce in the other ("foreign") country.[5] In the absence of government intervention, these firms are identical except for their country of operation. Assume that the number and location of firms is fixed and that firms produce at a constant marginal cost of $c > 0$. Profits from the production of q units of output are

$$\pi = (p - c)q$$

where p is the product price.

Consumers are assumed to reside in a third country. This assumption allows us to separate the profit shifting motives of a government from actions to influence the welfare of consumers. We comment in the conclusion about extensions of our results to a model

---

4. As in the classic literature on tariffs vs. quotas (see Bhagwati (1965)), these policies lead to identical outcomes in the case of unilateral intervention without uncertainty. This equivalence fails when more than one government intervenes (see Rodriguez (1974) or when there is market uncertainty (see Dasgupta and Stiglitz (1977) or Fischelson and Flatters (1975)). Our setting differs from those in that the motivation for government intervention stems from imperfectly competitive product markets. As a consequence, quotas have a strategic value not present in competitive markets.

5. We will denote country i variables with the subscript i for $i = 1, 2$. In some cases, we refer to country 1 firms as the domestic firms and country 2 firms as foreign firms.

COOPER & RIEZMAN   OLIGOPOLISTIC TRADE POLICY   131

with domestic consumption. For simplicity, assume that the inverse demand curve is

$$p = a - bQ + \theta$$

where Q is the total output of this homogenous commodity. The parameters a and b are both positive and θ is a random variable with mean zero. Let $G(\theta)$ represent the cumulative distribution function for θ.

In the absence of government intervention, these F firms would determine quantities non-cooperatively. The outcome of this interaction would be the Cournot-Nash equilibrium with output per firm of

$$\bar{q} = \frac{a + \theta - c}{b(F+1)}. \tag{1}$$

We assume that $a + \theta > c$ with probability one so that the numerator is positive. The equilibrium price level and profit level, respectively, are given by

$$\bar{p} = \frac{a + \theta + cF}{F+1} \quad \text{and} \quad \bar{\pi} = \frac{(a + \theta - c)^2}{b(F+1)^2}.$$

This equilibrium provides a basis for exploring the policy decisions of the two governments as they seek to shift profits in favour of their domestic firms. To do so, consider the following multi-stage game. In the first stage, governments decide on the *form* of intervention. This choice is restricted to either the use of subsidies or direct quantity controls.[6] The governments in the two countries are assumed to choose the form of intervention simultaneously. In the second stage of the game, governments choose the *level* of intervention. At this stage each government takes the policy levels chosen by the other government as given. Once these decisions have been made, the state of nature (θ) is revealed to the firms. Finally, after θ is known, firms in each country select output levels to maximize profits subject to the constraints imposed upon them by their governments. If a government intervenes with subsidies, its firms will have an opportunity to select their own output level. Alternatively, if governments intervene with direct quantity controls, the outcome of this last stage of the game is determined by the government actions directly in the prior stage. Prices are determined so that the market clears ex post.

The timing of moves and the resolution of uncertainty is displayed in Figure 1. Three aspects of this structure are critical. First, governments select the class of policies *prior* to the determination of the policy levels. This reflects our desire to understand the form of intervention separately from its level.

Second, governments are required to select non-contingent policies *prior* to the determination of θ. This reflects our view that firms are better informed than governments about the state at the time of their decisions. The crux of the restriction is that governments are not allowed to design mechanisms for inducing firms to reveal to them the true state

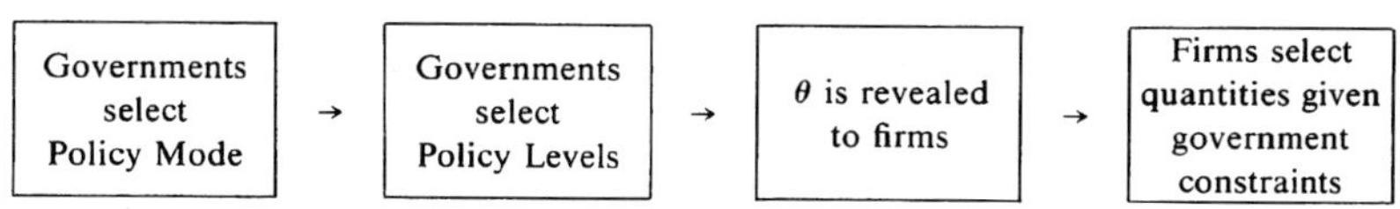

FIGURE 1

6. It is possible, of course, to consider mixtures of these two policies. In the literature following Weitzman (1974), combinations of price and quantity incentives have been shown to dominate either of the two extremes. Eventually, one would wish to solve for the optimal form of intervention in this market structure. Our intention is to shed some light on that problem by considering the costs and benefits of the extreme cases examined in this paper. Yohe (1981) discusses an example of a mixed policy.

of nature. Extensions of this model to allow revelation would be potentially quite interesting.

Third, the governments are assumed to move simultaneously and prior to the firms. This sequence of moves is common to this literature, see Brander and Spencer, Eaton and Grossman (1986) and Dixit (1984, 1986). The assumption that governments move simultaneously is quite natural as it is difficult to see that either has a basis for moving first. That governments move before private agents is a common assumption in models of policy intervention though it is important to understand the basis of the government's power to commit. This literature does not directly address the basis for the government's ability to commit though mention is often made of reputation effects as a source of discipline on government's actions. To facilitate comparison with these earlier results, we follow the now standard structuring of moves.

To characterize the perfect Nash equilibria of this game, we solve the two-stage bilateral policy game between the governments and the firms for each feasible pair of modes of intervention. There are four of these and this analysis is discussed in the following section. Given these four levels of payoffs, the form of government intervention is selected in the first stage of the game. This is discussed in Section IV of the paper. This method of solution guarantees that the equilibrium will be perfect.

III. NASH EQUILIBRIUM AND THE CHOICE OF POLICY MODE

Bilateral subsidies

To begin the analysis, assume that the governments have chosen an export subsidy, s_i. Then profits for a country i firm, π_i are

$$\pi_i = \{a - b(N_1 q_1 + N_2 q_2) - c + \theta + s_i\} q_i \tag{2}$$

where q_i is the output per firm in country i. Firms are assumed to set quantities given conjectures on the quantities chosen by all other firms. In a Nash equilibrium, these conjectures will be confirmed. As noted above, each firm knows the value of θ when they make their output decisions. Since firms are identical within a country, we solve for the best response of an arbitrary firm in each country as a function of conjectured per firm output level in the other country given that firms in each country are producing the same level of output. These conditions are

$$q_i = \frac{a - c + s_i + \theta - bN_{-i}q_{-i}}{b(N_i + 1)} \quad \text{for} \quad i = 1, 2. \tag{3}$$

In this expression, and hereafter, the notation $-i$ will denote the variable for the country other than country i. Nash equilibrium outputs per firm for given s_1 and s_2 are determined by solving (3) for q_1 and q_2 yielding

$$q_i = \frac{a - c + \theta + s_i + N_{-i}(s_i - s_{-i})}{b(F + 1)} \quad \text{for} \quad i = 1, 2. \tag{4}$$

These equations characterize the Nash equilibrium in the product market for given values of (θ, s_1, s_2). Notice that higher values of θ and/or s_1 lead to increased output by domestic firms, while higher values of s_2 causes output to fall. This latter interaction is important because governments recognize that increased subsidy levels lead to output expansions by home firms and output reductions by foreign firms.

COOPER & RIEZMAN   OLIGOPOLISTIC TRADE POLICY   133

The governments choose their subsidy prior to knowing the value of θ, taking into account the response of firms in both countries. Formally, a government's problem is to choose a value for the ex post subsidy that maximizes the expected value of its firms' profits net of subsidies. This objective function is appropriate as we assume there is no domestic consumption of the commodity, firms are risk neutral and the income distribution is not an important determinant of social welfare. For country i we have

$$\max_{s_i} E_\theta\{[a - c + \theta - b(N_1 q_1 + N_2 q_2)]q_i\} \tag{5}$$

where q_1 and q_2 are defined by (4) and are functions of (θ, s_1, s_2). Country i's optimal subsidy is

$$s_i = \frac{(1 - N_i + N_{-i})(a - c - s_{-i})N_{-i}}{2N_i(1 + N_{-i})} \quad \text{for} \quad i = 1, 2. \tag{6}$$

The two equations in (6) are reaction functions of the two governments and can be solved to obtain the Nash equilibrium level of subsidies of

$$s_i = \frac{(a - c)(1 - N_i + N_{-i})}{N_i(F + 3)} \quad \text{for} \quad i = 1, 2. \tag{7}$$

The Nash equilibrium subsidies are the same as in the certainty case. As discussed in Cooper and Riezman, in the equilibrium of the bilateral subsidy game, if the home country has a small domestic production sector (i.e. $N_1 < (1 + F)/2$), it will subsidize the output of its firms. Alternatively, if the home country has a large number of domestic firms, it will choose to tax the output of its firms.[7] These results carry over to the case of uncertainty as modeled here.

As we shall see shortly, the equilibrium outputs and profits do reflect the presence of uncertainty. Substituting (7) into (4) yields the output at Nash equilibrium subsidy levels of

$$q_i = \frac{(a - c)(1 + N_{-i})}{bN_i(F + 3)} + \frac{\theta}{b(F + 1)} \quad \text{for} \quad i = 1, 2. \tag{8}$$

Total output is given by

$$Q = \frac{(a - c)(F + 2)}{b(F + 3)} + \frac{\theta F}{b(F + 1)}. \tag{9}$$

Notice that expected output is the same as the deterministic output levels. However, because firms are free to select output ex post, these quantities respond to the state of demand. In states of high demand, all firms respond by increasing output.

We next compute welfare for the two countries. Expected per firm profits net of subsidies for country i are

$$E\pi_i = \frac{(a - c)^2(1 + N_{-i})}{bN_i(F + 3)^2} + \frac{\text{var } \theta}{b(F + 1)^2} \quad \text{for} \quad i = 1, 2. \tag{10}$$

Expected profits are composed of deterministic profits plus a term that includes the variance of θ. Increasing the variance of θ increases expected profits because firms choose output after observing θ.

---

7. These results extend those reported in Dixit (1984) to the bilateral subsidy case.

134   REVIEW OF ECONOMIC STUDIES

Bilateral quantity game

Suppose that instead of using subsidies, both governments elect to control their firms directly by setting output levels for each firm. The uncertainty is resolved after the governments determine output levels, so that the government in country i will select q_i to maximize

$$E\pi_i = E\{a - c + \theta - b(N_1 q_1 + N_2 q_2)\}q_i. \tag{11}$$

In solving this problem, country i takes the output level for country $-i$ as given. Hence, the problem is equivalent to a duopoly problem with multiple plants under uncertainty. The solution is given by

$$q_i = \frac{a - c}{3bN_i} \quad \text{for} \quad i = 1, 2. \tag{12}$$

From (12), note that both countries produce the same amount of total output though the levels of output per firm reflects the number of firms in each country. The per firm levels are again those that would be chosen in a deterministic environment. Given these quantities, the ex post price is influenced by the realization of θ. Expected profit levels for country i firms are

$$E\pi_i = \frac{(a - c)^2}{9bN_i} \quad \text{for} \quad i = 1, 2. \tag{13}$$

Quantity/subsidy mixtures

Finally, consider the equilibrium if country 1 chooses to intervene with subsidies while country 2 elects to use quantity controls. (The last case in which country 1 uses quantity controls and 2 uses subsidies is determined symmetrically.) In this case, country 1 selects a subsidy level at the same time as country 2 selects output levels for its firms so that country 1 does not anticipate any variation in q_2 as it varies s_1. In contrast, country 2 takes the response of country 1 firms into account when selecting q_2. The reaction of country 1 firms to variations in q_2 is given by (3).

The optimal subsidy in country 1 is

$$s_1 = \frac{(a - c)(1 - N_1) - q_2 bN_2(1 - N_1)}{2N_1}. \tag{14}$$

The optimal level of output firm in country 2 is given by

$$q_2 = \frac{(a - c) - N_1 s_1}{2bN_2}. \tag{15}$$

These two reaction curves can be solved to determine the equilibrium policy variables for the two countries, given by

$$s_1 = \frac{-(a - c)(N_1 - 1)}{N_1(N_1 + 3)} \tag{16}$$

and

$$q_2 = \frac{(a - c)(N_1 + 1)}{bN_2(N_1 + 3)}. \tag{17}$$

COOPER & RIEZMAN   OLIGOPOLISTIC TRADE POLICY   135

Note that country 1 always chooses to *tax* firms. This is in contrast to the results discussed above in which the choice between taxing and subsidizing firms depended on relative industry size. When foreign governments control quantities, the home industry is qualitatively "bigger" than the foreign industry since there is essentially a single firm in the other country. So, the best response of the domestic government is to tax firms exports as a means of restricting output.

Using these values of the policy variables, the expected level of profits (per firm) in the two countries is given by

$$E\pi_1 = \frac{(a-c)^2}{bN_1(N_1+3)^2} + \frac{\text{var }\theta}{b(N_1+1)^2}, \tag{18}$$

$$E\pi_2 = \frac{(a-c)^2(N_1+1)}{bN_2(N_1+3)^2}. \tag{19}$$

With these cases in mind, we are now ready to consider the government's choice of policy type. That is, should governments intervene by setting subsidies or controlling the output of firms directly? The analysis in this section indicates that these alternative modes of intervention do not lead to the same outcomes for two reasons. First, countries that use subsidies allow their firms to respond to the state of nature while those that employ quantity controls do not allow firms this flexibility. Second, countries that use subsidies cannot prevent their firms from responding to the policy actions of other governments. This strategic disadvantage of flexibility, which is explained in more detail below, is overcome by direct quantity controls. The resolution of the costs and benefits of flexibility will determine the mode of government intervention.

IV. FORM OF INTERVENTION

Table 1 summarizes the results of the previous section by displaying the *expected* payoffs for country 1 for the four possible combinations of government intervention. There are analogous payoffs to country 2 in these situations which can be derived by interchanging N_2 and N_1 in Table 1.

One key aspect of the choice of policy intervention is the variability of θ, measured by var θ. Variations in var θ are key to the tradeoff between the strategic advantages of quantity controls and the gains to flexibility from the use of taxes and subsidies. We proceed by first considering the extreme cases of large and small values of var θ and then discuss intermediate possibilities.

TABLE 1

Expected profits for country 1 firms

Country 1	Country 2	
	Subsidy/Taxes	Quantities
Subsidy/Taxes	$\dfrac{(a-c)^2(1+N_2)}{bN_1(F+3)^2} + \dfrac{\text{var }\theta}{b(F+1)^2}$	$\dfrac{(a-c)^2}{bN_1(N_1+3)^2} + \dfrac{\text{var }\theta}{b(N_1+1)^2}$
Quantities	$\dfrac{(a-c)^2(1+N_2)}{bN_1(N_2+3)^2}$	$\dfrac{(a-c)^2}{9bN_1}$

Case 1: Var θ *small*

When var $\theta = 0$, the use of quantity policies by each government is a dominant strategy. That is, regardless of whether country 2 uses a subsidy/tax policy or direct quantity controls, the government in country 1 will always prefer to directly control the output decisions of domestic firms. That quantity controls become a dominant strategy can be seen from Table 1 by setting var $\theta = 0$.

This result is due to the strategic advantage of preventing domestic firms from responding to the policies of foreign governments. To understand this, suppose that the domestic government adopts subsidies to control its firms. In doing so, the domestic government recognizes that its firms will respond to the policies chosen by foreign governments—a fact which foreign governments recognize as well. As a consequence, the foreign government will find it advantageous to increase the output of its firms, either through an increased subsidy or an increase in the export quota. Domestic firms will respond to this by reducing their output levels. This latter movement along the reaction curve of domestic firms is undesirable and can be avoided by the adoption of direct quantity controls. It is in this sense that the use of quantity controls provides the domestic government with a strategic advantage.

So, when var θ equals zero, there is no loss of flexibility from using quantity controls, this form of intervention is dominant. By continuity of the expected payoffs in the game, quantity controls remain a dominant policy for small values of var θ. Further, this result is *independent* of the number of firms in each of the two countries.

An implication of the strategic loss associated with the adoption of subsidies is that output is much lower when both governments use direct quantity controls than when they adopt subsidies. Multiplying (12) by the respective number of firms in each of the two countries and then adding these sums yields the total output when both countries use quantity controls. This total is $2(a-c)/3b$ and, by the nature of this policy, must be independent of θ. Total output in the case of bilateral subsidies (given by (9)) clearly exceeds this sum on average (i.e. when $\theta = 0$) since $F > 0$.

To understand this result, suppose that the subsidies of the two countries were set so that their firms produced at the duopoly levels given by (12). Further suppose for the moment that $\theta = 0$ with probability one. Then, as argued above, both governments have an incentive to increase their subsidies since the response by firms in the other countries to these subsidies makes them profitable. Hence, in equilibrium, output with bilateral subsidization will be higher than when both countries control export quantities directly.

The equilibrium in the bilateral policy intervention game is therefore the ex ante duopoly solution with relatively low levels of output and high industry prices on average. This is a favourable equilibrium for producers as it dominates the outcome in which governments do not intervene in the product markets. Consumers may be worse off than in the absence of intervention as the average level of output is lower.

This result is important in that the equilibrium predicted by the profit shifting literature in which subsidies are used to control firms (e.g. Brander and Spencer) has no predictive power in this environment. Once the policy space is expanded to allow governments to intervene through direct quantity controls, they do not choose to utilize subsidies in an environment with low uncertainty.

Case 2: Var θ *large*

The introduction of a sufficient amount of uncertainty over the state of demand alters these conclusions by creating a benefit from the use of subsidies. From Table 1, we see

COOPER & RIEZMAN   OLIGOPOLISTIC TRADE POLICY   137

that for a sufficiently large level of var θ , subsidies will be a dominant policy for both countries regardless of the size of their domestic industries. That is, when the environment is sufficiently uncertain, governments are willing to trade the strategic advantage of quantity controls for the flexibility of subsidy policies.

In this environment of bilateral subsidies, a characterization of the equilibrium is given in Section III of this paper. First, note that the number of firms in each country (the size of the domestic industry in this symmetric model), is a critical determinant of the choice between subsidization and taxation. As reported in Brander and Spencer, if the industry structure is symmetric (i.e. $N_1 = N_2 = N = F/2$), then both countries wish to subsidize exports. In an asymmetric setting, (7) implies that countries with few firms will elect to subsidize exports while countries with many firms will tax them. To understand this result, note that an increase in the subsidy increases domestic firm output and reduces the production of foreign firms. The net effect on total output and hence the price depends on the relative numbers of domestic and foreign firms. When there are many firms in the home country, then a reduction in output through a tax is desirable as the resulting price increase is large. Alternatively, if the home industry is small, then a subsidy leads to more output and prices will not fall much given the response of the more numerous foreign firms.

The ex post aggregate industry level of output in this equilibrium always exceeds that which would arise in the absence of intervention. Aggregate output in the case of bilateral subsidies is given by (9) while that in the case of no intervention is given by multiplying the per firm level of output given in (1) by F. Comparing these output levels, it is clear that the outcome in which governments intervene with subsidies has a higher level of aggregate output for each realization of θ. So, consumers are better off (in each state of nature) when governments attempt to shift profits through subsidies than in the absence of such intervention. This result extends that reported in Brander and Spencer, Proposition 5, to the more general case of asymmetric industry structure since we have not assumed that there are an equal number of firms in each of the two countries.

Further, the country with fewer firms gains from the bilateral policy game between the governments since it gains a larger share of the market through its subsidies. However, countries with many firms are actually worse off in the equilibrium relative to the no intervention case because their market share is lower as is the price of the good. The country with many firms would be better off if export subsidies were not allowed but, in the absence of such restriction, will impose an export tax in response to the policies chosen by exporting countries with fewer firms.

So in comparing the two extreme environments of small var θ with that of large var θ, a number of critical differences emerge. First, for large var θ subsidies are a dominant policy while quantity controls dominate in environments with little or no variability in demand. Second, on average industry output is higher when governments use subsidies rather than direct quantity controls.

Case 3: var θ intermediate

For intermediate values of var θ, the results are not as clean as in the extreme cases discussed above. To start, suppose that the economy is symmetric so that $N_1 = N_2 = N$. We comment below on the implications of asymmetric industry sizes in the two countries.

If country 2 decides to use subsidies, the payoffs for country 1 are then given by the first column of Table 1 with $N_i = N$ for $i = 1, 2$. When country 1 uses subsidies, then it gains in terms of ex post flexibility from its firms responding to realizations of θ and this gain increases with the variance of θ. However, direct quantity controls still confer the strategic advantage noted above. Thus there will be a critical level of the variance of θ, denoted by $\text{var}^*(S)$ such that if country 2 uses subsidies, the government in country 1 will be indifferent between using a subsidy/tax policy and direct quantity controls. When $\text{var}\,\theta > \text{var}^*(S)$, country 1 will choose to use a subsidy/tax policy and when $\text{var}\,\theta < \text{var}^*(S)$, country 1 will select quantity controls. This critical level of the variance of θ is given by:

$$\text{var}^*(S) = \frac{(2N+1)^2(1+N)}{N}\left[\frac{1}{(N+3)^2} - \frac{1}{(2N+3)^2}\right]. \tag{20}$$

These costs and benefits are also present even if country 2 elects to use direct quantity controls. Again from Table 1, there is a critical value for the variance of θ, denoted by $\text{var}^*(Q)$, such that if country 2 uses direct quantity controls, country 1 is indifferent with regards to its own mode of intervention. As before, if $\text{var}\,\theta$ exceeds this bound country 1 will use subsidies while if $\text{var}\,\theta$ is less than $\text{var}^*(Q)$, quantity controls will be utilized. This critical level of the variance of θ is given by

$$\text{var}^*(Q) = \frac{(N+1)^2}{N}\left[\frac{1}{9} - \frac{1}{(N+3)^2}\right]. \tag{21}$$

Note that both $\text{var}^*(Q)$ and $\text{var}^*(S)$ are positive and finite. Thus there will exist values for $\text{var}\,\theta$ such that quantity policies are dominant as described above. Further, $\text{var}\,\theta$ can become large enough so that subsidy/tax policies dominate for both of the countries. For intermediate values of $\text{var}\,\theta$, the form of the equilibrium will depend on the ordering between $\text{var}^*(S)$ and $\text{var}^*(Q)$.

If $\text{var}^*(S) > \text{var}\,\theta > \text{var}^*(Q)$, then there will be two asymmetric equilibria. If country 2 selects a subsidy/tax policy, then the best response of country 1 is to use quantity controls. Alternatively, country 1 will respond to country 2's use of quantity controls by selecting a subsidy/tax policy. By symmetry, country 2's responses to country 1 are the same, implying the existence of two asymmetric equilibria.

If $\text{var}^*(S) < \text{var}\,\theta < \text{var}^*(Q)$, then for intermediate values of $\text{var}\,\theta$ there will be multiple symmetric equilibria. That is, country 1 will select the same policy as country 2 regardless of the policy chosen by country 2. By symmetry, country 2 will do the same and multiple symmetric equilibria will arise. Note that these equilibria are in fact ordered from the perspective of the governments: they strictly prefer to be in the equilibrium in which both governments select quantity controls. Yet it is possible that the governments will be in the undesirable (from their perspective) equilibrium in which subsidy/tax policies are chosen. Of course, consumers in the importing country would prefer that the subsidy/tax policies are used.

Using (20) and (21) and the maintained assumption of symmetry, $\text{var}^*(S)$ and $\text{var}^*(Q)$ can be ordered as a function of N. Since $F = 2N$, increasing N can be interpreted as increasing the number of firms in the industry and hence the competitiveness of the market. One can show that for low values of N, $\text{var}^*(Q) < \text{var}^*(S)$ while for sufficiently large values of N, $\text{var}^*(Q) > \text{var}^*(S)$. So for sufficiently small values of N there will be asymmetric equilibria for intermediate values of $\text{var}\,\theta$. For N big enough, there will be multiple symmetric equilibria for intermediate values of $\text{var}\,\theta$.

When the economy is not symmetric, there will be country-specific critical values of the variances which determine the choice of the form of intervention in response of the choice of the other country. As above, these will determine the nature of the equilibria

COOPER & RIEZMAN　　　OLIGOPOLISTIC TRADE POLICY　　　139

for intermediate values of var θ. Still, as suggested above, for extreme values of var θ, the domination of either direct quantity controls or subsidies will hold even in asymmetric environments.

V. CONCLUSION

The literature on trade policies under imperfect competition points to a variety of means by which governments can gainfully intervene but provides little insight into the form of intervention. The point of this paper was to analyze the costs and benefits of two important modes of intervention. In particular, we focused on the tradeoff between the strategic gains of direct quantity controls and the flexibility provided by a policy of subsidies.

Our principle result is that the mode of intervention depends on the variability of the environment, and that the mode of intervention is an important determinant of the profitability of profit shifting policies. In more uncertain settings, the value of flexibility is high and governments should use subsidies. When the uncertainty is not too severe, the strategic gains of direct quantity controls outweighs the loss of flexibility. On average, industry output is higher (and price lower) when governments use tax/subsidy policies instead of directly controlling quantities. Thus, exporting countries do better when var θ is low.

Throughout we have assumed that the distribution of θ is exogenously given. One of the interesting implications of our analysis is that countries care about the variability of θ. Namely, when var θ is small, exporting countries use quantity controls and enjoy higher profits. If however, var θ is large, exporting countries use subsidy policies, and at least one of the countries will have smaller profits than the non-intervention case. This suggests that if we considered an enlarged strategy space to include policies that could affect var θ, exporting countries would have an incentive to adopt policies that reduce the variance of θ.

Our analysis rests heavily on a number of simplifying assumptions. These include: the specification of the demand structure, the source of the uncertainty, restrictions on the set of admissible government policies and the simple specification of governments' objectives. With regards to the specification of demand, we have generated a number of the results reported here for more general demand structures. In particular, when var $\theta = 0$, one can show that quantity controls are a dominant strategy for a fairly general demand structure. Further, the results in the bilateral subsidy game in which countries with many (few) firms tax (subsidize) exports hold in more general settings as well. Extensions of this general model to explore the tradeoffs illustrated here will be more difficult. The analysis should also be extended to consider richer environments of uncertainty including country and firm specific shocks to technology.

Finally, we have assumed that in neither of the two countries in the model consumed is the commodity being exported. This is appropriate if the good is produced solely for export *or* if the domestic market can be insulated from trade policies by the use of consumption subsidies/taxes. If it is impossible to use domestic policies to insulate domestic consumers, then subsidization policies which lower prices would be relatively more attractive and taxation and quantity controls policies would have an additional cost associated with them.

All of these issues need to be dealt with before firm conclusions can be reached. Nonetheless, we conjecture that the key tradeoff explored here between strategic advantages and flexibility will remain in more general models.

140   REVIEW OF ECONOMIC STUDIES

Acknowledgement. We are grateful to Wilfred Ethier for comments on an early draft of this manuscript and to Jon Eaton and Robert Staiger for informative discussions. Charles Bean and two anonymous referees provided helpful comments and suggestions as well.

REFERENCES

BHAGWATI, J. (1965), "On the Equivalence of Tariffs and Quotas", in Baldwin, R. E. et al. *Trade, Growth and the Balance of Payments-Essays in Honor of G. Haberler* (Chicago: Rand-McNally).

BRANDER, J. A. AND SPENCER, B. J., (1985), "Export Subsidies and International Market Share Rivalry", *Journal of International Economics*, **18**, 83–100.

COOPER, R. AND RIEZMAN, R. (1986), "Optimal Trade Policy with Oligopoly" (University of Iowa Working Paper No. 86–8).

DASGUPTA, P. and STIGLITZ, J. (1977), "Tariffs vs. Quotas as Revenue Raising Devices Under Uncertainty", *American Economic Review*, **67**, 975–980.

DIXIT, A. (1984), "International Trade Policy for Oligopolistic Industries", *Economic Journal*, **94**, (Supplement), 1–16.

DIXIT, A. (1986), "Strategic Aspects of Trade Policy" (Paper delivered at the Fifth World Congress of the Econometric Society).

EATON, J. and GROSSMAN, G. (1986), "Optimal Trade and Industrial Policy Under Oligopoly", *Quarterly Journal of Economics*, **101**, 383–406.

FISCHELSON, G. and FLATTERS, F. (1975), "The (Non)Equivalence of Optimal Tariffs and Quotas Under Uncertainty", *Journal of International Economics*, **5**, 385–393.

HUFBAUER, G. (1983), "Subsidy Issues after the Tokyo Round", in Cline, W. R. (ed.) *Trade Policy in the 1980's* (Washington, D. C.: Institute for International Economics).

KRISHNA, K. (1984), "Trade Restrictions as Facilitating Practices" (Harvard Institute of Economic Research, Discussion Paper No. 1119).

RODRIGUEZ, C. (1974), "Optimal Quotas and Retaliation", *Journal of International Economics*, **4**, 295–298.

WEITZMAN, M. (1974), "Prices vs. Quantities", *Review of Economic Studies*, **41**, 50–65.

YOHE, G. (1981), "Should Sliding Controls Be the Next Generation of Pollution Controls?", *Journal of Public Economics*, **15**, 251–68.

An Experimental Investigation of the Patterns of International Trade

By CHARLES N. NOUSSAIR, CHARLES R. PLOTT,
AND RAYMOND G. RIEZMAN *

This paper studies a laboratory economy with some of the prominent features of an international economic system. The patterns of trade and output predicted by the law of comparative advantage are observed evolving within the experimental markets. Market prices and quantities move in the direction of the competitive equilibrium, but the quantitative predictions of the (risk-neutral) competitive equilibrium are rejected. Considerable amounts of economic activity occur as disequilibria. Factor-price equalization is observed, but there is a universal tendency for factors of production to trade at prices below their marginal products. (JEL D50, F00, F30)

This study is the first attempt to create and study a laboratory economy with some of the prominent features of an international economic system. The purpose is to investigate some of the economic profession's fundamental assumptions about the nature of international trade. The concept of multiple "countries" in which each country has its own technology, preferences, and resource endowments, is introduced and operationalized. The questions posed in the study are related to the law of comparative advantage, factor-price equalization, terms of trade, efficiency in production, and exchange as guided by multiple and interacting markets and the effects of tariffs on international transactions. The study builds on previous work in the experimental study of general equilibrium phenomena.[1]

Because this paper carries laboratory experimental research to a new dimension of complexity and into a new field, it might be useful to address what would be the obvious concern of a skeptic. Since the world's international economies are vastly more complicated than the economies created for this study, of what relevance are laboratory-generated data? The answer is that laboratory experiments are not attempts to simulate field situations, as that question of the skeptic seems to presume. Laboratory research deals with the general theories and the general principles that are supposed to apply to all economies, the economies found in the field as well as those created in a laboratory. The laboratory economies are very simple and are special cases of the broad class of (often complex) economies to which the general theories are supposed to be of relevance. If a general theory does not work successfully to explain behavior in the sim-

*Noussair: Department of Economics, Krannert School of Management, Purdue University, West Lafayette, IN 47907; Plott: Humanities and Social Sciences—m/c 228-77, California Institute of Technology, Pasadena, CA 91125; Riezman: Department of Economics, College of Business Administration, W210 PBAB, University of Iowa, Iowa City, IA 52242. We acknowledge the financial support of the National Science Foundation and the Caltech Laboratory for Experimental Economics and Political Science. The comments of Charles Holt have been useful. The comments of Mahmoud El-Gamal were especially helpful and resulted in the econometric model used extensively in the paper.

[1] Jessica Goodfellow and Plott (1990) investigate the simultaneous determination of input and output prices. Peng Lian and Plott (1993), create a macroeconomy which includes one input and one output as well as fiat money and bonds.

ple and special cases of the laboratory, then it is not general. When a model is found not working, opportunity exists to modify the theory to account for the data or to reject the theory. Thus, the laboratory provides an arena in which competing notions and theories about the nature of human (and market) capacities can be joined with data. Clearly laboratory experimental work is constrained by technology and by background experimental work. When very little background work exists, the experimental research strategy is first to explore what seem to be the most basic and general theoretical ideas. Then, as technology permits, successful ideas can be challenged with increasingly complex experimental environments in follow-up experiments. Any laboratory experiment should be viewed as only one of the many steps needed to learn what we would like to know. This study is no different.

The focus of the study is the behavior of the entire economic system, rather than the behavior of individual agents. Two behavioral models, "competitive equilibrium" and "autarky," can be applied to the experimental environments. Both models make precise predictions of the magnitude of every variable in the system, which number in the dozens. The existence of such a large number of predictions creates methodological and expositional problems. With a large number of predictions, some predictions will almost certainly be wrong. The sheer size of the undertaking makes it very easy to reject the models statistically. Therefore, after making a clear statement of the negative result that the models are rejected, the analysis of the data focuses on the general properties of interdependent markets that are suggested by the models, as opposed to a focus on the accuracy of the specific predictions of each model. In the context of the broad implications of the models, a number of results are stated.

The paper is organized in the following manner. We begin by discussing in Section I the existing support found in field data for the basic principles we test. In Sections II and III, the design of the experiments is described. In Section IV, the theoretical models are discussed. In Section V, the data are presented and analyzed, and in Section VI, the conclusions are summarized.

I. Field-Data Support for Major Principles

The propositions that we propose to explore are so basic to accepted theory and are applied so universally, that some might wonder why we would bother. Is it the case that the law of comparative advantage and the principle of factor-price equalization are well documented and not controversial? We think not. Nagging doubts linger because no direct evidence exists. Empirical results in support of the most basic principles of international-trade theory are clouded as they always are when the data are from field sources. As Michael P. Porter (1990 p. 12) writes, "Evidence hard to reconcile with factor comparative advantage is not difficult to find."

In his handbook chapter on testing trade theories, Alan Deardorff (1984) discusses the general problem of testing trade theories using field data. He cites two types of problems. First, simple trade models omit important features of the world economy, so model specification is an inherent problem. For example, the models usually assume only two countries, and they typically ignore transport costs. On the other hand, field data are generated by countries trading with many other countries in a world in which transportation costs exist and are often thought to be important. The second general problem is that theories tend to be stated in terms of variables that are not observable, so that testing these theories directly with field data is not possible. An example is the theory of comparative advantage.

The theory of comparative advantage is a general theory which states that countries will export that good which has the lowest relative price in autarky. However, attempts to test and assess the theory have only been indirect. In principle, this theory cannot be tested directly with field data because conditions of autarky and thus autarky prices are rarely, if ever, observed. In order to cope with this problem, researchers have developed more specific models like the Ricardian and Heckscher-Ohlin models. The purpose of these models is to build theoretical relationships from observables, like labor productivity or endowments, that can be extended to nonobservables, like autarky prices, and then to use the latter as the benchmarks against which trade flows are measured. Thus, tests of the Ricardian model, or the Heckscher-Ohlin model, are actually joint tests of comparative advantage and the particular specification (i.e., the Ricardian model or the Heckscher-Ohlin model).

Unfortunately, these indirect tests have failed to distinguish between competing theories. For example, empirical tests of the Ricardian trade model (and the related law of comparative advantage) using field data date back to the early work of G. D. A. MacDougall (1951, 1952). His procedure was to look at U.S. and U.K. exports to third countries and to see whether the pattern of exports is explained by differences in the two countries' labor requirements. He found that the ratios of U.S. to U.K. exports and U.S. to U.K. labor productivity are highly correlated, which is consistent with the predictions of the Ricardian model and, therefore, suggests the operation of the law of comparative advantage. But, as observed by Deardorff, the tests fail to distinguish between the Ricardian model and the Heckscher-Ohlin model, and as a result, the role and support for the law of comparative advantage remained unclear.

Thus, from the beginning there has not been a clear test of the comparative advantage that is so fundamental to theory. Similarly, there have been relatively few studies testing factor-price equalization theory. Alfred Tovias (1982) and Hans Gremmen (1985) look at the EEC countries to see if there is evidence that factor prices converge as trade becomes freer within the EEC. Their results are quite mixed. They find periods in which factor prices seem to converge, but later, as the economies become more integrated, factor prices do not seem to be converging. A later paper by Manouchehr Mokhtari and Farhad Rassekh (1989) looks at a bigger sample of countries and gets more positive results. They con-

sider all of the OECD countries and use more sophisticated techniques. Their findings suggest that factor prices are converging within the OECD if countries are properly grouped into high-wage and low-wage countries. Furthermore, their evidence suggests that it is trade liberalization that accounts for much of this convergence. The evidence on factor-price equalization is far from conclusive.

The experimental data do not have many of the problems that are associated with field data. The experimental data are generated by only two countries. Transportation costs are under the control of the experimenter. The underlying structure is known. Variables unavailable in the field, like autarky prices, are known in the experiment. Factor prices can be observed under autarky and under free trade. In the field, neither can be observed. The field data on labor, for example, involves a great deal of aggregation across different types of labor. This means that one actually compares average wages of a group of workers in one country with the average wage of a different group in another country. If there is much variation across countries in groups, or if these groups change over time, a bias is introduced which may affect the results. No such problems exist in experiments.

Of course, experimental data are generated by much simpler economic environments than those found in the field. The preconditions for the operations of the principles have been introduced by the experimenters. The experiments are able to provide some insights into how models, based on the basic principles, are able to organize the data, given that the situation is one in which the model can be meaningfully applied. The experiment cannot, however, answer the equally important questions about the relative likelihood that nature has created a situation for which the parametric and institutional features of the model are relevant.

II. Experimental Design: Parameters

This section consists of a description of the market conditions within which the economic activity occurs. The description in-

TABLE 1—EXPERIMENTAL PARAMETERS

Preferences:[a]
Consumers, environment 1:
$$U(Y, Z) = 600Y - 40Y^2 + 700Z - 40Z^2$$

Consumers, environment 2:
$$U(Y, Z) = 600Y - 100Y^2 + 600Z - 100Z^2$$

Producers, environment 2:
$$U(L, K) = 600L - 100L^2 + 600K - 100K^2$$

Parameter	Environment 1	Environment 2	Franc/dollar conversion rate, experiment numbers:				
			030591 040191	041191	041391A	032091 041091 041391B	112890 113090 011891
Endowments:							
Consumers, country 1	$L_1 = 2, L_2 = 0$	$L_1 = 5, L_2 = 0$ $K_1 = 3, K_2 = 0$	1,000	800	900	800	800
Consumers, country 2	$L_1 = 0, L_2 = 2$	$L_1 = 0, L_2 = 3$ $K_1 = 0, K_2 = 5$	1,000	800	900	800	800
Producers, country 1	$L_1 = 1, L_2 = 0$	$L_1 = 0, L_2 = 0$ $K_1 = 0, K_2 = 0$	1,000	400	400	300	300
Producers, country 2	$L_1 = 0, L_2 = 2$	$L_1 = 0, L_2 = 0$ $K_1 = 0, K_2 = 0$	1,000	400	400	1,000	300
Production:							
Country 1	$Y = 3L, Z = L$	$Y = L, Z = K$					
Country 2	$Y = L, Z = 2L$	$Y = L, Z = K$					
Number:[b]							
Consumers, country 1	4	4					
Consumers, country 2	4	4					
Producers, country 1	4	4					
Producers, country 2	4	4					

[a]Utility functions are in franc units.

[b]The experiments in environment 1 involved either a 16-person design or 8-person design. In the 16-person design, consumers and producers were all different people. In the 8-person design, each factor owner in country i was also a producer and a consumer of final goods in country $j \neq i$. Thus, the number of agents identified by function was 16, but the number of people was 8.

cludes the environment, the parameters, and the form of market organization used to facilitate transactions. There are two environments: the first is motivated by the environment of the Ricardian Model of international trade;[2] the second is a similar environment, within which the robustness of results can be investigated and in which the properties of input markets can be considered in greater detail. All markets were organized through the computerized multiple unit double auction (MUDA). For details of the operation of this form of market organization, the reader can consult Plott (1991).

Money exists in both environments. Thus, the first environment, although similar to that of the Ricardian model, differs in that the purchase of any good requires money. Money is included in the design because it is an obvious feature of any well-functioning market process, including international economies, and it is certainly useful in experimental environments in facilitating equilibration. In both environments, there is

[2]For a clear exposition of the Ricardian model see Richard Caves et al. (1990 Ch. 5). For a fascinating account of the development of the Ricardian model see John S. Chipman (1965).

TABLE 2—REDEMPTION VALUES, ALL AGENTS, TWO ENVIRONMENTS, ONE COUNTRY (IDENTICAL COUNTRIES), ALL UNITS

Environment 1			Environment 2					
Consumer	Y	Z	Consumer	Y	Z	Producer	L	K
1	600	620	1	600	450	1	600	450
	520	540		250	400		250	400
	440	480		200	50		200	50
	360	400						
	280	320	2	550	500	2	550	500
	200	240		300	350		300	350
	120	160		150	100		150	100
	40	80						
2	560	660	3	500	550	3	500	550
	480	580		350	300		350	300
	400	500		100	150		100	150
	320	420	4	450	600	4	450	600
	240	340		400	250		400	250
	180	260		50	200		50	200
	100	180						
	20	100						
		20						
3	560	660						
	480	580						
	400	500						
	320	420						
	240	340						
	180	260						
	100	180						
	20	100						
		20						
4	520	700						
	440	620						
	360	540						
	280	460						
	200	380						
	120	300						
	40	220						
		140						
		60						

only one currency, and it has value as a commodity. All experimental currency held by subjects at the end of the experiment could be converted into dollars that the subject keeps as compensation for participation in the experiment. Since the focus of experimentation is international trade rather than finance, the complicating feature of multiple currencies has been omitted from the design.

Table 1 presents the experimental parameters for both of the environments that will be discussed below. Continuous approximations of the utility functions of both consumers and producers are quadratic and additively separable as shown in Table 1. The actual redemption values that were induced are contained in Table 2. Production technologies are linear as in Table 1. In the tables, valuations are given in francs (a common name for an experimental currency). The francs are converted into dollars according to ratios known privately to agents. These conversions can differ across agents and are contained in Table 1. The variables L_i and K_i refer to the factors L and K residing in country i and Y_i and Z_i refer to the outputs Y and Z produced in country i. The endowment listed in the table is the amount each individual agent possesses at the beginning of each market period. A country's total endowment is then four times the amount listed in the table, since each of the same type of agent has the same endowment.

A. *Environment 1*

Environment 1 is motivated by the Ricardian model. In environment 1, there are two output goods (final goods) called Y and Z and an input called L. There are two types of agents: consumers and producers. Consumers are owners of the factors of production and have induced preferences for consuming the outputs Y and Z. Producers also have an initial endowment of the input and can earn profits by using the input L to produce and then sell Y and Z. All agents can also attempt to earn profits by speculating in any input or output. Neither consumers nor producers have preferences for L other than its value as an input.

Agents are divided in equal numbers into two countries. Each country includes as members equal numbers of consumers and producers. The factor of production is not mobile between countries. The final goods Y and Z can be traded in either country, not only the one in which they were produced. The two countries differ only in their production technologies.

The economy works in the following way. Consumers sell their endowment of L to producers in their own country and then buy units of Y and Z produced in either country. Consumers get utility (U.S. dollars) from consumption and any profits made in price speculation. Producers in each country buy L from the consumers in their own country and can use L to produce Y and Z which they can sell to consumers in either country. Producers get utility (dollars) from profits earned from market and production activities.

In some experiments, free international trade was permitted; in others a tariff was imposed on the imports of Z to country 1. When a tariff was in effect, it took the form of a tax of 400 francs on international transactions of the final goods. The tariff revenue was not redistributed to citizens in either country but instead was taken by the experimenter. Thus, the tariff operated similarly to a transportation cost.

B. *Environment 2*

In environment 2, the two countries have different endowments of the inputs. In addition, the inputs are endogenously and elastically supplied to producers in the sense that resources could also be consumed. Environment 2 operated as a control on environment 1 to ensure that any properties of input markets observed in environment 1 were not simply due to the completely inelastic supply of the input. The endogenous-resource property of environment 2 is a natural feature to add as a check on robustness of a model's ability to capture observed behavior because it is a general property of the field economies in which the competitive and autarky models are regularly applied.

In environment 2 there are two output goods called Y and Z and two inputs called L and K. There are also two types of agents: consumers and producers. As in environment 1, consumers are also owners of the factors of production. Consumers are endowed with some of both of the inputs L and K. Consumers have induced preferences for consuming the outputs Y and Z. Producers of the final goods are also consumers of the factors of production. They have no initial endowment but have preferences induced for consuming the inputs L and K and also for the money they might get by producing Y from L and Z from K and selling the output.

Participants are divided equally into two countries. Each country has an equal number of consumers and producers. Both types of agents can trade the inputs L and K only with agents in their own country. The final goods Y and Z can be traded internationally. No tariffs existed in any of the experiments in which environment 2 was implemented.

TABLE 3—SUMMARY OF EXPERIMENTS

Experiment number (date)	Tariffs Y/N	Periods	Environment	Subject pool	Number of subjects
030591	N	11	1	Caltech	8
040191	N	10	1	Caltech	8
041191	N	9	1	U. Iowa	16
041391A	N	10	1	U. Iowa (exper.)[a]	16
032091	Y	10	1	Caltech	8
041091	Y	9	1	U. Iowa	16
041391B	Y	10	1	U. Iowa (exper.)[a]	8
112890	N	9	2	Caltech	16
113090	N	11	2	Caltech	16
011891	N	10	2	Caltech	16

[a] Subjects had experience in one of the earlier experiments listed here.

Consumers sell their endowment of inputs to producers in their own country, and consumers buy units of Y and Z produced in either country. Producers can buy L and K from consumers in their own country. Producers can consume any part of the purchases of L and K and can use the remainder to produce Y and Z, which they can then sell in either country.

III. Experimental Design: Procedures

A total of ten experiments were conducted. Table 3 provides a summary of treatments. Experiments are indexed by the date of the experiment. Two subject pools were used. The experiments involved either 8 people or 16 people. The use of 8 people for some experiments was dictated by cost and difficulties in recruiting subjects.

In the conditions of environments 1 and 2, there were six and eight markets, respectively, operating simultaneously.[3] Each variable had its own market (e.g., output Y_i, Y produced in country i, had its own market). The production process allowed subjects to transfer units from and to inventories of certain markets in fixed ratios. Production was accomplished through a series of keystrokes. To consume units, subjects held them in their inventory at the end of a market period.

Subjects, undergraduates at the California Institute of Technology and at the University of Iowa, had at least one half hour of prior training in use of MUDA.[4] The MUDA software is accompanied by a tutorial that explains the key functions to subjects and lets subjects practice using the keys in an environment containing randomly behaving robots. The Appendix contains instructions read to subjects. During period 0 and period 1, accounting records were checked carefully for mistakes, and spot checks were conducted in later periods.

The experiment was divided into trading periods or trading "days." At the beginning of each, subjects received new endowments and redemption values which were the same each period. At the beginning of the experiment there was a long practice period (period 0) for 15 minutes in which no money was paid. Market periods averaged 10 minutes in length.

---

[3] The names L and K were not used to label the markets in any experiments because they might suggest behavior to the subjects if they thought that L and K represented labor and capital. The labels used in markets are explained in the Appendix.

[4] Although Caltech subjects were only allowed to participate in one experiment in this particular line of experimentation, some of the Caltech subjects had been in other market experiments. None of the University of Iowa subjects had been in other market experiments previously, although experiments 041391A and 041391B used only subjects who had been in one of the previous experiments in the series.

IV. Models

The models described below rely on strong assumptions. The complex environments of the experimental markets are much richer than those that the models describe. However, experimental economics has demonstrated that models frequently have surprising power even when applied to environments much more complex than the structure of the models. The questions that will ultimately be posed concern the identification of models that can provide intuition needed for help with the interpretation of market data.

A. *The Competitive Model*

This section contains a brief elaboration and review of the competitive model. The computation and description of the competitive equilibria for both environments are in a technical appendix which is available from the authors upon request. Recall that the first environment has two outputs, both of which can be produced with the same input, paralleling that of the Ricardian model of international trade. In the Ricardian environment there are two final goods, Y and Z, each of which is produced using one factor, L. There are two countries which may differ in their endowments of the factor. The factor cannot cross national boundaries and is supplied inelastically to the markets. The two countries are assumed to have different production functions so that each country has a comparative advantage in production of one of the goods. Without loss of generality, call the country with a comparative advantage in the production of Y country 1. The two countries have identical aggregate demand for both goods. In autarky, the price ratio P_Z/P_Y should be greater in country 1 than in country 2. That is, country 1 can produce good Y more cheaply in terms of good Z then can country 2. If trade between the two countries is permitted, then comparative advantage dictates that country 1 specializes in and exports good Y. Similarly, country 2 specializes in and exports good Z. If the final goods are traded without restrictions, the prices of the final goods,

Y and Z, will be the same across countries and the price of L generally will be different in each country.

Thus, for environment 1, the competitive model predicts that countries 1 and 2 would produce exclusively goods Y and Z, respectively, and that each of the two countries would be a net exporter of the output which it produces. In particular country 1 would produce only Y, and country 2 would produce only Z. The prices of the outputs would be equal in each country according to the model, and the prices of inputs would equal their marginal revenue products.

If a tariff were imposed on the country-1 imports of Z in environment 1, then according to the competitive model international trade of Z would decline. The price of Z in country 1 would increase, and the price of Z in country 2 would fall. The input price in country 2 would also decline, since its marginal revenue product would be lower. The tariff imposed was 400 francs.

In environment 2, the competitive model predicts that each country would produce both output goods. Country 1, however, would be a net exporter of Y, and country 2 would be a net exporter of Z. Under conditions of free trade, the prices of outputs would be equal across countries. Since derived demand would be identical in both countries, then the factor prices would also be the same and would equal the factors' marginal revenue product. The price of each of the four types of goods in country 1 would equal its price in country 2. The prediction of the equality of input prices across countries in environment 2 will be referred to as the factor-price equalization principle. Notice that for the parameter values imposed in this environment, factor-price equalization is predicted even though the factors cannot be traded internationally.

B. *Autarky*

A natural alternative model to use is the autarky model. It is useful because it characterizes one benchmark of the potential behavior which a system might exhibit. Its predictions are based upon the proposition that no trade will occur across national

470 THE AMERICAN ECONOMIC REVIEW *JUNE 1995*

TABLE 4—SPECIFIC PREDICTIONS OF THE TWO MODELS: PRODUCTION AND EXPORT QUANTITIES AND PRICES IN FRANCS WITH AND WITHOUT TARIFFS

| | Environment 1 | | | | Environment 2 | |
| | Competitive | | Autarky | | | |
Variable	With tariff	No tariff	With tariff	No tariff	Competitive	Autarky
Production:						
Y_1	36	36	21	21	12	10
Y_2	0	0	5	5	4	6
Z_1	0	0	5	5	4	6
Z_2	32	32	22	22	12	10
Exports:						
Y_1	18	18	0	0	4	0
Y_2	0	0	0	0	0	0
Net Y (from 1 to 2)	18	18	0	0	4	0
Z_1	0	0	0	0	0	0
Z_2	16	6	0	0	4	0
Net Z (from 2 to 1)	16	6	0	0	4	0
Prices:						
L_1	720	720	600	600	200–250	150
L_2	760	360	520	520	200–250	300–350
K_1	—	—	—	—	200–250	300–350
K_2	—	—	—	—	200–250	150
Y_1	240	240	200	200	200–225	150
Y_2	—	—	520	520	200–225	300–350
Z_1	—	—	600	600	200–225	300–350
Z_2	380	180	260	260	200–225	150

boundaries. This model predicts the prices and production levels in each country which would occur in a competitive equilibrium with no international transactions permitted. This model thus offers specific predictions of prices, patterns of production, international trade, and the effects of tariffs.

For environment 1, the autarky model predicts that specialization would not occur in either country, and that there would be no international trade or payment imbalances. Since there is no trade across national boundaries, the predictions of this model are unaffected by the imposition of tariffs. According to the autarky model, prices of all goods would be different in the two countries.

The autarky model also makes predictions concerning production and trade in the two countries in environment 2. Both countries produce both goods but in different quantities than in the competitive equilibrium. Autarky predicts that there will be no international trade and that both input and output prices will be different across countries. The wage–price ratio predictions are identical to those predicted by the competitive model. There should be no payment imbalances. The predictions of the autarky model are computed in a similar way to the competitive model. The computations are available from the authors upon request.

The specific predictions of the two models in the two environments are given in Table 4. An illustration of the autarky model and the competitive model is given in Figure 1 from an individual's point of view for environment 1. In the figure, if trade between countries does not occur, an individual in country 1 achieves his highest indifference curve given initial endowments, by consuming 5.25 units of Y and 1.25 units of Z. Similarly, an individual in country 2 reaches his highest possible utility level by consuming 1.25 units of Y and 5.5 units of Z. In the experimental environment, money, which has value to all agents, may be borrowed costlessly in large quantities from the experimenter. For this reason, there is no budget constraint. The optimal consumption bundle is determined by the prices of Y and Z and by the consumer's utility for Y, Z, and money. The autarky consumption bundles of individual consumers in the two countries are labeled with A's in the figure. If free trade occurs, then each country can achieve a higher utility level by specializing in the commodity in which it has a comparative advantage and then trading internationally at the world competitive equilibrium price. The competitive-equilibrium individual consumption bundles are labelled with C's. In the competitive equilibrium, each country consumes 18 units of Y and 16 units of Z.

C. *Efficiency*

The efficiency measurements in our experiments were first developed by Plott and Smith (1978). In a single market the system is operating at 100-percent efficiency if the total profit that all subjects make in an experiment is at a maximum. It is similar to maximizing consumer plus producer surplus.

In a general-equilibrium system the problem becomes a little tricky. Because of the single currency in these experiments, the gains from exchange are exhausted at the maximum of system profits in terms of the experimental currency, francs. Actual profits divided by the maximum possible becomes the measure of system efficiency. Efficiency is 100 percent if the competitive equilibrium is attained. When tariffs were imposed, the government revenues were treated the same as were the profits of individuals and, therefore, included as part of the "consumer surplus" that was created by exchange.

V. Results

The principal observations are summarized in Results 1–9. A typical price time series from environment 1 (no tariffs) is represented in Figures 2 and 3. The vertical

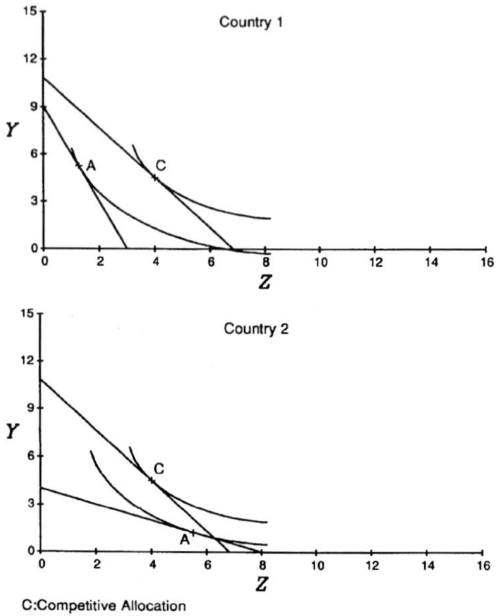

FIGURE 1. CONTINUOUS APPROXIMATION OF REPRESENTATIVE CONSUMER'S INDIFFERENCE CURVE AND RELATIVE PRICES UNDER AUTARKY AND FREE TRADE

axis measures price in terms of the currency of the experiment. The horizontal axis measures time in seconds. All markets were organized electronically with the bids, asks, and contracts made via computerized interactions. Thus market activity took place in real (clock) time, and the data are recorded in terms of the second at which actions took place. Thus, "Clock (sec)" on the horizontal axis means the exact second that the action took place. Vertical lines represent the beginning or the end of periods or "days" as described in Section III. Thus, the interval between the end of one period and the beginning of the next appears as an empty vertical band representing seconds in which nothing happened in the markets because the markets were closed while subjects did their accounting. Contract prices are represented as circles and are connected by lines so that the time sequence can be more easily identified. The input prices for each country separately are shown in Figure 2.

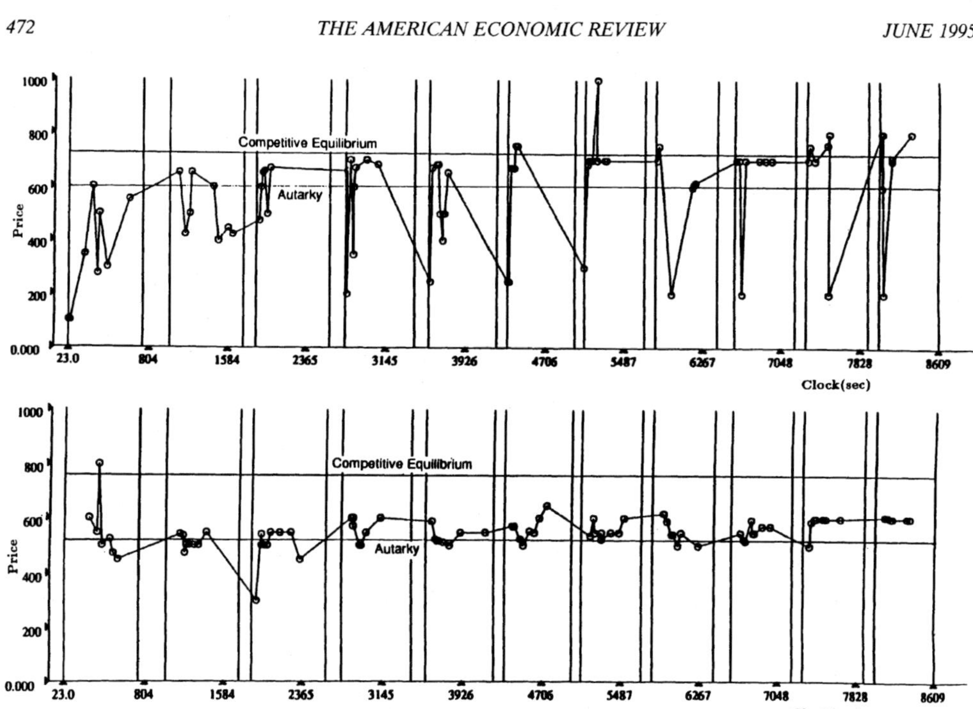

FIGURE 2. INPUT-PRICE TIME SERIES, EXPERIMENT 041391A: COUNTRY 1 (UPPER GRAPH) AND COUNTRY 2 (LOWER GRAPH)

The output prices are pooled across countries for each of the two outputs and are given in the two graphs of Figure 3. Horizontal solid lines are drawn at the level of the theoretical competitive prices and also the autarky prices as marked.

Several useful impressions can be drawn from the figures. First, the data are not automatically clustered at the competitive equilibria. This is perhaps no surprise to those who have studied the properties of experimental markets, but the fact that markets are not always automatically at the competitive equilibrium is of substantial importance to those who must use equilibrium theories as a specification tool in the interpretation of field data. Secondly, the prices over time move toward the competitive equilibria. This power of the competitive-equilibrium model in predicting the direction of the movement in these complicated

markets is also observed in simpler economic environments. The formal statements of results in this section will make these general impressions precise.

The analysis of the data of this section encounters some classical problems that exist in the analysis of almost all data produced in experimental markets. Markets exhibit a convergence process that is not understood theoretically. From a practical point of view, this means that serial correlation is present, and heteroscedasticity may be present. In the absence of a well-developed theory of a convergence process, such statistical complications create substantial problems with any attempt to summarize succinctly the patterns that may exist in the data. With these qualifications in mind, the following model, motivated by the model of Orley Ashenfelter et al. (1992), is used repeatedly to analyze the effect of time

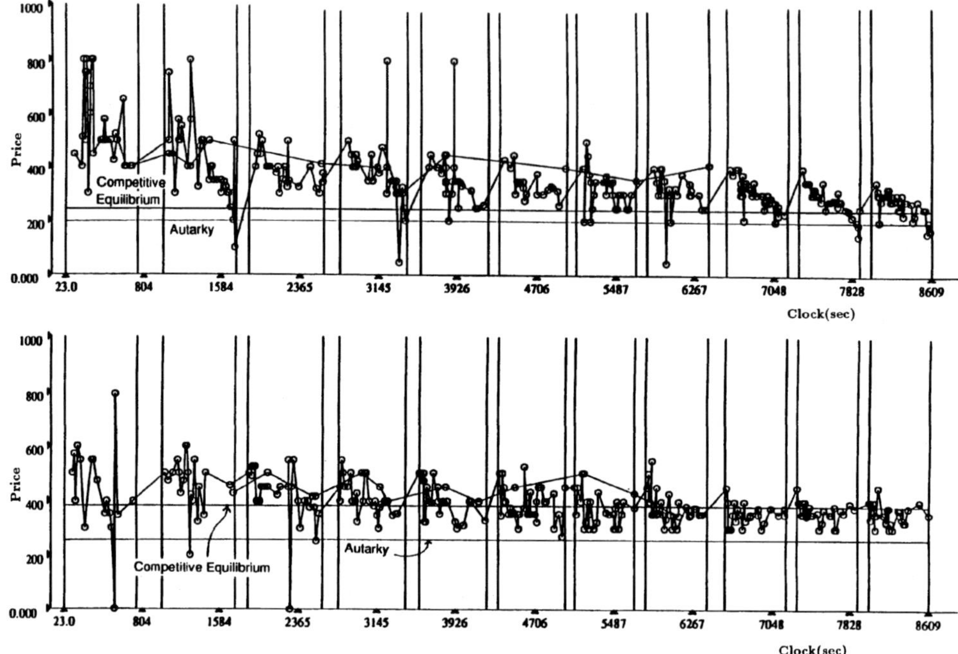

FIGURE 3. OUTPUT-PRICE TIME SERIES, EXPERIMENT 041391A: PRICES OF Y IN BOTH COUNTRIES (UPPER GRAPH) AND PRICES OF Z IN BOTH COUNTRIES (LOWER GRAPH)

on the outcome variables in the experiments:[5]

$$(1)\quad y_{it} = B_{11}D_1(1/t) + B_{12}D_2(1/t)$$
$$+ \cdots + B_{1i}D_i(1/t) + \cdots$$
$$+ B_{1n}D_n(1/t) + B_2(t-1)/t + u$$

where i indicates the particular experiment, t represents time as measured by the number of market periods in the experiment, D_i is a dummy variable that takes a value of 1 for i and a value of 0 otherwise, and B_{1i} is the origin of a possible convergence process. Notice that if $t = 1$ then the value of the dependent variable is equal to B_{1i} for experiment i. B_2 is the asymptote of the dependent variable. As t gets large the

present within the experimental sessions. In addition to the estimates of the equations given in the text, two alternative specifications were also used to analyze the data. They were

$$z = B_{11}D_1\frac{1}{t} + \cdots + B_{1k}D_k\frac{1}{t} + B_{21}D_1\left(\frac{t-1}{t}\right)$$
$$+ \cdots + B_{2k}D_k\left(\frac{t-1}{t}\right) + u$$

and

$$z = B_{11}D_1\left(\frac{1}{t}\right)^{\alpha_1} + \cdots + B_{1k}D_k\left(\frac{1}{t}\right)^{\alpha_k}$$
$$+ B_2\left(\frac{t-1}{t}\right)^{\gamma} + u$$

where z is any of the dependent variables, such as quantity produced, quantity exported, or price of a commodity. Refer to the last two equations as specifications 1 and 2, respectively. Specification 1 assumes a linear functional form but allows the time series to

---

[5]We benefited from several discussions with Mahmoud El-Gamal who suggested the specification that we used, along with others. The estimates in the tables are corrected for first-order autocorrelation, which is

TABLE 5—CONVERGENCE PATTERNS OVER TIME OF PRODUCTION, EXPORTS, AND MARKET PRICES, ENVIRONMENT 1 (NO TARIFF)

$$y = B_{11}D_1\frac{1}{t} + \cdots + B_{14}D_4\frac{1}{t} + B_2\frac{t-1}{t} + u$$

Dependent variable	B_{11}	B_{12}	B_{13}	B_{14}	B_2	Competitive equilibria		Autarky			
						Model predictions	Significance (p)	Model predictions	Significance (p)	ρ	R^2
Production:											
Y_1	17.73	21.56	13.44	28.15	32.70	36	< 0.005	21	< 0.005	0.13	0.69
	(3.32)	(1.32)	(2.10)	(1.86)	(0.70)						
Y_2	4.81	6.92	2.68	3.29	0.68	0	ns	5	< 0.005	0.45	0.71
	(0.85)	(1.11)	(1.16)	(0.42)	(0.47)						
Z_1	4.81	4.90	7.73	2.28	0.87	0	< 0.005	5	< 0.005	0.02	0.66
	(0.92)	(0.32)	(0.70)	(1.00)	(0.18)						
Z_2	18.73	18.10	26.84	25.42	30.93	32	ns	22	< 0.005	0.48	0.76
	(1.20)	(2.28)	(2.50)	(0.87)	(1.04)						
Net exports:											
Y	1.93	5.88	11.78	14.16	14.35	18	ns	0	< 0.005	0.58	0.73
	(2.62)	(2.05)	(2.47)	(2.80)	(2.14)						
Z	5.32	9.08	15.72	12.48	16.06	16	ns	0	< 0.005	0.49	0.62
	(2.78)	(1.47)	(4.47)	(1.77)	(1.61)						
Market prices:											
P_{L_1}	429.7	501.7	600.1	420.6	700.9	720	ns	600	< 0.05	0.42	0.48
	(79.3)	(66.0)	(231.1)	(43.0)	(49.8)						
P_{L_2}	415.1	300.9	580.6	501.3	601.9	760	< 0.005	520	< 0.05	0.59	0.69
	(91.0)	(65.1)	(48.6)	(47.0)	(44.7)						
P_{Y_1}	405.4	279.3	812.6	439.7	295.9	240	< 0.005	200	< 0.005	0.33	0.89
	(29.6)	(40.1)	(59.0)	(25.8)	(12.8)						
P_{Z_2}	439.6	484.6	745.7	426.8	439.6	380	< 0.005	260	< 0.005	0.34	0.77
	(26.9)	(28.8)	(76.9)	(33.6)	(14.6)						

Note: Estimates were corrected for AR(1).

weight of B_{i1} is small because $1/t$ approaches zero while the weight of B_2 is large because $(t-1)/t$ approaches 1. Notice that B_2 is common to all experiments. Finally, u is the random error term that is distributed normally with mean zero. We

converge to a different value for each experimental session. Specification 2 is nonlinear; we estimate the B, α, and γ terms. The functional form was based on an *ex post* inspection of the data. It allows the time series to converge at different rates in the different experimental sessions but requires all of the data to converge to a common asymptote. The estimates of the alternative specifications are not given here, because they do not improve upon the specification used in the text. Specification 1 yields adjusted R^2's, estimated coefficients, and standard errors close to those of the specification given in the text. The nonlinear specification 2 also yields comparable adjusted R^2's but very large standard errors, especially for the price variables, so that usually neither the competitive model nor the autarky model could be rejected.

allow for heteroscedasticity and first-order autocorrelation.

The model is equipped to answer questions about the direction of convergence. Each experiment might have a different starting point, but according to the intuition of competitive-market theory, the processes should converge, and the ultimate point of convergence should be the same (the competitive equilibrium quantities). For purposes of describing the data, the term "weak convergence" is used when the start of the data, as measured by B_{1i}, is further from the predictions of the model than is the asymptote, as measured by B_2.

The model was estimated for each of the relevant dependent variables, and the results of the estimates are contained in Tables 5, 6, and 7. The standard errors are corrected for heteroscedasticity using White's method (see Halbert White, 1980), as well as first-order autocorrelation. The model was estimated for each of the treat-

TABLE 6—CONVERGENCE PATTERNS OVER TIME OF PRODUCTION, EXPORTS, AND MARKET PRICES, ENVIRONMENT 1 (WITH TARIFFS)

$$y = B_{11}D_1\frac{1}{t} + \cdots + B_{13}D_3\frac{1}{t} + B_2\frac{t-1}{t} + u$$

| Dependent variable | B_{11} | B_{12} | B_{13} | B_2 | Competitive equilibria | | Autarky | | ρ | R^2 |
					Model predictions	Significance (p)	Model predictions	Significance (p)		
Production:										
Y_1	27.17	32.33	14.42	27.97	36	ns	21	ns	0.61	0.62
	(3.37)	(4.67)	(5.48)	(5.45)						
Y_2	2.13	9.14	9.56	3.96	0	< 0.005	5	ns	0.40	0.63
	(1.41)	(0.93)	(2.23)	(0.87)						
Z_1	3.06	1.26	7.03	2.57	0	ns	5	ns	0.64	0.66
	(1.22)	(1.74)	(1.67)	(1.82)						
Z_2	25.60	5.56	11.79	24.51	32	< 0.01	22	ns	0.56	0.77
	(1.94)	(1.99)	(4.31)	(2.70)						
Net exports:										
Y	7.16	14.05	-1.77	13.06	18	ns	0	< 0.005	0.52	0.57
	(1.82)	(5.11)	(3.41)	(3.28)						
Z	1.23	1.85	0.72	1.42	6	< 0.005	0	ns	0.43	0.31
	(1.03)	(1.57)	(0.75)	(1.20)						
Market prices:										
P_{L_1}	500.8	391.5	413.7	677.5	720	ns	600	ns	0.51	0.42
	(56.9)	(130.5)	(68.1)	(75.6)						
P_{L_2}	268.4	247.0	-24.3	473.3	360	ns	520	ns	0.88	0.68
	(646.5)	(959.9)	(938.2)	(964.5)						
P_{Y_1}	297.9	1,002.9	434.0	289.2	240	< 0.01	200	< 0.005	0.22	0.84
	(37.0)	(103.5)	(48.4)	(18.7)						
P_{Z_2}	166.4	1,003.0	606.5	283.6	180	< 0.005	260	ns	0.00	0.73
	(38.1)	(140.6)	(95.7)	(21.7)						

ment environments and for each of the variables, separately. The significance levels for various hypothesis tests are also in the tables.

Notice from Figures 2 and 3, that the transaction prices seem to be moving toward the competitive-equilibrium prices over time. While this tendency of convergence will ultimately be shown to be true, the first pass at the data holds to strict standards. As can be seen the prices are not at the competitive equilibrium. As we indicated earlier, in economic systems as complicated as these, it is very easy to statistically reject the benchmark models. This indeed proved true.

The first result is important because it shapes the entire discussion. It demonstrates that neither the competitive model nor the autarky model accurately represents the data generated by the experiments. Such a result is not particularly surprising to those who have studied the behavior of experimental markets. The market prices and quantities traded, as predicted by the competitive model, are often rejected, and the autarky model is usually rejected as well. The models are static, while the actual markets exhibit considerable dynamic and adjustment behavior, the very existence of which is sufficient to reject the models. However, Result 1 is especially interesting because of the power brought to the analysis by the econometric model introduced above. The result says that, even after the model has been modified to incorporate differential adjustment rates in different experimental sessions, both models can still be rejected.

RESULT 1: *Both the competitive model and the autarky model can be rejected as accurate representations of the data.*

SUPPORT:

Rejection of the models rests on the fact that each of the models makes numerous predictions. Of course, rejection only re-

TABLE 7—CONVERGENCE PATTERNS OVER TIME OF PRODUCTION, EXPORTS, AND MARKET PRICES, ENVIRONMENT 2

$$y = B_{11}D_1\frac{1}{t} + \cdots + B_{13}D_3\frac{1}{t} + B_2\frac{t-1}{t} + u$$

Dependent variable	B_{11}	B_{12}	B_{13}	B_2	Competitive equilibria		Autarky		ρ	R^2
					Model predictions	Significance (p)	Model predictions	Significance (p)		
Production:										
Y_1	6.69	7.79	7.68	11.53	12	ns	10	< 0.05	0.29	0.41
	(1.86)	(0.66)	(0.86)	(0.72)						
Y_2	5.74	7.58	3.11	4.72	4	< 0.05	6	< 0.005	0.13	0.25
	(1.87)	(0.84)	(0.93)	(0.39)						
Z_1	6.23	4.20	4.78	6.15	4	< 0.005	6	ns	0.09	0.06
	(0.83)	(1.82)	(1.54)	(0.51)						
Z_2	6.44	11.76	5.06	10.50	12	< 0.05	10	ns	0.16	0.27
	(0.92)	(2.04)	(2.96)	(0.64)						
Net exports:										
Y	−2.68	0.14	4.96	3.72	4	ns	0	< 0.005	0.12	0.48
	(1.16)	(1.42)	(1.70)	(0.49)						
Z	0.68	3.80	2.65	4.16	4	ns	0	< 0.005	0.30	0.19
	(1.89)	(1.68)	(2.45)	(1.11)						
Market prices:										
P_{L_1}	408.6	187.8	388.8	227.4	200–250	ns	150	< 0.005	0.12	0.89
	(16.9)	(8.5)	(15.7)	(5.6)						
P_{L_2}	390.9	307.9	514.4	220.8	200–250	ns	300–350	< 0.005	0.35	0.62
	(12.7)	(35.6)	(82.3)	(15.1)						
P_{K_1}	327.1	227.2	260.2	233.5	200–250	ns	300–350	< 0.005	0.37	0.58
	(44.6)	(7.2)	(34.5)	(11.0)						
P_{K_2}	349.4	301.7	281.8	220.0)	200–250	ns	150	< 0.005	0.27	0.47
	(23.8)	(28.0)	(49.2)	(9.9)						
P_{Y_1}	583.9	322.9	497.7	256.7	200–225	< 0.005	150	< 0.005	0.37	0.92
	(15.0)	(23.2)	(32.9)	(10.5)						
P_{Y_2}	525.2	382.9	534.5	255.6	200–225	< 0.005	300–350	< 0.005	0.31	0.87
	(18.9)	(34.9)	(17.8)	(10.0)						
P_{Z_1}	528.6	342.0	475.5	257.0	200–225	< 0.005	300–350	< 0.005	0.24	0.24
	(40.9)	(17.0)	(18.5)	(8.2)						
P_{Z_2}	448.3	377.0	331.5	276.7	200–225	< 0.005	150	< 0.005	0.00	0.71
	(13.2)	(18.6)	(16.8)	(5.3)						

quires that one prediction be wrong, but we reject the model's predictions of many of the outcome variables. Testing of the models is focused only on the variable B_2, which represents the long-term (asymptotic) tendency of the magnitude of the variables. The estimates are in Tables 5, 6, and 7 for each of the treatment conditions, environment 1 with and without tariffs, and environment 2. A summary of significance tests of the two models and variables is provided in each of the tables. As can be seen in Table 5, the autarky model is rejected for every variable in environment 1 (no tariff) at the $p < 0.005$ level of significance for eight of the ten variables and at the $p < 0.05$ level for the other two variables. As shown in

Table 7, all price predictions of the autarky model are incorrect in environment 2, as are its predictions of exports and of production of Y in both countries. The autarky model performs best under environment 1 (tariff), as shown in Table 6, but even in this case, two of the variables are significantly different from the predictions of the model at the 0.005 level of significance.

Under the conditions of environment 1 (no tariff) the competitive model fails to predict two of the four production variables, the prices of L_2, Y, and Z. Under the conditions of environment 1 (tariff), the competitive model fails to predict three of the six aggregate production and export levels, as well as the prices in two of the four markets. In all cases, the significance level supporting rejection is at least 0.05. As for environment 2, the competitive model is rejected for seven of the 14 variables at the 0.05 level of significance.

It is important to note, as is clear from the tables, that the competitive model has some merit when one compares the coefficients B_{1i} to B_2. The remaining results are attempts to summarize those aspects of the competitive and autarky models that are successful. The general theme is that convergence of the data over time, with replication of the market, is in the general direction of the competitive equilibria and that the autarky model is firmly rejected. In particular, several qualitative features of the competitive model are very prominent in the data and are described by the next series of results.

Result 2 summarizes observations concerning whether or not the law of comparative advantage can be seen in operation. The notion is that countries export the output in whose production they have a comparative advantage. Recall that when applied to the parameters of environment 1, the law of comparative advantage holds that country 1 should specialize in and be a net exporter of good Y. Country 2 should specialize in and be a net exporter of Z.

RESULT 2: *The law of comparative advantage accurately predicts trade patterns.*

SUPPORT:
Refer to Tables 5, 6, and 7. Under the conditions of environment 1 (no tariff), neither the net exports of Y nor the net imports of Z by country 1 are statistically different from the predictions of the competitive model of 18 units and 16 units, respectively. Thus, within this environment, the flow of international trade is not only in the direction predicted by the law of comparative advantage, but the actual magnitudes are converging to near those predicted by the competitive model. Net exports of Y and net exports of Z are 14.4 units and 16.1 units, respectively. Under the tariff condition, the directions of trade patterns are those predicted by the law, but exports of Z are significantly less than predicted by the competitive model. That is, the net exports of Y by country 1 are 13.1 units as opposed to the 18 predicted by the competitive model. Exports of Z by country 2 are 1.4, as opposed to the 6 units predicted by the competitive model. Under the conditions of environment 2 the net exports are not significantly different from those predicted by the competitive model (i.e., 3.7 units net exports of Y by country 1, compared with the competitive equilibrium of 4; 4.2 units of net exports of Z by country 2, compared with the 4 units predicted by the competitive model). In summary, under all conditions, the patterns of trade are consistent with the directions predicted by the law of comparative advantage.

Implicit in the discussion above is the fact that the law of comparative advantage can be viewed as an independent principle or it can be viewed as a consequence following from the assumptions of the general competitive model. Thus, since the result lends support to the competitive model, it is natural to inquire about other features of the model. The competitive model not only predicts the direction of net exports, as captured by the law of comparative advantage as discussed in Result 2, it also predicts patterns of production. For environment 1 the competitive model predicts that no units of Y would be produced in country 1 and that no units of Z would be produced in country 2. Result 3 reflects considerations of those precise implications of the competitive model under both tariff and no-tariff conditions.

The support for Result 3 can be seen in Figures 4 and 5 for environment 1. The figures contain world aggregate production for early periods and for later periods. The world production frontier is shown in the figure. The competitive model predicts that world production will be at the "kink" in the frontier. Figure 4 contains data from environment-1 experiments in which there were no tariffs. Figure 5 contains the data from environment-1 experiments in which tariffs existed. As can be seen in both

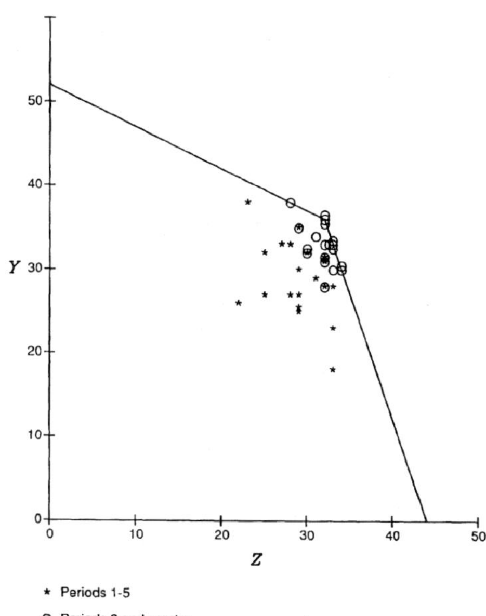

FIGURE 4. TOTAL SYSTEM PRODUCTION: ALL
EXPERIMENTS, ENVIRONMENT 1, NO-TARIFF
CONDITION

FIGURE 5. TOTAL SYSTEM PRODUCTION: ALL
EXPERIMENTS, ENVIRONMENT 1, TARIFF
CONDITION

of the figures, aggregate production is nearer the competitive equilibrium in the later periods.

RESULT 3: *Aggregate production patterns are converging toward those predicted by the competitive model under free trade.*

SUPPORT:

As was mentioned at the beginning of this section, a weak definition of the phrase "converging toward" is that the data are either at (statistically) the competitive equilibria at the end of the experiment or closer to the competitive equilibria at the end of the experiment than they were at the beginning. A stronger definition is that the data are converging to quantities that are not significantly different from the competitive-equilibrium predictions. As we stated in Result 1, we reject the notion that the outcome variables are converging to the competitive predictions in the strong sense. However,

under the environment-1 (no-tariff) condition Result 3 holds in the weak sense for most experiments and countries and variables. In every case B_2 is closer to the competitive equilibrium than all of the B_{1i}'s. The results under the conditions of environment 1 (tariff) are not so uniformly supportive of the result. For example, the production of Y_1 is converging in only two of the three experiments for which coefficients B_{11} and B_{13} equal 14 and 27, respectively, B_2 is 28, and the competitive equilibrium is 36 units produced. In summary, for the tariff experiments, of the 12 cases (two countries, two commodities, and three experiments), only eight support the result. In environment 2, the movement in nine of the 12 cases is toward the competitive equilibrium. As for the autarky model, in environment 1, without tariffs, none of the 16 production levels is converging in the weak sense. Under tariffs, however, nine of the 12 variables converge to autarky in the weak sense. In

TABLE 8—DEVIATIONS OF INDIVIDUALS' HOLDING FROM COMPETITIVE-EQUILIBRIUM PREDICTIONS (BY PERIOD)

Output	Statistic	Period								
		1	2	3	4	5	6	7	8	9
Y	μ	−0.91	−0.46	−0.58	−0.45	−0.46	−0.40	−0.24	−0.18	−0.28
	σ	1.63	1.49	1.29	1.38	1.09	1.11	0.91	0.98	1.05
Z	μ	−0.95	−0.79	−0.60	−0.40	−0.30	−0.31	−0.21	−0.23	−0.39
	σ	1.84	1.64	1.15	1.55	1.25	1.26	1.06	1.07	1.16

Notes: The statistics reported in the table were calculated as follows:

$$\mu = \sum_i (x_i - \hat{x}_i)/N$$

$$\sigma = \left[\sum_i (x_i - \hat{x}_i)^2/N \right]^{1/2}$$

where x_i = actual holdings of agent i, $\hat{x}_i$ = competitive equilibrium holdings of agent i, and N = total number of observations (consumers times experiments).

environment 2, 11 of the 12 variables are moving toward autarky.

Result 3 is focused on production. The next result considers consumption patterns. Do individual consumption levels converge with replication of periods to the competitive-equilibrium model? For this result a different statistical model is chosen for convenience. For each individual in each experiment, the difference between actual consumption and the competitive equilibrium is computed for each variable. These deviations are then pooled across all the experiments.

RESULT 4: *Individual consumption patterns are converging to those predicted by the competitive model.*

SUPPORT:

The deviation in individual consumption from the quantities predicted in the competitive model are diminishing over time (see Table 8). In the table, the data are pooled for all of the experimental sessions. From the table, it is evident that the absolute values of the deviations are smaller in the later periods than in the earlier periods. For example, the mean deviations from the competitive equilibrium fall consistently over the first four periods for both Y and Z.

Similarly, the standard deviations during the first periods are higher than those in the last periods. The hypothesis that the absolute value of the deviations for periods 1–3 are smaller than or equal to those for periods 7–11 can be rejected at $p < 0.01$.

The addition of tariffs on imports of country 1 changes the predictions of the competitive model. According to the model, the tariff discourages the export of Z by country 2 and encourages the home consumption of Z by country 2. Figure 6 demonstrates the differences in consumption patterns in environment 1 that were caused by the tariff. The figure shows aggregate consumption for each country, with the top panel containing data from country 1 and the bottom panel containing data from country 2. The production-possibilities curve is shown for each country as a point of reference. Note that the consumption of Z is shifted from country 1 to country 2 with the imposition of the tariff.

The change in consumption that is apparent in the figure reflects a deep interaction between principles of economics and the parameters of these economies. The tariff, 400 francs per unit of Z imported by country 1, is not so high as to prevent specialization in both countries in the same levels of output as would occur under free trade

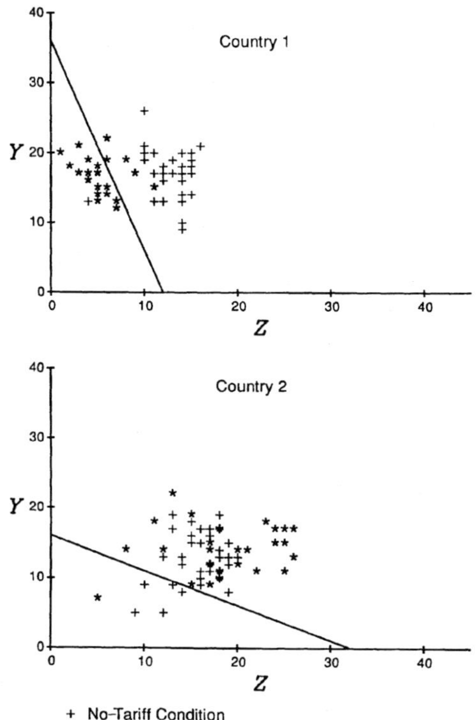

FIGURE 6. CONSUMPTION BY COUNTRY:
ENVIRONMENT 1, ALL EXPERIMENTS, ALL
PERIODS, TARIFF AND NO-TARIFF CONDITIONS

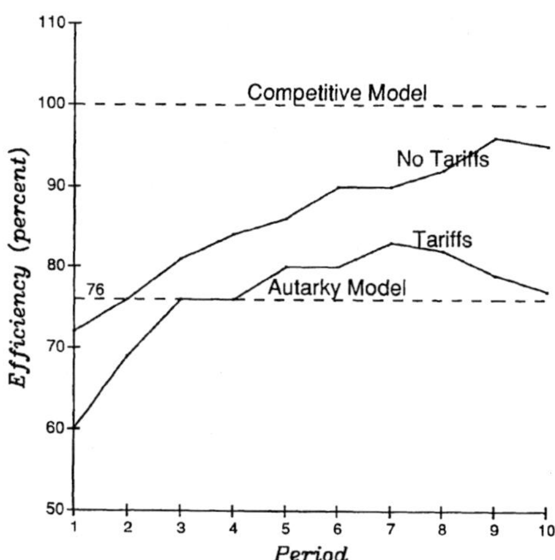

FIGURE 7. PREDICTED AND OBSERVED SYSTEM
EFFICIENCIES: ENVIRONMENT 1, ALL
EXPERIMENTS, ALL PERIODS, TARIFF
AND NO-TARIFF CONDITIONS

according to the competitive model. That is, the world patterns of production should not be altered by the tariff in this version of the Ricardian model. However, the competitive model predicts that the reduction in exports of Z would lead to lower system efficiency.[6] The impact of the tariff is to block some gains from international exchange. System efficiency thus falls due to the imposition of a tariff. This property is captured by the next result. Generally, we find that the tariff affects trade volume, efficiency, and prices in the way that the competitive model predicts.

RESULT 5: *Tariffs reduce international trade and market efficiency, as predicted by the competitive model. Prices also differ in the manner predicted by the competitive model.*

SUPPORT:

The relevant data are for environment 1. Average net exports per period are 10.3 without the tariffs and 2.8 under tariffs. We reject the hypothesis at the $p < 0.01$ level that exports of Z are lower or equal under free trade than under tariffs. Refer again to Figure 6, which depicts consumption in the two countries in all experiments in the condition of environment 1 with and without tariffs. Market efficiency under tariffs is compared to that without tariffs for the pooled environment-1 data in Figure 7. As can be seen for each period, average efficiency under the no-tariff condition is higher than average efficiency of the tariff condition. We reject the hypothesis that efficiency is equal in the two conditions or

---

[6] System efficiency is measured as actual social income (in francs) divided by social income at the competitive equilibrium under free trade. The tariff revenue is included as social income in our calculation of actual social income. See Plott and Smith (1978) for a discussion of this concept in a single-market economy. In a multiple-market economy the measure can be influenced by scale choices.

TABLE 9—THE EFFECTS OF TIME ON INPUT/OUTPUT PRICE RATIOS: ALL ENVIRONMENTS

$$y = B_{11}D_1\frac{1}{t} + \cdots + B_{14}D_4\frac{1}{t} + B_2\frac{t-1}{t} + u$$

| Environment | Dependent variable | B_{11} | B_{12} | B_{13} | B_{14} | B_2 | Competitive equilibria | | Autarky | | ρ | R^2 |
							Model predictions	Significance (p)	Model predictions	Significance (p)		
1 (NT)	P_{L_1}/P_{Y_1}	1.157 (0.207)	1.919 (0.388)	0.696 (0.237)	0.837 (0.184)	2.232 (0.235)	3	< 0.005	3	< 0.005	0.56	0.66
1 (NT)	P_{L_2}/P_{Z_2}	0.947 (0.243)	0.616 (0.190)	0.865 (0.197)	1.141 (0.101)	1.383 (0.114)	2	< 0.005	2	< 0.005	0.54	0.69
1 (T)	P_{L_1}/P_{Y_1}	1.611 (0.334)	−0.058 (0.451)	1.300 (0.448)	— —	2.090 (0.432)	3	< 0.025	3	< 0.025	0.62	0.66
1 (T)	P_{L_2}/P_{Z_2}	1.324 (0.087)	0.220 (0.305)	0.344 (0.343)	— —	1.383 (0.301)	2	< 0.025	2	< 0.025	0.64	0.71
2	P_{L_1}/P_{Y_1}	0.711 (0.060)	0.571 (0.076)	0.763 (0.048)	— —	0.873 (0.028)	1	< 0.005	1	< 0.005	0.25	0.49
2	P_{L_2}/P_{Y_2}	0.731 (0.057)	0.815 (0.041)	0.863 (0.176)	— —	0.884 (0.041)	1	< 0.005	1	< 0.005	0.28	0.17
2	P_{K_1}/P_{Z_1}	0.640 (0.045)	0.662 (0.046)	0.561 (0.040)	— —	0.868 (0.036)	1	< 0.005	1	< 0.005	0.34	0.52
2	P_{K_2}/P_{Z_2}	0.783 (0.037)	0.795 (0.086)	0.868 (0.189)	— —	0.799 (0.040)	1	< 0.005	1	< 0.005	0.29	0.12

Note: For environment 1, NT denotes no tariffs, and T denotes tariffs.

higher under tariffs ($p < 0.05$). We also reject the hypothesis, using the rank-sum test, that the prices of L_2 or the prices of Z_2 are equal under the tariff and in the absence of the tariff. The average prices of L_2 and Z_2 are 550 and 467, respectively, under no-tariff conditions and are respectively 402 and 380 under tariffs. As the competitive model predicts, they are both lower in the tariff case.

Result 5 can be viewed as a type of comparative-static result, but the comparisons are not exactly like those that are studied in theory. In the theory of comparative statics, a comparison is made between the equilibrium state before a tariff and the equilibrium state after a tariff. The comparison made in Result 5 is between the disequilibrium states as opposed to equilibrium states, with and without tariffs. The next results initiate an inquiry about the nature of this disequilibrium behavior. Result 6 is a statement about the behavior of output prices, the prices of Y and Z.

RESULT 6: *Output prices are converging (in the weak sense) toward the competitive equilibrium from above.*

SUPPORT:
Reference to Tables 5, 6, and 7 reveals that, for environment 1 (no tariff) and envi-ronment 1 (tariff), both output prices are above the competitive equilibrium (as well as the autarky prediction) during the late periods of the experiment. This is true for both outputs. The convergence path is revealed by a comparison of B_{1i}'s and B_2. In six of the eight possible cases under environment 1 (no tariff) and five of the six cases in environment 1 (tariff), the value of B_{1i}'s is above or equal to the value of B_2 and is not as close to the competitive equilibrium as is the value of B_2. For environment 2, prices are converging from above toward the competitive equilibrium in all 12 of the possible cases. Thus, the prices in early periods tend to be above the late-period prices, and the direction of movement over time is toward the competitive-equilibrium price.

While output prices move in a consistent way, as summarized by Result 6, input prices are more complex because of the nature of derived demand. The next result suggests that the deviation of factor prices from the competitive equilibrium is not only due to a lack of equilibrium in the output market prices, but factors have their own independent dynamic structure of adjustment. However, the direction of adjustment in the factor markets is toward the equilibria of the competitive model.

TABLE 10—CONVERGENCE PATTERNS OF INTERNATIONAL DIFFERENCES IN FACTOR PRICES, ENVIRONMENT 2

Dependent variable	B_{11}	B_{12}	B_{13}	B_2	Competitive equilibria		Autarky			
					Model predictions	Significance (p)	Model predictions	Significance (p)	ρ	R^2
$P_{L_1} - P_{L_2}$	10.44 (21.23)	−115.00 (42.10)	−126.59 (95.66)	6.37 (19.50)	0	ns	[−200, −150]	< 0.005	0.35	0.38
$P_{K_1} - P_{K_2}$	−15.46 (37.93)	−73.22 (28.79)	−23.62 (78.13)	12.92 (15.73)	0	ns	[150, 200]	< 0.005	0.32	0.27

Note: Estimates were corrected for AR(1).

RESULT 7: *Factor prices are below marginal revenue products. That is, all of the input/output price ratios are below marginal products. The convergence is in the direction of the competitive-equilibrium relationship.*

SUPPORT:

The condition for profit maximization under competitive conditions is simply that factor price equals marginal physical product times output price. Since production technologies are linear, the marginal physical product is a constant. It follows that the ratio of factor price to output price, when compared to marginal products, can then be used to determine whether the input conditions are satisfied.

Table 9 contains estimates of the time path of ratios of output prices to input prices. The econometric model is of the same form as described earlier. The B_{1i} variables measure the ratio during the first period, which is permitted to differ among experiments. The variable B_2 measures the ratio as time goes to infinity. In 25 of the 26 possible cases, the B_{1i}'s are less than B_2, and B_2 is less than the competitive equilibrium. This indicates that, convergence to the competitive-equilibrium input/output price ratio, in the weak sense, is always present.

Two reasonable explanations of the observed input/output price behaviors summarized in Result 7 are consistent with behaviors found in other experimental markets. The first is that the asymmetry of rents received by sellers and buyers of the factors (sellers receive more rents) leads to lower transaction prices because rents are split (see Smith and Arlington W. Williams, 1982). However, if this is the explanation, then the factor prices should approach equilibrium from below. In all environments, as long as output prices are at or above the competitive-equilibria prices, producer surplus is greater than consumer surplus in the appropriate partial-equilibrium model. As is evident in Table 6, factor prices in environment 2 do not approach the competitive equilibria from below.

Since factor prices do not approach equilibria from below in environment 2, this first (rent-splitting) explanation must be rejected. The other possible explanation is that the buyers of the factors face a market risk. The buyer may not be able to sell the final goods produced with the factor. In the experiments, producers must buy the input, then produce and sell the output. This takes time, and the possibilities that prices could change or that time could run out create real risks for producers. As a compensation to the producer for bearing this risk, a "return for risk-bearing," the factor/output price ratio starts low and adjusts upward. Risk of this type might be a general property of interdependent markets, and if it is, then the input/output price adjustments observed in the experiments might also be observed in the field. Regardless of the interesting separate dynamics, the most fundamental theoretical property derived from the competitive-equilibrium model still holds, as is captured by Result 8.

RESULT 8: *Factor prices adjust across countries (in environment 2) as predicted by the factor-price-equalization principle.*

SUPPORT:

In environment 2, competitive-equilibrium output prices are all the same (200–250), and competitive equilibrium in-

TABLE 11—CONVERGENCE PATTERNS OF PRODUCER PROFITS OVER TIME: ALL ENVIRONMENTS

$$y = B_{11}D_1\frac{1}{t} + \cdots + B_{14}D_4\frac{1}{t} + B_2\frac{t-1}{t} + u$$

| | | | | | | Competitive equilibria | | Autarky | | | |
| | | | | | | Model predictions | Significance (p) | Model predictions | Significance (p) | | |
Environment	B_{11}	B_{12}	B_{13}	B_{14}	B_2	predictions	Significance (p)	predictions	Significance (p)	ρ	R^2
1 (NT)	7,479	6,93	24,200	13,778	5,798	0	< 0.005	0	< 0.005	0.54	0.82
	(817)	(2,953)	(1,935)	(879)	(1,381)						
1 (T)	5,300	35,336	12,699	—	1985	0	< 0.005	0	< 0.005	0.07	0.87
	(875)	(3,713)	(2,550)		(648)						
2	3,730	3,085	3,179	—	1271	0	< 0.005	0	< 0.005	0.20	0.47
	(378)	(868)	(1,128)		(188)						

Notes: For environment 1, NT denotes no tariffs, and T denotes tariffs. Estimates were corrected for AR(1).

put prices are all the same (200–225). A natural test is, thus, whether or not the difference between the factor prices in the two countries is zero. Table 10 contains the estimates which show that, for both input factors, the hypothesis that the prices are equal as t gets large cannot be rejected.

The equality of factor prices for our parameters in environment 2 is a theoretically sound result. Since the outputs trade internationally they must trade at the same price in the two countries. Therefore, because production technology is linear and identical in the two countries, the marginal revenue product of the inputs and therefore their wages should be the same even though the inputs themselves do not trade internationally. Interestingly, in our experiment, we observe equality of input prices across countries even though these input prices are not equal to the marginal revenue product of the inputs.

Since profits can be viewed as a return to a special input (risk-bearing), the pattern of profits is worthy of special investigation. In the competitive model, equilibrium profits from production are zero. The next result demonstrates that the patterns of profits follow the laws suggested by the competitive model.

RESULT 9: *Profits from production are positive but fall over time.*

SUPPORT:
Table 11 contains estimates of the time path of profits. As can be seen the B_{1i}

terms in every experiment are greater than the B_2 term. Furthermore, B_2 is significantly greater than zero. Since the B_{1i} terms measure initial profits and the B_2 term measures profits as time goes to infinity, the conclusion is obtained. Profits are higher at the beginning than later, and profits are positive.

Finally, we make three observations. The first is a summary about the autarky model which is included for completeness. Observations 2 and 3 are different. Neither observation has particular foundation in theory. However, following the statement of the observations, we provide a conjecture about the nature of the dynamics at work in these markets. If the conjecture is correct, then the third observation can be explained.

OBSERVATION 1: *The competitive model explains the data better than does the autarky model.*

SUPPORT:
The support is contained in previously stated results. In Results 2 and 3 the production data from environment 1 reveal that the systems of production and export for all goods are moving toward the competitive equilibrium and away from autarky. The production data from environment 2 seem to favor neither model. From Result 5, we see that tariffs had effects predicted by the competitive model, while autarky predicted that tariffs would have no effects. From Result 6 we find that output prices are converging to the competitive equilibrium,

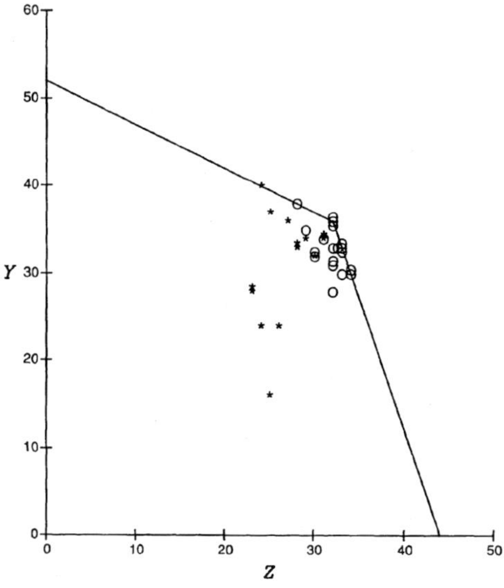

FIGURE 8. TOTAL SYSTEM PRODUCTION: ALL
EXPERIMENTS, ENVIRONMENT-1 TARIFF VERSUS
NO-TARIFF CONDITIONS, PERIOD 6 AND AFTER

as opposed to the autarky levels. The only input prices that move toward autarky and away from the competitive equilibrium are those for L_2 under the tariff condition.

OBSERVATION 2: *In the no-tariff condition, a large amount of exporting going back and forth between the two countries was observed. The trading appeared to be international speculation and seemed to help markets converge.*

SUPPORT:

Net exports constitute only 63.8 percent of total international trade under free trade in environment 1. The rest of the volume comprised units which had been or were being returned to their country of origin. When tariffs were imposed, the cross trading in Z was essentially eliminated.

OBSERVATION 3: *Contrary to the prediction of the competitive model, the tariff reduced production efficiency.*

SUPPORT:

Figure 8 contains world production data for the last few periods of experiments with tariffs and experiments without tariffs. These are periods after which some equilibration has taken place. Recall that in this version of the Ricardian model the tariff should have no influence on production. As is clear from the figure, production was less when the tariff existed.

Observation 3 indicates that the tariffs have costs beyond those predicted by the static competitive model. A review of some of the results presented above provides surprisingly strong support for a conjecture about the nature of the dynamics at work in these markets. Collecting Results 6, 7, 8, and 9, along with Observation 3, reveals a pattern of the disequilibrium dynamics. The system appears to be moving toward the competitive equilibria along a qualitatively distinctive path. The term "conjecture" is used because the path cannot be deduced from accepted theory, even though it is supported by much theoretical intuition.

An explanation of the dynamics, which we shall call the "risk-compensated input/output price-adjustment process," begins with the observation that markets have an inherent randomness as part of the general equilibration process. This randomness creates a risk for producers who must commit to the purchase of resources and who face the possibility of losses if the product produced from the resources cannot be sold at sufficiently high prices. Accordingly, producers restrict purchase of resources and thus restrict production as they gather information about market conditions. The results are higher (than equilibrium) market prices in output markets due to restricted supplies and lower (than equilibrium) input prices due to restricted input demand. As the experience that producers gain from the market advances with the repetition and stationarity of parameters, the uncertainty diminishes (due to the accumulation of information about the market) and the randomness decreases (due to equilibration). Output expands, output prices fall, and input prices rise. The results are an increasing input/output price ratio over time and falling profits. The conjecture that follows is simply that disequilibrium behavior is characterized by such a process.

CONJECTURE: *Equilibration in the experiments follows the risk-compensated input/output price-adjustment process.*

SUPPORT:

All of the properties of the path, as described, are contained in the market data. Output prices converge toward the competitive equilibrium from above (Result 6). Input prices converge toward the competitive equilibrium (Results 7 and 8). Finally, producers' profits fall over time (Result 9) as the input/output price ratio increases.

The fact that input prices converge to the competitive equilibrium from below in environment 1 and converge from above in environment 2 is also consistent with the hypothesis. In environment 1 producers faced greater risks than in environment 2. In environment 2 producers were also consumers of factors, so factors unused in production were valuable to them as consumption. In environment 1 producers had no such alternatives, so the "down side" losses to producers were greater in environment 1 than in environment 2. The greater risk to producers in environment 1 would then be manifest in lower input prices.

Observation 3 is also consistent with the hypothesis that the disequilibrium is characterized by such a path. A tariff imposed on the imports of Z in country 1 (which has a comparative disadvantage in Z and thus consumes only imported Z in equilibrium) constitutes a major perturbation of the system. The natural tendency is for the price of Z in country 1 to be higher as a result of the tariffs. The risk-compensated input/output price-adjustment process exacerbates the increase of the price of Z in country 1 in the early period of an experiment. With the price of imported Z very high in country 1 due to the combined effects, some Z gets produced in country 1. On the other hand, in country 2, market demand for Z is reduced because there is reduced demand for exports. Thus, in coun-

try 2 the price of Z falls, making Z less profitable for country-2 producers relative to the production of Y, whose market supply is reduced because some of the resources in country 1 are diverted to the production of Z. Some Y gets produced in country 2. Thus, along this disequilibrium path, country 1 (inefficiently) shifts production from a full specialization in the production of Y to include the production of some Z. Country 2 shifts from a complete specialization in the production of Z to include (inefficiently) the production of some Y. The resulting inefficiencies are captured in the data from the experiments as summarized by Observation 3 and are shown in Figure 8.

Of course, there is nothing theoretically new about profits being a return to producers for bearing market uncertainty. The new and difficult (theoretical) challenge stems from the fact that markets seem to have a natural but inexplicable random component that is not captured by modern theory. The intuition that should support a theory seems clear, but no formal statement of such a theory currently exists. The natural reaction of agents to the inherent randomness would seem to be similar for any portfolio adjustment. The system adjustment to the individual hedging behavior appears natural enough. Since the path has such clearly distinguishable features, it will be of interest to explore other experiments as well as field data to see whether system adjustments, along the risk-compensated input/output price path, is found in other places as well. It will also be of interest to learn whether the intuition captured by the explanation given above can be placed on solid theoretical footing.

VI. Conclusion

The main result of the paper is that we observe experimentally for the first time that the law of comparative advantage predicts patterns of trade and output. This result would not have been completely unanticipated by trade theorists, because it is so embedded in modern economic models.

However, the experiments, like naturally occurring economies, are complex, with mistakes, trading out of equilibrium, limitations on information, considerable uncertainty about the future, and other prominent features that are not present in existing stylized models. Furthermore, the recent debates on U.S. competitiveness suggest that many people outside the economics research community do not believe that the law of comparative advantage works and are prepared to base policy on much different principles of system behavior. We find it remarkable that this fundamental principle operates with such strength and robustness even though the competitive model is statistically rejected. Were it not found operating, we would be forced to reexamine one of the deepest aspects of modern theories of the nature of trade, and the existence of that very real possibility was an important consideration in the research design.

While there are many positive ways to look at these data, there is one fundamental fact that must not be overlooked. The competitive model is rejected. Considerable variation in these data remains to be explained. The quantitative predictions do not work so well.

Generally, the qualitative predictions of the competitive model are upheld. Convergence processes are present, so the competitive model receives better support in the later periods after equilibration takes place. This convergence takes place more quickly and strongly for quantities than for prices. The support of the competitive model extends itself to the qualitative impacts of a tariff. Support of this nature is very interesting since comparative-statics models generally assume that the system is moving from one established equilibrium to another. In real markets, such as those studied here, disequilibria exist. There is little support for the autarky model in these experiments. International trade occurs in a natural way and must be considered in the application of models to any of the interacting countries.

Factor-price equalization is a remarkable and unintuitive property. While this property is characteristic of only specialized environments, it is important in helping us to see and understand that the principles of economics can lead to unintuitive results. That wages should equalize as a result of competition in output markets alone is such a proposition. Under the strong conditions in which theory suggests it will exist, we actually found it.

Although it was diminishing over time, there was a universal tendency for the factors of production to trade at prices below their marginal revenue product. The most plausible explanation is that the output prices adjusted upward and the input prices adjusted downward to compensate producers for the risk they undertook in producing the output. In later market periods, as output prices stabilized and the natural randomness that exists in markets tended to diminish, the producers' risk declined, input prices increased, output prices decreased, and producer profits fell. The process is well described by the term "risk-compensated input/output price-adjustment process." This somewhat surprising pattern is so plausible in retrospect that it leads to a conjecture about whether it may be a general property of production economies observable in the field, especially those with extreme output-price uncertainty, such as centrally planned systems in transition to market economies.

APPENDIX

Several different instructions were used during the course of these experiments. Environments 1 and 2 differed because producers had redemption values for input goods in environment 2 but not in environment 1. There were also two input goods in environment 2 and only one input good in environment 1. The experiments with eight subjects had instructions that differed slightly from those with 16 subjects. In the 16-subject experiments, a distinction was made between agent "type" (type 1 or type 2), while no such distinction was made between agents in the eight-person experiments because the activities (producer and consumer) were combined. Then, there were the experiments in which an import tax

TABLE A1—LABELS OF OUTPUT AND INPUT ACTIVITIES
BY SOURCE: PAPER, INSTRUCTIONS, DATA SETS
(MARKETS)

Environment	Paper	Instructions	Data (market)
1	L_1	W	1
	L_2	X	2
	Y_1	Y_1	3
	Y_2	Y_2	4
	Z_1	Z_1	5
	Z_2	Z_2	6
2	L_1	W_1	1
	L_2	W_2	2
	K_1	Y_1	3
	K_2	Y_2	4
	Y_1	X_1	5
	Y_2	X_2	6
	Z_1	Z_1	7
	Z_2	Z_2	8

existed. In reviewing the material that follows, the reader should appreciate that each of these several instructions was generated by only a few word changes (e.g., "and/or" vs. "or"). A single paragraph added to the instructions explained the tariff in those experiments in which a tariff was operative.

The instructions hold two additional sources of potential ambiguity. The first is the labeling of markets. Three sets of labels exist throughout the series. For example, in the text of this paper the input from country 1 is labeled as L_1. However, in the instructions read to subjects, this input was called W, and the trading activity of W took place in market 1 and is recorded that way in the data sets. Table A1 lists all of the relationships. The word "paper" refers to the manuscript version of the text preceding this appendix; the word "instructions" refers to what subjects saw; and "data/markets" indicates the index as presented on computer screens during the experiment and in the data sets.

The second source of possible confusion is the assignment of subjects to agent types, such as consumer/producer. In 16-person experiments there is no confusion. Subjects in country i control resources and/or consume and/or produce in country i. In the eight-person sessions, the roles were different. The lack of subject numbers required functions of producer, consumer, and resource owner to be combined. Because of the small numbers, an oligopoly problem presented itself. If the producers own resources in their own country, then they could influence the activities of their competition by refusing to sell him/her the resources. In order to avoid this complicating factor, firms were producers/consumers in one country but owned resources in the other country. Thus, producers/consumers in country i were resource owners in country j. Of course resource owners still could not transport the resources from one country to another.

The set of instructions that follows is for the 16-person environment-1 experiments. The forms for the redemption value sheets (for consumption decisions) were the same for all treatments, as were the accounting forms. Blank examples of both are included at the end of the instructions. Of course, the redemption value sheets are filled in by the experimenter and the accounting sheets by the subject.

General Instructions [Exact Transcript]

This is an experiment in the economics of market decision-making. The instructions are simple, and if you follow them carefully and make good decisions, you might earn a considerable amount of money which will be paid to you in cash.

In this experiment, we are going to conduct a market in which you will be designated as one of two types of traders in a sequence of trading periods (either a type 1 or a type 2). Find your type at the top of the instructions. In your folder you have a sheet entitled Record Sheet. If you are a type 1, you will also have a Redemption Value Sheet. If you are a type 2 you will have a Production Schedule. These sheets will help you determine the value to you of any decisions that you might make. YOU ARE NOT TO REVEAL THE INFORMATION ON THESE SHEETS TO ANYONE. They are your own private information.

The currency used in this market is francs. All trading will be in terms of francs. Your final payoff will be in terms of dollars. The conversion rate is _________________ francs to 1 U.S. dollar. You will be paid at the end of the experiment.

There are four types of goods which can be traded in our market: W, X, Y, and Z. You may make profits in two ways, through consumption and through trading of the four goods.

Production Schedule

(Each Period)

Identification No: ____

Units of X (Input)	0	1	2	3	4	5	6	7	8	9	10	11	12
Unit Output (Y)	0	5	3	1	0	0	0	0	0	0	0	0	0
Total Output (Y)	0	5	8	9	9	9	9	9	9	9	9	9	9

Units of X (Input)	0	1	2	3	4	5	6	7	8	9	10	11	12
Unit Output (Z)	0	5	3	1	0	0	0	0	0	0	0	0	0
Total Output (Z)	0	5	8	9	9	9	9	9	9	9	9	9	9

Specific Instructions to Type-1 Traders [Exact Transcript]

CONSUMPTION

During each period you are free to purchase and sell as many units of W, X, Y and Z as you might want. Any units that you hold in your inventory at the end of the period are considered to be consumed by you. For the first unit of Y that you consume during a trading period you will receive the amount listed on your Redemption Value Sheet the column labelled Y Unit Value in the 1st row. If you consume a second unit you receive the amount listed in the column labelled Y Unit Value in the second row. The total amount that you receive from the consumption of both units is found in the column labelled Y Total Value in the second row. Notice that if you have unit values of zero in a space or a column that the corresponding units are worthless to you. The amount you receive from consumption of Z is found in exactly the same way. The redemption value received from consumption of W and X is always zero.

Specific Instructions to Type-2 Traders [Exact Transcript]

PRODUCTION

During each market period type two traders are free to produce units of Y and Z from units of W and X. This is done with the Transformation Key (F4). When producing units of Y and/or Z from units of W and X use the table labelled Production Schedule. This table reflects the number of units of Y and/or Z that you can produce from

REDEMPTION VALUE SHEET

(For Consumption Decisions)

Unit	W unit value	W total value	X unit value	X total value	Y unit value	Y total value	Z unit value	Z total value
1								
2								
3								
4								
5								
6								
7								
8								

given amounts of W and X for the whole period. You have already been instructed in how to read the production schedule, but the following hypothetical example may provide further clarification.

Example: Suppose that you have 2 units of X and you have the Production Schedule shown on the next page [previous page in this appendix]. You can produce either:

    a) 8 units of Y

    b) 5 units of Y and 5 units of Z

    c) 8 units of Z

Instructions to Both Types [Exact Transcript]

TRADING PROFITS

Another source of profits is from buying and selling the four types of goods. Selling increases your cash on hand by the amount of the sale price. Buying reduces your cash on hand by the amount of the purchase. Thus you can either gain or lose money on the purchase and resale of units.

EARNINGS

Your profits each period are computed by taking the redemption values of the units of W, X, Y, and Z that you consumed that period, adding the total sale price of the units of that you sold during the period and then subtracting the total of the prices you paid for the units that you bought during the period. The profits that you make exactly equal the change in your cash on hand from the beginning to the end of the period plus the redemption values of the units you consume.

At the end of the period enter the total number of units that you consume of W, X, Y, and Z at the top of your Record Sheet. Then, fill out the rest of your record sheet as follows. In line 2, fill in your Cash on Hand at the beginning of the period. In line 1, fill in your cash on hand at the end of the period. In line 3 fill in line 1 minus line 2. In lines 4–7 fill in your earnings from the consumption of W, X, Y, and Z. In line 8 add the total of lines 4–7. In line 9 add the total of lines 3 and 8. This amount is equal to your profits for the period (in francs).

ENDOWMENTS

1) At the beginning of each period you will be given an endowment of either W or X. This endowment will appear in your inventory and will remain the same every period. You are free to sell any part of this endowment to anyone who might want to buy it.

2) At the beginning of the experiment you will receive 100000 francs cash on hand.

Record Sheet

Period = 1

W __________　　X __________　Y __________ = __________

(1) Cash on hand at end of period　__________

(2) Cash on hand at beginning of period　__________

(3) Net change in cash on hand (1)-(2)　__________

Earnings from consumption

(4) W　__________

(5) X　__________

(6) Y　__________

(7) Z　__________

(8) Total earnings from consumption (4)+(5)+(6)+(7)　__________

(9) TOTAL PROFITS FOR THE PERIOD　__________

HOW THE SYSTEM WORKS

Type 1 people are endowed with W or X but would like to consume Y and Z. They can sell W or X to type 2 people to increase their cash in order to buy Y and Z. Type 2 people are endowed with W or X but may purchase additional units from type 1 people. They can produce Y and Z from W or X and sell them to type 1 people to increase their cash.

MARKET RESTRICTIONS

Some of you may not be able to trade in all markets. You may not trade in markets __________________. Unless you are informed otherwise these markets will be closed to you for the entire experiment.

You may be taxed for trading in market 6. The tax that you pay is __________________ francs for each unit that you buy or sell in that market. Unless you are informed otherwise, the tax will remain the same for the entire experiment.

REFERENCES

Ashenfelter, Orley; Currie, Janet; Farber, Henry S. and Spiegel, Matthew. "An Experimental Comparison of Dispute Rates in Alternative Arbitration Systems." *Econometrica*, November 1992, *60*(6), pp. 1407–33.

Caves, Richard; Frenkel, J. and Jones, R. *World trade and payments*, 5th Ed. Glenview, IL: Scott Foresman/Little Brown, 1990.

Chipman, John S. "A Survey of the Theory of International Trade: Part I, the Classical Theory." *Econometrica*, July 1965, *33*(3), pp. 477–511.

Deardorff, Alan. "Testing Trade Theories and Predicting Trade Flows," in Ronald W. Jones and Peter Kenen, eds., *Handbook of international economics*. Amsterdam: North-Holland, 1984, pp. 467–517.

Goodfellow, Jessica and Plott, Charles R. "An Experimental Examination of the Simultaneous Determination of Input Prices and Output Prices." *Southern Economic Journal*, April 1990, *56*(4), pp. 969–83.

Gremmen, Hans. "Testing the Factor Price Equalization Theorem in the EC: An Alternative Approach." *Journal of Common Market Studies*, March 1985, *23*(3), pp. 278–86.

Lian, Peng and Plott, Charles R. "General

Equilibrium, Macroeconomics, and Moneyin a Laboratory Experimental Environment." California Institute of Technology Social Science Working Paper No. 842, March 1993.

MacDougall, G. D. A. "British and American Exports: A Study Suggested by the Theory of Comparative Costs, Part I." *Economic Journal*, December 1951, *61*(244), pp. 697–724.

______. "British and American Exports: A Study Suggested by the Theory of Comparative Costs, Part II." *Economic Journal*, September 1952, *62*(247), pp. 487–521.

Mokhtari, Manouchehr and Rassekh, Farhad. "The Tendency Towards Factor Price Equalization Among OECD Countries." *Review of Economics and Statistics*, November 1989, *71*(4), pp. 636–42.

Plott, Charles R. "A Computerized Laboratory Market System and Research Support Systems for the Multiple Unit Double Auction." California Institute of Technology Social Science Working Paper No. 783, November 1991.

Plott, Charles R. and Smith, Vernon L. "An Experimental Examination of Two Exchange Institutions." *Review of Economic Studies*, February 1978, *45*(1), pp. 133–53.

Porter, Michael P. *The competitive advantage of nations*. New York: Free Press, 1990.

Smith, Vernon L. and Williams, Arlington W. "The Effects of Rent Asymmetries in Experimental Auction Markets." *Journal of Economic Behavior and Organization*, March 1982, *3*(1), pp. 99–116.

Tovias, Alfred. "Testing Factor Price Equalization in the EEC." *Journal of Common Market Studies*, June 1982, *20*(4), pp. 375–88.

White, Halbert. "A Heteroskedasticity-Consistent Covariance Matrix Estimator and a Direct Test for Heteroskedasticity." *Econometrica*, May 1980, *48*(4), pp. 817–38.

The Principles of Exchange Rate Determination in an International Finance Experiment

Charles N. Noussair

Purdue University

Charles R. Plott

California Institute of Technology

Raymond G. Riezman

University of Iowa

This paper reports the first experiments designed to explore the behavior of economies with prominent features of international finance. Two "countries," each with its own currency, were created. International trade could take place only through the operation of markets for currency. The law of one price and the flow of funds theory of exchange rate determination were used to produce general equilibrium models that captured much of the behavior of the economies. Prices of goods, as well as the exchange rate, evolve over time toward the predictions of the models. However,

We wish to acknowledge the financial support of the National Science Foundation and the Caltech Laboratory for Experimental Economics and Political Science. The cooperation of the Center for Research in Experimental Economics and Political Decision-Making at the University of Amsterdam was important for the conduct of experiments in Amsterdam. We also wish to thank Mark Olson for his assistance with the Amsterdam experiments. The help of Hsing-Yang Lee with the electronic market programs made the study possible. An earlier version of this paper was presented at the Allied Social Sciences Association annual meetings in January 1994. We thank Marianne Baxter for her helpful suggestions as discussant of the paper, and Lars Peter Hansen for his helpful suggestions.

[*Journal of Political Economy*, 1997, vol. 105, no. 4]

both the law of one price and purchasing power parity can be rejected for reasons that do not appear in the literature. Patterns of international trade were as predicted by the law of comparative advantage.

I. Introduction

The interdependencies inherent in the structure of international financial flows and international economic activity motivated some of the earliest attempts to develop the basic principles of economics. The theorizing predated Adam Smith by decades and has been the subject of almost constant evolution during the intervening centuries. Principles of economic behavior were isolated by partial equilibrium theories and were integrated over the years to construct the general competitive model. The overriding power of this model to provide consistency in sets of ideas and theories cannot be denied, and, as such, it stands as a remarkable intellectual achievement. However, the accuracy of the model might be challenged in special applications, and the specific quantitative predictions of the model might not be testable in the complicated setting of the naturally occurring world.

The experiments reported below were designed to explore the ability of the competitive equilibrium model to predict and track prices and exchange rates. The experimental economies are extraordinarily complex and contain some of the complexities about which decades, if not centuries, of theorizing have grappled. Of course, they are simple relative to the naturally occurring economies to which the competitive model is frequently applied.

The experiments deal with two broad questions. First, to what extent does the competitive model help explain the behavior of an international economic system? Does the system behave at all as one would expect from the study of a set of equilibrium equations? While the experimental economies are simple relative to the naturally occurring ones, they are nevertheless economies in which several of the assumptions of the competitive model are violated to one degree or another. The model is constructed from many "partial equilibrium components," and if one part fails, the whole model fails. The question addressed is which parts, if any, seem to work. We find overall that the model works rather well, but certain parts of the model do not. For example, we find that the exchange rate converges strongly to the predicted equilibrium value (see result 1), but the prices in some of the commodity markets do not (see result 3). This is quite remarkable since the foreign exchange market is used only to facilitate trading in the underlying commodity markets. The overall result is very important since it demonstrates that many aspects of the price discovery process can be accurately described by simple equilibrium equations even if other aspects of the data are inconsistent with equilibrium behavior.

A second question, which is closely related to the first, is, Do we see the same types of failures of the model that are found in the field? Variables thought to cause the failure of the model in the field are not present. As will be reported in the paper, similar failures are observed in the experiments; therefore, the theory may fail to explain the data in the field as a result of much more fundamental causes than was previously thought. Specifically, we find in the experiments that the law of one price (LOP) and purchasing power parity (PPP) do not work well at all. As it turns out, LOP and PPP do not work well in the field either (Meese and Rogoff 1983; Kimbrough 1987; Krugman and Obstfeld 1994). The failure of LOP and PPP to explain the field data has been met by an avalanche of models and theories.[1] This research has suggested a number of explanations for the failures of LOP and PPP to fit the data. Most prominent among them are the existence of governmental trade barriers and transportation costs, the presence of nontraded goods, imperfect competition, difficulties measuring national price indices accurately, and changes in the terms of trade. However, none of the factors suggested by this vast literature is present in our laboratory environments and therefore could not be responsible for the observed failures. This suggests that LOP and PPP could fail in the field as a result of more fundamental causes than has been previously supposed. Section VIII of the paper addresses this issue.

The paper is organized as follows. Section II describes the laboratory economies. The economic environments were designed to have a classical structure in which the competitive model could be naturally applied, with the equilibria easily computed and well separated from the predictions of other models in order that the results not be confused. The choice of design reflects practical difficulties associated with conducting complex experiments. Previous experimental results can be used as "baselines" of behavior, but the need to separate the predictions of various models is central to the design. Section III outlines the experimental design and procedures. The

---

[1] There has been an interest in the development of theoretical models that would produce departures from purchasing power parity as equilibrium phenomena (Sargent 1987; Grilli and Roubini 1992). However, the variables that can cause equilibrium departures in the models are not present in the actual economies we created.

EXCHANGE RATE DETERMINATION   825

models are discussed in Section IV, and the predictions are highlighted in Section V. A special statistical methodology is in Section VI. The results are listed in Section VII. Section VIII analyzes the reasons for the failure of LOP and PPP. Section IX summarizes our conclusions.

II. The Laboratory Economies

The experimental setup is consistent with requiring a type of cash-in-advance constraint, similar to that imposed by Lucas (1982). The parameters are set so that gains from exchange exist from international trade. That is, in the competitive equilibrium, foreign trade exists. However, the experimental environment requires that importers purchase foreign exchange in advance of their purchase of foreign goods. No agent is allowed to sell a good in a foreign country, so an agent cannot acquire foreign exchange by export and sale. Therefore, agents must acquire foreign exchange in advance of their purchases of foreign goods directly in the foreign exchange market. Of course, this activity creates a supply of home currency to the exchange market.

Two countries were indexed A and B. Each country produced two goods that were called x and y. Each country had three buyers of x and y who were indifferent between the source of supply. That is, a consumer in A received the same utility from x supplied from A as he received from x supplied from B, and similarly with y. Consequently, it will make sense to talk about a demand for and supply of x at either the country level or the world level. In addition, each country had three suppliers, each of whom supplied both x and y.

Buyers in each country had utility functions of the form U.S. dollars $= a[M_c - M_0 + R_x(x) + R_y(y)]$, where a is a scale factor; M_c is the currency of the country in which the agent resides; M_0 is the initial endowment of the home currency; x and y are the consumption by the individual, measured in the units of the two commodities; and R is denominated in terms of the home currency. Similarly, suppliers in a given country had an incentive function of the form U.S. dollars $= b[M_c - M_0 - C_x(x) - C_y(y)]$, where C is denominated in home currency units. All agents received a large initial endowment of home currency but had no endowment of foreign currency. Sellers received an endowment of x and y, and $C_x(x)$ and $C_y(y)$ represented the cost of sale. Buyers received no initial endowment of either x or y. Notice that individuals placed no value on the currency of the country in which they did not reside. So, this world had two countries with six agents in each, two commodities, and two currencies that had a value only to the agents of the home country.

Preferences were induced such that the aggregate demand and supplies were approximated by the following equations:

$$\text{country A:} \quad x \text{ demand: } 43 - .75x - p_x^A = 0,$$

$$x \text{ supply: } 2 + 2x - p_x^A = 0,$$

$$y \text{ demand: } 65 - 3y - p_y^A = 0,$$

$$y \text{ supply: } 11 + 1.5y - p_y^A = 0;$$

$$\text{country B:} \quad x \text{ demand: } 925 - 45x - p_x^B = 0,$$

$$x \text{ supply: } 127.5 + 15x - p_x^B = 0,$$

$$y \text{ demand: } 2{,}646 - 36y - p_y^B = 0,$$

$$y \text{ supply: } 150 + 180y - p_y^B = 0.$$

The notation p_k^i means the price of commodity k that exists in country i. These functions are shown in figure 1.

Constraints on trade were imposed to force the use of the international financial markets. First, all purchases and sales in a country had to be made in terms of the local currency. It was not possible to buy in a foreign country without having foreign currency first, and no agent was endowed with foreign currency. Second, no agent was allowed to export, but all agents could import. This meant that an agent who wanted to buy abroad could not sell abroad in order to get the exchange. The agent was required to go to the exchange market and purchase foreign currency with the home currency. Once purchases were made abroad, they could be transported to the home country without cost and either consumed or resold for home currency.

III. Experimental Design and Procedures

Four experiments were conducted. The subjects were students at the California Institute of Technology and the University of Amsterdam. Three sessions took place at the Laboratory for Experimental Economics and Political Science at Caltech, and one took place at the Center for Research in Experimental Economics and Political Decision-Making at the University of Amsterdam, in the Netherlands. A list of the experiments indexed by the date of the experiment can be found in table 1.

The experiments were conducted in English, and the subjects were paid in U.S. dollars at Caltech and in Dutch guilders at Amsterdam. All the Amsterdam subjects had participated in one pilot experiment of this series previously. This was intended to acquaint them

Country B
Country A
MARKET Y
MARKET X
2500
2000
1500
1000
500
0
120
100
80
60
40
20
0
5
10
15
20
25
30

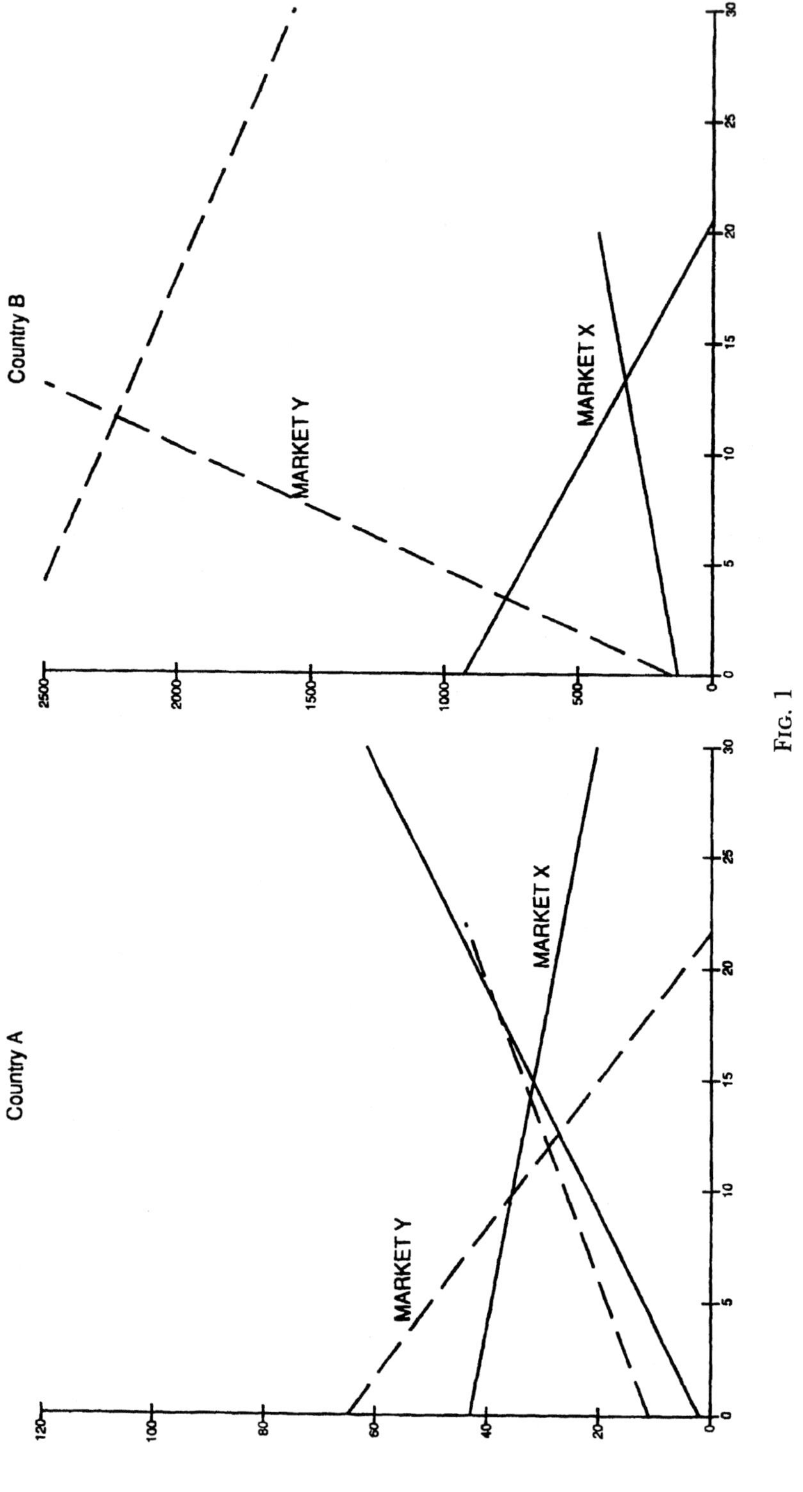

Fig. 1

828

828   JOURNAL OF POLITICAL ECONOMY

TABLE 1

EXPERIMENTS: LOCATION, SUBJECTS, AND EXPERIENCE

Index*	Location	Number of Subjects	Experience	Number of Periods
011393	Caltech	12	General market	10
011493	Caltech	12	General market	10
040793	Univ. Amsterdam	12	1 pilot experiment	10
042193	Caltech	12	General market	10

* Index corresponds to the date on which the experiment was conducted.

with the accounting procedures, the computer keys, and the general setting in which the economic activity takes place in an experiment. The Caltech subjects had not participated in international finance experiments previously, but a substantial fraction of these subjects had been in other market experiments before.

At the beginning of each experimental session, subjects went through an interactive computerized instructional program that took about 30 minutes. This program gave them instructions about the keys and the other functions of the computer.[2] Afterward, the experimenter read the specific instructions for this experiment aloud as the subjects followed along, reading from their own copy. Subjects were shown at the board an example of how to read a redemption value sheet and a cost schedule, the two sheets on which their incentive functions were displayed. They were also instructed on how to calculate their profits, which they were required to do on their end-of-period summary sheets. Examples of the written materials used can be found in the Appendix.

After the instruction was completed, the market was replicated 11 times, each replication constituting a period. Each was like a trading day, and each day was identical. The first period was used for practice and did not count toward subjects' cash earnings. Each individual kept the same "utility function" in each replication, although individuals' utility functions differed among agents. Thus the market environment was kept constant over the 10 periods following the practice period. All inventories of goods and currencies were reset at the same starting level each period. Nothing was carried over from period to period, except the earnings of the subjects.

In each of the experiments there were 12 subjects, six buyers and six sellers. There were three buyers and three sellers in each country.

---

[2] This program is part of the general multiple unit double auction (MUDA) program outlined in Plott (1991) and is contained in the diskette that accompanies the general market program used in the experiment.

EXCHANGE RATE DETERMINATION   829

As a resident of a country, each agent was endowed with an inventory of his or her home currency, and only the home currency had value to him or her. Consumption and home currency cash had value in U.S. dollars or Dutch guilders, depending on the location of the experiment. The foreign currency had no value, except as a means of buying the goods abroad, which could then be consumed or sold for home currency.

The market mechanism employed was a modified version of the computerized MUDA. The program was modified to allow for multiple countries, represented by different pages on the computer screen. Each page (country) contained three markets in which all trades took place in terms of the local currency. The page also listed the amount of that country's cash that the subject had on hand, which could be used to buy in the markets in that country. Sales in that country added to the amount of that country's cash that the subject had on hand. The three markets allowed trading of x, y, and the currency of the other country. So purchases and sales in these markets, as well as the purchase and sale of the currency of the other country, were made in terms of the currency relevant to the page, and all bids and asks were quoted in terms of the currency of that page. When the subject changed pages to the other country, the cash on hand of the first page became the inventory of foreign currency on the second page, and the inventory of foreign currency on the first page became the cash on hand on the second page. This convention automatically enforced the requirement that all transactions in a country took place in terms of the currency of that country.

Any agent could transport goods from another country into his own, but no individual could transport to the foreign country directly. The MUDA program allows for transformations of inventory in one group of markets (one country) to another group of markets (another country), possibly on different pages on the computer. This feature was used to implement international transport. Purchases in a foreign country, made with the currency from that country, were automatically credited to the inventory of the commodity held by the subject in the foreign country. The inventory of that commodity could be costlessly transformed into the inventory of the same commodity in the subject's home country. Once in the home country, the commodity could be sold at home for cash or consumed. Thus imports were allowed but exports were not. That is, no individual could transform inventories held at home to the inventory of the same commodity held in the foreign country. This restriction was needed to force the use of the currency markets. If transportation in both directions had been allowed, the subject could have exported a commodity and sold it for foreign currency, which could have then been used to purchase commodities for import and sale at home without ever using the foreign currency markets. Since the operation of the currency market was considered to be a fundamental purpose of the experiment, steps were taken to make sure that such markets had a function and would thus be used.

IV. Models

Two models are considered, competition and autarky. In the competitive model, agents make trades of commodities and corresponding purchases and sales of foreign exchange to permit these trades. There is no role for money, foreign or domestic, other than this transactions demand. Since the experimental agents receive payoffs for domestic (but not foreign) currency held at the end of each period, this is an economy in which demanders and suppliers have (domestic) money in their utility functions. In other words, the domestic money has commodity value, but not to foreigners.

The competitive outcome can be found by solving equations (1)–(7) below. There is also a possibility that autarky will occur. That is, traders will choose not to engage in foreign trade. This is not an unreasonable notion, as one might believe at first glance, considering the risks of participating in the foreign exchange market and the complexity of international transactions.

A. *The Competitive Model*

The competitive model has three components. Home market demand and supply give four equations that require that materials balance and that incentives to buy and sell be equated at existing prices. The second set of equations, which we call purchasing power parity, can be viewed as nonarbitrage conditions. They require that prices in the two countries, adjusted for exchange rates, be the same. The final component requires equilibrium in the foreign exchange market, given the special definitions of market demand and market supply based on imports and exports. Of course, these three components can be viewed as partial equilibrium models independently of any general equilibrium implications.

1. Home Market Demand and Supply

The law of supply and demand in the home markets captures the idea that home prices are determined by local demand, plus exports in relation to local supply, plus imports. In essence, the principles of demand and supply operate independently of the origin, ultimate destination, or use of the commodities. The theory is captured by the following equations:

$$D_x^A(p_x^A) = S_x^A(p_x^A) + \text{imports}, \tag{1}$$

$$D_y^A(p_y^A) = S_y^A(p_y^A) - \text{exports}, \tag{2}$$

$$D_x^B(p_x^B) = S_x^B(p_x^B) - \text{exports}, \tag{3}$$

and

$$D_y^B(p_y^B) = S_y^B(p_y^B) + \text{imports}, \tag{4}$$

where D_j^L and S_j^L equal the quantity demanded and supplied, respectively, of good j in country L.

2. Law of One Price and Purchasing Power Parity

In contrast to the home market demand and supply, the LOP theory generalizes the idea of market clearing to extend across international boundaries. In the absence of tariffs, taxes, transportation costs, and other complicating factors, the theory asserts that the prices of the goods will be the same in both countries after prices are factored by the exchange rates. It is the LOP theory that can be interpreted as governing the flow of imports and exports in response to relative prices and the exchange rate.

Let r be the exchange rate, that is, the price of currency A in terms of currency B. The equations for the LOP theory are

$$rp_x^A = p_x^B \tag{5}$$

and

$$rp_y^A = p_y^B. \tag{6}$$

Purchasing power parity theory is a similar relationship to (5) and (6) except that price indices are substituted for the prices of the goods. In Section VII we evaluate PPP using an appropriate price index for the experimental economy.

3. Flow of Funds Theory

It is the flow of funds theory that provides the final equation for exchange rate determination. Briefly, the theory is another way of saying that the exchange rate is determined by the demand for and supply of a currency. Formally the equation is

$$(\text{demand for imports of } x \text{ by A})\, p_x^B$$
$$= r(\text{demand for imports of } y \text{ by B})\, p_y^A. \tag{7}$$

The left-hand side of the equation is the international demand for currency B that results from the country A purchases of x from country B. Country A needs this amount of country B currency in order to make the purchases. The right-hand side of the equation is the supply of currency B in the international market. The imports of y by country B, when multiplied by the country A price of y, yield the total amount of country A currency that is needed by country B in order to purchase the imports. When multiplied by the exchange rate (the units of currency B needed to purchase a unit of currency A), the quantity on the right-hand side of the equation becomes the international supply of currency B.

Care must be exercised in interpreting equation (7). First, because the exchange rate r is measured in units of B per unit of A, an increase in the price of currency B is a decrease in r. Second, unless operational definitions are selected carefully, equation (7) can acquire the properties of a tautology. In particular, if "actual imports" are substituted for the "demand for imports," if all international exchange is spent on foreign goods (no unused exchange and no currency speculation), and if r is defined as an appropriate weighted average of transactions, then the equation must be satisfied by virtue of the definitions. In some of the analysis that follows, actual imports are used in the statistical analysis, so the degree to which the equation is not satisfied reflects the existence of speculation, wasted exchange, and the lack of appropriate weighting of individual transactions in the determination of the measure of r. The reader will be warned when this takes place.

Previous studies have consistently found that there is a strong tendency for double auction markets to converge to the competitive equilibrium with replication of the market period, even when there are multiple interdependent markets (Noussair, Plott, and Riezman 1995). However, the economy constructed here provides a very difficult test for the model. The cash-in-advance constraint and the existence of substantial international trade in the competitive equilibrium mean that importers must purchase foreign exchange for the model to predict correctly. Furthermore, agents must purchase enough foreign exchange to be able to import the competitive equilibrium amount of international trade and then sell all unused foreign exchange at the competitive equilibrium exchange rate.

B.   Autarky Model

The autarky model is one alternative to the competitive model. It predicts that international trade will not take place; instead, the economies will operate as though they were in isolation. The model

EXCHANGE RATE DETERMINATION   833

TABLE 2

PREDICTED PRICES OF THE COMPETITIVE EQUILIBRIUM MODEL AND THE AUTARKY
MODEL: COUNTRIES A AND B, COMMODITIES x AND y, AND EXCHANGE RATES
OF CURRENCIES A AND B

MODEL	COUNTRY A			COUNTRY B		
	x	y	Currency A/B	x	y	Currency B/A
Competitive equilibrium	15	40	1/47	682	1,888	47
Autarky	32	29	$\cdots$	327	2,230	$\cdots$

NOTE.—Prices in the table (except for the price of currency B in country B) are the values of the solution
to the continuous approximation of the experimental parameters rounded to the nearest integer.

should be taken seriously and not only as a benchmark. If the currency markets suffer from continuous disequilibrium, if the dynamics of adjustment are such that international trade is hazardous, if the transactions are too slow or fast, or if the market periods are too short, then international trade might not take place.

V. Predictions

Both the competitive and the autarky models predict the exact value of each of the variables in the system. That is, the models predict the prices in both countries and for all commodities, the exchange rate, the magnitude of imports and exports, and so forth. Some of these predictions are summarized in table 2.

The prediction of the competitive model is the solution to equations (1)–(7). The prediction of the autarky model is the solution to equations (1)–(4) with the value of all imports and exports constrained to be zero. The table displays the solutions to the equations rounded to the nearest integer. The exact demand and supply functions used in the experiment were discrete step functions that are approximated by the continuous functions listed in Section II and displayed in figure 1.

VI. Statistical Methodology

The application of statistical models to experimental market data is characterized by some classic problems. This section will facilitate an understanding of the methodology used in this paper and its possible limitations. Two problems appear not to have any good solution, given the current state of theory and estimation techniques, so all conclusions must be evaluated in light of the tenuous assumptions that are explicit and implicit in the statistical models. The first problem is that the models, such as the competitive model, make predictions of the magnitudes of a large number of variables. From an intuitive point of view, it is not surprising if the model fails on one or even several dimensions, but the statistical models that we have available are not forgiving of errors of any type.

The second problem occurs because the theoretical model is a static equilibrium model, whereas the data are clearly generated by a dynamic process. Furthermore, in simpler experiments the existence of a convergence phenomenon has been demonstrated on many occasions. Thus any statistical model must be sufficiently forgiving of the lack of theory of dynamics to allow some latitude for convergence.

The first problem is not addressed. Instead, each of the major predictions of a model is considered separately. Each variable is observed separately, and the question is posed about its magnitude in relation to the predictions of one or the other of the models.

The second problem is addressed by the application of a simple dynamic model.[3] This model assumes that, for any particular dependent variable, each experiment may start from a different origin but all markets will experience adjustment, as described by a common functional form. Furthermore, the model assumes that the variable will converge to a common asymptote. Formally, the model is

$$ z_{it} = B_{11}D_1\left(\frac{1}{t}\right) + \cdots + B_{1k}D_k\left(\frac{1}{t}\right) + B_2\left(\frac{t-1}{t}\right) + u_{it}, \quad (8) $$

where i is the index of the experiment, D_j are dummy variables that take the value one if $i = j$ and zero otherwise, t is time measured in terms of the number of the experimental period, k is the number of experiments, and u is a random variable distributed normally with zero mean.

Notice that the statistical model has some useful properties. It allows for the possibility that variables may take different values at the start of different experiments. The terms B_{1i} measure these different origins of the data for the different experiments. The model then captures the specification that the experiments are converging to a common asymptote. During the early periods the asymptote gets no weight because the term $(t - 1)/t$ is small; but as t gets large, the term goes to one whereas $1/t$ goes to zero. Thus the weight of the end of the experimental session is on the common term B_2.

Thus the model can be used to test the hypothesis that the data

---

[3] This model is called the Ashenfelter-El-Gamal model in Noussair et al. (1995), where it is first used.

are converging to the predictions of various models by testing whether or not the estimates of B_2 are significantly different from the predictions of the models. In addition, a notion of partial *convergence* can be used to assess the models. Comparison of the B_{1j} terms with the B_2 term reveals the direction of convergence. If the B_2 term is closer to the model's prediction than the B_{1j} terms are, we say that the data are *partially converging* to the model's predictions. If the B_2 term is not significantly different from a model's prediction, we say that the variable is *strongly converging* to the prediction.

VII. Results

Figures 2 and 3 contain time series for the two goods markets in each of the two countries for one of the experiments (experiment 042193). On the vertical axes are measured the prices in terms of the currency in which transactions took place. On the horizontal axes is measured the time in seconds at which actions occurred. These are the actual transaction price observations. Vertical lines indicate the start and end of periods. The data from the goods markets in country A are in figure 2 and the data from the goods markets in country B are in figure 3. One horizontal line represents the value of the competitive equilibrium for the appropriate variable, and another indicates the prediction of the autarky model. Both lines are labeled accordingly. Figure 4 contains the time series of the exchange rate for all four experiments, which corresponds to the prices in the market for currency A in country B. In addition, a market was opened for currency B in country A. Since the MUDA program allows trading only at integer prices, at a competitive equilibrium price of $1/47$, activity in the market for currency B in country A quickly ceased in every experimental session.

The data in figures 2 and 3 are typical of all the experiments. The prices seem to be moving toward the competitive equilibrium prices, although there is substantial variation in prices within periods. Early in the experiments, the prices for x in country A are higher than the competitive equilibrium levels, and the prices for x in country B are lower than the competitive equilibrium levels. As can be seen in figure 4, near the end of all the experiments, the exchange rate is close to the competitive equilibrium, although it tends to be lower early in each of the sessions.

Estimates of the parameters of the statistical model are contained in table 3. The standard errors are in parentheses. Each variable is estimated separately. In addition, separate tests are developed from the equations that define PPP theory and flow of funds theory. These tests are also contained in the table. The standard errors are cor-

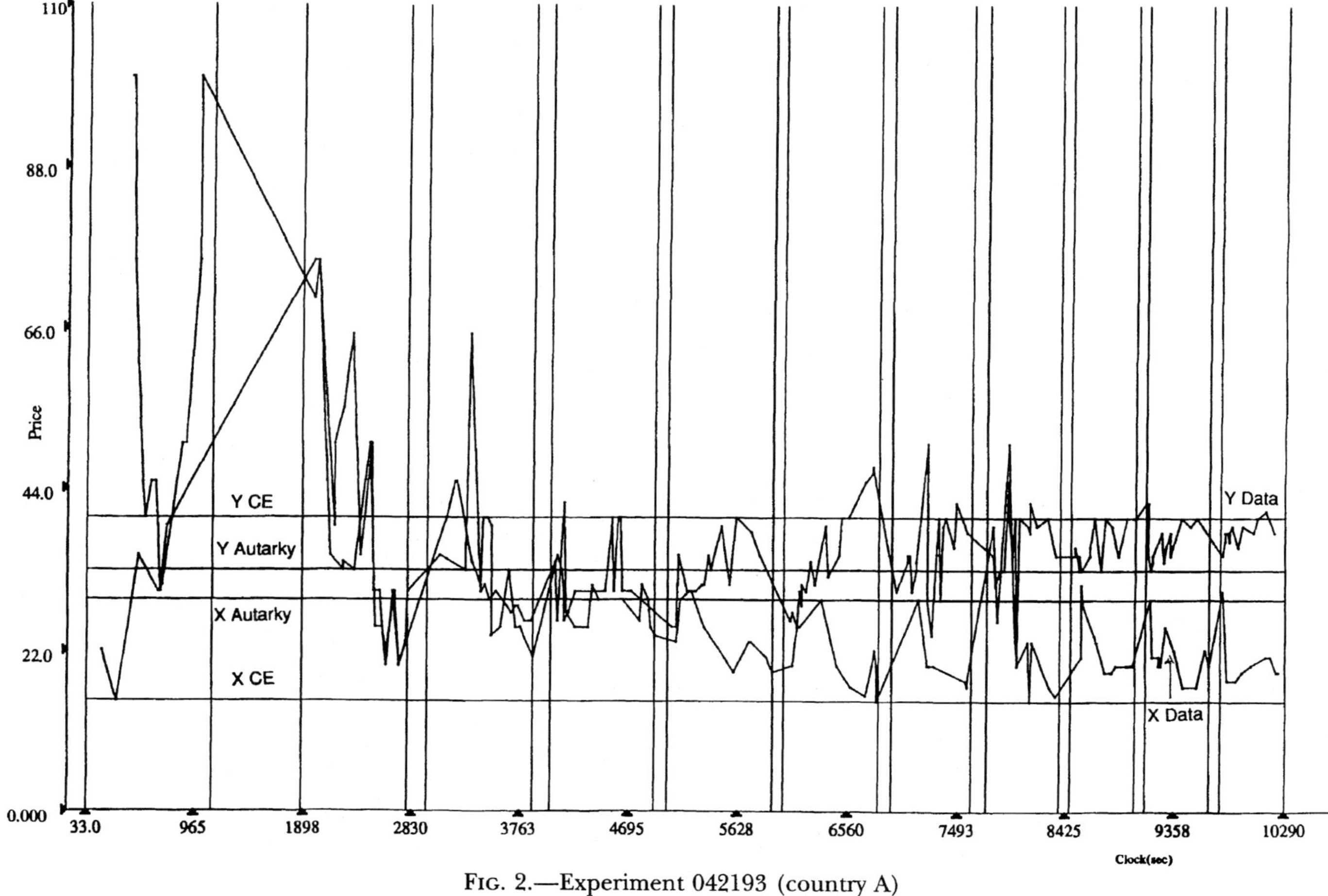

FIG. 2.—Experiment 042193 (country A)

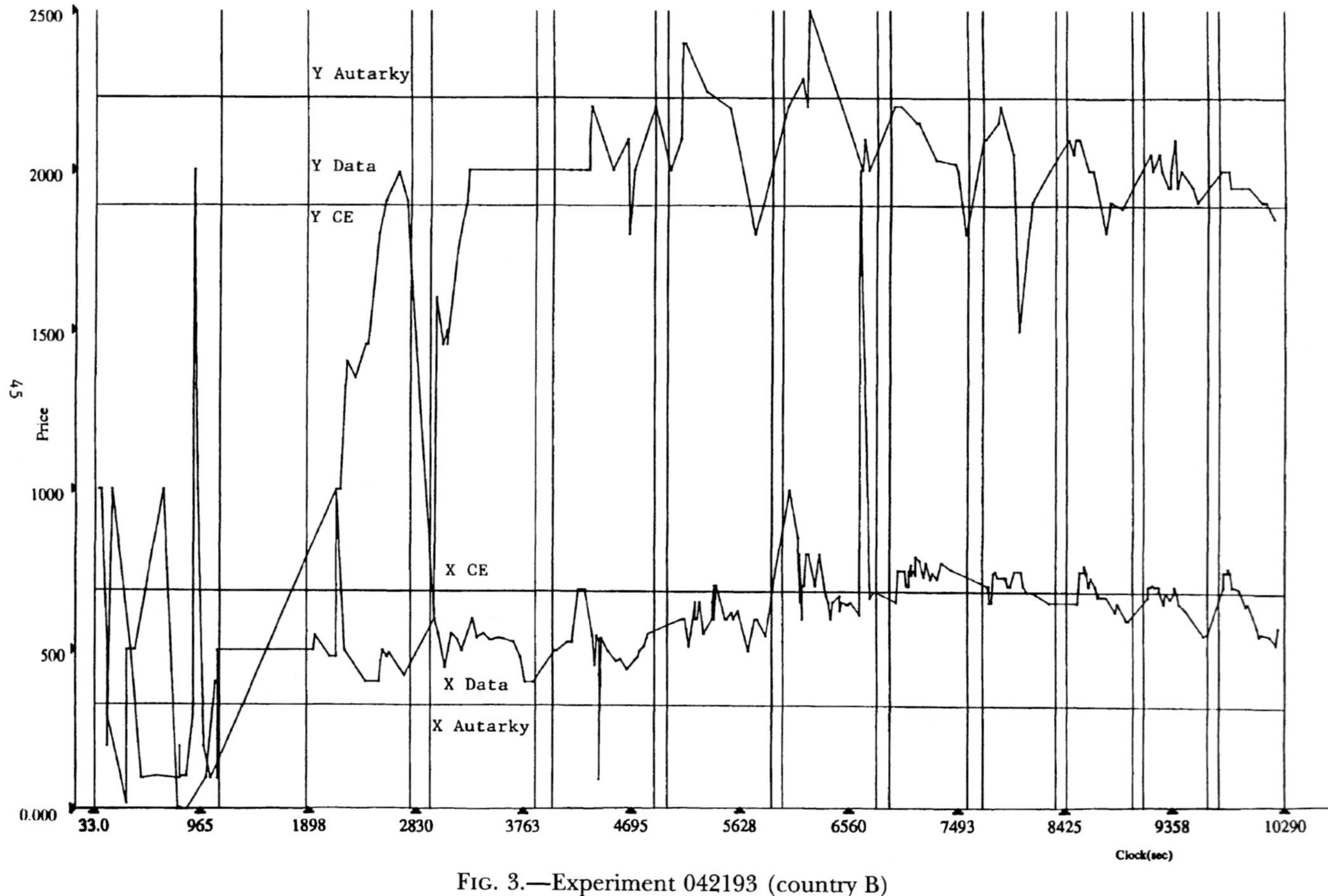

FIG. 3.—Experiment 042193 (country B)

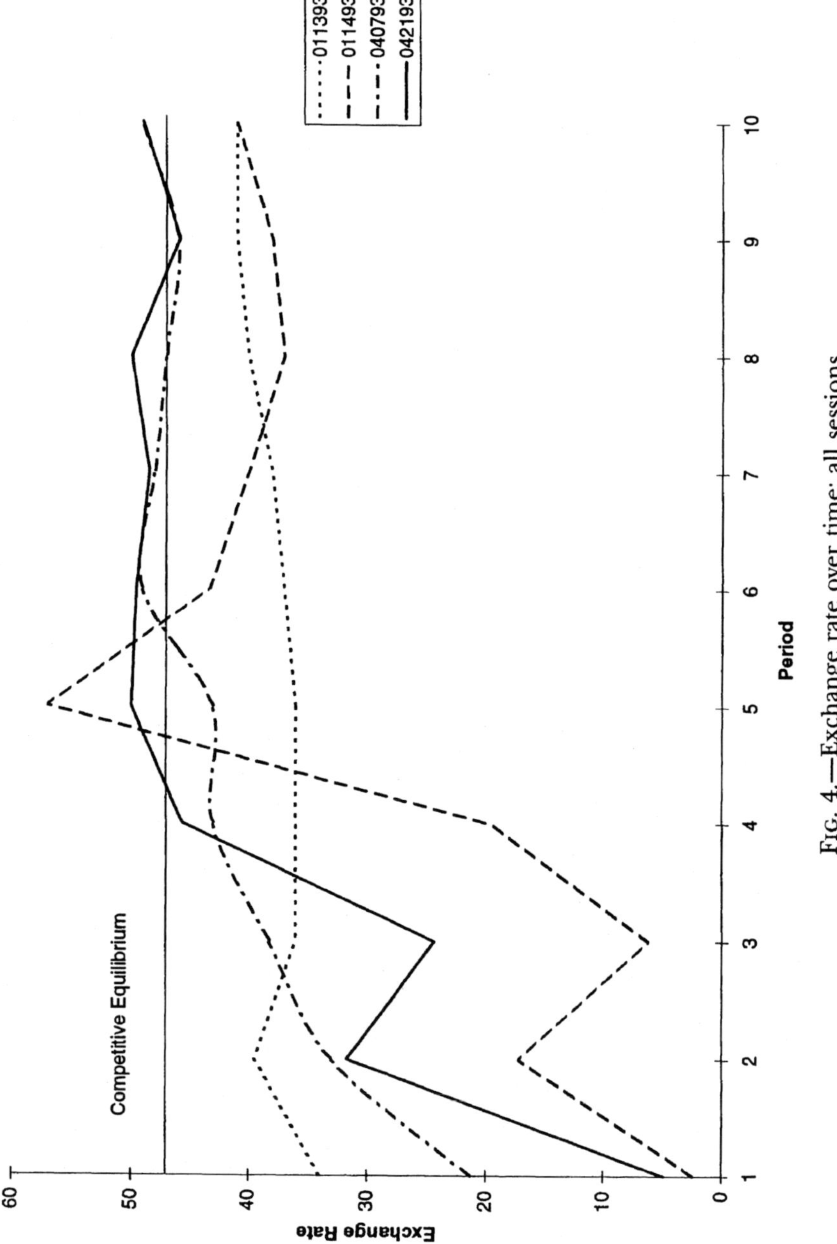

Fig. 4.—Exchange rate over time: all sessions

TABLE 3

Estimates of Statistical Model, Coefficient Estimates, and Standard Errors: Hypothesis Tests and General Statistics

| | | | | | | | | Prediction | | p-Value | |
| | | | | | | | | CE Model | Autarky Model | CE Model | Autarky Model |
Variable	B_{11}	B_{12}	B_{13}	B_{14}	B_2	R^2	Rho				
				A. Currency Markets							
r	29.238	−1.319	22.956	7.606	47.015	.69	.28	47		.4976	
	(5.158)	(8.762)	(1.983)	(5.825)	(2.381)						
V cur	582.65	1,423.36	78.47	372.48	351.48	.45	−.4	461	0	.0005**	.0000**
	(181.37)	(194.45)	(55.46)	(66.62)	(30.37)						
				B. Prices							
p_x^A	31.126	42.56	32.362	36.474	23.811	.66	.44	15	32	.0000**	.0000**
	(1.423)	(3.98)	(1.47)	(2.456)	(1.618)						
p_y^A	38.918	34.814	34.483	43.243	34.208	.42	.54	40	29	.0015**	.0034**
	(1.918)	(3.489)	(1.257)	(2.388)	(1.807)						
p_x^B	570.16	412.76	331.7	533.93	635.47	.48	.43	682	327	.1582	.0000**
	(34.76)	(110.91)	(101.66)	(38.8)	(45.77)						
p_y^B	2,177.5	757.7	1,931.1	1,582.2	1,984.3	.82	.36	1,888	2,230	.0267*	.0000**
	(182)	(202.8)	(42.9)	(142.4)	(48.1)						
p_x^A/p_y^A	.794	1.186	.932	.845	.707	.58	.53	.36	1.1	.0000**	.0000**
	(.056)	(.097)	(.059)	(.081)	(.07)						
p_x^B/p_y^B	.239	.499	.141	.317	.327	.47	.12	.36	.15	.0122*	.0000**
	(.033)	(.067)	(.065)	(.024)	(.014)						
$p_x^B/(r \times p_x^A)$	.819	3.295	.509	1.974	.404	.76	−.33	1		.0000**	
	(.163)	(.495)	(.099)	(.333)	(.061)						
$p_y^B/(r \times p_y^B)$	2.49	7.926	2.986	5.702	.693	.8	−.2	1		.0236*	
	(.53)	(1.2)	(.229)	(.999)	(.149)						
Z	.722	.108	.7747	.2805	1.157	.576	.099	1		.0003**	
	(.1427)	(.1565)	(.1464)	(.1658)	(.0418)						

TABLE 3 (*Continued*)

VARIABLE	B_{11}	B_{12}	B_{13}	B_{14}	B_2	R^2	RHO	PREDICTION		p-VALUE	
								CE Model	Autarky Model	CE Model	Autarky Model
				C. Excess Demands							
ED_x^A	−4.99	−3.15	−12.91	−8.57	−9.14	.34	.41	0	0	.0017**	.0017**
	(3.32)	(6.05)	(6.82)	(4.72)	(2.9)						
ED_y^A	−8.23	6.32	2.23	−8.91	3.62	.37	.31	0	0	.0115*	.0115*
	(4.6)	(5.36)	(3.98)	(2.77)	(1.52)						
ED_x^B	−15.16	−23.18	10.36	−18.72	−3.6	.5	.47	0	0	.2497	.2497
	(3.27)	(9.97)	(12.95)	(4.01)	(5.27)						
ED_y^B	−2.35	38.75	3.19	17.07	−.71	.67	.23	0	0	.33	.33
	(4.06)	(9.8)	(2.65)	(6.45)	(1.6)						
				D. Flow of Funds							
B_H^A	227.1	1,697.6	299.7	524.5	203.2	.35	.18	0	0	.0311*	.0311*
	(189.3)	(707.3)	(123.4)	(138.2)	(105.4)						
A_H^B	−.59	21.93	−6.47	22.65	17.45	.17	−.11	0	0	.0000**	.0000**
	(4.89)	(8.83)	(8.67)	(5.9)	(2.6)						
$p_x^B \times I_x^A$	3,186	−976.7	3,452.7	1,023.1	14,272	.67	.43	21,532	0	.0001**	.0000**
	(1,882.9)	(4,665.2)	(1,104.9)	(3,000.6)	(1,691.4)						
$p_y^A \times I_y^B$	99.2	410.9	269.7	177.1	298.5	.15	−.08	461	0	.0000**	.0000**
	(74.4)	(112)	(115.7)	(69)	(26.2)						

E. Production, Consumption, and International Trade

IMP_x^A	5.756	-17.999	12.077	.605	23.913	.78	.36	32	0	.0002**	.0000**
	(3.235)	(7.627)	(4.264)	(3.95)	(2.07)						
IMP_y^B	1.1	10.613	9.082	4.415	8.897	.15	$-.13$	11	0	.0016**	.0000**
	(2.492)	(3.519)	(3.406)	(1.568)	(.665)						
x_c^A	17.37	4.8	20.78	14.29	31.81	.78	.4	38	15	.0001**	.0000**
	(2.34)	(5.04)	(3.69)	(1.59)	(1.53)						
y_c^A	11.81	8.2	10.62	13.05	8.67	.26	$-.24$	8	12	.0072**	.0000**
	(.55)	(1.1)	(.91)	(.49)	(.26)						
x_c^B	14.27	21.95	11.88	15.19	6.1	.74	.22	5	13	.0209*	.0000**
	(1.3)	(2.03)	(.55)	(1.43)	(.52)						
y_c^B	14.65	15.3	20.4	15.25	18.97	.09	$-.11$	21	12	.0006**	.0000**
	(2.82)	(2.49)	(3.07)	(1.71)	(.58)						
x_p^A	11.85	23.07	9.3	13.91	7.79	.54	.23	6	15	.0159*	.0000**
	(1.84)	(3.43)	(1.13)	(2.68)	(.8)						
y_p^A	13.01	18.91	19.36	17.3	17.71	.12	$-.02$	19	12	.0063**	.0000**
	(2.14)	(2.49)	(2.51)	(1.47)	(.49)						
x_p^B	19.83	5.41	23.6	15.26	30.1	.66	.41	37	13	.0023**	.0000**
	(2.14)	(6.34)	(4.43)	(2.69)	(2.27)						
y_p^B	13.83	4.47	11.44	10.86	9.9	.68	$-.34$	10	12	.2236	.0000**
	(.26)	(.62)	(.34)	(.27)	(.13)						

NOTE.—Definitions of variables: r is the exchange rate, the price of currency A in terms of currency B; V cur A is the volume in the foreign exchange market, in terms of currency A; V cur B = rV cur A; p_y^A is the price of y in country A; p_x^A is the price of x in country A; Z is the ratio of the price level in country A to the price level in country B at actual exchange rates; ED_x^A is the excess demand for x in country A; ED_y^A is the excess demand for y in country A; B_H^A is the quantity of currency B held by residents of country A at the end of a period (recall that the currency has no value to them); A_H^B is the quantity of currency A held by residents of country B at the end of a period (recall that the currency has no value to them); $p_x^B \times I_x^A$ is the price of x in country B times max[0, IMP_x^A], which equals the quantity of currency B used to finance imports of x by country A; IMP_x^A is the net imports of x by country A; x_c^A is the consumption of x in country A; y_c^A is the consumption of y in country A; x_p^A is the production of x in country A; y_p^A is the production of y in country A; B_{1i} is the estimated value of the variable for period 1 of experiment i; B_2 is the estimated value of the variable as the number of periods grows large.

* Significant at the 5 percent level.
** Significant at the 1 percent level.

rected for heteroskedasticity using White's (1980) covariance matrix estimator.[4] The variables analyzed for prices and exchange rates equal the average transaction price during a market period, the unit of observation.

The analysis begins with the most central variables, the exchange rate and the volume of currency exchanged. If the response of these variables to the underlying economic conditions is not as predicted by theory, then the magnitudes of all other variables would be affected relative to theory. The first result is that the exchange rates are at a level anticipated by the competitive model. The second result is that the volume of exchange falls short of the competitive quantity.

RESULT 1. Exchange rates converge strongly to the competitive prediction.

Support. Refer to the row labeled r in panel A of table 3. The competitive equilibrium exchange rate is 47. The estimate of B_2 for r, the exchange rate variable, is 47.015 with a standard error of 2.381, as shown in the first row of the table. The hypothesis that the exchange rates are strongly converging to the predictions of the competitive equilibrium model cannot be rejected. Q.E.D.

The volume of exchange for country B is shown in figure 5. Since the volume of currency in country A is related to the volume of currency in country B by the exchange rate, only one country is shown. Panel A of table 3 has statistics for country A, whereas the figure has data for country B. For the most part, the figure shows that the competitive model is rejected because of insufficient trade, especially in one of the experiments (experiment 040793). The same conclusion is evident from the table.

RESULT 2. The volume of exchange in the international market falls short of the competitive equilibrium volume. In only one of the experiments is the volume partially converging to the competitive equilibrium. The autarky model can be rejected.

Support. The estimates from the model are in panel A of table 3, listed as the variable V cur. The estimated asymptote of the volume, B_2, is 351 compared with the competitive equilibrium volume, which should be at least 461. It could be more than 461 without being inconsistent with the model because of the possible existence of speculation. The hypothesis that the asymptotic value of the actual volume equals the theoretical value can be rejected. In addition, the

---

[4] The results are not substantially different without the correction for heteroskedasticity. Every coefficient B_2 that is significantly different at the 5 percent level from the competitive equilibrium or from autarky remains so if the correction is not performed. Likewise, every B_2 coefficient that is not significantly different from the predictions of one of the models at the 5 percent level with the correction is not significantly different from the model's prediction without the correction.

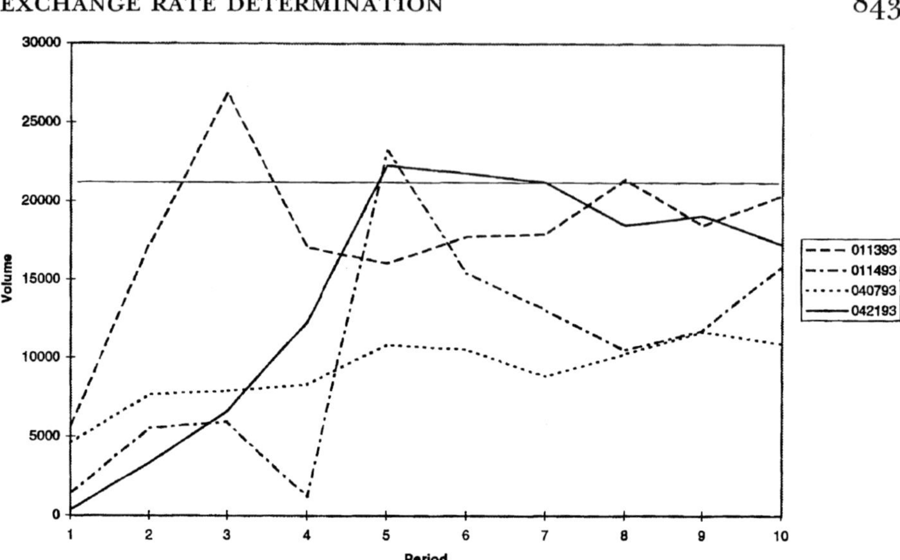

FIG. 5.—Volume in the currency B market over time: all sessions

B_{1j} terms for at least three experiments are closer to the competitive equilibrium than the asymptote. Since the B_{1j} terms are the measures of the beginning of the adjustment process, partial convergence is not observed. Q.E.D.

Though the volume of currency A is not converging toward the competitive equilibrium quantity, the amount of currency B traded increases from very low levels at the beginning of each session toward the competitive equilibrium quantity of 21,532 over the course of the session. This tendency is apparent in figure 5. The convergence of the volume of currency B, but not currency A, is associated with an increase in r, the exchange rate, over the course of each session.

Result 2 serves as a signal that these systems are not exactly on track as described by the competitive equilibrium model. Since the volume is not accurate, the simultaneous nature of the model's equation system suggests that inaccuracies are likely to exist elsewhere. The following results constitute an attempt to isolate the errors and find the fundamental causes. The prices that exist in each country are the obvious places to begin. They are addressed by the following result.

RESULT 3. Price patterns have the following properties: (i) Prices within countries partially converge to the competitive equilibrium predictions. (ii) Relative prices of x and y are converging in the partial sense toward the competitive equilibrium prediction in both countries. (iii) The competitive equilibrium is a better predictor than autarky is.

Support. Part i: Panel B of table 3 contains the estimates of the B_{1j} term for the prices of two countries, two commodities, and four experiments. It contains the estimate of the B_2 terms for each of the four prices (two countries and two commodities, p_x^A, p_y^A, p_x^B, and p_y^B). Three of the four B_2 terms, which are measures of the price asymptotes, are significantly different from the prediction of the competitive model, and all four are different from that of autarky. In all but five cases (four instances of p_y^A and one instance of p_y^B) of the 16 possibilities, the data are further from the competitive equilibrium at the start of the experiment than at the end. Part ii: Panel B of table 3 contains the test for the variables p_x^A/p_y^A and p_x^B/p_y^B. As can be seen, the hypothesis that B_2 is the ratio that is predicted by the competitive equilibrium can be rejected in both cases (two countries and two price ratios). The ratios seem close to 0.7 and 0.33 compared to the equilibrium predictions of 0.36, and the differences are statistically significant. The partial convergence is clearly present since, in all eight possible cases, the data at the beginning of the experiment are further from the competitive equilibrium than are the pooled data at the end. Part iii: In both cases the B_2 estimate is closer to the competitive equilibrium than it is to the autarky predictions. Q.E.D.

It is interesting to note that while the absolute prices are not at the competitive equilibrium, the movements are in that direction. Furthermore, the price ratios in both countries are not at the competitive levels, but the movement is in that direction. Thus the relative scarcities in a country are being reflected by prices even though the absolute levels of prices are off.

The previous result examined the data from the point of view of prices within a country. The next result views the data from the perspective of relative prices across countries and factors in the exchange rate. It indicates that the nature of the responses of the variables to the underlying economic conditions might differ according to the commodity.

RESULT 4. The law of one price, as defined by equations (5) and (6), receives some support in the market for y but is rejected in the market for x. Partial convergence is not present in the x market but is present in the y market.

Support. The test statistics are in panel B of table 3 for the variables $p_x^B/(r \times p_x^A)$ and $p_y^B/(r \times p_y^A)$. The hypothesis that the equation is satisfied in the y market can be rejected at the .025 level. The coefficient B_2 is 0.69, as opposed to the 1.0 predicted by the competitive model. Partial convergence is also present in every experiment. In the x market the coefficient B_2 is 0.4, as opposed to 1. As measured

EXCHANGE RATE DETERMINATION   845

by the variable B_{1i}, in the x market, two of the experiments are closer at the end than at the beginning.

The next result extends the analysis to a version of PPP theory. In order to cast the competitive model in the terms in which it is ordinarily applied, price indices are developed and used to reformulate LOP as PPP. Of course, this theory is sensitive to the choice of indices. The result is stated next.

RESULT 5. Purchasing power parity is not supported statistically in the data.

Support. Price indices were constructed using actual volume as weights. Consider the estimation of the following variable Z, where

$$Z = r \left[\frac{p_x^A(x_c^A + x_c^B) + p_y^A(y_c^A + y_c^B)}{p_x^B(x_c^A + x_c^B) + p_y^B(y_c^A + y_c^B)} \right].$$

The terms $[p_x^A(x_c^A + x_c^B) + p_y^A(y_c^A + y_c^B)]$ and $[p_x^B(x_c^A + x_c^B) + p_y^B(y_c^A + y_c^B)]$ are price indices in countries A and B, respectively. The prices of the two commodities x and y are weighted by the commodities' shares in the world consumption bundle. Under PPP, the exchange rate equalizes purchasing power in the two countries so that $Z = 1$. The estimates are given in panel B of table 3 in the row labeled Z.

As can be seen in the table, the estimated asymptotic value of Z, as measured by the variable B_2, is 1.157, and it is significantly different from one at the $p < .005$ level. Thus, since the estimated asymptote is about 15 percent off, the PPP model fails. Q.E.D.

Notice that PPP does not fail because of an inappropriate construction of price indices. The theory fails because the underlying and motivating LOP fails. Thus results 5 and 6 together demonstrate that a phenomenon found in the field data, the failure of PPP, is also found in the experimental economies.

The previous three results suggest that inaccuracies of the competitive model reside in both intercountry and intracountry comparisons. The next result is an attempt to focus more clearly on the behavior of the localities in which the price formation process takes place. Equations (1)–(4) are local market demand and supply equations. They say that, in each country and for each commodity, the local prices are set by the local conditions of demand and supply, together with the imports and exports. They are statements about the reaction of domestic economies to the underlying economic forces. The question posed is whether or not excess demand or excess supply, as defined by the actual parameters of the experiment and by the observed prices, exists in the local economies. Have the prices adjusted in the domestic economies, or are they adjusting to satisfy the partial equilibrium condition that demand equals supply? The result suggests that the two countries are adjusting much differently.

RESULT 6. Domestic excess demand for good x is not converging to zero in country A, but for y in country A, it is converging to zero in the partial sense. Domestic excess demand is converging strongly to zero in country B, for y and for x.

Support. Excess demand is defined by actual experimental parameters. Prices are average prices in a period. The estimated coefficients in panel C of table 3 provide the support. In the table, excess demand for m in country J is denoted by ED_m^J. In country A there is an excess supply of x at the asymptote B_2, of the adjustment path of 9.1 units. This is significantly different from zero. Furthermore, the asymptote is further from the equilibrium than the starting point in three of the four experiments. Similarly, there is a significant excess demand (3.6 units) for y in country A. However, the market is converging in the partial sense to an excess demand of zero in three of the four experiments. In country B the excess demand for both x and y is converging to zero in the strong sense. Q.E.D.

Result 6 indicates that the law of supply and demand is operating at the local levels, but an inexplicable asymmetry exists between the countries. The question to pose is whether there might exist a deeper problem as a result of the way the law is formulated at the international level to determine the exchange rate. The next result is fundamental. It says that the flow of funds theory is operating to determine the rate of exchange.

Two different types of models can be used to assess the flow of funds theory of exchange rate determination. The first rests on the fact that the international financial flows must satisfy the following accounting identity:

$$p_x^B \times I_x^A + p_y^B \times I_y^A + \mathrm{B}_H^A = r(p_x^A \times I_x^B + p_y^A \times I_y^B + \mathrm{A}_H^B), \quad (9)$$

where J_H^K is the quantity of currency J held at the end of a market period by residents of country K, and $I_m^J = \max[0, \mathrm{IMP}_x^J]$, where IMP_m^J is the net imports of m by country J. The left side of the equation is equal to the total amount of currency B purchased by residents of country A; the right side equals the total amount of currency A purchased by residents of country B, multiplied by the exchange rate, which is the price of currency A in terms of currency B. The equation does not include purchases and subsequent resale of currency, which is presumably due to speculation. Thus each side of the equation represents currency demanded and supplied for transaction purposes, plus wasted foreign exchange. In terms of the notation introduced above, B_H^A and A_H^B are the quantities of foreign exchange that are "wasted" in each of the countries A and B, respectively.

The competitive model predicts that

$$p_x^B \times I_x^A + p_y^B \times I_y^A + B_H^A = 21{,}532, \tag{10}$$

$$p_x^A \times I_x^B + p_y^A \times I_y^B + A_H^B = 461, \tag{11}$$

$$r = 47, \tag{12}$$

and

$$p_y^B \times I_y^A = B_H^A = A_H^B = p_x^A \times I_x^B = 0. \tag{13}$$

The first approach to flow of funds theory testing rests on interpretations of statistical tests of the last two equations. The data are captured by result 7.

RESULT 7. The international flow of funds is moving toward the competitive equilibrium prediction.

Support. The variable $p_y^B \times I_y^A = 0$ in every period of every experiment. The variable $p_x^A \times I_x^B = 0$ in every period of every experiment except for the first three periods of experiment 011493. It can be seen from panel D of table 3 that the variables B_H^A and $p_x^B \times I_x^A$ are converging in the partial sense to the competitive predictions in all four experiments, whereas r is converging strongly. The variable A_H^B is converging partially in two of the four experiments and $p_y^A \times I_y^B$ is converging partially in three of the four experiments. Q.E.D.

Result 7 indicates that the international flow of currency is converging toward the level predicted by the competitive model. It is obviously moving away from the autarky prediction of zero. Thus, even though the volume in the currency market is not moving to the competitive equilibrium prediction in result 2, the individual components of the demand for and supply of currency, as expressed in equation (9), are moving toward the predicted values. The poor performance of the competitive model in predicting the volume in the currency markets may be due to mistakes and speculation in the early periods of the experimental sessions. Now we consider the second approach, which is more deeply related to the dynamic relationship between r and the international demand for and supply of currencies.

The second approach to testing flow of funds theory is based on a hypothesis about the market. The test rests on the hypothesis that the direction of movement of the exchange rate from period $t - 1$ to period t is governed by the market conditions existing in period $t - 1$. If there was excess demand for currency A at the average exchange rate in period $t - 1$, we would expect r to rise in period

t. This idea is expressed in the following equation:

$$r_t - r_{t-1} = a + b(\mathcal{D}^A_{t-1} - \mathcal{S}^A_{t-1}), \tag{14}$$

where $\mathcal{D}^A_{t-1}$ and $\mathcal{S}^A_{t-1}$ can be interpreted as the excess demand for and excess supply of, respectively, currency A in period $t - 1$. Specifically,

$$\mathcal{S}^A_{t-1} = \left[D^A_x\!\left(\frac{p^B_x}{r}\right) - x^A_c \right] \times \frac{p^B_x}{r}, \tag{15}$$

where $D^A_x(p)$ is the market demand function for x by residents of country A evaluated at price p, and x^A_c is the total consumption of x by residents of country A. Thus $D^A_x - x^A_c$ is the additional amount of x that A could profitably import, given the foreign prices of x and its home consumption, which it did not import. When $D^A_x - x^A_c$ is multiplied by foreign prices and the exchange rate, it yields the amount of home currency that must be spent to import the desired additional amount; thus it is the excess supply of currency A to the international market.

Similarly,

$$\mathcal{D}^A_{t-1} = [D^B_y(p^A_y \times r) - y^B_c] \times p^A_y, \tag{16}$$

where D^B_y equals the demand for good y by residents of country B, which imports good y, measured at the actual country A prices and exchange rate. When consumption of home and foreign production is subtracted from desired consumption, a model of excess import demand is obtained. Multiplication by p^A_y yields the amount of currency A needed to make the purchases and thus yields a model of international excess demand for currency A.

The model rests on the hypothesis that $b > 0$. This maintains that the exchange rate increases in response to excess demand and decreases in response to excess supply of currency A. Furthermore, the concepts of demand and supply are those that are built from the flow of funds theory of international exchange rate determination. An examination of the data produces the finding contained in result 8.

RESULT 8. The movement of the exchange rate from one market period to the next is influenced by the international demand for and supply of currency as defined by flow of funds theory as captured in equation (14).

Support. The estimated coefficients and standard errors of equation (14) are given in table 4. Clearly $b > 0$, since the hypothesis that $b = 0$ can be rejected at the $p < .01$ level. A positive value for b means that excess demand for currency leads to a higher exchange

TABLE 4

ESTIMATES OF THE DYNAMIC MODEL OF EXCHANGE RATE ADJUSTMENT

Variable	Coefficient	Standard Error	t-Statistic
a	1.885	1.470	1.282
b	.000753	.000307	2.453

NOTE.—R^2 = .17; Durbin-Watson = 2.32.

rate in the next period. Although the coefficient is small, it indicates the change in r for each unit of excess demand of A, the magnitude of which was typically in the hundreds. The constant term is positive but not significantly different from zero, suggesting a weak upward trend over time, even when excess demand for and supply of currency are taken into account. Thus the dynamic pattern of movement follows the hypothesized property: an excess demand for a currency in the flow of funds sense in period t means an increase in the exchange rate in period $t + 1$. Q.E.D.

The issue of dynamics is pursued further by a conjecture about the direction of convergence. It is very clear from panel A of table 3 and figure 4 that the exchange rate is converging from below. Since this is the first experimental study of an economy with multiple currencies, any possible conjecture about the causes of the pattern of convergence is speculative, but it is tempting to draw an analogy with other market experiments. In single-market double auctions it has been observed that the direction of convergence of prices over time can be explained by the relative rents obtained by consumers and producers in the competitive equilibrium (Smith and Williams 1982). Rents tend to be divided more equally between both sides of the market at the beginning of the experiment than in the competitive equilibrium. The conjecture below generalizes this idea to the level of international economies.

Define the equal system surplus price adjustment path to be a movement of the exchange rate such that (i) the exchange rate begins at a level such that total gains from international trade are divided equally and (ii) the exchange rate is converging to the competitive equilibrium level. The concept of relative surplus of buyers and sellers in the currency market can be expressed as the relative gains in surplus of the two countries from international trade. For each country, the gain can be expressed as the sum of the profits (in terms of currency A) of the residents of the country in the competitive equilibrium minus the sum of the residents' profits in autarky. Explicitly the concept is the following.

Let CE equal the competitive equilibrium allocation and prices,

AUT the autarky equilibrium allocation and prices, and $\Pi^K(z, \mathbf{p})$ the consumers' surplus plus producers' surplus of country K in allocation z and at price vector $\mathbf{p}$ measured in terms of currency K. These magnitudes will be precisely defined when they are used in the discussion below.

The equal system surplus price adjustment path is an exchange rate path that begins with an exchange rate r that solves the equation

$$\Pi^A(\text{CE}) - \Pi^A(\text{AUT}) = [\Pi^B(\text{CE}) - \Pi^B(\text{AUT})]\,\frac{1}{r}.$$

The numbers for the experimental parameters are $[\Pi^A(\text{CE}); \Pi^A(\text{AUT})] = [949; 581]$ and $[\Pi^B(\text{CE}); \Pi^B(\text{AUT})] = [27{,}272; 19{,}697]$.[5] The equation thus becomes $369 = 7{,}575/r$. The r that equates the surpluses is thus 20.53. According to this model, one would expect the exchange rate to converge from below beginning near 20, moving upward and seeking a limit at the competitive equilibrium of 47.

CONJECTURE 1. The direction of convergence of the exchange rate over time is determined by the equal system surplus price adjustment path.

Support. A more equal division of the surplus than in the competitive equilibrium would imply that the exchange rate at the beginning of the experiment should tend to favor country B more than the

---

[5] The calculations of the surpluses are made possible because of the separability built into the experimental parameters. Inverse demand functions are well defined. Let the inverse of a function be indicated by lowercase letters. That is, the demand function $D_x^A(\cdot)$ has an inverse function designated by the notation $d_x^A(\cdot)$. Thus, for country A the difference between consumer plus producer surplus evaluated at the competitive equilibrium and the consumer plus producer surplus evaluated at the autarky equilibrium is

$$\int_0^{x_c^{A,\text{CE}}} [d_x^A(X) - p_x^{A,\text{CE}}]\,dX + \int_0^{y_c^{A,\text{CE}}} [d_x^A(Y) - p_y^{A,\text{CE}}]\,dY$$

$$+ \int_0^{x_p^{A,\text{CE}}} [p_x^{A,\text{CE}} - s_x^A(X)]\,dX + \int_0^{y_p^{A,\text{CE}}} [p_y^{A,\text{CE}} - s_y^A(Y)]\,dY$$

$$- \int_0^{x_c^{A,\text{AUT}}} [d_x^A(X) - p_x^{A,\text{AUT}}]\,dX - \int_0^{y_c^{A,\text{AUT}}} [d_y^A(Y) - p_y^{A,\text{AUT}}]\,dY$$

$$- \int_0^{x_p^{A,\text{AUT}}} [p_x^{A,\text{AUT}} - s_x^A(X)]\,dX - \int_0^{y_p^{A,\text{AUT}}} [p_y^{A,\text{AUT}} - s_y^A(Y)]\,dY,$$

where $x_c^{A,\text{CE}}$, $x_p^{A,\text{CE}}$, $y_c^{A,\text{CE}}$, and $y_p^{A,\text{CE}}$ are the quantities of x and y consumed and produced in country A at the competitive equilibrium. The amounts at the autarky equilibrium are indicated with the notation AUT replacing CE. Similarly, the equilibrium prices at the competitive equilibrium and autarky are indicated with the country as a superscript and the commodity as a subscript. A similar calculation can be made for country B. The actual numbers are obtained by substituting the inverse demand functions and supply functions from the formulas used as parameters in the experiment that are found in Sec. II.

competitive equilibrium exchange rate, indicating that currency B should have a higher value than in the competitive equilibrium. This implies an exchange rate less than 47 at the beginning of the experiment, with a pattern of convergence toward the competitive level. The equal system surplus price adjustment path begins with an exchange rate of 21. The estimates of the first-period exchange rates for the four experiments found in panel A of table 3 are 29.238, −1.319, 22.956, and 7.606, respectively (an average of about 15). Thus adjustment occurs from below in all experiments. The data support the conjecture. Q.E.D.

The results above suggest that patterns of international finance are similar but not exactly as predicted by the competitive model. For the most part the financial variables are moving in directions that would be suggested by the competitive equilibrium model. Either wasted exchange or speculation occurs at first but decreases over time. The next series of questions inquire about the real sectors of the economies and the underlying trade. Since the financial variables are moving in ways that the competitive model anticipates, it might be expected that the real sectors are responding accordingly also. The next result confirms this. It says that the patterns of trade are consistent with competitive theory.

RESULT 9. International trade patterns are consistent with the principle of comparative advantage.

Support. The competitive model predicts that country A will import x and country B will import y. As shown in panel E of table 3, net imports of x by country A, denoted by IMP_x^A in the table, are 23.9 units and net imports of y by country B are 8.9 units. These levels are short of the quantitative predictions of the competitive model of 32 units and 11 units, respectively; however, in all but two of the eight possible cases, the data are moving toward the competitive equilibrium quantities. These patterns are sufficient to support the result. Q.E.D.

Since trade is developing along the lines of comparative advantage and since the financial sectors are not far out of line, both consumption and production patterns should be conforming to the model. Since such conformity need not be the case, except as dictated by the principles of economics, which are under investigation, it is necessary to check. The next two results indicate that both are moving in the directions anticipated.

RESULT 10. Consumption patterns are moving toward the predictions of the competetive model.

Support. Two countries and two commodities represent four variables to consider. The variables are given as x_c^A, y_c^A, x_c^B, and y_c^B in panel E of table 3. All four of these variables are significantly different from the competitive equilibrium as measured by the B_2 term. But, in a sense, they are very close. For example, there are 8.67 units of consumption of y in country A (the competitive equilibrium is eight units) and 6.1 units of consumption of x in country B (the competitive equilibrium is five units). The variables are partially converging in all but two of the 16 possible cases (as measured by the B_{1i} estimates as opposed to the B_2 estimates).

RESULT 11. Production patterns are moving toward the predictions of the competitive equilibrium model.

Support. In 14 of the 16 cases (four variables and four experiments) the production levels are partially converging to the competitive equilibrium. See the rows marked x_p^A, y_p^A, x_p^B, and y_p^B in panel E of table 3.

In an earlier work (Noussair et al. 1995), we demonstrated that the patterns of production and trade predicted by the law of comparative advantage are observed in an experimental market. In those markets, members of different countries used the same currency. Results 9, 10, and 11 confirm that when members of each country use their own national currency to trade, the law of comparative advantage still works well.

VIII. The LOP and PPP Paradox

A phenomenon that has been widely observed in the field is also observed in the experimental economies. The equations derived from PPP theory fail to be satisfied in the data. How can that be? The experimental economies are much simpler than the field counterparts. None of the conditions that might be troublesome to the theory in the field is present in the experimental economies. One could surmise that the experimental economies operate under conditions that are very favorable to the theory. Indeed, not only does PPP fail, but also the underlying and more fundamental theory, LOP. Thus the experimental economies demonstrate that PPP and LOP can fail for more fundamental reasons than has been supposed in the literature.

We offer an observation and a conjecture about what the reason for the failure might be. The first is related to the inherent uncertainty in international finance. The second is related to the inherent interdependence in a multicountry and multicurrency economy.

Observation.—When trading in foreign economies, agents take unavoidable risks. All actions and prices must include a risk premium.

Trading in the experimental environment involves risks that are inherent in the trading technology. In the experimental economies, agents must buy foreign exchange before they can trade in the foreign commodity market. Thus agents must commit to buying the currency (which is worthless to them except to buy foreign goods) in the foreign market before they know at what price they will actually trade. This risk is not due to traders' lack of knowledge about the value of a system variable, but rather to uncertainty about whether the markets will adjust to their equilibrium values and exactly how and when this takes place. Thus there is not a way for them to hedge this risk, although it would presumably be small if the time lags were short. Nevertheless, previous experience in similar experiments leads us to believe that agents must be compensated for taking the extra risk. This could explain why even though the exchange rate market equilibrates, LOP and PPP fail.

The conjecture is a type of coordination hypothesis. It results from the nature of simultaneously interacting markets.

CONJECTURE 2. The law of one price fails because of the asymmetric speed of adjustments of the price discovery process of local markets.

That fact that markets converge at different speeds is well known to those that study experimental markets. This fact becomes important to the issue of LOP in international finance. In order for LOP (and to a lesser extent PPP) to be satisfied as an equilibrium condition, all markets have to be in equilibrium simultaneously. In fact, what happens in the experimental economies is that markets converge at different speeds, and within the time frames that were possible to observe, the simultaneous equilibration of all markets never occurred (see result 6). This phenomenon leads to the failure of LOP even when the exchange rate has converged to the level predicted by the competitive equilibrium model. Thus, if the same principles of economics operate in the field as are operating in the experimental markets, LOP and PPP may fail because there are multiple markets that are spatially separated, and the price discovery process in the different markets operates at different speeds.[6]

We are unaware of any coherent, general model that might be applied to capture all the complex adjustments that occur in the experimental economies and will help us make the point rigorously. However, the observation about risk premiums and conjecture 2 operate together with other results to form an impression of how the LOP failure occurs even under favorable circumstances. From conjecture 1 comes the proposition that the asymmetric gains from in-

---

[6] There are suggestions in the literature that LOP and PPP fail because trading takes time (Benninga and Protopapadakis 1988; Goodwin, Grennes, and Wohlgenant 1990). While we see no inconsistency between our observations and their models, the role of time in their models is difficult to make operational in the experimental economies.

ternational trade influence the exchange rate to converge from below. Similarly, international trade, because of the inherent risks, starts around the cautious, autarky level of zero and then moves upward. So if international trade approaches the competitive equilibrium levels, it will approach from below. That property is observed in the experimental markets.

Overall, the system is observed to move in the direction of the competitive equilibrium. Early in the experiment, currency A is selling for below its competitive equilibrium level and currency B sells for more than the competitive equilibrium. Thus, in this position of disequilibrium, it is expensive for country A to import x as it is supposed to, and with the lack of supply and competition from international sources, the prices of x in country A are high, relative to the competitive equilibrium. Similarly, in country B there is little international demand for x because of the low exchange rate, so the price is low relative to the competitive equilibrium. In both cases the prices of x respond according to this picture, with the x prices starting above the equilibrium prices in country A and converging downward and the x prices in country B starting below the competitive equilibrium and converging upward. The fact of risk buttresses these tendencies by decreasing the imports of x and thereby keeping the prices of x high in country A and low in country B.

The influence of these pressures on the prices of y is different. In country A the low exchange rate should place upward pressure on price because of the international demand, but this pressure is offset by the risk of international transactions. The excess demand at the disequilibrium exchange rate is not as strong as it would be if there were no risks, and thus the potential upward pressure on price is muted. Similarly in country B, the low exchange rate should be accompanied by substantial imports of y with an accompanying downward pressure on price. But the risk of international finance mutes the importation of y and thereby decreases the excess supply that would force prices down. These "cross pressures" result in ambiguous price movements of y in both countries.

IX. Conclusions

The autarky model can be solidly rejected by these experiments. It is not the case that the hazards of the foreign exchange markets are such that international trade stops or takes place at very low levels only. On the other hand, the competitive model is not perfect. In most instances the outcome variables are converging to the competitive prediction in the partial sense, but the model fails to predict the exact levels of activity in many instances, even when the asymptotic

EXCHANGE RATE DETERMINATION   855

tendencies are incorporated. Financial hazards of participation in international trade do exist and can appear in the form of "wasted" exchange. However, the equilibrating tendencies of the system serve to reduce the uncertainty and facilitate trade.

Generally speaking, the exchange rate seeks a level that is near that predicted by the competitive model. Although the volume in the currency market is less than the competitive level, the individual components of currency flows seem to be moving toward the model's predictions. The exchange rate movements from one period to the next respond to the excess demand and supply conditions prevailing in the currency market. Over the course of the experiment, the exchange rate moves in accordance with the equal system surplus adjustment path. The low volume in the foreign exchange market suggests that the full gains from trade are not being realized, and, indeed, international trade is below competitive levels. This relatively low level of international trade may be associated with the relative prices lying between the competitive and autarky predictions in both countries. Country A seems to be more problematic, with the price of x persistently much higher than the competitive equilibrium level.

The low level of international trade observed in the experiments may be due to the systemic risk resulting from the cash-in-advance constraint. The risk of possible losses from holding foreign currency when the market period ends, or having to sell it at a loss, requires the would-be importer to be compensated for engaging in international trade. Importing is worth it only for those units of x and y for which the gains from international trade are great and is not worth it for marginal units, which are therefore not imported. Thus the cash-in-advance constraint functions much like an excise tax or a tariff on international transactions, reducing the amount of international trade of x and y to below the competitive equilibrium level.

In general, prices within countries do not seem to be adjusting rapidly to local demand and supply conditions, although there is evidence of slow convergence to local market clearing. The adjustment is not taking place at all for market x in country A.

A perplexing phenomenon that has been observed in the field appears in the experimental markets. The law of one price and purchasing power parity fail. This failure of LOP and PPP can be traced to the differing speeds at which markets adjust in the different countries. Thus, in the economies studied here, the mystery of the failures resides in the nature of price dynamics in local economies. The problems do not reside with the complete apparatus of the competitive model. In these economies, PPP cannot fail because of problems with price indexes since accurate indexes were constructed. In addition, there are no trade barriers, nontraded goods, or transportation costs. Thus we are able to conclude that the phenomena can have another cause besides the variables that have been the focus of modern investigations. Violations of LOP and PPP arise naturally as disequilibrium phenomena, even in simple laboratory international economies.

Despite the behavior of local and international price ratios, which show departure from the competitive equilibrium levels, the real sectors of the economies are moving in the direction of the competitive equilibrium. Patterns of international trade are consistent with the law of comparative advantage. Local production and consumption levels are converging to the competitive equilibrium as well.

The competitive model is not perfect, in any sense, but the principles on which the general theory is based lead to a model that predicts the general movement of economic activity in a very complex and interdependent setting. When people discuss vague concepts of "economic forces," these data suggest that the formalization of the concepts with the competitive equilibrium model can be very useful. The forces are increasing the international trade between the two countries, with the result that the magnitudes of most outcome variables, especially net exports, production, consumption, and the exchange rate, move slowly toward the competitive equilibrium.

Appendix

Instructions and Forms

1. General Instructions

This is an experiment in the economics of market decision making. The instructions are simple and if you follow them carefully and make good decisions, you might earn a considerable amount of money which will be paid to you in cash.

In the experiment we are going to conduct a market in which some of you will be buyers and some of you will be sellers in a sequence of trading periods. Find a sheet labelled Buyer or Seller, which describes the value to you of any decisions you might make. You are not to reveal the information on this sheet to anyone. It is your own private information.

In the experiment there are two goods and two locations, which you could think of as separate countries. The goods are called X and Y and the locations are called A and B. In location A, there is a market for X and a market for Y. Also, in location B, there is a market for X and a market for Y. As will be explained later, the locations will be on different screens on the computer.

Each location has its own special currency. All transactions in location A will take place in currency A and all transactions in location B will take

EXCHANGE RATE DETERMINATION   857

place in currency B. Each unit of currency A is worth ______ guilders to you and each unit of currency B is worth ______ guilders to you.

2. *Specific Instructions to Sellers*

During each market period you are free to sell to any buyer or buyers as many units of X and Y as you might want. The first unit of X that you sell in a trading period, you obtain at a cost of the amount listed on the sheet in row (1) in the section of the sheet entitled Cost Schedule for X, in the column labelled unit cost. The second unit of X that you sell during the same trading period you obtain at a cost of the amount listed in row (2) in the column marked unit cost, etc. The profits from each sale, which are yours to keep, are computed by taking the difference between price at which you sold the unit and the cost of the unit. That is:

$$\text{Your Earnings} = \text{Sale Price of Unit} - \text{Cost of Unit}$$

Suppose, for example, that you sell two units of X and that the cost for the first unit of X is 140 and for the second unit is 160. If you sell the first unit at 200 and the second at 190, your earnings are

$$\text{Earnings from First} = 200 - 140 = 60$$

$$\text{Earnings from Second} = 190 - 160 = 30$$

$$\text{Total Earnings} = 60 + 30 = 90$$

The end of period summary will help you record your profits. On row A, record the total cost of X that you sold during the period. The X which you sold during the period is equal to your inventory of X at the beginning of the market period minus your inventory at the end of the market period. This total can be found in the row of the section labelled Cost Schedule for X corresponding to the amount of X you sold during the period in the last column, which is entitled total cost. For example, if you sold two units during the market period, the total cost can be found in row (2). Similarly, on row B, record the total cost of Y that you sold during the period.

On rows (C) and (D) record your beginning of period and end of period inventory of the currency which has value to you. On row (E), enter an amount equal to the amount in row (D) minus the amount in row (C). (E) indicates your net change in cash for the market period. On row (F) record your total profit for the period. The total profit equals the total cash obtained from sales of X and Y minus the cost of the X and Y sold. It also equals the amount in row (E) minus the amount in row (A) minus the amount in row (B). Subsequent periods should be recorded similarly.

3. *Specific Instructions to Buyers*

During each market period, you are free to purchase from any seller or sellers as many units of X and Y as you might want. For the first unit of X that you buy in a trading period, you will receive the amount listed in row (1) in the section of the page entitled redemption value schedule for X in the column marked unit value. If you buy a second unit during the trading period, you will receive the additional amount listed in row (2) in the column marked unit redemption value, etc. The profits from each purchase, which are yours to keep, are computed by taking the difference between the redemption value and the purchase price of the unit bought. That is:

$$\text{Your Earnings} = \text{Redemption Value} - \text{Purchase Price}$$

Suppose, for example, that you buy two units and that your redemption value for the first unit is 200 and for the second unit is 180. If you pay 150 for the first unit and 160 for the second unit, your earnings are:

$$\text{Earnings from First} = 200 - 150 = 50$$

$$\text{Earnings from Second} = 180 - 160 = 20$$

$$\text{Total Earnings} = 50 + 20 = 70$$

The end of period summary will help you record your profits. In row (A) enter the total value of X consumed. This amount can be found in the column labelled total value in the row corresponding to the total number of X held in your inventory at the end of the period.

Similarly, record the total value of Y consumed in row (B). On rows (C) and (D) record your beginning of period and end of period inventory of the currency which has value to you. On line (E), enter an amount equal to the amount in row (D) minus the amount in row (C). On line (F) record your total profit for the period, which equals your redemption values for having X and Y in your inventory at the end of the market period, minus the cash which you spent to acquire them.

4.　Currency

The locations are indicated by two computer screens. You can move from screen to screen by using the page up and page down keys. On each screen Cash on Hand is given in the upper right corner. On one screen, which represents location A, the Cash on Hand indicates your inventory of currency A. On the other screen, which represents location B, the Cash on Hand indicates your inventory of currency B.

While at location A, market 3 allows you to buy and sell currency B. Similarily, while at location B, market 6 allows you to buy and sell currency A.

All participants may transfer units of X and Y from one of the locations to the other. Some participants can transfer units of X and Y from location B to location A, but not from location A to location B. The rest of the participants can transfer units of X and Y from location A to location B, but not from B to A. To transfer units, use the F4 key.

5.　Trading Profits

A possible source of profits is from buying and selling X, Y, currency A, and currency B. Selling increases your cash on hand by the amount of the sale price. Buying reduces your cash on hand by the amount of the pur-

EXCHANGE RATE DETERMINATION 859

END OF PERIOD SUMMARY: PERIOD ______

(A)	Total Cost of X Sold (in Currency A)	______
(B)	Total Cost of Y Sold (in Currency A)	______
(C)	Beginning of Period Inventory of Currency A	______
(D)	End of Period Inventory of Currency A	______
(E)	Net Change in Currency A	______
(F)	Total Profit for the Period (E) − (A) − (B)	______

END OF PERIOD SUMMARY: PERIOD ______

(A)	Total Value of X in Final Inventory (in Currency B)	______
(B)	Total Value of Y in Final Inventory (in Currency B)	______
(C)	Beginning of Period Inventory of Currency B	______
(D)	End of Period Inventory of Currency B	______
(E)	Net Change in Currency B	______
(F)	Total Profit for the Period (E) + (A) + (B)	______

chase. Thus, you can either gain or lose money on the purchase and resale of units.

6. *Beginning of Period Inventories*

All sellers begin each period with inventory of X and Y. All buyers begin each period with no X or Y. All participants begin each period with a large inventory of either currency A or currency B. Beginning of period inventories are the same for each market period.

COST SCHEDULE FOR X

Unit	Unit Cost (in Currency B)	Total Cost (in Currency B)
(1)	150	150
(2)	195	345
(3)	240	585
(4)	285	870
(5)	330	1,200
(6)	375	1,575
(7)	420	1,995
(8)	465	2,460
(9)	510	2,970
(10)	555	3,525
(11)	600	4,125
(12)	645	4,770
(13)	690	5,460
(14)	735	6,195
(15)	780	6,975
(16)	825	7,800
(17)	870	8,670
(18)	915	9,585
(19)	960	10,545
(20)	1,005	11,550

860   JOURNAL OF POLITICAL ECONOMY

REDEMPTION VALUE SCHEDULE FOR Y

Unit	Unit Value (in Currency A)	Total Value (in Currency A)
(1)	42	42
(2)	39	81
(3)	36	127
(4)	36	163
(5)	33	196
(6)	30	226
(7)	27	253
(8)	27	280
(9)	24	304
(10)	21	325
(11)	18	343
(12)	18	361
(13)	15	376
(14)	12	388
(15)	9	397
(16)	9	406
(17)	6	412
(18)	3	415
(19)	0	415
(20)	0	415

7. Note on the System

You can imagine yourself at one of the two locations with an inventory of that location's currency. Should you find it advantageous, you could buy the currency of the other location and use it to buy X and/or Y there instead of buying X and/or Y at your location.

References

Benninga, Simon, and Protopapadakis, Aris A. "The Equilibrium Pricing of Exchange Rates and Assets When Trade Takes Time." *J. Internat. Money and Finance* 7 (June 1988): 129–49.

Goodwin, Barry K.; Grennes, Thomas; and Wohlgenant, Michael K. "Testing the Law of One Price When Trade Takes Time." *J. Internat. Money and Finance* 9 (March 1990): 21–40.

Grilli, Vittorio, and Roubini, Nouriel. "Liquidity and Exchange Rates." *J. Internat. Econ.* 32 (May 1992): 339–52.

Kimbrough, Kent P. "International Linkages, Exchange-Rate Regimes, and the International Transmission Process: Perspectives from Optimizing Models." In *International Economics*, edited by Lawrence H. Officer. Boston: Kluwer, 1987.

Krugman, Paul, and Obstfeld, Maurice. *International Economics: Theory and Policy*. 3d ed. New York: HarperCollins, 1994.

Lucas, Robert E., Jr. "Interest Rates and Currency Prices in a Two-Country World." *J. Monetary Econ.* 10 (November 1982): 335–59.

EXCHANGE RATE DETERMINATION   861

Meese, Richard A., and Rogoff, Kenneth S. "Empirical Exchange Rate Models of the Seventies: Do They Fit out of Sample?" *J. Internat. Econ.* 14 (February 1983): 3–24

Noussair, Charles N.; Plott, Charles R.; and Riezman, Raymond G. "An Experimental Investigation of the Patterns of International Trade." *A.E.R.* 85 (June 1995): 462–91.

Plott, Charles R. "A Computerized Laboratory Market System and Research Support Systems for the Multiple Unit Double Auction." Social Science Working Paper no. 783. Pasadena: California Inst. Tech., 1991.

Sargent, Thomas J. *Dynamic Macroeconomic Theory*. 2d ed. Cambridge, Mass.: Harvard Univ. Press, 1987.

Smith, Vernon L., and Williams, Arlington W. "The Effects of Rent Asymmetries in Experimental Auction Markets." *J. Econ. Behavior and Organization* 3 (March 1982): 99–116.

White, Halbert. "A Heteroskedasticity-Consistent Covariance Matrix Estimator and a Direct Test for Heteroskedasticity." *Econometrica* 48 (May 1980): 817–38.

Journal of Development Economics
Vol. 65 (2001) 55–80

JOURNAL OF
Development
ECONOMICS

www.elsevier.com/locate/econbase

Trade shocks and macroeconomic fluctuations in Africa

M. Ayhan Kose [a,*], Raymond Riezman [b]

[a] *Graduate School of International Economics and Finance, Brandeis University, Waltham, MA 02454, USA*
[b] *Department of Economics, University of Iowa, Iowa City, IA 52242, USA*

Received 1 December 1998; accepted 1 October 2000

Abstract

This paper examines the role of external shocks in explaining macroeconomic fluctuations in African countries. We construct a quantitative, stochastic, dynamic, multi-sector equilibrium model of a small open economy calibrated to represent a "typical" African country. External shocks consist of trade shocks, modeled as fluctuations in the prices of exported primary commodities, imported capital goods and intermediate inputs, and a financial shock, modeled as fluctuations in the world real interest rate. Trade shocks account for roughly half of economic fluctuations in aggregate output. Moreover, adverse trade shocks cause prolonged recessions since they induce a significant decrease in aggregate investment. © 2001 Published by Elsevier Science B.V.

JEL classification: F41; E31; E32; D58; F11
Keywords: Trade shocks; Dynamic stochastic quantitative trade model; African economies

1. Introduction

There is a large and expanding literature suggesting that highly unstable domestic macroeconomic environment is one of the primary reasons for the poor growth performance of African countries in the last 30 years.[1] The implication is that to

---

* Corresponding author. Tel.: +1-781-736-2266; fax: +1-781-736-2269.
E-mail addresses: akose@brandeis.edu (M.A. Kose), raymond-riezman@uiowa.edu (R. Riezman).

[1] Collier and Gunning (1999) provide a detailed survey of the literature examining the reasons of the slow growth in Africa. Sachs and Warner (1996) and Rodrik (1998) use a variety of growth regressions to study the determinants of economic performance, and conclude that macroeconomic stability is an important factor for the long-run growth in Africa. Ramey and Ramey (1995), using the data of developing and developed economies, find that countries with highly volatile macroeconomic environment have relatively lower growth.

0304-3878/01/$ - see front matter © 2001 Published by Elsevier Science B.V.
PII: S 0 3 0 4 - 3 8 7 8 (0 1) 0 0 1 2 7 - 4

56   *M.A. Kose, R. Riezman / Journal of Development Economics 65 (2001) 55–80*

improve growth performance in Africa, we need to understand why their economies are so volatile. That is the objective of this paper: using a dynamic, stochastic model we establish a link between external shocks and the highly volatile macroeconomic fluctuations in these economies. We study the effects of trade and financial shocks. Surprisingly, we find that, despite the fact that these countries are typically heavily indebted, trade shocks play a much more important role than financial shocks. In particular, it turns out that trade shocks explain almost half of the volatility in aggregate output.

International trade can induce macroeconomic fluctuations in a small open economy by two channels: one channel is through trade in goods and services, and the other one is by trade in financial assets. In African economies, these two channels have distinctively important roles in shaping domestic economic activity: first, the volume of international trade on average accounts for more than 70% of the aggregate output in these countries. Moreover, a narrow range of primary commodities constitutes a significant fraction of their exports, and their main import items are intermediate inputs and capital goods. Their export revenues are highly unstable due to recurrent and sharp fluctuations in the prices of primary commodities. Second, most of the African countries are heavily indebted, and a significant fraction of their export revenues are used to meet their debt service obligations. These make African countries extremely vulnerable to sudden changes in the world interest rate.

A thorough understanding of the sources of macroeconomic fluctuations in African economies requires a good grasp of the impact of trade shocks and financial shocks on domestic economic activity. Trade shocks are modeled as fluctuations in the prices of exported primary commodities, imported capital goods, and intermediate inputs, and financial shocks are fluctuations in the world real interest rate in our framework. We address the following questions to shed some light on these issues: first, do trade disturbances account for a significant fraction of macroeconomic fluctuations? Second, how are trade shocks transmitted and propagated through these economies?

We begin by documenting some of the major characteristics of industrial structure, composition of international trade, and dynamics of trade shocks to provide empirical evidence that there is a strong link between international trade disturbances and domestic economic activity in African countries. We, then, construct a multi-sector, dynamic, stochastic small open economy model which reflects the structural characteristics of a "typical" African economy. We compare the properties of the macroeconomic fluctuations generated by this model with those actually observed in African countries. We quantitatively evaluate the contribution of international trade shocks to domestic macroeconomic fluctuations.

Our paper contributes to the large literature examining the links between economic activity and trade shocks in developing economies and is particularly related to some recent papers studying the sources of macroeconomic fluctuations in African countries.[2]

---

[2] Feder (1983) and Basu and McLeod (1992) examine the relation between export instability and economic growth. Bevan et al. (1994) provide a computable general equilibrium model of an open economy to examine the economic experiences of Kenya and Tanzania after the major trade shock in 1976.

M.A. Kose, R. Riezman / Journal of Development Economics 65 (2001) 55–80 57

Deaton and Miller (1996) employ a vector autoregression (VAR) model to examine the importance of commodity price shocks. Hoffmaister et al. (1998) estimate a structural VAR model, where identifying restrictions are derived from a long-run small open economy model, to study the role of terms of trade and world real interest rate shocks. While the former study concludes that price shocks play an important role in driving macroeconomic fluctuations in African economies, the latter one finds these disturbances account for only a small fraction of the variation in output. Mendoza (1995) examines the importance of terms of trade shocks in a small open economy model calibrated for a typical developing economy and finds that these shocks account for almost half of the aggregate output fluctuations.[3]

This study extends the scope of this research program in several dimensions: first, we study the sources of macroeconomic fluctuations in African countries in a fully specified, stochastic, dynamic, open economy model reflecting the structural characteristics of these economies.[4] Since the model economy is dynamic, and involves endogenous labor–leisure choice, we are able to examine the link between trade shocks and fluctuations in aggregate investment, foreign asset holdings, and labor markets. The model economy employs domestically produced capital goods, imported capital goods, and imported intermediate inputs in two different sectors. This structure of differentiation in productive factors allows us to study the impact of different types of trade shocks on different sectors of the economy.

Second, our study considers a broader definition of trade shocks as it focuses on the price changes of the main export and import items instead of terms of trade disturbances. This is motivated by our empirical finding that the terms of trade do not fully reflect highly volatile movements in relative prices of the main export and import items of African countries. Third, while assessing the role of trade shocks, we investigate the impact of world interest rate fluctuations on domestic economic activity in African countries.

The organization of the paper is as follows: in Section 2, we review the empirical regularities. Following this, we present the model in Section 3. Model calibration is described in Section 4. In Section 5, we first examine the ability of the model in replicating major features of business cycle dynamics in a typical African country. Then, we quantitatively evaluate the importance of different types of shocks. The model dynamics are analyzed using impulse responses. Following this, the sensitivity of the results is briefly investigated. We conclude with a summary in Section 6.

---

[3] Praschnik (1993) studies the role of input price shocks in generating business cycles in developing countries using a closed economy model. Kouparitsas (1997a) investigates the transmission of business cycles from developed Northern countries to developing Southern economies in a two-country model. Mendoza (1991), using a small open economy model, examines the importance of world real interest rate shocks in driving business cycles in Canada.

[4] See Baxter (1995) for a survey on dynamic general equilibrium models of open economies. Kose (1999) examines the role of price shocks in driving business cycles in developing economies and provides an extensive review of the relevant literature.

58   *M.A. Kose, R. Riezman / Journal of Development Economics 65 (2001) 55–80*

2. Analysis of the data

2.1. Structural characteristics of the African economies

We begin with an examination of the decomposition of aggregate output to provide a better understanding of the structural characteristics of the African economies. Our analysis is based on the annual data of 22 non-oil exporting African countries for the 1970–1990 period.[5] We present information about the expenditure shares of aggregate output and industrial structure in Table 1a. The G7 average of each magnitude is also provided for comparison purposes. The major difference between these two groups is the role played by international trade in domestic economic activity. In African (G7) countries, exports account for almost 31 (20)% of total GDP while imports constitute more than 40 (18)% of it. Strikingly, the volume of trade on average accounts for more than 71% of GDP in African countries while only 38% of total GDP is attributable to the trade volume in the G7 countries. As Table 1a indicates, African countries have relatively large trade deficits: the average trade deficit is around 10% of the GDP in the African economies in our sample.

African economies' industrial structures also make them highly vulnerable to trade shocks: they have relatively smaller industry and service sectors, and, consequently, the share of agricultural sector is considerably larger in these countries. To be more specific, agricultural goods on average account for 28 (4)% of total GDP while industrial production constitutes roughly 18 (30)% of total domestic income in African (G7) countries.

Table 1b describes the structure of exports. As this table clearly illustrates, the African economies heavily depend on primary goods for their export revenues: the share of primary exports on average is 77% and ranges from 26% in Tanzania to 99% in Sudan. Interestingly, the average share of capital good exports is less than 2% in total exports. In order to examine the extent of diversification of exports at a more disaggregated level, we use two different criteria that are presented in the last two columns of Table 1b. Both of these measures suggest that the African countries in our sample seem to be much more concentrated in their exports than the G7 countries. First, we examine the number of commodities exported by the African economies: they export on average 54 different goods. This number is around 213 for the G7. Second, we use the Gini–Herschman coefficient to measure the concentration of exports. A higher value of this coefficient indicates a higher degree of export concentration. While the average

---

[5] We examine the data of 22 non-oil exporting African countries. Eighteen of these countries are Sub-Saharan African, four of them are Arab States: Burundi, Cape Verde, Egypt, Gambia, Ghana, Guinea Buissea, Kenya, Liberia, Madagascar, Malawi, Mauritania, Mauritius, Morocco, Seychelles, Sierra Lione, Sudan, Swaziland, Tanzania, Tunisia, Zaire, Zambia, and Zimbabwe. Egypt, Seychelles, and Tunisia receive a significant fraction of their export revenues from oil. However, these countries are not major oil exporters. When we considered a sample without these countries and repeated our calibration exercise, we saw that the results reported here were not affected in any significant way. See Kose and Riezman (1999) for a detailed documentation of the statistics reported here.

M.A. Kose, R. Riezman / Journal of Development Economics 65 (2001) 55–80   59

Table 1

(a) Decomposition of GDP (%)

Country	Expenditure shares[a]				Industrial structure[a]		
	Exp.	Imp.	T.V.	T.B.	Agr.	Ind.	Ser.
African							
Mean	30.8	40.4	71.1	−9.6	28.0	18.2	48.5
Median	26.8	34.8	60.8	−7.2	28.8	16.2	48.2
G7							
Mean	19.7	18.3	38.0	1.3	3.7	29.7	60.0
Median	20.3	20.3	40.7	0.7	3.7	28.0	62.0

(b) Decomposition of exports[b] (%)

Country	Food	Agr.	Metals	Prima.	Man.	Cap.	Inter.	Fuels	Total Inter.	Num. Exp.	Concen Index
African											
Mean	47.4	9.7	20.0	77.1	14.4	1.8	12.7	6.9	19.7	54.3	60.1
Median	52.4	4.6	6.9	82.6	9.8	0.9	7.8	1.3	11.4	44.0	64.4
G7											
Mean	8.9	3.2	4.6	16.7	76.8	40.7	36.2	4.5	40.7	213	9.6
Median	7.3	1.6	3.6	12.8	76.9	38.5	39.4	3.5	42.9	216	9.1

(c) Decomposition of imports[b] (%)

Country	Food	Agr.	Metals	Primary	Man.	Cap.	Inter.	Fuels	Total Inter.
African									
Mean	19.3	2.5	1.6	23.4	63.3	27.8	35.5	12.0	47.5
Median	17.8	1.9	1.5	24.7	62.5	26.8	36.6	11.6	48.3
G7									
Mean	12.6	5.3	7.1	25.0	57.1	26.9	30.3	16.4	46.6
Median	13.6	4.6	7.2	25.5	60.0	24.1	30.2	16.1	48.1

[a]Exp. = exports; Imp. = imports; T.V. = (Exp. + Imp.)/GDP; T.B. = (Exp. − Imp.)/GDP; Agr. = agriculture; Ind. = industrial activity (manufacturing + mining and quarrying + electricity + gas + water); Ser. = services. The mean and median values are calculated using the data of 22 non-oil exporting African economies and the G7 countries. For most of the countries in our sample, the data are averages over the years 1970, 1980, and 1990. Source: Handbook of International Trade and Development Statistics (various years).

[b]Agr. = agricultural raw materials; Primary = Food + Agr. + Metals; Man. = manufactured goods; Cap. = capital goods = machinery and equipment; Inter. = intermediate inputs (all manufactured items less machinery); Total Inter. = Inter + Fuels; Number Exp. = number of commodities exported; Concen. Index = export concentration index. The mean and median values are calculated using the data of 22 non-oil exporting African economies and the G7 countries. For most of the countries in our sample, the data are averages over the years 1970, 1980, and 1990. Source: Handbook of International Trade and Development Statistics (various years).

coefficient of export concentration is more than 60 for the African countries, it is less than 10 for the G7.

Table 1c provides information about the decomposition of imports. Two points about this table are noteworthy: First, the main import items of these countries are capital

Table 2
Debt indicators[a] (%)

	ED/GNP	IN/GNP	ED/EXP	TD/EXP	IN/EXP	SH/EXP	SH/ED
Mean	89.0	3.0	379.3	19.9	9.5	42.6	12.3
Median	76.8	2.6	263.0	19.7	8.6	27.5	9.3

[a]GNP = gross national product; ED = total external debt; IN = total interest payments; EXP = exports of goods and services; TD = total debt service; SH = short-term external debt. To get the mean and median values, we use the data of 22 non-oil exporting African economies over the years 1980 and 1990. The source of the data is the World Bank World Debt Tables (various years).

goods and intermediate inputs. While the imports of intermediate inputs account for almost half of the total imports, the average share of capital good imports is approximately 28%. Second, the share of agricultural goods is minor in total imports.

Movements in the cost of servicing external debt also seem to be an important source of macroeconomic fluctuations in several African countries, particularly highly indebted ones.[6] As Table 2 indicates, the average ratio of external debt to GNP is around 89% and the debt service to export ratio, which is a widely used measure of debt burden, is around 20% for the African economies in our sample.

2.2. Dynamics of prices

Since our ultimate objective is to evaluate the effects of trade shocks proxied by relative price fluctuations on macroeconomic dynamics of the African economies, we briefly examine the cyclical features of price series and provide empirical evidence about the relation between these series and macroeconomic fluctuations in these countries. Instead of analyzing the terms of trade dynamics only, we also examine a disaggregated measure of the terms of trade and look at the dynamics of relative prices of capital goods and intermediate inputs to primary goods. Table 3 documents our findings. The relative price of capital goods to primary goods, p_t^k, is calculated as the ratio of the US producer price index of capital equipment to the export price index of the domestic economy. The relative price of intermediate goods, p_t^v, is equal to the ratio of the US producer price index of intermediate materials to the export price index of the domestic economy. The terms of trade is calculated as the ratio of export price index to import price index of each country. Interestingly, the relative prices are more volatile and more persistent than the terms of trade. The relative prices of capital goods (intermediate inputs) to primary commodities are 1.23 (1.11) times more volatile than the terms of trade. The persistence of the terms of trade is 0.22 while the persistence of relative price of capital (intermediate) goods is 0.38 (0.35).

There are two major reasons why relative price series exhibit different cyclical dynamics than the terms of trade. First, as we found in the previous section, African countries heavily rely on a limited number of primary commodities for their export

---

[6] Fosu (1996) finds that the debt burden of Sub-Saharan African countries has a strong adverse impact on the growth performance of these countries using regression estimates.

M.A. Kose, R. Riezman / Journal of Development Economics 65 (2001) 55–80   61

Table 3
Properties of price fluctuations[a]

	Volatility			Persistence		
	σ_{p^k}	σ_{p^v}	σ_{tot}	ρ_{p^k}	ρ_{p^v}	ρ_{tot}
Mean	14.36	12.97	11.67	0.38	0.35	0.22
Median	13.62	11.81	11.36	0.40	0.36	0.26

	Comovement							
	$\rho_{p^k,\text{tb}}$	$\rho_{p^v,\text{tb}}$	$\rho_{\text{tot},\text{tb}}$	$\rho_{p^k,y}$	$\rho_{p^v,y}$	$\rho_{\text{tot},y}$	$\rho_{p^k,\text{tot}}$	$\rho_{p^v,\text{tot}}$
Mean	-0.26	-0.23	0.34	-0.08	-0.05	0.03	-0.67	-0.71
Median	-0.24	-0.28	0.41	-0.06	-0.02	-0.02	-0.70	-0.77

[a] σ_x is the percent standard deviation of the variable x. ρ_x is the first-order serial autocorrelation of the variable x. $\rho_{x,y}$ is the contemporaneous correlation between the variables x and y. p^k = the relative price of the capital goods to export price index; p^v = the relative price of the intermediate inputs to the export price index; tot = terms-of-trade; tb = trade balance; y = aggregate output. The data is logged and filtered using HP(100) filter. To get the mean and median values, we use the data of 22 non-oil exporting African economies.

earnings. Second, African countries' export and import patterns are quite heterogeneous. These two suggest that it is hard to accurately proxy the extent and duration of fluctuations in the prices of main export and import items of these countries with a single price index, like the terms of trade.[7]

3. The model economy

3.1. Preferences

The economy is inhabited by a large number of infinitely lived, identical households.[8] The representative household maximizes expected lifetime utility given by

$$U(c,l) = E_0\left\{\sum_{t=0}^{\infty} \beta^t \frac{[u(c_t,l_t) - 1]}{1 - \sigma}\right\} \qquad \sigma > 0, \beta > 0 \tag{1}$$

where the parameter β denotes the subjective discount factor of the household and σ is the risk aversion parameter. c_t is consumption of the non-traded final good and l_t represents leisure in period t.

We do not consider exported or imported goods as utility deriving goods in the model because of the following reasons: first, the empirical evidence provided in the previous

---

[7] Kouparitsas (1997b) provides extensive evidence that the relative prices are more volatile than the terms of trade and finds that the relative prices of non-fuel commodities to manufactured goods is 1.37 times more volatile than the terms of trade. Bidarkota and Crucini (2000) examine the commodity price fluctuations and find that commodity prices are much more volatile than the terms of trade.

[8] See Kose (1999) for detailed information about the small open economy model presented here.

62			*M.A. Kose, R. Riezman / Journal of Development Economics 65 (2001) 55–80*

section indicates that a significant fraction of exports comes from the primary goods sector in African countries. These exported primary goods are generally used as inputs in producing final goods, so the contribution of these goods to utility is via final goods. Second, recent empirical studies indicate that consumer goods are only a small fraction of the total imports of developing countries.[9]

The instantaneous utility function u has the form

$$u(c_t, l_t) = \left(c_t - \psi(1 - l_t)^v\right)^{1-\sigma} \qquad v > 1, \psi > 0 \tag{2}$$

v governs the intertemporal elasticity of substitution in labor supply, ψ is a parameter used to set the steady state level of labor hours.

3.2. Technology

The economy produces non-traded final goods and primary goods. Non-traded final goods production, y_t^f, uses labor, n_t^f, capital, k_t^f, and intermediate inputs, v_t:

$$y_t^f = z_t^f (n_t^f)^\alpha \left[s(k_t^f)^{-u} + (1-s) v_t^{-u} \right]^{-(1-\alpha)/u} \qquad 0 < \alpha, s, u < 1 \tag{3}$$

z_t^f represents the exogenous productivity shock. α is the share of non-traded output earned by labor and s is the relative weight of capital. The elasticity of substitution between intermediate inputs and capital is governed by u.

The primary goods sector produces output by using labor, n_t^p, capital, k_t^p, and land, L^p, which is assumed to be inelastically supplied. The production function in the primary goods sector is given as

$$y_t^p = z_t^p (n_t^p)^{\theta_1} (k_t^p)^{\theta_2} (L^p)^{1-\theta_1-\theta_2} \qquad 0 < \theta_1, \theta_2 < 1 \tag{4}$$

where z_t^p is the technology shock. θ_1 and θ_2 are the labor and capital income shares, respectively. Our modeling of primary goods production is quite different from earlier small open economy business cycle models: since production of primary goods requires substantial amount of land input in African economies, we introduce land into the primary production. This also reduces the variation of the primary sector output by limiting the substitution effects across different factors. This, in turn, decreases volatility of aggregate output, and helps the model to generate realistic volatility properties.

The production structure in this model also differs from those in earlier models. For example, Mendoza (1995) constructs a small open economy model where capital is perfectly substitutable between exportable and importable goods producing sectors, and domestically produced capital goods in the non-tradable goods sector are inelastically supplied. Since the only endogenous factor in the non-traded sector is labor, terms of trade disturbances have only an indirect effect on the dynamics of that sector in his model. By contrast, in our model, the supply of non-traded capital goods is endogenously determined. Moreover, we do not allow the perfect substitutability of capital

---

[9] See Ahearne (1997) and Hentschel (1992) for evidence suggesting that the share of imported consumption goods in aggregate consumption is quite small in developing countries.

M.A. Kose, R. Riezman / Journal of Development Economics 65 (2001) 55–80 63

across two sectors, as capital is sector specific in our model. In particular, we assume that primary sector capital is imported and capital used in the non-traded goods sector is domestically produced. These features of the model allow us to study the impact of the price shocks on the distribution of imported intermediate inputs and capital goods across two sectors. Further, we are able to examine the impact of different types of price shocks on different types of factors of production.

Capital accumulation is modeled as

$$k_{t+1}^{j} = (1 - \delta)k_{t}^{j} + \phi_{j}\left(\frac{i_{t}^{j}}{k_{t}^{j}}\right)k_{t}^{j} \qquad j = \text{f,p} \tag{5}$$

Here δ is the rate of depreciation, i_t^j is the amount of investment in sector j, and $\phi_j(\cdot)$ represents the concave adjustment cost function, with $\phi_j(\cdot) > 0$, $\phi_j(\cdot)' > 0$, and $\phi_j(\cdot)''$ < 0. Adjustment costs prevent excessive volatility of investment (see Baxter and Crucini, 1993).

The resource constraint for the non-traded goods sector is given by

$$c_t + i_t^{\text{f}} = y_t^{\text{f}} \tag{6}$$

The primary good is numeraire in the resource constraint of the primary good sector which is

$$p_t^k i_t^{\text{p}} + p_t^v v_t + nx_t = y_t^{\text{p}} \tag{7}$$

where nx_t represents the balance of trade. The household, who has a fixed time endowment normalized to one, faces the following labor–leisure allocation constraint

$$l_t + n_t^{\text{f}} + n_t^{\text{p}} = 1 \tag{8}$$

3.3. Financial markets

While each household has free access to world financial markets, these markets are incomplete in the sense that households can trade only a single financial asset, A_t, with a rate of return, r_t, from period t to $t + 1$. This market structure partly captures the fact that a number of African countries maintain a variety of capital controls. The holdings of financial assets evolve according to the formula

$$A_{t+1} = nx_t + A_t(1 + r_t) \tag{9}$$

The possibility of the household playing a Ponzi game is ruled out by imposing the condition:

$$\lim_{t \to \infty} E_0\left(A_t \frac{1}{(1 + r_t)^t}\right) = 0$$

In addition to this, we assume that $\beta = 1/(1 + r^*)$, r^* is the steady state level of interest rate. It is known that when the discount rate is smaller (greater) than the interest rate, the representative household accumulates (decumulates) assets in a deterministic version of this model. In other words, there is no steady state equilibrium in those cases. If the two are equal, the economy is at a steady state equilibrium which is compatible with any level of foreign asset holdings.[10]

3.4. Exogenous shocks and the numerical solution method

There are five shocks in the model: two shocks to the relative prices of imported capital and intermediate goods, a world interest rate shock, and two sectoral productivity shocks. The vector of exogenous shocks is represented by $Z_t = [\ln(p_t^k),\ \ln(p_t^v),\ r_t,\ \ln(z_t^f),\ \ln(z_t^p)]'$. The evolution of Z_t follows a first order Markov process and is given by

$$\ln Z_{t+1} = \Pi \ln Z_t + \varepsilon_{t+1} \tag{10}$$

The vector of innovations is denoted by $\varepsilon_t = [\varepsilon_t^k,\ \varepsilon_t^v,\ \varepsilon_t^r,\ \varepsilon_t^f,\ \varepsilon_t^p]'$ where $\varepsilon_t \sim N(0,\ \Sigma)$.

We solve the optimization problem of the representative household by maximizing the expected lifetime utility, Eq. (1), subject to the constraints (Eqs. (3)–(10)). We find an approximate solution to this problem using the log-linear approximation method of King et al. (1988).

4. Model calibration

4.1. Preferences

The risk aversion parameter, σ, is equal to 2.61 which is the GMM estimate from the panel study of a group of developing economies, some of which are African countries, by Ostry and Reinhart (1992). Prior empirical studies show that the value of the intertemporal elasticity of substitution in labor supply, $1/(\nu - 1)$, is between 0.3 and 3.2 (see Greenwood et al., 1988). We set the value of this parameter at 0.83 to produce reasonably volatile labor supply fluctuations. The value of ψ is selected so that the fraction of hours worked in the steady state is consistent with our assumption about the allocation of labor hours between the market and non-market activities.

As the world real interest rate measure, we use the LIBOR (the London Interbank Offer Rate) deflated by changes in the export unit value index of developing countries. The average world real interest rate, r^*, is found to be 3.5% annually. Since the interest rate is equal the discount rate at the deterministic steady state, the discount factor, β, is equal to 0.97.

4.2. Technology

The relative weight of capital, s, is set at 0.55. At the steady state, the capital goods and intermediate inputs shares are equal to 0.23 and 0.32, respectively. Following

---

[10] Kim and Kose (1999) show that a small open economy model with an endogenous discount factor produces business cycle dynamics that are very similar to those produced by a model with a fixed discount factor. Our formulation is also similar to the one in Correia et al. (1995).

M.A. Kose, R. Riezman / Journal of Development Economics 65 (2001) 55–80 65

Praschnik (1993) we set the share of labor, θ_1, at 0.37. By using sectoral data and the first order condition for primary capital, we find that the share of land, $1 - \theta_1 - \theta_2$, is equal to 0.45. We select the rate of depreciation at 0.10 that is a widely used value in the business cycle literature. The labor share for the non-traded final goods sector, α, is set at 0.45 to be in line with the earlier studies in the literature (see Mendoza, 1995). We choose a value of 0.58 for the Allen elasticity of substitution between capital and intermediate goods. This value is consistent with the estimates provided by Berndt and Wood (1975).

Following Baxter and Crucini (1993), we assume that $\phi(i_f/k_f) = \phi(i_p/k_p) = \delta$ and $\phi'(i_f/k_f) = \phi'(i_p/k_p) = 1$ at the steady state. The elasticity of the marginal adjustment cost function, $\eta = -(\phi'/\phi'')/(i/k)$, for each type of capital, is set so that the volatility of investment generated by the model is equal to that of the data. Since we assume the equality of the interest rate to the discount factor, the steady state value of foreign assets is a free parameter, which is determined by the trade balance to output ratio. This ratio is set at the average trade balance–output ratio in our sample (-0.096). Table 4b presents calibrated parameters of the model.

4.3. Exogenous shocks

4.3.1. Productivity shocks

We estimate the total factor productivity in the non-traded goods sector, z_t^f, using the formula of the Solow residual in logarithms

$$\log(z_t^f) = \log(y_t^f) - \alpha\log(n_t^f)$$

y_t^f is the total real value added of industry and service output. n_t^f is equal to the employment index since data on labor hours is unavailable for most of the countries in our sample. The capital stock and intermediate input usage are excluded from the formula for the following reasons: first, it is known that fluctuations in the capital stock are not large in the short-run. Second, the contemporaneous correlation between capital stock and output is negligible. Third, the data on intermediate input usage is not available. We fit an univariate AR(1) process to find the parameters of the productivity shock for each country and then take an average over the whole sample of these parameters. These averages are assumed to be the relevant parameters for the representative African economy. We use the data of agricultural value added and employment in manufacturing sector to estimate the shock process for the primary sector output. Table 4a presents the resulting specifications for exogenous processes.

4.3.2. Trade shocks

We determine the parameters of the processes of trade shocks by using an univariate AR(1) processes.[11] We do not have any data series or world price indices that are specifically designed for capital goods and intermediate inputs. However, this data is available at the country level. We conjecture that world prices of those goods closely follow the prices of the same goods produced in the US. So, the US producer price

---

[11] See Deaton and Miller (1996) for a similar AR(1) modeling of price series.

Table 4

(a) Exogenous shocks

	Description of the parameter	Value
Π	Persistence of shocks $Z_{t+1} = \Pi Z_t + \varepsilon_{t+1}$ $\varepsilon_t \sim N(0,\Sigma)Z_t = [\ln(p_t^k), \ln(p_t^v), r_t, \ln(z_t^f)], \ln(z_t^p)]'$ Sample standard errors are in parenthesis.	$\begin{bmatrix} 0.44(0.07) & 0 & 0 & 0 & 0 \\ 0 & 0.42(0.08) & 0 & 0 & 0 \\ 0 & 0 & 0.34 & 0 & 0 \\ 0 & 0 & 0 & 0.54(0.24) & 0 \\ 0 & 0 & 0 & 0 & 0.32(0.24) \end{bmatrix}$
Σ	Variance–covariance matrix of innovations. Sample standard errors for shocks estimated using the data of 22 non-oil exporting African countries are in parenthesis. The bold values represent the correlations between the innovations.	$\begin{bmatrix} 0.22^2(0.07)^2 & \mathbf{0.71} & \mathbf{0.35} & \mathbf{0.19} & \mathbf{-0.01} \\ 0.18^2 & 0.21^2(0.07)^2 & \mathbf{0.29} & \mathbf{-0.30} & \mathbf{-0.05} \\ 0.11^2 & 0.10^2 & 0.17^2 & \mathbf{-0.05} & \mathbf{-0.03} \\ -(0.04)^2 & -(0.04)^2 & -(0.02)^2 & 0.03^2(0.01)^2 & \mathbf{0.06} \\ -(0.01)^2 & -(0.02)^2 & -(0.01)^2 & 0.08^2 & 0.04^2(0.03)^2 \end{bmatrix}$

(b) Parameters of the model

Parameter	Description	Value
Preferences		
β	Discount factor	0.97
r	Real interest rate, $r = (1/\beta) - 1$	0.035
$1/(\nu - 1)$	Intertemporal elasticity of substitution in labor supply	0.83
σ	Coefficient of relative risk aversion	2.61
ψ	Level parameter for labor supply	5.35
Technology		
Primary goods sector		
θ_1	Share of labor income	0.37
θ_2	Share of capital income	0.18
η_p	Elasticity of marginal adjustment cost function $\eta_p = -(\phi'/\phi'')/(i_p/k_p)$	2.2
Final goods sector		
α	Share of labor income	0.45
s_k	Share of capital income	0.23
s_v	Share of intermediate input income	0.32
$1/(u + 1)$	Elasticity of substitution between intermediate and capital goods	0.77
$\sigma_{k,y}$	Allen elasticity of substitution between intermediate and capital goods	0.55
δ	Depreciation rate	0.10
$tb/(y^p + y^f)$	Trade balance to aggregate output ratio	-0.096
η_f	Elasticity of marginal adjustment cost function $\eta_f = -(\phi'/\phi'')/(i_f/k_f)$	2

See Section 4 for details about the calibration of the model.

indices of capital equipment and intermediate goods are used to represent the prices of imported capital and intermediate goods, respectively. The price series of primary commodities correspond to the export unit values of each country. This assumption is easily justified because a significant fraction of exports in African countries are primary commodities. The relative price of capital goods (intermediate inputs) to primary commodities is the ratio of the US producer price index of capital equipment (intermediate inputs) to the export unit value index for each economy. In order to estimate the world real interest rate, we use the 6-month LIBOR (the London Interbank Offer Rate) deflated by changes in the export unit value index of African countries. Table 4a presents the resulting specifications for exogenous processes.

5. Results

5.1. How successful is the model?

While it is not our primary objective to examine the ability of our model in terms of matching the main characteristics of macroeconomic fluctuations in African economies, we still think that this is an useful exercise since our model economy is the first one in its class designed to study economic dynamics of African countries. We present the major stylized features of macroeconomic fluctuations in these countries along with those of the model economy in Table 5a. All properties of the data refer to moments of Hodrick–Prescott (HP(100)) filtered variables (see Hodrick and Prescott, 1997). We consider the two main features of macroeconomic fluctuations: volatility, measured by standard deviation, and comovement, measured by correlations.

Columns 2, 3, and 4 reveal the following stylized features of business cycles in African countries: first, the volatility of output in the primary goods sector is roughly two times larger than that of aggregate output. Second, the volatility of consumption is two times greater than that of aggregate output since our consumption series includes durable goods, and African economies do not have well functioning financial markets that can create consumption smoothing opportunities. Third, while investment exhibits high cyclical volatility, the trade balance is the most volatile aggregate. Fourth, except for the trade balance, all macro aggregates are procyclical.[12]

We simulate our model with the specification described in the previous section. Each statistic we report is the sample average of across 1000 simulations of the same length as the data (23 years). The simulated data is also detrended with the HP(100) filter. In terms of matching volatility properties of macro aggregates, the model is quite successful as columns 5, 6, and 7 show: qualitatively, it replicates most of the features of actual data. Both trade balance and investment are more volatile than aggregate output. The model also captures the volatility ordering of outputs of production sectors: the primary sector output has the largest variability, and aggregate output is the least volatile series. From a quantitative perspective, the model is able to reproduce some of the stylized

---

[12] Kose and Riezman (1999) present a detailed examination of the features of macroeconomic fluctuations in African countries.

M.A. Kose, R. Riezman / Journal of Development Economics 65 (2001) 55–80   69

Table 5

(a) Business cycle properties

Variable	African average[a]			Model[*]		
	Volatility	Relative volatility	Comovement	Volatility	Relative volatility	Comovement
Output	4.10 (1.41)	1.00	1.00	4.93 (0.03)	1.00	1.00
Primary	7.99 (3.57)	1.95	0.51 (0.36)	6.20 (0.03)	1.26	0.57 (0.01)
Non-traded final	4.83 (1.53)	1.18	0.62 (0.33)	5.32 (0.03)	1.08	0.98 (0.00)
Consumption	8.28 (3.80)	2.02	0.39 (0.43)	4.98 (0.03)	1.01	0.77 (0.00)
Investment	15.69 (4.52)	3.83	0.46 (0.26)	15.69 (0.09)	3.18	0.69 (0.00)
Labor Hours	7.33 (4.48)	1.79	0.22 (0.45)	3.40 (0.02)	0.69	0.99 (0.00)
Trade Balance	16.45 (6.15)	4.01	−0.10 (0.30)	19.81 (0.11)	4.02	−0.72 (0.01)

(b) Business cycle properties[b] (model)

Variable	With productivity shocks		With trade shocks	
	Volatility	Comovement	Volatility	Comovement
Output	4.46 (0.03)	1.00	1.18 (0.01)	1.00
Primary	5.54 (0.03)	0.45 (0.01)	2.58 (0.02)	0.95 (0.00)
Non-traded final	4.97 (0.03)	0.97 (0.00)	0.93 (0.01)	0.98 (0.00)
Consumption	2.08 (0.01)	0.99 (0.00)	3.95 (0.02)	0.86 (0.00)
Investment	5.46 (0.03)	0.97 (0.00)	13.23 (0.07)	0.78 (0.00)
Labor hours	1.42 (0.01)	0.99 (0.00)	2.70 (0.01)	0.99 (0.00)
Trade balance	12.54 (0.07)	−0.66 (0.00)	14.04 (0.08)	−0.85 (0.00)

[a]Average moments of African country sample are averages over the moments of 22 countries. The data is in terms of real domestic prices, constructed for per capita quantities, logged and filtered using HP(100) filter. Trade balance refers to detrended exports minus detrended imports. Volatility is the percentage deviation from the HP trend. Relative volatility is the standard deviation of the respective variable relative to the standard deviation of the output. Comovement is the contemporenous correlation with the output. The sample standard errors of the averages are given in parenthesis. The data, for the period 1970–1992, is from the World Bank World Tables (1994). All model moments are averages over the 1000 simulations of the model each with 23 observations. The simulated data is also filtered by HP(100). The asymptotic standard deviations of the statistics are given in parenthesis. See text for details.

[b]See text for details.

facts. For example, it is able to mimic volatilities of sectoral outputs and aggregate output with a small margin. The predicted standard deviation of the trade balance is slightly higher than the actual one. We set the relevant elasticities of adjustment costs so the model can exactly replicate the volatility of investment.

The volatilities of consumption and employment relative to output are seemingly low in the model economy. This result should not be interpreted as a weakness of the model: first, the only available data on consumption in African countries, which we have access to, includes both non-durable and durable consumption expenditures. Unlike the data, our model does not take into account durability. It is widely known that the volatility of durable goods consumption is two to four times higher than that of non-durable consumption. Second, the labor supply variation in the model is captured only along the intensive margin. Conversely, we have employment data which measures the labor supply fluctuations only along the extensive margin. Earlier empirical studies indicate that the volatility of employment is two to three times higher than that of labor hours. Interestingly, the prediction of the model concerning employment fluctuations is also consistent with this empirical regularity.

We next evaluate the performance of the model in replicating comovement properties of the data. While quite closely matching the correlation between the primary sector output and aggregate output, the model overpredicts the aggregate output–final sector output correlation. The correlations between consumption and output, and between investment and output in the model are higher than those in the data. The output–labor hours correlation in the model is higher than the output–employment correlation in the data. Our preference formulation implies that the marginal rate of substitution between consumption and leisure depends only on labor supply inducing perfectly procyclical labor hours. One of the important features of the model economy is its ability to generate countercyclical behavior of the trade balance series. Interestingly, compared with the actual data, there is a relatively high negative correlation between the trade balance and aggregate output in the model. This result might be due to the coexistence of productivity and trade shocks that together generate prolonged trade deficits in the model. We further investigate this possibility in Section 5.4.

5.2. Variance decompositions

We apply the variance decomposition method, which is widely used in the vector autoregression literature, on the solution of the model to determine the relative importance of shocks in explaining economic fluctuations.[13] This method requires us to impose a certain information ordering on the shocks because the relative contribution of each disturbance to macroeconomic fluctuations is sensitive to its place in the shock specification. Since our model represents a small open economy, there is a natural ordering of shocks. By construction, the small open economy does not have any control over the external shocks it faces in the world markets. This implies that domestic shocks do not have any impact on the external shocks, i.e. the external shocks precede sectoral productivity shocks in our specification.

The results of the variance decompositions, which are obtained by using the information ordering in Eq. (10), are reported in Table 6. Strikingly, a significant fraction of macroeconomic fluctuations is explained by trade shocks. They account for roughly 45% of the variation in aggregate output. Our results indicate that shocks to the relative price of capital goods to primary goods play a more important role than shocks to the relative price of intermediate inputs. While almost 25% of variability in aggregate output is due to the changes in relative prices of capital goods, less than 20% of the

---

[13] In a multi-shock model, measuring the contribution of a single shock to business cycle fluctuations is difficult because the shocks are correlated with each other. Mendoza (1995) employs the standard "variance-ratio" approach, which examines each shock in isolation from the other shocks. Some recent papers (see Ingram et al., 1994; Cochrane, 1994) argue that the standard approach can yield misleading inferences about the relative importance of shocks. Our approach does not suffer from the problems of the standard variance ratio method.

M.A. Kose, R. Riezman / Journal of Development Economics 65 (2001) 55–80 71

Table 6
Variance decomposition[a] (%)

Variable	Trade shocks			World interest rate	Technology shocks		
	Capital Goods	Intermediate Inputs	Total		Final Goods	Primary Goods	Total
Output	24.72	19.92	44.64	0.87	52.77	1.71	54.49
Primary	37.94	15.77	53.71	2.15	9.44	34.70	44.15
Final	24.05	21.59	45.64	1.69	51.41	1.27	52.67
Consumption	43.6	35.54	79.14	2.89	15.77	2.20	17.97
Intermediate goods	49.78	42.42	92.20	1.83	4.48	1.48	5.96
Investment	52.77	33.59	86.36	0.46	12.81	0.37	13.17
Primary	98.7	0.7	99.40	0.15	0.32	0.12	0.44
Final	42.34	40.78	83.12	0.8	15.45	0.64	16.09
Labor hours	42.8	37.97	80.77	1.41	16.56	1.26	17.82
Primary	42.53	29.47	72.00	3.11	14.98	9.91	24.89
Final	43.44	35.79	79.23	3.22	14.91	2.64	17.55
Trade balance	41.18	32.54	73.72	4.57	12.87	8.84	21.71
Asset holdings	45.77	30.50	76.27	5.84	13.36	4.52	17.88

[a]The ordering of shocks is p_t^k, p_t^v, r_t, z_t^f, z_t^p, so world price shocks drive the domestic technology shocks. In each cell, the volatility of the respective variable explained by a particular shock is reported. For example, shocks to the prices of capital goods explain 24.72 percent of the output volatility.

fluctuations is due to the disturbances to relative prices of intermediate inputs. The domestic productivity disturbances also play an important role in driving economic activity: roughly 55% of the output variation is due to productivity disturbances. Interestingly, most of the variation explained by the productivity shocks is due to the domestic productivity movements in the final goods sector.

In our model, trade shocks have a direct impact on output fluctuations, since both sectors of the economy use imported goods as factors of production. A significant fraction of the macroeconomic volatility in the final goods producing sector, that heavily relies on imported intermediate inputs and domestic capital goods, is explained by the trade shocks. Roughly 46% of the output variation in the non-traded final goods producing sector is due to the trade shocks. Interestingly, trade disturbances play a more important role in explaining consumption fluctuations than they do in output variation: almost 80% of the variation in consumption is due to the trade shocks.

Our results also show that trade shocks have a large impact on macroeconomic fluctuations in factors of production: more than 86% of the volatility of aggregate investment is explained by trade disturbances. In particular, shocks to the relative prices of primary capital goods account for more than 98% of the variation in primary investment. This result can be explained by the fact that all investment goods in the primary good producing sector are imported capital goods. More than 42% of the variation in intermediate inputs is explained by the disturbances to the relative prices of intermediate goods. Shocks to the prices of capital goods and intermediate inputs also play an important role in inducing fluctuations in the labor market. Movements in the relative prices of capital goods (intermediate inputs) account for more than 42 (37)% of the variation in the total labor hours.

Trade balance dynamics and foreign asset holdings are also heavily affected by the price fluctuations in the world markets. This is an intuitively appealing result as it establishes the connection between highly volatile price shocks and trade balance dynamics: almost 74% of the fluctuations in the trade balance is accounted for by the trade shocks. Shocks to the relative prices of capital goods explain more than 45% of the volatility in the foreign asset holdings.

Deaton and Miller (1996) analyze the importance of international commodity prices in driving economic fluctuations in African countries using vector autoregression analysis. Their results suggest that while a sudden 10% increase in commodity prices results in a 6% increase in output, the price shocks most heavily affect investment dynamics in African economies. Hoffmaister et al. (1998) estimate a structural VAR model, where identifying restrictions are derived from a long-run small open economy model. They consider terms of trade, world output, domestic supply, fiscal policy, and nominal policy shocks. Their results suggest that terms of trade shocks play only a minor role in accounting for aggregate output fluctuations.

Mendoza (1995) uses a similar model to the one presented here and finds that terms of trade shocks explain roughly one half of the output volatility in developing countries. Our results regarding the link between trade shocks and price fluctuations are in line with those in Mendoza (1995) and Deaton and Miller (1996). However, these studies do not consider the importance of price shocks in inducing business cycles in different sectors and factors of production. One important contribution of this study is that it examines the impact of different types of price shocks on cyclical fluctuations in different sectors and different types of factors of production. In particular, our results show the substantial role played by these shocks in generating economic fluctuations in traded and non-traded sectors of the economy and all factors of production. For example, our findings suggest that changes in the relative prices directly affect the dynamics in the non-traded good sector, because the non-traded sector employs imported intermediate inputs. In particular, we find that roughly 46% of the output variation in the non-traded final goods producing sector is due to the trade shocks. Our findings also emphasize the importance of studying the impact of the fluctuations in the prices of the major export and import goods.

Interestingly, we find that world real interest rate shocks do not play a significant role in driving domestic economic activity in our model.[14] For example, they account for less than 1% of the output volatility. These shocks have a relatively more important role in driving the dynamics of asset holdings, but their influence is still very small compared to the role of other shocks: less than 6% of the variation in foreign asset holdings is explained by interest rate disturbances.

We consider four possible reasons why world real interest rate shocks play only a minor role in inducing macroeconomic fluctuations: first, we study a highly stylized

---

[14] This result is consistent with the findings in Mendoza (1991) and Correia et al. (1995). The former considers the importance of the world interest rate shocks in a one-sector small open economy model calibrated to represent Canada, the latter one examines the same issue in a similar model calibrated to represent Portugal.

M.A. Kose, R. Riezman / Journal of Development Economics 65 (2001) 55–80 73

incomplete asset market structure in our model. A more complex asset market construction, which includes borrowing constraints, might lead to different results. Second, our interest rate data suggests that there are only a few large interest rate changes over the time period we consider.[15] Capturing the effects of those large and short-lived interest rate fluctuations on economic activity might require the use of different techniques.[16] Third, since our sample size is quite small, it might be the case that the persistence coefficient of the world real interest rate shock we estimate is biased downwards. This, in turn, might reduce the effect of these shocks in generating business cycles.[17] Fourth, and probably the most important, it might be the case that since the ratio of foreign interest rate payments to output is not sufficiently large in our benchmark calibration, world real interest rate shocks unable to generate strong enough income and substitution effects to have a sizeable impact on economic fluctuations (see Mendoza, 1991). In Section 5.3 we study the last two possibilities and show that as the steady state trade deficit–output ratio gets larger world real interest rate shocks become more important in driving macroeconomic activity in African countries.

5.3. The dynamic effects of shocks

We study the dynamic effects of trade and productivity shocks by using impulse response analysis. We analyze the impulse responses of model variables to a 1% temporary shock. The results, presented in Figs. 1 and 2, are plotted as percentage deviations from the initial steady state.

We present the impulse responses of model variables to a temporary 1% increase in productivity of both sectors in Fig. 1. A sudden increase in productivity results in an economy-wide boom: output increases in both sectors. This causes a rise in demand for imported capital goods, intermediate inputs and labor supply. Since the increase in exports (primary goods) is less than the rise in imports (the sum of the imported investment and intermediate goods), the economy has a substantial trade deficit. The representative household increases its consumption. Qualitatively, the sectoral productivity shocks lead to more pronounced effects in investment and trade balance compared to those in output and consumption.

Fig. 2 shows the time paths of model variables in response to a 1% temporary increase in the relative price of capital goods and intermediate inputs. This type of adverse price shock pushes the economy into a recession. Investment in primary goods sector sharply drops; however this decrease does not lead to a significant decline in aggregate investment since the share of primary investment in the aggregate investment is relatively small since the decrease in imports is larger than that in exports.

Our results suggest that the magnitudes of labor supply responses in the traded and non-traded sectors of a typical African economy are comparable with those of the other

---

[15] Kose and Riezman (1999) provide an extensive analysis of the interest rate data.

[16] See Blankenau et al. (1999) for a methodology, which allows backing out world real interest rate shocks in a small open economy model. They show that interest rate shocks, which are perfectly consistent with the time series of major macroeconomic variables, are able to account for a significant fraction of output fluctuations.

[17] We would like to thank the referee for suggesting this exercise.

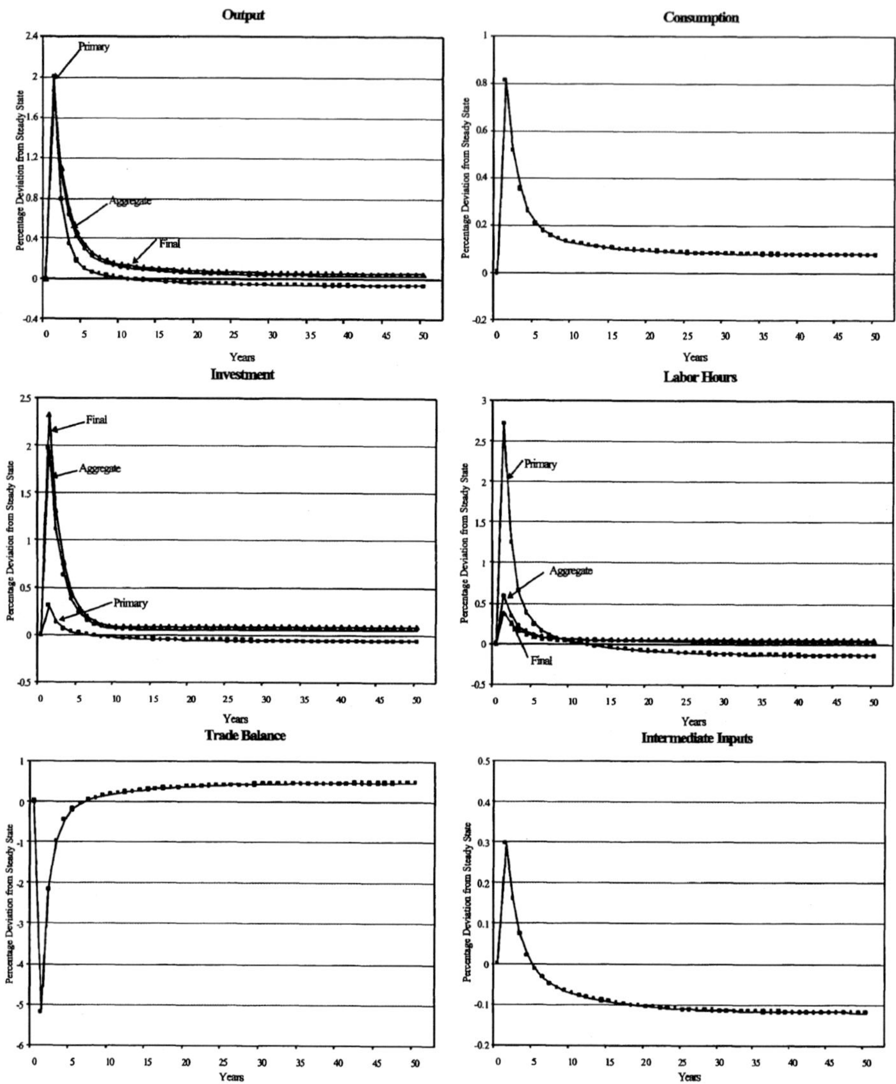

Fig. 1. Impulse response of a 1% shock to the productivity of both sectors.

variables when the model is subjected to domestic productivity and international trade shocks: in response to a 1% temporary productivity shock in the primary sector, there is a considerable increase in the labor supply in that sector, a decrease of labor supply in the non-traded goods sector, and an increase in the aggregate labor supply. Correspondingly, primary sector output increases and the production in non-traded final goods sector slightly decreases due to a shortage of productive inputs.

The overall effect of trade shocks in our model is the opposite of that of domestic productivity shocks since trade shocks act like negative productivity shocks. While

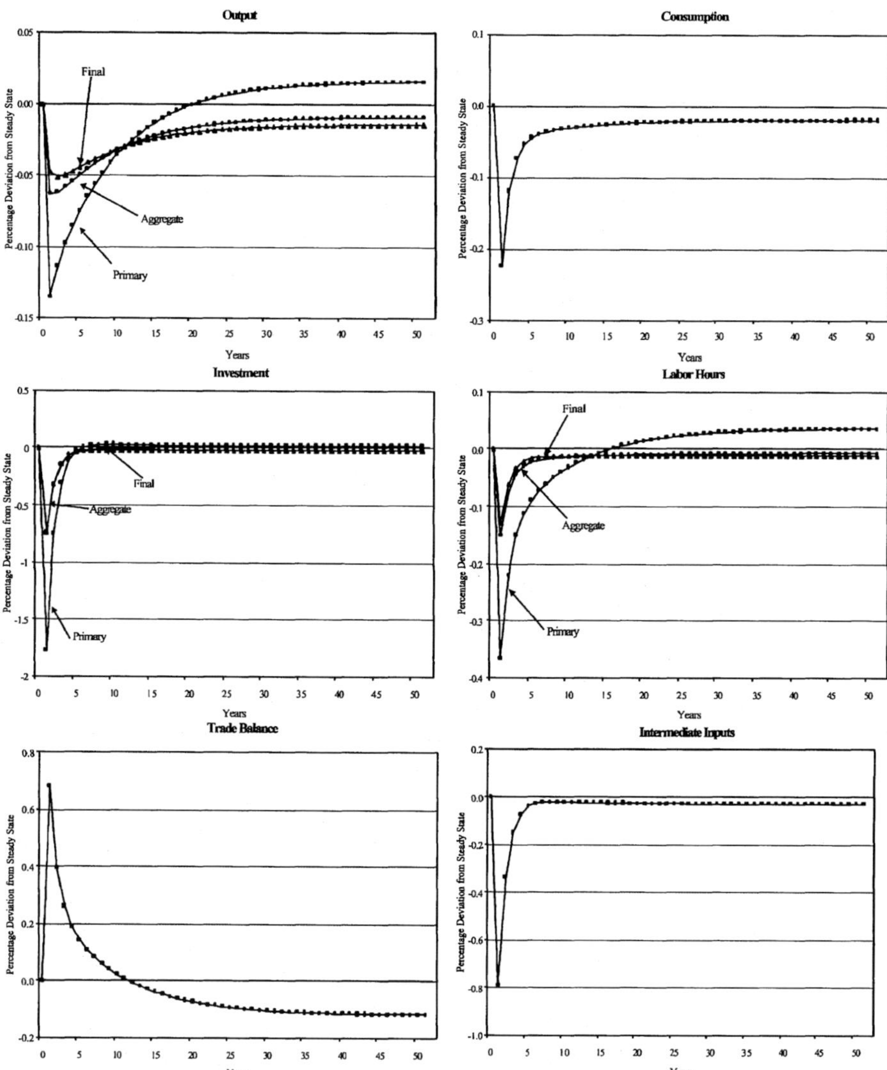

Fig. 2. Impulse response of a 1% shock to the prices of imported inputs.

positive productivity shocks stimulate the economy and result in short lived expansions, negative trade disturbances have adverse implications: they cause negative income effects which are accompanied by a fall in consumption, and a contraction in demand for productive inputs. Furthermore, trade shocks lead to prolonged recessions by having a detrimental impact on aggregate investment: in response to a positive productivity shock, aggregate output reaches its steady state level after 15 periods, in other words, the economic expansion generated by the improvement in domestic productivity lasts 15 periods. After receiving a negative shock to the relative price of intermediate inputs

76   *M.A. Kose, R. Riezman / Journal of Development Economics 65 (2001) 55–80*

(capital goods), it takes 25 (35) periods to attain the steady state level of aggregate output for the model economy.[18]

5.4. Sensitivity analysis

In this section, we first analyze the individual roles of productivity and trade shocks in our model. In Table 5b, the results of a simulation when only productivity shocks are present are reported. The model is not able to match the volatilities of aggregate output and its components. It underpredicts the volatility of primary sector output. It matches neither the variation of aggregate output nor the one of final sector output. Further, the model is not able to successfully replicate consumption, investment and labor dynamics when the trade shocks are absent. We then simulate the model with only trade shocks. The results of this experiment are also given in Table 5b. The model is not able to match the volatilities of aggregate output and its components. However, it does a better job in terms of capturing the volatility of consumption, investment, labor hours, and the trade balance. When the model is simulated with only trade (productivity) shocks, it predicts that the correlation between the trade balance and output is around -0.85 (-0.66). This suggests that both trade shocks and productivity shocks are responsible for the relatively high negative correlation between the two variables.

We briefly investigate the sensitivity of our results to the changes in the following parameters of the model: the elasticity of substitution in intermediate and capital goods, the intertemporal elasticity of substitution in labor supply, the risk aversion parameter, share of land in the primary sector, and the elasticity of marginal adjustment cost. When the elasticity of substitution in intermediate and capital goods increases, the volatility of the trade balance goes down and the other variables exhibit slightly larger variability. This result can be explained with the following intuition: the representative household uses international markets less often to buy intermediate inputs, and faces less fluctuations in the trade balance. The variability of other macro aggregates slightly increases, since the representative household substitutes domestic capital into imported intermediate inputs more often. Changes in the relative weight of capital, s, have also similar effects on the moments of model variables.

The other two parameters, ν and σ, do not play important roles in the dynamics of the model. An increase in ν causes a minor decrease in the variability of labor hours. The volatility of the trade balance decreases in response to an increase in the risk aversion parameter, σ. Inelastically supplied land limits substitution effects across factors of production in the primary goods sector. This dampens the impact of these factors of production on output and allows the model to produce realistic volatility properties. When the share of land, $1 - \theta_1 - \theta_2$, decreases, the model exaggerates the volatility of macroeconomic aggregates. Changes in the elasticity of marginal adjustment

---

[18] The impulse responses of a 1% temporary increase in the world interest rate are not presented here because of the space considerations. This shock does not generate significant movements in the model variables except the trade balance and foreign asset holdings.

Table 7
Sensitivity analysis variance decomposition of output[a] (%)

Change	Trade shocks			World interest rate	Technology shocks		
	Capital goods	Intermediate inputs	Total		Final goods	Primary goods	Total
Benchmark	24.72	19.92	44.64	0.87	52.77	1.71	54.49
Volatility of interest rate shocks ↑ 20%	24.36	19.88	44.24	1.23	52.82	1.71	54.54
Persistence of interest rate shocks ↑ 20%	24.53	19.89	44.42	1.07	52.79	1.71	54.50
Persistence of interest rate shocks ↑ 100%	22.86	19.48	42.34	3.66	52.3	1.70	54.00
Trade balance/Output = −51%	5.02	9.87	14.89	51.80	31.56	1.74	33.37
Trade balance/Output = 0.03%	27.02	19.33	46.35	0.10	51.03	2.51	53.54
$(1 - \theta_1 - \theta_2)$ ↓ 45% (share of land)	33.95	16.52	50.47	0.37	47.48	1.68	49.16

[a]See the notes in Table 6. ↑ sign refers to an increase. For example, in the fifth row volatility of interest rate shocks increases by 20%.

78   *M.A. Kose, R. Riezman / Journal of Development Economics 65 (2001) 55–80*

cost affects the volatility properties of model variables as higher elasticity values result in higher volatility of investment.

We also examine the sensitivity of our variance decompositions to changes in some of the parameters of the model and stochastic processes. Table 7 provides the results of some of our sensitivity experiments. We find that an increase in the volatility or persistence of productivity (trade) shocks, increases the importance of productivity (trade) shocks in explaining output variation. An increase in the elasticity of marginal adjustment cost has almost no impact. However, a decrease in the share of land increases the importance of relative price shocks of capital goods as imported primary capital goods and labor become more important in the production process.

We examine the impact of interest rate shocks by considering two different experiments: first, we study whether the changes in the persistence and volatility of interest rate shocks result in any changes. When the volatility of interest rate shocks is raised by 20%, the fraction of output volatility explained by these shocks rises from 0.9% to 1.3%. Increasing the persistence terms does not induce any major change either. For example, increasing the autocorrelation coefficient of the interest rate shocks by 100% causes the share of output fluctuations accounted by these shocks go up from 0.9% to 3.7%. Second, we examine whether changes in the trade balance output ratio affect the results. In particular, we run an experiment in which the trade deficit output ratio is equal to the largest one in our data set (-51%, Cape Verde). This makes world interest rate shocks quite important as they now explain 52% of output variation. When the trade deficit output ratio is equal to the smallest value in our sample (-0.3%, Zimbabwe), interest rate shocks account for only 0.1% of output volatility. In other words, as the ratio of foreign interest rate payments to output increases, world real interest rate shocks account for a much larger output variation by generating stronger income and substitution effects.

6. Conclusion

We examine the effects of trade shocks, namely fluctuations in the relative prices of capital goods to primary goods, and relative prices of intermediate goods to primary goods, on macroeconomic fluctuations in African countries using a dynamic, stochastic, multi-sector, small, open economy model. Our model is able to replicate volatility and comovement properties of sectoral outputs in African countries. Our estimations suggest that trade shocks have a significant role in driving macroeconomic fluctuations in African economies. In particular, more than 44% of the economic fluctuations in aggregate output is explained by trade shocks. More importantly, these shocks play a very important role in inducing business cycles in factors of production as they account for more than 86% of investment and 80% of labor supply fluctuations. While the world interest rate shocks have a minor effect on economic dynamics in our benchmark experiments, we find that these shocks are quite important in those economies that have to allocate a significant fraction of their export revenues to foreign debt payments.

As our model is the first dynamic model capturing main structural characteristics of these economies, we have not dealt with those issues associated with complex trade

M.A. Kose, R. Riezman / Journal of Development Economics 65 (2001) 55–80 79

policies, well documented market rigidities, and political economy considerations which are important aspects of African countries. Extensions of this model along these dimensions are important steps to be taken in future research.

Acknowledgements

We would like to thank an anonymous referee whose suggestions significantly improved the paper. We are grateful to David Bevan, Ahmed El-Softy, Simon Evenett, Jan Gunning, David Richardson, Linda Tesar, Kei-Mu Yi, and Kamil Yilmaz for their helpful comments. We also benefited from the suggestions of seminar participants at the University of Connecticut, Center for the Study of Globalization and Regionalization at the University of Warwick, 1998 Fall Midwest International Economics Conference at the University of Michigan, and 1999 Eastern Economic Association Conference in Boston. The usual disclaimer applies.

References

Ahearne, A.G., 1997. Trade liberalization and capital accumulation in developing economies. Working Paper, Carnegie Mellon University.

Basu, P., McLeod, D., 1992. Terms of trade fluctuations and economic growth in developing countries. Journal of Development Economics 37, 89–110.

Baxter, M., 1995. International trade and business cycles. In: Grossman, G., Rogoff, K. (Eds.), Handbook of International Economics, vol. 3, North Holland, Amsterdam, pp. 1801–1864.

Baxter, M., Crucini, M., 1993. Explaining saving-investment correlations. American Economic Review 83, 416–436.

Berndt, E.R., Wood, D.O., 1975. Technology, prices, and the derived demand for energy. Review of Economics and Statistics 57, 259–268.

Bevan, D., Collier, P., Gunning, J.W., 1994. Controlled Open Economies. Clarendon Press, Oxford.

Bidarkota, P.V., Crucini, M.J., 2000. Commodity prices and the terms of trade. Review of International Economics 8, 647–666.

Blankenau, W., Kose, M.A., Yi, K., 1999. Can world real interest rates explain business cycles in a small open economy? Journal of Economic Dynamics and Control, in press.

Cochrane, J.H., 1994. Shocks. Carnegie Rochester Conference Series on Public Policy 41, 295–364.

Collier, P., Gunning, J.W., 1999. Explaining African economic performance. Journal of Economic Literature 37, 64–111.

Correia, I., Neves, J.C., Rebelo, S., 1995. Business cycles in a small open economy. European Economic Review 39, 1089–1113.

Deaton, A., Miller, R., 1996. International commodity prices, macroeconomic performance and politics in Sub-Saharan Africa. Journal of African Economies 5, 99–191, Supplement.

Feder, G., 1983. On exports and economic growth. Journal of Development Economics 12, 195–218.

Fosu, A.K., 1996. The impact of external debt on economic growth in Sub-Saharan Africa. Journal of Economic Development 21, 93–118.

Greenwood, J., Hercowitz, Z., Huffman, G., 1988. Investment, capacity utilization and the real business cycle. American Economic Review 78, 402–416.

Hentschel, J., 1992. Imports and Growth in Highly Indebted Countries. Springer-Verlag, Heidelberg.

Hodrick, R.J., Prescott, E., 1997. Postwar US business cycles: an empirical investigation. Journal of Money Credit and Banking 19, 1–16.

Hoffmaister, A.W., Roldos, J.E., Wickham, P., 1998. Macroeconomic fluctuations in Sub-Saharan Africa. International Monetary Fund Staff Papers 45, 132–161.

Ingram, B., Kocherlakota, N., Savin, N.E., 1994. Explaining business cycles: a multiple shock approach. Journal of Monetary Economics 34, 415–428.

Kim, H., Kose, M.A., 1999. Dynamics of Open Economy Business Cycle Models. Working Paper. Brandeis University.

King, R.G., Plosser, C., Rebelo, S., 1988. Production, growth and business cycles: I. The basic neoclassical model. Journal of Monetary Economics 21, 195–232.

Kose, M.A., 1999. Explaining business cycles in small open economies. Working Paper. Brandeis University.

Kose, M.A., Riezman, R., 1999. Trade Shocks and Macroeconomic Fluctuations in Africa. Working Paper. Brandeis University.

Kouparitsas, M., 1997. North–South business cycles. Working Paper. Federal Reserve Bank of Chicago.

Kouparitsas, M., 1997. North–South terms-of-trade: an empirical investigation. Working Paper. Federal Reserve Bank of Chicago.

Mendoza, E.G., 1991. Real business cycles in a small open economy. American Economic Review 81, 797–889.

Mendoza, E.G., 1995. The terms of trade, the real exchange rate, and economic fluctuations. International Economic Review 36, 101–137.

Ostry, J.D., Reinhart, C., 1992. Private saving and terms of trade shocks. International Monetary Fund Staff Papers 39, 495–517.

Praschnik, J., 1993. The importance of input price shocks for business cycles in developing economies. Working Paper, University of Western Ontario.

Ramey, G., Ramey, V.A., 1995. Cross-country evidence on the link between volatility and growth. American Economic Review 85, 1138–1151.

Rodrik, D., 1998. Trade policy and economic performance in Sub-Saharan Africa. NBER Working Paper Series No. 6562.

Sachs, J.D., Warner, M., 1996. Sources of slow growth in African economies. Journal of African Economies 5, 335–376, Supplement.

Journal of International Economics 73 (2007) 421–433

Journal of INTERNATIONAL ECONOMICS

www.elsevier.com/locate/econbase

Trade and the distribution of human capital [☆]

Spiros Bougheas [a,1], Raymond Riezman [b,*]

[a] *School of Economics, University Park, University of Nottingham, NG7 2RD, Nottingham, UK*
[b] *Department of Economics, W360, PBAB, University of Iowa, Iowa City, Iowa 52242, USA*

Received 27 October 2005; received in revised form 30 June 2006; accepted 28 March 2007

Abstract

We develop a two-country, two-sector model of trade where the only difference between the two countries is their distribution of human capital endowments. We show that even if the two countries have identical aggregate human capital endowments the pattern of trade depends on the properties of the two human capital distributions. We also show that the two distributions of endowments also completely determine the effects of trade on income inequality. We also look at a simple majority voting model. It turns out autarky and free trade with and without compensation may be the voting outcome.
© 2007 Elsevier B.V. All rights reserved.

Keywords: Patterns of trade; Income distribution; Welfare; Political economy

JEL classification: F_1

1. Introduction

The impact of trade on income inequality has been a topic widely discussed in both academic and policy forums. What has triggered interest in this topic is a growing concern among industrialized nations about their ability to sustain high standards of wellbeing in the face of competition from low wage countries. These issues have been addressed theoretically by models

[☆] We would like to thank Rick Bond, Indraneel Dasgupta, Carl Davidson, Rod Falvey, Udo Kreickemeier, Steve Matusz, Doug Nelson, seminar participants at the Midwest International Economics Group meeting, the Kobe COE Conference on International Trade, the COE/RES Workshop on International Trade and Investment at Hitotsubashi University, Michigan State University, the SAET meetings in Vigo, Spain and the University of Nottingham for helpful comments. Financial support from the Leverhulme Trust (Programme Grant F114/BF) is gratefully acknowledged.

* Corresponding author.
E-mail address: raymond-riezman@uiowa.edu (R. Riezman).
[1] Tel.: +44 115 8466108.

0022-1996/$ - see front matter © 2007 Elsevier B.V. All rights reserved.
doi:10.1016/j.jinteco.2007.03.002

422 *S. Bougheas, R. Riezman / Journal of International Economics 73 (2007) 421–433*

in which trade occurs because of differences in technologies and endowments.[2] However, it has also been noted that a large volume of international trade takes place between rich countries and they have similar technologies and endowments.[3]

In order to address these issues in a way that accounts for these facts we develop a two-country, two-sector model of trade where the only difference between the two countries is in their *distribution* of human capital endowments.[4] Their technological capabilities and the preferences of their consumers are identical.[5] In each country there is a primary sector where output is produced using labor and a high-tech sector that uses human capital as its input. We will demonstrate that even if the two countries have identical aggregate human capital endowments they will trade with the patterns of trade depending on the properties of the two human capital distributions.[6]

We will also show that together, the two distributions of endowments also completely determine the effects of trade on income inequality. More specifically, we will find that inequality always rises in the country that exports the high-tech product and declines in the country that exports the primary commodity.

Next, we explore the welfare implications of our model. We compare total welfare under autarky with the corresponding welfare under free trade and find that, unless the marginal utility of income is constant, there exist free-trade equilibria that are welfare reducing. If we allow income redistribution, then there are always long-term gains from trade for each member of society as long as losers are compensated.[7]

Finally, we ask what outcome would emerge in a simple majority voting framework. We find that in the absence of redistribution, autarky or free trade could be the equilibrium choice of a majority of the population. There is also an equilibrium in which free trade is chosen but overall welfare declines. In that case, free trade is preferred by the majority but the losses of the losers outweigh the gains of the winners.

If, in addition to voting on free trade, we also allow voters to vote on whether there should be income redistribution that ensures no member of society loses from trade, then autarky can never be an equilibrium. However, there still is an equilibrium in which free trade is chosen, redistribution fails to be approved and overall welfare declines. We begin by developing the model.

---

[2] Both the theoretical and empirical literatures are extensive and have recently been reviewed by Feenstra and Hanson (2001).

[3] See Brander (1981), Davis (1995), Grossman and Maggi (2000) and Krugman (1979) for theoretical attempts to account for this observation.

[4] We consider differences in both means (aggregate endowments) and variances.

[5] Yeaple (2005) has a model in which worker heterogeneity, technology differences and trade costs jointly determine firm heterogeneity.

[6] Bond (1986) considered a trade model where firm heterogeneity arises because of variations in entrepreneurial ability. He analyzed the relationship between factor intensities, factor returns and patterns of trade, however, he kept the distribution of ability fixed throughout the paper. To our knowledge, Ishikawa (1996) was the first to explore the relationship between the distribution of human capital and the patterns of trade. However, he has restricted his attention to countries that differ in aggregate endowments while we are also interested in differences in the variance of the two distributions. Grossman and Maggi (2000) using production technologies where workers' talents can be complementary in some sectors and substitutable in others have also found that the distribution of human capital can potentially matter for a country's patterns of trade. This is in contrast with our paper where as long as the distributions differ the two countries can benefit from trade. In addition, both of the above papers focus on trade patterns while we are also interested on trade's consequences for inequality and welfare. Lastly, distributions also matter in Grossman (2004) but in his model firms are not perfectly informed about workers' productivity and their output is not verifiable by their employees.

[7] Here, we completely ignore any short-term adjustment costs as the economy moves from one regime to another. See Davidson and Matusz (2006, 2004) and Davidson, Matusz, and Nelson (2006) for interesting work in this area.

S. Bougheas, R. Riezman / Journal of International Economics 73 (2007) 421–433 423

2. The model

There are two countries: A and B. Each country is populated by a continuum of agents of measure 1. Each agent (i for country A and j for country B) is endowed with one unit of labor and some level of human capital, h_i (h_j), randomly drawn from the interval $[1, h_{\mathrm{MAX}}]$. Let f_A and f_B denote the density functions and F_A and F_B the corresponding human capital distribution functions of countries A and B respectively.

There are two goods X and Y. Good Y is a primary commodity and each unit produced requires one unit of labor. In contrast, good X is a high-tech product and each unit produced requires one unit of human capital. The amount of good X produced by an agent corresponds to their level of human capital. So, an agent with human capital h_i produces h_i units of good X.

All agents derive utility from the consumption of both goods and they have identical homothetic preferences.

2.1. Autarky

In this section, we derive the equilibrium under autarky. Without any loss of generality we concentrate on country A. We first derive the production possibilities frontier. The maximum amount of good Y that can be produced is equal to 1. Each agent uses her single labor unit endowment to produce one unit of the primary good. The slope of the PPF at the point where it intersects the x axis is equal to $-(1/h_{\mathrm{MAX}})$. This is because efficiency requires specialization according to comparative advantage, and the agent with the most comparative advantage in producing X is agent h_{MAX}. However, as production of the high-tech product increases the PPF gets steeper because the new producers have lower human capital endowments. The maximum amount of good X that the economy can produce, $\hat{h}_A$ is attained when all the agents produce good X, hence, is equal to the average endowment of human capital. That is,

$$\hat{h}_A = \int_1^{h_{\mathrm{MAX}}} h_i f_A(h)\mathrm{d}h$$

The marginal rate of transformation is equal to $\dfrac{\mathrm{d}Y}{\mathrm{d}X} = 1/h'$ where h' is equal to the human capital endowment of the agent with the highest endowment among those producing good Y.

2.1.1. Equilibrium

Define as p_A the relative price (i.e. the price of good Y measured in units of good X), $q_A(X)$ the quantity produced of good X and $q_A(Y)$ the corresponding quantity of good Y. Then,

Proposition 1. Equilibrium under autarky

The equilibrium price satisfies $1 < p_A < h_{MAX}$ and there exists a critical level of human capital endowment, h_A^*, such that $p_A = h_A^*$, all agents with $h_i < h_A^*$ produce good Y, all agents with $h_i > h_A^*$ produce good X, $q_A(Y) = \int_1^{h_A^*} f_A(h)\mathrm{d}h$, and $q_A(X) = \int_{h_A^*}^{h_{MAX}} h f_A(h)\mathrm{d}h$.

Proof. The proposition follows from straightforward arbitrage arguments. ☐

Notice that agents with human capital endowments equal to h_A^* are indifferent between producing X or Y.

2.1.2. Income distribution

Next we derive the economy's income distribution. In order to measure incomes we need a numeraire. It is clear that any income evaluation is affected by the choice of numeraire. However, as long as we are interested in changes in inequality this choice is inconsequential. With this in mind we use good X as the numeraire. Then, for each type of equilibrium we can derive the corresponding income distribution of the economy. Let z_i denote the income of agent i. Then,

Proposition 2. Income distribution under autarky

Under autarky, $z_i = h_A^*$ for all i such that $h_i \leqslant h_A^*$, and $z_i = h_i > h_A^*$ for all i such that $h_i > h_A^*$. The proportion of agents with income exactly equal to h_A^* is given by $F_A(h_A^*)$ and the proportion of agents with income higher than h_A^* ($h_A^* < h_i < h_{MAX}$) is given by $1 - F_A(h_A^*)$.

The intuition behind the above result is the following. Each agent's income is equal to the value of her marginal product. The marginal product of all agents employed in sector Y is equal to 1 and $p_A = h_A^*$. The marginal product of those agents employed in sector X is equal to their endowment of human capital h_i and the price of the high-tech product is equal to 1 (numeraire).

We next illustrate what autarky equilibrium looks like for a particular utility function.

Example 1. Suppose that preferences are described by the utility function: $U(X, Y) = U(X, Y) = AX^\gamma Y^\delta$. For a given price p_A, those agents with $h_i \geqslant p_A$ (producers of X) maximize the above utility subject to the budget constraint: $h_i - X - p_A Y = 0$ that yields the following demand functions:

$$X = h_i \frac{\gamma}{\gamma + \delta}, \quad Y = \frac{h_i}{p_A} \frac{\delta}{\gamma + \delta}$$

while those agents with $h_i \leqslant p_A$ (producers of Y) maximize the same utility subject to the budget constraint: $p_A - X - p_A Y = 0$ that yields the demand functions:

$$X = p_A \frac{\gamma}{\gamma + \delta}, \quad Y = \frac{\delta}{\gamma + \delta}$$

The equilibrium price h_A^* is such that the supply of Y (demand for X) is equal to the demand for Y (supply of X); in other words it satisfies the following equality:

$$\int_1^{h_A^*} \frac{\gamma}{\gamma + \delta} f_A(h) \mathrm{d}h = \int_{h_A^*}^{h_{MAX}} \frac{h_i}{h_A^*} \frac{\delta}{\gamma + \delta} f_A(h) \mathrm{d}h$$

Notice that each producer of Y produces 1 unit, consumes $\dfrac{\delta}{\gamma + \delta}$ units and supplies $\dfrac{\gamma}{\gamma + \delta}$ units of Y. Simplifying the above expression we get:

$$p_A = h_A^* = \frac{\delta}{\gamma} \frac{\int_{h_A^*}^{h_{MAX}} h_i f_A(h) \mathrm{d}h}{F_A(h_A^*)} = \frac{\delta}{\gamma} \frac{q_A(X)}{q_A(Y)} \tag{1}$$

2.2. Free trade

We next turn to consideration of opening up to international trade. In our two country models the only way that the two countries differ is in their *distributions* of human capital endowments. In general, this implies that $p_A \neq p_B$ ($h_A^* \neq h_B^*$) which means that autarky prices differ in the two countries. Different relative autarky prices imply that there are opportunities for trade. It is clear that the world price p_T will be between the two autarky prices and that the country with the higher autarky price will export good X and import good Y.

S. Bougheas, R. Riezman / Journal of International Economics 73 (2007) 421–433 425

2.2.1. Patterns of trade

Suppose that the two human capital distributions have the same mean which implies that the two countries have the same aggregate endowments. If the two human capital *distributions* are different then the autarky prices will be different. This implies that aggregate endowments may not be accurate predictors of the patterns of trade. This leads to two questions.

The first is under what conditions will a country that has a higher aggregate endowment in human capital export the human capital intensive good? The second question is what properties of human capital distributions provide reliable guides to predict trade patterns? We answer the first question with the following proposition.

Proposition 3. *Suppose that preferences are Cobb–Douglas the sizes of the two countries are equal and let $F_B(h)$ dominate $F_A(h)$ in the sense of first-order stochastic dominance. Then country B, that is the human capital abundant country, will export the human capital intensive good.*

Proof. We need to show that $h_A^* < h_B^*$. First-order stochastic dominance implies that $F_A(h) \geqslant F_B(h)$ and $\int_{h'}^{h_{\text{MAX}}} h_i f_A(h) \mathrm{d}h \leqslant \int_{h'}^{h_{\text{MAX}}} h_i f_B(h) \mathrm{d}h$ for every h'. Then the inequality follows directly from the autarky price equilibrium condition (1). $\quad\square$

This proposition identifies the patterns of trade for the case in which one human capital distribution dominates the other in the sense of first-order stochastic dominance. In this case the variances of the two distributions do not matter. Hence, the pattern of trade depends only on aggregate endowments as in the Heckscher–Ohlin–Samuelson model. Fig. 1 illustrates the above result.

Given that the populations of the two countries are equal both production possibilities frontiers intersect the y axis at the same point. However, if the two countries produce only the high-tech good then country B, that is the country with the higher endowment, will produce more. What the proposition demonstrates is that when the two production possibilities frontiers have the same slope then $\frac{q_A(Y)}{q_A(X)} > \frac{q_B(Y)}{q_B(X)}$. Thus, given homothetic preferences, country B exports the high-tech good.

The above result contrasts with the no-trade result that Grossman and Maggi (2000) derive under first-order stochastic dominance. In their model, both sectors exhibit constant returns to scale in talent (our human capital) and thus the slopes of the two PPFs at points where any ray

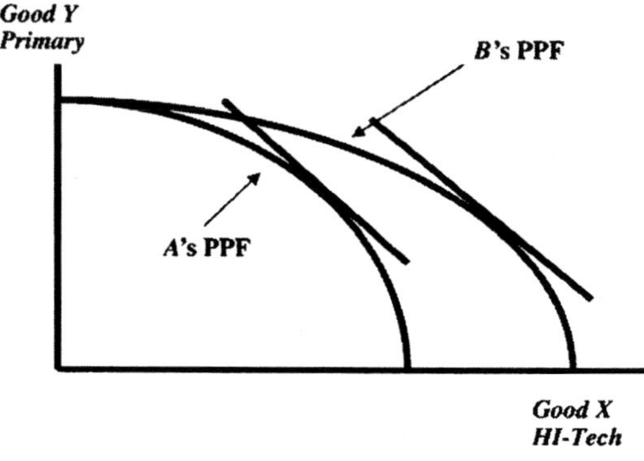

Fig. 1. Comparative advantage under first-order stochastic dominance.

426   *S. Bougheas, R. Riezman / Journal of International Economics 73 (2007) 421–433*

through the origin crosses them are equal. Then homotheticity implies that under autarky the two countries produce exactly the same ratio of quantities of the two goods and thus there is no comparative advantage and hence, no trade. In contrast, in our model the returns to human capital vary across sectors and thus, there are gains from trading.

To provide an answer to the second question we consider the case of two distributions of human capital that have the same mean but different variance (mean-preserving spreads) with the additional restriction that their cumulative distribution functions cross only once. Let the variance of country A's distribution be higher than that of country B's. In the terminology of Grossman and Maggi (2000) the country A's distribution is more *diverse* than country B's. Fig. 2 shows the two production possibilities frontiers.

Notice that the two PPFs share the same intercepts. This is because (a) the populations of the two countries are equal that implies that the maximum amount of good Y that they can produce is the same, and (b) aggregate endowments are the same which implies that the maximum amount of good X that they can produce is also the same. Notice that country B's PPF lies inside country A's PPF. This follows from the fact that if $F_A(h)$ is more diverse than $F_B(h)$ then $\int_{h'}^{h_{\mathrm{MAX}}} h f_A(h)\mathrm{d}h > \int_{h'}^{h_{\mathrm{MAX}}} h f_B(h)\mathrm{d}h$. That is, if the two countries produce both goods and also produce the same quantity of Y then country A will produce a higher quantity of X. The following proposition describes the patterns of trade.

Proposition 4. *Suppose that preferences are Cobb–Douglas and that country A's distribution is more diverse than country B's. Then if the demand for the primary good is relatively strong country A will export the high-tech product and if the demand for the high-tech product is relatively strong country A will export the primary commodity.*

Proof. (Use Fig. 2) First note that in the vicinity of the y intercept country A's PPF is flatter than B's while it is steeper in the vicinity of the x intercept. Then, continuity implies that there exists a unique ray through the origin $\left(\frac{q_A(Y^*)}{q_A(X^*)} = \frac{q_B(Y^*)}{q_B(X^*)} \right)$ such that at the points where it crosses the two PPFs their slopes are equal ($MRT_A = MRT_B = MRT^*$). If we are to the left of that ray (relatively strong demand for the primary commodity), i.e. $MRS < MRT^*$, then $\frac{q_A(Y)}{q_A(X)} < \frac{q_B(Y)}{q_B(X)}$ meaning that Country A exports X, the high-tech good. If we are to the right of that ray (relatively strong demand for the high-tech product), i.e. $MRS > MRT^*$, then $\frac{q_A(Y)}{q_A(X)} > \frac{q_B(Y)}{q_B(X)}$ and country B exports the high-tech good. $\qquad\square$

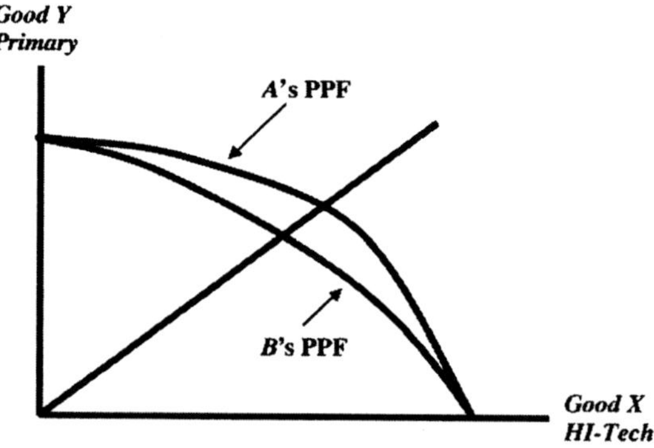

Fig. 2. Comparative advantage under mean-preserving spreads.

One implication of the above discussion is that when countries only differ in the distributions of their endowments, these distributions alone are not sufficient to determine the pattern of trade. We also need to know the exact specification of preferences even when they are the same for all agents. Once more, this result contrasts with the corresponding result in Grossman and Maggi (2000). In their model the more diverse country always exports the good that is produced using a process characterized by input substitutability while the less diverse country exports the good that is produced using a process characterized by input complementarity. Therefore, the two distributions completely determine the pattern of trade.

2.2.2. Trade and inequality

We compare the income distributions of each country under autarky and after trade. In this section, we are only interested in changes in inequality and thus the choice of numeraire does not matter. We begin with the following lemma.

Lemma 1. *Trade increases inequality in the country that exports the high-tech product and reduces inequality in the country that exports the primary commodity.*

Proof. Without any loss of generality, assume that $h_B^* < h_G^* < h_A^*$. therefore at the global equilibrium country A exports the high-tech product while country B exports the primary commodity. Using good X as the numeraire, we observe that, after trade, country A's income distribution is as follows: $z_i = h_G^*$ for all i such that $h_i \leqslant h_G^*$, and $z_i = h_i > h_G^*$ for all i such that $h_i > h_G^*$. Comparing this distribution to the corresponding one obtained under autarky we find that all agents with $h_i \leqslant h_G^*$ (proportion equal to $F_A(h_G^*)$) have experienced a decrease in income equal to $h_A^* - h_G^*$, those agents with $h_G^* < h_i < h_A^*$ (proportion equal to $F_A(h_A^*) - F_A(h_G^*)$) have experienced a decrease in income equal to $h_{A^*} - h_i$, while the income of the rest of the agents (proportion equal to $1 - F_A(h_A^*)$) has remained the same. Therefore, agents with low endowments of human capital have experienced the greatest relative loss in income, the loss of agents with moderate endowments group has been more moderate, while the incomes of those agents with high endowments has remained unchanged. Similarly, comparing country B's after trade income distribution to the corresponding one obtained under autarky we find that the income of agents with low endowments (proportion equal to $F_B(h_B^*)$) has increased by $h_G^* - h_B^*$, the income of those agents with moderate endowments (proportion equal to $F_B(h_G^*) - F_B(h_B^*)$) has increased by $h_G - h_i$, while the incomes of those endowments (proportion equal to $1 - F_B(h_G^*)$) has remained unchanged.[8]   □

We can now prove the main result of this section.

Proposition 5. Suppose that preferences are Cobb–Douglas

Part 1: Suppose that country A's distribution dominates country B's distribution in the sense of first-order stochastic dominance. Then trade will increase inequality in country A and decrease inequality in country B.

Part 2: Suppose that countries A and B have the same aggregate endowments but country A's distribution is more diverse than country B's. Then trade will increase inequality in country A if there is relatively strong demand for the primary good while inequality in country B will increase if there is relatively strong demand for the high-tech good.

---

[8] In general, we need to be cautious with inequality comparisons because one needs to take into account not only relative income changes but also absolute ones. For example, an increase in the gap between rich and poor does not necessarily imply an increase in inequality if it is also accompanied by an increase in per capita income that is uniformly distributed. Nevertheless, such concerns are clearly irrelevant for our model. When inequality increases, depending on the numeraire used either the rich get richer and the poor stay the same or the poor get poorer and the rich stay the same.

Proof. The proof of part 1 follows from Proposition 3 and Lemma 1 and that of part 2 follows from Proposition 4 and Lemma 1.   □

The above results suggest that trade has the opposite effect on the income inequality of the two trading partners. In contrast, Feenstra and Hanson (1996) and Zhu and Trefler (2005) find that inequality increases in both countries. The difference is that they are interested in trade between developed and developing nations where trade is driven because of a technological gap while we are interested in trade between countries with similar technologies.

Propositions 3, 4, and 5 together suggest that whether the gap between two countries' inequality measures increases or decreases after they trade depends on the patterns of trade which in turn, depend on the two endowment distributions and preferences.

3. Welfare

In this section we demonstrate that uncompensated trade does not necessarily enhance social welfare. We know that not all agents gain from trade. But here we are going to prove a stronger result; namely that if the losers are not compensated then trade might reduce social welfare. We measure welfare by using a standard additive social welfare function:

$$W(h,p) = \int_1^{h_{\text{MAX}}} U(X(h,p), Y(h,p)) f(h) \mathrm{d}h \tag{2}$$

Let p^a denote the equilibrium relative price under autarky. If trade is welfare improving then the following must be true:

$$p^a = \text{argmin}\left\{ \int_1^{h_{\text{MAX}}} U(X(h,p), Y(h,p)) f(h) \mathrm{d}h \right\}$$

That is, if trade is welfare improving then the social welfare must be minimized when agents trade at autarky prices. We can prove the following result:

Proposition 6. *Suppose that the preferences of agents are described by the utility function $U(X, Y) = AX^\gamma Y^\delta$. Then, unless $\gamma + \delta = 1$, there exists a set of prices such that if the country trades at those prices its welfare will decrease.*

Proof. See the Appendix.   □

To understand the intuition for this result consider the postulated 'weighted utilitarian' social welfare function. One can think of this welfare function as representing the expected utility of an agent whose endowment is randomly drawn from a distribution that is the same as the distribution of aggregate endowments. Suppose we change γ and δ but we keep the ratio $\frac{\gamma}{\delta}$ constant. We know that such a change will only affect the marginal utility of income leaving equilibrium prices and quantities unaltered. However, expected utility valuations are affected by changes in the marginal utility of income.

We next identify the relationship between the marginal utility of income and the social welfare minimizing prices to better understand the circumstances under which uncompensated trade can reduce social welfare. The next proposition completely characterizes the prices for which social welfare falls.[9]

---

[9] It will become clear that the result must hold for any atomless distribution with a convex domain. However, our method of proof cannot be applied for general specifications of distribution functions.

S. Bougheas, R. Riezman / Journal of International Economics 73 (2007) 421–433 429

Proposition 7. *Suppose that the preferences of agents are described by the utility function $U(X, Y) = AX^\gamma Y^\delta$ and that endowments are uniformly distributed on the interval [1, 2]. If $\gamma + \delta < 1$ then there exists an interval (p, p^a) such that if the country trades at a price in that interval its social welfare will be lower relative to autarky. Similarly, if $\gamma + \delta > 1$ then there exists an interval $(p^a, \bar{p})$ such that if the country trades at a price in that interval its social welfare will be lower relative to autarky.*

Proof. See the Appendix. ☐

Putting Propositions 6 and 7 together the intuition is straightforward. When $\gamma+\delta<1$ the marginal utility of income is decreasing in income. We know that when the equilibrium free trade price is below the autarky price inequality increases. What happens in this case is that trade transfers income from agents with low endowments of human capital to agents with relatively high endowments. But, given that agents' marginal utility of income is decreasing in income, the absolute value of the welfare losses of those agents with low endowments are higher than the welfare gains of those agents with high endowments. In contrast, when $\gamma+\delta>1$ the marginal utility of income is increasing in income. When the equilibrium free trade price is above the autarky price inequality decreases. In this case, trade transfers income from agents with high endowments to agents with relatively low endowments. But given that agents' marginal utility of income is increasing the absolute value of the welfare losses of those agents with high endowments are higher than the welfare gains of those agents with low endowments.

4. Trade and political economy equilibrium

In the previous section we showed that welfare results depend critically on whether or not there is redistribution of income to compensate those agents who suffer losses under free trade. In this section, we demonstrate that such policies might be ruled out in a political economy equilibrium. In addition, we are going to show that it is possible that the majority might vote for *trade without redistribution* even when trade reduces aggregate welfare. We adopt a very simple political economy model and assume that majority voting decides (a) the choice between autarky and trade, and (b) any redistribution policies.[10] Our work follows the median-voter approach to trade policy that was first employed by Mayer (1984) in his classic work on endogenous tariff formation.

We completely characterize the political economy equilibria for the case of diminishing marginal utility of income $(\theta < 1)$[11] and prices in the interval $(1, 2)$. Our proposition characterizes equilibria when redistribution is not on the political agenda. We then discuss how the results would change when redistribution is available. Let h^m denote the human capital endowment of the median voter; i.e. $F_A(h^m)=0.5$.

Remember that when the marginal utility of income is diminishing if $p<p_T<p_A$ uncompensated trade reduces social welfare. We need to consider three cases. The first case is when $1<p_T< p<p_A<2$. We know that the welfare of all those agents with human capital endowments such that $h>p_A$ is higher under trade and the welfare of all agents with human capital endowments such that $h<p_T$ is lower under trade. Since utility is weakly monotonic in endowments it implies that for those agents, with human capital endowments such that $p_T<h<p_A$ there exists a threshold level of endowment h_1 such that the welfare of all agents with human

---

[10] Implicitly, in the text we have assumed that when both votes are available they take place simultaneously. However, the results remain the same in the case of as sequential voting procedure.

[11] Similar results can be obtained when $\theta \geqslant 1$.

capital endowments such that $p_T < h < h_1$ is lower under trade and the welfare of all agents with human capital endowments such that $h_1 < h < p_A$ is higher under trade.

The second case is when $1 < \underline{p} < p_T < p_A < 2$. As in the previous case, there exists a threshold level of endowment h_2 such that the welfare of all agents with human capital endowments such that $p_T < h < h_2$ is lower under trade and the welfare of all agents with human capital endowments such that $h_2 < h < p_A$ is higher under trade.

The last case is when $1 < \underline{p} < p_A < p_T < 2$. Now, the welfare of all those agents with human capital endowments such that $\bar{h} < p_A$ is higher under trade and the welfare of all agents with human capital endowments such that $h > p_T$ is lower under trade. Using a similar argument as above we can show that there exists a threshold level of income h_3 such that the welfare of all agents with human capital endowments such that $p_A < h < h_3$ is higher under trade and the welfare of all agents with human capital endowments such that $h_3 < h < p_T$ is lower under trade.

When the political agenda does not include the option of redistribution we have the following proposition:

Proposition 8. *Characterization of Politico-Economic Equilibria without redistribution for $\theta < 1$.*

> *Let $1 < p_T < \underline{p}$*
> *If $h_1 > h^m$ then autarky*
> *If $h_1 < h^m$ then Trade (Social welfare increases)*
> *Let $\underline{p} < p_T < pA$*
> *If $h_2 > h^m$ then autarky*
> *If $h_2 < h^m$ then Trade (Social welfare decreases)*
> *Let $p_A < p_T < 2$*
> *If $h_3 > h^m$ then Trade (Social welfare increases)*
> *If $h_3 < h^m$ then autarky*

Now suppose the possibility of redistribution is included in the political agenda. In the above three cases that result in autarky, we will get trade with redistribution chosen and in these cases welfare increases. In the three above cases in which free trade is the equilibrium, it means that the majority of voters are better off under trade and that majority will vote for trade, but against redistribution. In those three cases, since redistribution will be voted down, the outcome is unchanged by introducing the possibility of redistribution. So, introducing the availability of redistribution always leads to free trade, and in some, but not all cases, to welfare improvement.[12] Interestingly, there is the possibility that free trade without redistribution is chosen and social welfare falls.

5. Conclusion

In this paper, we have assumed that the distribution of human capital is exogenous. One obvious extension would be to allow for endogenous accumulation of skills. This can be accomplished by considering an economy in which 2-period lived agents spend their first period of their lives investing in skill accumulation while during the second period produce, trade and consume. In such a model, the agents' investment in skills will depend on their expectations about

---

[12] Mayer (1984) restricted his analysis to the case of a constant marginal utility of income and thus in his model uncompensated trade is always welfare increasing.

S. Bougheas, R. Riezman / Journal of International Economics 73 (2007) 421–433 431

both government policies and the trade regime. Because of the associated costs with skill accumulation, underemployment of human capital becomes a much more serious issue.

There are two types of government policies that would be worthwhile to consider; namely redistribution policies and educational subsidies. There is a growing literature that examines issues related to the relationship between skill accumulation and income inequality but the majority of the work in this area has ignored government policies. Two exceptions are Deardoff (1997) and Janeba (2000). However both papers focus on the optimality of government policies ignoring their potential implementation in systems where decisions are not taken by a social planner but rely on a majority rule.

Another possible extension is to consider the problem that governments face when they decide how to allocate a fixed budget for investments in human capital accumulation. In this case government policies completely determine the distribution of human capital (there is no initial distribution to begin with) which in turn will determine the patterns of trade and post-trade income distribution.

A third extension would be to apply our model to immigration issues. As it stands our model cannot explain immigration because we obtain factor price equalization.[13] However, by adding a third factor, say physical capital, that is complimentary to human capital factor price equalization might fail. Our analysis suggests that immigration or emigration of agents will affect both welfare and income distribution.

Appendix A

A.1. Proof of Proposition 6

Using the demand functions that we derived in Example 1, we find that we can write the indirect utility function V of an agent with income h who trades at price p as

$$V = c \frac{h^{\gamma+\delta}}{p^{\delta}}$$

where $c = A \left(\frac{\gamma}{\gamma+\delta}\right)^{\gamma} \left(\frac{\delta}{\gamma+\delta}\right)^{\delta}$. Notice that the income of an agent who produces the primary commodity is equal to p.

Then, using (2), social welfare is given by:

$$p^{\gamma} \int_{1}^{p} f(h)\mathrm{d}h + p^{-\delta} \int_{p}^{h_{\mathrm{MAX}}} h^{\gamma+\delta} f(h)\mathrm{d}h$$

The f.o.c. condition for a minimum is given by:

$$p^{-1}\left(\gamma p^{\gamma} F(p) - \delta p^{-\delta} \int_{p}^{h_{\mathrm{MAX}}} h^{\gamma+\delta} f(h)\mathrm{d}h\right) = 0$$

---

[13] In Ishikawa (1996) immigration is possible because national economies of scale with respect to human capital imply that an individual's efficiency units change with migration and factor price equalization obtains only in terms of efficiency units.

Notice that the s.o.c. is also satisfied. Rearranging the above expression we find that if the social welfare minimizing price is given by the solution of the following equation:

$$p^{\gamma+\delta} = \frac{\delta}{\gamma} \frac{\int_{p^a}^{h_{MAX}} h^{\gamma+\delta} f(h)dh}{F(p)}$$

The proof is completed by adding the observation that unless $\gamma+\delta=1$ the solution of the above equation will not be equal to p^a.

A.2. Proof of Proposition 7

Let $\theta=\gamma+\delta$ and $k=\frac{\delta}{\gamma}$. From Proposition 6 we know that the price that minimizes social welfare is given by the solution to the following equation

$$p^\theta = k \frac{\int_p^2 h^\theta dh}{p-1}$$

In order to prove the proposition we need to show that this price increases with θ, i.e. the marginal utility of income. The reason that this step is sufficient follows from (a) Proposition 6, where we have shown that when $\theta=1$ the minimum is attained at the autarky price, and (b) the continuity of the social welfare function with respect to p. After solving the integral and rearranging the above expression we get

$$p^{1+\theta}\left(1+\frac{k}{1+\theta}\right) - p^\theta = k \frac{1}{1+\theta} 2^{\theta+1} \tag{A1}$$

The left-hand side of (A1), denoted by L, is strictly increasing in p while the right-hand side, denoted by R, is independent of p. Then to complete the proof we need to show that $\frac{dL}{d\theta} < \frac{dR}{d\theta}$. Now,

$$\frac{dL}{d\theta} = p^{\theta+1}\left(1+\frac{k}{1+\theta}\right)\log p - p^{\theta+1}\frac{k}{(1+\theta)^2} - p^\theta \log p$$

and

$$\frac{dR}{d\theta} = -\frac{k}{(1+\theta)^2} 2^{\theta+1} + \frac{k}{1+\theta} 2^{\theta+1}\log 2$$

thus

$$\frac{dR}{d\theta} - \frac{dL}{d\theta} = \frac{k}{1+\theta}\left(2^{\theta+1}\log 2 - p^{\theta+1}\log p\right) - \frac{k}{(1+\theta)^2}\left(2^{\theta+1} - p^{\theta+1}\right)p^\theta(p-1)\log p \tag{A2}$$

From (A1) we find that

$$\frac{k}{1+\theta} = \frac{p^\theta(p-1)}{2^{\theta+1} - p^{\theta+1}}$$

S. Bougheas, R. Riezman / Journal of International Economics 73 (2007) 421–433 433

We can substitute this expression in (A2) to get

$$\frac{dR}{d\theta} - \frac{dL}{d\theta} = \frac{p^\theta(p-1)}{2^{\theta+1} - p^{\theta+1}}\left(2^{\theta+1}\log 2 - p^{\theta+1}\log p\right) - \frac{1}{1+\theta}p^\theta(p-1) - p^\theta(p-1)\log p$$

$$= \frac{2^{\theta+1}\log 2 - p^{\theta+1}\log p}{2^{\theta+1} - p^{\theta+1}} - \frac{1}{1+\theta} - \log p$$

$$= (1+\theta)2^{\theta+1}(\log 2 - \log p) - (2^{\theta+1} - p^{\theta+1})$$

But this last expression is monotonically decreasing in p for $1 < p < 2$ and it is equal to 0 for $p = 2$ which completes the proof. $\qquad\square$

References

Bond, E., 1986. Entrepreneurial ability, income distribution and international trade. Journal of International Economics 20, 343–356.

Brander, J., 1981. Intra-industry trade in identical commodities. Journal of International Economics 11, 1–14.

Davidson, C., Matusz, S., 2004. International Trade and Labor Markets: Theory, Evidence and Policy Implications. W.E. Upjohn Institute, Kalamazoo.

Davidson, C., Matusz, S., 2006. Trade liberalization and compensation. International Economic Review 47, 723–747.

Davidson, C., Matusz, S., Nelson, D., 2006. Can compensation save free trade. Journal of International Economics 71, 167–186.

Davis, D., 1995. Intra-industry trade: a Heckscher–Ohlin–Ricardo approach. Journal of International Economics 39, 201–226.

Deardoff, A., 1997. International externalities in the use of domestic policies to redistribute income. . Discussion Paper, vol. 405. University of Michigan.

Feenstra, R., Hanson, G., 1996. Foreign investment, outsourcing, and relative wages. In: Feenstra, R., Grossman, G. (Eds.), The Political Economy of Trade Policy: Papers in Honor of Jagdish Bhagwati. MIT Press, Cambridge.

Feenstra, R., Hanson, G., 2001. Global production sharing and rising inequality: a survey of trade and wages. NBER Working Paper 8372.

Grossman, G., 2004. The distribution of talent and the pattern and consequences of international trade. Journal of Political Economy 112, 209–239.

Grossman, G., Maggi, G., 2000. Diversity and trade. American Economic Review 90, 1255–1275.

Ishikawa, J., 1996. Scale economies in factor supplies, international trade, and migration. Canadian Journal of Economics 29, 573–594.

Janeba, E., 2000. Trade, income inequality, and government policies: redistribution of income or education subsidies? NBER Working Paper, vol. 7485.

Krugman, P., 1979. Increasing returns, monopolistic competition, and international trade. Journal of International Economics 9, 469–479.

Mayer, W., 1984. Endogenous tariff formation. American Economic Review 74, 970–985.

Yeaple, S., 2005. A simple model of firm heterogeneity, international trade, and wages. Journal of International Economics 65, 1–20.

Zhu, S., Trefler, D., 2005. Trade and inequality in developing countries: a general equilibrium analysis. Journal of International Economics 65, 21–48.